India's National Security Annual Review 2004

India's National Security Annual Review 2004

Editor-in-Chief
Satish Kumar
Former Professor of Diplomacy
Jawaharlal Nehru University
New Delhi

India Research Press
New Delhi

India Research Press
B-4/22, Safdarjung Enclave,
New Delhi – 110 029.
Ph.: 24694610; Fax: 24618637
bahrisons@vsnl.com
contact@indiaresearchpress.com
www.indiaresearchpress.com

ISBN : 81-87943-82-3

Cataloguing in Publication Data
Includes bibliographical references and index.
1. National Security 2. India 3. South Aisa Security
I. Title II. Author

Printed in India at Focus Impressions, New Delhi – 110 003.

Preface

India's National Security Annual Review 2004 is the fourth volume in the series, which was launched in September 2000 to make an integrated assessment of India's national security concerns every year. India's post-Pokhran II experience necessitated that the growth of India's full potential as a power must not be dissipated by external or internal constraints of any kind. The Kargil War further validated this realization.

It became necessary to undertake an annual assessment of India's national security by factoring in political, military, economic, technological and internal security aspects. It was also realized that questions of higher defence management and issues related to military/nuclear doctrines must be addressed and debated regularly. In course of time, taking into account long-term security concerns, it was felt that non-traditional issues should be addressed too. With this holistic perspective in view, a proposal to prepare an annual volume to assess India's national security was approved by the National Security Council Secretariat. This independent project later came to be supported by the Confederation of Indian Industry also.

In the present volume, the analytical section has been divided into two parts. Part I contains essays reviewing various aspects of India's national security in the year 2003–4. Part II focuses attention on critical aspects of national security that have remained neglected or that would require more urgent attention in the coming years. Attention has been drawn to some operational and doctrinal aspects of India's defence, the importance of India's maritime security, the challenges facing India's trade diplomacy, the complexity of the North East situation, the need to manage India's diversity, the critical importance of understanding Pakistan's strategic thinking, the emerging importance of ASEAN for India, the nature of modern warfare and its implications. The contributors are eminent scholars and specialists in respective fields.

This year's National Security Index is an improvement on last year's Index in the choice of variables, sources of information and methodologies employed. A new feature in this volume is an assessment of the Security and Foreign Policy Initiatives taken by India during the year. A continuing feature is a survey of Arms and Military Technologies acquired by India and its neighbours. The reference section contains the regular features, i.e., Chronology of Major Events, Select Documents and Basic Statistics.

The *INSAR* series has emerged as a vital source of information and analysis on issues pertaining to India's national security. It is being widely used by scholars and administrators, parliamentarians and journalists in India and abroad to seek clarifications and authentic viewpoints on major national security issues. Foreign publishers of repute have shown interest in co-publishing this series for the world market.

We are grateful to the National Security Council Secretariat and the Confederation of Indian Industry for their continued support and guidance. It must, however, be stated that the views expressed in this volume are not necessarily those of the NSC Secretariat, any government agency, or the Confederation of Indian Industry.

We are grateful to Amb. M. Rasgotra, Chairman, and other members of the Editorial Board for providing invaluable guidance in the preparation of this volume. S. Kaushik, a Ph.D. scholar in the Centre for Study of Regional Development, School of Social Sciences, Jawaharlal Nehru University, assisted in the preparation of the National Security Index. Bibhu Prasad Nayak, a Ph.D. scholar also in the Centre for Study of Regional Development, JNU, worked on Basic Statistics. Samuel C. Rajiv, Joseph Kuba, and Namrata Goswami, Ph.D. scholars in the Centre for International Politics, Organization and Disarmament, School of International Studies, JNU, in their capacity as Research Assistants for *INSAR* worked hard for long hours throughout the year for the completion of this volume. Mukesh Pokhriyal and Anil Kumar Singh, Computer-cum-Office Assistants, worked with a deep sense of commitment. My grateful acknowledgement of the extremely valuable support provided by all of them.

August 2004 **Satish Kumar**

Contributors

Tarun Das is the Chief Mentor, Confederation of Indian Industry (CII), New Delhi. He was its Chief Executive from 1974 until June 2004. He was educated at Calcutta University and Manchester University, and was awarded an Honorary Degree of Doctorate in Science by the University of Warwick, UK. He was conferred an Honorary CBE by Her Majesty the Queen for his contribution to Indo-British relations. He is also the non-executive Chairman of The Associated Cement Companies Ltd., India, and Haldia Petrochemicals Ltd, India; non-executive Director on the Boards of John Keells Holdings Ltd., Sri Lanka, and GIVE Foundation.

Sudhir T. Devare was a member of the Indian Foreign Service (1964-2001). He served as Secretary, Ministry of External Affairs from 1998 to 2001, as well as Ambassador to South Korea, Ukraine and Indonesia (1994-2001). He was Visiting Professor at the Jawaharlal Nehru University in 2002. He served as a member on the National Security Advisory Board in 2002 and 2003. He was also Vice-Chairman of the Research and Information System of Non-Aligned and Other Developing Countries. He is currently a visiting Senior Research Fellow at Institute of South East Asian Studies, Singapore.

Wilson John is Director, Observer Research Foundation, New Delhi. With an experience of over two decades in journalism, his areas of research include strategic studies, information warfare, terrorism and Pakistan. He is a columnist for *The Pioneer*. He has authored two books, *Karachi: A Terror Capital in the Making* (ORF-Rupa, 2003) and *An Admiral's Fall* (Har Anand, 1999).

Air Vice Marshal Kapil Kak, after a 34-year long career in the Flying Branch of the Indian Air Force, in a range of command, staff and instructional assignments joined the Institute for Defence Studies and Analyses, New Delhi, where he was Deputy Director. He is currently Adviser, Strategic Studies, University of Jammu and Additional Director, Centre for Air Power Studies, New Delhi. His writings on security and defence issues are frequently published in books, professional journals and newspapers. He is also a regular commentator on TV and radio networks.

Lt Gen (Retd.) V.K. Kapoor, PVSM, was commissioned on 9 February 1964 in 17 HORSE, called "Fakhre Hind" by the Indian Army and retired on 31 March 2003. He has taken part in the 1965 and 1971 wars. He is an alumnus of Defence Services Staff College (DSSC), the Higher Command Course at Mhow and the National Defence College Course at Delhi. He also served as Deputy Director General of Military Operations, Instructor at the DSSC and Commandant, Army War College, Mhow. He has contributed articles to professional journals.

Dr Nagesh Kumar is Director-General, Research and Information System (RIS) for the Non-aligned and Other Developing Countries, New Delhi. He obtained his PhD in Economics from the Delhi School of Economics. He has held teaching and research positions at the University of Delhi, IIPA and NISTAD. He served on the faculty of the UNU Institute for New Technologies, the Netherlands (1993-98). He has been Consultant to the World Bank, UNDP, UNCTAD, UNIDO, UN-ESCAP, ILO, the Commission on Intellectual Property Rights, and other organizations.

Maj. Gen. Ashok K. Mehta (Retd.) is a commentator on strategic affairs specializing in India's neighbourhood. He took his training from Fort Leavenworth, USA, and the Royal College of Defence Studies, UK. He belongs to 5 Gorkha Rifles and has trekked extensively in Nepal for which he was awarded the fellowship of the Royal Geographical Society and the Ati Vishist Seva Medal.

Jaideep Saikia is a leading security analyst having published and presented over two dozen academic papers. His books include *Contours: Essays in Security and Strategy,* and *Development Challenges in India: Assam in the 21st Century*. He was granted the prestigious ACDIS-Ford Fellowship, University of Illinois at Urbana-Champaign, USA. He was educated at the Rashtriya Indian Military College, Dehra Dun, and St. Stephen's College, Delhi. His present positions include Senior Adviser, SAPRA, New Delhi, Senior Adviser, Policy Alternatives for the North East, Shillong, and Senior Consultant, Institute for Conflict Management, New Delhi.

Brigadier (Dr.) Arun Sehgal is Senior Fellow at the Institute for Defence Studies and Analyses. He is also a Distinguished Fellow at the School of Geo-Politics, Manipal Academy of Higher Education. In a career spanning over 36 years in the Indian Army, he has held a number of important Command, Staff and Instructional appointments. His most distinguished service assignment included Director of the Office of Net Assessment, Integrated Defence Staff (Ministry of Defence). His important works include *Conflict Escalatory Dynamics: A Case Study of South Asia* and *Systems Approach to National Security Management*.

Kanwal Sibal retired as Foreign Secretary in November 2003 after 37 years in the Indian Foreign Service. He has served as India's Ambassador to Turkey (1989-92), Egypt (1995-98) and France (1998-2002). He has been Deputy Chief of Mission in Indian Embassies in Washington (1992-95) and Kathmandu (1982-85). During his career he has done stints at Paris, Dar-es-Salaam and Lisbon. He is currently India's Ambassador to Russia. As Foreign Secretary, he co-chaired the High Technology Cooperation Group with the United States.

Vice Admiral R. B. Suri (Retd.) is the Executive Director, Forum for Strategic and Security Studies, and Editor, *Agni*. He was President, Navy Foundation, Delhi Chapter (1999-2002), Member, Executive Council, Institute for Defence Studies and Analyses. He also served as Controller of Warship Production and Acquisition (1991), Chief of Staff, Southern Naval Command (1989), Assistant Chief of Naval Staff, Operations (1987), and Director, Naval Plans (1983). He co-authored the book *National Security– Military Aspects* (2003) and authored the United Services Institute paper on *Shape and Size of the Indian Navy in the 21st Century* (1997).

B.G. Verghese is columnist and author, associated with the Centre for Policy Research, New Delhi. He was educated at Delhi and Cambridge Universities. He was the Editor of the *Hindustan Times* and the *Indian Express* and worked with the *Times of India*. He was Information Adviser to the Prime Minister (1966-68), Information Consultant to the Defence Minister (2001), Member, National Security Advisory Board, 1998-2000, and Member, Kargil Review Committee. He received the Magsaysay Award for Journalism in 1975. His books include *Reorienting India: The New Geo-politics of Asia*, *India's Northeast Resurgent*, and *Waters of Hope*.

Contents

Editor's Overview xix

I. National Security Review

II. Perspectives on National Security

III. Chronology of Major Events, 2003

IV. Select Documents

V. Basic Statistics

Compiled by INSAR Research Staff

Editor's Overview

For the third year in succession, the National Security Index, which is a measure of the national power of 50 richest countries of the world, makes the point that India belongs to the league of top 10 countries. In this year's National Security Index, India ranks 9th in cumulative national power. India's national income rank is 11th, while its defence capability rank is 3rd. In effective population, which takes into account the percentage of adult literacy and the percentage of population above poverty line, India ranks 2nd, next only to China. India's population is thus an asset rather than a liability. However, India needs to pull itself up in the fields of technology, wherein it ranks 25th, health with rank 46 and environmental vulnerability, also with rank 46.

India's external security environment registered an improvement, with a general relaxation of tension with China and Pakistan and considerable improvement of relations with the United States. The peace process with Pakistan culminated in a summit meeting between the Prime Minister of India and the President of Pakistan in January 2004. This summit meeting in turn led to the resumption of the composite dialogue, which had remained suspended since 1998. Further, indications in China's maps of its recognition that Sikkim is an integral part of India and the opening of border trade between India and China via Sikkim were a significant landmark in the upward movement of relationship between the two countries. There remained, however, certain anxieties about the immediate neighbourhood, like continued cross-border infiltration from Pakistan, illegal immigration from Bangladesh, sanctuaries of anti-India insurgents in Bangladesh, Maoist rebellion in Nepal and its backlash in India, and the suspended peace process and the spate of assassinations in Sri Lanka.

India's internal security situation caused continuous concern. There was no significant reduction of violence in Jammu and Kashmir. Similarly in the North East, the situation with regard to various insurgent groups did not register any marked improvement, and there was no progress towards resolution of respective conflicts. Politics in some parts of the country tended to aggravate communal tensions. Left-wing extremism continued to pervade large parts of India. Economic hardships led to farmers' suicides. However, the government's endeavours to tackle many of these areas of unrest, especially Jammu and Kashmir and the North East were noticeable.

With regard to higher defence management, there was general appreciation of the fact that recommendations of the Group of Ministers of February 2001 were being implemented. But there was criticism as to why the appointment of the Chief of Defence Staff (CDS) was being withheld. In the absence of a CDS, the thrust and coherence in military planning he was required to provide as the Principal Military Adviser to the Defence Minister is missing. It has also been noted that in the functioning of the Cabinet Committee on Security (CCS), the Chiefs of Staff are invited on "as required" basis. They have no permanent political interface. Given India's complex national security situation, which may require the application of military force at short notice, it is necessary to have an institutionalized politico-military interface involving the Prime Minister with the Chiefs of Staff Committee, and not merely the Defence Minister. The steps taken so far to integrate the Service Headquarters into the Government have been found unsatisfactory. The seriousness with which the functioning of the newly formed Strategic Forces Command (SFC) is being attended to has also been questioned.

In the field of economic security, there was considerable optimism. On the part of the government, the taxation policy and the exchange rate policy helped the growth of the economy. Agriculture witnessed massive growth in 2003 and became the principal propeller of the Indian economy's growth impulse taking it to an unprecedented 8 per cent GDP growth figure. The industry, whether in the public sector or private sector or small and medium enterprises, showed a new courage, confidence and competitiveness. In services, the Information Technology sector was faced with new challenges of difficult markets and protectionist trends. But other services like Tourism, Healthcare, Media, Entertainment, R&D, Training, Banking, Insurance, Financial Services, Maintenance and Repairs, Engineering and Education, steadily grew within India and also built their international presence. Infrastructure sectors showed a mixed performance. Although there was a new focus on technology development, it was yet not done in a mission mode. Overall, 2003 was an incredible year for the Indian economy and the pace of change was rapid. It will, however, take time for perceptions about India to change.

According to another assessment, in 2003, India's external economic security was better assured than its internal economic security. The continued accretion to foreign exchange reserves, a stable exchange rate and reduced dependence on debt and aid flows with increased capital inflows and earnings from invisible exports contributed to a more robust external economic profile. India, however, continued to be a laggard on foreign direct investment. In the internal field, in 2004 the government will have to pay more attention to employment generation, assuring stability of prices and improving the fiscal health of central and state governments. The reform of the public sector, in areas where privatization is not likely to happen or is unwarranted, as in healthcare, education and urban transportation, is also of vital importance.

A special area of interest in 2003 was Indo–US relations. Although the relations had started moving upward in the later part of the Clinton years, they acquired a sharper focus during the Bush years with high technology and defence cooperation occupying a prominent place. In November 2002, India and the US had announced the establishment of a High Technology Cooperation Group (HTCG), the first that the US set up with any country. In February 2003, both sides agreed on the Statement of Principles that would govern trade in high technology. At the first meeting of the HTCG held in July in Washington, it was agreed to concentrate on four broad industry sectors, namely, information technology, bio-technology, nano-technology and defence technology. A meeting in November in Bangalore and Delhi followed the July meeting. The US side was keen that the private sector lend support to the deliberations of the HTCG, arguing that if the US private sector developed a stake in such commerce between India and the US, the existing barriers on the US side would be easier to overcome. The private sector participation from both sides in these meetings was impressive. In 2003–04, the approval rate of export licences increased and the volume of high-technology trade between the two countries grew. Even though the figures were modest, they indicated how much scope there was for expansion.

The Maoist violence in Nepal became a source of serious concern because of the linkages it developed with left-wing extremism in India. India's inability to shape events in Nepal despite its support for multi-party democracy and constitutional monarchy as the twin pillars of stability was noticeable. The United States' increasing involvement in the affairs of Nepal was another development of strategic significance.

In Bangladesh, Islamic fervour was noticeably replacing secular Bengali nationalism. There was also evidence of growing linkages between Bangladeshi extremist and Pakistani terror networks. The Pakistan High Commission in Dhaka was accused by India of having become the nerve centre of the Inter Services Intelligence (ISI) of Pakistan. The 4100 km long porous border facilitated massive illegal immigration from Bangladesh, which continued to be denied by that country.

The peace process in Sri Lanka, despite the ceasefire which had held since February 2002, came to a halt in April 2003. Sri Lankan politics entered a turbulent phase when, in the wake of differences between the government and the LTTE on the question of an administrative structure for the North East, President Chandrika Kumaratunga dismissed the Ministers of Defence, Interior and Mass Communication. The President felt that Prime Minister Wickremasinghe had allowed the LTTE to become stronger during the ceasefire. Her Senior Adviser on Foreign Affairs, Lakshman Kadirgamar, pointed out that the security situation around Trincomalee harbour had worsened and the LTTE had made encroachments there in violation of the ceasefire. Kumaratunga even suggested that India could not afford to "stand aloof" or wait "till the situation became irreversible".

The only redeeming development in the neighbourhood was the action taken by the Royal Bhutan Army, code-named 'Operation All

Clear', to oust anti-India insurgents from its territory. These groups from India's North East had well-established sanctuaries in Bhutan. The Bhutanese action was highly appreciated by India, which cited it as an example to other neighbours in jointly combating terrorism.

The situation within Pakistan gave no reason to hope that internal imperatives would make the country more conducive to peace with India. The constitutional amendments proposed by General Pervez Musharraf in the form of the Legal Framework Order (LFO) and adopted in December 2003 ended up consolidating the army's hold and his personal grip over the politics of the country, rather than democratizing the polity. The clout of religious/fundamentalist parties combined as Muttahida-Majlis-e-Amal (MMA) tended to grow and the nexus between these parties and terrorist groupings like al-Qaeda and the Taliban remained as strong as ever. General Musharraf was found to be quite comfortable in dealing with the ambitious Maulanas of the MMA and sharing power and influence with them, completely sidelining the mainstream political parties in the process. Despite his declaration of intent to step down as Chief of Army Staff (COAS) by December 2004, the general feeling was that Pervez Musharraf could not be taken on his word in this respect. Pakistan's economy continued to record steady improvement.

In January 2003, India released the main elements of its Nuclear Doctrine and the details of its Command and Control structure. The Doctrine adhered to the concept of 'No First Use' and of 'Non-Use' of nuclear weapons against non-nuclear weapon states (NNWS). India's strategic Command and Control structure would vest in the Nuclear Command Authority (NCA) comprising a Political Council and an Executive Council, the former chaired by the Prime Minister and the latter by the National Security Adviser. The Political Council alone would authorize the use of nuclear weapons while the Executive Council would provide inputs for decision-making and would implement the decisions taken by the Political Council. India's strategic forces will be managed and administered by the Strategic Forces Command (SFC) headed by a Commander-in-Chief.

I

National Security Review

Global Security Trends

Satish Kumar

Introduction

The invasion of Iraq by the US-led coalition in March 2003 was the defining event in the post-Cold War history. In one stroke, it shattered the framework of international peace and security so laboriously built after World War II. Institutions of collective security represented by the United Nations completely lost their credibility, weakened as they were by the exercise of superpower veto in the days of the Cold War. Rule of law gave way to supremacy of force.

The doctrines that had been propounded by the US Administration in the previous year, namely, the concept of unilateralism and the doctrine of pre-emption, were actually given effect to in this war. The colossal loss of human life and massive ill will among cultures and religions that resulted from the war did not yield a single weapon of mass destruction in Iraq, the main pretext for the pre-emptive war. Nor did it produce any evidence that the dispossessed Iraqi regime of Saddam Hussein had an obvious and direct link with al-Qaeda, the main source of global terrorism.

Going by the trend up to the middle of 2004, the highly asymmetric war, which resulted in the defeat of Saddam Hussein, led many would-be proliferators to believe that possession of WMDs was the best way of ensuring their security. North Korea and Iran were the examples, notwithstanding their protestations to the contrary. Terrorism, which was meant to be rolled back by this war, did in fact spread its tentacles far and wide.

The war widened the gulf between the United States and Europe and stimulated Europe's desire to strengthen its independent military capability. It led China and Russia to rethink their defence postures and military doctrines. What is worse, it left the people of the world guessing as to what exactly was the purpose of this war.

The Iraq War

By including Iraq among the countries which constituted an "axis of evil" in his State of the Union address on 29 January 2002, President Bush had put Iraq on notice. Iraq, North Korea and Iran were said to "pose a grave and growing danger". North Korea was arming itself with WMDs and missiles. Iran was pursuing WMDs and exporting terror. Iraq was developing WMDs and disallowing international inspections in violation of its commitments. It continued to "flaunt its hostility towards America and to support terror". The President warned that "all nations should know: America will do what is necessary to ensure our nation's security". And he added, "I will not wait on events, while dangers gather".[1]

Bush's "axis of evil" speech led to concerns among America's allies in Europe that after winning the "anti-terror" war in Afghanistan, the US was considering extending it to Iraq, and even to Iran or North Korea. Countries like UK, Germany and France drew a distinction between the war against Afghanistan (which had been justified under article 51 of the UN Charter) and war against any other country without compelling evidence linking its government to the events of 11 September 2001. To reassure the allies, the US Secretary of State Colin Powell told the Senate Budget Committee on 12 February: "with respect to Iran and North Korea, there is no plan to start a war with these nations". However, "with respect to Iraq, it has long been, for several years now, a policy of the US government that regime change would be in the best interests of the region".[2]

Another sign of the hardening of the US position was the leakage by the Bush Administration of the Pentagon's Nuclear Posture Review of January 2002 in early March. This review indicated that the US was considering adapting its nuclear doctrine to allow the use of low-yield "bunker busting" nuclear weapons in pre-emptive strikes against non-nuclear adversaries believed to be developing nuclear, chemical or biological weapons.[3] If so, this would be a violation of the Non-Proliferation Treaty of 1968, which prohibited the use of nuclear weapons against non-nuclear treaty signatories.

President Bush upped the ante further in his speech delivered to

West Point military graduates on 1 June. He said that he reserved the right to take pre-emptive action against any rogue nation suspected of involvement in terrorism, and repudiated the Cold War policies of deterrence and containment. He felt that the US must take the battle to "the enemy" and "confront the worst threats before they emerge".[4]

By the time this speech was delivered, it seems the battle had already been taken to "the enemy". The *Washington Post* of 16 June reported that Bush had signed an intelligence order earlier in the year directing the CIA to use "all available tools" to overthrow Saddam. These included the supply of money, weapons, equipment, training and intelligence information to Iraqi opposition groups; greater efforts to collect information from within the Iraqi government; and authorization to deploy special forces to eliminate specific targets. Congress, apparently, had been consulted about this move.[5]

The *New York Times* of 5 July published details of a highly classified leaked document intended to reveal that the US was planning a three-pronged invasion of Iraq, involving air, land, and sea forces attacking from different directions. The plan called for the involvement of 250,000 US soldiers and Marines, with land forces invading from Kuwait.[6]

On 26 September, the US Defence Secretary Donald Rumsfeld offered the most detailed account to date of alleged links between Iraq and Osama bin Laden's al-Qaeda network. Rumsfeld said that the USA had evidence of "increasing contacts" between Iraq and al-Qaeda and claimed that al-Qaeda members had received training related to biological and chemical weapons.[7]

The US House of Representatives approved by 296 votes to 133 a resolution on 10 October authorizing President Bush to take military action to deprive Iraq of WMDs if the administration failed to resolve the issue by diplomacy under UN auspices. Next day, the same resolution was approved by the Senate by 77 votes to 23. The approval of the resolution, however, became possible after several amendments demanded by the Democrats, which had the effect of authorizing military action only against Iraq and not other countries or individuals. Also, the amendments made it obligatory for the Administration to exhaust various diplomatic means before taking military action.[8]

On 24 September, the UK government had published a long-awaited dossier entitled "Iraq's Weapons of Mass Destruction: The Assessment of the British Government." The dossier outlined what Prime Minister Tony Blair called an "overwhelming" case against Saddam Hussein's regime. According to the dossier, Iraq could deploy chemical and biological weapons at 45 minutes notice. The regime could develop a nuclear bomb too within two years should it secure essential components from foreign sources.[9]

The UN Security Council unanimously passed Resolution 1441 on 8 November 2002 giving President Saddam Hussein a last chance to comply with commitments to disarm or face "serious consequences". The text represented a compromise between France and Russia on one side and the US and the UK on the other. Although the resolution did not provide the US with overt authority to attack Iraq, it amounted to sending a very strong message to Saddam that if he was perceived to be not cooperating with the UN Weapons Inspectors, he could be attacked.[10]

The Iraqi government officials delivered to the UN Monitoring, Verification and Inspection Commission (UNMOVIC) on 8 December 2002 a 12,000-page declaration on weapons of mass destruction and dual-use equipment. Delivery of the declaration by 8 December had been one of the key demands of Security Council Resolution 1441. Handing over the Declaration to UNMOVIC officials, Amer al-Saadi, senior weapons adviser to Saddam Hussein, insisted that the "complete and accurate" declaration would show that Iraq had no illegal weapons programme.

After its officials had examined the Declaration, the US on 19 December declared Iraq to be in "material breach" of Resolution 1441. Secretary of State Colin Powell said that the Iraqi Declaration failed to meet the UN demand for accurate and complete information on its weapons programmes and brought Iraq closer to the day when "it would have to face the consequences" threatened in Resolution 1441.[11]

In January 2003, the US and the UK pushed ahead with a large-scale military build-up in the Gulf in preparation for a possible attack on Iraq. On 1 January, the US ordered more than 11,000 US troops from the Georgia-based 3rd Infantry to move towards the Gulf. About 60,000 US troops were already in the region. On 20 January, the UK announced plans to send 30,000 troops to the Gulf. Responding to these developments, France and Germany expressed concern. France argued that Iraq could be disarmed through peaceful means. Germany warned that military strike against Baghdad would involve unprecedented risks. Both France and Germany said that they would not support military action at that stage. Differences between the US and Europe over Iraq hardened on 22 January when US Defence Secretary Donald Rumsfeld bluntly described France and Germany as a "problem" and said that they represented "old Europe".[12]

The US and the UK stepped up diplomatic efforts in early February to secure a second UN Security Council Resolution authorizing a US-led attack against Iraq. President Bush, during his meeting with Prime Minister Tony Blair on 31 January had said that while he would "welcome" a second resolution, he would not be prepared to wait for long, and that Resolution 1441 already gave the US authority to strike at Iraq. The countdown began on 24 February when the US, the UK, and Spain tabled a new resolution asking the Security Council to take action. The resolution was countered by an alternative plan from France, Russia and Germany, proposing a timetable that would give Iraq more time to disarm.[13] The French President Jacques Chirac stated explicitly on 10 March that he would veto a Security Council resolution authorizing war against Iraq.[14]

The war began on 20 March, when the US and the UK invaded Iraq. The opening of hostilities was greeted by condemnation from around the world, and by large anti-war demonstrations and protests. Both the US and the UK insisted that they had legal authority for the war, while France, Russia, China, and other countries were equally adamant that they did not. The UN Secretary General Kofi Annan also questioned whether the invasion was "in conformity" with the UN Charter.[15]

The foregoing account would suggest that the Bush Administration had made up its mind to bring about a regime change in Iraq by use of force with or without UN support. The US administration discerned early enough that even its traditionally strong allies were reluctant to support the invasion of Iraq because of inadequate evidence that Saddam Hussein had WMDs or that he was not cooperating with the UN inspectors or that he had links with al-Qaeda. Nevertheless, it coined the concept of the "coalition of the willing" and went ahead with its plans with very limited international support.

Indeed, the Bush Administration had announced in its National Security Strategy on 20 September 2002 that it would not hesitate to "act alone" and to act "pre-emptively" to defend the country against the threat of terrorism. Obviously, President Bush was making allowance for the possibility that his plans to overthrow Saddam Hussein might not get the kind of spontaneous international support that he got while attacking Afghanistan in the wake of 9/11.

In this process, George W. Bush laid bare the foundations of a strategy which came to be regarded as a watershed in the post-Cold War US approach to world politics. "Unilateralism" and "pre-emption", combined with his Nuclear Posture Review of January 2002, sent a message to nations big and small that exercise of brute force irrespective of legal justification could be expected from the militarily, technologically, and economically most powerful country in the world. When such an exercise of force was actually witnessed in Iraq, the security discourse all over the world started changing, even as most nations thought it wise to continue to maintain a façade of friendship with the United States.

Weapons of Mass Destruction

The world has no reason to believe that it was any more successful in 2003-4 to come closer to the goal of controlling the spread of nuclear weapons. And this, despite the defeat inflicted on Saddam Hussein in April 2003 ostensibly to contain the proliferation of weapons of mass destruction. Partly, of course, the United States itself is to be blamed for this situation. Its withdrawal from the ABM Treaty and decision to pursue the programme of ballistic missile defences created a sense of all-round insecurity and set nations thinking on how to counter the proposed US anti-missile shield by building their own nuclear and missile arsenals. Its Nuclear Posture Review

(NPR), leaked in January 2002, also tended to re-legitimize the use of nuclear weapons as weapons of war.

For instance, the Chinese had a very negative reaction to the NPR. Until then, the Chinese appeared to believe that the nuclear weapons were becoming less relevant in the modern world and would never be used. Also, they thought that a conflict with the United States over Taiwan would not involve nuclear weapons. But the Chinese were rattled by the fact that the NPR mentioned a possible use of nuclear weapons over a conflict in the Taiwan Strait, and also that the US would pursue the development on earth-penetrating tactical nuclear weapons. In this context, the Chinese felt that the US might even consider restarting its nuclear tests.[16]

A rather grim picture of the prospects of WMD proliferation was presented by the Director of CIA George Tenet and the Director of Defence Intelligence Agency Vice Admiral Lowell Jacoby on 11 February 2003 in their separate reports to the Senate Select Committee on Intelligence. George Tenet said that "the 'domino theory' of the 21st century might well be nuclear". He said that it was becoming increasingly difficult to control the spread of WMD technology and equipment to and from non-state actors, and that there was a "continued weakening of the international non-proliferation consensus". The desire for nuclear weapons was on the upsurge. New nuclear states were able to deter threats from more powerful states, he said, apparently referring to the stand-off between North Korea and the US.[17]

Admiral Jacoby said that some twenty-five countries possess or are actively pursuing WMD or missile programmes. According to him, "secondary proliferation—today's technology importers become tomorrow's exporters" is likely to worsen as these countries' technological sophistication increases. For instance, Iran was exporting missile technology to Syria. Reference was also made to Russian and Chinese entities continuing to supply WMD programmes to countries like Iran and Pakistan. Also, terrorist groups like al-Qaeda were seeking chemical, biological, radiological and nuclear weapons.[18] The international community was seriously concerned about WMD proliferation and assessed the situation from time to time at various levels. For instance, the G-8 summit held on 1-3 June 2003 in Evian, France, described WMD proliferation as "the pre-eminent threat to international security". It said that diplomatic non-proliferation tools such as inspections, export controls and treaties should be accorded high value. If necessary, "other measures in accordance with international law" should be resorted to.[19]

The Bush Administration took extensive recourse to proliferation-related sanctions. It levied penalties against foreign companies and individuals 34 times in 2002 and 21 times (until September) in 2003. This was many times more than the sanctions imposed under the Clinton Administration. The policy became controversial at home. Robert Einhorn, Assistant Secretary of State for Non-Proliferation in the Clinton Administration, said that the Bush Administration did not always explain to China why its entities were being sanctioned. "The frequent imposition of sanctions", he said, "has diluted their value as a means of influencing Chinese behavior".[20]

The United States launched another highly controversial measure to tighten the noose around would-be proliferators, called the Proliferation Security Initiative (PSI). President Bush unveiled this Initiative in a speech in Poland on 31 May 2003. Under this measure, the US and other countries which joined it would be enabled to "search planes and ships carrying suspect cargo and to seize illegal weapons or missile technologies." As of mid-2004, the members of this initiative included Australia, Canada, France, Germany, Italy, Japan, the Netherlands, Norway, Poland, Portugal, Russia, Singapore, Spain, the United Kingdom and the United States. The controversy pertained to the extent to which this initiative would stand the test of prevailing international law, which permits "innocent passage" to all ships through national waters.[21]

In addition to Iraq, North Korea and Iran had been singled out for special attention in the "axis of evil" speech of President Bush in January 2002. North Korea announced its withdrawal from the NPT on 10 January 2003. The US and North Korea held talks in Beijing on 23-24 April. The talks broke down when the North Korean representative stated not only that North Korea already had nuclear weapons but that it had almost finished the reprocessing of 8,000 spent fuel rods which would provide it with the plutonium for eight more warheads. He also hinted that North Korea might conduct a nuclear test or export weapons.[22] The North Korean nuclear crisis could not be resolved even though six-party talks involving South Korea, Japan, Russia and China, in addition to North Korea and the United States, were held in Beijing in August 2003, February 2004 and June 2004.

After Iran's President Mohammed Khatami announced on 9 February 2003 that Iran had extracted uranium for the production of nuclear energy, the US State Department spokesman Richard Boucher said on 10 February that the US had "grave concerns" that Iran was using its supposedly peaceful nuclear programme as a pretext for advancing a nuclear weapons programme.[23]

In its report dated 6 June, the IAEA said that Iran had failed to meet its "safeguards" obligations under the NPT by processing nuclear material without notifying the IAEA. Earlier on 2 June, the leaders of G-8 states after a meeting in France had issued a warning to Iran over its nuclear programme and called for inspections by the IAEA. The IAEA Board adopted a resolution on 12 September giving Iran 31 October as the deadline to provide information and access necessary to prove that it was not diverting nuclear material to weapons production. It was only when the Foreign Minister of the UK, France, and Germany visited Iran and held talks with it on 21 October that it agreed to sign the "additional protocol" of the IAEA which would allow the IAEA unfettered and surprise inspections of its nuclear facilities. Iran also agreed to suspend its uranium enrichment programme.[24] Iran signed the "additional protocol" in Vienna on 18 December.

Libya was another country of concern to the international community, particularly the West, with regard to proliferation of WMD. After nine months of secret negotiations between the US, the UK, and Libya, the US and the UK announced on 19 December 2003 that Libya had agreed to disclose and dismantle its programme to develop weapons of mass destruction. It would sign international treaties restricting nuclear and chemical weapons, and would destroy all missiles with a range greater than 300 km.[25]

Talks between the three countries began in March after a deal had been reached to compensate the families of the victims of the 1988 Lockerbie bombing. Libya had agreed to pay US$2.7 billion to the families and to renounce terrorism. This led to the lifting of all UN sanctions in September. Libya was anxious to see US sanctions lifted as well, which would allow US oil companies to develop the country's oil reserves.

Mohammed El-Baradei, the Director General of IAEA, in his interview with Miles Pomper, the Editor of *Arms Control Today* on 21 October 2003 drew attention to some critical aspects pertaining to curbing nuclear proliferation. He went beyond the clichéd argument of strengthening the non-proliferation regime and emphasized the need to de-legitimize nuclear weapons. "You cannot just continue to have the privileged few relying on either nuclear weapons or the nuclear weapons umbrella and others are told 'you cannot have nuclear weapons,' " said El-Baradei.[26]

Referring to the problem of withdrawal from NPT, he said that if you want a treaty from which no one withdraws it should be a "universal treaty". In other words, you must "have a regime which prohibits nuclear weapons, which is universally applied and which is regarded as a preemptory norm of international law, which means that whether you are in or out, you are bound by that regime."[27] The present regime, according to him, is not universal. There are countries outside it. But even those inside it continue to have nuclear weapons. Therefore, countries need to keep this opting-out clause because their security might be threatened. He also suggested "multilateralization" of the fuel cycle to curb proliferation. This might be achieved by an additional protocol to the NPT, which would limit the right of a member-state to have certain parts of the fuel cycle.[28]

International Terrorism

International terrorism showed no signs of abatement, despite military actions, diplomatic endeavours, resolutions, declarations, and statements all over the world. Ethnic tensions, religious fundamentalism, separatist movements, xenophobia, other anxieties and insecurities, became breeding grounds for terrorist organizations. Major terrorist incidents of the year included the 12 May bombings in

Riyadh, attacks on US properties abroad like the Consulate bombing in Karachi on 28 February, bomb attacks in South East Asia like the one in Davao city international airport in the Philippines on 4 March, another one on 2 April, spate of bombings in Myanmar in May attributed to the Karen National Union (KNU) and the Shan State Army (SSA), suicide bombings in Casablanca, Morocco on 16 May, suicide bombings in Russia that included one on a bus in the North Ossetia province on 24 June, another one in Moscow on 5 July at a rock festival, bomb attack on a military hospital in North Ossetia on 1 August, killing of Jews in Morocco in September by radical Islamic groups, Maoist insurgency in Nepal that claimed hundreds of lives, especially after the breakdown of the ceasefire in late August, and suicide bombings on synagogues in Istanbul on 15 November.

The arrest of Riduan Isamuddin, alias Hambali, the operations chief of Jemaah Islamiyah (JI), on 14 August after a two-year manhunt in the Thai town of Ayutthaya, was testimony to the organic linkages that al-Qaeda had developed with South East Asian radical Islamic groups. Hambali, also known as 'Baby Bin Laden', was arrested as a result of painstaking investigation by the Thai police and the US CIA. The agencies got valuable inputs from the arrest of the man who was acting as a courier to transfer money between Khalid Sheikh Mohammad of al-Qaeda and Hambali.[29] Khalid Sheikh, the alleged mastermind of the 11 September attacks, was arrested in March in Rawalpindi. The arrest of Hambali removed a crucial financial link between al-Qaeda in West Asia and the JI organization in Malaysia and Indonesia. US intelligence, however, suspects that there are over 750 JI activists operating in South East Asia, thus giving the JI the ability and the manpower to strike at will.[30]

These terrorist incidents occurred in spite of the efforts of the governments and security agencies to prevent them. In South East Asia, for example, over 200 persons suspected to belong to JI had been arrested. In order to better respond to terror threats, President Bush announced the creation of the Terrorist Threat Integration Center (TTIC) in his State of the Union address on 28 January. The TTIC would compile a daily 'threat matrix' for the US President and analyse threat assessment after inputs from various organizations like the FBI, CIA, Pentagon's Defence Intelligence Agency (DIA), and Department of Homeland Security (DHS), among others.[31]

It was also decided to allow DHS to open offices in Muslim countries to process visa applications, like the ones which opened in Saudi Arabia in August 2003. US Attorney General John Ashcroft announced on 16 September the decision of the Administration to establish a counter-terrorism screening centre to collate and coordinate the 'watch lists' of suspected terrorists.[32] Recognizing that terror networks grew in the absence of a proper education system, the US decided to invest $157 million on education in Indonesia, a decision announced when President Bush visited Bali on 22 October. He also designated the Philippines as a Major Non-NATO Ally (MNNA).[33] The US also decided to station teams of inspectors at the seaports of Muslim countries or countries with sizeable Muslim populations to prevent the smuggling of WMD.[34]

EU countries took steps to stop the terror finance networks, strengthen their immigration and asylum policies, and define terrorism so as to place it within the penal code to invite the maximum deterrent punishment. Britain, for example, put in place a slew of legislations that included the Anti-Terrorism Act, and the Crimes of Terrorism Bill, among other measures. More than 200 people have also been arrested in Europe since 11 September 2001.[35]

The UN initiated efforts to better understand the scourge of global terrorism. UN Secretary General Kofi Annan, addressing a conference on "Fighting Terrorism for Humanity", in New York on 22 September, stressed the need to address "the political disputes and long-standing conflicts that generate support" for terrorism. The summit was called to discuss the findings of the Oslo panel that was constituted in June 2003 to examine the root causes of terrorism. The panel found that the reasons for terrorism included lack of democracy, failed or weak states, rapid modernization, extreme ideologies, political violence, corrupt governments, inequality, repression and discrimination.[36] The UN Monitoring Group on al-Qaeda network in a report released on 26 June urged all states to tighten controls to cut off terrorists' access to finance. It also recommended that all states should sign the Chemical Weapons Convention (CWC), the Biological and Toxin Weapons Convention (BTWC), and the Convention on the Physical Protection of the Nuclear Material.[37]

The US bilateral initiatives to reinforce defence mechanisms include support to Nepal in the form of military assistance and training worth $17 million, help to South East Asian governments in the form of material support and training, US-Philippines joint exercises named Balikantan 03-01, the presence of about 300 US troops in the Philippines, with a core of 70 Special Forces troops to help in training and surveillance, US cooperation with Colombia for anti-narcotics assistance, and US-Venezuela anti-narcotics cooperation agreement. Anti-terrorism cooperation agreement between Australia and the Philippines was another effort undertaken by governments to cope with the terrorist threat.[38]

Individually also, governments strengthened their anti-terrorist measures. The Australian Senate, for example, passed legislation on 25 June that gave new powers to the Australian Security Intelligence Organization (ASIO) to detain a terrorist suspect, or one having information about terrorist activities, for up to three days without charge.[39]

After 11 September 2001, there has been an increased level of cooperation between the US, Russia, and China in the Central Asian region to curb terrorist activities. The Central Asian region is a hotbed of ethnic and religious divides. Groups like the Islamic Movement of Uzbekistan (IMU), the Hizb-ut-Tahrir al-Islami (HTI), active in the Ferghana valley, and which is against US bases on Central Asian territory and the US war on Iraq, the Eastern Turkestan Islamic Movement (ETIM) of the Uighur separatists in the Xinjiang province of China, among others, are very active in the region.[40]

The US got basing rights from Uzbekistan, Kyrgyzstan, and Tajikistan. Worried about the active presence of the US in the region, Russia and China moved in to better involve regional security initiatives in the fight against terrorism. The Collective Security Treaty Organization (CSTO) was formed on 28 April 2003, comprising Armenia, Belarus, Kazakhstan, Kyrgyzstan, Russia, and Tajikistan. A regional anti-terrorist centre was expected to open in the Uzbek capital, Bishkek, in January 2004, under the initiative of the Shanghai Cooperation Organization (SCO), with the active involvement of Russia and China.

In South Asia, there were growing indications that militants belonging to the Taliban and al-Qaeda had relocated to the North West Frontier Province (NWFP) of Pakistan, and were grouping for renewed attacks against targets in Afghanistan. On 1 October, the Pakistan government launched army action against the Taliban and al-Qaeda in the Federally Administered Tribal Areas (FATA) of NWFP.[41]

The arrest of the alleged mastermind of the 11 September attacks, Khalid Sheikh Mohammad, was very instructive. He was arrested along with Mustafa Ahmed Fawsawi, alleged to have funded the attacks, and Ahmed Abdul Qadoos, a member of the Jamaat-i-Islami party, a leading constituent of the Muttehida-Majlis-e-Amal (MMA). The arrests pointed to the close nexus that had developed between radical elements of indigenous Islamic parties and transnational terrorist organizations.

Such nexus could be seen in other parts of the world like East Africa and South East Asia as well. Al-Qaeda has been able to find a ready recruiting ground for its activities in East Africa, where the rapid growth of the Muslim population combined with the phenomenon of drug trafficking and transnational crime have made the Horn of Africa a fertile ground for its activities. Reports talk of Islamic militants driven out of Afghanistan having moved to mosques in Tanzania.[42] The botched attempt to blow up an Israeli Arkia airliner at Mombasa airport in Kenya with a Russian-made 9M32M Strela 2M man-portable air defence system (MANPADS) in February was testimony to the ability of terrorists to find the necessary resources and organization to carry out their plans as far as East Africa.[43]

A new trend that is receiving increasing attention from security agencies is the vulnerability of nuclear power stations and energy infrastructure to terrorist attacks. Attacks on energy infrastructure have been reported from Baluchistan province in Pakistan and also from Nigeria.[44] According to the IAEA, there were 175 cases of trafficking in nuclear material since 1993 and 201 instances of smuggling of other radioactive sources.[45] Attempts to damage or penetrate nuclear reactors were reported to the IAEA from Western Europe, Argentina, Lithuania, South Korea, and South Africa.

America versus the World

The military action taken by the United States against Iraq without credible international support inside or outside the United Nations did create concern in the international community about how secure the world order was. Even those nations who admire the United States and value good relations with it felt somewhat disillusioned. In interviews conducted by the *New York Times* correspondents from Africa to Europe to South East Asia, one point emerged clearly:

"The war in Iraq has had a major impact on public opinion, which has moved generally from post-9/11 sympathy to post-Iraq antipathy, or at least to disappointment over what is seen as the sole superpower's inclination to act pre-emptively, without either persuasive reasons or United Nations approval."[46]

The Economist, while examining the question whether America was becoming a problem for the world, commented: "The United States is now inherently assertive and unilateralist, and so can no longer be trusted to lead the world. Instead, it should be feared."[47]

The United States was opting out of international regimes and institutions, or weakening those regimes if they conflicted with its interests. This happened in the case of the International Criminal Court, the World Trade Organization, and the Kyoto Protocol on Environment.

On 1 July 2003, the Bush Administration suspended American military assistance to thirty-five countries because they refused to pledge to give American citizens immunity from trial before the International Criminal Court.[48] The court, created to prosecute individuals accused of genocide, war crimes and crimes against humanity in cases where the accused's home country is unable or unwilling to do so, was launched in March 2003. President Clinton had signed the treaty creating the court but President George W. Bush revoked it and started pressing the United Nations to grant American troops on peacekeeping missions a permanent exemption from prosecution by the ICC. Meanwhile, America has been getting a series of temporary exemptions.

Although the ICC will try cases against individuals, not states, Mr. Bush feared that it will be used to bring trumped up, politically motivated cases against American troops and even senior government officials. His administration started applying severe pressure on many countries to sign agreements granting immunity to American citizens. The measure to stop military aid to those that do not cooperate was inserted into an anti-terrorism bill that the US Congress passed in 2002. More than fifty countries are said to have given in to this pressure and signed immunity agreements. The European Union tried to stop America pressuring its current and prospective members to sign but failed.[49]

Similarly, the United States was perceived as pursuing a go-it-alone policy in matters of international trade, thus threatening the world trade regime. According to a report in the *New York Times*, the WTO officials were complaining that the US had compiled a long record of violating trade rules and had single-handedly blocked an agreement to provide medicines for the world's poorest nations through exemptions from trade rules. This was done to safeguard the interests of the American pharmaceutical industry. Trade diplomats felt that while Europe was willing to stand up to its pharmaceutical industry and support the agreement, the United States was not.[50]

European officials were said to have complained the loudest about the United States breaking trade rules. In one such dispute, Europe was awarded the right to impose $4 billion worth trade sanctions against the United States for giving tax breaks to American exporters through foreign sales corporations. WTO officials were also worried about the US attitude when President Bush imposed steel tariffs and approved a dramatic increase in farm subsidies. As the world's largest trading power, what was expected of the United States was to lead the movement for more liberal trading rules rather than obstructing the implementation of existing rules.[51]

Another instance of the US role in weakening international regimes was its attitude towards the Kyoto Protocol to the United Nations Convention on Climate Change. The Protocol, intended to reduce emissions of carbon dioxide and other greenhouse gases, was negotiated in Kyoto, Japan, in December 1997. It opened for signatures on 1 March 1998 and closed on 15 March 1999.

Under this legally binding agreement industrialized countries will reduce their collective emissions of greenhouse gases by 5.2 per cent compared to the year 1990. The national targets range from 8 per cent reductions for the European Union and some others to 7 per cent for the US, 6 per cent for Japan, 0 per cent for Russia, and permitted increases of 8 per cent for Australia and 10 per cent for Iceland.[52]

Before the Protocol negotiations were complete, the US Senate had passed a resolution in June 1997 conveying the sense that the US should not be a signatory to any protocol that did not include binding targets for developing as well as developed countries, or would harm the US economy. And yet, Vice-President Al Gore signed the Protocol on 12 November 1998. However, the Clinton Administration never submitted the Protocol for ratification.

President Bush, reversing a position he had taken during the election campaign, announced on 29 March 2001 that he would not do anything that would harm the American economy. His spokesman, Ari Fleischer, said: "President Bush does not support the Kyoto Treaty. It is not in the United States' economic best interest." In a letter to several Senators, the President said on 13 March that he would withdraw support for CO2 controls, that he was opposed to the Kyoto Protocol, and that the science of climate change was questionable. Regulating carbon dioxide emissions, he told reporters, would hinder the efficiency of coal-burning power plants which were the source of 56 per cent of the nation's electricity.[53]

The prospect of the US staying outside the agreement influenced a number of other countries, including Australia, Japan and Canada, to discuss whether they should ratify the agreement. While Japan and Canada ultimately decided to ratify the protocol, Australia has said it will not ratify. Russia, having indicated on 2 December 2003 that it would not ratify the protocol "in its present form", reversed its position when President Putin said on 21 May 2004 that Russia would quickly move to ratify the protocol, perhaps as a concession to the European Union in exchange for the EU's support for Russia to join the WTO.[54]

Europe's Widening Rift with America

Europe's alliance with America, which was born during World War II and matured during the Cold War, was described by US Senator John McCain as "the greatest political military alliance in the history of mankind".[55] This was true, given the number of years for which it endured and the challenges that it overcame. While the alliance did come under strain from time to time, it was the Iraq War that sowed the seeds of its destruction.

It all began with the refusal of France, Germany, and Belgium, the three NATO allies of America, to agree to the American request that NATO should plan for the defence of Turkey, while Turkey prepared its territory to be the launching ground for a war on Iraq. France and Germany were none too happy with the US Defence Secretary Donald Rumsfeld's earlier remark referring to them as "Old Europe", and another comment comparing Germany to Libya and Cuba. As the timetable for the invasion of Iraq drew closer, differences sharpened between France and Germany on one side and the United States and United Kingdom on the other. France and Germany wanted Iraq to be given more time to prove its innocence on the question of WMD proliferation. In any case, they were opposed to military action without proper United Nations authorization. The US and UK, on the other hand, seemed to have made up their mind to take military action irrespective of any other consideration. The US, frustrated with France and Germany, reached out to countries like Poland and Spain to seek support.

Such was the impact of "old Europe" feeling ignored and of US "unilateralism" being pursued as a strategic doctrine that Europeans started feeling uncomfortable about America's global leadership. A survey conducted by the German Marshall Fund of the United States and Compagnia di San Paolo of Turin, Italy, found that as against 64 per cent Europeans who favoured a strong American presence in the world in 2002, the number dropped to 45 per cent in 2003. In France, 7 out of 10 respondents said that American global leadership was "undesirable", and 5 out of 10 Italians and Germans agreed. The poll came to the conclusion that Americans are more likely than Europeans to resort to use of force to rid nations of dangerous weapons, and are more willing to circumvent the United Nations if their vital interests are at stake. The survey sampled the views of 8,000 Americans and Europeans in June 2003.[56]

The most glaring example of Europe's alienation from the United States was the concretization of a proposal, for long under consideration, that Europe should have a common security strategy and a joint military planning staff separate from NATO. The decision was taken by leaders of the 15-nation European Union at a meeting in Brussels on 12 December 2003. A common security strategy, the leaders felt, would enable Europe to have a "share in the responsibility for global security, and in building a better world".[57]

The 14-page strategy paper, based on a draft by the European Union's foreign affairs chief, Javier Solana, departed from the security thinking of the Bush Administration by pointing out that none of the current threats to peace—including terrorism, weapons of mass destruction, the collapse of government institutions and organized crime—was purely military, "nor can they be tackled by purely military means".[58] The document represented the culmination of many years' effort by European nations to formulate a defence policy separate from NATO, which is dominated by the United States. The movement gained force after the Treaty of Maastricht, which took effect in 1993, mandating gradual progress from mere economic integration to common policies in defence and foreign affairs. The adoption of a common security strategy was preceded by weeks of intense diplomatic effort to lessen American resistance to the adoption of an independent European security strategy.

Changing Military Geography after 9/11

The end of the Cold War was a defining moment in world history. For the next ten years, there was an interregnum, when the world was without "any enemy". Then came September 2001. Suddenly, there was "the enemy" which provided contours to world politics. The new enemy was international terrorism, personified as al-Qaeda and its affiliates. For a while, the whole world admired and supported the will of the United States to confront this enemy. No one questioned the military reach of the United States to achieve victory in Afghanistan. But the global consensus broke down when it came to attacking the next outpost of terrorism (and WMD proliferation), namely, Iraq.

Despite the breakdown of consensus, the United States went ahead with the invasion of Iraq. But in the process, and by the time of the invasion, the United States had perfected the conceptual constructs and strategic justifications for restructuring its global military presence. The military deployments meant against the Soviet threat were to be relocated to counter the threat of terrorism to America's vital national interests, whether from state actors or non-state actors. The process took roots in America's Quadrennial Defence Review of 2001. It was mentioned in President Bush's National Security Strategy of 2002. It culminated in the Global Posture Review announced by President Bush on 16 August 2004.[59]

The troops redeployment strategy is based on the American perception that there exists an "arc of instability"—a sweep of poor, roughed-up countries that runs from South East Asia through the Middle East on to North Africa. Most of the sources of international terrorism are embedded in this arc. (It so happens that most of the known reserves of oil and natural gas are also embedded in this arc.) At the moment, some of America's biggest overseas bases are far from that arc. Germany has 68,000 American troops. Many more are there in Italy and Britain. Japan hosts 41,000 troops, and South Korea 37,000.[60]

The threat from terrorists can come "from anywhere at any time". This threat will require nimbler armies rather than "big, clunky bases deep in friendly territory". "Much better would be to develop a network of smaller 'forward operating bases' around the world, which could serve as a springboard for troops monitoring a threat or responding to trouble."[61] In the words of President Bush,

> Over the coming decade, we will deploy a more agile and more flexible force... We will move some of our troops and capabilities to new locations, so they can surge quickly to deal with unexpected threats. We'll take advantage of 21st century military technologies to rapidly deploy increased combat power. The new plan will help us fight and win these wars of the 21st century. It will strengthen our alliances around the world ...[62]

America already has considerable number of small global outposts and military presence, e.g. Guam in the Pacific, Bosnia and Kosovo in Central Europe, Egypt in the Middle East, apart from tens of thousands afloat in foreign seas. But there are many vacant spots still, e.g. Sub-Saharan Africa, where Kenya has already had its share of al-Qaeda attacks, and Somalia, which has a perennial potential of lawlessness. Besides, America wants to establish bases in Mali and Algeria, apart from sorting out refuelling rights for its planes in Uganda and Senegal. There was also the possibility of an American peacekeeping contingent in Liberia.[63]

In Asia the US Global Posture Review visualized, apart from some redeployment within South Korea, the shifting of troops to Singapore and Australia, trusted allies in the war against terrorism, and also to Vietnam. The Philippines already has more than 1000 American troops sent in 2002 to train Filipino troops as part of the joint counter-terrorism strategy. It refused to host American combat troops due to constitutional constraints, when approached in this regard. In Europe, there were moves to replace Germany with Bulgaria and Romania, both of whom were too eager to have American troops, much to the chagrin of the Russian Federation.

As *The Economist* commented,

> If even some of these changes happen, America's military map will probably look very different in just a few years. Its new alignments, no longer so wedded to Cold-War geography, will probably be more effective. But simply creating a more agile force, backed by the latest technology, may not be enough.[64]

The point, however, is that America has launched itself on a historic new role. Max Boot, a scholar at the Council on Foreign Relations in New York said, "America's destiny is to police the world." Michael Ignatieff, a Canadian scholar at Harvard argued, "Imperialism doesn't stop being necessary just because it is politically incorrect." Niall Ferguson, a Scottish historian at New York University said, "What the British empire proved is that empire is a form of international government that can work—and not just for the benefit of the ruling power."[65]

On the other side of the Atlantic, however, there were grave reservations: "The 'war against terrorism' is certainly an excuse, and an organizing principle, but not in and of itself a primary motive for a strategic new direction in international relations and American world policy", said Stefan Frolich, a German scholar and a Professor of International Politics at the Friedrich Alexander University in Erlangen. "In this sense, the war against Iraq can be seen as a logical and necessary defence of American predominance", he continued.[66]

Russia's Defence Posture

Russia's Defence Minister Sergei Ivanov addressed a meeting of the military and political top brass in Moscow in the presence of President Putin on 2 October 2003. He unveiled the latest thinking of Russia on defence policy and military restructuring in a report titled "Immediate Tasks of Development of the Armed Forces of the Russian Federation".[67] The report, which was described by the media as the new "Defence Paper" or "White Paper", tended to revise and develop the ideas contained in the Russian Military Doctrine published in 2002. This report is a carefully thought out response to America's Nuclear Posture Review of January 2002, National Security Strategy of September 2002, and National Strategy to Combat Weapons of Mass Destruction of December 2002.

The Defence Minister's report specifies three types of threats whose "neutralization" to one degree or another is the function of the armed forces of Russia: external, internal and trans-border. The classical external threats are now imbued with fundamentally new aspects. For instance, interference in the internal affairs of Russia by foreign states, or organizations supported by foreign states; 'instability' in the "near boundary" [near abroad] countries generated by the weakness of their central governments. The special features of contemporary external threats require of the Russian armed forces the accomplishment of missions of different nature in "different regions of peace". The report then declares, "We cannot absolutely exclude *the preventive application of force*, if the interests of Russia or her allied obligations require this"[68] [Emphasis added].

Elaborating on the nature of trans-border threats, it says these threats include those that have the "manifestation" of being internal, but "in essence" are external. For instance, the activities of "structures" in the territory of Russia which are connected with international terrorist organizations; preparation in the territory of other states for actions by armed units in the territory of Russia or its allies; or trans-border criminality which includes contraband and other unlawful activity. The report says that it would be senseless to separate terrorist activity into "internal" and "international". We have learnt this from the experience of Chechnya. It emphasizes then that it would be "irresponsible" for Russia that in a situation which is "so complex", the "prerogatives of the activity of the army" should be limited only to the "external sphere".[69]

The most interesting part of the Defence Minister's report pertains to Russia's revised thinking on the use of nuclear weapons. The report emphasizes that Russia should consider the "possibility of the return to nuclear weapons of the properties of real military tool". It says that Russia has noted that due to technological achievements, there are attempts "to convert nuclear weapons from the tool of restraining [deterrence] into the weapon of battlefield". "We consider that this is the [an] extremely dangerous tendency, which undermines global and regional stability", says the report. The Defence Minister said that the given processes are being thoroughly tracked, for even an "insignificant reduction in the threshold of the application of nuclear weapons will require from Russia the readjustment of the troop command and control system and principles of their combat employment". The report also deals with the likely emergence of future threats and says that Russia should be ready not simply to defend itself in the case of external aggression "but also to transfer war shooting in one manner or another on the territory of the enemy".[70]

Crisis of the International System

The invasion of Iraq, disregard of the United Nations, unilateralist approach, strategy of pre-emption, no progress in controlling WMD proliferation, no success in preventing the spread of international terrorism, all these made 2003 a year of soul searching for many at the United Nations, including its Secretary General, Kofi Annan. Addressing a wide-ranging news conference in New York on 30 July 2003, he called for a rethinking of "the international institutions that were largely sidelined during the Iraq war". "Many of us sense", the Secretary General said, "that we are living through a crisis of the international system." The war and other recent events "force us to ask ourselves whether the institutions and methods we are accustomed to are really adequate to deal with all the stresses of the last couple of years". He then asked, "If we are going to make preventive action, or war, part of our response to these new threats, what are the rules? Who decides? Under what circumstances?"[71]

Elaborating his views at another news conference at the United Nations on 8 September, Mr. Kofi Annan suggested enlarging the Security Council to make it more representative of the 21st-century geopolitical realities. "Events have shaken the international system", Mr. Annan said. "Member states have been sharply divided about some of the most fundamental issues that this organization was set up to deal with." Although this issue had been simmering for more than a decade, "the Iraqi crisis brought this to the fore".[72]

Presenting his annual report to the UN General Assembly at its 58th session on 16 September 2003, the Secretary General criticized it for conducting "repetitive and sterile" debates on issues that are irrelevant to most of the world's people. All the important stuff, he said, is decided by the much smaller Security Council, which lacks legitimacy, especially in the eyes of the developing world.[73]

The Secretary General appointed on 4 November a 16-member group to review the role of the United Nations, including its rules, institutions, and strategies, in the wake of the diplomatic failures in the run-up to the Iraq War. The panel was headed by Anand Panyarachum, former Prime Minister of Thailand, and included Qian Qichen, former Vice Premier and Foreign Minister of China, Yevgeny Primakov, former Prime Minister of Russia, Gen. (Retd.) Brent Scowcroft, National Security Adviser to former US President George Bush, and Gareth Evans, former Foreign Minister of Australia, among others.[74]

Non-traditional Security Concerns

The *World Water Development Report*, released by UNESCO on 5 March, revealed that 1.1 billion people lacked access to clean water. It warned that while water consumption doubled during the last fifty years, water supplies per capita reduced by about one-third during the decades between 1970 and 1990.[75] Moves to privatize water resources, the 'blue gold', which the Camdessus Report of 2003 recommends, also came in for sharp criticism from the developing world.

UNICEF's report on the *State of the World Children, 2003*, noted that while 150 million children in developing countries are underweight, another 120 million are not going to primary school, of which 53 per cent are girls.[76] *The World Population Report, 2003*, focusing on the rights of young people, stated that 238 million young people are living in extreme poverty. The UNDP's *Human Development Report*, while being optimistic about the UN's Millennium goal of halving the number of people living on less than US$1 per day by 2015, warned that a total of 54 countries were poorer than they were in 1990.[77] FAO's annual report, *The State of Food Insecurity*, released on 25 November, noted that the 1996 target set by the World Food Summit of reducing the number people suffering from hunger by half by 2015, was looking "increasingly remote".[78] The WHO, in a report published on 11 December, estimated that 150,000 deaths could be occurring due to climate change every year.[79]

While these reports sharply remind us of how distant we are from the goals of human security, there has been no consensus on the steps that need to be taken to achieve these goals. Forums like the Asian Social Forum held in Hyderabad from 2-7 January, the World Social Forum held in Porto Allegre from 23-27 January, and Peoples World Water Forum held in New Delhi, were efforts to develop alternative approaches as against the prevailing neo-liberal paradigm of globalization and free trade. The topics discussed at these forums included the global security environment, the dangers of Pax Americana, environmental concerns, the problems of marginalized and excluded groups, and alternative energy resources, among other concerns.[80]

Among the positive developments witnessed in the year were the adoption of the Framework Convention on Tobacco Control (FCTC) by the WHO in May that would ban tobacco advertising, sponsorship, and promotion within five years of the treaty coming into force. 4.9 million people die due to smoking-related diseases every year.[81] The Multilateral Nuclear Environmental Programme of the Russian Federation (MNEPR), adopted on 21 May, provided a legal framework for handling spent atomic fuel, and also had provisions for cleaning up nuclear waste from decommissioned nuclear submarines.[82] The agreement, negotiated between Russia, the US, the UK, Norway, Sweden, and Euratom over a five-year period, would go a long way in making the environment of Russia safe for future generations.

The year also witnessed the scourge of the Severe Acute Respiratory Syndrome (SARS), which originated in China and affected Hong Kong, Singapore and Taiwan, among other countries in South East Asia. By 1 May, 372 people had died and thousands were infected. ASEAN called an emergency meeting on 29 April and agreed to take "collective responsibility" to tackle the spread.[83] China officially declared on 18 August that there were no more cases of SARS. The global economic consequence of the spread of the disease was estimated at around $30 billion.[84] Another epidemic that struck the region was the Avian Influenza (AI), which affected Vietnam, Thailand, China, South Korea, Japan, Laos, Indonesia, Pakistan, and Bangladesh. India was not affected as the country does not fall into the migratory routes of the water fowl, the carrier of the virus, and food habits do not include exotic and wild birds. Nearly 25 million poultry were slaughtered to contain the disease.[85]

The deadly AIDS continued to ravage parts of the world, especially Africa. While 11 per cent of the population of South Africa was suffering from the disease, India had the second highest number of patients (4.58 million). The CIA in September 2003 projected that the number of HIV-infected people in India would reach 25 million by the end of the decade.[86]

Notes

1. http://www.whitehouse.gov/news/releases/2002/01/20020129-11.html.
2. *Keesings Record of World Events*, February 2002, p. 44606.
3. Ibid., March 2002, p. 44662.
4. Ibid., June 2002, p. 44873.
5. Ibid.
6. Ibid., July 2002, p. 44919.
7. Ibid., September 2002, p. 45009.
8. Ibid.
9. Ibid., October 2002, pp. 45028-9.
10. Ibid., November 2002, p. 45114.
11. Ibid., December 2002, p. 45161.
12. Ibid., January 2003, p. 45216.
13. Ibid., February 2003, p. 45264.
14. Ibid., March 2003, p. 45314.
15. Ibid., p. 45313.
16. Joanne Tompkins, "How US Strategic Policy is Changing China's Nuclear Plans", *Arms Control Today*, January/February 2003, p. 13.
17. "Intelligence Chiefs Paint Grim Picture of Proliferation", *Arms Control Today*, March 2003, p. 19.
18. Ibid.
19. "Western Governments Assess Non-Proliferation Measures", ibid., July/August 2003, p. 27.
20. "Bush Emphasis on Proliferation Sanctions Stirs Debate", ibid., September 2003, pp. 3-5.
21. "US Pushes Initiative to Block Shipments of WMD, Missiles", ibid., July/August 2003, p. 26; George Perkovich et al., "Universal Compliance: Strategy for Nuclear Security" (A Draft Paper), Carnegie Endowment for International Peace, Washington, DC, June 2004, p. 60.
22. *Keesing's Record of World Events*, April 2003, p. 45342.
23. Ibid., February 2003, p. 45267.
24. Ibid., October 2003, p. 45672.
25. Ibid., December 2003, p. 45764.
26. *Arms Control Today*, November 2003, p. 4.
27. Ibid., p. 5.

28. Ibid.
29. "The Geography of Terror", *Economist.com*, 21 August 2003.
30. Anthony Davis, "Southeast Asia Fears New Terrorist Attacks", *Jane's Intelligence Review*, November 2003, pp. 15-19.
31. John Daly, "USA Centralises Terror Threat Assessments", *Jane's Intelligence Review*, March 2003, pp. 4-5.
32. *Keesing's Record of World Events*, November 2003, p. 45588.
33. Ibid., October 2003, p. 45645.
34. Ibid., June 2003, p. 45454.
35. Frank Gregory, "The EU's Role in the War on Terror", *Jane's Intelligence Review*, January 2003, pp. 14-17; Tamara Makarenko, "Europe Adapts to New Terrorist Threats", ibid., August 2003, pp. 24-7.
36. Gorill Husby, "Defining the Causes of Terrorism", ibid., November 2003, p. 55.
37. *Keesing's Record of World Events*, June 2003, p. 45500.
38. Ibid., January 2003, p. 45194; ibid., March 2003, p. 45296; ibid., August 2003, p. 45547.
39. Ibid., June 2003, p. 45474.
40. Tamara Makarenko, "Foreign Bases Complicate Terror Assessments in Central Asia", *Jane's Intelligence Review*, June 2003, pp. 32-5.
41. *Keesing's Record of World Events*, October 2003, p. 45649.
42. Gorill Husby, "Islam Gains Ground in East Africa", *Jane's Intelligence Review*, May 2003, pp. 30-1.
43. David A. Kuhn, "Mombasa Attack Highlights Increasing MANPADS Threat", ibid., February 2003, pp. 26-31.
44. Tamara Makarenko, "Terrorists Threat to Energy Infrastructure Increases", ibid., June 2003, pp. 8-13.
45. Robert Hutchinson, "The Struggle for Control of Radioactive Sources", ibid., March 2003, pp. 32-4.
46. Richard Bernstein, "Foreign Views of US Darken since September 11", *New York Times*, 11 September 2003.
47. "America Versus the World: Greatest Danger or Greatest Hope", *Economist.com*, 6 November 2003.
48. *New York Times*, 2 July 2003.
49. *Economist.com*, 2 July 2003.
50. "US Unilateralism Worries Trade Officials", *New York Times*, 17 March 2003.
51. Ibid.

52. "Kyoto Protocol", *WorldIQ.com.*
53. "President Bush: Adios Kyoto—US Economy First, World CO2 Concerns Secondary", http://www. solcomhouse.com/bush.htm.
54. "Kyoto Protocol", n. 52.
55. "As Cold War Link Itself Grows Cold, Europe Seems to Lose Value for Bush", *New York Times*, 12 February 2003.
56. "Study Finds Europeans Distrustful of US Global Leadership", *New York Times*, 4 September 2003.
57. "Europeans Approve New Security Strategy", *New York Times*, 13 December 2003.
58. Ibid.
59. Defense Department Background Briefing on Global Posture Review, www.globalsecurity.org/military/library/news/2004/08/mil-040816-dod02.htm.
60. "Patrolling the World", *Economist.com*, 15 July 2003.
61. Ibid.
62. The White House, "Fact Sheet; Making America More Secure by Transforming Our Military", 16 August 2004, www.globalsecurity.org/military/library/news/2004/08/mil-040816-whitehouse01.htm.
63. "Patrolling the World", *Economist.com*, 15 July 2003.
64. Ibid.
65. "Manifest Destiny Warmed Up?", *Economist.com*, 14 August 2003.
66. Richard Bernstein, "Echoes of Empires Past", *New York Times*, 14 April 2003.
67. Nikolai Sokov, "Russian Ministry of Defense's New Policy Paper: The Nuclear Angle", *CNS Reports*, Monterey Institute of International Studies, http://cns.miis.edu/pubs/reports/sok1003.htm.
68. "Sergei Ivanov's Appearance at the Conference in the Defense Ministry RF", 2 October 2003, http://babelfish.altavista.com/babelfish/urltrurl?lp=ruen&zural=http%3a%2www.old.mil.ru%2fprint.php.
69. Ibid.
70. Ibid.
71. "Annan Warns of World 'Crisis' ", *New York Times*, 31 July 2003.
72. "Annan Wants Security Council to Grow to Better Reflect World", *New York Times*, 9 September 2003.
73. "Nations United in Discontent", *Economist.com*, 17 September 2003.
74. *Keesing's Record of World Events*, November 2003, p. 45725.

75. Ibid., March 2003, p. 45325.
76. T.K. Rajalakshmi, "Focus on the Rights of Children", *Frontline*, Vol. 20, No. 2, 18-31 January 2003, pp. 77-8.
77. *Keesing's Record of World Events*, July 2003, p. 45540.
78. Ibid., November 2003, p. 45725.
79. Ibid., December 2003, p. 45767.
80. Sukumar Muralidharan, "Globalising Resistance", *Frontline*, Vol. 20, No. 5, 1-14 March 2003, Vol. 20, No. 2, 18-31 January 2003, pp. 4-8; Sharmini Peries, "Heralding Another World", *Frontline*, Vol. 20, No. 5, 1-14 March 2003, pp. 28-30; Angela Saini, "Scarce 'Blue Gold' ", *Frontline*, Vol. 21, No. 3, 31 January-13 February 2004, pp. 37-8.
81. *Keesing's Record of World Events*, May 2003, p. 45443.
82. Ibid., May 2003, p. 45430.
83. P.S. Suryanarayana, "ASEAN Summit and China's Case", *Frontline*, Vol. 20, No. 10, 10-23 May 2003, p. 25.
84. R. Ramachandran, "The SARS Epidemic", *Frontline*, Vol. 20, No. 9, 26 April-9 May 2003, pp. 122-5.
85. Idem, "Avian Epidemic", *Frontline*, Vol. 21, No. 4, 14-27 February 2004, pp. 48-51.
86. Siddharth Narain, "A Health Care Emergency", *Frontline*, Vol. 20, No. 19, 13-26 September 2003, pp. 82-3; Asha Krishnakumar, "For a War on Many Fronts", *Frontline*, Vol. 20, No. 26, 20 December 2003-2 January 2004, pp. 92-4.

External Security Environment

Satish Kumar

Introduction

India's external security environment was marked by a gradual improvement in some respects, although without any specific breakthrough. With both China and Pakistan there was a thaw, but no clear sign that the issues of the border and Kashmir respectively would be resolved any time soon. However, a process of engagement on these two issues was set in motion, in the case of China during Prime Minister Vajpayee's visit in June 2003 and in the case of Pakistan during the Indo-Pak summit in Islamabad in January 2004.

A much deeper engagement, however, was undertaken with strategic partners like the United States, Russia, and France, further strengthening multi-dimensional defence ties, whose range was significantly expanded. Besides, India's international horizon was widened by developing critical ties with important regional powers like Israel, Brazil, and South Africa. Considerable importance was also given to maintaining the momentum of India's developing relationship with the ASEAN region.

Despite these endeavours, India has a long way to go to carve a commanding position for itself economically and politically. Problems with China and Pakistan apart, there also persist the conditionalities and constraints in the flow of high technology from advanced countries. However, the process of engagement has opened many roadblocks. This process should enable the country to negotiate its way forward in the international system more dynamically.

United States

The US-led war in Iraq and the efforts to stabilize the post-war situation provided the context for relations of most major powers with the United States. India took a dim view of the need for military action to disarm the Iraqi leader of his weapons of mass destruction (WMDs), which of course have remained untraced till today. India's

Parliament passed a resolution on 8 April condemning the war (using a Hindi word 'ninda'), and called for an immediate end to the war and a quick withdrawal of the 'Coalition' troops.[1]

The US was keen that the Indian army participated in "stabilization and security" duties in Iraq. The request, however, suffered from vagueness on the part of the US on the extent of its stay in Iraq and the "ambiguities" and the "grey areas" associated with the UN Security Council resolution 1483, which called for the disarmament of Iraq, failing which it warned of military action. Besides, Indian troops had never operated abroad under any command other than that of the United Nations. The Cabinet Committee on Security (CCS) decided on 14 July that unless there was an explicit UN mandate for this purpose, India would not send its troops to Iraq. The Indian decision caused some disappointment in Washington.[2]

India contended that the reasons given by the United States to justify its attack on Iraq could equally be applied to Pakistan to justify a pre-emptive strike by India. The Minister for External Affairs, Yashwant Sinha, told the Rajya Sabha that Pakistan was a "fitter case" and "in a much worse category" if possession of weapons of mass destruction, export of terrorism, and absence of democracy were the criteria by which Iraq was attacked.[3]

Indian concerns with respect to Pakistan's support for cross-border terrorism were not adequately addressed. India continued to remind Washington of the commitments that Pakistan made to it to end its support for terrorist activities. Christina Rocca, Assistant Secretary of State for South Asia, told a Congressional Sub-Committee on Asia-Pacific that the Administration would "hold Pakistan's feet to the fire"[4] on infiltration, but not much was seen in tangible results.

The US continued to rely on Pakistan for support in the war on terror, with National Security Adviser Condoleezza Rice praising the Pakistan President as a "strong fighter in the war on terror".[5] Pakistan did in fact hand over as many as 500 al-Qaeda activists to the United States. The US wrote off a debt of $5 billion to Pakistan in April and pledged an aid of $1.5 billion starting from October 2004.[6] The

Bush Administration's efforts to prop up the military regime of President Musharraf were disillusioning for India.

There was an increased interaction between the armed forces of the two countries. Eric K. Shinseki became the first US Army Chief to visit India in February 2003. India and the US conducted joint exercises to increase interoperability between their respective forces. "Shantipath 03", seventh of the series of multinational peacekeeping military exercises, was held for the first time in the Asia-Pacific region in February. In April, there was an exercise at the Army's Counter-Insurgency and Jungle Warfare School at Varangate, Mizoram. From 5-20 June, a 31-member Indian Air Force (IAF) team was in Alaska for "Cooperative Cope Thunder", a multinational exercise involving the UK, Canada, Japan, Thailand, Malaysia, and Singapore. A three-week joint exercise, codenamed "Balance Iroquois/Vajra Prahar" was held in September in Ladakh. These were followed in October by the Malabar exercises, three days of joint Indo-US naval exercises 100 nautical miles from Kochi.

Defence cooperation between the two countries was deepened in various other ways as well. The Defence Policy Group (DPG), the highest forum of bilateral defence cooperation, met in Washington on 6 August. The Defence Secretary Ajay Prasad led the Indian side while the Under Secretary of Defence Douglas Feith led the US delegation. The two sides agreed that "global terrorism, state sponsors of terrorism, and the proliferation of weapons of mass destruction" were the key threats to international peace and security. The two sides also discussed measures to end curbs on the transfer of dual-use technology items. The Master Information Exchange Agreement, initialled by Prasad and Feith, addressed US concerns over security of technology being given to India. India also placed its request for light arms for its Special Forces, deep submergence rescue vessels for the Indian Navy, ground sensors and chemical suits.[7]

The two sides made rapid progress in attaining greater clarity of each other's positions as regards the so-called "trinity" issues. These included issues related to civilian space cooperation, nuclear energy, and dual-use high-technology transfer. Both sides agreed to follow the 'Glide Path' agreement under which New Delhi committed itself to strengthen the domestic export control laws in exchange for enhanced market opportunities within the US.[8] On 12 January 2004, the US President issued a statement expressing his country's resolve to carry forward this dialogue for cooperation in those three areas plus on the issue of missile defence under the new name Next Steps in Strategic Partnership (NSSP).

The first meeting of the High Technology Cooperation Group (HTCG) was held in Washington on 2 July, co-chaired by Foreign Secretary Kanwal Sibal and the US Deputy Secretary of Commerce, Kenneth Juster. The HTCG discussed issues concerning information technology, life sciences, nano-technology and defence technology.[9]

The year also saw the US extending an invitation to India to be a part of the Proliferation Security Initiative (PSI) to curb the proliferation of WMDs. Ten other nations have joined this initiative. They are the UK, France, Germany, Italy, Spain, Portugal, Poland, the Netherlands, Japan, and Australia.[10]

Europe

Europe made further strides towards unity and self-assertion, although on the question of the Iraq War there were differences among some leading powers. While countries like Germany and France were resolutely opposed to the idea of disarming Iraq by force, Spain and Portugal were firmly on the side of the United States-led coalition. President George Bush declared at the Azores summit attended by the US, UK, Spain, and Portugal on 16 March that the "Iraqi regime will disarm itself or the Iraqi regime will be disarmed by force."[11] Britain agreed with the US. The British Foreign Secretary Jack Straw said that there was no option left "but to use force".[12] On the other hand, the French President Jacques Chirac strongly held the view that a war against Iraq jeopardized "future methods of peaceful disarmament in crises linked to the proliferation of weapons of mass destruction".[13]

The European Convention, charged with the task of writing a constitution for Europe, presented a 300-page draft in Brussels on 13 June. The Convention was chaired by former French President Valery Giscard d'Estaing. The draft was hailed as "historic" and a "legal revolution, with no precedent".[14] The draft generated heated debate over issues like the inclusion of the mention of Christianity as a common European heritage, and differences over the proportion of voting rights each member state could have. Countries like Italy, Spain, Ireland, and Poland were in favour of mentioning the common Christian heritage while secular nations like France were opposed to the move.[15] On the question of voting rights, Spain and Poland wanted to retain their voting rights secured under the controversial Nice Treaty of 2000. Under that treaty, both countries, having a population of less than 40 million, were granted 27 votes each, whereas countries like Germany (82 million) and France (60 million) were granted only 29 votes each. The talks at the heads of government meeting in Brussels on 12 December collapsed over irreconcilable differences on the matter.[16]

The debates over the new constitution, and discussions to set up a new Central European military headquarters in 2004 by France, Germany, Belgium, and Luxembourg, took place in the backdrop of the imminent expansion of the European Union by the addition of ten member-states by 1 May 2004 at Athens. The inclusion of the Czech Republic, Estonia, Cyprus, Latvia, Lithuania, Hungary, Poland, Slovenia, Slovakia and Malta would result in the addition of 75 million people to the population of EU, which would touch a total of 450 million, having 25 per cent of the world's GDP and 20 per cent of the world trade.

The other developments that had a pan-European bearing included the Russia-NATO Council meeting in Moscow on 13 May that approved the first phase of a cooperation programme to deploy a non-strategic anti-missile defence in Europe.[17] "Enlarged Dialogue" between the G-8 and twelve developing countries on questions of globalization and international governance took place at Evian, France. The countries represented were India, China, Malaysia, Saudi Arabia, Brazil, Mexico, South Africa, Algeria, Egypt, Nigeria, Senegal, and Morocco.[18]

A rapid-reaction joint land, air, sea and special operations force, called the NATO Response Force (NRF) was created. The NRF would be under the command of the British General Jack Deverell.

The Force is expected to reach its full strength of 21,000 troops from its present level of 9000 in the year 2006. It would be designed in such a way that it could be deployed around the globe within five days. Supreme Allied Commander, Europe (SACEUR), General James Jones, remarked that the Force represents an "unambiguous commitment of the Alliance's intent to stay militarily relevant in a global context".[19]

India's interaction with Europe was fruitful, with the year witnessing a number of mutual bilateral visits, strategic dialogues, and the India-EU summit in New Delhi. The dignitaries who visited India included the French Prime Minister Jean Pierre Raffarin in February, French Defence Minister Michelle Alliot-Marie in April, German President Johannes Rau in April, British Chief of Defence Staff General Michael Walker in September, President of the European Commission Prof. Romano Prodi for the India-EU summit, Hungarian Prime Minister Peter Medgyessey (the first visit of a Hungarian Prime Minister in twenty-nine years), Polish Prime Minister Leszek Miller, and the Foreign Minister of Bosnia-Herzegovina, Mladen Ivanic.

During the visit of Mr. Raffarin, a $2 billion deal to buy 43 Airbus aircraft was finalized. An MoU was also signed between France's Snecma and HAL (Hindustan Aeronautics Ltd.) to make French aircraft engines, and another MoU with Turbomeca to develop "Shakti Ardien" engines for India's Advanced Light Helicopter (ALH). HAL would also export $6 million worth of products to Snecma.[20] During Ms. Alliot-Marie's visit, proposals for the manufacture of six Scorpene diesel-powered attack submarines at Mazagon docks, costing about $1.8 billion, were discussed.[21] The year also saw the ninth and tenth rounds of Indo-French Strategic Dialogue between National Security Adviser Brajesh Mishra and the Diplomatic Adviser to the French President, Maurice Goudault-Montagne. President Jacques Chirac expressed, on 24 September in the UN General Assembly, his country's support for India's candidature for a permanent seat in the UN Security Council.[22]

Prime Minister A.B. Vajpayee visited Berlin in May, where he stressed that Germany and India shared a vision of a "cooperative multi-polar world".[23] He also addressed the German Parliament.

An Indo-British Parliamentary Forum (IBPF) was set up, chaired by Rajya Sabha member Praful Patel and co-chaired by Lok Sabha MP Renuka Chaudhury, with assistance from the Federation of Indian Chambers of Commerce and Industry (FICCI). The year witnessed the Indian decision to buy British-made Hawk jet trainers, in a deal worth one billion pound sterling.[24] General Walker, the British Chief of Defence Staff, on his visit to Jammu and Kashmir, described the violence in the region as a "terrorist campaign".[25] The new British High Commissioner Michael Arthur reported that trade between India and the UK stood at $7 billion and that India was the eighth largest investor in Britain.

The fourth India-EU summit was held in New Delhi on 29 November. Two agreements, one on trade and investment development, and the other on customs procedures, were signed. At the India-EU Business Summit, the Minister of External Affairs, Yashwant Sinha, urged investors to discard the old image of India and promised further reduction of the high tariff rates to facilitate trade. EU Commissioner Chris Patten, in his turn, highlighted the problems of "excessive red tape, poor infrastructure, and rigid labour laws" as impeding the business climate in India.[26]

The visit of the Polish Prime Minister Leszek Miller marked the fiftieth anniversary of the establishment of diplomatic relations between the two countries. The visit saw an agreement between the Defence Committee of the CII (Confederation of Indian Industry) and the Polish Chamber of National Defence Manufacturers. The agreement facilitates the exchange of defence experiments and expertise, and products and technologies available in the respective countries. Addressing the CII and FICCI, Prime Minister Miller stressed that the current level of economic cooperation between the two countries, worth about $250 million, was "insufficient".[27] The two countries also signed an extradition treaty.[28]

In a development that could have far-reaching consequences, India, China, and the EU joined hands to develop a global navigation system called 'Galileo'. While India would contribute $350 million to the project estimated to cost $3.2 billion, China would pitch in with $230 million. The system, expected to be in place by 2008, would challenge the American GPS system in commercial terms.[29]

Russia

The year saw the pro-Kremlin party, United Russia, sweeping the elections held on 7 November for the State Duma, the lower house of parliament. The party eventually won 300 seats in the 450-member house, thus ensuring an overwhelming control of the house for President Vladimir Putin and making his position strong for the presidential elections in March 2004.

Reacting to the altered strategic environment in the region as a consequence of the US-led war on terror in Afghanistan and Iraq, Russia took decisions to strengthen itself strategically. One of these decisions was the opening of a new air base 25 km from the capital of Kyrgyzstan, Bishkek, at Kant,[30] the first such military outpost established since the collapse of the Soviet Union. Russia bought 30 RS-18 long-range missiles from Ukraine.[31] These missiles, code-named SS-19 by NATO, were part of the arsenal of 160 missiles Ukraine had inherited after the break-up of the Soviet Union. Russia also decided to retain its multiple-warhead missiles. In response to the US withdrawal from the 1972 ABM Treaty, on 25 May, President Putin revealed to parliament that Russia was building strategic weapons capable of destroying the missile shield of the United States.[32] Russia also held its first war games in ten years in the Caucasus mountains in April. Mobile nuclear forces took part in the exercises that included the test-firing of an ICBM (Intercontinental Ballistic Missile). Russia also inducted six new 10,800-km range Topol-M nuclear missiles. These missiles purportedly cannot be shot down by existing missile defence systems and are immune to electronic jamming.[33]

Defence Minister Sergei Ivanov told presspersons on 14 April that the war in Iraq should remind the Russians of the words of Czar Alexander III, who had remarked that Russia had only two reliable allies, the Army and the Navy.[34] Russia was resolutely opposed to the use of military force against the regime of Saddam Hussein. President

Putin categorically said that there was no justification for this military action.[35]

The viewpoints of India and Russia converged considerably over the issues of Iraq and Afghanistan. Both the countries wanted a quick transfer of political authority to the Iraqis themselves and a greater involvement of the United Nations in the decision-making process. They constituted a joint working group (JWG) on Afghanistan, later renamed as the Indo-Russian Joint Working Group on New Global Challenges. At the meetings of the JWG, Vyacheslav Trubnikov, First Deputy Foreign Minister and co-chair of the JWG[36] expressed concern over the resurgence of the Taliban and the help being provided to them by Pakistan. Concern was also expressed at the efforts of certain forces in Pakistan "to turn Afghanistan into a staging area for counteracting India".

Russia was also sympathetic to Indian concerns on cross-border terrorism and the role of Pakistan in abetting it. During the visit of President Musharraf to Moscow in February, the Russian Foreign Ministry spokesman told presspersons that Russian concerns over the "threats of terrorism, extremism and illegal drug trafficking emanating from Afghanistan and Pakistan have been made known to Islamabad".[37]

India's interaction with Russia during the year was fruitful, the highlight of which was the successful visit of Prime Minister Vajpayee to Moscow on 11-13 November. As many as ten agreements were signed in varied fields, testifying to the strength of the relationship. In a seven-page declaration titled "Global Challenges and Threats to World Security and Stability", both sides vowed to "resist terrorism with their full might".[38]

Both sides discussed ways to boost bilateral trade, which had not progressed beyond the $1.5 billion mark for the past few years. Satisfaction was expressed at the cooperation between the two sides in the field of nuclear energy, with Russia helping build two 1000 MWe reactors at Koodankulam, Tamil Nadu and ONGC Videsh investing $1.7 billion in the Sakhalin oil and gas project.[39]

The year witnessed hard negotiations between the two countries over the sale of the aircraft carrier *Admiral Gorshkov*. The carrier is being offered for free but the negotiations were over the price of the refit and refurbishment, and the type of missile systems on board, among other things. The Russians were quoting a price of $1 billion for the refit but at the end of the year, the Chief of Naval Staff Admiral Madhvendra Singh announced that the deal had been finalized at $650 million for the carrier, the MiG-29 K aircraft, and the Kamov helicopters.[40] It was later clarified that negotiations were still continuing for other weapon systems and the missile systems.[41]

An interesting event was a "Trialogue" that took place between India, Russia and China on the sidelines of the UN General Assembly in New York on 23 September. Issues discussed at the meeting between the foreign ministers included Iraq, Afghanistan and the need to strengthen the United Nations.[42]

Japan

Japan came out strongly in support of the war in Iraq. Prime Minister Koizumi promised that Japan would work together with the United States and Britain to do as much as possible to rebuild Iraq.[43] The Japanese parliament approved a bill authorizing the use of Self-Defence Forces to help in the reconstruction of Iraq. In spite of hiccups which delayed the deployment of troops in 'non-combat' duties, like the killing of 26 people including 16 defence personnel of Italy at Nassiriyah on 13 November, a 40-member contingent of the Japan Air Self-Defence Force (JASDF) left for deployment in Kuwait on 26 December.[44]

Indo-Japanese interaction witnessed a remarkable growth, with both sides rediscovering each other's strategic importance. Foreign Minister Yoriko Kawaguchi set the tone of the interaction with her visit in January, during which she remarked that Japan "attaches considerable importance to developing relations with India from a strategic point of view".[45] The importance of the Indian Navy in securing the sealanes of communication (SLOC) in the Indian Ocean and across the Straits of Malacca, an issue of immense importance to Japan, which is heavily dependent on external sources of oil, was advertised as an area where India's strategic importance was manifested.[46]

Analysts also pointed out the increasingly dominant role being played by Beijing in the region and the importance of India as a possible check on its influence. Sino-Japanese tensions over Diayou Islands, three of which Japan had leased from a private owner and which China termed as "invalid", tensions over the North Korean nuclear programme, common interests in ensuring a peaceful solution to the Sri Lankan ethnic problem, in which Japan is taking a keen interest, and mutual concerns as regards the threat of international terrorism, cooperation in the UN, and the development of advanced technologies, among other issues, brought a closer understanding between the two countries during the year.[47]

Indo-Japanese concerns on Pakistan also converged, especially as regards the spread of terrorism and Pakistan's well-documented support to North Korea and its nuclear weapon programme. Pakistan's support to North Korea, the Japanese contend, has complicated Japan's security environment.[48]

Indo-Japanese strategic dialogue took place in April with National Security Adviser Brajesh Mishra holding talks with the Minister-in-Charge of the Japanese Defence Agency, Shigeru Ishiba, and the Chief Cabinet Secretary, Yasuo Fukuda. Addressing the Japanese Institute for International Affairs, Mr. Mishra said, "with our shared values and complementarities, we can together make a major impact virtually everywhere".[49]

While there was convergence in strategic issues, India and Japan did show certain differences especially with regard to trade issues. Japan wanted India to discuss the "Singapore issues", related to market access and agricultural access, among others, at the Cancun Ministerial Conference of the World Trade Organization (WTO), an idea to which India was opposed.[50]

China

China experienced a glorious year with Yang Liwei becoming the first Chinese astronaut to enter space on 15 October 2003. He did fourteen orbits in a Shenzhou V spacecraft in a mission that President Hu Jintao described as a "millennial dream".[51] Hu Jintao was himself elected as the sixth President of the People's Republic of China. The change of guard took place at the 10th National People's

Congress held in March. Jiang Zemin was re-elected Chairman of the Central Military Commission.

At the 54th Anniversary celebrations of the founding of the People's Republic of China in October, the Communist Party of China (CPC) Central Committee dealt with two draft proposals to modernize the socialist market economic system and to incorporate the thought of "three represents", as enunciated by the outgoing President, Jiang Zemin. The theory commits the party to the advanced production forces, the cultural forces and the majority of the people.[52] The Standing Committee of the National People's Congress that met on 28 December formally incorporated the thought into the constitution.[53]

International events that engaged the Chinese leadership during the year included Iraq and North Korea. The Chinese walked a fine line and adopted a very cautious approach with regard to the US efforts to topple the regime of Saddam Hussein. While on the one hand China as a nuclear weapon power tried to express solidarity with the US in its attempts to dispossess Saddam Hussein of his weapons of mass destruction, on the other hand China was highly sceptical of America's "unilateral overdrive" in this respect.[54]

Given its proximity to North Korea, China was involved in efforts to help reduce the danger of North Korean nuclearization. These included the "Beijing Process" of trilateral talks involving the US, China, and North Korea, and the Six-Party talks, involving Russia, Japan, South Korea along with the US, China, and North Korea. Foreign Minister Jiaxuan called for "direct dialogue" between Pyongyang and Washington to bring about denuclearization of the Korean peninsula.[55]

Indian engagement with China touched a new high during the visit of Prime Minister A.B. Vajpayee to Beijing and Shanghai from 22-27 June, the fourth Indian Prime Minister to visit China. The Chinese side stressed the elements of "mutual understanding, mutual accommodation, and mutual adjustment" in order to conclude an agreement on the vexed border question amicably.[56] A highlight of the visit was the conclusion of a border trade agreement that implied that the Chinese would henceforth acknowledge Sikkim as a part of the Indian Union.[57] Prior to the bilateral meeting between Prime

Ministers Vajpayee and Wen Jiabao at the Indo-ASEAN Summit at Bali, Indonesia on 8 October, the Chinese Foreign Ministry removed the part mentioning Sikkim as an "independent country" from its official website.[58] India on its part reaffirmed the Tibet Autonomous Region as a part of the territory of the People's Republic of China.[59]

Both sides agreed to take steps to increase the volume of trade to $10 billion by the year 2005, from the current levels of about $5 billion.[60] China also decided to set up a $500 million corpus fund for investments in India. The two sides initialled the "Declaration on Principles for Relations and Comprehensive Cooperation".

One of the most important outcomes of the visit was the setting up of Special Representatives to fine-tune the process of finding a solution to the border problem. National Security Adviser Brajesh Mishra and Chinese Executive Vice-Foreign Minister Dai Bingguo were appointed "to explore, from the political perspective of the overall bilateral relationship, the framework of a boundary settlement".[61] The two Representatives met in October to take the process forward.[62]

Other high-profile visits exchanged during the year included that of the Defence Minister George Fernandes in April, when the two countries decided to step up military-to-military exchanges, hold a counter-terrorism dialogue, and increase confidence-building measures along the Line of Actual Control (LAC). Mr. Fernandes held talks with Defence Minister Cao Gangchaun, Foreign Minister Li Zhaoxing, Prime Minister Wen Jiabao, and the Vice-Chairman of the Central Military Commission (CMC) General Guo Boxiong, as also the Chairman Jiang Zemin.[63]

Consequently, the two countries decided in June that they would hold joint naval exercises off the eastern coast of India later in the year. Also, a 50-member Air Force team of the Chinese People's Liberation Army (PLA) visited India in July for talks with the Indian Air Force's Directorate of Concepts and Doctrines.[64] Joint naval exercises were held off the Shanghai coast in November, in which three Indian ships—INS *Ranjit*, a guided missile destroyer, INS *Kulish*, a guided missile corvette, and INS *Jyothi*, a replenishment tanker—took part along with two Chinese vessels, *Jia Xing* and *Feng Chang*.[65] Sino-Indian Dialogue Mechanism on Counter-Terrorism was held in Beijing on 13 June to strengthen cooperation at bilateral and multilateral levels.[66]

However, increased Chinese presence in the Bay of Bengal, and its electronic surveillance installations in islands off the Myanmar coast have been a source of concern to India.[67] Besides, the Chinese committed a blatant act of violation of the sanctity of the LAC when a ten-member Indian team comprising members of the Intelligence Bureau (IB) and Special Security Bureau (SSB), on a routine mission 10 km inside the LAC in Arunachal Pradesh's Upper Subansiri district was detained, disarmed, and interrogated, and later released.[68] Reacting to newspaper reports of the incursion, Chinese Foreign Ministry spokesman Kong Quan affirmed, "China does not recognize the so-called Arunachal Pradesh".[69] Prime Minister Vajpayee described the Chinese behaviour as "not dignified".[70]

Pakistan

The 11 September 2001 terror strikes in New York and the subsequent war on terror launched by the US in Afghanistan continued to define and dominate Pakistan's strategic environment in the year 2003. The US and the Western powers firmly believed that President Pervez Musharraf was the best bet to ensure a stable Pakistan, re-establish democracy, control religious fundamentalism, capture terrorists wanted in connection with the 9/11 terror strikes, and deliver on his repeated promises to stop the infiltration of terrorists across the Line of Control (LoC) into Kashmir. To this end, the international community rewarded the Pakistani government abundantly. While Pakistan obtained nearly $900 million as compensation from the US for its cooperation, the donor countries of the Paris Club rescheduled loans amounting to $12.5 billion.[71]

While reminding General Musharraf to be true to his word to stop cross-border terrorism, the Bush Administration did its best to keep the General in good humour. On his visit to the US in June, General Musharraf became the first leader from South Asia to be invited to the Presidential retreat of Camp David. President Musharraf managed to get an economic/security assistance package worth $3 billion, to commence from fiscal year 2005.[72] The military assistance came with the rider that it would be disbursed only if the US was satisfied with the General delivering on his promises of handing over power to a democratically elected government and curbing cross-border infiltration.[73]

Internally, President Musharraf had a tough year. He survived two attempts on his life in December, on the 14th and the 25th. The attacks were carried out in Rawalpindi, a few kilometres from his house in the second instance. The attacks reinforced the vulnerability of the President and the strength of the terrorist groups who wanted to eliminate him. The extremists held General Musharraf responsible for the foreign policy orientation of Pakistan and the alignment with the US in its war on terror, and were themselves at the receiving end of the crackdown on fundamentalism and extremism within Pakistan.

Reforms were also initiated to modernize Madrassa education, long considered the breeding ground for the militants. A ban on militant organizations was imposed, especially on those that had been declared as international terrorist organizations by the US State Department. These included the Jaish-e-Mohammad (JeM), the Hizb-ul-Mujahideen (HuM), and sectarian outfits like the Shia group Tehreek-e-Islam Pakistan, and the Sunni Millat-e-Islam.[74] Restrictions were imposed on the movement of militant leaders like Masood Azhar, head of the JeM. However, reports did note the fact of Azhar flouting the ban and visiting Pakistan-occupied Kashmir (POK). Pakistan handed over nearly 500 terrorists wanted by the US in an attempt to advertise its sincerity of cooperation on the anti-terror front.[75]

Politically, President Musharraf faced a tough time with the six-party alliance of religious parties, the Muttahida Majlis-e-Amal (MMA) threatening a boycott of Parliament if General Musharraf continued to hold dual posts of the President and Chief of Army Staff (COAS). They threatened to go on mass public protests and strikes, with General Musharraf not relenting on the issue.[76] Controversy also surrounded the set of laws promulgated by General Musharraf, called the Legal Framework Order (LFO), also known as Musharraf laws. The LFO incorporates all the amendments made by General Musharraf to the Constitution. These include the extension of his tenure as COAS till 2007, and election as President on the basis of the April 2002 referendum. An extremely controversial provision in the LFO was the establishment of a National Security Council that would tend to institutionalize the supremacy of the military leadership over the civilian in all matters of national importance. A compromise was reached on 24 December whereby Musharraf agreed to shed his uniform by 31 December 2004, and agreed that the National Security Council would be set up under an Act of Parliament.

The year witnessed a gradual thawing of the relationship between India and Pakistan that culminated in Prime Minister A.B. Vajpayee travelling to Islamabad to participate in the SAARC Summit in January 2004. The thaw began with Prime Minister Vajpayee extending "a hand of friendship" to Pakistan during his speech at Srinagar on 18 April. He emphasized that "both sides should decide they have to live together".[77] He maintained, however, that Pakistan must deliver on its promise to end support to terrorists operating in India and stop cross-border infiltration. Pakistan insisted that it was doing everything possible to stem the tide of militants crossing into India, in spite of evidence to the contrary. Reports talked of the ranks of the militants and their training camps having in fact increased during the year.[78]

Shiv Shankar Menon took over as India's envoy to Pakistan while Aziz Ahmad Khan was appointed Pakistan's High Commissioner to India in a move meant to bring back a sense of normalcy to the ties hurt by the audacious attack on the Indian Parliament on 13 December 2001. The ban on overflights was lifted and a series of confidence-building measures were announced to inject dynamism to the relationship. These included the proposal to restart the Lahore-Delhi bus service, introduce a Srinagar-Muzaffarabad bus service, a Sindh (Khokrapar)-Rajasthan (Munabao) train service, medical treatment to Pakistani children, and restoration of India-Pakistan sporting encounters.[79] In an important development, both sides also agreed, during the last week of November, to maintain ceasefire along the 198 km International Border (IB), the 778 km Line of Control (LoC), and the 150 km Actual Ground Position Line (AGPL).[80]

Increasing trade and business interaction was also held as an important tool to bridge the gap between the two countries. Official trade between India and Pakistan during the year 2001-2 stood at $204 million while unofficially, it was believed to be anywhere in the range of $1-6 billion. Gas pipeline proposals like those connecting Turkmenistan-Afghanistan-Pakistan and Iran-Pakistan-India held the promise that they would promote trust and regional economic cooperation. Pakistan, in fact, invited India to be part of the project involving Turkmenistan and Afghanistan and financed by the Asian Development Bank (ADB).[81] The India-Pakistan CEOs' Business Forum was launched in September, which decided to meet at least once in six months.[82] The Minister for External Affairs, Yashwant Sinha, launching the Forum, urged a quick progress towards the realization of the South Asian Free Trade Agreement (SAFTA).

The Pakistani itch to highlight the Kashmir issue at international fora rubbed India the wrong way. General Musharraf, in New York to attend the UN General Assembly, termed the efforts to equate the Kashmiri freedom struggle with terrorism as a "travesty". He even called upon the UN to promote a solution for Kashmir, as it did for East Timor.[83] Prime Minister Vajpayee, in a hard-hitting reply, asserted that India would never let "terrorism become a tool of blackmail". He added: "Just as the world did not negotiate with al-Qaeda or the Taliban, we shall not negotiate with terrorism".[84]

While the unstable nature of the Pakistani polity posed a threat to the region, Pakistani actions like the overt support to terrorists operating across the border in Kashmir and Afghanistan, nuclear cooperation with countries like Iran, and repeated missile tests added to make it a dangerously destabilizing factor in the subcontinent.[85] If possession of weapons of mass destruction (WMD), lack of democracy, support to terrorists, and the dangers of missile and nuclear proliferation were the criteria that justified an American pre-emptive attack against Iraq, India contended that Pakistan was in a far worse category and India was well within its rights to launch a pre-emptive strike against Pakistan.[86] The US cautioned India against undertaking or entertaining such thoughts.

The year also witnessed Pakistan flex its strategic muscle with the test-firing of nuclear-capable ballistic missiles and the induction of the first indigenously built submarine, constructed with French help.[87]

Nepal

The year held hopes that the negotiations between the Nepal government and the Maoists would result in a common ground between the two sides in conflict with each other. The Government of Nepal had stopped terming the Maoists as "terrorists" and withdrew international arrest warrants as well as monetary rewards put on the heads of important leaders as early as in November 2001.[88] Maoist leader Baburam Bhattarai offered a Sihanouk-like role to the King, where the people would draft a constituent assembly and define the role of the Monarch.[89] The government constituted a six-member committee under the leadership of Deputy Prime Minister B. Prasad Mandal to deliberate upon the offer of the Maoists. Mr. Mandal belongs to the Madhesia community, Nepalese of Indian origin, who constitute about 40 per cent of the population of Nepal. Maoists have demanded autonomy for them and other ethnic communities as well.[90]

The peace talks, held on 27 April, were boycotted by the Nepali Congress and the Communist Party of Nepal (Unified-Marxist-Leninist), who alleged that they would be marginalized in a deal between the Maoists and the government.[91] Prime Minister Lokendra Bahadur Chand stepped down from his post on 30 May, under pressure of agitation by mainstream parties for restoration of real democracy. He was a palace appointee. The Nepali Congress, the Communist Party of Nepal (Unified-Marxist-Leninist), Jan Morcha, Nepal Mazdhoor Kisan Party, and the Nepal Sadhbhavana Party threatened to call for the establishment of a republican form of government if the King did not establish democracy.[92] The King eventually selected Surya Bahadur Thapa as Prime Minister on 4 June. This was Mr. Thapa's fourth innings as the Prime Minister.

India has all along maintained that the dialogue in Nepal should be based on a "national consensus", and asserted that its "deep interest lay in Nepal's stability".[93] India also helped the Nepal government militarily by supplying weapons at concessional rates.[94] During Prime Minister Thapa's visit to New Delhi in November, Prime Minister Vajpayee stressed the need to take urgent broad-based measures to check the Maoist threat.[95] This was after the Maoists had unilaterally suspended the peace talks on 27 August, following which the Nepal government re-branded them as "terrorists".[96] The Maoists indulged in large-scale killing and looting following the suspension of the talks.[97] They did declare a nine-day ceasefire from 2-10 October to observe Nepal's biggest festival, Dashain.

The Nepal government also received military help from the United States. Not only did the US train its personnel and provide arms and ammunition, it also gave Nepal an amount of $14 million for military assistance.[98] The role of the US came in for sharp criticism from the Maoists. They contended that the US involvement was creating "unnecessary confusion". They also alleged that the US was utilizing the opportunity provided by the situation in Nepal to realize its "imperial ambitions" in the South Asian subcontinent and control the activities of India and China.[99] US Ambassador to Nepal Michael Malinowski called for cooperation between India and the US "with the approval of Nepal and in a spirit of cooperation and not interference", to tackle the Maoist threat.[100] Taking exception to these remarks and the growing role of the US, the Maoists called for a three-day strike beginning from 18 September. They called for the expulsion of all US military advisers from Nepal and gave a five-day deadline for the government to do so on 28 July. The US clarified that there were no military advisers in the country.[101]

India decided to open a railway link between Kolkata and Kathmandu from March 2004. The 36-hour journey as against the six days it would take by road would reduce the transportation costs by around $16 million per annum for the people of the two countries.[102] Nepal also assured India that its territory would not be allowed to be used by anti-India elements to wage activity inimical to India's interests. Finance Minister Prakash Chandra Lohani gave this assurance while addressing a workshop on "Indo-Nepal Economic Cooperation" in Kathmandu.[103]

Bangladesh

India-Bangladesh relations went through a difficult phase. Illegal migrations, the active presence of anti-India elements on Bangladesh territory, and Bangladeshi concerns over India's river-linking plans were among the issues that created tension between the two countries. The incident in February when nearly 200 Bangladeshis were stranded on the border in the Cooch Behar district of West Bengal and Bangladesh Rifles (BDR) refused to allow them to cross over into Bangladesh, insisting that they produce proof of residence/citizenship, illustrated the dangers of illegal migration. The incident threatened to become a major problem between the two countries, with the Border Security Force (BSF) reportedly calling in reinforcements and ordering the evacuation of people living in the area. It took the intervention of the Minister for External Affairs, Yashwant Sinha, who spoke with his Bangladeshi counterpart, Morshed Khan, to defuse the situation and let the Bangladeshis return to their country. Bangladesh had characterized this incident, prior to Mr. Sinha's intervention, as yet another attempt by the BSF to infiltrate "Bangla-speaking Indians" into Bangladesh.[104]

It was reported that close to 20 million Bangladeshis were in the country illegally. The Intelligence Bureau (IB) characterized these immigrants as posing a threat to the country.[105] The Union Home Ministry, taking cognizance of the threat, planned to introduce multi-purpose National Identity Cards (NIC) as a pilot project initially in thirteen states from 1 April, and proposed the setting up of a Multi-Agency Centre (MAC). This was meant to be a nodal agency for counter-terrorist activities and to coordinate the activities of the Research and Analysis Wing (RAW), IB, and the Defence Intelligence Agency (DIA).[106]

Indian concerns over Bangladesh becoming a haven for anti-India elements were another major irritant in the bilateral relationship. India was unhappy with the presence in Bangladesh of Pakistan's Inter-Services Intelligence (ISI), of the activities of militant organizations operating in India's North-East, of their leaders and training camps of whose presence India provided documentary evidence, and the revelation that the plot to hijack the Indian Airlines flight IC-814 in 1999 was hatched in the Sabzi Mandi area of Dhaka.[107] The Bangladesh government countered with the argument that no militant was operating in Bangladesh "with the knowledge of the Bangladeshi government" and that even RAW had a presence in Bangladesh.[108]

Acting on India's concerns, Bangladesh did ban a militant outfit, the Shahdat-e-al-Hikma, which was being funded by the Karachi-based Dawood Ibrahim.[109]

The process of dialogue was kept going between the two countries. The Bangladesh Foreign Minister asserted at the beginning of the year that Dhaka would "fully engage in a constructive dialogue" with India. The visits of the respective Foreign Ministers, talks on the border issues, on trade and economic concerns, and over the sharing of the waters of the border rivers constituted the effort of both countries to address areas of concern. India shares the waters of 54 rivers with Bangladesh. India maintained that its plan of interlinking of rivers was only at a "conceptual stage" and that Bangladesh had nothing to worry about the project. Bangladesh expressed concern as it was a lower riparian country and contended that any plan to link the rivers would hit it adversely.[110]

India-Bangladesh trade relations were also subject to the insecurities surrounding other aspects of their bilateral relationship. Bangladesh had not taken any decision on the supply of gas and oil, that it has in abundance, to the region's biggest market. Bangladesh had a trade deficit of $1 billion with India. It wanted India to open its borders for six months on "an experimental basis as a way of redressing the trade imbalance.[111] India had meanwhile proposed a Free Trade Arrangement (FTA) with Bangladesh, after experiencing its success with Sri Lanka. The first round of talks on the FTA was held from 20-22 October, where the issues relating to time-frame, rules of origin, and negative lists, among others, were discussed.[112] When the Minister for External Affairs, Yashwant Sinha, met the Bangladesh Prime Minister Khaleda Zia in July, both the countries decided to increase cooperation in the fields of Science and Technology (S&T), Information Technology (IT), agriculture, and in the management of natural disasters.[113]

The United States was also not happy with the Bangladeshi territory becoming a haven for international terrorists.[114] There were reports that terrorists of the Jemaah Islamia (JI) of Indonesia were being provided safe houses in Dhaka.[115] Washington even included Bangladesh in a list of countries that would face stricter immigration control. Following the action of the Royal Bhutan Army (RBA) in flushing out anti-India insurgents from its territory, India expressed the hope that Bangladesh would follow suit.[116]

Domestically, the government of Begum Khaleda Zia completed two years in power. She called upon all the political parties to come to a consensus on democratic norms and principles, on the development strategy, and foreign and defence policies. Leader of the Opposition Sheikh Hasina termed the ruling government as a "corrupt, terrorist, and oppressive regime".[117]

Sri Lanka

The year began with the promise that a solution to the intractable ethnic problem troubling the island nation would be found with the fourth round of peace talks between the Sri Lankan government and the Liberation Tigers of Tamil Eelam (LTTE), being held from 6-9 January in Thailand.[118] The talks hit a roadblock over the sensitive issue of demilitarizing the High Security Zones in northern Jaffna peninsula. The government insisted that unless there was complete and verifiable de-commissioning of arms by the LTTE, it would not be in a position to withdraw its forces from the area. The talks, which started with the ceasefire agreement of 22 February 2002, were by themselves a step forward in that the rebels agreed to put aside their demand for a separate "Eelam" and find a formula to share power under a federal administrative set-up.

However, the LTTE unilaterally pulled out of the peace process on 21 April 2003. On the Wickremasinghe government's proposals for an interim administrative structure put forward in the last week of May, the LTTE countered that it wanted an "innovative administrative structure, vested with adequate authority and legal status having greater participation in decision-making, rebuilding the war-damaged economy, and restoring normalcy in the Tamil-speaking homeland."[119]

The government offered the LTTE a fresh set of proposals on 17 July. In these, the government offered the LTTE a provisional administrative structure, a "development-oriented structure", but without power to collect revenue, and no authority over law and order.[120] After much deliberation within the organization itself and with other Tamil groups, the LTTE put forward its counter proposals on 31 October. The LTTE proposed the setting up of an Interim Self-Governing Authority (ISGA), which would have power over the subjects of revenue, land, and law and order, areas over which the July proposals of the government had not given the LTTE control.[121]

In effect, the LTTE wanted complete control over the affairs of the Tamil-dominated North-East. They also wanted power over marine resources, which would imply access to the seas and authority to maintain a navy (the Sea Tigers), authority to engage in external economic relations, and full administrative powers for the Tamil majority of the North-East, among other demands.[122] They also wanted access to close to $2 billion that was pledged at the Tokyo Donors Conference in June, a conference that the LTTE had boycotted. Prime Minister Wickremasinghe asserted that there was "nothing federal" about the LTTE proposals.[123]

President Kumaratunga had her apprehensions about the peace process entered with the LTTE by the Wickremasinghe government. She held that the LTTE was using the cover of the peace process to increase its numbers and rearm.[124] It was reported that the LTTE had increased its cadre strength from around 9000 before the ceasefire to about 19,000 after the ceasefire.[125]

President Kumaratunga's disagreement with the Wickremasinghe government was precipitated by her action in dismissing the Ministers of Defence, Interior, and Mass Communication, and proroguing Parliament on 4 November.[126] The President even declared a "short-term emergency" and asserted that the "sovereignty, territorial integrity, and unity of Sri Lanka" was not negotiable.[127] She even proposed the coming together of political parties to form a "National Government of Reconstruction and Reconciliation".[128]

The Wickremasinghe government, in its turn, held that it would not be possible to "accept responsibility" for the peace process without having authority over the defence and media portfolios.[129] The political uncertainty provided the LTTE another opportunity to state its lack of confidence in the Sinhala political leadership.[130]

India held a consistent position that a solution to the Sri Lankan problem had to be found without compromising the territorial unity and integrity of the island nation. The LTTE proposals differed fundamentally from not only what the Sri Lankan government had offered them but also from the stated positions of the Indian government.[131] India and Sri Lanka issued a joint statement after the conclusion of the visit of Prime Minister Wickremasinghe to New Delhi in the third week of October. New Delhi stated that it was in favour of a "negotiated settlement acceptable to all sections of Sri Lankan society within the framework of a united Sri Lanka and consistent with democracy, pluralism, and respect for individual rights."[132] The LTTE on its part maintained that it would not in any way "act prejudicial to India's geopolitical, strategic, and economic interests."[133]

India also took steps to strengthen the hands of the Sri Lankan government. During the visit of Prime Minister Wickremasinghe, the two countries agreed to increase their defence cooperation. Commercial relations were robust following the successful working of the Free Trade Agreement (FTA). Bilateral trade had crossed $1 billion in the year 2001-2. Both countries were working out the modalities of a Comprehensive Economic Partnership Agreement (CEPA), an FTA+ arrangement that would include, besides other sectors of economic cooperation, the services and investment sectors. The two Prime Ministers directed their officials to conclude a CEPA by 31 March 2004.[134]

India was also the third largest investor in Sri Lanka with approved investments totalling $392 million.[135] During the visit of the Minister for External Affairs, Yashwant Sinha, to Colombo to participate in the Fifth Indo-Sri Lanka Joint Commission meeting, India decided to release an amount of $30 million as a second tranche of a $100 million line of credit, which it had committed to rebuild the country.[136] Talking to newspersons, Mr. Sinha stated that the Indian government was pursuing the extradition of the LTTE chief Prabhakaran through "legal and diplomatic channels".[137]

The year also saw the Indian Oil Corporation (IOC) take over the oil tanks of the China Bay Oil Farm in Trincomalee. The step fulfilled a provision of the Indo-Sri Lanka accord of 1987. IOC was also expected to invest $100 million to develop the energy infrastructure of the island nation.[138] In order to sidestep the objections of the Tamil Nadu government to a Colombo-Tuticorin ferry service, Mr. Wickremasinghe proposed a Colombo-Kochi service.

Bhutan

The crackdown by the Royal Bhutan Army (RBA) on the militant infrastructure operating from Bhutan's territory against India was the dominating event in the Indo-Bhutanese relationship during the year. The Government of Bhutan cracked down on the militants after repeated requests/warnings from the Government of India to do so.[139] India could convince Bhutan of the nuisance being posed by these outfits to it as well as the dangers to Bhutan's unity and territorial integrity itself. More importantly for the Drukpa monarchy, these groups were developing organic linkages with groups like the Bhutan Communist Party (BCP), which were against the monarchy.

After six years of negotiations, the latest of which were held in the months of October and November 2003, the Bhutanese government launched "Operation All-Clear" on the morning of 15 December to smash the militant infrastructure. The militant groups targeted by the RBA included the United Liberation Front of Asom (ULFA), fighting for a separate homeland in Assam, the National Democratic Front of Bodoland (NDFB), a militant outfit fighting for a separate 'Bodoland' north of the Brahmaputra river, and the Kamtapur Liberation Organization (KLO), fighting for a separate 'Kamtapur' state encompassing north Bengal and some parts of Assam. The ULFA reportedly had 13 camps, NDFB 12, and the KLO 5 camps. These camps were being operated for more than a decade in the southern districts of Samtse, Kalikhala, Sarpang, Nganglam, Samdrup Jongkhar, Bhangtar, and Daifam.[140]

There were reports that the top-rung leadership of these organizations had an inkling of the impending action and had fled the country to Nepal and Bangladesh. However, the operation succeeded in destroying the central headquarters of ULFA at Phukaptong in Samdrup Jongkhar district, its general headquarters at Merengphu in the same district, NDFB camps in Tikri, Samdrup Jongkhar and Nganglam, and KLO camps in Samtse. The operation also resulted in the death, surrender, or capture of over 150 militants. The leaders captured included the publicity secretary of ULFA, Mithinga Daimary, and KLO leaders Tom Adhikari and Milton Barman.[141]

The Cabinet Committee on Security (CCS) meeting in New Delhi on 19 December appreciated the role of the Royal Bhutan Army in carrying out the operation.[142] There was much speculation about the actual role played by the Indian Army in the RBA action. The Indian Chief of Army Staff asserted that the role of the Indian Army was limited to sealing off the international border with Bhutan. There were reports, however, of the Indian Army providing logistical support to the 6,000-strong RBA and of Indian Army helicopters transporting the injured Bhutanese soldiers to hospitals.[143]

The militant outfits declared a 48-hour bandh from 19 December and ordered Bhutanese nationals living in Assam and Bengal to quit the states or face dire consequences.[144] Reports noted the killing of two Bhutanese businessmen at Bijni in Bongaigaon district of Assam. ULFA 'Chairman' Arabinda Rajkhowa appealed to the Government of Bhutan to halt the operations and requested the Chinese to permit the fleeing fighters to enter the country. Bhutan, however, rejected the appeal.[145]

India and Bhutan also signed an MoU for the 870 MW Punatsangchu hydroelectric power project during the visit of the King of Bhutan Jigme Singye Wangchuk to India in September.[146] Prior to the King's visit, the Indian government approved of an aid amounting to Rs. 1,464 crore to Bhutan and designated as 'non-plan' expenditure for the Ministry of External Affairs.[147] The King also requested Indian help to draft his country's constitution that would be "indigenous" and "beneficial" to the Bhutanese people.[148]

Major Regional Developments

East Asia

The North Korean missile standoff continued to remain grim, with repeated acts of brinkmanship by Pyongyang that included missile tests on three occasions (24 February, 10 March, 21 October) and the scrapping of the 1992 Agreement with South Korea meant to keep the Korean Peninsula free of nuclear weapons. In early April, however, multilateral efforts at bringing Pyongyang to the negotiating table paid off, with North Korea shifting its position from an insistence on purely bilateral negotiations with the US to a stated willingness to consider "other formats of dialogue". This eventually translated into acceptance of the "six-way proposal" by Pyongyang. The six-party talks began in Beijing on 27 August, with China setting the tone as both the host and the chief interlocutor. However, no conclusive formula was worked out and the six nations decided to meet again within two months.

North Korean Deputy Foreign Minister Kim Yong Il's statement on 29 August that his country may test an atomic bomb in the near future to prove its nuclear capability clouded the possibility of a breakthrough at future talks.[149] On 2 October the North Korean Vice-Foreign Minister, Choe Su-Hon, was quoted as saying that Pyongyang was not interested in attending any more six-party talks. A few weeks later, on 20 October, after it test-fired a ground-to-ship missile, North Korea again reiterated that it was determined to strengthen its nuclear deterrent force.[150]

In late October, prospects to rein in North Korea again brightened with reports that North Korea was willing to consider the US offer of written security assurances in exchange for its weapon programme.[151] In December, North Korea offered to freeze its nuclear weapon programme if the US lifted economic sanctions, provided fuel aid and removed its name from the list of state sponsors of terrorism.[152] Meanwhile the US, although saying that the proposals were "steps in the direction", held back from calling them as 'breakthroughs' and continued attempts at bringing the major powers in North-East Asia together to thrash out an agreement to pave the way for a second round of six-party talks.

South East Asia

India's engagement with the nations of South East Asia focused on cementing the already burgeoning ties in economic and security-related areas. Significant during the year were the three accords, a framework agreement towards a free trade area by 2011, a joint declaration against terrorism and New Delhi's accession to the ASEAN Treaty of Amity and Cooperation (TAC), signed between India and the Association of South East Asian Nations (ASEAN) during their second summit in Bali, Indonesia, on 8 October. On the sidelines of the summit, the Indian leadership was also able to meet individual heads of government of ASEAN. While terrorism featured in most of the discussions, enhancing security through greater economic interaction constituted the essence of the meetings.

India raised the question of terrorism in South Asia and pushed for bigger trade and economic exchanges during meetings with the South Korean President, Roh Moo-Hyun and the Vietnamese Prime Minister, Phan Van Khai. Prime Minister Vajpayee also met the Philippines President Gloria Macapagal and discussed the possibilities of cooperation between the two in combating terrorism through the exchange of information and speeding up the signing of the mutual extradition treaty that was already underway. With Thailand, the signing of the Framework Agreement on Free Trade Area on 9 October was a significant development.[153] It may be also be noted that earlier in January, India and Thailand had identified the areas of extradition, mutual legal assistance on criminal matters, joint work on security issues and the drive against narcotics as broad areas for cooperation to address their security concerns.[154]

India's distaste for doing business with an undemocratic Myanmar was less evident, as was indicated by the number of official-level visits during the year. High-level visits included those of the Indian Naval Chief, Admiral Madhvendra Singh, Telecommunications Minister, Arun Shourie, and Vice-President, Bhairon Singh Shekhawat.[155]

India did announce that it was closely watching "with concern" the "recent developments" in Myanmar, referring to the detention of the National League for Democracy (NLD) leader Aung San Suu Kyi on 30 May. Suu Kyi had been arrested following bloody clashes between her, followers and groups opposed to her, in which four persons were killed and 50 injured. The Nobel laureate's detention had brought in criticism from all quarters, including ASEAN.

The declaration of intent on the India-Singapore Comprehensive Economic Cooperation Agreement calling for liberal trade ties was signed on 8 April during the visit of Singapore Prime Minister Goh Chok Tong to India. The agreements to fashion a legal framework for India's anti-terror cooperation with Indonesia, the move to enhance the security-related coordination between their defence forces and a proposal to take new initiatives for mutual benefit in the energy sector on 1 September at the first ever Joint Commission meeting in Jakarta may be seen within the focus of India's "Look East" policy.

Central Asia

Major powers vying for a stake in oil- and gas-rich Central Asia have rendered the region a hotbed of power politics, with serious security implications. In what has been termed as the "new big game" in Central Asia, the US has been seen as attempting to entrench itself through the Baku-Ceyhan pipeline project through Georgia and Turkey, bypassing Russia. It is also trying to revive GUUAM, an economic and security group made up of five former Soviet states, Georgia, Ukraine, Uzbekistan, Azerbaijan and Moldova. Russia, meanwhile, responded to the US moves by boosting its military presence and building multilateral security structures. These included the transformation of the ten-year old Collective Security Treaty into a full-fledged regional defence pact.[156] China also pledged to convert the Shanghai Cooperation Organization (SCO) into a full-fledged regional security body by the end of 2003.

India's policy thrust in Central Asia must be seen in this context. The new initiatives included India's promise to actively participate in building the trans-Afghanistan road and rail links between Uzbekistan's Termez and Iran's Chahbahar Port in the Gulf, stationing of troops and air platforms in Ayni, 10 km from the Tajik capital, and setting up of a joint working group on counter-terrorism with Tajikistan. India also reached out to Kyrgyzstan and Uzbekistan for meaningful dialogue and partnership. The statement of the Minister for External Affairs, Yashwant Sinha, that the region constituted India's extended neighbourhood, exemplified the significance of the strategically important region both in economic and security terms.[157]

West Asia

Israel

The Israeli Cabinet on 25 May endorsed a new internationally brokered "road map" for peace, brightening the hopes of an end to the Israeli-Palestinian conflict.[158] This endorsement entailed an acceptance in principle of the creation of an independent Palestinian state by 2005. The peace plan, initiated by the US and backed by Russia, the European Union and the United Nations, envisaged the independent state on condition that suicide attacks on Israeli civilians end. With Israeli Prime Minister Ariel Sharon and the Palestinian leader Mahmoud Abbas politically backing the peace plan, the stage was set for the cessation of violence and the resumption of the stalled dialogue.

A few weeks into the peace initiative, however, Israeli helicopters fired missiles at a car carrying Abdel Aziz Rantisi, a senior Hamas leader, wounding him and killing his bodyguard and a bystander. In a retaliatory attack in Jerusalem on 11 July, a Palestinian suicide bomber killed 16 persons and injured 70 others in an attack on a bus. Even as both parties attempted to salvage the peace process, it became evident that the road to peace was not going to be easy.

India consolidated its strategic ties with Israel on the occasion of the visit of the Israeli Prime Minister, Ariel Sharon, on 9-10 September. The visit was a landmark event in the context of the common threat of terrorism faced by the two "embattled democracies". In the joint statement issued at the end of the visit, Israel offered all "material" support to destroy the roots of terrorism. This included specialized surveillance equipment, training of personnel, cooperation in intelligence gathering, joint exercises and cooperation to stop money laundering and terror funding.[159]

The discussions between the two delegations centred on defence cooperation, including the sale of "Phalcon" early warning radars worth nearly $2 billion, which had been recently cleared by the United States.[160] In fact, Israel was believed to have offered to India the integrated defence system comprising Greenpine and Phalcon radars and the Arrow Missile Defence.[161] Other items discussed were co-production of unmanned aerial vehicles (UAV) and installation of electronic warfare systems.[162]

South West Asia

Iran

The United States' accusations against Iran that Tehran was secretly attempting to build a nuclear bomb, that it was supporting international terrorism by giving haven to top al-Qaeda leaders and was attempting to destabilize Iraq in the post-US occupation period by positioning a pro-Tehran Shia regime gave indications that the United States' next target, after Iraq, could possibly be Iran.[163] With pressure mounting on Iran both from the US and the international community and the 31 October deadline given to open up its nuclear facilities for inspection, Iran relented in September by allowing UN inspectors to examine thousands of imported uranium enrichment machinery parts.[164] The IAEA, on 11 November, in a 29-page report gave a clean chit to Iran saying that there was "no evidence" so far that Iran sought to build a nuclear bomb.[165] The US, however, declared that it was not convinced and contended that the nuclear ambitions of Iran could not be dismissed.

Iran's strategic importance to the US was evident by the fact that it was the neighbour of Iraq and Afghanistan, the locale of the United States' most important post-Cold War engagements. Some observers felt that the country, branded an "axis of evil" state by the US, could very well be the next hot spot of superpower engagement.[166]

Afghanistan

With efforts to reintegrate all the regions of Afghanistan making no significant headway, the country continues to be a mess of war-lord-dominated enclaves hostile to one another. Until late 2003, the national army was yet to take shape and communication facilities yet to be put in place, making it difficult for the government to make inroads into interior regions. President Hamid Karzai's influence was also seen as being not allowed to stretch to provinces outside of Kabul.[167]

Meanwhile, in late August the US introduced Provincial

Reconstruction Teams (PRT) comprising Special Forces and aid officials to penetrate all provincial capitals. It was also announced in early October that NATO, which was recently made responsible for the International Security Force in Kabul, would soon move to other areas in the interior.[168] Despite these efforts, there were fears that provincial warlords, who had already been complaining that they had only a "modest stake" in the political and economic reconstruction process, might not be too keen to welcome the new intrusion.

India's relations with Afghanistan saw an upward trend during the year. From a modest participation in aid and relief materials, India contributed towards the creation of the Afghan army by supplying vehicles and equipment and training of the forces.[169] India also signed a Preferential Trade Agreement with Afghanistan and pledged a grant of $70 million for the Zaranj-Dilaram road project.

SAARC

What may be termed as a positive development in SAARC distinct from the perennial India-Pakistan squabbling was the engagement of the member countries in trade negotiations that had reached the fourth round during 2003 after the coming into force of the SAARC Preferential Trade Agreement (SAPTA).[170] This raised hopes that the proposed South Asian Free Trade Area (SAFTA) was on track and could be negotiated particularly during the 12th SAARC Summit that was to be held in January 2004. Economic cooperation has been seen as one of the most important ways to rescue SAARC from the political muddle. An Additional Protocol to the SAARC Convention on Terrorism was also most likely to be negotiated and added to the agreements during the January Summit in Islamabad. However, the future of the protocol remained uncertain until the end of December, with serious differences between India and Pakistan on the "definition of what constitutes terrorism".[171]

The 12th SAARC Summit was held in Islamabad in January 2004 amidst positive developments such as the approval of the draft SAFTA framework treaty as well as an additional protocol to the existing regional convention on the suppression of terrorism. At the opening session, a positive note was also struck with the Indian Prime Minister, A.B. Vajpayee, and his Pakistani counterpart, Mir Zafarullah Khan

Jamali, avoiding mentioning contentious issues such as the Kashmir dispute or cross-border terrorism.

Africa and Latin America

The formation of the "Trilateral Commission" in June 2003 under the India-Brazil-South Africa (IBSA) Forum saw India's engagement with these major countries of Africa and Latin America reach new heights. The focus of the new tripartite cooperation included enhancing liberal trade ties, a common stand at multilateral forums such as WTO and advocating the three countries" positions as "natural candidates to enter the United Nations Security Council" as permanent members.[172] At the bilateral level too there were a number of diplomatic exchanges between the three. India hosted visits of delegations from both countries. On 16 October, India signed a number of agreements with South Africa, which included an extradition treaty, documents on defence cooperation and an accord on cultural cooperation.[173] A joint declaration between the Indian Prime Minister, A.B. Vajpayee, and the South African President, Thabo Mbeki the following day, also saw renewed efforts at fighting terrorism.

Conclusion

Despite the peace process started by Prime Minister Vajpayee in April 2003, Pakistan remained the most difficult area of conflict resolution. Much more would have to be done by India by way of ameliorating discontent in Kashmir and devising a suitable strategic response to Pakistan's machinations, to drive home the message that resort to terrorism can not help resolve the Kashmir problem.

India was pleased by China's declaration of intent that Sikkim would be recognized as part of India and the subsequent removal of Sikkim as an "independent country" from the official website of China's Foreign Ministry. However, despite the two rounds of talks between the special representatives of the Prime Ministers on the border question, China is perceived to be less active in the articulation of principles that should govern the resolution of the border question.

The strategic partnership with the United States acquired a much deeper and larger meaning through joint military exercises and a sustained dialogue on cooperation in defence and technology-related issues. The behind-the-scenes role played by the US in bringing India and Pakistan to the conference table was appreciated.

There was a deepening of strategic ties with France and Russia. India, France and Russia have more or less similar perceptions of the international situation and aim to work for a multipolar world. India has a highly valuable strategic relationship with Russia. The recent economic and military revival of Russia provides further scope for building on that relationship. France and India have tended to strengthen their relationship in the field of defence production. The future seems to hold promise in this direction.

In India's neighbourhood, Bhutan's cooperation in flushing out anti-India militants from its soil in December set a good example of how neighbours can handle common threats. But the Maoist insurgency in Nepal poses a complex challenge. Simplistic approaches like helping the Monarchy with arms and money may not lead to durable solutions.

Bangladesh has proved to be an enigmatic neighbour. Carving out a positive framework of relationship with Bangladesh on a host of issues and reducing its anti-Indian potential will require fresh and innovative approaches. Stagnation of Sri Lanka's peace process was a source of worry. India needs to develop a strong, consistent and consensual approach to the Sri Lankan conflict so that it is not taken unawares by the adverse fallout of this conflict on its own security interests.

On the whole, India needs to acquire greater economic and military clout and demonstrate a stronger political will to derive the best from the existing international environment.

Notes

1. "Resolution Calls for End to War", *The Hindu*, 9 April 2003.
2. Sridhar Krishnaswami, "We Would Have Liked to See Indian Troops in Iraq: Powell", *The Hindu*, 30 September 2003.
3. "Elders too Deplore War against Iraq", *Hindustan Times*, 10 April 2003.
4. Sridhar Krishnaswami, "Ending Infiltration into J & K is Our Key Goal:

Rocca", *The Hindu*, 22 March 2003.

5. Vir Sanghvi, "Bush, Vajpayee Walked Tightrope on Iraq, Terror", *Hindustan Times*, 26 September 2003.
6. S. Rajagopalan, "Sibal may Take up Aid Issue with US", *Hindustan Times*, 30 June 2003.
7. Idem, "Indo-US Defence Talks Begin", *Hindustan Times*, 7 August 2003; Sridhar Krishnaswami, "India, US to Step up Defence Cooperation", *The Hindu*, 9 August 2003.
8. Sridhar Krishnaswami, "US, India Close to Agreement on 'Trinity' ", *The Hindu*, 6 October 2003; Manoj Joshi, "Indo-US Ties Set to Take a Hi-Tech Flight", *Times of India*, 7 October 2003.
9. Sridhar Krishnaswami, " 'Grey Areas' in UN Resolution on Iraq: Sibal", *The Hindu*, 4 July 2003.
10. K. Subrahmanyam, "US Security Initiative", *Times of India*, 13 October 2003.
11. "Bush Promises a 'Moment of Truth', Saddam Ready", *Indian Express*, 17 March 2003.
12. Hasan Suroor, "Geoff Hoon Warns of Long War", *The Hindu*, 21 March 2003.
13. Vaiju Naravane, "France to Veto Resolution", *The Hindu*, 12 March 2003.
14. "Accord on EU Constitution", *The Hindu*, 14 June 2003.
15. Vaiju Naravane, "Italy to Push for Reference to Christianity in EU Statute", *The Hindu*, 3 October 2003.
16. Idem, "Deadlock Persists over Constitution", *The Hindu*, 13 December 2003; idem, "Talks Collapse over Voting Rights", *The Hindu*, 14 December 2003.
17. Vladimir Radyuhin, "Russia-NATO Defence Pact for Europe", *The Hindu*, 14 May 2003.
18. Amit Baruah, "India Included in G-8's 'Enlarged Dialogue' ", *The Hindu*, 7 May 2003.
19. "NATO Launches New Global Force", *Times of India*, 16 October 2003.
20. Vishal Thapar, "$2 Billion Airbus Deal with IA Sealed: France", *Hindustan Times*, 7 February 2003; Vaiju Naravane, "France for Strategic Ties with India: Raffarin", *The Hindu*, 3 February 2003.
21. Vishal Thapar, "France Favours Strong Military Ties with India", *Times of India*, 29 April 2003; "French Minister Asks India to Join Hands Against America", *Times of India*, 29 April 2003.
22. Sridhar Krishnaswami, "Chirac Backs India's Case for Council Seat", *The Hindu*, 25 September 2003.

23. Amit Baruah, “Ready for Dialogue on All Issues with Pakistan: PM”, *The Hindu*, 29 May 2003.
24. Rashmee Z. Ahmed, “Hawk Sale to India Worries UK's ‘Doves’ ”, *Times of India*, 5 September 2003.
25. “J and K Militants Have Outside Support”, *The Hindu*, 27 September 2003.
26. “Verbal War at India-EU Summit”, *Times of India*, 29 November 2003.
27. “Miller Invites Indian Investors”, *The Hindu*, 18 February 2003.
28. Ibid.
29. Saurabh Shukla, “India, EU in Space Partnership”, *Hindustan Times*, 17 November 2003.
30. “Russia's New Kyrgyz Base”, *Times of India*, 24 October 2003.
31. Vladimir Radyuhin, “Russia Boosts Strategic Arsenal”, *The Hindu*, 31 July 2003.
32. Idem, “Russia Builds Anti-Missile Defence Weapons”, *The Hindu*, 26 May 2003.
33. Idem, “Russia to Build Powerful Missile”, *The Hindu*, 23 December 2003.
34. Idem, “Russia Sees a Threat in US Presence in Republics”, *The Hindu*, 15 April 2003.
35. Idem, “A Mistake: Putin”, *The Hindu*, 21 March 2003.
36. Idem, “Pak. Abetting Taliban: Russian Minister”, *The Hindu*, 15 September 2003.
37. Amit Baruah, "Putin Calls up Vajpayee", *The Hindu*, 5 February 2003.
38. Dadan Upadhyay, "Vajpayee, Putin Sign Declaration on Global Terror", *Indian Express*, 13 November 2003.
39. Vladimir Radyuhin, "Russia's Priority for Economic Ties", *The Hindu*, 12 November 2003.
40. Vishal Thapar, “*Gorshkov* Deal Struck”, *Hindustan Times*, 3 December 2003.
41. “Ministry Clarifies on *Gorshkov* Deal”, *The Hindu*, 4 December 2003.
42. K.K. Katyal, “Beijing-Moscow-New Delhi Trialogue”, *The Hindu*, 22 September 2003.
43. P.S. Suryanarayana, “Role in Iraq under UN, US Auspices”, *The Hindu*, 20 July 2003.
44. Idem, “Japan Defers Dispatch of Troops”, *The Hindu*, 14 November 2003; idem, “Japan's SDF Team Leaves for Iraq”, *The Hindu*, 27 December 2003.
45. Amit Baruah, “India, Japan Close Partners, Says Kawaguchi”, *The Hindu*, 8 January 2003.

46. P.S. Suryanarayana, "India a Strategic Partner: Japan", *The Hindu*, 2 January 2003.
47. C. Raja Mohan, "India, Japan to Discuss N. Korea-Pak. Nuke Ties", *The Hindu*, 4 January 2003; P.S. Suryanarayana, "Japan to Work with India on Sri Lanka Peace", *The Hindu*, 5 January 2003; C. Raja Mohan, "India, Japan Launch Strategic Dialogue", *The Hindu*, 19 April 2003.
48. Sandeep Dikshit, "Japan May View Pak. Export of N-Tech 'Seriously' ", *The Hindu*, 3 May 2003.
49. C. Raja Mohan, "India, Japan Launch Strategic Dialogue", *The Hindu*, 19 April 2003.
50. "Japan Differs with India on 'Singapore Issues' ", *The Hindu*, 6 July 2003.
51. P.S. Suryanarayana, "China Puts Man in Space", *The Hindu*, 16 October 2003.
52. Idem, "China to Focus on Market Economics", *The Hindu*, 1 October 2003.
53. Idem, "NPC Panel Adopts Constitutional Changes", *The Hindu*, 29 December 2003.
54. Idem, "China Walks a Fine Line with US", *The Hindu*, 8 February 2003.
55. Idem, "China Calls for Dialogue with US", *The Hindu*, 10 January 2003.
56. Idem, "We Will Never Seek Hegemony: Wen Jiabao", *The Hindu*, 22 June 2003.
57. Manoj Joshi, "Walking the Talk on Sikkim", *Times of India*, 24 June 2003; Amit Baruah, "Accord on Opening Border Trade Through Sikkim", *The Hindu*, 24 June 2003.
58. Amit Baruah, "Sikkim No Longer an 'Independent Country' on Official Chinese Website", *The Hindu*, 9 October 2003.
59. Vir Sanghvi, "India, China Warm up to Each Other", *Hindustan Times*, 24 June 2003.
60. P.S. Suryanarayana, "India, China to Act in Concert on WTO Issues", *The Hindu*, 26 June 2003.
61. Idem, "Special Representatives to Address Border Issue", *The Hindu*, 25 June 2003.
62. Shishir Gupta, "Brajesh, Dai Push Limits for Early Border Solution", *Indian Express*, 24 October 2003.
63. "For George, It's Hindi-Chini Bhai Bhai Again", *Indian Express*, 22 April 2003; P.S. Suryanarayana, "India, China to Sustain Bilateral Cooperation", *The Hindu*, 22 April 2003; idem, "China for Expanding Defence Ties", *The Hindu*, 27 April 2003.

64. "India, China Joint Naval Exercises Soon", *The Hindu*, 28 June 2003; Vishal Thapar, "India-China Military Exercises on Cards", *Hindustan Times*, 1 July 2003.

65. P.S. Suryanarayana, "India, China Hold Naval Exercises", *The Hindu*, 7 November 2003.

66. Idem, "India, China to Step Up Counter-Terror Cooperation", *The Hindu*, 14 June 2003.

67. Rajat Pandit, "Fernandes to Visit China", *Times of India*, 2 April 2003.

68. Sudhi Ranjan Sen, "As PM Visited China, its Army Visited Arunachal", *Hindustan Times*, 24 July 2003; "India Confirms Chinese Transgression of LAC", *The Hindu*, 25 July 2003.

69. "Arunachal Pradesh Not Part of India, says Beijing", *The Hindu*, 26 July 2003.

70. "Differences Exist with China on Boundary Demarcation: PM", *The Hindu*, 1 August 2003.

71. B. Muralidhar Reddy, "Pak. Gets $891 Million Compensation", *The Hindu*, 9 March 2003.

72. S. Rajagopalan, "Bush Gives Musharraf $3 Billion, but No F-16s", *Hindustan Times*, 25 June 2003.

73. Chidanand Rajghatta, "Pak Has to Earn its $3 Billion Aid", *Times of India*, 26 June 2003.

74. B. Muralidhar Reddy, "Pak. Bans Renamed Militant Groups", *The Hindu*, 16 November 2003; idem, "Offices of Militant Units Sealed in Pakistan", *The Hindu*, 17 November 2003.

75. "Musharraf Helped Capture over 500 Terrorists, Says Bush", *The Hindu*, 26 June 2003.

76. "Islamists Ask Musharraf to Quit Army by Mid-August", *Times of India*, 22 May 2003; B. Muralidhar Reddy, "MMA Threatens 'Million March' ", *The Hindu*, 6 June 2003.

77. "India, Pak Tone Down Rhetoric", *Hindustan Times*, 19 April 2003.

78. Mohammad Shehzad, "Militant Ranks Swell under Gen's Nose", *Indian Express*, 26 July 2003; Press Trust of India, "ISI Reviving Terror Camps, Set to Push in 1600 Ultras", *Hindustan Times*, 29 September 2003.

79. "India Offers Pak 12 Steps to Peace", *Hindustan Times*, 23 October 2003; B. Muralidhar Reddy, "Pak Accepts Many CBMs, Attaches Riders to Others", *The Hindu*, 30 October 2003.

80. Saurabh Shukla, "India, Pak. Agree to Stop Shelling, Buy Time for Peace", *Hindustan Times*, 23 November 2003; Amit Baruah and Sandeep Dikshit, "Ceasefire in Place", *The Hindu*, 26 November 2003.

81. Sanjay Datta, "Pak Wants India in the Pipeline", *Times of India*, 22 July 2003.

82. "Indo-Pak Business Forum Launched", *Hindustan Times*, 15 September 2003.

83. Sridhar Krishnaswami, "Get over the Annual 'Itch' on Kashmir, India Tells Pak.", *The Hindu*, 24 September 2003.

84. S. Rajagopalan, "PM Trashes Pak's Peace Rhetoric", *Hindustan Times*, 26 Septemebr 2003.

85. Dadan Upadhyaya, "Pak. Helping Taliban Regroup: Russia", *Indian Express*, 16 September 2003; Press Trust of India, "Pak Minister Says Dawood has Base in Karachi", *Hindustan Times*, 22 September 2003; Chidanand Rajghatta, "Pak-Iran Nuke Links Out in the Open", *Times of India*, 28 September 2003; Joby Warrick, "Pak Hand in Iran N-Plan: UN Body", *Indian Express*, 28 September 2003.

86. Gargi Parsai, "Pak in a Much Worse Category", *The Hindu*, 10 April 2003.

87. B. Muralidhar Reddy, "Pakistan Test-fires N-capable Missile", *The Hindu*, 4 October 2003; idem, "Pakistan Conducts Another N-capable Missile Test", *The Hindu*, 9 October 2003; "Pak. Launches First Indigenous Submarine", *Times of India*, 13 December 2003.

88. Suman Pradhan, "Nepal to Hold Talks with Maoists Soon", *Times of India*, 31 January 2003.

89. Keshav Pradhan, "Nepal Maoists Offer Sihanouk-like Role to Monarch", *Hindustan Times*, 13 April 2003.

90. Idem, "Nepal Team for Rebel Talks", *Hindustan Times*, 17 April 2003.

91. Suman Pradhan, "Nepal Government Begins Talks with Maoists", *Times of India*, 28 April 2003.

92. Keshav Pradhan, "Nepal PM Steps Down", *Hindustan Times*, 31 May 2003.

93. "Nepal Dialogue Should be Based on Consensus", *The Hindu*, 31 January 2003; Amit Baruah, "Nepal Needs to be Transparent for Better Ties", *The Hindu*, 4 February 2003.

94. "Army Chief's Nepal Visit from Today", *Times of India*, 2 April 2003.

95. "India, Nepal to Strengthen Ties", *The Hindu*, 26 November 2003.

96. Keshav Pradhan, "Nepal Maoists Call off Truce", *Hindustan Times*, 28 August 2003; idem, "Nepal Re-brands Maoists as Terrorists", *Times of India*, 29 August 2003.

97. Suman Pradhan, "Nepal Maoists Attack Police Post, 38 Killed", *Times of India*, 12 October 2003; idem, "Fresh Maoist Violence Kills 63 in Nepal", *Times of India*, 14 October 2003.

98. "Nepal Maoists Say No to US Interference", *Times of India*, 1 April 2003.

99. "Maoists Allege US Plot", *The Hindu*, 3 November 2003; K.P.M. Basheer, "US Presence in Nepal a Threat to India", *The Hindu*, 30 November 2003.

100. Keshav Pradhan, "Nepal Maoists Resent US, Indian Role", *Hindustan Times*, 10 September 2003.

101. Suman Pradhan, "Maoists Issue 5-Day Ultimatum to Nepal Government", *Times of India*, 29 July 2003.

102. "India to Open Railway Link to Nepal", *The Hindu*, 9 November 2003.

103. "Nepal Will Not Allow Anti-India Activity", *The Hindu*, 22 December 2003.

104. Debasis Sarkar, "Bangla Border Tense, 213 Still Stranded", *Times of India*, 3 February 2003; "Bangla Migrants Go Back", *The Hindu*, 7 February 2003.

105. Chandan Nandy, "Bangla Migrants Pose Threat: IB", *Hindustan Times*, 7 November 2003.

106. "Bangladeshis to be Traced, Thrown Out", *Indian Express*, 8 January 2003.

107. "India Gives a Wanted List of 88 to Dhaka", *The Hindu*, 29 January 2003; Rajnish Sharma, "IC-814 Hijack Plot was Hatched in Dhaka", *Hindustan Times*, 28 October 2003.

108. Amit Baruah, "Illegal Immigration on Both Sides, Says Bangla Minister", *The Hindu*, 16 February 2003.

109. Bhavna Vij-Aurora, "Bangladesh Acts on India List, Bans Outfit", *Indian Express*, 18 February 2003.

110. Gargi Parsai, "Bangladesh Makes an Issue of India's River-linking Plans", *The Hindu*, 30 September 2003; Haroon Habib, "Khaleda Hopes for 'Acceptable Solution" to Water Issues", *The Hindu*, 12 October 2003.

111. Haroon Habib, "Dhaka Wants Delhi to Open Border", *The Hindu*, 24 May 2003.

112. "Indo-Bangla Trade Accord Soon", *The Hindu*, 29 October 2003.

113. Haroon Habib, "Khaleda Stresses Need to Reduce 'Trade Imbalance' ", *The Hindu*, 16 July 2003.

114. Idem, "US Action Sparks Panic in Bangladesh", *The Hindu*, 18 April 2003.

115. Chandan Nandy, "Indonesian Jehadis Get Refuge in Bangla", *Hindustan Times*, 31 March 2003.

116. "India Wants Similar Action from Dhaka", *Times of India*, 9 December 2003.

117. Haroon Habib, "Khaleda Hopes for 'Acceptable Solution' to Water Issues", *The Hindu*, 12 October 2003.

118. V.S. Sambandan, "Peace Process has Reached a Decisive Stage", *The Hindu*, 6 January 2003.
119. Idem, "LTTE Rejects Wickremasinghe Offer", *The Hindu*, 31 May 2003.
120. Idem, "Central Issue Not Addressed: LTTE", *The Hindu*, 5 June 2003.
121. Idem, "A Historic Document: LTTE", *The Hindu*, 1 November 2003.
122. Idem, "Proposals, Govt. Offer Differ in Fundamental Respect", *The Hindu*, 2 November 2003.
123. "Nothing Federal about This", *The Hindu*, 4 November 2003.
124. Amit Baruah, "Chandrika Conveys 'Concerns' about Peace Talks", *The Hindu*, 11 April 2004.
125. Iqbal Athas, "The LTTE and the 'KP' Factor", *The Hindu*, 15 October 2003.
126. V.S. Sambandan, "Chandrika Takes over Defence, Two Other Portfolios", *The Hindu*, 5 November 2003.
127. Idem, "Chandrika Declares 'Short-Term Emergency' ", *The Hindu*, 6 November 2003.
128. P.K. Balachandran, "Chandrika Proposes National Government", *Hindustan Times*, 8 November 2003.
129. V.S. Sambandan, "Ranil Govt. Says It is Not in a Position to Deal with the Peace Process", *The Hindu*, 10 November 2003.
130. Idem, "Tamils' Confidence Eroded: Prabhakaran' ", *The Hindu*, 14 November 2003; Press Trust of India, "Tigers Demand Guarantee of Truce, Political Stability", *Indian Express*, 14 November 2003.
131. See Iqbal Athas, "Implications of the LTTE Proposals", *The Hindu*, 3 November 2003.
132. Iqbal Athas, "The Unfolding Indian Role in Sri Lanka", *The Hindu*, 1 November 2003.
133. V.S. Sambandan, "LTTE Wants Radical Change in India's Attitude", *The Hindu*, 9 December 2003.
134. Amit Baruah, "India, Sri Lanka Talks Soon on Economic Agreement", *The Hindu*, 21 October 2003.
135. Idem, "Private Indian Airlines to be Allowed to Fly to Colombo", *The Hindu*, 22 October 2003.
136. V.S. Sambandan, "India Commits $30 Million to Colombo", *The Hindu*, 16 October 2003.
137. Idem, "India Pursuing LTTE Chief's Extradition", *The Hindu*, 16 October 2003.
138. "To Trincomalee at Last", *The Hindu*, 31 May 2003.
139. Pramit Pal Chaudhuri, "India Puts Bhutan on Notice", *Hindustan Times*,

30 March 2003.

140. "Bhutan Cracks down on Anti-India Militants", *The Hindu*, 16 December 2003; "Major Bhutan Offensive Against Militants", *Hindustan Times*, 16 December 2003.

141. "ULFA Central Command Captured in Bhutan", *The Hindu*, 17 December 2003; Jaydeep Majumdar and Rahul Karmakar, "ULFA HQ in Bhutan Smashed, 25 killed", *Hindustan Times*, 17 December 2003.

142. "Bhutan Has Set an Example for Dhaka: Govt.", *Times of India*, 20 December 2003.

143. PTI/HTC, "All 30 Insurgent Camps Smashed", *Hindustan Times*, 20 December 2003.

144. Rahul Karmakar, "Quit Assam: ULFA to Bhutanese", *Hindustan Times*, 21 December 2003.

145. "Bhutan Rejects ULFA's Ceasefire Call", *The Hindu*, 19 December 2003.

146. "Bhutan's Assurance on Tackling Militants", *The Hindu*, 17 September 2003.

147. Amit Baruah, "Bhutan King Arrives Tomorrow", *The Hindu*, 13 September 2003.

148. Saurabh Shukla, "Bhutan Seeks Help in Drafting Constitution", *Times of India*, 18 September 2003.

149. "North Korea May Hold Nuclear Test", *Hindustan Times*, 30 August 2003.

150. P.S. Suryanarayana, "North Korea Test-fires Ground-to-Ship Missile", *The Hindu*, 21 October 2003.

151. "N. Korea Contacts US on Nuke Talks", *Times of India*, 27 October 2003.

152. "North Korea Deal", *Hindustan Times*, 11 December 2003.

153. Kanwar Sandhu, "India, Thailand Sign Free Trade Agreement", *Hindustan Times*, 10 October 2003.

154. P.S. Suryanarayana, "India-Thailand Ready for Extradition Treaty", *The Hindu*, 1 February 2003.

155. C. Raja Mohan, "India Avoids Isolating Myanmar", *The Hindu*, 4 September 2003.

156. Vladimir Radyuhin, "The New Big Game in Central Asia", *The Hindu*, 18 July 2003.

157. Atul Aneja, "Central Asia is Our Extended Neighbourhood, says Sinha", *The Hindu*, 2 February 2003.

158. Idem, "Israel Approves Plan for Palestinian State by 2005", *The Hindu*, 26 May 2003.

159. "India, Israel Tie up to Combat Terror", *Hindustan Times*, 11 September

2003.

160. "India, Israel Seek to Peak Defence", *Indian Express*, 10 September 2003; "In Defence, Israel to Give Russia Run for its Money", *Times of India*, 10 September 2003.

161. "Tel Aviv Offers an Integrated Radar, Missile Defence System", *Hindustan Times*, 10 September 2003.

162. "India, Israel Discuss Defence Deals", *The Hindu*, 10 September 2003.

163. Atul Aneja, "Pressure Mounting on Iran", *The Hindu*, 31 May 2003.

164. "Iran Allows UN to Inspect Machinery", *Indian Express*, 29 October 2003.

165. Joby Warrick and Glenn Kessler, "UN Body's Clean Chit to Iran over Atomic Bomb Charges", *Indian Express*, 12 November 2003.

166. M.H. Ansari, "Iran after Iraq?", *The Hindu*, 25 June 2003.

167. M.K. Bhadrakumar, "Manipulating Afghanistan", *The Hindu*, 20 August 2003.

168. K.K. Katyal, "Multinational Force to Move to Interior Afghanistan", *The Hindu*, 12 October 2003.

169. Saurabh Shukla, "Afghan Army to Get Indian Equipment", *Hindustan Times*, 7 March 2003.

170. K.K. Katyal, "Saving SAARC", *The Hindu*, 16 October 2003.

171. Saurabh Shukla, "Terror Clause, Trade Deadlock Queer Pitch Before SAARC", *Hindustan Times*, 25 December 2003.

172. Amit Baruah, "India, Brazil, South Africa Natural Candidates for Security Council Seat", *The Hindu*, 22 October 2003.

173. "India, S. Africa Sign Extradition, Other Treaties", *Hindustan Times*, 17 October 2003.

Internal Security Situation

Satish Kumar

Introduction

In a vast and plural society like India, the internal security situation can never be said to be normal. The year 2003 was no exception. There was a definite improvement in atmospherics in both Jammu and Kashmir and the North East. Prime Minister Vajpayee's peace initiative taken in Srinagar in April facilitated the start of a dialogue between the central government and the All Party Hurriyat Conference (APHC). In the North East, the ceasefire with NSCN (IM) held and the level of violence remained low. But there was no real breakthrough on any of the basic issues. A detailed survey of these and other aspects of internal security is undertaken below.

Jammu and Kashmir

The situation in Jammu and Kashmir remained disturbed despite positive indications that the cumulative number of casualties (deaths) from terrorist violence was relatively low as compared to the preceding two years (2001 and 2002).[1] The most gruesome incident took place on 24 March when militants gunned down 24 Kashmiri Pandits in Nadimarg village, about 65 km from Srinagar. Although no organization came forward to claim responsibility for the killings, the police suspected that it could have been the handiwork of any of the three groups active in the area—Laskar-e-Toiba (LeT), Hizbul Mujahideen (HuM) or Jaish-e-Mohammad (JeM). It was also suspected that the reasons behind the attack could have been the killing of Abdul Majid Dar, a former commander of the Hum by unidentified gunmen at Sopore in north Kashmir the previous day, or an attempt by separatist elements to undo the peace effort initiated after the government of Mufti Mohammad Sayeed took office in 2002.[2] It may be noted that on 3 April the chief of Pakistan-based LeT, Hafiz Saeed, in an interview to a Pakistan weekly, the *Friday Times*, said that India "only understands the language of jihad. We have no choice but to respond by killing Hindus as they are killing Muslims."[3]

There were several incidents of attacks on police and army personnel. On 22 July, a group of three fidayeen terrorists attacked the camp of the Electrical and Mechanical Engineers at Tanda, near the border town of Akhnoor. Brigadier V.K. Govil and six soldiers were killed in the attack. Lt. Gen. Hari Prasad, Lt. Gen. T.P.S. Brar, Maj. Gen. T.K. Sapru, Maj. Gen. D. Khanna and Brig. Baldev Singh were all injured in the attack. Al-Shuhda Brigade, suspected to be a front organization of the LeT, claimed responsibility for the attack. Brig. S.C. Chopra, head of the Gulmarg-based High Altitude Warfare School, also nearly lost his life in a massive car bomb explosion at the Parimpora fruit and vegetable market in Srinagar on 6 September, triggered by the HuM. In a similar kind of attack on 15 August, 20 persons were injured in a grenade blast at a Special Operations Group camp at the Charar-e-Sharif area in central Kashmir. In other incidents of terrorist violence, nine policemen were killed on 16 March, and 12 Army jawans were killed on 29 June.

Revenge killings by terrorists targeted both army convoys and family members of security personnel. On 2 September, terrorists carried out a series of attacks on the security forces, killing 19 persons and injuring several others across Jammu and Kashmir reportedly in retaliation to the killing of Gazi Baba, Chief Commander (Operations) of the JeM. Earlier on 30 August, Gazi Baba, who was also allegedly the mastermind behind the 13 December 2001 attack on the Parliament building and the 1 October 2001 attack on the Jammu and Kashmir Assembly, had been killed in an encounter with the security forces in Noorbagh, a residential area in Srinagar. On 19 May, JeM cadres beheaded six members of an army staffer's family in Chowikan Kotedara village of Rajouri district in Jammu. The killing was reportedly in retaliation to the killing of JeM "Divisional Commander", Saifullah Shirazi, by the Army.

Several instances of attacks on government buildings were also reported. There was an attempt to storm the residence of the Chief Minister, Mufti Mohammad Sayeed on 17 October. Three persons, which included two Border Security Force (BSF) guards, were killed and four others were injured. On 26 April, a group of Fidayeen militants attempted to blow up the office of Radio Kashmir by detonating an explosives-laden car on the building. Two security personnel were killed and eight others injured. A BSF jawan was killed and nine others, including a BSF Deputy Inspector General (DIG) were injured as heavily armed members of Al Mansooren outfit made an attempt to storm the Bharat Sanchar Nigam Limited office (BSNL) building in Srinagar on 27 August. In a second attack on the building, on 28 October, a grenade was lobbed at the office, resulting in the killing of one person and injuring 37 others.

A pioneer of the counter-insurgency movement in J&K and Chairman of the Jammu Kashmir Awami League, Mohammed Yosuf, better known as Kuka Parrey, along with his two associates was gunned down in Hajin village in Baramullah district on 13 September. He was regarded as an important emblem of pro-Indian forces in the state. Attacks on public figures and those close to the government, especially in the recently initiated peace process were carried out. On 10 May, terrorists killed eight people including three Peoples Democratic Party leaders in Jammu and Kashmir hours after the Chief Minister Mufti Mohammad Sayeed appealed for a cease-fire.

As in previous years, attacks on pilgrims on their way to holy shrines in the state were carried out. Two powerful explosions (IED blasts) at Bal Ganga near Katra on 21 July killed seven pilgrims and injured 38 others on their way to the Vaishno Devi shrine. Authorities blamed the LeT for the attack. The two blasts reportedly took place in a span of ten minutes in a community kitchen owned by the late music baron Gulshan Kumar.

The peace initiatives, first by Mufti Mohammad Sayeed's government and subsequently by the Central government, on the occasion of the visit of Prime Minister Vajpayee to the state in April, captured a lot of attention during the year. Although the Centre, earlier in January, announced that it was in "no hurry to hold Jammu and Kashmir talks" because the first "priority" before holding any talks was tackling "Pakistan-sponsored terrorism" which had shown no signs of decline, it later in October said that it was ready for talks including with the All Party Hurriyat Conference (APHC).[4] The

APHC announced that it was ready for talks with the Centre although its initial response was cautious.

The Centre's decision to hold talks with the APHC was preceded by a couple of positive developments. The Prime Minister, A.B. Vajpayee's announcement of 18 April in Srinagar of the Centre's willingness to talk to the "people of Jammu and Kashmir" was followed up by the visit of the Centre's chief interlocutor, N.N. Vohra, to Kashmir. Vohra's attempt to bring in various groups into the peace process reportedly included "secret" parleys with separatist groups.[5] Another positive development in this regard was the replacement of APHC chairman Abdul Ghani Bhat by Moulvi Abbas Ansari, a moderate, on 12 July. This replacement was seen as a severe blow to the Islamic right and indicated a rejection of the leadership of the hardliner, Syed Ali Shah Geelani, within the conglomerate.[6]

Anti-dialogue forces in Jammu and Kashmir, however, made it clear that they were against any move by the APHC centrists to strike a deal. Armed groups such as the Jamait-ul-Mujahideen and the Hizbul Mujahideen threatened to kill anyone "walking away with the fruits of their jihad". The Geelani faction of the APHC and the Jammu and Kashmir Liberation Front (JKLF) also indicated that they would not allow any deal that betrayed the "secessionist" cause. The success of any dialogue in Kashmir was contingent on reining in of armed groups in Kashmir by Pakistan. Pakistan's continued support of such groups and indications that it would not allow a successful dialogue without its involvement created pessimistic speculations about the future of the talks. The arrest on 6 February of Anjum Zamrud Habib, an activist of the AHPC while she was coming out of the Pakistan High Commission in New Delhi allegedly after collecting Rs. 3 lakh for terrorist funding, was evidence enough that Pakistan's intentions were anything but questionable. The diary recovered from the lady reportedly revealed detailed disbursement details of amounts to be given to various terrorist organizations. Owing to this the APHC office in Delhi was closed by the government.

North East Insurgency

The North Eastern region saw a number of healthy developments during the year 2003. In what was considered a landmark meeting between the leaders of the National Socialist Council of Nagalim (Isaac-Muivah) and the Indian leadership in New Delhi on 11 January, the Naga leaders assured the government that there would be complete cessation of hostilities. After talks with the Prime Minister, A.B. Vajpayee, Deputy Prime Minister, L.K. Advani and Defence Minister, George Fernandes, the Naga leaders, Isaac Swu and Thuingaleng Muivah announced: "There will be no more fighting between Indians and Nagas. That is the understanding we have reached after our talks with Vajpayee and other top leaders."[7] This assurance by the Naga leaders was expected to result in relative peace in two major conflict-prone areas, Nagaland and the hill districts of Manipur. The Naga leaders also reportedly met different political parties, including Congress (I) president Sonia Gandhi.

Although no substantial agreement was reached during the ten-day talks, many observers agreed that a positive environment had been created for a political settlement of the long-standing Naga insurgency. Both sides had agreed that the peace dialogue would continue.[8] The main issue that remained to be settled was reportedly the demand of the Nagas for integration of all Naga-inhabited areas in the adjoining states of Manipur, Assam and Arunachal Pradesh into one administrative unit.[9] These states, however, made it clear that any settlement of the Naga issue should not affect their territories.[10] The strongest protests came in from Manipur where the Nagas inhabit four of the eight districts. It may be recalled that in July 2001, when the ceasefire agreement between the Central government and the NSCN (IM) was extended to Manipur, there were riots in Imphal, the state's capital, resulting in a number of deaths and burning of the state Assembly building. NSCN (IM)'s position, however, that there could be no settlement outside this framework, could very well derail the peace process and the resumption of armed hostilities.

The result of the 26 February elections to the Nagaland Assembly that dislodged the Congress (I) and installed the Democratic Alliance of Nagaland (DAN) government under the leadership of Neiphiu Rio was also seen as aiding the peace process.[11] Ex-Chief Minister and Congress (I) leader, S.C. Jamir, considered a hardliner, had consistently refused any peace dialogue with the NSCN (IM). He had argued that for any peace process to be successful the government had to talk to all Naga insurgent groups, including NSCN Khaplang group and the Naga National Council (NNC). He had also earlier announced that if Swu and Muivah entered Nagaland they would be arrested on charges pending in courts in Nagaland.

The peace attempts made it possible for the Prime Minister, A.B. Vajpayee, to pay a two-day visit to Nagaland on 27 October—the first by a head of the central government in several years. The visit was significant in the backdrop of the peace talks initiated by Delhi for two reasons. First, the Prime Minister was able to meet various public leaders, thus enhancing his image as a viable peace broker. Secondly, the pakage of Rs. 510 crore offered by the Prime Minister for infrastructure development, including the proposed creation of 25,000 jobs, was seen as a much-needed economic intervention for the infrastructure-starved state.

In Assam, the dissolution of the Bodo Liberation Tigers (BLT) and the installation of the Interim Executive Council of the Bodo Territorial Council (BTC), headed by Hagrama Basumatary (former Commander-in-Chief of the BLT), at the Kokhrajar District Sports Association stadium on 6 December, signalled the end of 17 years of armed struggle by the BLT.[12] The formation of a BTC in Assam was agreed upon between the government and the BLT on 10 February 2003 although the process had started back in February 1993.

The formation of the new political unit, however, did not go well with all parties. Non-Bodo people living within the proposed BTC argued that the agreement would benefit only the Bodo community in the ethnically mixed region comprising caste Hindu Assamese, the Adivasis and the immigrant Muslim communities. The Sanmilita Janagosthiya Sangram Samity (SJSS), the apex body of several non-Bodo organizations, called for a 100-hour bandh after the new Council assumed office. The National Democratic Front of Bodoland (NDFB), opposed to BLT, rejected the formation of the Council. They vowed to continue the struggle for an independent

Bodoland by attacking the "Indian occupational forces" and "foreign immigrants".[13]

The United Liberation Front of Asom (ULFA), on the other hand, were involved in several cases of attacks on security personnel and public utility facilities, including railway lines and oil installations. On 8 March, ULFA struck simultaneously at four places in Assam targeting oil installations and police posts. Two persons were killed and six injured. A tank containing 4500 kilolitres of oil was destroyed. A few days later on 16 March, six persons were killed and 50 injured when a truck carrying security personnel was attacked in Goalpara district of Assam. On 17 June again, a Major of the 14 Field Regiment of the Army was killed in an encounter with ULFA at Neogpara in Darrang district of Assam.

The situation in Tripura evoked serious concern during the year 2003 for the spate of killings of innocent people by the National Liberation Front of Tripura (NLFT) and the All Tripura Tiger Force (ATTF). In a bloody run-up to the elections, which was held on 26 February, cadres of the banned NLFT killed 11 supporters of the Communist Party of India (Marxist) in West Tripura's Bankim Nagar.[14] On 7 May, in another gruesome incident the NLFT butchered 31 non-tribals including eight children and six women and injured six others in the Moharcherr market area in West Tripura district. And on 14 August, hours before Independence Day, the All Tripura Tiger Force (ATTF) shot dead 18 persons and wounded 26 in Baralunga village in West Tripura district. All the victims were non-tribals and immigrants. In recent years, there has been a consistent attack on "outsiders" in the state.

On the morning of 15 December, Bhutan launched a massive offensive against militant camps belonging to the ULFA, NDFB and the Kamtapur Liberation Organization (KLO), along its 360 km border with India.[15] According to official reports from Bhutan, the ULFA headquarters complex at Phukaptong in Samdrup Jongkhar and its secondary headquarters at Merengphu were overrun. The NDFB's biggest camp in Tikri, another NDFB camp in Nganglam sub-district and KLO camps in Samtse district were also destroyed. A Bhutan Foreign Ministry statement said that of the 30 camps destroyed, 13 belonged to the ULFA, 12 to the NDFB and five to the KLO. Further, it was reported that during the operations, the Royal Bhutan Army (RBA) was able to capture top leaders of the organizations including Bhimkanta Burugohan, one of the founder leaders of the ULFA. The KLO suffered the most serious setback with the arrest of five of its most senior leaders, Joydeb Roy alias Tom Adhikari, Milton Burman alias Mihir Das, Sanjoy Adhikari, Bhim Dakua and Pabitra Sinha. During the operations, over 100 cadres of the various organizations were reportedly killed and over 500 captured and handed over to the Indian authorities.

The crackdown by Bhutan was seen as being extremely important for India in terms of the security of the North Eastern region. The India-Bhutan border was a preferred base for groups, particularly those operating in Assam and North Bengal, even though they had hideouts in Bangladesh and Myanmar. The crackdown not only secured this stretch of geo-strategic location but also assured India that Bhutan would not allow such activities in the future. It may be recalled that the National Security Adviser, Brajesh Mishra, had warned Bhutan in March 2003 to close down the militant camps. During the official visit of the King of Bhutan to India on 14-18 September, he had announced in New Delhi that Bhutan had already sent warnings to the various groups that a severe crackdown on the camps would follow if the groups did not disband their camps and the cadres left Bhutanese soil on their own. The December crackdown was seen as a follow-up of this warning.

The operation, that resulted in the capture of top leaders of the various organizations, the killing of a large number of their cadres and the destruction of their most important strongholds, reportedly severely demoralized not only these groups but other insurgent groups who had relied heavily on hideouts in the region. This also sent out strong signals of a similar crackdown in the future involving other neighbouring states. Meanwhile, there were reports that the groups were frantically trying to recover from the onslaught. The ULFA, for example, proposed peace talks in the aftermath of the crackdown, which the Centre rejected saying that the "proactive policy against the insurgents" would continue.[16] The "Chairman" of the ULFA,

Aurobindo Rajkhowa, was also reported to have approached China for "sanctuary and shelter" for all those affected, including the Arunachal Dragon Force (ADF), which had its camp in Bhutan.

On 18 December, the ULFA attacked a Central Reserve Police Force (CRPF) unit in Sibsagar district of Upper Assam seriously injuring two jawans, indicating the possibilities of increased attacks in retaliation to the crackdown and as an attempt to regroup. Meanwhile, Indian security forces were reportedly manning transit points to stop the groups' cadres from re-entering India or transiting to Myanmar or Bangladesh.

Communal Tension/Polarization

The communal scenario in the country remained a source of concern during the year 2003. The country was yet to recover from the mortifying experience of the Gujarat riots in the previous year—an event that had firmly polarized the Hindu and Muslim communities in the state. The Gujarat riots generated a severe form of insecurity and communal tension perceivable in a host of subsequent communal flare-ups in sensitive parts of the country even for minor reasons. On 6 January, an indefinite curfew was clamped on Lunawda town in Gujarat following communal violence that was triggered by reports of a Hindu girl eloping with a Muslim boy. Sensitive Godhra and Vadodara towns in Gujarat witnessed a series of avoidable "knee-jerk" incidents during the Holi and Muharram festivals in March in which police had to be called in and curfew imposed. Communal violence was also reported from Hyderabad, Bhopal, Kerala and other places. On 2 May in the area of Marad in Kozhikode district in Kerala violence erupted between the Hindu and Muslim communities in which nine people were killed and property worth about one crore rupees destroyed.

Post-Gujarat initiatives by the government, including police action and judicial rehabilitation were severely criticized by several political commentators as further widening the divide between the two communities in the long run.[17] On 27 June in the first judgement on the Godhra communal riots, all the 21 accused in the Best Bakery carnage, in which 12 persons were burnt alive, were acquitted and set free by the Vadodara fast-tract court citing "lack of evidence" after all the witnesses turned hostile. A month or so later, however, the key witness, Zahira Sheikh, in a press conference in Mumbai said that she had turned hostile and lied in court under pressure and threat and demanded that the case be reopened again outside Gujarat. (This has since been done under orders of the Supreme Court).

Communal harmony was also vitiated by the sustained determination of the Vishwa Hindu Parishad (VHP) to pursue the Ram temple agenda despite painful social and political costs. During the early part of 2003, the VHP went on record on several occasions saying that it would give a further "impetus to its Hindutva movement" by introducing more militancy into its activities.[18] The trishul diksha (distribution of the trishul) to the youth, it announced, was part of the campaign. On 22 February, in New Delhi, a nationwide agitation through dharnas and satyagrahas in support of the demand for the construction of the Ram temple at Ayodhya was announced at a VHP-led dharma sansad and a 27 March deadline was given to the Centre to decide to hand over the undisputed land to the Ram Janmabhoomi Nyas, failing which the organization(s) threatened militant agitation.

In an attempt to find a legal solution, on 5 March, the Lucknow Bench of the Allahabad High Court ordered the Archaeological Survey of India (ASI) to undertake excavations at the disputed site to ascertain whether a temple existed at the spot where the Babri Masjid was built. It may, however, be noted that on 10 March, VHP leader, Praveen Togadia, announced that the organization would not give up the claim on the disputed Masjid site in the event of the ASI excavation failing to establish the existence of a Hindu structure. By 15 June, the Court's deadline to the ASI for coming up with a final report, it was reported that the ASI had not yet been able to establish the evidence of a Hindu structure below the Mosque.[19]

On 1 July, the Sankaracharya of the Kanchi Kamakoti Peetam, Jayendra Saraswati, came up with a proposal to the Chairman of the All India Muslim Personal Law Board (AIMPLB), which envisaged "gifting" the disputed land in Ayodhya to the Hindus. The AIMPLB, however, not only firmly ruled out any bargain on the disputed land but also went on record saying that it looked upon the Acharya's proposals as "thinly veiled threats" to Muslims to submit and surrender themselves unconditionally to the demands of the Sangh Parivar.[20] The Board, on the other hand, was reported to have requested the government to involve itself in "sincere" negotiations and said that the scope for an "honourable" compromise still existed.[21]

According to observers, the above two issues, the inability of the ASI to come up with the physical basis for the construction of the temple and failure of the Sankaracharya's "negotiated" settlement resulted in "a new phase of adventurism" whereby the VHP vowed to take the campaign to the streets and pressure the government into enacting a law on Ayodhya.[22] This, they argued, was clearly a further hardening of stance by the VHP. It was also reported that VHP leader, Ashok Singhal, gave enough hints that the issue would be a major plank of the Sangh Parivar for the forthcoming elections. Meanwhile, the AIMPLB unambiguously stood by its previous statement that the Babri Masjid was the property of Allah and could not be alienated by sale, gift or otherwise. In answer, the VHP leader, Pravin Togadia, on 27 September, was reported to have told a meeting of the Bharatiya Janata Party Minority Morcha in New Delhi that Muslims must give up all claims to the disputed site in Ayodhya and if they did not do this, Ayodhya would be "taken by force" closing forever the possibility of Hindu-Muslim amity. This standoff between the two was expected to define the communal health of the country in the near future.

Left-wing Extremism

An in-house data reportedly generated by the Intelligence Bureau showed that while there had been a relative decline in the number of civilians killed in major theatres of violence in India during 2003, deaths due to left-wing extremist violence had on the other hand increased compared to the previous year.[23] While reports of the Naxalite violence had come in mainly from Andhra Pradesh, the problem, according to another report, was much larger and in the past couple of years spread to Maharashtra, Madhya Pradesh, Karnataka, Tamil Nadu and even to Kerala, Punjab, Delhi and Haryana.[24] This steady spread was also believed to be the result of the resurgent Maoist influence from neighbouring Nepal. It had been reported that a border committee comprising representatives of the People's War (PW), the Maoist Communist Centre (MCC) and the Communist Party of Nepal was formed and they were also earlier known to support each other.

The activities of these organizations included kidnapping, execution of people alleged to be criminals or police informers, attacks on police convoys, particularly through the use of landmines, assassination attempts and attack on banks and other public utility structures like railway stations and tracks. Some of the severest attacks on police personnel included the 15 April ambush by the MCC where eight policemen were killed on the Fatehpur-Govindpur Road of Nawada district in Bihar. In a similar attack on 30 July, 10 police personnel were killed in a landmine blast triggered by the PW in Orissa's Malkangiri district. And on another occasion 12 police personnel, all travelling in a jeep, were killed in a landmine blast triggered by Naxalites near Dabua Mod in Rohtas district of Bihar.

In many rural areas of Naxalite-affected states, the various organizations acted virtually like policemen, arresting, meting out "justice" and in some cases even executing the guilty. For example, on 8 February, the MCC executed three persons in Pipra Village in Gaya district of Bihar allegedly for committing crimes after being held guilty by a MCC "kangaroo court". Corrupt village leaders, political activists and others were targeted for colluding with the government in corrupt practices or for informing the police about the activities of the group. On 22 September cadres of the PW killed the Sarpanch of Ganthimarri village of Ramagiri Mandal in Anantapur district, Andhra Pradesh, on charges of being a police informer.

On 1 October, the PW attempted one of its most determined attacks when they targeted the Andhra Pradesh Chief Minister, Chandrababu Naidu. PW activists triggered a series of nine powerful claymore mines on the Tirumala Ghat road near Tirupati, the route that the Chief Minister's convoy was to take. The Chief Minister and his entourage had a providential escape. The incident, however, brought to the fore the growing reach of the Naxalite groups and their ability to penetrate even the most stringent of security cordons.

After the attack, in a statement by Ramakrishna, the Secretary of the State Communist Party of India (Marxist-Leninist) Committee of the People's War, said that "Chandrababu Naidu and the state police" were "enemies of the people" and "deserved to be eliminated".[25] The group also accused Mr. Naidu of being submissive to international funding agencies to whom the interests of the state had been mortgaged in utter disregard of the welfare of the people. It may be noted that the PW has issued death warrants against West Bengal Chief Minister, Buddhadeb Bhattacharjee and the former Chief Minister of Jharkhand, Babulal Marandi, for being "anti-people".

After the attacks, it was reported that Chief Minister Chandrababu Naidu called upon the Naxalites to lay down arms and join the mainstream. Secretary of the Nalgonda district unit of the PW, Naveen, however, speaking to a select group of journalists in the forests of Nallamala on 4 November, rejected the offer made by the Mr. Naidu and ruled out holding talks with the Andhra Pradesh government. He said that the PW had initiated talks three years earlier by announcing a unilateral ceasefire but the government had scuttled the talks and further talks would only "expose the hollowness of the government programmes".[26]

Corruption

Revelation of corrupt practices at the highest level shook the country again on several occasions during the year 2003. During January/February a planned operation of fraud and cheating in the results of the Karnataka Public Service Commission examination was uncovered in which ten candidates, the chief examiner and the then Secretary of the Commission were found involved.[27] Although impartial and transparent internal inquiry was conducted under the directions of the Karnataka High Court and prompt action was taken against the culprits, it was reported that public confidence in the institution was seriously affected. A host of scandals involving persons responsible for conducting examinations of various types were also uncovered during the year.

On 4 March, the Lok Sabha witnessed uproarious scenes over allegations that the Uttar Pradesh (UP) Chief Minister, Mayawati, had asked her party Members of Parliament to give to the party fund a percentage of the "commission" they got on works done by spending the constituency fund of Rs. 2 crore. Although the UP government denied the accusation, reports indicated that such a demand had been made. A few weeks later, on 27 March, in a major corruption case, the Central Bureau of Investigation (CBI) unearthed a major scam involving the Delhi Development Authority (DDA). In subsequent raids, a total of Rs. 43.7 lakh was recovered from senior officials of the DDA and on 3 April the CBI arrested the Vice-Chairman of the DDA, Subhash Sharma, on the charge of abusing his official position and taking bribe for showing favours to a construction company and a private school. The official was later removed from office. The scam also saw the arrest of a former Delhi High Court Judge, Shameet Mukherjee, on 30 April for his alleged role in the DDA corruption scam. Mr. Mukherjee had resigned as judge a month before the scam came to light.

A host of other corruption cases were also reported from various parts of the country. On 12 May, a senior Indian Administrative Officer belonging to the Jharkhand Cadre, Ashok Singh, was arrested on charges of corruption and abuse of power when he officiated as the Managing Director of the State Finance Corporation. On the same day in Chandigarh, Punjab, a judicial magistrate (first class), S.S Bhardwaj, and a district and sessions judge, R.M. Gupta, were arrested by the CBI for accepting a bribe from a litigant and in Hyderabad, the axe fell on 55 persons including 19 former Directors of the Vasavi Cooperative Urban Bank for being involved in a scam. A few days later on 17 May, close on the heels of the arrest and detention of two judges in Punjab, two judges of the lower court in Patna, Bihar, were suspended for alleged dereliction of duty and showing undue favours in granting bail. On 24 May, the CBI unearthed a racket dealing in bogus non-judicial stamp papers worth Rs. 8 crore and postage stamps worth Rs. 25 lakh in Ahmedabad. In Orissa on 27 May, the Vigilance Department registered corruption cases against an IAS officer, Prafulla Chandra Mishra, for allegedly committing large-scale financial irregularities while he was Chairman-cum-Managing Director of the Orissa State Beverages Corporation. And in Nagaland on 3 July, the

CBI charge-sheeted former Union Minister for Urban Development, P.K. Thungon, for allegedly embezzling Rs. 50 lakh meant for developing irrigation facilities.

On 6 December, the Congress Party suspended the outgoing Chhattisgarh Chief Minister, Ajit Jogi, following allegations by the Bharatiya Janata Party (BJP) that he had attempted to bribe newly elected BJP Members of the Legislative Assembly (MLA) in Chhattisgarh to engineer a split in the party and prevent its government from taking office. The following day, Union Law Minister, Arun Jaitley, at a late night press conference in Raipur, played a tape purportedly containing the conversation of the deal and displayed currency to the tune of Rs. 45 lakh alleged to have been given to BJP members, Virendra Pandey and Balliram Kashyap. The case was subsequently handed over to the CBI and on 9 December, the CBI filed cases under the Prevention of Corruption Act against Mr. Jogi, his son Amit Jogi and Congress Member of Parliament, P.R. Kunte.

The Union government also suffered two serious cases of corruption during the year. On 22 May, a personal assistant of the Minister of State for Finance, Gingee Ramachandran, was arrested by the CBI while accepting a bribe from a senior Indian Revenue Service officer, Anurag Vardhan, for facilitating a posting of his choice. And on 17 November, the *Indian Express* exposed the Union Minister of State for Environment and Forests, Dilip Singh Judev, for accepting a bribe. The Minister was caught on camera accepting wads of money from an unknown person in return for favours to an Australian mining company. The government's handling of the "Judev episode" came in for severe criticism when it was alleged that the CBI had focused its investigation on the anonymous "bribe-giver" rather than the "taker".[28]

Anti-Dalit/Anti-Tribal

Caste prejudices in the country have often translated not only into physical attacks on the so-called "lower castes" but also attempts to forcibly appropriate the property of this group of people by vested interests. In a serious case of attack on tribals in a protected forest land at Muthanga in Wayanad district in Kerala, on 19 February, police clashed with the tribal population when they refused to leave the forest land after eviction orders.[29] Two tribal persons were killed and several were injured during the incident. On 27 April, it was reported by a Dalit organization that 200 Dalit families were evicted by members of the "upper castes" in Harsoula village in Haryana. In similar incidents, on 13 August, in an outbreak of caste violence, over 70 Dalits were injured when members of the Thakur community opened fire on them following a dispute over a piece of land at the Tejopur village in Mau district of Uttar Pradesh and on 2 October, the tribals of Pachwara Panchayat in Pakur district were up in arms protesting against the central government and the Jharkhand government and two business firms, which they alleged, were illegally seeking to usurp their land for coal mining.

Dalits and tribal population in many parts of the country, especially in rural areas, have been the targets of upper-caste people for various and often minor reasons. On 9 February, a Dalit woman and her son were beaten up by upper-caste men in a dispute over filling of drinking water from a public hand pump in Shivpuri, Madhya Pradesh. On 8 March, two Dalit youths were killed by persons belonging to an upper caste near Sattukheda near Aligarh allegedly for killing an upper caste man. And on 3 July two tribal women were burnt to death in public by the Mahuasosle and Auratand villagers in Godda district allegedly for practising witchcraft.

Punjab saw one of the most serious clashes between the upper castes and Dalits in recent years.[30] From April through October tension between Jat landlords and Dalits was simmering. The bone of contention had been a pond in the middle of Hasanpur village in Sangrur district. On 11 October, it exploded into violent clashes, first in Hasanpur and later in various parts of the state, in which one person was killed and 24 others, mostly Dalit women, were injured. Earlier in April, there had been clashes at Talhan in Jalandhar.

Anti-Minority Incidents

There was a sustained attack on minority communities, particularly Christians, during the year 2003. In total disregard for secular values, certain Hindu fundamentalist groups targeted leaders and institutions of the Christians in various parts of the country. In a serious case of minority-bashing, it was reported on 3 July that an Indian Administrative Service official in Kerala ordered a detailed study of churches and mosques in the state. Not only was this strongly condemned by the affected communities but it generated considerable tension among the minorities in the state. In a similar case, on 26 May, in disregard of the Gujarat High Court's orders, the Patan district police launched a survey of Christians and the institutions run by the community even as the state authorities denied issuing any such instructions. It may be noted that during the last couple of years, Christians had been at the receiving end in Gujarat.

Other serious cases included the 14 January attack on Joseph Cooper, an American missionary, and five others, seriously injuring them, by a ten-member gang of RSS activists at the Koppam Harijan colony in Thiruvananthapuram. They were attacked for allegedly "communally inflammatory" speeches that Cooper had made at a Christian convention. In similar attacks, on 8 June, the Hindu Jagran Manch and VHP youth wing activists disrupted a Christian religious meeting at St. John's College in Agra and on 21 November in Deogarh town in western Orissa, a church was attacked, a Catholic nun abused and the house of a preacher was ransacked by suspected VHP and Bajrang Dal activists.

Drug Trafficking

Various parts of the country have for long served as transit points for drug smugglers, especially those originating from the Golden Triangle in Myanmar and some regions in Afghanistan. Customs sleuths in Delhi made some of the biggest catches of drugs during the year 2003 and also uncovered some cases of nexus between certain government officials and drug smugglers. On 22 April, 16 kg of heroin packed in almond shells were recovered from a passenger who came in by an Ariana Afghan Airlines flight from Kabul at the Indira Gandhi International (IGI) airport. A total of 21.6 kg of high purity heroin was recovered from different parts of Delhi in a span of four days (25-29 August), which included recovery of 1.6 kg from the IGI airport from a Nigerian woman.

On 19 May, a former Additional Director of the CBI, U.N. Biswas, landed in a thick controversy when officials of the Narcotics Control Bureau recovered 24 kg of a psychotropic substance, used in the making of a heroin substitute and valued at Rs. 5 crore in the international market, from five foreigners staying with his tenants in Kolkata. Although, he denied any links with the arrested persons, this incident brought into serious focus other cases of nexus between government officials and drug smugglers.

Underworld Operations

Underworld dons have in the near past been able to direct most of their activities in India from their hideouts in neigh bouring states. These criminals have been able to get not only refuge but even state protection despite India's demand that they be handed over to face charges. Most of their activities have been financed by funds transacted through the Hawala route. For example, on 6 February, the Enforcement Directorate sleuths in Chennai uncovered a major Hawala operation running to nearly Rs. 100 crore run by Dubai-based Shareef and his counterpart C.K. Mustafa in Kozhikode. In a major blow to the police and the investigations in the Mumbai blast case, Dubai reportedly released associates of the underworld don, Dawood Ibrahim, including his brother Noora and others who were all accused in the Mumbai blasts and who were earlier taken into preventive custody.

Illegal Migration

Anti-migration sentiments, particularly in the North East, have for long been an important contributory factor to the rising ethnic tension in the region. Bangladeshi migrants on the look-out for economic opportunities, particularly in Assam, have put considerable demographic pressures on the local populace and of late clear signs of revolt against these migrants have become rampant. Despite efforts to control these illegal entries, it has not been possible for the authorities to check all the transit routes. Deputy Prime Minister

L.K. Advani, while addressing a conference of Chief Secretaries and Directors General of Police at New Delhi on 7 January, pointed out that there were 11,500 Pakistanis and half a crore Bangladeshis who had remained in India after the expiry of their visa.

Farmer Suicide Incidents

Suicide by farmers due to economic hardship has been a persistent reflection on the country's failure with regard to food security. In a report in *The Hindu* on 9 September, the Development Commissioner of the Karnataka government told presspersons that the government had received information about 208 cases of suicide by farmers since April 2003. The government had instituted an investigation after hearing reports that the farmers had killed themselves due to their inability to repay agricultural loans taken from the government. The official said that of the 156 cases taken up for investigation 93 cases were rejected while attempts to compensate were made in the genuine cases.

Political Kidnapping and Assassination

A few instances of kidnapping for ransom or political rivalry and political assassination attempts were reported. On 20 February, the Deputy General Manager of the Bharat Sanchar Nigam Limited (Manipur Branch) was kidnapped by suspected Kuki militants in Thoubal district of Manipur reportedly for ransom. And in a similar case on 26 March, the Vice-President of Bihar unit of the Nationalist Congress Party along with five of his associates were kidnapped for ransom by members of the Ramchandra Choudhary gang for ransom.

Former Gujarat Minister of State for Home and Revenue, Haren Pandya, whose differences with the Chief Minister, Narendra Modi, had cost him the BJP Assembly ticket was shot dead by unknown assailants on 26 March. While the government instituted an inquiry into the killing, commentators pointed out that the killing was motivated by political rivalry. On 4 July the Jammu and Kashmir Rural Development Panchayati Raj Minister, Peerzada Mohammed Sayeed, escaped an attempt on his life in Anantnag district allegedly by militants. One person was killed and 16 were injured in the attack.

Conclusion

In Jammu and Kashmir, even though the infiltration of militants from across the Line of Control (LoC) declined in some months, the level of violence remained high throughout the year. The presence of a large number of terrorists was also manifest throughout. The possibility of terrorists infiltrating into Kashmir from Nepal and Bangladesh could not be ruled out. There were also reports that the infrastructure of terrorism on the Pakistani side remained intact. The area south of the Peer Panjal range became the new focus of militancy. At the same time, India's security forces displayed greater efficiency in tackling terrorism. A number of prominent "commanders" were killed by security forces through better intelligence and coordination. Even though the APHC opened a dialogue with the Centre, it remained buffeted between the militants on one side and moderates on the other. Its support base remained narrow.

In the North East, the situation despite the ceasefire with the NSCN (IM) remained a matter of concern. The insurgency was getting criminalized. There was no real progress in resolving the Naga issue. The demand for "Greater Nagaland" had a destabilizing effect on neighbouring Manipur. A number of Khaplang supporters moved over to NSCN (IM) and Khaplang was somewhat isolated. ULFA continued to maintain its sanctuaries in Bangladesh, which continued to deny their presence. The action of the Royal Bhutan Army in December weakened ULFA but did not crush it. Insurgent camps continued to exist in Myanmar. The links between insurgent groups in the North East and China also remained intact.

Violence emanating from left-wing extremism escalated but government agencies did not seem to appreciate the scale of the threat well enough. There was also evidence of growing links between Indian left-wing extremists and Maoists in Nepal. Socio-economic factors and governance issues causing left-wing violence need to be addressed urgently.

Illegal immigration from Bangladesh also continued to be a serious internal security threat. Bangladesh continued to deny the existence of such a problem. India's relations with Bangladesh need to improve considerably to safeguard India's security in the eastern sector.

Notes

1. See Union Ministry of Home Affairs, "Comparative Killings, 2001-2003", cited in Praveen Swami, "Peace and War", *Frontline*, Vol. 20, No. 23, 8-2 November 2003, p. 30.
2. See Praveen Swami, "The Nadimarg Outrage", *Frontline*, Vol. 20, No. 8, 12-25 April 2003, pp. 38-40. Also see "Militant Strikes Expose Govt's Vulnerability" *Hindustan Times*, 25 March 2003, p.13.
3. *Friday Times*, 11-17 April 2003, p. 5.
4. The decision was reportedly taken after a meeting of the Cabinet Committee on Security on 22 October chaired by the Prime Minister, A.B. Vajpayee. See "Delhi to Hold Talks with Hurriyat", *The Hindu*, 23 October 2003.
5. Vohra was reported to have met about 30 organizations and 117 individuals during his visit to the state in April. He also indicated that he had held talks with separatist groups secretly although he did not give out names. See "Vohra Hints at Secret Parleys", *Indian Express*, 30 April, 2003.
6. A detailed examination of this aspect has been done by Praveen Swami. See "The Battle Within", *Frontline*, Vol. 20, No. 15, 19 July - 1 August 2003, pp. 32-4.
7. See Kalyan Chaudhuri, "Promise of Peace", *Frontline*, Vol. 20, No. 2, 18-31 January 2003, p. 126.
8. The first meeting of the government negotiators and the Naga leaders after the Delhi talks was held in Bangkok on 23 May. See "Derailing the Naga Peace Process", *The Telegraph*, 23 May 2003.
9. See "Greater Nagaland the Key Issue", *The Hindu*, 26 January 2003.
10. For more details, see Kalyan Chaudhuri, "Territory Tussles", *Frontline*, Vol. 20, No. 4, 15-28 February 2003, pp. 45-7.
11. See for more details "A Few Reasons to Hope", *The Telegraph*, 18 March 2003.
12. See for details "Bodoland Council Sworn in", *The Hindu*, 8 December 2003.
13. During the past year, although the NDFB was involved only in one major incident of violence on 21 June in which four persons were killed, it may be noted that in 2002 between January and November, 89 people including security forces were killed by this militant group. See M.S. Prabhakara, "Another Round in Assam", *Frontline*, Vol. 19, No. 23, 9-22 November 2002, pp. 28-9.
14. For a detailed report on this, see Kalyan Chaudhuri, "In the Shadow of Violence", *Frontline*, Vol. 20, No. 4, 15-28 February 2003, p. 32.
15. For details see "Crackdown in Bhutan", *Frontline*, Vol. 21, No. 1, 3-16 January 2004, pp. 4-16.

16. See M.S. Prabhakara, "An ULFA Manoeuvre", *Frontline*, Vol. 21, No. 1, 3-16 January 2004, p. 9.
17. For example, see Dionne Bunsha, "Cases of Injustice", *Frontline*, Vol. 20, No. 15, 19 July - 1 August 2003, pp. 25-8.
18. See "Unconcealed Aggression", *The Hindu*, Wednesday, 8 January 2003.
19. For details, see Sukumar Muralidharan, "Excavating Truth", *Frontline*, Vol. 20, No. 15, 19 July-1 August 2003, pp. 8-9.
20. Purnima S. Tripathi, "A Failed Mission", *Frontline*, Vol. 20, No. 15, 19 July -1 August 2003, p. 11.
21. Ibid., p. 10.
22. For example, see Sukumar Muralidharan, "A New Phase of Adventurism", *Frontline*, Vol. 20, No. 15, 19 July -1 August 2003, pp. 4-8.
23. See Praveen Swami, "Fewer Terror Attacks, Yet Little to Cheer About", *The Hindu*, 31 December 2003. The total civilian deaths in Maoist violence during 2002 were 482 and the total deaths projected in 2003 were 488.
24. K. Srinivas Reddy, "Red Terror", *The Hindu*, 4 February 2003. Also see K. Srinivas Reddy, "Extremist Resurgence", *Frontline*, Vol. 20, No. 21, 11-24 October 2003, pp. 20-1.
25. For more details, see S. Nagesh Kumar, "A Blast and its Shock", *Frontline*, Vol. 20, No. 21, 11-24 October 2003, pp. 18-22.
26. K. Srinivas Reddy, "People's War Rules out Talks with A.P. Govt.", *The Hindu*, 6 November 2003.
27. For a detailed report on the case, see Parvathi Menon, "Marked Manipulation", *Frontline*, Vol. 20, No. 4, 15-28 February 2003, pp. 51-2.
28. See V. Venkatesan, "A Flawed Inquiry", *Frontline*, Vol. 20, No. 25, 6-19 December 2003, p. 33.
29. For a detailed story, see T.J. Rajalakshmi, "A Carnage and a Clean Chit", Vol. 20, No.1, 4-17 January 2003, pp. 41-2.
30. For the complete story, see Praveen Swami, "Growing Dalit Resistance", *Frontline*, Vol. 20, No. 25, 6-19 December 2003, pp. 45-6.

Defence Modernization: Higher Defence Management, Procurement and Equipment Issues

V.K. Kapoor

Introduction

Modernization of defence systems is a complex and time-consuming process. Its first prerequisite for success is a well-informed and visionary political leadership, quick to grasp national security issues and able to conceptualize a national security doctrine and convey clear strategic directions to the Armed Forces. Based on such political directions, future threats and likely strategic settings, the higher military leadership, in turn, envisions and evolves future war-fighting doctrines, military strategy, and long-term perspective plans of the three services. These provide the orientation and thrust to technological development and equipment procurement/production. The recommendations of the Group of Ministers (GOM) pointed out the deficiencies and weaknesses in the defence planning process, defence R&D, defence acquisition process, synchronization between the departments of the Ministry of Defence (MOD) and the functioning of the Chiefs of Staff Committee (COSC)[1] and made certain specific recommendations at the macro level on each of these issues.

Regarding the defence modernization and planning process, the GOM recommended (a) the establishment of a Chief of Defence Staff (CDS) and a Vice Chief of Defence Staff (VCDS), (b) the integration of Service headquarters into the Government, (c) enhancement of "joint-ness" in the Armed Forces, (d) the creation of a Defence Procurement Board, (e) the preparation of an integrated long-term defence perspective plan (LTDPP) for a period of fifteen to twenty years, (f) the five-year defence plan of the Services to be transformed into joint Services plan by the VCDS in consultation with both the CDS and the Defence Secretary, (g) reforms in defence budgeting procedure, (h) private sector participation in defence production, (i) reforms in the Department of Defence R&D, and (j) the establishment of a National Defence University (NDU).[2]

By withholding the appointment of the CDS, the Government has weakened the pace, the content and the quality of military reforms recommended by the GOM. Most of the other reforms that have been undertaken have acquired a purely theoretical appearance, in the absence of the overall thrust and coherence that the CDS would have provided as the Principal Military Adviser to the Defence Minister and the VCDS would have executed. Government intervention in nominating a CDS at the earliest to carry forward the reforms recommended by the GOM is inescapable.

The aim of this article is to discuss certain pertinent issues concerning higher defence management, the defence procurement system, and give a brief update regarding the equipment aspects of the three Services during the year 2003.

Higher Defence Management

Higher defence management in India continues to have a loose, ad-hoc structure, without an effective apex body. For meetings of the Cabinet Committee on Security (CCS), the Chiefs of Staff are invited on "as required" basis.[3] Therefore they have no permanent political interface. Without direct access to the executive head of state, namely the Prime Minister, higher defence management remains unsatisfactory, especially in the Indian style of governance, often with a multi-party alliance. A regular politico-military interaction is essential in a country like India which faces a large variety of military and non-military threats that need a constant watch and evaluation, and may require the application of military force at short notice. The National Security Council (NSC), which at the apex has a composition similar to the CCS, seldom meets; its second and third tiers, namely the Strategic Planning Group and the National Security Advisory Board, are merely coordinating and advisory bodies. Therefore, an institutionalized politico-military interface involving the Prime Minister with the Chiefs of Staff Committee, and not merely the Defence Minister, is vital for the nation's security. India's political leadership will have to evolve a suitable method for ensuring this within the NSC, in which regular meetings with COSC could be arranged. India requires to demonstrate political resolve to handle security issues. Partly, this resolve would be demonstrated by having a senior political leader of strong character, with proven capability of vision and a quick grasp of security issues, which involves long-term national investments, to head the Defence Ministry. A candidate sifted only through political compromise must never fill the post.

The move to transform the status of Service Headquarters from "Attached Offices" to "Integrated Headquarters" has not made much difference in the functioning of the Services Headquarters vis-à-vis the MOD. The former still function outside the apex structure of the Government.[4] Much greater delegation of financial powers (capital and revenue expenditure) and administrative powers to the Service Headquarters and lower formations are necessary to achieve greater speed, higher levels of efficiency and accountability. Attitudinal change to negate the near-combative mentality that tends to develop between the Services Headquarters and the MOD can be achieved by measures such as joint training of Armed Forces officers with their civilian counterparts at middle and senior levels, and through proper integration through cross postings in the Services Headquarters and in the MOD.

Another disturbing aspect of higher defence management is the unclear status of the Strategic Force Command (SFC). The constitution of the SFC was announced, on 4 January 2003, "to manage and administer all strategic forces", but it is still to find a location for its Headquarters and a role for itself in the employment of nuclear weapons. It appears that the Government, the scientists and the three Services have little time for the SFC. All nuclear delivery systems of all three Services should be held with the SFC. Its Commander-in-Chief should have complete knowledge of the technical capabilities and details regarding the procedure and time needed for operationalization of nuclear weapons and he should be in the chain of control of the use of nuclear weapons.[5] With contradictory pulls and pressures, at best a temporary arrangement prevails in this vital field of higher defence management.

Defence Procurement System

The aim of a defence procurement system is to ensure that procurement/production is timely, is qualitatively acceptable, provides value for money in the provision of defence equipment and leads to modernization of the Armed Forces. The GOM recommendations on "Reforming the National Security System—February 2001" had observed that the current procurement structure operative since 1992 had led to sub-optimal utilization of funds, long delays in acquisition, and had not been conducive to the modernization of the Services. They recommended the creation of a separate and dedicated institutional structure to undertake all procurement functions to ensure a higher degree of professionalism and cost-effectiveness.

Similar observations had been made by the Standing Committee of Parliament on Defence in their 10th, 11th, 15th, 18th, and 19th reports. This led to the establishment of the Defence Acquisition Council (DAC) and the Defence Procurement Board (DPB). The former is chaired by the Raksha Mantri. Its members are Rajya Raksha Mantri, CDS/COSC, Service Chiefs, VCDS, Secretaries Defence, Defence Production, Defence R&D, Defence Finance, and Special Secretary Acquisition (SSA). The primary role of the DAC is to accord, in principle, approval of long-term perspective plans; acceptance of necessity for capital acquisition plans (five years), identify "make", "buy", and "make & buy" projects, and monitor progress of three boards under it, that is, the Defence Procurement Board, the Defence Production Board, and the Defence R&D Board.[6]

The Defence Procurement Board under the Defence Secretary with a Special Secretary Acquisition (SSA) will have the primary role of capital procurements and coordination. The Board has as its members the Services Vice Chiefs, VCDS, other Secretaries, Financial Adviser (FA), and the SSA. The acquisitions are made based on provisional approval of the DAC.

The Acquisition Wing is the third tier under the SSA, and has separate land, maritime, air and systems divisions, besides a separate finance division. Revenue acquisitions are to be delegated to the integrated Services Headquarters. Each division (for land, maritime and air) has an Acquisition Manager (Joint Secretary) and Technical

Managers (Two Star Officers). Negotiations and contract management is overseen by the Acquisition Manager, while the trials, evaluations, and equipment selection is handled by the Technical Managers. Each Service has Equipment Induction Cells (EIC) to facilitate induction and management of weapons and equipment. All qualitative requirements are approved by the respective Services Headquarters.

The Defence Production Board has a composition similar to the Procurement Board, except that Secretary Defence Production and Supplies heads it, with the Defence Secretary as a member, along with the other members of the Board. The Board oversees all activities related to indigenous manufacture; progresses "make" projects, and provides support to DAC.

The Secretary Defence (R&D) chairs the Defence R&D Board. Its composition is similar to the Defence Production Board. It will have other members such as the Chief Controller R&D and distinguished scientists on an "as required basis". Services Deputy Chiefs are invited members. The R&D Board progresses, monitors and reports on all indigenous R&D proposals, in consultation with user Service and the Production Board. The board also recommends and evaluates technology transfer to the DAC.

In addition to creating these boards, DAC monitors their functioning and also resolves inter-Services disputes, wherever the CDS (when nominated) fails to do so. Special Secretary Acquisition provides the permanent secretariat to the Defence Production Board.

Current Weaknesses in the System[7]

Merely setting up a new structure will not make the system more efficient or effective. Of far greater importance is streamlining the procedures and organizations, and a positive attitude among the officials concerned to the changes instituted. Attitudinal change is the most difficult to effect, and offers tremendous scope for the military and civil bureaucracies, charged with such responsibilities, to reflect on. The current weaknesses and shortcomings of the system are:

- Decision-making process is neither structured nor accountable. Despite operational urgency as expressed by the Services, there is indecisiveness and vacillation at times. Moreover, the Defence

Acquisition Council meetings are not regular and are not backed by a dedicated secretariat. This has resulted in non-utilization of capital budget fully.

- Financial powers are centralized with the MOD. The financial powers of Competent Financial Authorities (CFAs) are marginal. Delegation of capital expenditure, up to Rs. 25 crore, to the Services, has not yet been implemented. All cases have to be routed through the Defence Procurement Board. The delegation of powers to the SSA needs to be enhanced.
- The need for repeated examination of proposals at various levels in the MOD and MOD (Finance) should have been eradicated by the creation of DAC and the Defence Procurement Board. Unfortunately, this continues. This must be arrested, and the officials concerned held accountable for delays caused by lethargy and inaction.
- Qualitative Requirements (QRs) prepared by the Services continue to be stringent and unrealistic, and require waiver by the Defence Procurement Board.
- Inability of the Defence Research and Development Organization (DRDO) to deliver indigenously developed equipment in time defeats the purpose of these projects, and due to rapidly advancing technology, makes the equipment near-obsolescent even before it is introduced into service. DRDO should carefully consider each project, before accepting/promoting it.
- There is no single agency to handle drawing up of contracts and coordinate post-contractual obligations.
- There should be flexibility in applying the rules, so as to be more responsive to operational needs.
- The production agencies, both in the defence public sector and in the ordnance factories, need to have greater freedom to select new technologies, management techniques and financial investment. They must have the freedom to discard excess staff and unproductive manpower. Military modernization should not become a prisoner of the weaknesses in the system, and it is in such areas that political leadership needs to intervene.

Privatization of Defence Production

If India aspires to be a global/regional power, it must seek a strong participation of the private sector in defence production. While this is a vast subject, this entry is merely intended to highlight the importance of this aspect.

The growth of India's industry over the past four decades has been diverse. The private sector has acquired the capability of manufacturing a wide range of products of interest to the defence industry, and with closer institutional linkages, this partnership can become mutually beneficial. Indian industry has not shown any interest in manufacturing heavier calibre equipment, such as tanks, artillery guns, ships, aircraft, etc., but this could change with Government participation in the R&D and in allowing greater foreign direct investment (FDI) in the defence sector. The current policy of 26 per cent FDI is a welcome step. In the meantime, *Jane's Defence Weekly* (26 March 2003) reports that the MOD has awarded licences to two private companies, namely Larsen and Toubro (L&T), and Mahindra and Mahindra (M&M). Five licences have been awarded to L&T to build warships, submarines, weapon platforms (off-shore, floating and submerged), high-speed boats, radar, sonar, electronic warfare equipment, armoured and combat vehicles, including associated systems and sub-systems. M&M has been awarded a licence to supply the Army vehicles developed with foreign assistance, possibly from an Israeli company.[8]

The growth strategy for privatization should be to employ commercial off-the-shelf technology (COTS) for defence use so as to cut down costs of R&D, use commercial specifications, have universal standards, and acquire technology through joint R&D with civil industry, including foreign manufacturers. Government should extend financial support to initiate the private sector into defence, and grant liberal tax/duty exemptions. Procedural and labour reforms should follow to ensure productivity and effectiveness. With these measures, India could be in a position to galvanize the partnership with the private sector, and take it to its culmination.[9]

Non-Lapsable Defence Allocations, 2004-5

In the defence budget (vote on account) for the year 2004-5, the

Government has committed Rs. 25,000 crore as a non-lapsable defence modernization fund, to cater for the procurement needs of the Armed Forces. With this long-awaited and positive step, it is to be hoped that paucity of funds will not come in the way of the defence establishment in implementing modernization and weapon acquisition plans. The process of defence procurement often extends to over three years. Adequate and a committed availability of funds, over such a period, for defence modernization and weapon systems acquisition need a satisfactory resolution. The fund will be made available to the Ministry of Defence from the new financial year", said the then Finance Minster, Jaswant Singh, in his interim budget speech on 4 February 2004. The fund will not lapse annually, but would be a permanent source that can be tapped by the Defence Ministry when the need arises, because the Ministry is often unable to utilize its entire allocation in a short time-frame due to the long process of procurement. In the past, it has had to surrender substantial funds under the "Capital Expenditure" head.[10]

Equipment Aspects

It is widely known that India's defence expenditure slumped from an all-time high of 3.59 per cent of GDP in 1987-88 to 2.09 per cent during 1996-97 and though it picked up somewhat thereafter, it has never exceeded 2.6 per cent of GDP in the ensuing years. The break-up of the Soviet Union compounded the problem, which resulted in disruption of maintenance and supply of spare parts. "The defence sector bore the brunt of austerity and no worthwhile modernization of defence systems took place during the last two decades or so resulting in erosion of combat edge."[11] Consequently, an emboldened Pakistan launched the Kargil intrusion in May 1999 followed by the Kargil conflict.

The momentum of equipment modernization and procurement picked up somewhat after the GOM Recommendations in February 2001 started getting implemented. Some critical equipment inductions and equipment-related decisions, in respect of the three services, discerned through reports, are highlighted in the ensuing paragraphs.

Army

The Standing Committee on Defence, in 2003, in its 19th report made some pertinent remarks with regard to Army equipment. It expressed deep concern at the major shortfall of nearly 2.5 lakh bulletproof jackets for the operational role of the Army along the Line of Control and in its counter-insurgency operations. It went on to adversely comment on the delayed induction of the Arjun tank for which government approval had been accorded in February 1999 and indent for 124 tanks was placed by the Army on 30 March 2000. The delivery is now likely to be completed by 2006-7. In reply to a question by the Committee, the MOD stated that T-90 will remain the main battle tank of the Indian Army till the end of the 12th Plan period. The programme for the induction of T-90 tanks is to have 124 fully formed tanks, 186 to be manufactured from semi-knocked-down kits and fully knocked down kits and import of transfer of technology (TOT) for manufacture of 1000 T-90 tanks at the Heavy Vehicles Factory, Avadi. The cost of transfer of technology is US$ 70,900,000.[12]

Media reports indicate that a formal "acceptance of necessity for procurement" was approved by the MOD in January 2004 for procurement of 18 medium-range air defence systems. The current KVADRAT system, procured in the 1970s, is considered obsolete. Under consideration are the Patriot system of US origin, BUK MI-2 of Russian origin and Aster-30 from European Missile House MBDA.[13]

The Government has cleared the acquisition of two regiments each of indigenously developed Pinaka multi-barrel rocket launchers (MBRL-90) with a range of 35 km and the Russian Smerch MBRL with a range of 90 km. A total of 36 numbers Pinaka and 24 Smerch are likely to be inducted in 2004. Negotiations are also taking place for procurement of 155 mm self-propelled (SP) medium guns drawn from Denel of South Africa.[14] The total deal involves nine regiments of 155 mm (SP) guns for employment with the mechanized and armoured formations of the Army and possibly with the Artillery Divisions.

Government approval has also been accorded for acquisition of nine Israeli HERON and 12 additional SEARCHER-2 unmanned aerial vehicles (UAVs).[15]

The delivery of 12 ANTPQ-37 weapon locating radars for the Artillery, from the US, will start from September 2004 onwards.

The upgradation of 20 regiments of existing 130 mm medium guns of the Artillery to 155 mm calibre by Soltam of Israel has started, in phases, after the successful firing trials concluded in July 2003. Talks are also being held with Russia to upgrade the existing BM-21 Grad free-flight multiple rocket systems which were inducted in 1972 from the erstwhile Soviet Union.[16]

The Army unveiled its Rs. 3000 crore infantry modernization plan to equip infantry battalions with anti-material rifles, automatic grenade launchers, flame throwers, hand-held thermal imagers, battlefield surveillance radars, unattended ground sensors, better communication equipment and high-resolution binoculars. This modernization is well under way with priority being given to units in Jammu and Kashmir.

Air Force

After more than two decades the Government finally signed a $1.75 billion MOU with UK's Defence Export Services Organization (DESO) to procure an initial 66 tandem-seat HAWK Mk 155y, lead-in fighter trainers (LIFT) from BAE Systems for the IAF. Of this amount $1.3 billion is payable to BAE Systems and the rest is to be spent on upgrading state-owned HAL for undertaking licensed production. An initial 24 LIFT will be procured from BAE Systems and the remaining 42 will be license-built by HAL. Delivery of the aircraft will begin 35 months after contract signature. All 66 LIFT will join service within the next six years.[17]

The Standing Committee on Defence (2003) in its 19th report made scathing comments on non-utilization of some of the funds for the IAF under capital and revenue heads. The Committee reiterated the need for fully utilizing the funds for all Services and for the IAF in the thrust areas of modernization, viz. direct acquisition/transfer of technology or indigenous development of the state-of-the-art weapon system, aircraft, sensors, and radars so that obsolescence in this respect is obviated.

As regards the light combat aircraft (LCA), the Committee noted that a huge investment of nearly Rs. 5000 crore has been made on the project initiated in 1983. There have been considerable cost and time overruns due to embargoes of critical components, including GE-404 engines. Induction of LCA in a time-bound manner is a critical requirement of the IAF in its 15-year plan. The LCA will replace the MIG-21, which are likely to phase out of service in the near future.[18]

PHALCON airborne early warning and control system (AWACS) will be based on new IL-76 TD of Tashkent Aircraft Production Company (TAPC). These aircraft will undergo structural modifications and will be re-engined with more powerful PS-90 engines in Russia. The overall cost proposed by ELTA, Israel, is $1290 million. In view of Russia's stand a tripartite agreement (between India, Russia and Israel) has been considered necessary. The contract was signed on 5 March 2004.[19]

Due to operational necessity, three more squadrons of UAVs are to be acquired for the IAF on a fast track basis from IAI Malat of Israel. The entire equipment will be delivered within twelve months of signing of the contract. The total cost is Rs. 657.3 crore.[20]

Navy

The MOD has stated that in order to ensure optimum capacity utilization, particularly in regard to shipbuilding and submarine construction and also meet the requirements of the Indian Navy in terms of shorter intervals at which successive ships of each project are to be delivered, the existing facilities at Mazagon Docks Ltd. (MDL), Mumbai, Garden Reach Shipbuilders & Engineers Ltd. (GRSE), Kolkata and Goa Shipyard Ltd. (GSL), Goa are in urgent need of upgradation and augmentation. The Navy's 15 Years Shipbuilding Plan, awaiting approval, envisages construction of 26 ships, 21 ships and 24 ships, including major warships/submarines, at MDL, GRSE and GSL respectively. Action has already been initiated by the shipyards for modernization of the facilities through project-aided funds to be given by the Indian Navy. The estimated cost for the modernization of the three shipyards is, MDL Rs. 281 crore, GRSE Rs. 180 crore, and GSL Rs. 241 crore.[21]

The acquisition of the Russian aircraft carrier *Admiral Gorshkov* has been under consideration since 1994. The MOD has informed the Standing Committee on Defence that four Indian delegations have since assessed the state of the ship and eleven Russian delegations have since visited India. Inter-Government Agreement between India and Russia was signed on 4 October 2000. Technical and price negotiations were held from March 2002 and the deal was finalized by end 2003. The repair and re-equipping, training and extensive trials are scheduled to take about 52 months from the commencement of repairs. The ship is being redesigned to operate the MIG-29K.[22]

In the recent past the Navy has acquired unmanned aerial vehicles (UAVs), it has inducted a sophisticated anti-missile system like the BARAK-M in its ships and has successfully test-fired Prithvi and BrahMos missiles for installation on ships and submarines. Maritime reconnaissance aircraft are now getting sophisticated sensors.

Data links are now being provided for sharing real-time information between platforms. Some important additions in the past have been three Delhi-class destroyers; three Talwar-class frigates purchased from Russia; and assorted missile corvettes.[23] Three XFAC (extra fast attack craft) built by Goa Shipyard Ltd. in collaboration with IAI Rama of Israel have been inducted. They are designed for putting to sea in the shortest possible time for day-night coastal surveillance and reconnaissance, coordinated sea-air search and rescue (SAR), beach insertion/extraction of commando forces and high-speed interception of small manoeuvrable intruder craft over territorial waters. With a displacement of 60 tons, it is the fastest combatant in the Indian Navy.[24]

The lead-time for inducting a platform in the Navy is ten years and more and hence a long-term plan of the Navy has to be drawn up, sanctioned by the Government, and pursued vigorously. It is alarming that hardly any vessels have been sanctioned in the past five years. The penalties to be paid in the future are obvious. Even programmes sanctioned by the previous governments have slowed down due to indecision and bureaucratic delays. The acquisition of *Admiral Gorshkov*, for example, was sanctioned in 1997, but the contract was signed in December 2003. Had the process been faster it would have been commissioned by now at a much lower cost. Two other programmes of the Navy have been subjected to similar treatment. These first pertains to the submarines to be built indigenously whose letter of intent was issued in 1997. The second programme concerns the Air Defence Ship to be built in the country whose letter of intent was issued more than six years ago.[25] The Standing Committee on Defence has adversely commented upon this issue in its 19th Report.

It is seldom appreciated that after the 1962 War, for nearly sixteen years the capital expenditure on defence procurement had grown at an average rate of 16.7 per cent. During the next nine years the growth rate had gone up to 20.4 per cent. However after 1987, the average annual growth rate of capital expenditure came down to 11.96 per cent.[26] For the last three years, the MOD could not spend the allocations. The Non-Lapsable Fund Account should be of considerable help in overcoming this difficulty. However, the most significant role will continue to be played by the Defence Procurement Board whose initiative, vision, and diligence will help in equipping the Services adequately.

Notes

1. Group of Ministers (GOM) Recommendations on *Reforming the National Security System—February 2001*, pp. 97-8.
2. Ibid.
3. Ibid., p. 102.
4. B.D. Jayal, "India's Military Modernisation", in Satish Kumar (ed.), *India's National Security Annual Review, 2003*, p. 100.
5. Pravin Sawhney, "Bombed", *FORCE*, February 2004, pp. 8-9.
6. Yogendra Narain, "Defence Procurement", *Indian Defence Review*, October-December 2003, pp. 25-6.
7. Chandra Shekhar, *Arming the Defence Forces*, Manas, New Delhi, 2003.
8. B.D. Jayal, n. 4, p. 108.

9. T.J.S. Gill, "Privatisation of Defence Production: Strategy for Defence Forces", *CDM Papers*, 1/2003 Volume 1, pp. 46-51.
10. Yogendra Narain, n. 6, p. 30.
11. Chandra Shekhar, n. 7.
12. Standing Committee on Defence, 19th Report, 13th Lok Sabha, p. 29.
13. Vivek Raghuvanshi, "Will India Replace Air Defense", *Defense News*, 23 February 2004, p. 28.
14. Pravin Sawhney, "All Dressed up But Not Partying Yet", *FORCE*, February 2004, pp. 28-9.
15. Pravin Sawhney, "The New Firepower", *FORCE*, November 2003, p. 36.
16. Ibid.
17. Prasun K. Sengupta, "India Signs Hawk MOU", *FORCE*, April 2004, pp. 9-10.
18. Standing Committee on Defence, n. 12, p. 40.
19. Prasun K. Sengupta, "Deal for Phalcon Inked", *FORCE*, May 2004, pp. 38-9.
20. Standing Committee on Defence, n. 12, p. 41.
21. Ibid., p. 31.
22. Ibid.
23. P.S. Das, "Not Shining at Sea", *FORCE*, April 2004, p. 44.
24. "Naval Systems", *Defence & Technology*, December 2003, p. 10.
25. P.S. Das, n. 23, p. 44.
26. Yogendra Narain, n. 6, p. 32.

Economic Security—I

Sanjaya Baru

Conceptualizing Economic Security

There is, as yet, no established concept of "economic security" in mainstream economics, much less a framework of analysis to define the elements that contribute to it. In the absence of a "theory" of "national economic security", there are no quantitative indicators and hence no official database. Economists have more recently tried to develop the concept of "human security", based on the concept of "human development", drawing attention to access to basic needs and access to "entitlements" and provision of "capabilities", all of which go to enhance the security of life for all people.[1] There are other, more focused concepts of economic security pertaining to energy security, environmental security, financial security, and so on. Yet economic theory has not yet come forward with a comprehensive view of what exactly constitutes the economic security of nations. The matter is further complicated by the increased "globalization" of all national economies in recent years, with more open trade and capital flows. Thus, the concept of "economic security" is in a flux.

In the absence of an established, widely understood and accepted conceptual framework, official data are not available on what may be regarded as indicators of economic security, whether at the national or international level. Neither national governments nor multilateral organizations like the United Nations, the International Monetary Fund or the World Bank put out any estimates of trends in economic security or the economic security status of countries. The UNDP's *Human Development Report* tries to capture trends in "human security" through measurement of human development.

More recently, security and strategic policy analysts have tried to estimate national economic security through the prism of national power, with power expressed and estimated in terms of economic and non-economic national capabilities.[2] Developing the idea of economic power as national power, Tellis has constructed a framework for the measurement of trends.[3] From such studies and estimates analysts in China, the United States and India have constructed an index of "national security".[4] It is a moot point whether it can be presumed that there is in fact a positive correlation between economic "power" and economic "security". The assumption that "power" guarantees "security" can be questioned for a variety of reasons. Hence, an index of national power need not be relevant to measuring national security. Yet this is what has been attempted by analysts in the US, China and India.

Analysts at the China Academy of Military Sciences have attempted a measurement of Comprehensive National Power (CNP), defining it as the weighted sum of military, economic, scientific and technological power. The eight variables used are natural resources (with a weight of 0.08), domestic economic capability (0.28), external economic capability (0.13), scientific and technological capability (0.15), social development level (0.10), military capability (0.10), government capability ((0.08) and foreign affairs capability (0.08).[5] It is possible to collect quantitative data for each variable and try and measure year-to-year changes in CNP and extrapolate from that changes in the level of economic security of a country. Note that purely economic indicators as also indicators with a high economic content have a high share in the CNP index, of more than 50 per cent.

Based on such concepts, the INSAR's National Security Index (NSI) for India is an attempt to construct a simpler index based on five variables, namely, defence capability, gross domestic product, human development levels, research and development levels, and the quantity and quality of population. Regrettably, annual and up-to-date statistical information is not available on all these components. The leads and lags in data, especially with respect to human development, demographic trends and even R&D capability make accurate year-to-year estimates of the index of national security difficult. Even so, it is possible, on the basis of available data, to come to some tentative conclusions in a medium-term framework.

For India, the improvement in the economy's performance in 2003-4, with acceleration in the rate of growth of national income, should have enabled a marked improvement in the GDP indicators in the NSI. Similarly, a good monsoon, a moderation in rates of inflation, and increased budgetary allocations for education and defence should normally suggest an improvement in NSI.

The Economics of Economic Security

However, the NSI does not capture other dimensions of "economic security" that may be equally important for a large continental economy like India in a globalized world. What these missing dimensions could be was discussed in the Economic Security sub-group of the National Security Advisory Board of India in 1999-2001. A paper prepared for the sub-group defined "economic security" thus:

> The concept of economic security is wide-ranging and comprehensive. It implies political and economic sovereignty and autonomy of decision-making, albeit in an increasingly interdependent world characterized by the "globalization" of economic activity. It implies the assurance of economic well-being and social justice as reflected in particular by generalized access to food, clothing, shelter, education and employment. It implies the acquisition of skills and knowledge aimed at acquiring technical and technological capabilities required for sustained and self-reliant economic development and the assurance of defence capability.

There are "external" and "internal" dimensions to economic security. Internal economic security requires a sustained growth of per capita income, based on a higher investment and savings ratio and productivity; general economic well-being of all people, assurance of minimum economic needs; stable macroeconomic policy, sustainable fiscal and monetary policy and moderate inflation; economic viability of domestic business, particularly in the financial sector, competitiveness of domestic firms; and a reduction in inter-regional, inter-sectoral (urban/rural and industry/agriculture), inter-class, inter-communal and inter-caste inequalities in development.

External economic security entails viability of the balance of payments, manageable current account deficit, reasonable stock of foreign exchange reserves, growing external trade, manageable external debt with minimum dependence on short-term debt, prudent management of foreign assets and a market-based exchange rate policy within the parameters of an open trade and investment regime, with active participation in multilateral, regional and bilateral trade agreements. The NSAB paper observed that:

> The economic security challenge for India is to pursue above average national income growth at the annual rate of at least 7.0 per cent to 8.0 per cent so that India's share of world GDP is commensurate with her population size, and a larger economic base can more truly reflect India's status in the global arena. Increasing the size of India's national income will enable the country to better address the aspirations of the mass of the people, and also generate resources required to address the external and internal security challenges confronting the nation. While the assurance of peace and security is necessary to pursue higher economic growth, the pursuit of economic growth is also a means of ensuring peace and security.

This conceptual framework should enable one to construct a more comprehensive index of external and internal economic security, if the required data are available. Much of the macroeconomic data are now readily available, though there are inordinate time-lags in data availability and the quality of data is uneven. This framework allows us to list the economic variables that would define and determine changes in "economic security" for India. These could be divided into (a) indicators of internal economic security; and (b) indicators of external economic security.

(a) *Indicators of internal economic security*

— per capita income growth
— GDP growth
— employment generation
— rate of inflation
— foodgrain production and per capita availability
— foodgrain stocks
— revenue and fiscal deficits
— investment and savings rate
— literacy, especially female literacy
— per capita consumption of electricity and steel.

(b) *Indicators of external economic security*

— foreign exchange reserves
— trade deficit
— current account deficit
— exchange rate stability
— real effective exchange rate
— external debt and debt service indicators.

Trends in Economic Security, 2003

After five years of close to 7.0 per cent economic growth, between 1992-97, the rate of growth of the Indian economy slipped closer to 5.0 per cent in the subsequent five years of 1998-2003. This deceleration of growth was partly on account of the preceding "overheating" of the economy in 1995-97, and the decision of the authorities to pursue a deflationary monetary policy in 1996-98. This was compounded by a clutch of external problems like the Asian financial crisis, the global economic slow down, the increase in oil prices, and so on. Finally, a weak monsoon in 2002 worsened matters and dragged down the growth rate to 4.0 per cent. Lacking data on employment one can only surmise that employment, whether in the organized or unorganized sectors, stagnated in 2003.

The slow down did contribute to a worsening of fiscal indicators and the fiscal and revenue deficit of the states and the Centre increased to over 10.0 per cent, a level earlier reached in the early 1990s at the time of the external payments crisis. Table 1 gives trends in major macroeconomic variables and indicates that the domestic economy did weaken in 2003. The weak monsoon also exerted pressure on prices and the rate of inflation went up from such lows as 1.0 per cent and 3.0 per cent to over 5.0 per cent in 2004. The weak monsoon also contributed to a drawing down of food stocks and a consequent increase in food prices. Industrial production did begin to pick up after nearly five years of virtual standstill, but gross capital formation continued to be limited at around 23 per cent of GDP. The continued political discord on price reform in the power sector stymied new private investment, even though some new power projects were taken up in the public sector to augment supply.

Table 1. Macroeconomic Trends, 2000-4

	2000-1	2001-2	2002-3	2003-4
GDP at factor cost (constant prices)	4.4	5.8	4.0	8.7
GDP per capita (constant prices)	2.1	3.4	2.8	—
Gross domestic savings (% GDP)	23.7	23.5	24.2	—
Gross domestic capital formation (% GDP)	24.3	23.1	23.3	—
Private capital formation (% GDP)	17.9	17.3	17.6	—
Public sector capital formation (% GDP)	6.4	5.8	5.7	—
Index of industrial production	5.1	2.6	5.8	7.0
Index of agricultural production	–6.4	6.8	–15.1	19.6
Per capita availability of foodgrains (kg/annum)	151.1	—	—	—
Wholesale price index (% change)	7.1	3.7	3.4	5.4
Consumer price index ind. workers (% change)	3.8	4.3	4.0	—
Exports as per cent GDP	10.4	10.0	11.1	10.0
Imports as per cent GDP	11.8	11.7	13.8	12.9
Current Account Balance (% GDP)	–0.8	0.2	0.8	0.1
Debt Service Ratio	16.2	13.6	—	—
Foreign Exchange Reserves (US$ bn)	42.28	54.11	74.81	110.32
Combined Fiscal Deficit (% GDP)	9.4	10.0	10.0	9.0
Combined Domestic Liabilities (% GDP)	64.1	67.6	75.5	76.9

Source: Economic Survey, Ministry of Finance, Government of India (various issues).

Persistently weak government budgets, notwithstanding the reassurance provided by the enactment of the Fiscal Responsibility and Budget Management Bill, high fiscal deficits, slow power sector reforms, slow employment generation and persistent inter-regional inequalities in economic development and growth remain areas of concern with respect to internal economic security.

Among other summary measures of domestic economic

performance that capture a country's developmental status and thereby mirror its national power, capability and security, consumption of steel or electricity is one, just as literacy, especially female literacy. On both counts India fares poorly, even by comparison with China, and has a long way to travel. India's per capita steel consumption was only 29 kilograms in 2002 compared to a world average of 150. China improved its steel consumption per capita remarkably from 103 in 1999 to 163 kilograms in 2002. On indicators such as per capita electricity consumption and female literacy also the gradual improvement in recent years takes India nowhere near East Asian levels, as yet.

While such domestic economic challenges constrain India's internal economic security, its external economic security is today more robust. Indian economic policy has always been mindful of "external economic security" and many elements of the ancien regime in economic policy that goes under the rubric of "inward oriented" industrialization were based on the paramount need for such external security. These policies were framed within the political paradigm of "self-reliance". The importance of such external self-reliance was underscored by the 1991 payments crisis and the experience with economic sanctions imposed by some developed industrial economies in 1998 in response to India's decision to conduct nuclear tests. The need to reduce dependence on aid, to minimize the risk of external default, to minimize the need to approach multilateral and bilateral donors for financial assistance and the need to steer clear of global economic shocks transmitted through open capital markets led to the pursuit of a set of economic policies on the external front that increased India's economic security in the 1990s and early 2000s.

The continued accretion to foreign exchange reserves, with almost a 50 per cent increase in reserves in 2003-4, albeit with implied costs of sterilization of reserves to limit their monetary impact in the home economy, a stable exchange rate regime and reduced dependence on debt and aid flows with increased capital inflows and earnings from invisibles exports contributed to a more robust external economic profile, even though India continued to be a laggard on foreign direct investment.

Thus, in 2003 India's external economic security was better assured than its internal economic security. In 2004, the government will have to pay more attention to employment generation, assuring stability of prices and improving the fiscal health of the central and state governments. The reform of the public sector, in areas where privatization is not likely to happen or is unwarranted, as in health care, education and urban transportation, is also an area of vital importance.

Fortunately, the rate of inflation remained subdued in 2003 at levels below 5.0 per cent. However, indications are that in 2004-5 new inflationary pressures may develop both on account of an increase in commodity prices, especially oil prices, and also on account of increased demand. The Indian economy has moved to a new "inflationary threshold" of around 5 per cent from the long-term average "threshold" rate of around 8.0 per cent. Reduced inflation tolerance is a global phenomenon and policy-makers in India must remain alive to the fact that world inflation rates are still below India's current levels. Hence, any increase in inflation rates is likely to erode the competitiveness of Indian industry.

Table 2 presents the sectoral growth rates for 2002-3 and 2003-4.

Table 2. Sectoral Growth Rates, 2002-3

	Fiscal Year	
GDP at factor cost	**2002-3***	**2003-4****
	4	8.1
Agriculture, forestry and fishing	–5.2	9.1
Mining and quarrying	8.8	4
Manufacturing	6.2	7.1
Electricity, gas and water supply	3.8	5.4
Construction	7.3	6
Trade, hotels, transport and communication	7	10.9
Finance, insurance, real estate, business services	8.8	6.4
Community, social and personal services	5.8	5.9

* Quick Estimates; **Advance Estimates.

Source: Economic Survey (various issues).

According to a study prepared by economists at the Delhi School of Economics,[6] the growth rates for 2003-4 and 2004-5 would be 7.6 per cent and 6.6 per cent respectively. This forecast is based on assumptions relating to the performance of the economy set out in Table 3. What this forecast shows is that while the growth rate of the economy over the next two years is likely to be above the long-term average of 5.8 per cent for the period 1980-2002, it will not as yet touch the Tenth Plan target rate of 8.0 per cent in the next two years. This will require domestic economic reforms aimed at increasing the productivity of investment at home and increasing gross capital formation.

The industry break-up of the aggregate GDP shows that the agricultural sector, estimated to grow at 8.6 per cent during 2003-4, is forecast to grow at 2.5 per cent in 2004-5 and 2.66 per cent in 2005-6 on the assumption that normal weather conditions would prevail in both years. However, without new investment in agriculture and infrastructure it will be difficult to sustain an acceleration of growth, nor can the required employment be created in urban, semi-urban and rural areas. The recent decline in food stocks on account of drought also necessitates replenishment of stock to ensure price stability and food security. In recent years food prices have remained under check thanks to huge stocks and lower tariffs. However, if growth acceleration continues the demand for food may well increase, exerting pressure on food prices.

Finally, an important economic security challenge for India is the uneven levels of economic development between regions and the sharp differences in inter-regional trends in economic growth (see Table 4). Recent trends do not point to a reduction in this differential. Unless the laggard states invest in human development, infrastructure and urbanization they will continue to lag behind the rest of the country, creating major economic distortions and posing a challenge to political management of the country. The central government has to develop a road map for reduced regional imbalances, but much of the effort will remain at the level of the state government. Unless governments in the backward regions embrace economic reforms, assure better governance and raise the resources for development they will be faced with an insurmountable development challenge that can pose a threat to national security. The problem also has an intra-state dimension in large states where the development problems

Table 3. Forecasts for Major Economic Indicators

Variable	Level 2002-3	Forecast level 2002-3	Y-O-Y Increase (%)		
			2003-4	2004-5	2005-6
Real GDP: Rs bn. (at 1993-94 prices)	13183.21	13045.48	7.59	6.56	6.80
Value Added in Industry: Rs bn. (at 1993-94 prices)	4783.77	4687.88	6.55	7.44	7.70
Real Private Consumption: Rs. bn. (at 1993-94 prices)	8972.43	8931.64	5.37	5.31	5.52
Real Government Consumption Expenditure: Rs. bn. (at 1993-94 prices)	N.A	1825.73	6.36	7.01	6.98
Real Private Corporate Investment: Rs. bn. (at 1993-94 prices)	840.92	822.80	5.06	11.74	11.87
Wholesale Price Index: (at 1993-94 prices)	166.8	166.22	5.54	5.07	5.11
(Wholesale Price Non-fuel at 1993-94 prices)	154.96	154.04	5.23	4.96	5.14
Consumer Price Index (at 1993-94=100)	186.8	186.66	3.77	3.30	3.05
Exports: DGCI & S (US$ bn)	52.72	52.46	17.73	14.73	14.80
Imports: DGCI & S (US$ bn)	61.41	62.70	25.01	19.93	20.73
C/A Balance: RBI* (US$ bn)	4.14	4.21	4.88	4.16	3.24

Source: *Economic Outlook India 2004-6*, Prepared by Centre for Development Economics and Delhi School of Economics Research Team, University of Delhi, 2004.

Table 4. State-wise Per Capita Gross Domestic Product and Rate of Growth of GSDP

State	Per Capita GSDP (Constant Rs), 2001-2	Rate of Growth of Per Capita GSDP, 1980-98 (%)
Punjab	17326	3.0
Maharashtra	17029	4.5
Gujarat	16923	4.3
Haryana	16263	3.1
Tamil Nadu	14911	4.3
Karnataka	13294	3.6
Kerala	12338	3.1
Andhra Pradesh	11549	2.9
West Bengal	11386	3.3
Rajasthan	10008	3.8
Madhya Pradesh	8704	2.5
Uttar Pradesh	6829	2.0
Orissa	7039	1.7
Bihar	3757	1.0
All India	13305	—

Source: Col. 1. *National Income Statistics, 2004*, Centre for Monitoring Indian Economy.

Col. 2. J. Sachs, N. Bajpai and A. Ramiah, "Understanding Regional Economic Growth in India", *Asian Economic Papers*, Vol. 1, Issue 3, 2002.

of backward districts require urgent attention to prevent deterioration of the security environment. Breaking up states into smaller states may not always address the problem. Rather, good governance and institutional mechanisms to deal with agrarian and social backwardness of regions must be evolved.

Conclusion

While there are conceptual imponderables in analysing year-to-year changes in a country's economic security, recent trends in the Indian economy suggest that challenges relating to India's external economic security, in terms of the sustainability of balance of payments, quantum of foreign exchange reserves, exchange rate stability and external debt flows, have been more convincingly addressed than internal economic security challenges in terms of capital formation, employment, food security, inter-regional imbalances in growth and infrastructure development.

Clearly, public policy must address the domestic economic security challenge as convincingly as it has tried to address the external economic security challenge.

Notes

1. See Mahbub ul Haq, *Reflections on Human Development* (New York, Oxford University Press, 1995); S Fukuda-Parr and A.K. Shiva Kumar, *Readings in Human Development* (Delhi, Oxford University Press, 2003).
2. See Michael Pillsbury, *Chinese Views of Future Warfare* (Washington DC, National Defense University, 1997); Indian edition, Lancer, 1998.
3. Ashley J. Tellis et al., *Measuring National Power in the Postindustrial Age*, Rand-Arroyo Centre, n.d.
4. See Satish Kumar, "National Security Index", in S. Kumar (ed.), *India's National Security Annual Review, 2003* (Delhi, India Research Press, 2004).
5. Michael Pillsbury, *China Debates the Future Security Environment*, (Washington DC, National Defense University Press, 2000).
6. *Economic Outlook India 2004-2006*, Prepared by Centre for Development Economics and Delhi School of Economics Research Team, University of Delhi, 2004.

Economic Security—II

Tarun Das

The year 2003 witnessed a further reinforcement of the process of economic security in India on several fronts, thus building renewed domestic and international confidence in India.

Government Policies

In terms of government policies that helped the process along, the first set of measures concerned taxation policy. Traditionally, India has followed a policy of high levels of tax, direct and indirect, to generate revenues for government expenditure requirements. There has been a gradual shift in this policy, and significantly in 2003. The central budget reflected a commitment to fuel demand and growth through lower levels of tax, customs duties, excise duties, and direct taxes. The rules and procedures were also made simpler. The economy and industry responded with a surge in growth.

A corollary to this tax policy was the exchange rate policy where the Reserve Bank of India allowed the market to determine the exchange rate. Through 2003 there was a steady appreciation of the rupee vis-à-vis the US dollar, again reflecting a stronger domestic economy. This can have an adverse impact on export competitiveness but Indian exporters and manufacturers maintained export growth essentially through higher levels of competitiveness, lower margins and reduced costs.

The continuing drive to become increasingly competitive in global markets was an important factor in Indian industry in 2003. This drive came from a strong internal effort in industry to enhance its competitive ability and recognition that there is limitless potential to reducing costs through innovative and creative efforts. Industry, therefore, carried on the process of internal reform and restructuring, avoiding complacency.

2003/04 also witnessed a new phenomenon of Indian companies—both manufacturing and service sectors—investing globally, acquiring companies through competitive bids and showing their ambition to go beyond the market and boundary of India. Pharmaceutical, information technology, automotive components and commercial vehicles sectors witnessed overseas investments and acquisitions by Indian corporates. This reflects that Indian industry is not only adopting a new vision of a global player but has the resources and capability to implement that vision. The government facilitated the process by relaxing controls on foreign exchange, overseas remittances, international borrowing, etc.

Public Sector

In 2003/04, a number of public sector companies grew in autonomy and freedom through substantial and successful disinvestments. This freedom, with diminishing levels of government intervention combined with a different kind of accountability to private and foreign investors as well as the capital market will enable the public sector to grow and compete. 2003/04 was clearly a turnaround year in terms of disinvestment, moving from promise and potential to actual performance.

India's public sector has been, is and can be a source of great strength to India's economic security if it is given the desired policy support, freedom and environment to perform. The successful disinvestment initiatives of 2003/04 augur well for the future, adding to the public sector's capability to contribute through production, technology, exports, employment, ancillarization and other ways.

The SME Sector

In the 1990s, the small and medium enterprises (SMEs), which form a large expanse of industry representing huge employment, went through enormous pain because of their uncompetitiveness, the government policy of reservations and fragmented capacities which inhibited competitiveness. Indian SMEs are generally located in clusters around the country, with each cluster focused on a particular product group. For example, auto components in Gurgaon, Pune, Chennai; textiles in Tirupur, Coimbatore, Ludhiana; bicycle components in Punjab, and so on. During 2003/04, these clusters took a cooperative initiative to reorganize themselves, develop new levels of competitiveness and not only survive but prosper. The past year could therefore represent a turning point for SMEs showing the ability to face competition, match the expectations and demands of their principal buyers and restructure themselves to be globally competitive.

Service Sector

The services sector, which had established itself in the 1990s as a new star on the Indian economic horizon, faced differing situations and challenges. The Information Technology software/BPO (business process outsourcing) sector continued to meet new challenges of difficult markets and protectionist trends with new benchmarks of competitiveness. Especially, the leading companies in software met the difficulties and achieved improved results. Concurrently, this sector recognized the need to enhance value addition to its portfolio of technology and invested increasingly in research and development (R&D). Gone were the complacent years of the late 1990s, but this sector, buoyed by outstanding leadership, added new depth to its capability in 2003.

Side by side, the other services sectors grew and established their reputation and capability. Tourism, healthcare, media, entertainment, R&D, training, banking, insurance, financial services, maintenance and repairs, engineering, education, and many other services steadily grew within India and also built their international presence. These services sectors were not recognized earlier as "industry". The new developments in terms of economic space and opportunity have given rise to a whole range of new services and, with it, new employment as well as self-employment.

2003 has been a landmark year for the evolution of the services sector in India but the best is yet to come. With 54 per cent population in India below the age of 25 years, the Indian services sector is emerging as a global resource.

Infrastructure

2003 showed a mixed performance in the infrastructure sectors, which are the underpinning required for high growth and a greater degree of economic security. Telecom showed boom conditions with 2 million new cellular telephones being added each month. In terms of telecom growth, India achieved the first rank in the world in terms of growth. The next few years should show sustained growth because the people of the country are hungry for telecom services, which are becoming increasingly affordable.

Highways and roads are being implemented but not at the pace required to support 10 per cent GDP growth. What has been implemented already is showing a new face of India, speeding up transportation services, increasing productivity and reducing waste. However, greater resort to concrete roads would avoid recurrent costs on repairs and ensure long-term stability of the road transport network across the nation and in its 600,000 villages.

The newer private sector ports displayed efficiency comparable to Dubai and Singapore. This was a new star on the infrastructure scene. But the older ports, especially in the government sector, continued to languish.

In the power sector, it was a mixed performance. The Electricity Act 2003 provided enabling legislation to generate a framework and structure where payment for power supply was imperative. However, this sector still continued to be short on investment and, therefore, quality capacity for generation, transmission and distribution. 2003 could have been a turning point, but since past hopes have not materialized, the forecast is cautious.

Airports also continued to be a source of concern. The international airports were woefully short on capacity and quality of facilities and services. Domestic, smaller airports were equally deficient. Many very small airstrips remained unutilized. Airport infrastructure could transform development and growth in India, but remains a bottleneck.

The greatest cause of anxiety in the infrastructure sector is the Indian Railways, the past backbone of the economy and transportation. The performance of this sector—which continues to be a critical component for movement of the common person and basic commodities—was dismal in terms of efficiency, safety record, and competitiveness. With huge employment within, and support through its patronage to a wide range of manufacturing and services outside, the railways can add or subtract a clear one per cent to or from GDP. Currently, the railways is a minus factor.

Agriculture

Agriculture witnessed massive growth in 2003 and became the principal propeller of the Indian economy's growth impulse, taking it to an unprecedented 8 per cent GDP growth figure. Essentially, this dramatic turnaround had its base in excellent monsoons and a poor previous year. A repeat performance is unlikely.

Agriculture and food could add strength to the economy if reforms, in terms of deregulation of distribution, production, prices, movement, export and import, etc. could happen. There is growing attention to agriculture reforms but it has been slow, blocked by vested interests and hampered by the lack of political will especially at the state level. There is a huge agenda ahead to transform the agriculture sector, on which 60 per cent of India's population still depends.

Technology

2003 certainly witnessed a new focus on technology development but not in a mission mode across all the key technologies. Space, nuclear technology and defence production have been successful examples of a mission approach but many other sectors deserve the same priority, e.g. IT hardware, renewable energy, capital goods.

Unless it gets its technology act together, India will suffer because the world outside is cautious about sharing and transferring technology. Even when it does so, the technology is never state-of-the-art and up to date. There is another angle to this. Many developing countries are starved of technology and the ability of India to develop technologies at competitive cost would be very helpful to their development.

Education

Another area of concern is skills development for employability of Indian youngsters who come out of schools and colleges and training centres. With a huge additionality of new people coming into the employment force, the country faces enormous challenges to create employment and self-employment opportunities. India's human resources are an asset but the numbers alone will not create employability. There is a severe mismatch between demand and supply, not in numbers but in quality and actual skills. 2003 continued the poor record. The required spirit of a nationwide mission to impart appropriate skills to people is still absent.

Another area of concern continues to be the inadequate number of people going for science studies. In this age of technology and knowledge, India is seen as a knowledge resource. To maintain this position and leadership, it is critical that increasing numbers of students are attracted to study the sciences.

Competition

Since 1991, competitive pressures have steadily increased, alternative choices are available to the consumer and the economy benefits from this process. However, in many sectors—for example, capital goods—competition is sometimes tilted against domestic manufacturing. There are other sectors, e.g. energy, where competition may be inadequate; and there are sectors where monopolies continue.

2003 brought about some change but not enough. A judicious stepping up of competition and its pressures on industry—the producer—is important and essential. This does not happen in a consistent and planned manner, impacting the nation as a whole. The situation may work to the advantage of a few but not to the benefit of the many. The nation needs to address this issue of fostering competition, sector by sector.

E-governance

The application of technology, especially IT, to all decision-making, especially in central and state governments, local authorities, etc. would bring about speed, transparency and efficiency. E-governance is being applied but with differing degrees of success. Unless the implementation of IT is expedited across all aspects of governance, the nation's ability to cope with complex challenges with speed and efficiency will be impacted. In 2003 the process continued but far too slowly.

False Perceptions

There have been many positive aspects, but because of the size and scale of India and its challenges, many areas remain that need higher priority and action. Overall, 2003 has been a good year for India and the pace of change has been rapid. It will, however, take time for perceptions about India to change. First, take the perception of India being protectionist, not wanting to engage the world on trade issues, holding back the WTO (World Trade Organization), working for the failure of the Cancun process, and so on. India actually had a progressive, forward-looking mandate for Cancun which covered both Agriculture and the Singapore issues. Unfortunately, Agriculture was never discussed, and on the Singapore Issues, the Cancun meeting was aborted. The outdated view of India forgets that the same India has concluded a free trade area agreement with Thailand and ASEAN and is in advanced negotiations with Singapore.

Second, the perception of India being "in a corner", somewhat defensive about globalization and not managing it well. The then Prime Minister Atal Bihari Vajpayee personally led India's engagement with the world. He visited Germany, China, Turkey, USA, Russia, Indonesia, Thailand, Tajikistan and Syria in a whirlwind round of visits, towing Indian business interests along. These visits helped bring India centre stage on global affairs.

Third, the perception of an isolationist India. Curiously, the same critics have also voiced their anger that India, together with Brazil, South Africa and China played a part in the Agriculture G-21 coalition for Cancun. So, is India isolationist or global? The latter, of course, because it has embarked upon a series of coalitions that herald a new foreign and economic diplomacy strategy. G-21 was one example. The Brazil-South Africa-India coalition is another. The BIMST-EC is a third. India-ASEAN is a fourth. The list goes on.

Fourth, that India is Fortress India with high tariff walls, reluctant to open its markets. The trade data with China is useful to show this is not so. Bilateral trade in 2002 stood at US$5 billion. In 2003 it stood at US$7 billion plus. This was in tandem with a huge growth in imports from China. The problem for the competition is that East Asian economies are more competitive than India's.

Fifth, that India is running scared of globalization. This was true in the 1990s as the first pain of liberalization and competition were felt by industry in India. But over the last three years there has been enormous restructuring, cost cutting, downsizing and efficiency building. Today, Indian business is by and large competitive and confident. Corporates are in fact venturing out into other markets, acquiring companies, investing globally and building a new breed of Indian multinational corporations (MNCs).

Sixth, Foreign Direct Investment (FDI) levels are low in India compared to China, which reflects poorly on India. This a very simplistic view, because India's development model is different. Growth comes from both domestic resources and external investments, not one or the other. India is showing to the world a way to growth and development different from the standard formulae churned out in the 1990s that FDI is the only route to growth. FDI no doubt is important but so is domestic resource and financing coming from the rich abundance of Indian enterprise. Our entrepreneurs can generate wealth with innovation and creativity.

India 2003 is very different from the past, but its speed of development and growth can be faster. That is the challenge for 2004 and beyond so that 600,000 villages and 600 million people living in the rural areas can be part of India's new development story. In the process of building growth rates of 8 per cent and more over the next ten to fifteen years, India's economic security will look very different.

High Technology as a Thrust Area in Indo-US Relations

Kanwal Sibal

Background

India has had serious differences over the years with the United States over its nuclear and space programmes. Ironically, US assistance in India's civilian nuclear (Tarapur) and space (Thumba) programmes was very notable at the early stages. After India refused to sign the Nuclear Non-Proliferation Treaty (NPT) in 1968, exploded its peaceful nuclear device in 1974 and began its Integrated Missile Development Programme in the mid-1980s, US cooperation in these areas ceased. India became a target of sanctions under the US non-proliferation legislation, besides being denied access to high technology through restrictive regimes such as the Nuclear Suppliers Group and the Missile Technology Control Regime. India also became the target of regimes originally directed against the Communist bloc, such as the Wassenaar Arrangement. Under these regimes, technology clearly intended for military nuclear and missile programmes is barred altogether, while technology which can be used both for military and genuinely civilian purposes is severely restricted through complex export control arrangements. The US has the most elaborate and stringent laws in this regard and is the most difficult to access for so-called "sensitive" technologies. The motive force behind all these highly restrictive regimes is the United States.

In this background, any effort to develop a strong political and economic relationship between India and the United States must address the technology denial issue. No worthwhile strategic relationship can be built between the two countries unless the strategic issues involving India's nuclear and missile programmes are resolved in a manner consistent with India's dignity, security and sovereignty. India is not hoping or trying to obtain technology from the US for its non-civilian nuclear and space programmes. The problem is in the area of dual technologies, as these technologies have clear and beneficial civilian uses, and as such are valuable for development purposes. How does one reach a mutually satisfactory arrangement with the US which ensures that specific technologies that could also have military uses will be used only for declared civilian purposes? This is where the US export control laws, with separate lists controlled by the State Department and the Commerce Department, with their complex presumptions of denial and approval, of entities lists (those under sanctions) and end-use verification come in. To add to the complexity of the subject, the US denies technology for legislative, policy and administrative reasons. Overcoming legislative hurdles is the most difficult, unless for high political reasons the US Administration seeks waiver from Congress. There is greater flexibility in the policy and administrative areas, but, in practice, here too flexibility depends on the political relationship between the US and a particular country at any given point in time.

Whenever India and the US have decided at the highest political level to stimulate their bilateral relationship, the one issue that raises its head is that of high-technology trade. After Prime Minister Indira Gandhi's fruitful meeting with President Ronald Reagan at Cancun, India and the US signed a memorandum of understanding in 1984 on facilitating trade in high technologies, one concrete result of which was the sale of the Cray super computer to India, although under onerous conditions. Subsequent efforts, especially in the early 1990s, to breathe fresh life into the MoU proved disappointing. When Prime Minister Atal Bihari Vajpayee and President George W. Bush decided to qualitatively transform Indo-US relations, high-technology commerce came under focus inevitably and figured in the November 2001 joint statement by the two leaders.

Current Issues

Unlike in the past, this time there is a more meaningful and intensive effort by both sides to address the high-technology issue. In November 2002, India and the US announced the establishment of a High Technology Cooperation Group (HTCG), the first that the US set up with any country, and in that sense, an earnest of US commitment to deal seriously with this long-standing bottleneck in Indo-US relations. While India's original intention was to focus on stimulating strategic trade through the easing of US export controls, the agenda of the discussions has been enlarged to include high-technology commerce more broadly defined. Progress since November 2002 has been fairly quick. In February 2003 both sides agreed on the Statement of Principles that would govern such trade and the first meeting of the HTCG followed in July that year in Washington. It was agreed at that meeting to concentrate on four broad industry sectors: information technology, bio-technology, nano-technology, and defence technology. The US side was keen that the private sector lend support to the deliberations of the HTCG, arguing that if the US private sector developed a stake in such commerce between India and the US, the existing barriers would be easier to overcome. The US cites the example of US-China trade in high technology which is larger than Indo-US trade in this sector even though, according to the US side, China is subject to greater export controls by the US than India is. Both in the July meeting in Washington as well as the November (2003) meetings in Bangalore and Delhi, the private sector participation from both sides was impressive.

To ensure that HTCG discussions are pointed and purposeful, an Action Plan was also agreed upon in the July meeting covering areas such as Customs and Trade Facilitation, Tariffs, E-Commerce, Data Protection, Standards, E-Education, Telehealth, Outsourcing/Offshoring/H1B visas/Equalization Agreement. Other issues for discussion are Policy Review for Dual Use Exports, End-Use Verification, Outreach Activities, Indo-US Bilateral Export Control Programme including strengthening India's export controls, etc. The HCTG's agenda is well balanced, with the concerns of both sides finding place. The US side is interested in opening up the Indian market for US technology by having India address tariff and intellectual property issues. There is agreement, however, that India should concentrate on the middle ground between high policy issues of the World Trade Organization (WTO) variety and micro-level company-specific issues. Through this engagement the US side seeks to promote its non-proliferation goals by having India strengthen its export controls to their satisfaction. India is keen to see the easing of the unduly restrictive US export controls on dual-use technology items. India sees the HTCG as a forum for advancing high-technology commerce through specific, tangible, realistic, and achievable steps. India would like the focus to be on regulatory and policy issues related to high-technology trade.

As a result of lifting of post-Pokhran US sanctions in 2001 and "outreach" activities undertaken by the US Commerce Department to diffuse information about liberalization of the licence regime for India, the approval rate of export licences has increased and the volume of high-technology trade between the two countries has grown. But the figures remain quite modest and show how much scope there is for expansion. In US Fiscal Year 2003 licences worth $57 million were approved; in the first four months of FY 2004, the figure has already reached $51 million. Interestingly, for the Indian Space Research Organization (ISRO), which is one of the two major entities still under sanctions, the value of licences approved for FY 2003 was $9 million and for the first four-month FY 2004 the figure has reached $7 million. The case of ISRO would show that although, to India's disappointment, the organization has not yet been removed from the entities list, the US side is taking pragmatic decisions to license sale of technology for ISRO's satellite programme, which is vital for India's development and communication needs, besides exploring seriously possibilities of space cooperation between the two countries. The Indo-US Space Cooperation and Commerce Seminar in Bangalore in June 2004, although not held under the auspices of the HTCG, saw the participation of US Under Secretary for Commerce Kenneth Juster who co-chairs the HTCG along with the Indian Foreign Secretary, besides a whole host of US scientists and academics, indicating the considerable evolution that has taken place in attitudes and environment relating to trade in sensitive areas. More than the civilian nuclear field, space provides better prospects for India-US cooperation as the political and legal issues involved are relatively less complex and commercial possibilities more immediately attractive.

The US considers two issues as particularly important in the context of high-technology trade: strengthening India's export controls and end-use verification procedures. India's political commitment to maintain and strengthen export controls is unquestionable. It is firm about prohibiting export of WMD-usable technologies or their delivery systems. India is aware of responsibilities arising from possession of advanced technologies and is sensitive to international concerns in a way that would enhance global security while preserving national security interests. As mentioned in the Statement of Principles, India is committed to strengthening its system and bringing it up to "modern export control standards". There have been fairly extensive discussions on end-use verification. It is important to have a clear understanding on procedures. The vital difference between "end-use verification" and "inspections" has to be recognized and questions of sovereignty sensitively dealt with. The November 2002 joint statement clearly affirms the shared commitment and common interest of the two countries in preventing proliferation of strategic goods and technology and further enhancing their export control cooperation.

Strategic Trade

There is a clear synergy between strategic trade and high-technology trade in India's discussions with the US. The US side has undoubtedly made efforts at the highest levels to advance cooperation on "quartet issues". Although the dialogue on this subject is taking place separately, as part of the Next Steps in Strategic Partnership (NSSP), the issues are linked to the HTCG and the Statement of Principles. In fact, in the HTCG, discussions are held both on Facilitating and Promoting High Technology Trade as well as Strategic Trade. There is clearly some overlap in these two forums for discussions, though in the HTCG there is no discussion on non-proliferation regimes and India's relationship with them.

India's record on non-proliferation has been impeccable, indeed superior to many countries that are otherwise very vocal about the dangers of proliferation. India's nuclear and missile capabilities are entirely defensive in nature. India is not selective in its approach to non-proliferation, recognizing or ignoring proliferation activity in the light of its global or regional relationships. While India can understand theoretical concerns about "onward proliferation" from India if Indo-US trade in high/strategic technologies develops, it would be undesirable if the political objective behind the current exercise between India and the US is derailed by excessive and misguided zeal of the non-proliferation lobby in the US on the export control and end-use verification front.

India and the US are currently trying to lay firm foundations for opening up high/strategic technology trade between the two countries. In view of the political sensitivity of the subject and its linkage to the issue of non-proliferation on which India has been at odds with the US and other countries for decades, progress is bound to be slow. While the Indian side should not look for spectacular results, it may note with some satisfaction that the seriousness with which the current exercise is being undertaken is unprecedented.

Strategic Neighbourhood: Nepal, Sri Lanka, Bangladesh, Bhutan

Ashok K. Mehta

There are certain unchangeable and inescapable regional realities in India's strategic neighbourhood. The Himalayas and the Indian Ocean encompass South Asia. Probably, no other region in the world presents such an integral security zone. Given its preponderance and centrality within the region, India may justifiably regard any alien presence or influence in it without India's consent as a potential threat to its security.[1]

Nepal

Four main events have shaped the current power struggle in Nepal between the monarchists, political formations and Maoists—the Palace massacre in June 2001, Maoist attack against the Royal Nepal Army (RNA) in November 2001, suspension of democracy in October 2002, and the gradual decline of the economy. In a bid to run a totalitarian state, the Maoists have challenged both the political formations and the King, who has either directly or indirectly exercised from absolute to real power in Nepal, over the last half century. After the failure first, of the party-less Panchayat system and later, democracy, the Maoists appealed to the people to give them a chance to govern the country. "Try us" was their slogan. King Gyanendra trying to usher in a new monarchy, more proactive than under his brother late King Birendra, took over power in October 2002 under Article 127 of the 1990 Constitution.[2] In so doing, he has put the Constitution in suspended animation. The stalemate favours the interest of the King instead of the country.

The year 2003 saw the three-way power struggle narrow down to a struggle between the King and the Maoists. Traditionally, Nepal has had only one power, the King. Power poles proliferated with the advent of democracy. State power now resides with the King with the help of the RNA, though there is a nominated government. The

Maoists have not only occupied the political space vacated by democratic forces but also control more territory than the state apparatus. They run a parallel government in the hinterland and have been giving the security forces—the RNA, the armed police and the civil police—a run for their money.

Conflict resolution and formation of a national government were tried throughout 2003. A seven-month-long ceasefire, January to August, provided a peace dividend that benefited the economy. King Gyanendra and the Palace filled the political void by appointing Prime Ministers and nominating governments from the royalist Rashtriya Prajatantra Party (RPP). Between them, Prime Ministers Lokendra Bahadur Chand and Surya Bahadur Thapa held three rounds of peace talks with the Maoists during the ceasefire. The talks failed, the peace dividend did not stick and the Nepalese people were once again caught in the crossfire. Periodically, the King held talks with leaders of political parties in a bid to form a national government.

The other prominent developments in the year under review were the uncertain status of the constitution, renewed agitation led by political parties for restoration of democracy, speculation that the Supreme Court might revive Parliament and the role of outside players in the internal dynamics of Nepal.

For India, land-locked Nepal comprises its front yard. Its security concerns flow from the external and internal power play in Nepal. In 1919, a British Foreign Office document had noted, "Nepal is in a position to exercise powerful influence on India's internal stability and if it were disaffected, the anarchy would spill over." Attending the annual Asian Security seminar at the Institute for Defence Studies and Analysis (IDSA), New Delhi in January 2003, Nepalese security analyst Dhruba Khanal posed this teaser: why had India not intervened in Nepal following the Maoist revolt by invoking the 1950 Treaty of Peace and Friendship?

India acted with traditional restraint and in a spirit of maximum cooperation. After the Maoists caught the RNA on the wrong foot in November 2001, Nepal declared a state of emergency. Under existing agreements, India provided substantial military assistance to refurbish the RNA and other security forces. India's annual aid to

Nepal has averaged around Rs. 160 crore (IC). India started in 1990 a Rs. 460 crore modernization package for the RNA. Since the start of the Maoist insurgency, it has supplied more than Rs. 200 crore worth of military hardware.[3] Counterinsurgency training and relevant military expertise have also been provided. With the defence budget more than double, the RNA has added considerable manpower and firepower to its capability in dealing with the Maoist threat. Two new Brigades (a third is underway), three Divisional Headquarters and nearly 30,000 men in police forces have been added. The RNA has grown in strength from 53,000 to 70,000. A new Unified Headquarters has enhanced the operational performance of the security forces.

The Maoists have suffered serious reverses after ceasefire broke down on 27 August 2003. In a change of strategy the Maoists, who have a hard core of 6,000 armed cadres, have started operating in the Terai but studiously avoided the RNA. They continue to face shortages in ammunition, weapons and manpower, mounting casualties and limited sources of replenishment. Nearly 7,000 lives have been lost since November 2001, of which at least 4,000 are civilians. Official figures are much lower.

Between 2000 and 2003, four Prime Ministers have engaged the Maoists in negotiations. These efforts at conflict resolution were unstructured and ad hoc though the Nepalese congratulated themselves for keeping the peace talks internalized—no third-party involvement. The first formal ceasefire, a 22-point code of conduct for its observance and the most comprehensive summary of proposals by the Maoists came about in 2003 because both sides needed the ceasefire: the government due to the pressure from donor countries to hold elections; and the Maoists as they felt they were in a sound bargaining position and that time was not on their side. The absence of any confidence-building measures and a ceasefire monitoring mechanism broke down the negotiations. The immediate provocation for the Maoists terminating the ceasefire was the massacre by the RNA of 19 Maoists in Ramechhap in East Nepal. The Maoist supremo Prachanda gave three other reasons—the government's lack of sincerity, not honouring previous agreements, and refusal of the demand for a constituent assembly.

Although the Maoists were keen to talk directly with the King, they held discussions with the Palace-approved teams of negotiators belonging to governments which the Maoists had called unconstitutional. The current status of the constitution of Nepal is uncertain. Daman Dhungana, who was associated with the formulation of the constitution, says that the constitution is "brain-dead": it was imperfect when it was made. As it had conceded wide powers to the King, real transfer of power from the Palace to the people did not take place. How else can one explain the King's refusal to act on his Prime Minister's advice to mobilize the RNA against the Maoists—as stipulated in Article 118(2) of the Constitution—before 26 November 2001?[4] The extraordinary delay in employing the RNA against the Maoists will remain one of Nepal's bigger mysteries, like the Royal massacre.

One anomaly of the constitution of Nepal is in not clearly articulating "civilian control" of the RNA. The current debate in Nepal is over the method of meeting the aspirations of the people and the Maoists—should it be through a new constitution or by a Constitution Reforms Commission?

The war has severely damaged the economy. The economy had grown at an average of 5 per cent for a decade: but in 2001-2 it registered a negative growth. Per capita income fell from $240 to $224. According to the World Bank, Nepal will spend Rs 14 billion on security from a revenue estimate of Rs 62 billion.[5] Development aid has not been utilized in areas affected by the war. Worse, the Maoists have systematically destroyed infrastructure in areas under their control.

The Government of India has periodically stated that the stability of Nepal rests on the twin pillars of multiparty democracy and constitutional monarchy. It went a step further when it emphasized the need for a national government. Western countries, notably the US and the UK, were initially in favour of "stability first and democracy later", ostensibly to prevent Nepal from becoming a failed state. They are now coming closer to the Indian position. 9/11 and the imposition of emergency in Nepal saw the Western countries play a more proactive role, which included substantive US military assistance programmes for Nepal. At times, some of them tried to upstage India. On its part, India has not been able to shape events in Nepal though bilateral relations have been sound.

India can ill afford another full-blown insurgency in the North, leading directly into the strategic Indo-Gangetic Plains, already afflicted by Maoists and the People's War Group. The bulk of the nearly 8 million Nepalese in it are part of the Akhil Bharat Nepal Ekta Samaj (ABNES) that is sympathetic to the Maoists.

Nepal is facing its worst ever political crisis. Some steps are necessary for reviving a political process and providing stability—establishing a national government, addressing Maoist demands about constitutional changes, and holding elections. The international community would need to make development and military aid contingent upon steps for the restoration of democracy. On 11 April 2003, the leading Maoist ideologue, Baburam Bhattarai, said: "Our basic agenda is to form a Republican state. If the King abdicates voluntarily, we will offer him some position. It will be good if he agrees to play the role of Norodom Sihanouk."[6]

King Gyanendra, by all accounts, is perceived to have acted in the larger interest of the monarchy than that of the country. This is part of the internal contradictions of Nepal's Third Revolution, holding up the transfer of power to the people. King Gyanendra is hardly likely to volunteer to become a King Norodom Sihanouk.

Sri Lanka

At the end of the Oslo meeting on 5 December 2002, Sri Lankan Prime Minister Ranil Wickremasinghe said that the peace process—making remarkable progress after the Memorandum of Agreement on a ceasefire between the Liberation Tigers of Tamil Eelam (LTTE) and the Sri Lankan Government on 23 February 2002—"would reach a point of no return in 2003". Analysts noted at the time that things were moving too fast and that the Norwegian facilitators, as they had done during the Middle East peace process, "were putting aside difficult political issues with an emphasis on development".[7]

Barring minor glitches, the ceasefire has held out for nearly two years mainly because of a stable and effective regime supervised by a

Sri Lanka Monitoring Mission (SLMM) consisting of nearly sixty officers from Scandinavian countries. The first palpable signs of discord emerged, however, ironically, after an outline of an agreement was claimed on the core political issue of regional self-rule (or internal self-determination) based on a federal structure within a united Sri Lanka (instead of Eelam).

After six rounds of talks the LTTE pulled out of the peace process in April 2003, refusing to attend the international donors' conference in Tokyo two months later. The official reason stated was that the Sri Lankan Government had not honoured agreements made in earlier rounds, specifically the vacation by Sri Lankan Security Forces (SLSF) of the High Security Zone in Palaly in Jaffna so that Tamils displaced from those areas could be resettled. There were two other reasons. The first had to do with the preparatory to the Tokyo conference in Washington under the aegis of the US State Department to which the LTTE had not been invited as it was on the US Foreign Terrorist Organizations (FTO) list. But the real reason for the LTTE's anger and impatience was the delay over handing over the interim administration of the North East to them, an arrangement widely believed to have been made with the United National Party (UNP) before the elections in 2001.

After initial euphoria over the momentum of the peace process, the year 2003 was largely one of setbacks at two levels: conflict resolution or the transformation of the political process into a peace process; and chasms in Sinhalese consensus over power sharing with the LTTE. This manifested in the failure of political cohabitation between President Chandrika Kumaratunga of the Sri Lanka Freedom Party (SLFP) and her arch rival, Prime Minister Wickremasinghe from the UNP. The only ray of hope came from the peace dividend that had partly turned around the economy of the war-ravaged island and good and sound relations with India.

Most experts had predicted that political cohabitation was unlikely to work though the ceasefire would certainly hold and the LTTE would not be the first to break it. This was for two reasons: the $4.5 billion international safety net for development and reconstruction of the North East and the prospect of the LTTE legitimizing their de facto control of the North East. Eric Solheim, a key Norwegian facilitator, has said that the road to peace had three obstacles: political cohabitation, the Muslim-Tamil factor and the transformation of the LTTE from a military force into a political entity.

Cracks in the political cohabitation appeared when the Supreme Court shot down the 19th amendment curbing the powers of the Executive President. Chandrika Kumaratunga is not only head of state, but also head of government and cabinet and supreme commander of the armed forces. In the past she had kept the defence and finance portfolios with her but did not do so in the new government. But she did not refrain from publicly criticizing her government of a sellout to the LTTE. Just before the Oslo accord her party questioned the wisdom of giving control over the North East to the LTTE without their renouncing violence and agreeing to decommission weapons.[8]

She criticized Norway for ignoring Sri Lanka's national interest for the success of the talks and the US and the UK, who had proscribed the LTTE, for rewarding terrorism by committing funds. On at least two official visits to New Delhi during 2003, she lambasted the UNP government for ignoring violations of the ceasefire by the LTTE and letting them improve their defences and war preparedness. She warned the diplomatic community in Colombo and India that the LTTE had not given up Eelam and that the peace process and funding must be linked with decommissioning.[9] She complained that the LTTE had grown from 6,000 armed cadres to nearly 18,000 fighters with regular shipment of arms and recruitment of children. The SLSF, meanwhile, had little to show by way of upgradation of firepower or manpower. She said that while she realized that India, which was "militarily once bitten" was now "twice shy", it could not afford to "stand aloof" or wait "till the situation became irreversible".[10]

Writing in *The Hindu* on 5 August 2003, the former foreign minister and senior advisor to the President on foreign affairs, Lakshman Kadirgamar, described the worsening security situation around Trincomalee harbour, where he said the LTTE had encroached in violation of the ceasefire. Later the same month he visited New Delhi and briefed Indian leaders and officials about the threatening political and security situation in Sri Lanka.[11]

Meanwhile, the Government on 17 July made its proposal for a Provisional Administrative Structure with a majority stake for the LTTE to run the North East. The proposal, which kept Land, Revenue, Police and Security with Colombo, was rejected as "inadequate" by the LTTE.[12] LTTE counter-proposals for an Interim Self-governing Authority (ISGA), made on 31 October, sought sweeping powers covering nearly all aspects of governance that are a blueprint for a separate state, far removed from some kind of federal solution within a united Sri Lanka.[13] The ISGA, representing a maximalist position, would extend for five years before a final settlement. The government was quick to observe that the LTTE offer "differs in fundamental respects" from the proposals made by Colombo for resuming the stalled peace talks.[14] Through the years, the LTTE's strategy has been to maximize the divisions in the Sinhala-dominated Sri Lankan political establishment. The ISGA was clearly meant to deepen the rift between President Kumaratunga and Prime Minister Wickremasinghe, who represent two opposite camps.

For President Kumaratunga, bitterly opposed to the numerous concessions already made to the LTTE, the latter's counterproposals acted as the proverbial red rag to a bull. On 4 November she suddenly but not unexpectedly took three steps that amounted to a presidential coup. She assumed control of the ministries of Defence, Interior and Mass Communications, prorogued Parliament and declared an island-wide emergency. The last two measures were denied or revoked subsequently. The President justified her actions in "national interests" to "safeguard the sovereignty, security and territorial integrity of the country".[15]

President Kumaratunga had several reasons for her actions. She wanted to reassert her authority as executive President and be counted in the peace process. Most of all, as Supreme Commander she wished to exercise full control over the armed forces. Her efforts at reconciling differences with her Prime Minister failed as the latter was unwilling to resume talks with the LTTE without the return of the Defence portfolio. Despite the differences neither wanted the ceasefire or the peace process to go asunder. By the end of the year, President Kumaratunga had reworked the previously failed electoral alliance with the Marxist radical hardline Janata Vimukthi Peramuna (JVP).[16] A snap election, the third in four years, was most likely despite the Government, the LTTE and the donors trying to prevent it.

India-Sri Lanka relations were characterized as the best that India had with any other country in the region. The core for an emerging strategic partnership was bilateral economic ties and Sri Lanka's appreciation of India's security concerns. After decades of disuse, Trincomalee's historic oil tank farms in the harbour were entrusted in May 2003 to Lanka-India Oil Corporation, a wholly owned subsidiary for a 35-year lease and $30 million modernization plan.[17] Similarly, India is being awarded the contract of the modernization of the Palaly airbase. A defence cooperation agreement, which was in the making in 2003 and to which the LTTE were opposed, was expected to be signed in 2004. This could be followed by the SLSF at long last getting the go ahead for the construction of a memorial for the Indian Peace Keeping Forces (IPKF).

The success of the framework Comprehensive Economic Partnership Agreement (CEPA), prepared by a joint study group appointed in April 2003, would depend on the willingness of the two countries to open up their markets bilaterally by careful phasing out of existing barriers.[18] CEPA came against a backdrop of the bilateral trade crossing $1 billion under the India-Sri Lanka Free Trade Agreement. In addition to trade cooperation, Sri Lanka requested Indian assistance in the modernization of railways and support for a gas or coal power plant. New Delhi has extended $100 million line of credit and agreed to consider diversification of product ranges covered under the facility.[19]

India has high strategic stake in a just, fair and peaceful resolution of the ethnic conflict. The North East is hyphenless thanks to the 13th Amendment courtesy the India-Sri Lanka Accord (1987), which merged the two provinces temporarily for one year. Ever since, a proclamation is issued each year, allowing the merger to continue in the interest of conflict resolution. India extended the ban on the LTTE on 13 May 2002 for two years. The forthcoming elections in India will see a change of alliances affecting the key state of Tamil Nadu. This could give a future government in Delhi greater flexibility to influence events in Sri Lanka. India must not be seen to be vacating its strategic space in the Indian Ocean region centred around Sri Lanka due to the bitterness of history. Sri Lankans now openly acknowledge India's pre-eminence in the region and recognize that their prosperity rests in the nature of relations with India. Most of all, that there can be no resolution of the ethnic conflict without India's involvement.

Bangladesh

Maj. Gen. Nazir Husain Shah, one of Pakistan's most experienced soldiers of the 1971 War in East Pakistan, said soon after the surrender of Pakistan's forces and the creation of Bangladesh that he feared that Bangladesh would turn into a Disturbed Desh.[20] Many experts would today agree with his prediction. Bangladesh represents a serious security concern for India and the region, particularly the North-East. Indian strategic experts regard Bangladesh as the main sanctuary for Indian insurgent groups and Islamic terrorists, including al-Qaida and Taliban. Next to Pakistan, India considers Bangladesh its most difficult and worrisome neighbour. The year 2003 represents the lowest point in the history of bilateral relations. The irony is that India helped in the separation from Pakistan and the creation of Bangladesh. The paradox is that it was a Bengali Muslim leader, Abdul Kasem Fazlul Haq, who first moved the Lahore-Pakistan resolution.[21]

A more telling irony is that whereas India-Bangladesh relations are going downhill, Bangladesh-Pakistan ties are on the mend. An Islamic resurgence is palpable especially after 9/11, the October 2001 elections and Gen. Pervez Musharraf's Dhaka visit in 2002. Bangladesh was established on the four principles of democracy, socialism, secularism and Bengali nationalism. It was Bangladesh's two military leaders—Gen. Ziaur Rehman (1975) and Lt. Gen. H.M. Ershad (1987) who amended the constitution, removed secularism as its cornerstone, introduced Islam as State religion and brought back pro-Pakistan fundamentalist parties and sidelined heroes of the freedom struggle.

In the past decade Bangladesh has undergone a fundamental social and political transformation with a new brand of nationalism and Islamic fervour replacing secular Bengali nationalism.[22] The Khaleda

Zia-Bangladesh Nationalist Party-led coalition government includes the fundamentalist Jamaat-e-Islami (JeI) and Islamic Oikyo Jote (IOJ). Aziz ul Haque, the IOJ chairman, is a member of the advisory council of Harkat ul Jehadi al Islam (HuJI), Bangladesh's main terrorist group. The HuJI has ties with Islamic militants in Pakistan and has been declared a terrorist organization by the US. The Islamist groups that have come up in Bangladesh are JeI, Islamic Chhatra Shivir—youth wing of JeI, IoJ, HuJI (who also call themselves the Bangladeshi Taliban), the Jehad Movement, the Arakan Rohingya National Organization and Rohingya Solidarity Organization.[23]

Bangladesh intelligence services and armed forces are not insulated from local and foreign terrorist groups with bases in Bangladesh. The Directorate General Field Intelligence (DGFI), Bangladesh's premier intelligence agency, has strong ties with Pakistan's Inter Services Intelligence (ISI). There are nearly thirty terrorist outfits that operate in North-East India and have bases in Bangladesh.

On 27 November 2002, India's Minister of External Affairs, Yashwant Sinha, stated publicly that the Pakistan High Commission in Dhaka had become the nerve centre of the ISI. On 28 October 2003, the Director General of the Border Security Force (BSF) handed over details of 88 insurgent leaders and 99 camps to his Bangladeshi counterpart. These camps belonged to the National Liberation Front of Tripura (25), All Tripura Tiger Force (20), National Socialist Council of Nagaland-IM (18), United Liberation Front of Assam (17), People's Liberation Army (10), Achik National Volunteer Council (3), Muslim United Liberation Tigers of Assam (2), National Democratic Front of Bodoland (2), Chakma National Liberation Front (1), and Dima Halim Daogah (1). After Bhutan's military operations in December 2003 against thirty camps of Indian insurgent groups on its soil, India has been pointedly suggesting that Bangladesh and Myanmar follow suit.

The history of bitterness and hostility between Dhaka and Islamabad is being slowly revised partly to spite India and partly due to vigorous efforts by Pakistan in conjunction with China and Saudi Arabia to exploit conflictual relations between Bangladesh and India. Reconciliation with Pakistan will take time and require an apology for 1971, repatriation of stranded Pakistanis and division of liabilities and assets, notwithstanding the historic first visit of a Pakistani President, General Musharraf in July 2002.[24] Pakistan-Bangladesh annual trade amounts to a mere $130 million though a Joint Business Council recently estimated that the potential is for $4.5 billion.

Bangladesh has against India its list of grouses: taking away valuables after the military victory in 1971, failure to resolve the Farakka dispute, lack of demarcation of some border areas and dumping of Indian goods in Bangladesh markets.[25] The anti-India feelings, rise of the Islamists and resurgence of Bangladeshi nationalism have combined to further whittle down Indian influence in Bangladesh. The single biggest problem for India 28 years after the India-Bangladesh land border agreement is management of the 4100 km long boundary. Bangladesh's borders abut West Bengal, Assam, Meghalaya, Myanmar and Tripura. The demarcation is inadequate: 51 Bangladesh enclaves and 101 Indian enclaves have to be exchanged while 6.5 km of border have yet to be demarcated.[26] Another problem of the porous border is smuggling. Speaking in the Rajya Sabha on 24 April 2003, Minister of State for External Affairs, Vinod Khanna, stated that unofficial exports to Bangladesh are estimated at Rs 11.65 billion annually.

At the latest meeting in October 2003 between the BSF and Bangladesh Rifles (BDR), the two sides agreed on joint inspection to determine defensive structures forbidden within 150 yards on either side of the international border. Only 650 km of the border has been fenced so far. In April 2003, India had proposed joint patrolling of the common border to prevent smuggling, unauthorized cross-border activity and illegal immigration.[27] The Indian proposal was rejected. Nearly 6,000 people from Bangladesh cross over daily to India in search of work.

The most serious problem is that of illegal immigration. Thousands of Bangladeshi nationals have been arrested trying to cross the border. While the BSF prefers a quick handover, the BDR prefers deportation through consular access. Cross-border movement of terrorists results in incidents of firing. The export of manpower, both legal and illegal, appears to have become part of Bangladesh's foreign policy. A group of intellectuals in Dhaka has sought to justify and even legitimize the migration of its people to the north-east region of India by invoking the theory of Lebensraum (living space).[28] Similarly, fundamentalists in Bangladesh are advocating that the borders defined at the time of partition are no longer relevant and need to be changed on account of demographic alterations brought about by large-scale illegal immigration. To counter Bangladesh's policy of destabilizing India's north-east, more innovative schemes for border management would be needed.

In 1971, India was forced to go to war to push back 10 million refugees from East Pakistan. According to a statement from the Ministry of Home Affairs, as many as 20 million Bangladeshis are known to have infiltrated into India of which 10 million are in Assam and West Bengal alone. The demographic bomb is ticking away. The problem is so serious that in November 1998, the Governor of Assam Lt. Gen. S.K. Sinha had to submit a special report to the President of India. The Illegal Migration Detection Tribunal (IMDT) Act of 1983 has proved highly impractical and only five of the sixteen district tribunals are functional. Between 1983 and 2000, just 10,000 illegal residents were identified and only 1400 deported.[29]

At the bilateral level relations are at a nadir since 1971. Differences are manifest in a number of areas, especially on water sharing, trade issues and export of gas. The only good news came from the appointment of a joint technical group on the sharing of the Teesta waters and six other common rivers.[30] The BNP-led government is historically antagonistic to India and uses the external factor to leverage India. The rising tide of fundamentalism, Islamic fervour and increasing presence of insurgent groups and terrorists are likely to result in a not too distant future in a backlash in Bangladesh as in Pakistan, which would have the potential of spilling over into India.

Bhutan

Bhutan has continued to rely on the philosophy of Gross National Happiness rather than Gross National Product. It has factored four areas of activity: economic growth and development, preservation and promotion of cultural heritage, preservation and sustainable use of environment, and good governance.[31] Bhutan has become an oasis of political and economic stability in the region, enjoying the highest per capita income of US$800 in South Asia. Water power generates Bhutan's relative affluence and contentment. Of the estimated potential of 38,000 MW of electricity, nearly 2000 MW would have been realized by 2005 due to the Chukha and Tala (and Ruksom) projects.

Relations between Bhutan and India are the most stable, friendly and cooperative and guided by the 1949 Indo-Bhutan Treaty of friendship, according to which Bhutan has agreed to be guided on defence and foreign affairs by India. The Treaty is observed more in spirit than in text. It was in this spirit of cooperation that the Royal Bhutan Army launched its first and most successful Operation All Clear on 15 December 2003 to evict insurgents belonging to ULFA, NDFB and KLO holed up in thirty camps in East Bhutan.[32] More than 50 per cent of the 2000 insurgents were neutralized while 500 had surrendered. Although Bhutan took its own time responding to the strategic challenge posed by the insurgents, by its decisive action it demonstrated a determination not to allow the use of its sovereign territory to be used by insurgents operating in neighbouring India. Their presence in Bhutan was a threat not only to Bhutan's own security but also to the stability of the region.

The bold, courageous, and independent action by Bhutan augurs well for security cooperation in South Asia and will act as an example that Bangladesh, Pakistan, and Myanmar could emulate in dealing with terrorists who have sought sanctuary on their soil. At the 12th SAARC summit at Islamabad in January 2004, Bhutan was commended for its military operations. Bhutan has to resolve the contentious issue of 90,000 of its refugees in Nepal and the border dispute with China. India, it has been suggested, should consider steps to lower the visibility of the military training and border construction teams deployed in Bhutan.

Notes

1. Lakshman Kadirgamar, "Securing South Asia", *The Hindu*, 29 December 2003.
2. Constitution of the Kingdom of Nepal 2047 and Electoral Laws, Article 127, Power to Remove Difficulties. "If any difficulty arises in bringing this

Constitution into force, His Majesty may issue necessary orders to remove these difficulties. The orders so issued shall be placed in Parliament." In the view of many experts, the King has removed democracy rather than the difficulties.

3. Ashok K. Mehta, "The Maoist Insurgency in Nepal and State Response", paper presented at the Institute for Defence Studies and Analyses (IDSA), New Delhi, May 2003.
4. Constitution of the Kingdom of Nepal 2047 and Electoral Laws, Article 118(2), "His Majesty shall perform the operation and deployment of Royal Nepal Army on the recommendation of the National Defence Committee". The Prime Minister chairs this committee.
5. Baleshwar Agarwal, quoting World Bank estimates for 2003-4 in *Friends of Nepal*, a fortnightly summary of background material on Nepal, 15 January 2004.
6. Maoist Website, www.maoist.org, 11 April 2003.
7. Ashok K. Mehta, "LTTE: Benefit of the Doubt", *The Pioneer*, 18 December 2002.
8. Ibid.
9. Press Release, Presidential Secretariat—Democratic Socialist Republic of Sri Lanka, 31 March 2003 and her briefing in New Delhi to a select group on 9 April 2003. Also see press release of 16 August 2003 at New Delhi by Lakshman Kadirgamar containing a critique of the ceasefire and its violations.
10. President Chandrika Kumaratunga's briefing in New Delhi to a select group on 9 April 2003.
11. Lakshman Kadirgamar, press release at New Delhi, 16 August 2003.
12. V.S. Sambandan, "LTTE Rejects Proposals", *The Hindu*, 21 July 2003.
13. Editorial, *The Hindu*, 4 November 2003.
14. V.S. Sambandan, "Government Offer Differs in Fundamental Respects", *The Hindu*, 2 November 2003.
15. Dipankar Banerjee and N. Manoharan, "Constitutional Crisis and the Peace Process in Sri Lanka", Institute of Peace and Conflict Studies, issue brief no. 15, December 2003.
16. The pact was signed on 19 January 2004 with five basic objectives. The SLFP and JVP combined to form the United People's Freedom Alliance. President Chandrika Kumaratunga's previous alliance was called People's Alliance.
17. V.S. Sambandan, "Modernisation Work Begins at Sri Lanka's Oil Tank Farm", *The Hindu*, 28 May 2003.
18. Nisha Taneja and Arpita Mukherjee, "The Failure of Indo-Lanka CIPA", *Business Standard*, 23 October 2003.
19. V.S. Sambandan, "Ranil to Focus on Economic Partnership", *The Hindu*, 19 October 2003.

20. These remarks were made to Ashok K. Mehta in conversation on 17 December 1971 at Bogra, East Pakistan/Bangladesh.
21. Dr Moonis Ahmar, "Pakistan and Bangladesh: From Conflict to Cooperation", Bangladesh Institute of Strategic Studies, Paper 19, March 2003.
22. Bertil Lintner, "Extremist Islamist Consolidation", *Faultlines*, Vol. 14, April 2003.
23. Ibid.
24. Dr Moonis Ahmar, n. 21.
25. Ibid.
26. Kanchan Lakshman and Sanjay K. Jha, "Restoring Sovereignty on Neglected Borders", *Akrosh*, July 2003.
27. Anand Kumar, "It Takes Two to Manage a Border", *Indian Express*, 9 November 2003.
28. Ibid.
29. Lakshman and Jha, n. 26.
30. Pioneer News Service, "Indo-Bangla Watersharing Meet", *The Pioneer*, 22 January 2004.
31. Window on Bhutan 2003, Roots Advertising Services, New Delhi.
32. Dipankar Banerjee and Bidhan S. Laisharan, *Bhutan's Operation All Clear—Implications for Insurgency and Security Cooperation*, Institute of Peace and Conflict Studies, New Delhi, February 2004.

Pakistan under Islamist Siege

Wilson John

Pakistan is a nation with dwindling options. The military's attempts at democracy by holding elections, forging alliances with religious parties and enacting new laws to circumvent the Constitution have only deepened the political vacuum in that country. This could have serious consequences for South Asia in the near future. Despite the crackdown on terrorist groups after the two assassination attempts on President Pervez Musharraf and a US-led operation against terrorist elements in the tribal areas, Pakistan faces the threat of jihadis more than ever before, this time with a lurking fear that they may have gained access to nuclear or radioactive materials, if not nuclear weapons.

There has been a dramatic change in the fortunes of President Musharraf since 12 January 2002, when he, in an address to the nation, outlined his resolve to put down extremist elements and create an atmosphere of peace and reconciliation within Pakistan and with its neighbours, particularly India.[1] Notably strident on Kashmir on other occasions, President Musharraf called for a peaceful means of resolving the dispute.[2] Pragmatism and more than a little nudge from the United States prompted him to strike this conciliatory posture. He was aware that the US did not intend to limit its operations to Afghanistan if his country continued to harbour the fleeing al-Qaida and Taliban elements. What caused General Musharraf and his Army serious concern was the ready support the fleeing al-Qaida and Taliban elements were drawing from homegrown terrorists and religious extremist networks. Even the US intelligence agencies were becoming alarmed by this growing nexus. Intelligence reports from Central Intelligence Agency (CIA) and Federal Bureau of Investigation (FBI) operatives in Pakistan increasingly reported the regrouping of al-Qaida and the Taliban elements with local religious and extremist groups like Sipah-e-Saheba Pakistan (SSP) and Lashkar-e-Jhangvi (LeJ). Reports also spoke of al-Qaida elements staging attacks on US troops operating in Afghanistan from their bases in Pakistan's Frontier and tribal areas.[3] President Musharraf himself, the reports warned, was in extreme danger of being ousted either in a coup engineered by religious extremist elements in the Army or assassinated by extremist groups who were changing under the pressure. Giving testimony to this effect before Congress Vice Admiral Lowell Jacoby, Director of the US Defense Intelligence Agency, warned: "Islamist opponents of the current government, or religious extremists, could try to instigate a political crisis through violent means. Coup or assassination could result in an extremist Pakistan."[4]

Rise of Religious Parties

The rise and growth of religious parties after the October 2002 general elections has been phenomenal. The birth of Muttahida Majlis-e-Amal (MMA) is a representative case study. The MMA is a six-party alliance of religious parties and groups. The two factions of Jamait-ul-Ulema Islam (JUI), the more important of these six groups, have been on and off the fringes of domestic politics but boast strong influence in matters of religion, mainly in the vast, impoverished, illiterate hinterland of Pakistan. Some leading lights of the alliance—Maulana Fazlur Rehman, Maulana Samiul Haq and Qazi Hussain Ahmed—have been involved in creating and propagating the mujahideen culture, providing recruits and sanctifying it as a Jihad or Holy War. While the President and his men were cobbling together a King's Party—the Pakistan Muslim League Qaid-e-Azam (PML-QA)—by cannibalizing outright opportunist politicians from other parties, the MMA won just enough seats in the provincial Assemblies and the National Assembly to put them in a jockeying position for power. The MMA is today the third largest party in Parliament, has a government in the North West Frontier Province and a coalition government in Balochistan. Never before had the religious groups come so close to ruling from Islamabad.

The political clout of the MMA has had a dramatic morale boosting effect on the religious extremist groups, which were reeling under a series of ban orders issued by the Musharraf government and monitored by US intelligence and security forces. Groups like SSP and LeJ, officially banned, operated under various new names, providing shelter to al-Qaida and Taliban elements. The first evidence of the latter regrouping surfaced just two months after the US began carpet-bombing Afghanistan to dismantle the Taliban,[5] in the killing of six Shiite SUPARCO (Space and Upper Atmosphere Research Commission) employees in Karachi in September 2003 and the subsequent revenge killing of SSP chief Azam Tariq in Islamabad the next month.[6]

It would be presumed, rightly, that in some instances at least, a few organs of General Musharraf's government were aware of these alliances and were actively encouraging them. In the much-publicized crackdown on extremist and terrorist organizations, the leaders of terrorist and extremist organizations were kept under house arrest and charged only under the Maintenance of Public Order Act, 1960, and not under a more severe anti-terrorism law. All of them were released subsequently since three months in the maximum detention stipulated by the law. Emboldened by this pusillanimity of the government, the MMA became vociferous in its twin demand for General Musharraf's ouster and withdrawal of the Legal Framework Order (LFO).[7] It held nation-wide protests and rallies, staged walk-outs from the National Assembly and generally created an atmosphere of uncertainty by imposing restrictions on women, education and entertainment in the name of Sharia. The Army unequivocally stood by General Musharraf, as was evident in the arrest of a senior al-Qaida leader, Khaled Mohammad Sheikh from the Rawalpindi house of Ahmed Abdul Quddus, a member of Qazi Hussain Ahmed's JUI. The Qazi has been particularly vocal in the demand for General Musharraf's ouster. In quick succession, as the MMA announced a series of anti-US rallies across the country, two other al-Qaida operatives, Abu Omar and Abu Humza, were arrested from the house of another JUI leader in Karachi, Sahiba Ali Khan. The message was clear to the MMA leaders.

Constitutional Amendment

For the MMA, a coalition riddled with over-ambitious leaders and retrogressive ideologies, the LFO provided the only highway to Islamabad. The LFO was a quasi-constitutional amendment which

General Musharraf had promulgated in August 2002 disguised as a notification for the general elections but with the primary objective of keeping a check on the Opposition parties from threatening his position. It was obviously an Army law in character, blanketing all civilian participation in governance and making the Chief of Army Staff the final arbiter of Pakistan's destiny. It fitted well with the Army's scheme of "democratizing" Pakistan, a Presidential form of government with the Chief of Army Staff as the President with over-arching powers over the civilian establishment. The second step in that process was the Seventeenth Amendment, passed, ironically with the help of the MMA, on 29 December 2003. From the outset it was clear to the MMA leadership that General Musharraf was not a push over nor was there any chance of the Army rebelling against him. The Pakistan Army has never brooked opposition from the civilians. The MMA, therefore, came up with a more realistic demand: either General Musharraf give up his uniform or quit as the President.

General Musharraf, and the Army, were more comfortable in dealing with the MMA rather than other political parties in the Opposition. An instance of their deft handling of the Maulanas in the past was inviting some of them for a special briefing at the Foreign Ministry in the initial stages of the US operations in Pakistan. The Maulanas, in the Army's perception, would never enjoy the kind of national support that the other political parties could, given a freer space to operate in Pakistan's polity. With their narrow interpretation of the Islamic way of life, the Maulanas are seen by a large majority of people as retrogressive, an anachronism at a time of increasing globalization and rising aspirations for a better and prosperous future. The World Bank's refusal to disburse a grant of US$100 million sanctioned for women empowerment programmes in the North West Frontier Province ruled by the MMA drove this message home. General Musharraf found it convenient to negotiate with the Maulanas alone, dividing what otherwise would have been a formidable Opposition even without former Premiers Nawaz Sharif and Benazir Bhutto. He also banked on the fact that the leadership of the MMA was too ambitious to remain united in the days to come. In fact, the passing of the Constitution (Seventeenth Amendment) Bill, 2003, saw the sidelining of smaller parties in the MMA who resent the fact that Qazi Hussain Ahmed and Maulana Fazlur Rehman are calling the shots without consulting the other alliance partners. The top brass of the Army meanwhile has vocally backed General Musharraf at least on three occasions in the past two years: they have expressed the view that given the present geo-strategic environment, General Musharraf would best serve the interest of the nation and not a new General in Islamabad.[8]

There are indications that in return for signing an agreement on 24 December 2003 to allow the government to incorporate the LFO into the Constitution, the government had offered to the MMA leadership a deal, negotiated over six months. The nature of its secrecy implies substantial concessions to the religious parties and their affiliate extremist and secessionist organizations. Both the military regime and the Maulanas were acting out a charade before the world since most of the provisions in the Seventeenth Amendment were agreed to in July 2003 itself, including the controversial Article 58(2)(b), the discretionary power of the President to dismiss the National Assembly.[9] General Musharraf, on his part had, by September 2003, declared his intention to step down as the Chief of Army Staff by December 2004.[10] These concessions were announced piecemeal with the objective of enticing the other alliance, the Alliance for Restoration of Democracy (ARD), to the side of the regime. The MMA even floated the idea of gathering all political parties under one umbrella by holding briefings for the members of the Opposition on the progress of the talks. Interestingly, three days later when the Bill was tabled in the National Assembly, the MMA baulked; Maulana Fazlur Rehman, during the debate on the Bill, said they would only agree to vote if the Bill amended the 1973 Constitution as it was before the LFO. It was a clear attempt to extract maximum mileage from General Musharraf, a fact which became clear the next day when the government and the MMA re-entered an agreement which said both the parties would allow the Bill as tabled in the Assembly to be passed with the condition that it could be changed if there was a violation of their mutual agreement. By then, it was clear that the other opposition parties would not back the President.

General Musharraf, at the end of the day, gained political legitimacy, a critical factor in his equation with the United States, and a reprieve from the constant political badgering on the issue of LFO and Uniform in return for a solo concession of agreeing in principle to shed his uniform by December 2004. The Seventeenth Amendment reveals the scope of power he now enjoys. Article 58(2)(b) gives him the power to dissolve the National Assembly with a caveat that he will have to refer the matter to the Supreme Court which "shall decide the reference within thirty days, whose decision shall be final". In other words, this clause bars a Prime Minister or any member of the Cabinet or anyone else from challenging the presidential decision in a court of law. Similar powers have been bestowed upon the Governors in respect of provincial Assemblies (Article 112) except that it would require presidential approval. The new law also gives the President the discretionary authority (Article 152A) to make appointments of the Service Chiefs with a rider that he would consult the Prime Minister. Two other significant clauses are those that bar two-time Prime Ministers from holding the same office for a third term (Qualification to hold Public Office Order—Chief Executive Order No. 19 of 2002) and an amendment to the National Accountability Bureau Ordinance. The seventeenth Amendment disallows their amendment without the approval of the President.

Fractious Mullahs

The momentary discord within the MMA, however, betrayed a division within the alliance since the decision to oppose the Bill in the Assembly on the first day of the debate was taken at the behest of Qazi Hussain Ahmed, who was abroad when the agreement was signed. A factor that might have caused consternation in the Qazi faction of the JUI was the manner in which Maulana Fazlur Rahman made himself a part of the two-member negotiating committee of Liaqat Baloch of JUI and Hafiz Husain Ahmed of JUI-F and signed the agreement. The divisions within the MMA have been known for quite some time, especially among the top leadership. The Qazi and the Maulana have often struck diametrically different notes on issues like Kashmir, peace talks with India and President Musharraf. During the early stages of the talks with the government, the JUI-F and JUI had serious differences over the charter of demands. In fact, an agreement brokered by PML-QA leader Chaudhary Shujaat Hussain and JUI-F had to be abandoned in the face of stiff opposition from the Qazi. On 22 October 2003, the dissension broke out in the open when several Members of the National Assembly belonging to JUI-F and JUI confronted MMA chief Ahmad Noorani on the issue of LFO and asked him to spell out the party's stand. The meeting convened by Noorani also witnessed a boycott by JUI-Samiul Haq members. There were also indications that the MMA, despite its anti-US rhetoric, was following the diktat of the United States. The agreement between the MMA and the government was, in fact, one of the talking points when Prime Minister Mir Zafarullah Jamali and President Musharraf visited the United States in September 2003.[11]

This only lent further credence to the belief that the MMA was hand in glove with the Musharraf government and was pursuing a peace agenda with India, a factor that may have prompted extremist groups to launch two assassination attempts on President Musharraf. Lashker-e-Toiba, in particular, had been critical of Maulana Fazlur Rahman visiting India on a Track II mission to expedite the thaw in Indo-Pak relations. Lashkar chief Hafiz Sayed termed it as "sabotaging" the Kashmir jihad.[12] A London-based terrorist group, Hizbul Tehreer, engaged in the recent past in expanding its activities in Pakistan, warned several Senators through letters against voting in favour of President Musharraf.[13] In September 2003, Ayman al-Zawahari, a key aide to Osama bin Laden, in a taped broadcast had called President Musharraf an enemy and directed that he be eliminated. As the investigations have subsequently proved, several groups were involved in the two attacks on President Musharraf (14 and 25 December 2003); the use of C4 explosive and suicide bombers revealed meticulous planning, infiltration of local police and intelligence agencies and the involvement of an expanding local network of terrorists with international connections,[14] especially al-Qaida and the Taliban.

It was against this background that two significant events unfolded. First, the surprisingly swift thaw in India-Pakistan relations with President Musharraf shedding his traditional rhetoric on Kashmir and expressing a clear willingness to sit across the table with India. Second, his decision to launch an Army operation in the tribal areas against al-Qaida and other terrorist groups regrouping against the US security forces. This unprecedented decision could have immediate and serious implications for General Musharraf in the days to come if the operations were to continue for a longer duration. The JUI-F faction in the MMA has already criticized the operations in Wana, terming them as "terrorism". Early January 2004, at least four Pakistani soldiers were killed as cornered terrorists launched a rocket attack on the Army Brigade Headquarters. The Army has lost sixteen of its soldiers in south Waziristan since June 2002. Not only had the Army rushed 500 commandos to the site to control the situation, the administrator of south Waziristan, Mohammad Azam Khan, spelt out a warning to the jirga (an assembly) of 250 tribesmen, to either back the Army operations or face serious repercussions. Either way, it would spell a period of uncertainty and anxiety for President Musharraf and, in no less measure, the international community increasingly dismayed at the extent of nuclear proliferation orchestrated by a handful of nuclear scientists, politicians and Army officials for more than a decade. The chain of events and misdemeanours, being uncovered by a worldwide investigation, is disclosing that the fear of nuclear materials falling into the hands of extremist elements in Pakistan or elsewhere is a very real threat.

A Dim Prospect

What lies in store for Pakistan is certainly not peace and prosperity. A progressive nation draws its strength from its political, judicial and social institutions. In Pakistan, these institutions have long been subservient to the military with occasional flirtations with the idea of civilian democracy. In the past four years of his rule, President Musharraf has only strengthened the military stranglehold over these institutions by systematically compromising first the judicial institutions, beginning with the Supreme Court and high courts, filling up civilian positions with retired and serving military officers and then rendering the political establishment vulnerable and brittle by a series of political blackmail and horse-trading. The much-touted rapprochement with the MMA, acclaimed by the United States and others, was another of his expedient strategies to buy time to consolidate his position within the military establishment after allowing the US security forces a free hand to operate in the tribal areas of Pakistan, and, no less significantly, prevent any attempts on the part of political parties to unite against his rule. But this strategy has the potential to boomerang on him. The two major opposition parties—the Pakistan People's Party and the Pakistan Muslim League-Nawaz—have been forcibly sidelined from the political spectrum, which would prove to be the fatal flaw in President Musharraf's professed attempts at democratization.[15] The MMA is a mercurial alliance, led by highly ambitious Maulanas who have their feet firmly on the religious ground with their sight on Islamabad. Their past alliances, strong and traditional, with extremist groups, including the Taliban, cannot simply be wished away. Not long ago, they would have been locked up behind bars; at least one of the Maulanas was charged with sedition in the early months of President Musharraf's regime.

There are no visible signs of Pakistan emerging from this state of negatives[16] in the foreseeable future; it is, and will remain, a state incapable of building an enduring political system, a factor which, coupled with an ever-increased threat from extremist elements in the madrasa-military complex in Pakistan, a rapidly decreasing economic opportunity and a booming birth rate, would continue to blight the possibility of an enduring peace and stability within a nuclearized Pakistan, with consequential fallouts in its neighbourhood.

Notes

1. "Text of President Musharraf's Address to Nation", *Dawn* (Karachi), 12 January 2002. http://www.dawn.com/2002/01/12/speech020112.htm
2. "The Kashmir problem needs to be resolved by dialogue and peaceful means in accordance with the wishes of the Kashmiri people and the United Nations resolutions. No organisation will be allowed to indulge in terrorism in the name of Kashmir". See ibid.
3. "Testimony of Vice Admiral Lowell Jacoby, Director, Defense Intelligence Agency, before the US Senate Committee on Intelligence, 11 February 2003", http://fas.org/irp/congress/2003_hr/021103jacoby.html
4. Ibid.
5. A Kenyan trucking firm operator, Sheikh Ahmed Salim, an al-Qaida activist involved in the 1998 bombing of US embassies in Nairobi and Dar es-Salaam, when arrested in July 2002 from Karachi, revealed the regrouping

of al-Qaida and the Taliban in Pakistan with the help of religious extremist groups like LeJ and SSP. Salim said he had collected several million dollars with the help of LeJ and SSP (extortion is an important source of revenue for extremist elements in Pakistan). One of Salim's conduits in Karachi was a LeJ activist named Fazl Karim. He was picked up for questioning in March 2002 for the murder of American journalist Daniel Pearl. Karim was one of the three who held Pearl and slit his throat. Karim told his interrogators about the regrouping and merger of various sectarian and extremist groups within Pakistan. The two Yemenis who slit Pearl's throat were associates of Ramzi Yousef, a key al-Qaida operative who was caught in Karachi early 2003. Karim had aligned with two others, Naeem Bokhari and Zubair Chishti, in plotting Pearl's killing. Bokhari was an al-Qaida sympathizer and member of SSP. Chishti, another SSP activist, had fought against the Northern Alliance in Afghanistan.

6. "Azam Tariq: the man who was", *Friday Times*, 10-16 October 2003. Intelligence officials have uncovered another link in the chain that binds these groups. During the investigations of various secessionist and terrorist activities during the past two years it was noted that every time there was a crackdown on terror groups in areas bordering Pakistan and Afghanistan, Shia Muslims were targeted promptly. Such incidents have happened in Quetta twice in July 2003. The Karachi killings followed crackdowns on terror groups in south Waziristan. More than Karachi (since most of the al-Qaida cells were wiped out in the past two years under the United States' pressure), it is Quetta which reveals the return of the al-Qaida-Taliban combine with the active assistance of JuI, which is a coalition partner in the provincial government in Balochistan. The new terror groups, which operate under various names (one new addition was Muslim United Army), draw sustenance, both moral and material, from madrasas run by JuI in Balochistan; one such madrasa is Shaldara madrasa run by Maulana Nur Mohammed, known to be a prominent training and shelter house for the new Taliban-al-Qaida combine.
7. "Text of Legal Framework Order, 2002", *Dawn*, 22 August 2002, http://dawn.com/2002/08/22/ top3.htm
8. "Army Wants Musharraf to Stay As President, COAS", *The News* (Lahore), 17 May 2003.
9. "Govt.-MMA Accord on Four LFO Issues", *The News*, 30 July 2003.
10. "Musharraf to Quit as COAS by December 2004", *The Nation*, 10 September 2003.
11. "Govt.-MMA Talks Have US Backing", *The News*, 18 September 2003.
12. "Jehadi Groups Unhappy with JUI, JI", *Friday Times*, 18-24 July 2003.
13. "Senators Get Threatening Letters from Banned Outfit", *The News*, 27 December 2003.
14. "48 Religious Outfits with 'Terror Links' Identified", *Daily Times*, 27 December 2003.

15. "Stability or Instability Ahead?", *Daily Times*, 27 December 2003.
16. Stephen Cohen, "The Nation and the State of Pakistan", *Washington Quarterly* (Washington), Summer 2000.

National Security Index

Satish Kumar

This year's National Security Index is an improvement on last year's index in the choice of variables, sources of information and methodologies employed. What we have is a fairly dependable estimate of India's national power in comparison with forty-nine other countries of the world. These fifty top countries of the world have been selected on the basis of their national income rather than defence expenditure which was the basis of selection for last year's Index.

It should be interesting to note that for the third year in succession, India occupies a position among the top ten countries of the world in the composite National Security Index, which takes into account all plausible quantifiable variables. The National Security Index 2004 is based on an assessment of national income, defence capability, effective population, technological strength, national health and environmental vulnerability of 50 countries. While India occupies the 9th position in the composite index, it is preceded by the United States, which tops the list and China, Japan, Sweden, Finland, Russia, Canada, and South Korea in descending order. There are important countries like Germany, Switzerland, Australia, Norway, France and United Kingdom, which are placed below India and occupy the 10th to 15th positions respectively.

Significantly, India is well placed with regard to national income, defence capability and effective population, with the rank of 11 in national income, 3 in defence capability and 2 in effective population. India is somewhat moderately placed in technological strength holding the 25th rank, and very poorly placed in health and environmental vulnerability, holding the 46th rank in each.

The index on National Income is based on Gross National Income (GNI) of each country in 2002 and the growth rate of GNI over the previous year. The size of GNI and the growth rate are assigned a weightage of 60 per cent and 40 per cent respectively in the calculation of the index. The Defence Index is calculated from two indicators, viz., defence expenditure in 2002 and the size of the army. Both the indicators are given equal weightage in the calculation of this index.

The Technology Index is calculated from three indictors, viz., research and development (R&D) expenditure as percentage of Gross Domestic Product (GDP) during 1996-2000; patents granted per million residents in 1999; and scientists and engineers in research and development per million residents during 1999-2000. R&D expenditure as percentage of GDP is assigned 60 per cent weightage, and the other two indicators are assigned 20 per cent weightage each. The Population Index consists of three variables, viz., size of the country's population, adult literacy rate and the proportion of the population above the poverty line. The size of the population is multiplied by the adult literacy rate and the proportion of population above the poverty line to obtain the size of effective population.

The Health Jndex is computed from three variables, viz., life expectancy at birth—2001, incidence of tuberculosis, and incidence of HIV/AIDS. These three variables are given equal weightage. The Environment Vulnerability Index is obtained from the South Pacific Applied Geo-Science Commission Report, which computed the index for 235 countries based on 54 indicators covering a variety of aspects like environmental degradation, meteorological, geological, anthropogenic and biological factors and intrinsic resilience of the country.

The composite National Security Index combines the above six indices with the weightage given against each:

National Income	:	25
Defence Capability	:	25
Effective Population	:	15
Technological Strength	:	15
National Health	:	10
Environmental Vulnerability	:	10

Computation of the Indices

The index has been constructed to standardize the indicators on a scale of 0 to 100 and make it unidirectional. The index of a positive variable (where a higher value indicates greater strength) like national income and size of the army is calculated as:

$$Index = \frac{(Country\ Value - Minimum\ Value)}{(Maximum\ Value - Minimum\ Value)} \times 100$$

For instance, the value of the index for GNI of India is computed as follows:

$$\frac{\text{501,532 (India's GNI) - 48,462 (Lowest GNI among the 50 countries)}}{\text{10,110,087 (Highest GNI) - 48,462 (Lowest GNI)}} \times 100$$

$= 4.5$

The index of growth rate of GNI for India has been similarly computed and found to be 74.7.

The cumulative index of national income (with a weight of 60% for GNI and 40% for growth rate of GNI) for India is:

$= (0.60 \times 4.5) + (0.40 \times 74.7)$

$= 32.58$

For a negative indicator (where a lower value indicates greater strength) like incidence of tuberculosis and AIDS, the index is calculated as:

$$\text{Index} = \frac{(Maximum\ Value - Country\ Value)}{(Maximum\ Value - Minimum\ Value)} \times 100$$

Table 1. National Security Index

Country	Composite Index	Rank
United States	**68.51**	**1**
China	**52.93**	**2**
Japan	40.61	3
Sweden	36.33	4
Finland	35.91	5
Russian Federation	35.40	6
Canada	35.13	7
Korea, Rep.	34.92	8
India	**34.73**	**9**
Germany	34.40	10
Switzerland	33.36	11
Australia	33.14	12
Norway	32.87	13
France	32.55	14
United Kingdom	30.67	15
Israel	29.89	16
New Zealand	29.58	17
Saudi Arabia	27.79	18
Denmark	27.43	19
Mexico	27.24	20
Ireland	27.07	21
Czech Republic	26.90	22
Brazil	26.81	23
Turkey	25.96	24
Belgium	25.94	25
Netherlands	25.87	26
Austria	25.87	27
Spain	25.59	28
Chile	25.51	29
Poland	25.40	30
Italy	25.34	31
Greece	24.99	32

Country	Composite Index	Rank
Algeria	24.86	33
Egypt, Arab Rep.	24.10	34
Hungary	23.91	35
Iran, Islamic Rep.	23.83	36
Colombia	23.57	37
Portugal	23.56	38
Thailand	22.35	39
Peru	22.27	40
Indonesia	22.27	41
Malaysia	21.92	42
Venezuela, RB	21.40	43
Singapore	21.34	44
Pakistan	**20.78**	**45**
Hong Kong, China	20.68	46
Argentina	18.72	47
Bangladesh	17.18	48
Philippines	16.09	49
South Africa	11.47	50

Table 2. Ranks of Constituents of the National Security Index

Country	Rank						National Security Index
	National Income	Defence Capability	Effective Population	Technological Strength	National Health	Environmental Vulnerability	
United States	**1**	**1**	**3**	**5**	**16**	**11**	**1**
China	**5**	**2**	**1**	**27**	**40**	**38**	**2**
Japan	2	12	5	1	2	47	3
Sweden	36	43	39	2	1	12	4
Finland	40	45	45	3	10	3	5
Russian Federation	3	6	7	19	43	9	6
Canada	9	35	23	16	7	1	7
Korea, Rep.	13	4	17	4	31	44	8
India	**11**	**3**	**2**	**25**	**46**	**46**	**9**
Germany	8	9	9	8	13	34	10
Switzerland	22	11	42	7	4	26	11
Australia	26	32	27	18	5	2	12
Norway	16	44	45	14	3	4	13
France	14	13	11	9	9	32	14
United Kingdom	6	14	11	15	18	40	15
Israel	31	21	44	6	6	41	16
New Zealand	10	49	48	22	11	8	17

Saudi Arabia	4	20	29	49	29	9	18
Denmark	41	47	45	10	20	33	19
Mexico	7	22	8	35	30	16	20
Ireland	21	48	48	20	19	18	21
Czech Republic	23	37	36	21	25	19	22
Brazil	43	16	6	31	41	13	23
Turkey	24	7	10	32	36	31	24
Belgium	28	40	36	13	14	43	25
Netherlands	27	34	31	12	12	47	26
Austria	39	39	41	17	15	37	27
Spain	19	24	19	23	21	36	28
Chile	38	33	33	33	24	5	29
Poland	15	26	25	29	27	28	30
Italy	17	17	13	24	8	45	31
Greece	32	23	35	30	17	22	32
Algeria	18	25	30	49	35	7	33
Egypt, Arab Rep.	42	10	24	40	38	19	34
Hungary	12	46	40	26	33	35	35
Iran, Islamic Rep.	34	8	15	43	37	23	36
Colombia	44	19	22	39	34	17	37
Portugal	33	41	38	28	26	26	38

(Continued)

Table 2 Continued

Country	Rank						National Security Index
	National Income	Defence Capability	Effective Population	Technological Strength	National Health	Environmental Vulnerability	
Thailand	29	18	14	44	42	21	39
Peru	20	31	34	42	44	15	40
Indonesia	25	15	4	46	48	29	41
Malaysia	35	28	28	36	39	23	42
Venezuela, RB	48	42	32	38	28	14	43
Singapore	49	30	50	11	22	50	44
Pakistan	**37**	**5**	**18**	**47**	**45**	**42**	45
Hong Kong, China	46		43	37	23	30	46
Argentina	50	36	26	34	32	6	47
Bangladesh	45	27	21	48	49	39	48
Philippines	30	29	16	45	47	49	49
South Africa	47	38	20	41	50	25	50

Annexure 1. Gross National Income $mn (GNI) Index

Country	GNI 2002 ($ mn)	GNI 2001 ($ mn)	Growth Rate of GNI	Index GNI 2002	Index of Growth Rate	Cumulative Index of National Income
Algeria	53,814	50,400	6.8	0.1	76.4	30.6
Argentina	154,145	261,000	-40.9	1.1	0.0	0.6
Australia	386,623	383,300	0.9	3.4	66.9	28.8
Austria	190,400	194,500	-2.1	1.4	62.2	25.7
Bangladesh	48,462	49,900	-2.9	0.0	60.9	24.4
Belgium	239,949	239,800	0.1	1.9	65.7	27.4
Brazil	497,393	528,500	-5.9	4.5	56.1	25.1
Canada	700,454	661,900	5.8	6.5	74.9	33.8
Chile	66,318	66,900	-0.9	0.2	64.2	25.8
China	**1,209,528**	**1,131,000**	**6.9**	**11.5**	**76.7**	**37.6**
Colombia	80,101	82,000	-2.3	0.3	61.8	24.9
Czech Republic	56,717	54,100	4.8	0.1	73.3	29.4
Denmark	162,743	166,300	-2.1	1.1	62.1	25.5
Egypt, Arab Rep.	97,607	99,400	-1.8	0.5	62.7	25.4
Finland	122,231	124,200	-1.6	0.7	63.0	25.6
France	1,342,735	1,377,400	-2.5	12.9	61.5	32.3

(Continued)

Annexure 1 continued

Country	GNI 2002 $ mn	GNI 2001 $ mn	Growth Rate of GNI	Index GNI 2002	Index of Growth Rate	Cumulative Index of National Income
Germany	1,870,383	1,948000	-4.0	18.1	59.2	34.5
Greece	123,906	124,600	-0.6	0.7	64.7	26.3
Hong Kong, China	167,600	176,200	-4.9	1.2	57.7	23.8
Hungary	53,702	48,900	9.8	0.1	81.3	32.5
India	**501,532**	**474,300**	**5.7**	**4.5**	**74.7**	**32.6**
Indonesia	149,879	144,700	3.6	1.0	71.3	29.1
Iran, Islamic Rep.	112,098	112,900	-0.7	0.6	64.4	26.1
Ireland	92,552	88,400	4.7	0.4	73.1	29.5
Israel	104,128	104,100	0.0	0.6	65.6	26.6
Italy	1,097,944	1,123,500	-2.3	10.4	61.9	31.0
Japan	4,265,616	4,574,200	-6.7	41.9	54.8	47.0
Korea, Rep.	473,050	447,700	5.7	4.2	74.6	32.4
Malaysia	85,956	86,500	-0.6	0.4	64.5	26.0
Mexico	596,703	550,500	8.4	5.4	79.0	34.9
Netherlands	386,774	385,400	0.4	3.4	66.1	28.5
New Zealand	53,055	47,600	11.5	0.0	83.9	33.6
Norway	171,770	160,600	7.0	1.2	76.7	31.4
Pakistan	**59,205**	**59,600**	**-0.7**	**0.1**	**64.5**	**25.9**

Peru	54,734	52100	5.1	0.1	73.6	29.5
Philippines	81,453	80800	0.8	0.3	66.8	26.9
Poland	176,616	163900	7.8	1.3	78.0	32.0
Portugal	108,709	109200	-0.4	0.6	64.8	26.3
Russian Federation	307,913	253400	21.5	2.6	100.0	41.5
Saudi Arabia	181,066	149900	20.8	1.3	98.8	40.3
Singapore	86,150	99400	-13.3	0.4	44.2	17.9
South Africa	113,492	125500	-9.6	0.6	50.2	20.5
Spain	594,114	586900	1.2	5.4	67.5	30.3
Sweden	221,508	225900	-1.9	1.7	62.4	26.0
Switzerland	274,157	266500	2.9	2.2	70.2	29.4
Thailand	122,240	120900	1.1	0.7	67.3	27.4
Turkey	173,979	168300	3.4	1.2	71.0	29.1
United Kingdom	1,486,194	1451400	2.4	14.3	69.4	36.3
United States	**10,110,087**	**9900700**	**2.1**	**100.0**	**68.9**	**87.6**
Venezuela, RB	102,577	117200	-12.5	0.5	45.6	18.6

Source: World Bank, Washington D.C., *World Development Report, 2004 and World Development Report, 2003.*

Annexure 2. Defence Index

Country	Defence Expenditure ($ bn)	Size of Army ('000)	Index of Defence Expenditure	Index of Size of Army	Cumulative Index
Algeria	3.1	110	0.86	6.23	3.54
Argentina	1.5	41.4	0.41	2.18	1.30
Australia	8	26.6	2.21	1.31	1.76
Austria	1.8	34.6	0.50	1.78	1.14
Bangladesh	0.675	110	0.19	6.23	3.21
Belgium	3.6	24.8	0.99	1.20	1.10
Brazil	10.2	189	2.82	10.89	6.85
Canada	8.2	19.3	2.26	0.88	1.57
Chile	2.7	47.7	0.75	2.55	1.65
China	**51**	**1700**	**14.08**	**100.00**	**57.04**
Colombia	3	178	0.83	10.24	5.53
Czech Republic	1.5	39.85	0.41	2.09	1.25
Denmark	2.7	14.7	0.75	0.61	0.68
Egypt, Arab Rep.	3.3	320	0.91	18.61	9.76
Finland	2.1	19.2	0.58	0.87	0.73
France	40.2	137	11.10	7.82	9.46
Germany	33.3	191.35	9.20	11.02	10.11
Greece	6.5	114	1.79	6.46	4.13

Hungary	1	23.6	0.28	1.13	0.70
India	**13.8**	**1100**	**3.81**	**64.61**	**34.21**
Indonesia	6.6	230	1.82	13.30	7.56
Iran, Islamic Rep.	5.1	350	1.41	20.38	10.89
Ireland	0.759	8.5	0.21	0.24	0.22
Israel	9.9	125	2.73	7.11	4.92
Italy	25.6	116	7.07	6.58	6.82
Japan	39.5	148.2	10.91	8.48	9.69
Korea, Rep.	13.3	560	3.67	32.77	18.22
Malaysia	3.4	80	0.94	4.46	2.70
Mexico	5.6	144	1.55	8.23	4.89
Netherlands	7.7	23.15	2.13	1.10	1.62
New Zealand	0.667	4.43	0.18	0.00	0.09
Norway	3.6	14.7	0.99	0.61	0.80
Pakistan	**2.7**	**550**	**0.75**	**32.18**	**16.46**
Peru	0.914	60	0.25	3.28	1.76
Philippines	1.6	66	0.44	3.63	2.04
Poland	3.6	104.05	0.99	5.88	3.43
Portugal	3.1	26.7	0.86	1.31	1.08
Russian Federation	50.8	321	14.03	18.67	16.35
Saudi Arabia	22.2	75	6.13	4.16	5.15

(Continued)

Annexure 2 Continued

Country	Defence Expenditure ($ bn)	Size of Army ('000)	Index of Defence Expenditure	Index of Size of Army	Cumulative Index
Singapore	4.6	50	1.27	2.69	1.98
South Africa	1.8	36	0.50	1.86	1.18
Spain	8.7	95.6	2.40	5.38	3.89
Sweden	4.2	13.8	1.16	0.55	0.86
Switzerland	3	320.4	0.83	18.64	9.73
Thailand	1.8	190	0.50	10.94	5.72
Turkey	9.2	402	2.54	23.45	12.99
United Kingdom	37.3	116.67	10.30	6.62	8.46
United States	**362.1**	**485**	**100.00**	**28.34**	**64.17**
Venezuela, RB	0.0011	34	0.00	1.74	0.87

Source: International Institute of Strategic Studies, London, *Military Balance, 2003-04*

Annexure 3. Effective Population Index

Country	Population (in millions) 2002	Adult Literacy Rate 2001	Population above Poverty Line (%)	Measure of Effective Population	Index of Effective Population
Algeria	31	67.8	77.4	16.3	1.2
Argentina	38	96.9	70.1	25.8	2.1
Australia	20	100	100	20.0	1.6
Austria	8	100	100	8.0	0.4
Bangladesh	133	40.6	66.3	35.8	3.1
Belgium	10	100	100	10.0	0.6
Brazil	174	87.3	82.6	125.5	11.7
Canada	31	100	100	31.0	2.6
Chile	16	95.9	83	12.7	0.9
China	**1281**	**85.8**	**95.4**	**1048.5**	**100.0**
Colombia	44	91.9	82.3	33.3	2.8
Czech Republic	10	100	100	10.0	0.6
Denmark	5	100	100	5.0	0.1
Egypt, Arab Rep.	66	56.1	83.3	30.8	2.6
Finland	5	100	100	5.0	0.1
France	59	100	100	59.0	5.3
Germany	82	100	100	82.0	7.5

(Continued)

Annexure 3. Continued)

Country	Population (in millions) 2002	Adult Literacy Rate 2001	Population above Poverty Line (%)	Measure of Effective Population	Index of Effective Population
Greece	11	97.3	100	10.7	0.7
Hong Kong, China	7	93.5	100	6.5	0.3
Hungary	10	99.3	82.7	8.2	0.4
India	**1048**	**58**	**71.4**	**434.0**	**41.2**
Indonesia	212	87.3	72.9	134.9	12.6
Iran, Islamic Rep.	66	77.1	100	50.9	4.5
Ireland	4	100	100	4.0	0.0
Israel	6	95.1	100	5.7	0.2
Italy	58	98.5	100	57.1	5.1
Japan	127	100	100	127.0	11.8
Korea, Rep.	48	97.9	100	47.0	4.1
Malaysia	24	87.9	84.5	17.8	1.4
Mexico	101	91.4	89.9	83.0	7.6
Netherlands	16	100	100	16.0	1.2
New Zealand	4	100	100	4.0	0.0
Norway	5	100	100	5.0	0.1
Pakistan	**145**	**44**	**67.4**	**43.0**	**3.8**
Peru	27	90.2	51	12.4	0.8
Philippines	80	95.1	63.2	48.1	4.2

Poland	39	99.7	76.2	29.6	2.5
Portugal	10	92.5	100	9.3	0.5
Russian Federation	144	99.6	69.1	99.1	9.1
Saudi Arabia	22	77.1	100	17.0	1.3
Singapore	4	92.5	100	3.7	0.0
South Africa	44	85.6	100	37.7	3.3
Spain	41	97.7	100	40.1	3.5
Sweden	9	100	100	9.0	0.5
Switzerland	7	100	100	7.0	0.3
Thailand	62	95.7	86.9	51.6	4.6
Turkey	70	85.5	100	59.9	5.4
United Kingdom	59	100	100	59.0	5.3
United States	**288**	**100**	**100**	**288.0**	**27.2**
Venezuela, RB	25	92.8	68.7	15.9	1.2

Source: World Bank, Washington DC, *World Development Report, 2004 and World Development Report, 2003*. UNDP, New York, *Human Development Report, 2003*.

Annexure 4. Technology Index

Country	R&D Expenditures (% GDP) 1996-2000	Patents Granted to Residents (per million people) 1999	Scientists and Engineers in R&D (per million people) 1996-2000	Index of R&D Expend-itures	Index of Patents	Index of Scientists and Engineers in R&D	Cumulative Index on Technological Strength
Algeria	0	0	0	0.0	0.0	0.0	0.00
Argentina	0.4	4	713	10.5	0.4	14.0	9.19
Australia	1.5	65	3353	39.5	6.1	65.8	38.08
Austria	1.8	159	2313	47.4	15.0	45.4	40.51
Bangladesh	0	0	51	0.0	0.0	1.0	0.20
Belgium	2	103	2953	52.6	9.7	58.0	45.12
Brazil	0.8	3	323	21.1	0.3	6.3	13.96
Canada	1.8	44	2985	47.4	4.2	58.6	40.97
Chile	0.5	1	370	13.2	0.1	7.3	9.37
China	**1**	**2**	**545**	**26.3**	**0.2**	**10.7**	**17.97**
Colombia	0.3	0	101	7.9	0.0	2.0	5.13
Czech Republic	1.4	22	1349	36.8	2.1	26.5	27.82
Denmark	2.1	67	3476	55.3	6.3	68.2	48.07
Egypt, Arab Rep.	0.2	1	493	5.3	0.1	9.7	5.11
Finland	3.4	1	5059	89.5	0.1	99.3	73.56

France	2.2	195	2718		57.9	18.4	53.3	49.10
Germany	2.5	229	3161		65.8	21.7	62.0	56.21
Greece	0.7	1	1400		18.4	0.1	27.5	16.57
Hong Kong, China	0.4	4	93		10.5	0.4	1.8	6.76
Hungary	0.8	30	1445		21.1	2.8	28.4	18.87
India	**1.2**	**1**	**157**		**31.6**	**0.1**	**3.1**	**19.58**
ndonesia	0	0	130		0.0	0.0	2.6	0.51
Iran, Islamic Rep.	0	2	590		0.0	0.2	11.6	2.35
Ireland	1.2	66	2184		31.6	6.2	42.9	28.77
Israel	3.6	71	1563		94.7	6.7	30.7	64.32
Italy	1	113	1128		26.3	10.7	22.1	22.36
Japan	3	1057	5095		78.9	100.0	100.0	87.37
Korea, Rep.	2.7	931	2319		71.1	88.1	45.5	69.35
Malaysia	0.4	0	160		10.5	0.0	3.1	6.94
Mexico	0.4	1	225		10.5	0.1	4.4	7.22
Netherlands	2	187	2572		52.6	17.7	50.5	45.21
New Zealand	1.1	86	2197		28.9	8.1	43.1	27.62
Norway	1.7	97	4112		44.7	9.2	80.7	44.82
Pakistan	**0**	**0**	**69**		**0.0**	**0.0**	**1.4**	**0.27**
Peru	0.1	0	229		2.6	0.0	4.5	2.48
Philippines	0	0	156		0.0	0.0	3.1	0.61

(Continued)

Annexure 4 Continued

Country	R&D Expenditures (% GDP) 1996-2000	Patents Granted to Residents (per million people) 1999	Scientists and Engineers in R&D (per million people) 1996-2000	Index of R&D Expend-itures	Index of Patents	Index of Scientists and Engineers in R&D	Cumulative Index on Technological Strength
Poland	0.7	26	1429	18.4	2.5	28.0	17.15
Portugal	0.7	9	1576	18.4	0.9	30.9	17.41
Russian Fed.	1	105	3481	26.3	9.9	68.3	31.44
Saudi Arabia	0	0	0	0.0	0.0	0.0	0.00
Singapore	1.9	12	4140	50.0	1.1	81.3	46.48
South Africa	0	0	992	0.0	0.0	19.5	3.89
Spain	0.9	45	1921	23.7	4.3	37.7	22.60
Sweden	3.8	285	4511	100.0	27.0	88.5	83.10
Switzerland	2.6	203	3592	68.4	19.2	70.5	58.99
Thailand	0.1	0	74	2.6	0.0	1.5	1.87
Turkey	0.6	0	306	15.8	0.0	6.0	10.67
United Kingdom	1.9	76	2666	50.0	7.2	52.3	41.90
United States	2.7	298	4099	71.1	28.2	80.5	64.36
Venezuela, RB	0.3	0	194	7.9	0.0	3.8	5.50

Source: UNDP, New York, *Human Development Report, 2003*

Annexure 5. Health Index

Country	Life Expectancy at Birth 2001	Incidence of TB (per 100,000 people) 2000	Prevalence of HIV (% of adults)	Index of Life Expect-ancy	Index of Tuber-culosis	Index of HIV	Cumulative Health Index
Algeria	71	46	0.1	70.6	92.1	99.5	87.4
Argentina	74	48	0.7	79.4	91.7	96.5	89.2
Australia	79	8	0.1	94.1	99.4	99.5	97.7
Austria	78	15	0.2	91.2	98.1	99.0	96.1
Bangladesh	62	242	0.1	44.1	54.5	99.5	66.0
Belgium	78	14	0.2	91.2	98.3	99.0	96.2
Brazil	68	68	0.7	61.8	87.9	96.5	82.1
Canada	79	7	0.3	94.1	99.6	98.5	97.4
Chile	76	25	0.3	85.3	96.2	98.5	93.3
China	**70**	**107**	**0.1**	**67.6**	**80.4**	**99.5**	**82.5**
Colombia	72	50	0.4	73.5	91.4	98.0	87.6
Czech Republic	75	19	0	82.4	97.3	100.0	93.2
Denmark	77	13	0.2	88.2	98.5	99.0	95.2
Egypt, Arab Rep.	68	39	0	61.8	93.5	100.0	85.1
Finland	78	11	0	91.2	98.8	100.0	96.7

(Continued)

Annexure 5 Continued

Country	Life Expectancy at Birth 2001	Incidence of TB (per 100,000 people) 2000	Prevalence of HIV (% of adults)	Index Life Expect-ancy	Index of Tuber-culosis	Index of HIV	Cumulative Health Index
France	79	15	0.3	94.1	98.1	98.5	96.9
Germany	78	12	0.1	91.2	98.7	99.5	96.4
Greece	78	22	0.2	91.2	96.7	99.0	95.6
Hong Kong, China	80	91	0.1	97.1	83.5	99.5	93.4
Hungary	72	41	0.1	73.5	93.1	99.5	88.7
India	**63**	**184**	**0.8**	**47.1**	**65.6**	**96.0**	**69.6**
Indonesia	66	280	0.1	55.9	47.2	99.5	67.5
Iran, Islamic Rep.	69	53	0	64.7	90.8	100.0	85.2
Ireland	77	14	0.1	88.2	98.3	99.5	95.3
Israel	79	11	0.1	94.1	98.8	99.5	97.5
Italy	79	9	0.4	94.1	99.2	98.0	97.1
Japan	81	36	0	100.0	94.0	100.0	98.0
Korea, Rep.	74	62	0	79.4	89.1	100.0	89.5
Malaysia	73	111	0.4	76.5	79.7	98.0	84.7
Mexico	73	38	0.3	76.5	93.7	98.5	89.5
Netherlands	78	9	0.2	91.2	99.2	99.0	96.5

New Zealand	78	11	0.1	91.2	98.8	99.5	96.5
Norway	79	6	0.1	94.1	99.8	99.5	97.8
Pakistan	**63**	**175**	**0.1**	**47.1**	**67.4**	**99.5**	**71.3**
Peru	70	212	0.4	67.6	60.3	98.0	75.3
Philippines	70	330	0	67.6	37.6	100.0	68.4
Poland	74	36	0.1	79.4	94.0	99.5	91.0
Portugal	76	52	0.5	85.3	91.0	97.5	91.3
Russian Federation	66	132	0.9	55.9	75.6	95.5	75.7
Saudi Arabia	73	45	0.01	76.5	92.3	100.0	89.6
Singapore	78	48	0.2	91.2	91.7	99.0	94.0
South Africa	47	526	20.1	0.0	0.0	0.0	0.0
Spain	78	34	0.5	91.2	94.4	97.5	94.4
Sweden	80	5	0.1	97.1	100.0	99.5	98.9
Switzerland	80	11	0.5	97.1	98.8	97.5	97.8
Thailand	69	140	1.8	64.7	74.1	91.0	76.6
Turkey	70	36	0	67.6	94.0	100.0	87.2
United Kingdom	**77**	**12**	**0.1**	**88.2**	**98.7**	**99.5**	**95.5**
United States	78	5	0.6	91.2	100.0	97.0	96.1
Venezuela, RB	74	42	0.5	79.4	92.9	97.5	89.9

Source: World Bank, Washington D.C., *World Development Indicators, 2003.*

Annexure 6. Environmental Vulnerability Index (EVI)

Country	EVI Values	Index of Environmental Vulnerability
Algeria	2.59	74.0
Argentina	2.54	76.2
Australia	2.03	97.9
Austria	3.53	34.0
Bangladesh	3.58	31.9
Belgium	3.78	23.4
Brazil	2.74	67.7
Canada	1.98	100.0
Chile	2.5	77.9
China	**3.55**	**33.2**
Colombia	2.92	60.0
Czech Republic	3	56.6
Denmark	3.36	41.3
Egypt, Arab Rep.	3	56.6
Finland	2.31	86.0
France	3.33	42.6
Germany	3.38	40.4
Greece	3.1	52.3
Hong Kong, China	3.31	43.4
Hungary	3.43	38.3
India	**3.87**	**19.6**
Indonesia	3.3	43.8
Iran, Islamic Rep.	3.15	50.2
Ireland	2.97	57.9
Israel	3.72	26.0
Italy	3.85	20.4
Japan	3.92	17.4
Korea, Rep.	3.79	23.0
Malaysia	3.15	50.2

Country	EVI Values	Index of Environmental Vulnerability
Mexico	2.89	61.3
Netherlands	3.92	17.4
New Zealand	2.6	73.6
Norway	2.38	83.0
Pakistan	**3.75**	**24.7**
Peru	2.82	64.3
Philippines	4.03	12.8
Poland	3.27	45.1
Portugal	3.18	48.9
Russian Federation	2.62	72.8
Saudi Arabia	2.62	72.8
Singapore	4.33	0.0
South Africa	3.16	49.8
Spain	3.46	37.0
Sweden	2.64	71.9
Switzerland	3.18	48.9
Thailand	3.05	54.5
Turkey	3.32	43.0
United Kingdom	3.66	28.5
United States	**2.63**	**72.3**
Venezuela, RB	2.79	65.5

Source: South Pacific Applied Geoscience Commission (SOPAC), Technical Report No. 356, Fiji, 2003.

India's Security and Foreign Policy Initiatives

INSAR Research Staff

Defence Reorganization and Force Structuring

India's security posture, in terms of defence reorganization and force structuring, particularly in the post-Kargil period, has focused on three aspects: integrating the three services for better coordination, service personnel participation in decision-making processes, and creation of specialized force units within the plans for a leaner, more modernized military force. Among the more notable initiatives in this direction, the first was the creation of the post of Chief of Integrated Defence Staff (CIDS). This is to be an interim arrangement pending the appointment of a Chief of Defence Staff (CDS). Also two years ago, the first ever tri-service command was established in the Andaman and Nicobar Islands.

Towards upholding the principle of rotation in inter-service appointments for the purpose of promoting better coordination among the three arms of the military, the Government named Vice-Admiral Raman Puri, Commander-in-Chief of the Eastern Naval Command, as the new Chief of Integrated Defence Staff (CIDS) on 20 September. It was reported that the Army had been keen to retain this post.[1] Admiral Puri was slated to take over command after the incumbent Lt. Gen. Pankaj Joshi of the Army retired on 30 September after a two-year stint. In a similar fashion, the joint command in the Andaman and Nicobar Islands got an Army officer as its Commander-in-Chief with the appointment of Lt. Gen. Bhupender Singh Thakur to the post. So far only the Navy had commanded this joint command—with predominantly maritime orientations—with elements from the three services and the Coast Guard.

Towards better personnel participation in decision-making processes, the Indian Navy Headquarters were renamed the Integrated Headquarters of the Ministry of Defence (Navy) on 20 November.[2] The transition was reportedly a follow-up of the report of the Group of Ministers on revamp of the national security apparatus. The post-Kargil report had recommended that service headquarters be no longer treated as attached offices of the Ministry of Defence but integrated with the Ministry for better defence management. This recommendation envisaged a greater degree of participation and involvement of service personnel in the decision-making process in defence and strategic affairs. Earlier, the Government's decisions and directives used to be communicated to the service headquarters through civilian officers in the Ministry.

The Government's intentions at better force structuring, during 2003, concentrated on setting up specialized force units rather than taking steps towards creating "leaner, meaner and younger" services as recommended by the Bagga Committee in the post-Kargil period. Army Chief Gen. N.C. Vij was reported to have ordered the raising of special operations forces along the lines of the US Special Forces for offensive operations in enemy territory.[3] Earlier in December 2002, four battalions of Special Forces for counter-insurgency purposes had been raised. In a similar way, the Army Chief was reported to have decided to raise four more battalions to work outside India. The Directorate of Military Operations and the Army Training Command were asked to work out a doctrinal underpinning for India's Special Forces and a detailed blueprint about how India could best use such forces.

The Government was also reported to have cleared the setting up of specialized regiments for the intermediate-range ballistic missiles (IRBM). According to a report based on the journal *Force*, the CCS had approved the raising of two Agni missile groups.[4] Control of the shorter-range Agni-I (range 700 km) was to be vested with the Army's 334 Rocket Missile Group, and the medium-range 1,500 km Agni-II was to be handled by the 335 Missile Group. The Government also cleared the raising of two Prithvi groups, to be named as the 444 and 555 Missile Groups. Administratively, the GOC-in-C of the Southern Command was to be in-charge but the operational directives were to come from the tri-service Strategic Forces Command.[5]

The Chief of Air Staff, Air Chief Marshal S. Krishnaswamy, also indicated a specialized "air and space" role for the IAF in the future. On 6 October, in New Delhi, he was reported to have said that work had begun to have a weapon platform in space. He said, "Any country on the fringe of space technology like India has to work towards such a command as advanced countries are already moving towards laser weapon platforms in space. The IAF has started work on conceptualizing such a weapon system and its operational command system".[6] In a closed-door meeting with his commanders the previous year, a presentation on the subject was made and the IAF Chief said that the IAF could aspire to transform itself into an air and space force. Although the Defence Ministry has not confirmed initation of such a project, the IAF Chief is known to have initiated preliminary work.

Meanwhile, the Government was reported to have temporarily put on hold its plans for a leaner, meaner and younger service as per the Bagga Committee recommendations on account of massive reorganization problems and their far-reaching implications. Defence Minister George Fernandes, in reply to questions in the Rajya Sabha in July, said, "Since the recommendations encompass a wide spectrum of service-related issues, no time-frame for implementation can be indicated".[7] The Minister was also said to have suggested that the recommendations be forwarded to the Air Force and Navy before the Ministry took a final decision on the subject.

Nuclear Doctrine and Strategic Command and Control Structures

Following a meeting of the Cabinet Committee on Security (CCS) on 4 January 2003, India made public the main elements of its Nuclear Doctrine and details of its Command and Control structure. The former presented no surprises and is clearly built around pronouncements made by the Government over the years following Pokhran-II. It is also much along the lines of the Nuclear Doctrine suggested by the National Security Advisory Board (NSAB) in August 1999. The Doctrine embraces the concept of "No First Use" and of "Non-Use" of nuclear weapons against Non-Nuclear Weapon States (NNWS). It elaborates that India would use nuclear weapons only in retaliation against a nuclear attack on Indian territory or on Indian forces abroad and it would retain the option of using such weapons in the event of a major attack against India or Indian forces abroad by biological or chemical weapons. While underlining that the use of nuclear weapons could be authorized only by the civilian political leadership, it unambiguously asserts that retaliation to a first strike would be massive and designed to inflict unacceptable damage. The fact that India will be a mature and responsible nuclear weapon state is borne out not only by the incorporation in its Nuclear Doctrine of elements such as "No First Use" and "Non-Use" of nuclear weapons against Non-Nuclear Weapon States but also by a clear indication that India would continue to observe a moratorium on nuclear tests, maintain strict control on export of nuclear and missile-related technologies and participate in the Fissile Material Cut-off Treaty (FMCT) negotiations. The doctrine furthermore reiterates India's continued commitment to the goal of nuclear weapon-free world through global, verifiable and non-discriminatory nuclear disarmament.

India's strategic Command and Control structure vests in the Nuclear Command Authority (NCA) comprising a Political Council and an Executive Council, the former chaired by the Prime Minister and the latter by the National Security Adviser. The Political Council alone can authorize use of nuclear weapons while the Executive Council provides inputs for decision-making and is the former's executive arm. India's strategic forces are managed and administered by the Strategic Forces Command (SFC) headed by a Commander-in-Chief. The CCS at its meeting of 4 January approved the appointment of Air Marshal T.M. Asthana as the first Commander-in-Chief of the tri-service SFC.

With regard to India's declared Nuclear Doctrine, it may be noted that the NSAB in its 160-page recommendation submitted to the National Security Adviser, Brajesh Mishra, on 20 December 2002, had advised against the retention of India's stated policy of "No First Use" and its self-imposed moratorium on nuclear tests.[8] The Government, however, decided to retain both commitments made earlier in the Draft Nuclear Doctrine. The NSAB's contention was that most other nuclear weapon states had not accepted the policy of "No First Use" and hence India should "consider withdrawing from this commitment" and further, that India should break its self-imposed moratorium on nuclear tests should the US resume testing. The NSAB had also suggested that India should take note of the US Nuclear Posture Review, which listed even non-nuclear weapon states as targets. Defence Minister George Fernandes, however, said on 13 January that India had no intention of reviewing its policy of "No First Use". He said, "We have a nuclear doctrine. A nuclear and strategic force command chain is in position. So we stand by the 'No-First-Use' policy."[9]

On 1 September, the Political Council of the Nuclear Command Authority (NCA) met for the first time in the Cabinet Committee room of the Prime Minister's Office (PMO).[10] Headed by the Prime Minister, the Council reviewed the arrangements in place of the nuclear weapons programme. The review indicated that the Command and Control (C2) and Indications and Warning (I&W), as well as the infrastructure for the strategic nuclear force were yet to be in place. The Council was said to have told the operational and planning wings of the NCA to accelerate work on all these areas and to ensure that the systems, commensurate with India's strategic requirements, were ready by the end of 2003. The Council also approved the decision to build two nuclear bunkers to shield the Cabinet in case of a nuclear attack.[11]

Weapon System Acquisitions/Inductions

With continued focus on air-based weapon systems, India kept up the programme of missile and aircraft development and acquisition of sophisticated airborne early warning systems. A number of tests were conducted of the various missile systems with plans to induct a number of them as early as possible.

Missile Development/Induction

India successfully test-fired its 800 km range Agni-I missile with a one tonne payload on 9 January.[12] Official sources said that the missile was tested from a mobile platform, which meant that it had been nearly configured for use in real-life setting. The Railways were also reported to have already manufactured special wagons to carry the missile disguised as regular commercial goods. Meanwhile, both officials of the Defence Research and Development Organization (DRDO) and the Defence Ministry announced that improved versions of the Agni missile were being developed and would attain deployable status during 2003. DRDO chief, V.K. Aatre, announced that the Agni-III ballistic missile with a strike range of 3500-4000 km was ready to be tested by the end of 2003.

The short-range surface-to-air missile Trishul was successfully test-fired twice in June and December from the Interim Test Range (ITR) at Chandipur on Sea. Earlier reports had indicated that the Trishul programme was "as good as dead" and that the Government had allowed the Navy to buy Israeli-made Barak missiles due to the infeasibility of the Trishul missile system.[13] A top DRDO official clarified in Bangalore that the Navy was given the green signal to buy the Barak because the Government did not want the Navy to wait for the Trishul system.[14] The DRDO had promised to deliver Trishul for evaluation after nullifying the snags in command guidance, he said.

Ever since the Trishul project became part of the country's Integrated Guided Missile Development Programme (IGMDP)— July 1983, it has come a long way. The solid fuel-propelled missile, with a range of 500 m to 9 km and a 15 kg warhead, was developed to provide a triple battlefield role for the Army, Air Force and Navy. The test-firing on 22 June and 19 December was from a mobile launcher. After the December tests a DRDO official said "there was consistent engagement of the targets in all the four flights. This showed that the design as a whole—the missile system, the ground system and the interfaces—was proved".[15] Though the missile had 65 development flights already, it is still to become operational.

Prithvi, the tactical surface-to-surface missile with a strike range of 150 km and one tonne payload, was also successfully test-fired from the Chandipur test range on 26 March and 29 April. Defence Ministry officials said that the tests were to fine-tune the missile that had already been fully inducted into the Army. The missile reportedly has the latest on-board computers and an advanced inertial navigation and is capable of carrying nuclear warheads. Defence Minister George Fernandes told the Rajya Sabha on 7 May that production of a second version of the Prithvi had already started and assured the House that it would attain deployable status by the end of 2003.[16]

India also test-fired successfully a prototype of the beyond visual range (BVR) air-to-air missile, Astra, from the Chandipur test range. Once it became fully operational, Astra was slated to be used to arm all the fighters in the IAF inventory, including the light combat aircraft (LCA) being developed by Hindustan Aeronautics Limited (HAL), Bangalore, when it became fully operational.

BrahMos (codenamed PJ-10), a supersonic anti-ship cruise missile with a 290 km range and a cruising speed of Mach 3 at an altitude of 15,000 m, under development by India and Russia jointly, was successfully launched from the Chandipur test range on 29 October. This was the third launch from land and was reported to have achieved cent per cent success. Officials of the DRDO said that the launch was an important development as the missile had been launched in a surface-to-surface role. In a brief statement in the Lok Sabha on 11 December, the Defence Minister, George Fernandes, said that the supersonic cruise missile BrahMos had "proved its performance" and was ready to be deployed on the Navy's frontline destroyers, frigates and submarines.[17] The Navy was reportedly given the green signal for the induction of the Brahmos. The BrahMos has a long flight range, fire-and-forget principle of operation, low radar signature, variety of flight trajectories and high destructive capabilities. It has been touted to be three times superior to other current subsonic anti-ship missiles in terms of velocity, flight range and seeker range.

Progress in the development of Akash and Nag missiles, however, appears disappointing as of now. It has been reported that the Army and the Air Force may not find it feasible to induct the medium-range surface-to-air missile Akash. Apparently, the delay in its development made the Akash prohibitively expensive.[18] It has been reported that one Akash group comprising four missile batteries is likely to cost Rs 2000 crore, too large a portion of the Army's budget for fresh procurement. DRDO Chief, V.K. Aatre, however, is optimistic of the future of the Akash. He is reported to have announced that the missile had not been altogether shelved and that it would be ready for user-trials by the end of 2004. Similarly, he said that the anti-tank guided missile Nag was also under development and would be under user trial soon.

AWACS/Air Defence System

In a major boost to the IAF, final hurdles were cleared for the transfer of the Israeli Phalcon Airborne Early Warning and Control System (AWACS) to India, paving the way for India to become one of the few countries to possess AWACS.[19] The transfer became possible with the US dropping objections to the transfer after keeping the decision on hold for about a year and a half on account of the tension between India and Pakistan. A trilateral deal on principles of cooperation on the Phalcon AWACS system was signed on 10 October between the Indian Defence Secretary, Ajay Prasad, and officials from Israel and Russia. Since the Phalcon system is to be mounted on the Russia-made Il-76 aircraft, Russia will be called upon to modify the Il-76 aircraft that will become the AWACS platform.

An indigenous, DRDO-developed air defence system with a centralized command, control and communication structure and linked to several mission control units throughout the country to detect all incoming missiles and enemy aircraft was expected to be operational by the end of 2004. V.K. Saraswat, Director, Research Centre Imarat, a DRDO institution and the focal centre for developing the defence system in collaboration with other defence laboratories, said that a part of the system was already operational and was being tested with simulated batteries and radars.[20]

Sea-based Systems

On 8 January, at the end of the third meeting of the Indo-Russian Inter-Governmental Commission (IRIGC) for Military Technical Cooperation in Moscow, the Defence Minister announced that negotiations had been almost finalized for the acquisition of the aircraft carrier *Admiral Gorshkov* and the procurement of the MiG-29K aircraft that were to be a part of the *Gorshkov* package. Meanwhile, the Indian Navy announced that it would revive production of the indigenous Air Defence Ship (ADS), a smaller version of an aircraft carrier, by May-June 2004. The project had been approved in 1999 at an estimated cost of Rs 1700 crore but had been much delayed. The 35,500 tonne ADS would be 252 metres long and capable of achieving a speed of 28 knots. It would have a 14 degree ski-jump with a

STOBAR (short take-off but arrested recovery) design for the MiG-29Ks and the naval variant of the indigenous LCA.

Aircraft

The Cabinet Committee on Security (CCS), chaired by the Prime Minister, on 3 September approved the much-needed purchase of a total of 66 Hawk-115Y advanced jet trainers (AJT) from the United Kingdom at an expense of Rs. 12,460 crore. For the past thirty years, India had depended on the Kiran (HJT-16) basic trainer jet for training its Air Force pilots. In deciding on the British Hawk, the CCS reportedly overlooked a price advantage of up to Rs. 41.42 crore per aircraft, which was offered by the Czech-American competitor, Aero Vodochody for its L-159B trainer. Defence Secretary Ajay Prasad while announcing this decision said, "We recently evaluated the American-Czech aircraft. One of the factors in favour of the Hawk was its reliability and acceptance by 17 countries".[21] Another reason for favouring the Hawk was its ability to double as a combat vehicle in case of emergency. The CCS meeting also approved the acquisition of five EMB-145 jets from Brazil to equip the IAF's VIP transport squadron at an expense of Rs. 730 crore.

India's own production of jet trainers achieved a milestone when the HJT-36 intermediate jet trainer (IJT), designed and developed by HAL in record time (the project was sanctioned in July 1999), made its maiden 20-minute flight at the Bangalore airport on 7 March.[22] Although the flight was termed "unofficial" since the Defence Minister was not there to witness the flight, HAL officials present at the test flight announced that all the systems had worked excellently. The HJT-36 is expected to replace the IAF's 200-odd Kirans (HJT-16) and to supplement the AJTs to be acquired by India.

On 4 May, the indigenous light combat aircraft (LCA) was christened Tejas at a ceremony in Bangalore by the Prime Minister after a successful technology demonstrator flight by two LCAs.[23] On 1 August, Tejas made its maiden supersonic flight at Mach 1.08 and flying at an altitude of 11 km. Powered by an American GE 404 engine, the flight reportedly lasted for 35 minutes. The flight made aviation history as this was for the first time that an Indian-designed fighter aircraft was able to accelerate to supersonic speed and hold on at that speed.

HAL announced on 1 April that it was making major investments in setting up machinery and infrastructure to better manage and quicken the pace of development of the three projects in its charge—the Sukhoi-30MKI, the LCA and IJT. The HAL Company Manager said that HAL was setting aside Rs. 900 crore in the next two to three years for the purpose. HAL also announced that the state-of-the-art Sukhoi fighter would be ready to roll out of the Indian factory by the end of 2004.

Defence Budget

On 28 February the Finance Minister, Jaswant Singh, proposing a marginal increase in the defence budget over the previous year, said: "The Government is fully committed to modernizing the armed forces and equipping them with the best available. This is non-negotiable. Therefore, during the next year, any additional requirement that may emerge on account of modernization needs of the three armed services or on account of married accommodation project, will be fully met. There will be no shortage of funds for defence."[24] The proposal envisaged an increase in defence budget from Rs. 65,000 crore in 2002 to Rs 65,300 crore in 2003.

However, political indecisiveness to come up with planned acquisitions during the previous year had resulted in severe under-utilization of the capital expenditure allotted in 2002-3. It was reported that the defence forces had to surrender nearly Rs. 6,499 crore or 30 per cent of the budget, with the two most striking failures being the inability to close the AJT deal and the *Admiral Gorshkov* deal.[25]

A Parliamentary Committee report, tabled on 22 April, said that there was a strange paradox in the echelons of the Government dealing with national security.[26] While there was continued under-utilization of funds, steep projections were made by the defence services with no proper planning. The report identified as the main cause for the under-utilization of funds, the weak monitoring system for spending allocated funds within the prefixed target dates and lack of an effective system for identifying the causes of delay in decision-making and implementation stages. The Defence Minister, on 17 March, also said that India was unable to purchase essential defence equipment due to a number of factors such as the Central Vigilance Commission's order asking the Ministry to look for better deals whenever rival variants were offered at lower prices, scare among decision-makers after the Tehelka episode and unspent funds being surrendered annually to the Finance Ministry.[27]

External Constraints

India's plans to acquire military hardware and software have suffered from various forms of external constraints. For example, India could get spare parts for the Navy's 25-strong fleet of Sea King MK 42 anti-submarine warfare and utility helicopters only after the US lifted sanctions in 2003—nearly four years after they became due. It was also reported that the US intervened to block preliminary negotiations between New Delhi and Tel Aviv on the sale of the Arrow anti-missile system to India. Tel Aviv was reported to have said that since the US had extensively funded the Arrow system, Washington's consent for the transfer became necessary and that Israel's capacity to ignore the US persuasion was limited because it was seeking more US funding for the larger induction of the Arrow missiles into its own arsenal.

Speaking on Technology Day on 11 May in New Delhi to leading defence scientists, the Prime Minister hit out at the West's three-decades-old endeavour to impair India's quest to become self-reliant in hi-tech defence technologies while turning a blind eye to covert attempts in this by its neighbours.[28] He also said that India's contribution in turning down lucrative export offers to maintain the regional security balance and comply with international treaties also went unacknowledged.

Operation Parakram

Operation Parakram, launched within days of the 13 December attack on the Parliament building was reported to have resulted in the death of 798 army personnel till July 2003. This was disclosed by Defence Minister George Fernandes in the Lok Sabha on 31 July. In comparison, the Kargil War had caused 527 casualties.[29] Operation

Parakram involved the forward deployment of over 5 lakh troops along the Indo-Pakistan border for almost a year.

India and the Iraq War

India was opposed to the manner in which US President George W. Bush handled the Iraqi question arising out of Iraq's defiance of UN resolutions with regard to weapons of mass destruction. Prime Minister Vajpayee called upon the United States on 28 January to avoid war with Iraq. Speaking at the Non-Aligned Movement (NAM) summit in Kuala Lumpur on 25 February, Mr. Vajpayee said that India could not support the US war moves in Iraq. He said that the NAM provided a platform in which controversial issues were resolved through dialogue. India also stressed the centrality of the United Nations in resolving the Iraq crisis.

India set up a Crisis Management Group (CMG) on 18 March headed by a Secretary in the Ministry of External Affairs to ensure that Indian nationals in the Gulf would not be stranded if war broke out. The Civil Aviation Minister, Shahnawaz Hussein, said that the Government had drawn up a contingency plan to evacuate 50,000 Indians from Kuwait within a week. The Minister also said that a war in Iraq would cause large financial losses to civil aviation and tourism in India as the air space of three airports in the Middle East—Damman, Kuwait and Bahrain—would be closed.

Parliament passed a resolution on 8 April condemning the war and seeking withdrawal of occupation forces from Iraq. There was considerable debate in the country whether India should accede to the US request to send troops to Iraq. After careful deliberation, the Cabinet Committee on Security decided on 14 July not to send Indian troops to Iraq.

Bangladeshi Immigrants

The large influx of illegal migrants from Pakistan and Bangladesh has of late been recognized as a major internal security threat in the states of the North-East. Deputy Prime Minister L.K. Advani, while addressing a conference of Chief Secretaries and Directors General of Police at New Delhi on 7 January, pointed out that there were

11,500 Pakistanis and half a crore Bangladeshis who had remained in India after the expiry of their visas.[30]

The central government delegated the power to deport these illegal residents to the state governments and Union Territories. The Centre and states also decided to introduce National Identity Cards to combat the problem. A pilot project for issuance of Identity Cards was launched in thirteen states from 1 April at a cost of Rs. 14 crore. The states included in the plan were Jammu and Kashmir, Gujarat, Uttaranchal, Rajasthan, Uttar Pradesh, Assam, Andhra Pradesh, West Bengal, Tripura, Tamil Nadu, Goa, Pondicherry and Delhi.

Notes

1. Vishal Thapar, "Navy Takes over Integrated Defence Staff", *Hindustan Times*, 21 September 2003.
2. Idem, "In Post-Kargil Revamp, Navy Hq. Gets New Name", *Hindustan Times*, 21 November 2003.
3. Aditya Sinha, "Indian Army to Raise US-type Special Forces", *Hindustan Times*, 20 April 2003.
4. "Raising of Two Agni Missile Groups Cleared", *The Hindu*, 24 September 2003.
5. "Artillery Division Raised to Handle Strategic Missiles", *Hindustan Times*, 29 September 2003.
6. "IAF Working on Weapon Platforms in Space", *The Hindu*, 10 October 2003.
7. Saikat Datta, "Plans for a Leaner, Younger Army on Hold", *Indian Express*, 4 November 2003.
8. Vishal Thapar, "Scrap Nuclear No-First-Use Policy, Advises Security Panel", *Hindustan Times*, 10 January 2003.
9. "India Not to Review No-First-Use Policy", *The Hindu*, 14 January 2003.
10. Sandeep Dikshit, "N-deployment Systems by Year-end", *The Hindu*, 2 September 2003.
11. Ibid.
12. Idem, "Agni Missile Test-fired Successfully", *The Hindu*, 10 January 2003.
13. "Development of Short-range Trishul Missile on Backburner", *Times of India*, 13 March 2003
14. "DRDO: Trishul Alive and Kicking", *The Hindu*, 8 July 2003.
15. T.S. Subramaniam, "Successful Trishul Tests Boost DRDO", *The Hindu*,

21 December 2003.

16. "Agni Missiles to be Deployed This Year", *The Hindu*, 8 May 2003.
17. Rajat Pandit, "Brahmos on Deployment Track", *Times of India*, 13 December 2003.
18. Aditya Sinha, "Army, Air Force Set to Dump Akash", *Hindustan Times*, 17 August 2003.
19. Vishal Thapar, "India Inks Deal for IAF's Eye in Sky", *Hindustan Times*, 11 October 2003.
20. Y. Mallikarjun, "Indigenous Air Defence System to be Operational Next Year", *The Hindu*, 15 December 2003.
21. "Hawk's Reliability Tipped the Scale", *Hindustan Times*, 4 September 2003.
22. Manoj Joshi, "Jet Trainer Takes off", *Times of India*, 8 March 2003.
23. "LCA is Now Tejas", *The Hindu*, 5 May 2003.
24. Saikat Datta, "Marginal Increase in Defence Outlay", *Indian Express*, 1 March 2003.
25. "Finance Willing but Defence Remains Shy", *Times of India*, 1 March 2003.
26. "Defence Funds Under-utilised, Says Committee", *The Hindu*, 23 April 2003.
27. "Defence Purchases Hit, Says Fernandes", *The Hindu*, 18 March 2003.
28. "PM Flays Double Standards in Imposing Sanctions", *The Hindu*, 12 May 2003.
29. "Parakram Killed More than Kargil", *Times of India*, 2 August 2003.
30. "Pak, Bangla Overstayers Should be Deported: Advani", *The Hindu*, 8 January 2003.

Acquisition of Arms and Military Technology by India and its Neighbours

INSAR Research Staff

India

India-Russia

India has been among the Russian defence industry's biggest clients, accounting for nearly 30 per cent of Russian arms exports. Defence cooperation between the two countries is wide ranging, and includes all aspects of defence equipment, aircraft, missiles, ships and defence technology. The visit of the Indian Defence Minister, George Fernandes, to Russia in early January, reportedly signalled further expansion of defence cooperation. *Aviation Week & Space Technology* reported on 27 January 2003 that at the end of the third meeting of the Indo-Russian Inter-Governmental Commission (IRIGC) for Military Technical Cooperation, on 8 January, in Moscow, the Indian Defence Minister announced that the visit was intended to clear the way for completing several long-awaited contracts, which included the acquisition of the aircraft carrier *Admiral Gorshkov* and the "related" lease-purchase of two Akula (Bars)-class Type 971 nuclear-powered submarines (SSN) and four Tu-22M strategic bomber/maritime strike aircraft by the end of fiscal year 2003-4. The Minister also visited the MiG Corporation facilities for a detailed review of the MiG-29K/KUB naval fighter programme, since MiG-29K aircraft were to be procured as part of the *Gorshkov* package.

Aviation Week & Space Technology reported on 9 June 2003 that in a $300 million contract with a conglomerate of Russian organizations, including Sokol Aircraft Manufacturing and Phazotron-NIIR Co., India was upgrading 72 of its ageing MiG-21 Bis fighters with FK-04 Kopyo radars. The upgrade programme, according to the report, was being carried out by Hindustan Aeronautics Limited (HAL). The FK-04 Kopyo radar has a 57 km detection and a 40 km lock-on range that allows pilots to track eight targets and launch two air-to-air missiles simultaneously. In a major defence deal between the two countries, *Defense News* reported on 14 July, India had signed a $455 million contract with Russia to buy 36 Smerch multiple-rocket launchers. Smerch with its volley of 12 rockets can hit targets in a 67-hectare area (165 acres) up to 90 km away. Its 9M55K rockets measure 300 mm in diameter, 7.5 m in length and weigh 800 kg and carry sensor-fuzed submunitions and other advanced conventional warheads.

On 18 June, more than a year behind schedule, India finally received the first of three Talwar-class stealth frigates built by Russia for the Indian Navy. The frigate was commissioned into service at the Baltiysky Zavod shipyard in St. Petersburg. In a related transfer, on 16 October, India began receiving the second batch of 12 Su-30MKI multi-role fighter aircraft from the NPK Irkut IAPO plant in Irkutsk, Russia. The aircraft were shipped in semi-disassembled form on Volga-Dnepr Antonov AN-124-100 planes. India had already received 18 Su-30K aircraft and 10 Su-30MKI with guarantees of long-term uninterrupted spares supply as well as technical assistance in the production of critical items. The remaining 10 Su-30MKIs were expected to be delivered by the end of 2004.

BrahMos (codenamed PJ-10), a supersonic anti-ship cruise missile under development by India and Russia, was successfully launched for the first time from a mobile complex at a test range on India's eastern coast on 9 November. Brahmos is a 290 km range missile designed to attain a cruising speed of Mach 3 at an altitude of 15,000 m.

In the nuclear field, Russia, after having assisted India in building two power reactors at Koondakulam in Tamil Nadu the previous year, assured a continuous supply of fuel. *The Hindu* reported on 22 March that a fuel supply agreement for the two 1000 MWe nuclear power plants was signed. The agreement envisaged fuel supply for the two plants for their entire life, be it 30 years or 60 years.

India-Israel

Defence cooperation between India and Israel is multifaceted. *Jane's Defence Weekly* reported on 15 January 2003 that India concluded an estimated $20 million agreement with Israel Military Industries (IMI) for the acquisition of an unspecified quantity of Tavor 21 5.56 mm assault rifles and Galil 7.62 mm sniper rifles. The contract included the provision of 5.56 mm ammunition, night-vision sights, laser rangefinders and other targeting equipment.

In a major boost to the Indian Air Force (IAF), final hurdles were reportedly cleared for the transfer of the Israeli Phalcon Airborne Early Warning and Control System (AWACS) to India, paving the way for India to become one of the few countries to possess AWACS. According to the reports on 23 May, the transfer became possible with the United States dropping objections to the transfer after keeping the decision on hold for about eighteen months on account of the tension between India and Pakistan. However, in another report by the Israeli daily *Haaretz* in September, the United States was reported to have intervened to block preliminary negotiations between New Delhi and Tel Aviv on the sale of the Arrow anti-missile system to India. The daily said that since the United States had extensively funded the Arrow system—and Israel was seeking more US funding for the larger induction of the Arrow missiles into its own arsenal—Washington's consent for the transfer became necessary.

In December, the Indian Navy was reportedly negotiating the purchase of additional Barak anti-missile defence systems worth $100 million from the Israel Aircraft Industries (IAI). The Barak provides 360 degree defence against sea-skimming missiles, cruise missiles, smart bombs and fixed - or rotary-wing aircraft. It also features a vertical launcher, command-to-line-of-sight guidance, all-weather day/night operation and an intercept range from a minimum of 500 m to 10 km. Earlier in September, the Indian Government had reportedly approved the purchase of electronic warfare systems for Indian warships from the Israeli company Rafael under a package estimated at $105 million.

India-US

Defence cooperation between India and the United States has seen major improvements in recent times. Nearly four year after the US stalled military contacts after India's nuclear explosions in May 1998, the two countries renewed their defence cooperation particularly through the Defence Policy Group that has been having regular meetings in Washington and New Delhi. In one of the earliest indications of the changed atmosphere, *Jane's Defence Weekly* reported on 12 February 2003 that an initial shipment of spare parts for the Indian Navy's 25-strong fleet of Sea King MK 42 anti-submarine warfare and utility helicopters had been released by the US.

The Hindu reported on 11 June that India and the US were discussing the sale of hi-tech military equipment and modules of the missile defence shield, including the P-3-C Orion sought by the Indian Navy for long-range reconnaissance, and nuclear, biological and chemical warfare equipment like protection suits. These military deals were among the first major agreements after the two countries got back to cooperating in defence-related matters. In an indication of yet increased collaboration, *Jane's Defence Weekly* on 23 July reported that India had received the first two AN/TPQ-37 firefinder weapons-locating radar systems it had ordered from the United States more than five years earlier under a $190 million Foreign Military Sales (FMS) contract. Over the next three years India was to receive another 10 of the long-range artillery and rocket locators.

On 6-7 August, a meeting of the Defence Policy Group was held in Washington. The meeting discussed various issues related to potential FMS accord. Another meeting of the Defence Policy Group was held in New Delhi in September.

India-Other Countries

Among European countries, France has been India's largest supplier of defence equipment. *Jane's Defence Weekly* reported on 12 February 2003 that India and France signed an agreement on 6 February to jointly develop and manufacture an improved version of the TM 333B helicopter engine (Shaki) to power the locally designed, twin-engine Advanced Light Helicopter (ALH) in operation with the three armed services. The agreement to build 300-350 Shaki engines worth $400-500 million in India was reportedly signed between France's Turbomeca and HAL. On 7 February, the French MBDA Missile Systems and India's Bharat Dynamics Limited (BDL) also reportedly signed an agreement to acquire and produce anti-tank missiles. The French Ambassador to India, Dominique Girard, said in New Delhi that a deal to assist India to locally build six

Scorpene submarines at an estimated cost of between $1.8 billion and $2 billion was in the final stages of discussion.

On 3 September, New Delhi approved the purchase of Hawk-115Y advanced jet trainers (AJT) from the United Kingdom for training IAF pilots. The deal is worth Rs. 12,460 crore spread over several years. The Cabinet Committee on Security (CCS), chaired by the Prime Minister, reportedly took the decision and a total of 66 Hawks were expected to be acquired. During the CCS meeting a deal to acquire five EMB-145 jets from Brazil to equip the IAF's VIP transport squadron at an expense of Rs. 730 crore was also approved.

Indigenous Production

On 7 March, HAL completed the first flight of the HJT-36 Intermediate Jet Trainer from its Bangalore factory. The two-seat aircraft was flown for 20 minutes. The aircraft is powered by a 3,825 lb (17kN) Snecma Larzac 04H20 turbofan engine. In a similar achievement, on 1 August, *Tejas*, the indigenously built Light Combat Aircraft (LCA) powered by an American GE 404 engine made its maiden supersonic flight at Mach 1.08, flying at an altitude of 11 km. The flight reportedly lasted for 35 minutes.

The Defence Ministry announced in July that its first indigenously assembled Russian Main Battle Tank (MBT) T-90S was ready to roll out of the Avadi Heavy Vehicle Factory. *Jane's Defence Weekly* reported on 27 August that the ordnance factory in Medak had developed a new 81 mm Carrier Mortar Tracked Vehicle (CMTV) based on the chassis of the Sarath Infantry Combat Vehicle (ICV). The turret had been modified for its new role. The new 81 mm CMTV was the latest in a long line of Sarath variants developed by the Medak ordnance factory for the Indian Army. In an announcement in July, the Government said that it was going to induct 36 improved version of the Pinaka multiple-rocket launchers from its ordnance factory in Kanpur. Defence officials said that the guidance system of the Pinaka launchers had to be perfected after it was used in the Kargil War.

In a major achievement for the Indian Navy, on 18 April India launched INS *Shivalik*, its first locally built Project 17 stealth frigate at the Mazagon Docks in Mumbai more than two years behind schedule.

India has reportedly planned a Rs. 3000 crore programme to equip the *Ghatak* or lethal platoons in infantry units with enhanced firepower, night fighting, surveillance and communications capabilities by 2007. The project was approved at the Cabinet Committee on Security (CCS) meeting on 3 September.

China

China has been focusing on indigenous upgradation and production of weapon systems. In early January, Beijing's aspiration to field a new generation of stealth fighter aircraft was reportedly confirmed when its Chengdu No. 611 Institute completed the conceptual design work on two advanced variants of its J-10A fighter. On 22 January, the production of the FC-1 lightweight fighter was formally launched at the Chengdu No. 132 factory. *Jane's Defence Weekly* said that the FC-1 fighter programme also involved Pakistan and China would supply the first batch of 12 aircraft to Islamabad during 2004 for test and evaluation. Meanwhile, China's AVIC I organization, in October, was also reported to have received the authorization to promote an upgraded version of the attack fighter to potential export customers.

In June 2003, China was reported to have developed to prototype stage a new and highly advanced infantry fighting vehicle (IFV) that boasts significant improvements in key areas of armour, mobility and firepower over vehicles currently employed by the People's Liberation Army (PLA). In July, China reportedly unveiled a new version of its HJ-73 anti-tank guided weapons that can penetrate Explosive Reactive Armour (ERA). This penetrating capability is reported to be more than twice that of the original warhead against conventional armour.

Jane's Defence Weekly reported that the PLA had boosted its amphibious capabilities by modernizing its Type 63 amphibious armoured personnel carrier (APC) and Type 63A light amphibious tank. The original versions of the amphibious vehicles had operational capabilities only in lakes and slow-flowing rivers but the improved versions could be deployed further off shore and in rough seas. The report also said that the PLA had been upgrading part of its fleet of Type 59 main battle tanks (MBT) to enhance their firepower and battlefield survivability. The latest version, Type 59D (or WZ120C), was upgraded with the latest Chinese 105 mm Type 83-I rifled gun as well as a new computerized fire-control system with image intensification sights for the commander and the gunner.

In a span of three months, beginning July, China launched two advanced guided-missile destroyers into its Navy, both of them being launched from the Jiangnan shipyard in Shanghai. The first, Type 052B, began contractor's sea trials on 24 July. The ship was reportedly fitted with the Shtil-1 medium-range air defence system (with 3S90 single-arm launchers and four MR-90 Orekh radar illuminators) and the Frega M2EM surveillance and target indication radar. The second, Type 052C, was launched on 29 October. This destroyer, although similar to Type 052B, in its hull design and specification was said to be fitted with vertical launchers associated with the HQ-9 theatre air defence missile system.

China has been one of the biggest importers of Russian weapons. *Jane's Defence Weekly* reported on 15 January 2003 that China was ready to sign a new contract with Russia's Sukhoi Corporation for the supply of 24-28 Su-30MKK multi-role fighters apart from other defence equipment. The new contract, worth $2 billion, would be the third since 1999. *The Hindu* on 20 December reported that the accord between Russia and China came at the end of a one-day session of the Russia-China Inter-Governmental Commission for Military-Technical Cooperation. The report said that the sale of weapons was to commence the following year.

Jane's Defence Weekly on 1 October 2003 reported that the Chinese People's Liberation Army Air Force (PLAAF) was in an advanced stage of negotiations with Russia to acquire up to 20 Il-76 heavy transport aircraft worth more than $500 million to boost its airlift capabilities. The PLAAF's acquisition of the aircraft was believed to be for a new airborne corps being established, to be located in the Nanjing Military Region, responsible for military operations dealing with Taiwan.

In recent years, China has been assessing and implementing vigorous electronic-based programmes into its military modernization agendas. *Jane's Defence Weekly* reported on 20 August that China was engaged in at least six simultaneous programmes aimed at bolstering its airborne electronic warfare (AEW) capabilities. Four of the programmes involved new variants of the SAC Y-8 medium transport/

multi-role aircraft. The fifth was a version of Russia's Beriev A-50 AWACS and the sixth, a modified Il-76 strategic transport. The Il-76 programme was reported to be focusing on a platform fitted with the BAE Systems Argus radar. The A-50 programme centred on the A-50Eh early warning system developed by Russia after the plan to acquire the Israeli Phalcon system was blocked by the US. The first two programmes involving the SAC Y-8 were said to be operational already and had been deployed in China's south-eastern coastal areas to collect electronic intelligence and the other two Y-8 programmes were expected to enter service the following year.

China's quest for an enhanced status in space programme has been unmistakable in recent years. *Aviation Week & Space Technology* reported on 24 November that for the fourth time in a month China launched a major space flight, the latest being a ChinaSat communication satellite to be operated by the Ministry of Post and Telecommunications. Meanwhile, it was reported that China had confirmed its $232 million investment in the $3.7 billion European Galileo global navigation satellite system. Galileo has been scheduled to be operational in 2008, with 30 satellites operating in medium earth orbit and two ground control centres.

Pakistan

Much of US-Pakistan defence collaboration comes with riders, such as that the US should be satisfied that Pakistan is collaborating wholeheartedly in the United States' "war on terrorism", that Pakistan is ensuring that there will be no onward proliferation and that it is moving towards democracy. These were reflected during the visit of President Pervez Musharraf to the US on 24 June. The US Government reportedly promised a financial package of $600 million a year for five years (a total of $3 billion), beginning in fiscal year 2005. The aid was to be evenly split between foreign military financing and economic assistance. US Administration officials said that the aid was part of a pledge between the two countries to "make a long-term commitment to build a relationship that is fundamentally different from what we have seen in the past". The package reportedly did not include new F-16 fighters, though the US declared that it was willing to consider requests for the upgradation of existing

F-16s as well as spares already in the Pakistani inventory.

The Hindu reported on 21 August that the US Ambassador to Pakistan, Nancy J. Powell, called on the Chief of Air Staff Kaleem Sadat to announce the sale of six C-130 aircraft to Pakistan from the Lockheed Martin Company at an estimated cost of $75 million. The sale was also a part of the Foreign Military Finance Programme that provided grants to eligible foreign governments.

The Pakistan-China defence cooperation has particularly focused on missiles, aircraft and nuclear technology. One of its major programmes has been co-production of the FC-1/JF-17 fighter aircraft by the Pakistan Aeronautical Complex and the Chinese Chengdu Aircraft. On 24 August, the FC-1/JF-17 fighter aircraft was reported test-flown for the first time. The 17-minute flight, according to the report, was successful although it came after years of delay with the avionics suite for the aircraft yet to be chosen. Earlier on 26 March, a Pakistan Atomic Energy Commission (PAEC) spokesman said that the PAEC signed a Memorandum of Understanding (MoU) with China for a second 300 MW nuclear reactor at Chashma. The unit was expected to be built within six years.

Pakistan's thrust in arms acquisition and defence preparedness has been evident from the reported increase in defence allocation from PRs. 146 billion for 2002-3 to P Rs. 160.3 billion for 2003-4. Although mobilization along the India-Pakistan border throughout 2002 was reportedly the reason for the increase in allocation, it also envisaged the purchase of new defence equipment and systems. The Government had reportedly authorized the Navy to negotiate the procurement of four F-22P frigates from China and also consider buying some Chinese corvettes. The Air Force was also asked to examine the acquisition of AWACS, while the Army was considering improving its surveillance capabilities.

On 8 January, the Pakistan Army's Strategic Force Command formally introduced the 1300 km Ghauri medium-range ballistic missile (MRBM), also known as Half-V, into service. President Pervez Musharraf accepted the Ghauri on behalf of the Army at a ceremony held at the Kahuta Research Laboratories in Rawalpindi. The Pakistan Navy's second Agosta 90B diesel-electric submarine, Saad, was reportedly ready for operational service before the end of the year after completing its deep-test drive on 19 September. This was the first ocean-going submarine built in Pakistan at the Karachi Shipyard & Engineering Works.

Iran

Plagued by reports that Iran had failed to inform the International Atomic Energy Agency (IAEA) of a number of nuclear activities, including research and development for Iran's uranium enrichment gas centrifuge programme at an undisclosed facility in Tehran called Kalaye Electric, Tehran got itself into a tight spot with sections of the international community, which warned that its behaviour was "a matter of concern". US officials called it a violation of the 1967 Nuclear Non-Proliferation Treaty (NPT) to which Iran is a signatory, and asked Russia, with which Tehran had been cooperating in the nuclear field, to suspend all such cooperation. The Russian Government, however, gave the green signal for Iran's acquisition of nuclear fuel for its nuclear project, announcing that the first shipment of the fuel would be dispatched immediately after an additional protocol on the return of spent fuel to Russia was signed. The fuel was meant for the Russian-built nuclear reactor in Bushehr.

Iran's force modernization programme has largely depended on the purchase of Russian-made arms and military equipment. Iran was reported to have sought Russia's help to upgrade its air defence system around Tehran and other key industrial centres with the Almaz S-300PMU long-range and Tor-M1 short-range surface-to-air missiles. The report by ***Flight International*** in November-December 2003 also said that it was interested in upgrading its Sukhoi Su-24MK strike aircraft to extend their night attack capability and converting its MiG-29 air defence fighters to the MiG-29SMT multirole variant.

Jane's Defence Weekly reported on 5 February 2003 that Iran had confirmed its possession of the single-stage solid-fuel Fateh A-110 (formerly Mershad) short-range ballistic missile built by the Iranian Aerospace Industries Organization. The confirmation came from a picture of the missile on Iranian Television. Tehran also revealed, in early April, an enhanced composite armour package for its locally made Boraq Armoured Personnel Carrier (APC). This included an armour that could be rapidly fitted to the front of the hull to protect against 30 mm armour-piercing ammunition. Iran was also reported to be already exporting the Boraq APC.

Afghanistan

The first and second brigades of the new Afghan National Army (ANA) were officially activated on 22 March 2003 after assistance from international donors, particularly Bangladesh, China, Germany, India, Iran, Italy, Pakistan, Turkey, the United States and the United Kingdom and recruitment drives that also focused on educated Afghans. The brigades were the first two of the three that would form the ANA's Central Corps. In March, the Netherlands was reported to have transferred several hundred RT 3600 combat net radios to the fledgling ANA at no cost to Afghanistan. Until then the ANA had reportedly no communication equipment and much of their communication network depended on post-to-post bicycle runs.

In July 2003, Russia announced that it would expand deliveries of military equipment and spare parts to Afghanistan to replenish the Afghan defence inventory, which constituted close to 100 per cent of Russian-made weapons. Defence Minister Sergei Ivanov, who made this announcement, said however, that the supply would not include new weapons due to the "vague" political future of the country.

Myanmar

Myanmar was reportedly expanding its naval facilities on the Great Coco Island near India's strategically important Andaman and Nicobar Islands with significant Chinese support. The project was reported to have been inaugurated on 4 November 2002 and was expected to be completed by the end of 2003. The project involved the construction of a jetty measuring 85m x 70m at a cost of $11 million. In the early 1990s, the Great Coco Island was the site of a major signals intelligence facility built by China.

Nepal

Jane's Defence Weekly reported on 2 July that Nepal had received 3,000 M16A2 assault rifles from the United States for its army. The shipment completed the 2001 purchase of 5000 rifles worth approximately $4.7 million. The US was also to supply another 8,000 M16s as part of a military assistance package to better equip Nepalese forces to combat the Maoist insurgency.

II

Perspectives on National Security

Operational Management: Nature of Wars and Military Technology and a Joint Doctrine for the Armed Forces

V. K. Kapoor

Higher Operational Management

"The COSC (Chiefs of Staff Committee) has not been effective in fulfilling its mandate. It needs to be strengthened by the addition of a CDS (Chief of Defence Staff) and a VCDS (Vice-Chief of Defence Staff)." This was stated by the Group of Ministers (GOM) in their recommendations on "Reforming the National Security System" in February 2001. The fact, however, is that the COSC was not organizationally equipped to handle integrated planning, training and conduct of joint operations. With greater emphasis on joint and integrated operations in the future, the system had to be reorganized with a CDS, and a VCDS together with an integrated staff, to render "single point military advice" to the Government, to administer the Strategic Forces, to enhance the efficiency and effectiveness of the planning process through intra- and inter-service prioritization, and to ensure the required "jointness" in the Armed Forces. Ironically, no operational role has been currently envisaged for the CDS. The Chiefs of Staff have retained their roles of Operational Commanders-in-Chief of their respective services, despite the reformation.

To elaborate further, say the CCS (Cabinet Committee on Security) issues a "CCS Directive" to the COSC. The latter, after analysing the requirements and after converting the political aims and objectives to military strategic aims and objectives, would prepare a "COSC Directive" for the Services. The Chiefs of Staff, thus wearing two hats, would receive their own directive for operational implementation and prepare operational instructions for their respective regional commands. Each Service plans exclusively and attempts to coordinate later with the other Services. This is unsuited to a future operational environment where close integration of all elements would be vital. Taking the Service Headquarters out of the chain of operational command and creating integrated regional commands can correct this operational anomaly. The "COSC Directive" could be sent directly to the integrated regional commands, ensuring joint planning at that level before further implementation. This is also economical.[1] The GOM, it may be noted, had stated categorically, "This is likely to be the first step in a series of structural reforms to be implemented incrementally."[2]

The Service Headquarters can then look after equipment, administration and welfare, operational logistics and training needs of their respective forces, instead of micro-managing operations from South Block or Vayu Bhawan. The Service Chiefs would then have more time to manage their own organizational, political and bureaucratic environment in the capital. Operational responsibility and accountability will rest with the CDS and the Commanders-in-Chiefs of the integrated theatre commands. Pruning the inflated size of each Service Headquarters and strengthening the Headquarters of the Integrated Defence Staff will also achieve efficiency and economy. The CDS, who is currently charged with the responsibility of prioritizing equipment, force levels and budgets within the Services, and to promote "jointness" in training and operations would then, as the Chairman COSC, be responsible for evolving the military strategic plan of the nation, together with the other Service Chiefs, with the secretarial support being provided by the Headquarters of the Integrated Defence Staff.

This article briefly examines the nature of war in the future in order to identify the type of capabilities and technologies required by the Indian Armed Forces and recommends doctrinal precepts for a joint warfighting doctrine.

Nature of Wars and New Technologies

Nature of Wars in the Future

Induction of new technology requires consideration of trends in warfare and must be tailored to the type of force structures and organizations that we require. It needs to be fused with our future war fighting doctrine, force development, organization and training. Superior technology alone cannot win wars.[3]

The first generation of warfare pertained to the era of smoothbore muskets and tactics of lines and columns. The second generation was characterized by the use of breach loaders, barbed wire, machine gun and indirect fire. Tactics were based on fire and movement. Operations were linear, sequential and attrition oriented. The third generation of warfare was also a result of increase in battlefield firepower. The Germans developed radically new tactics to offset the disadvantage of smaller force levels imposed by the Treaty of Versailles after World War I. The first attempt at truly non-linear tactics emerged. The attack now relied on infiltration or on wide outflanking movements to bypass and collapse the enemy's combat forces rather than seeking to close with and destroy him. The use of tanks and aircraft brought about a major shift at the operational level. The Germans termed it Blitzkrieg (the lightning war) and achieved outstanding victories till their opponents learnt how to execute and counter such tactics. Military analysts are now deliberating and reflecting on a "fourth generation" of warfare, in which the target will be the whole of the enemy's society (ideology, culture, political setup, infrastructure and civil society). This generation of warfare, they say, will be characterized by dispersion, increased importance of actions by small groups, decreased dependence on centralized logistics, high tempo of operations and more emphasis on manoeuvre. Masses of men and firepower may become a disadvantage, being easy to target. Small, highly manoeuvrable, agile forces will tend to dominate. The aim would be to cause the enemy to collapse internally, rather than physically destroy him. There will be little distinction between war and peace. It will be non-linear, possibly to the point of having no definable battlefields or fronts. Major military and civil facilities will become targets. Success will depend heavily on joint operations. If we combine these general characteristics with new technology, we see one possible outline of the new generation.[4]

The Indian armed forces are still taught to employ second- and third-generation tactics. However, in our context too, with the nuclearization of South Asia, the likelihood of large-scale all-out conflict has reduced considerably, though short-duration limited conventional conflicts cannot be ruled out. Even within this framework there are a large number of operations that the armed forces may be called upon to undertake. Moreover, the threat may not be from a different country. It could be within, and would therefore remain ill defined and unknown. The size of the threat would not pose a problem, but the fact that it would be nimble, focused and highly motivated, knowledge-intensive, and capable of achieving strategic and tactical surprise needs to be noted.

We cannot know precisely when, where, and for what ends war will be waged. This dilemma becomes even more acute if the animosity against our traditional adversaries disappears. Thus, the issues related to methodology and technologies have to be examined in relation to the total spectrum of war. Wars in the future have to be viewed conceptually to identify the types of technologies needed to accomplish the likely future missions economically and precisely, with least amount of collateral damage.[5] If India were to fight such wars, the changes, in our own context, are likely to be in the detailed constitution of the war waging apparatus and methodology, covering the entire gamut of warfare, as under:

- Method of preparing for war
- Method of planning for and conducting war
- Technologies employed
- Force structures and organizations

Spectrum of War: The Future

The total spectrum of war in the future, in our context, covers various types of military operations, involving land, air and naval forces. Some that can be anticipated are:

- Limited conventional conflicts fought on land, sea and in the air with a nuclear, biological, chemical (NBC) backdrop.
- Border skirmishes.
- Counter-insurgency and counter-proxy wars (insurgency aided by neighbouring state(s)) operations.
- Punitive actions (against erring states).
- Counter-terrorism, involving non-state actors, on land, at sea, and in the air.

- Maintaining maritime superiority in the approaches to the Indian Peninsula, up to a range of 1500 miles against all contingencies.
- Defence of own sealanes of communications (SLOCs) and interdicting enemy SLOC.
- Battle space dominance over enemy's littoral and engaging in joint operations against the littoral.[6]
- Anti-piracy operations at sea.
- Power projection to assist friendly countries and preserve regional stability.
- Defence of disputed territory, island territories and a long coastline.
- Air superiority and even dominance over selected regions.
- Air operations with multi-role platforms and precision munitions.
- Military reaction (offensive or defensive) to unforeseen contingencies on land, at sea, and in the air.
- UN peacekeeping operations.
- Other forms of warfare such as information warfare, psychological warfare, and space warfare.

Capabilities

In view of the paradoxical nature of threats and challenges in the future, it would be prudent to plan for capability-based force structures, and not threat-based structures.[7] In the field of conventional warfare, with the type of imponderables that face the nation, we should plan on fully integrated (tri-service) conventional forces for future conflicts. The structure and organizations should be, incrementally, technology-driven, with corresponding reductions in manpower, but with greater lethality and mobility. They should be capable of undertaking short and swift operations through any or all mediums (land, sea, air, ether and space), under unified command structures enabled through integrated regional commands. Some of the other vital military capabilities that we need to develop, through re-engineering of the current force levels are:[8]

- **Rapid Deployment Forces** to replace the current ground-holding formations of the Army. These forces are intended to be smaller in manpower, but superior in firepower, mobility (ground and air), and other support components.

- **Strike Forces (tri-service)**, comprising smaller, tailor-made, fully integrated task forces, operating under unified command structures at operational levels (integrated theatres).
- **A high-technology, but manpower-intensive counter-insurgency force** for fighting insurgencies, proxy wars (insurgencies aided by other states), and for internal employment.
- **Air Power**, capable of deterring any potential adversary, defending the Indian air space, and capable of conducting integrated operations, with land and naval forces at strategic (national), operational (theatre), and tactical levels (below theatre) with multi-role platforms and precision munitions.
- **Naval Power** to have a credible ocean presence, capable of deterring all potential adversaries and capable of achieving operational missions at sea and in joint operations against the enemy's littoral.
- **A Strategic Force (tri-service) with a triad capability** (land, sea and air components) with an effective C4I2 (command, control, communications, computers, information and intelligence) with a wide range of nuclear weapons, capable of deterring all potential adversaries in the future.
- **Sophisticated intelligence, surveillance and reconnaissance capability**, to provide complete situational awareness about own and enemy troops at all times.
- **Defence Communications**, which are networked and secured.
- **Strategic and tactical transportation of troops and material**, by air, as per operational compulsions.
- **Integrated Power Projection** capability in India's sphere of influence.
- **Integrated Special Forces**, trained, equipped and organized to undertake counter-terrorist operations in all their manifestations, including weapons of mass destruction (WMD), against state and non-state actors, which threaten the sovereignty and stability of the nation.

- **Anti-ballistic missile capability.**
- **Cruise missile capability** to hit hinterland targets of potential adversaries.
- **An Amphibious Task Force** (tri-service) redesigned and reorganized, using high-speed sealift technologies.
- **An Air Assault Formation** capable of conducting airborne and helicopter-borne operations in any type of terrain, which is also the mainstay for the power projection capability.

Technology

To acquire the capabilities discussed in the above paragraphs, the Indian Armed Forces will need to focus on some key areas. The technologies needed to develop and produce the systems are:[9]

- **Digital communication** networks linking sensors, communication devices and weapons, for real-time response. The defence communications being currently designed will have to cater for this requirement of C4I2.
- **Ground and airborne surveillance** with an array of manned and unmanned aircraft and UAVs (unmanned aerial vehicles) sending data direct to the integrated command headquarters with intermediate units and formations receiving the data simultaneously.
- **Situational Awareness with Identification Friend and Foe (IFF)** for own troops, combat vehicles and tanks.
- **Digital imaging with GPS** will allow commanders to draw up fresh battle plans with accurate and up-to-date information of enemy movements through situational awareness with IFF.
- **Precision-guided munitions**, sub-munitions, smart mines and smart munitions used along with situational awareness will markedly reduce collateral damage.
- **Networked logistics** and networked tracking system for functioning in a mobile and dynamic environment.
- **Transportation for rapid movement** of troops, equipment and logistics at strategic, operational and tactical levels.
- **Accurate long-range firepower** with field guns and MBRLs

(multiple barrel rocket launchers), with a variety of munitions, including precision munitions.

- **Advanced air-defence systems.**
- **AEW (airborne electronic warfare)** technology and AWACS (airborne warning and control systems).
- **Underwater sensors and weapons.**
- **New generation of combat aircraft and helicopters.**
- **New generation of tanks**, which are lighter but have heavier firepower and are capable of strategic mobility.
- **High-speed sealift technologies.**
- **Electronic and Information Warfare Systems.**
- **Satellite-based surveillance, intelligence and communication systems.**
- **Underwater and anti-submarine warfare systems.**
- **Missile warfare and anti-ballistic missile defence.**

The DRDO Interface and Future Technologies

The DRDO (Defence Research and Development Organization) needs to focus on frontier technologies rather than developing technologies that are available off - the - shelf. The latter can be acquired. The long-term plans of DRDO need to be formulated keeping in mind the long-term perspective plans of the Services, which should be synthesized and prioritized by the Headquarters of Integrated Defence Staff.

Some key areas that DRDO needs to concentrate on, in the long term, are:

- **Directed Energy Weapons**. The specific area of high-energy physics that promises the maximum pay-off is laser technology. Laser, particle beams, and high-power pulse weapons come in this category. The role of such weapons in the future for destruction of satellites, missiles and aircraft will be critical.[10]
- **Nano-Technologies**. These technologies are associated with manufacturing processes at the molecular level. One area where nano-technology is used is in micro-electronics mechanical systems

(MEMS), where small groups of atoms are manipulated by microscopic machines to produce, say, a data storage facility wherein a set of 500 Encyclopedia Britannica would fit on a single square centimetre chip. This technology has also resulted in the advent of "army ants"—a class of micro-size mobile robot that performs physical tasks and takes cooperative decisions as a coordinated homogeneous team. Their group actions denote their usefulness. Their uses range from clearing minefields to carrying out damage control actions in a hazardous environment to identification and transportation of inventories in large ammunition or ordnance depots.[11]

- **Bio-technology**. It has a wide range of applications besides bio-warfare. It takes only Rs. 2000 to produce enough anthrax spores to depopulate an area of one square kilometre. Another area is bio-molecular electronics. The ability to design protein molecules that are organized in predetermined three-dimensional structures gives the prospect of growing circuits. With semiconductor molecules included in the protein framework, the biochip could be self-reproducing, regenerative and of high capacity. Militarily, the added advantage could be resistance to EMP (electronic magnetic pulse) effects, as well as a very compact size for a given capacity. Additionally, this technology could be harnessed to manufacture very sensitive and selective biosensors, which would be engineered to act as rapid and cheap bio-chemical agent detectors. Biotechnology also promises breakthrough in the area of non-lethal technologies.
- **Space-based Systems**. High-resolution imagery, satellite-based surveillance, and communications will play a vital role in the future.
- **Propulsion Technologies**. Cruise missiles, long-range torpedoes, artillery shells and rockets, hyper-velocity aircraft and anti-ballistic missile systems.
- **Sensor Technology**. If miniature devices, as discussed earlier, can detect, process information, move and communicate, they can provide a very fine battlefield sensor network. Some predict the development of small robots, a few inches in size, scattered

over the battle space to provide continuous, real-time surveillance. Others foresee the development of "surveillance dust", a cloud of microscopic airborne sensors that could gather and report data over extended periods over large areas. Some writers envision "fire ant warfare", with the battlefield dominated by millions of small machines networked together, recognizing a friend from foe, and able to make large areas impassable to the enemy.[12]

- **Advanced Soldier Protection Concepts**. The US Institute for Soldier Nano-Technologies visualizes integration of a wide range of functionalities, including multi-threat protection against ballistics, sensory attack, chemical and biological agents; climate control (cooling, heating and insulating), possible chameleon-like garments; bio-medical monitoring; and load management. The aim is to achieve a revolutionary advance in soldier survivability, through development of advance materials for integration into the "Objective Force Warrior System".[13]

A Joint Doctrine for the Armed Forces

What is a Doctrine

A military doctrine is basically evolved from the national security doctrine and its formulation takes into account key factors such as historical experience, trends in warfare, current/future technologies and national ethos and culture. In the absence of the latter, the military formulate their doctrine based on existing policy letters and pragmatic assumptions as has been, ostensibly, done by the three Services while formulating their respective current doctrines.

A doctrine reflects the will and philosophy of an organization and specifies premises and convictions to sustain it in all its endeavours. It is influenced by the past and takes note of the future. Thus it is a constantly maturing process and its value lies in it being relevant, achievable, acceptable and adaptable.[14]

From the military point of view, a doctrine is a system of views adopted in a given period on the aims and character of a possible war, on the preparation of a country and its armed forces for such a possibility as well as on the method of waging war should it break out. Changing circumstances, e.g. global/regional backdrop, threat, demography and technological changes, must be constantly evaluated because they can modify beliefs and necessitate changes to doctrine.[15]

The Need for Change in the Indian Context

Indian military thinking has traditionally favoured deliberate, set-piece military operations that are attrition oriented and hence with a tactical bias. These have not been cost-effective. The outstanding military victory in the 1971 War with Pakistan in the Eastern theatre was made possible by favourable strategic factors like geography, air supremacy, people's support in erstwhile East Pakistan and poor enemy morale, whereby the Indian forces could afford to take risks in operational conduct. In the Western Theatre, however, due to India's proclivity for more traditional methods, the operations remained deadlocked.

The enlarged spectrum of conflict, with conventional war with a nuclear backdrop on one end and terrorism and insurgency at the other and the need to apply the multi-dimensional aspects of war (such as psychological warfare, information warfare and strategic and operational-level deception) to win decisively and swiftly necessitates the formulation of a new military doctrine. The nuclear backdrop brings in the strong possibility of international pressure to prevent a war in the region, and if it does take place, to keep it short. Our political and military leadership will therefore have to be very clear on war objectives. Attempts to fight attritional battles over territory per se are likely to result in stalemate and heavy casualties. Secondly, in terms of the political aims of war, it must enable the country to achieve the strategic objectives quickly and yet not escalate the war beyond the conventional realm. The political aims and military objectives of war would therefore have to be carefully calibrated and the senior military commanders would have to be clear, confident and convinced regarding the method of war fighting in the future. The basic tenets adopted must also guide the country in reshaping its organizations and force structures for the future. These issues need to be internally debated, discussed and war-gamed at strategic (national and military strategic) and operational (integrated theatre) levels so that the country's political and military leaders fully comprehend the constraints under which they would be required to function in the future.

Another concern is about the procedure to be adopted when an adversary adopts nuclear brinkmanship as a strategy. Operational-level commanders (Army Commanders and equivalents) must be aware of the implications of their operational decisions on the overall war effort, the likely reactions of the opponent and the country's counter-reactions and hence have to be part of the strategic decision-making process, including nuclear response. Unawareness of the strategic realm can lead to operational embarrassments and even disasters.

The next parameter relates to the rapid advances in technology in recent times. Technology drives the change in the method of war fighting. We face an entirely new technology era but have not been able to integrate new technologies at military strategic levels or evolve a suitable joint doctrine for the armed forces. Moreover, higher technology confers the advantage of being able to hit almost anywhere, which requires even lower tactical-level commanders to understand the operational and strategic logic and implications of their actions. This also demands a re-look at the training of our military leaders.

Operational and military strategic levels demand the maximum skills from a military professional because they require of him to be equally competent in all three levels of war, i.e. strategic, operational and tactical. All military officers who aspire to reach higher ranks must therefore study and understand Operational Art as an important ingredient of the art of war. This is, currently, a weak area of training of our officer cadre in all three Services. Moreover, an over-centralized command and staff culture prevails in India's military, which inhibits intellectual growth and maturity. This calls for an introspection of the culture that prevails in India's Armed Forces.

Wars are fought for a purpose. The political leadership provides this purpose since, as Clausewitz said, "War is an extension of politics by other means". The Indian way of going to war must be studied and formalized. The higher direction of war and the system of issuance of directives/instructions from the highest strategic bodies to the lower tactical formations must be formalized as a part of the joint operational methodology.

In the twenty-first century, India's armed forces are still planning for conflicts, service-wise essentially, the way it was done in World War II. They have not even begun the journey for integrated warfare in the twenty-first century.[16]

Doctrinal Precepts

Considering the enlarged spectrum of war and the new dimensions of warfare, some guiding principles or doctrinal precepts that are central to India's requirements of war fighting in the future are being highlighted for inclusion in India's Joint Doctrine:

- **Indian Way of Going to War** There should be an Indian way of going to war. As citizens and soldiers of this great nation, we conduct military business in a peculiar Indian way. This needs to be formalized. Currently there is no formal procedure followed.

  > "Our security environment is characterized by insufficient overall direction; too many ad-hoc structures and responses; poor inter service and inter agency coordination; shortages of appropriate equipment and material; inappropriate support systems; cumbersome regulatory systems; serious institutional resistance to change; limited dedicated resources; peacetime oriented security plans; and lack of joint doctrine and training."[17]

  India's political leadership, perhaps for political reasons, shies away from giving written directives to Service Chiefs. On receipt of such a political directive, the COSC is required to convert the abstract political aim(s) of war to achievable military aim(s) and objectives. If after analysis it comes to the conclusion that the political aim(s) set forth are not achievable, it must have the courage to say so. The nation must not go to war for an unachievable political aim. This process is a part of the higher direction of war.

- **The Approach to Warfare**. The methodology advocated by operational art should be adopted. This approach advocates the employment of all military forces (tri-service in India's context) to achieve strategic goals in a theatre of operations or a theatre of war through a unique contextual design, organization and conduct of operations. It is the intermediate level of warfare which connects strategy (policy) to tactics. The essence of operational art is to convert the given political objective (strategic goals) into achievable military objectives and to achieve these goals most skillfully, with least cost to own side. Hence this approach recommends innovative use of technology, firepower and manoeuvre as opposed to attrition to fight and win wars. A new, unique and creative operational design is conceived for every situation confronted so as to achieve the strategic goals with maximum efficiency and least cost. It involves a tri-service approach to an emerging or existing operational problem and therefore advocates integration of all elements functioning in a theatre under a single commander and hence the conduct of the campaign, its sequence, methodology and procedures are jointly evolved.[18]

- **Effects Based Operations (EBO)**. These are enabled by "network centric warfare". Improved and updated knowledge of the enemy through situational awareness along with the ability to generate accurate and lethal firepower and non-lethal effects against multiple targets in close succession allows defeating the enemy without the need for complete destruction of his forces or infrastructure. This demands a complete understanding of enemy sources of strength and coherence whereby use of relatively smaller number of strikes or manoeuvre forces will have disproportionately greater effects on his will and his ability to conduct future operations. EBO looks at own force structures from the perspective of achieving the effects desired. At the strategic level EBO requires close integration of military means with diplomatic, economic and other elements of national power. In other words, EBO sets those conditions which defeat an enemy's ability to wage war rather than focusing on attriting his war fighting capability. EBO requires superior military capabilities, to be built into the force structures, through the use of technology coupled with innovative Operational Art, to achieve these effects.[19]
- **Integrated Operations**. We should transcend from joint operations to integrated operations to unleash the full potential of combat power of joint operations. This demands integrated command structure at military strategic and operational levels in the context of the campaigns in the future. We must progress to

integrated regional theatres to achieve the type of synergy required to win wars in a short time-frame.

- **Shared Fighting Culture**. Currently the planning for war is peculiar and exclusive to each Service. Advocates seem to argue from a single-Service perspective and there is a tendency to underplay a single-Service weakness while overplaying its strengths. In the 2001 offensive that destroyed the Taliban regime in Afghanistan, air power could not have succeeded on its own. Even if all structural targets had been destroyed from ramshackle command posts to the handful of ammunition depots and fighter aircraft and so on, the Taliban would not have been weakened significantly. Yet the bombing was effective all the same. Information networking was the key to this responsiveness but the final resolution and discrimination for targeting was provided by small, mobile land forces that had secure satellite communications and accurate positional data to cue the weapon systems. Such employment and deployments will demand a shared fighting culture, a complete change in the way we plan and conduct military operations. This can be done through joint training and intense joint war-gaming.
- **Address the Vulnerabilities and Weaknesses of the Opponent**. To avoid attritional warfare and to use the asymmetry of even a superior opponent to our advantage, we should concentrate on his vulnerabilities/weaknesses. To learn this art we have to have detailed knowledge of our potential adversaries that is kept updated at all times, even during the conduct stage of war, through situational awareness. We have to prepare our senior commanders for all contingencies, through intensive joint war-gaming.
- **Rapid Deployment and Environmental Mobility**. Future wars will demand the capability of rapid deployment and environmental notability to be used for proactive missions or as a reactive response to any developing situation. This capability will be required across the board at strategic, operational, and tactical levels.[20]
- **Directive Style of Command**. For successful application of innovative Operational Art, in future wars, the command style cannot be rigidly centralized. A more flexible style, which

encourages risk taking and maximum initiative by subordinate commanders, will have to be adopted. This change of culture will also allow subordinates to conceptually grasp the higher commanders' intention and the higher framework of war and facilitate the adoption of the manoeuvre approach to warfare in the Indian context, through all mediums (air, sea, land, space and ether) and in all types of terrain.

- **Manoeuvre**. There is an imperative need to evolve manoeuvre approach as the key element underpinning our approach to war fighting, through all mediums and in all types of terrain, including our mountainous regions, because it targets vulnerabilities rather than mass. Our force development and organizations will have to cater for this capability, which in the future will involve close integration of air, ground and naval forces and other dimensions of warfare such as information war and psychological war.[21]
- **Transformation Through Technology**. We should achieve faster transformation through use of new technologies and innovations coupled with Operational Art. This will not only change the method of war fighting but also confer distinct advantages, which could be maximized through fusion of technology with training, organizational structure and force development.
- **Information Superiority**. Information superiority confers a competitive advantage in the transformation of the operational capabilities of a joint/integrated force. It is transitory in nature and must be created and sustained through conduct of information operations. The information revolution is progressing at such a rapid pace that there is a risk of being left behind if we are not constantly studying the phenomenon to examine how to use new findings to evolve new military concepts of exploiting information superiority for military gains.
- **Non-Linearity**. This calls for an attitudinal change in the military mindset with regard to conventional/unconventional ground, air, sea and space operations. We should be able to translate our idea of fighting the close, intermediate and deep battles, in all five dimensions, in near simultaneity and synchronize the destructive effects of battles on the ground, at sea, and in the air. This will require fusion of new technologies mentioned above and a

thorough understanding of operational art to psychologically unbalance the opponent and achieve cognitive effects targeted against his will.

- **Operational War-Gaming**. A tri-service war-gaming centre should be established for strategic and operational-level war games, with gaming software, to analyse issues such as emerging threats, new settings, new technologies, new concepts and war fighting methodologies. Without such a facility we will not be able to validate the concepts and doctrines that should be adopted in the future. This is the most urgent requirement.
- **Close Politico-Military Interaction**. Given the restrictive aspects of short-duration wars, nuclear backdrop and other factors, destruction of the adversary's strategic forces or capture of large tracts of territory will neither be possible nor desirable. War aims will have to be modulated, tempered and calibrated according to the environmental constraints. Therefore, translation of political aim(s) to achievable military objectives of war and skilful conduct of war will require a close politico-military interaction throughout.
- **Visionary Leadership.**[22] Yet another requirement of the future is the need for enlightened leadership at military, strategic and operational levels with a large enough vision to fully comprehend the entire perspective of strategic and operational level of warfare without over-identification with tactical objectives. This mandates sound training and selection procedures and unbiased policies, in which our track record is not flawless. The key attributes of operational and strategic-level leaders are considered to be as under:
    - Professionally astute (Possess a penetrating intellect)
    - Vision
    - Wisdom
    - Contemplative/reflective approach
    - Self-restraint/self-control
    - Self-knowledge
    - Ability to inspire/is a role model
    - Sacrifice of personal interest
    - Possesses all attributes of intelligence (IQ, emotional intelligence and spiritual intelligence).

The transformation of the Armed Forces through technological improvements coupled with innovative operational art and application of combat power through joint and integrated operations should be the essence of our war fighting doctrine, which will confer distinct advantages over a potential adversary. We must acknowledge the genuine strengths and weaknesses of the three Services' capabilities and achieve a level of integration, which will allow us to unleash the full potential of joint combat power. This is vital for preserving and furthering our national interests as a global/regional power in the future.

Conclusion

A paradigm shift in the definition of national security occurred when Frank Traegar defined national security as "that part of Government policy having as its objective the creation of national and international political conditions favourable to the protection or extension of vital national values/interests against existing and potential adversaries." Robert McNamara and Indira Gandhi added another dimension by stating that "Security is Development and Development is Security". Thus it is seen that national security encompasses a nation's political, diplomatic, economic, intellectual, technological, and military power. An indicator of National Power has been suggested by Cline in his book *National Power in 1990* where he states:

$$PP = (C + E + M) X (S + W)$$

where

PP = Perceived Power

C = Critical Mass = Population + Territory

E = Economic Capability

M= Military Capability

S = Strategic Purpose

W = Will to Pursue Strategy

It is obvious that strategic purpose and will are vital factors, which multiply manifold the perceived power of a nation. Unless the political leadership evolves and articulates its national vision and provides strategic directions to its own functionaries and shows a strong political will to pursue its national strategy, firmly and decisively, its credibility will remain low.

India faces tough security challenges in the future but with its vast resources and brain power it has the potential to be among the most powerful nations in the world, in not too distant a future. For this to become a reality, among other measures, in the security arena, the following needs to be done at the earliest:

- The political leadership (CCS) should articulate a Vision and provide Strategic **Directions** periodically to the military establishment.
- CCS instructions on operational matters should invariably be issued as a written **"CCS Directive"** to the COSC to avoid ambiguity and misunderstandings.
- An institutionalized and functional security framework at the strategic levels, which permits and indeed encourages constant security assessment and dialogue **between the Prime Minister and the Service Chiefs** and is responsive to the operational needs of the Services should be created out of the existing structure of NSC.
- **A CDS should be nominated** and the higher operational management should be reorganized to **preclude the current exclusive planning method followed by each Service Headquarters**.
- Restructure regional commands as integrated theatres to ensure integrated planning and conduct of war.
- Design **capability-based** and, where feasible, integrated force structures for the future.
- Evolve, adopt and articulate a **new joint operational doctrine** for the Armed Forces for the future.
- **Remove** the drawbacks and **weaknesses** noticed in the system of **defence procurement** and modernization.
- Identify and acquire technologies needed now and in the future, especially those technologies **that will help us to fight with greater precision.**
- **Integrate Services Headquarters** with the Ministry of Defence to avoid delays and ease the pressure of work at the MOD.
- Make all **officials (civil and military) strictly accountable for their actions/inaction.**

Notes

1. V.K. Kapoor, "Operational Art in the Indian Context", *USI Journal*, October-December 2003, pp. 564-5.
2. Group of Ministers (GOM) Recommendations on "Reforming the National Security System", p. 101.
3. Milan N. Vego, *Operational Warfare*, Naval War College, USA, NCW 1004, p. 619.
4. William S. Lind and Others (US Army and Marine Corps), "The Changing Face of War: Into the Fourth Generation", *Defence and Technology*, February 2002, pp. 10-11.
5. V.K. Kapoor, "Army 2020: Force Structuring and Doctrine", Paper presented at the Centre for Land Warfare Studies (CLAWS) Seminar, New Delhi, 4-5 March 2004.
6. Raja Menon, "Technology and India's Maritime Defence", *Defence and Technology*, July 2003.
7. Kapoor, n. 5.
8. Ibid.
9. Ibid.
10. Chandra Shekhar, *Arming the Defence Forces*, Manas, New Delhi, 2003.
11. R.K. Mehta, *Leveraging Technology as a Change Vehicle for National Security*, CDM Papers 1/2003, p. 85.
12. Ibid.
13. Ibid.
14. Army Training Command, *Fundamentals, Doctrines and Concepts—Indian Army*, August 1998.
15. V.K. Kapoor, "Fundamentals of Operational Art", *Combat Journal*, March 2001, p. 9.
16. Kapoor, n. 1, pp. 554-7.
17. Vijai Oberoi, "Air Power and Joint Operations: Doctrinal and Organisational Challenges", *USI Journal*, January-March 2003, p. 8.
18. Kapoor, n. 16.
19. Geoff Hoon, "Britain's Armed Forces for Tomorrow's Defence", *RUSI Journal*, June 2003, pp. 3-4.
20. General Sir Mike Jackson, "The Future of Land Warfare, Defence and International Security", *RUSI Journal*, August 2003, p. 56.
21. Robert Leonhard, *The Art of Manoeuvre*, English Book Depot, Dehra Dun, 1998.
22. Kapoor, n. 16, pp. 566-7.

India's Maritime Security

R.B. Suri

Introduction

A self-confident, economically strong and resurgent India stepping into the new millennium has already become a regional power of some consequence. With growth in status and power, competition will also grow and challenges will be encountered. With growing power would also come greater responsibility. In the maritime sector, essential to India's growth and development, threats would emerge in the long term. It is also in the ocean areas surrounding India that it can provide the much-needed stability and tranquillity. This essay will examine India's maritime interests and analyse the geopolitical situation and emerging security scenario in the Indian Ocean.

Guarding the Sealanes

India's vast maritime interests, its geography, heritage, trade and the exclusive economic zone that is nearly as big as the land mass and millions of seafaring people and thousands of islands make the country a great maritime nation. To these compelling imperatives and the growing importance of the seas India will turn in the years ahead. With 15 per cent of the world's population, India's energy consumption is only 3 per cent of the global total. The per capita annual energy consumption in the United States is 8.55 TOE (tonnes oil equivalent). The global average is 1.68 TOE. The corresponding figure for India is 0.32 TOE. We have only 0.5 per cent of the world's oil and gas reserves. West Asia in contrast holds 65 per cent of the oil and 36 per cent of gas reserves. At current level of consumption every percentage point represents a little over one million tonnes of oil and gas. India's present oil imports of 80 million tonnes represent slightly over two-thirds of its requirements. At current growth trends this will double by 2020. We will therefore continue to be a net importer and heavily dependent on energy transported mostly over the seas. Several thousand tankers would bring our energy supplies in the years ahead to our ports.

The security of the maritime energy lifelines over the sealanes would need to be adequately provided for. India's oil reserves are located in 26 sedimentary basins covering more than 3 million sq. km. Our current production comes from less than 20 per cent of this area. More than 50 per cent of the area is either unexplored or poorly explored. The biggest discovery of gas and oil in the world in 2002 was made in the Krishna Godavari offshore area. The next big discoveries are also expected to be located in deep waters on the western and the eastern coasts. In time, huge offshore oil production and processing platforms similar to Bombay High would be erected around our coast in the EEZ. Their security would have to be catered for.

As much as 97 per cent of India's trade is conducted through its 11 major and 184 minor ports, which handled 313 million tonnes of cargo in 2002-3, as compared to 252 million tonnes four years earlier. Greater awareness of the role that ports and harbours play in the economy of the country has led to the inception of the Sagar Mala project. The project aims at the integrated development of ports, shipping and inland waterways to optimize seaborne trade. It envisages an investment of over Rs. 10,000 crore over the next 8-10 years through public-private partnership for setting up new ports, modernizing existing ones and improving their productivity. The government claims to have already improved the turn around time of vessels from 6.03 days to 3.67 days. The Jawaharlal Nehru Port Trust (JNPT) handled more than one million tonnes equivalent units (TEUs) and was ranked 29th in the container handling ports of the world. Dahej and Ennore manifest the growing importance of the maritime sector. Thirty-eight projects for creating 123.52 million tonnes additional port capacity have been identified and nearly half of these have been approved by the Government. Export target for the current year (2003-4) aims at 12 per cent growth. If this momentum can be maintained, India's seaborne trade will cross 1000 million tonnes by 2020. Security of ports would therefore become even more important.

Indian merchant shipping has lagged behind the country's growth. It is ranked 17th in gross registered tonnage and 15th in dead weight tonnage in the world. To provide incentives to shipping, all type of ships can now be imported through open general licence and depreciation rates have been enhanced from 20 per cent to 25 per cent. Four Aframax tankers of 110,000 tonnes DWT capacity and two of 93,000 DWT crude oil tankers have been inducted into the Shipping Corporation of India. Orders for two Ultra Large Crude Carriers (ULCC) have also been placed. With the recognition of the importance of the maritime infrastructure greater tasks will arise for its security.

Transnational Threats

India's vast EEZ of over 2 million sq. km. contains untapped seabed wealth. In the years ahead, when it becomes commercially viable to tap such resources, the scope of conflict will increase. Even today more than 150 million Indian citizens living on the coast and in the island territories depend for their livelihood on the seas. Most of the fishing activity, being non-mechanized, is confined to territorial waters. There is tremendous potential in this area, especially in depths beyond 100 m but this would require modern and large mechanized fishing vessels. If adequate measures are not taken, poaching—prevalent largely in the Bay of Bengal—will continue to deplete our resources. Smuggling was once a commercial activity. Its nexus with narco-terrorism has increased the vulnerability of our long coastline. India, located between the Golden Crescent and the Golden Triangle, is especially exposed to such activity. When one adds the al-Qaida and Jehadi fundamentalism on the western borders with Jamaal-e-Islamiya (JEI) of Indonesia and the Philippines to the east with the LTTE in the south, the dimensions of maritime security become more complex.

The peace dividend that the end of the Cold War promised has not materialized. Rather, the code of conduct in international order that had maintained stability for nearly half a century has weakened. Civil wars, ethnic strife and religious fundamentalism, long suppressed, erupted the world over virulently as terrorism. Nine-Eleven brought it to the entire stage of the world. Neo-conservatism gathered force in the United States as a backlash, which further eroded world order. The war in Iraq was started presumably to rid the world of despots and purportedly to spread democracy but the pre-emptive action of the sole superpower has made its allies and friends uneasy. Multilateral action is preferred to unilateral action and the world order should be evolved through consensus.

Most of the conflicts threatening global security originate in Asia. Asia is also the economic powerhouse of the new millennium. It generates more than half of the world's economy. If the present momentum is maintained, by 2020 Asia would account for nearly 60 per cent of the world's GDP. Most of the goods and services generated by the Asia-Pacific region, Japan, China, India among others, along with their energy requirements would be transported through the Indian Ocean. The security of its sealanes would therefore be an important strategic objective for the great powers as well as emerging powers of the region. The Indian Ocean region would also be an area of power rivalry since here the influences of the United States come in direct contact with its main competitors, China and Russia. The energy reserves of the Persian Gulf and Central Asian Republics would ensure its strategic importance for the western world. The hub of terrorism is also in this region.

The security scenario in the Indian Ocean has witnessed major changes in the post-Soviet area. It is here that forces were concentrated in the Gulf wars of 1991 and 2003 to unleash the power of the modern military machine. The presence of the United States in this area is a reality and is likely to be permanent. The Chinese, who consider themselves as the emerging challenge to the United States at least in Asia, are not far behind in exerting influence in the Indian Ocean.

Operating facilities provided by the friendly countries could in the long term enable the PLA (Navy) to extend its operations in this region. In the west, China is not only supplying and building warships for Pakistan but also building a deep-water port at Gwadar, which overlooks the Persian Gulf energy sealanes. A coastal highway would join Gwadar to Karachi. In the east, China has longstanding relations with Bangladesh and has offered to develop Chittagong harbour. In the south, China has supplied ships to the Sri Lankan Navy. In Myanmar China has had a long relationship of building infrastructure like ports and roads. The Naval base at Hainggi Island was reportedly designed to support Chinese nuclear submarines. The media has also reported plans of connecting southern Yunan in China to Yangon province in Myanmar by road and waterway. Listening posts set up in Coco Island could help China monitor Indian Naval activity in the Bay of Bengal and missile testing facilities in Balasore and Chandipur. The PLA (Navy) has undertaken major plans of modernization for achieving blue-water capability. Western sources surmise that though the PLA (Navy) cannot challenge the might of the US Navy currently, it could in the next 10-15 years. Even today it has the largest submarine force in Asia.

Most other maritime nations in the region have also been developing their navies. Thailand, Malaysia and Singapore in the east possess modern navies, some with three-dimensional capabilities. Indonesia supports one of the largest naval amphibious forces. Pakistan has a strong sea-denial capability. Saudi Arabia, Iran and South Africa have the potential of growing into naval powers.

Their flexibility and mobility enables naval forces to concentrate in any part of the world at short notice. Since oceans have no borders, threats can materialize where none appear to exist today. Hence the presence of regional and extra-regional powers would influence maritime security in the Indian Ocean. While there are colossal opportunities in maritime activities, the attendant risks need to be guarded against.

Apart from such risks of the naval capability, most countries of the region face problems such as piracy, insurgency, narco-terrorism and small-arms proliferation. Transnational terrorism has flourished in the Philippines and Indonesia in the east, Sri Lanka in the south and Pakistan, Afghanistan and West Asia in the west. Links between terrorists and smugglers have exposed our vulnerability in guarding our coast. Terrorist killings have become common in Jammu and Kashmir but such action at sea can have disastrous results. A war game recently played focused on such a scenario. A Chinese tanker was on passage from the Persian Gulf destined for Guangzhou in China. The ship encountered rough weather near the western coast of India and had to slow down. A small but sturdy boat pulled up alongside the ship and ten hijackers climbed on board. They overpowered the crew and took charge of the vessel but not before the ship was able to flash a message to the Indian Coast Guard.

Another ship carrying oil was successfully hijacked south of Sri Lanka. Both these tankers made their way towards east. The terrorists sank one of the ships south of Car Nicobar, causing huge oil spill and panic. Simultaneously, the second ship was sunk in the narrow Malacca Straits. This impeded the merchant ship traffic there. As the countries in the region were grappling with the environmental crisis, Lloyds raised the insurance rates of seagoing merchandise. The consequent increase in freight spiralled oil prices upward. It had been easy to overpower an unarmed scantily manned merchant ship. Soon, terrorists struck at other sites, including an oil platform and a passenger ship, and anarchy spread at sea.

How does one deal with the emerging maritime threats in the Indian Ocean? Though the Cold War rivalries have abated, the region is too important a strategic space for important powers, regional and extra-regional, to allow it to remain benign in character. The idea of the Indian Ocean as a zone of peace has been a non-starter. Collective security, European style, would also be difficult to achieve in view of the myriad differences in the political, economic, social and ethnic fabric of the countries in the region. An increase in regional cooperation through trade and commerce like the recent Free Trade Area announced between Thailand, Myanmar, Sri Lanka, Nepal, Bhutan and India of the BIMSTEC (Bangladesh, India, Myanmar, Sri Lanka, and Thailand Economic Cooperation) group could perhaps bring about a more conducive atmosphere for building a security framework. But even this would take a long time. Alliances between powers would also not be a sound proposition. Self-reliance and expansion of its maritime capabilities must therefore remain for India a key option for protecting its maritime interests. Bilateral arrangements with different maritime countries could be progressed on need-based issues to offer reciprocal arrangements and facilities, against common threats. The threat of terrorism at sea could persuade the affected countries to take measures against it. But for such initiatives, mindsets have to alter. India, a dominant maritime power in the region, must itself adopt a more active focused policy on maritime security. Do we have a comprehensive perspective on this subject? Do we have a formulation of a proactive Oceanic vision statement that covers not only scientific aspects but also political, economic and military aspects?

Have we changed and adapted to the new realities of this changing world? The answer is a hesitant and tentative affirmative. For example in the 1980s, any mention of Diego Garcia sent us into a tizzy. Today, we are talking of beginning a strategic relationship with the US. Missile defence, high dual-use technology, civil nuclear and space cooperation are part of the roadmap ahead. Defence cooperation is growing with countries like Israel and South Africa, with whom we had no diplomatic relations a few decades ago. Our Look East policy has made us a dialogue partner in the Asian Regional Forum (ARF). Similarly, in the maritime dimension, in the 1980s, a handful of India's naval ships used to undertake goodwill visits to the neighbouring countries. Today, this number exceeds 40. There was little of naval exercises with foreign navies in those days. Today we are exercising with all the major navies, including the Chinese PLA(N). Joint patrolling in the Malacca Straits, earlier unthinkable, is today a reality. Similarly, the Indian Navy being asked to provide security to the recent African Summit showed that the presence of a responsible regional maritime power adds to the stability of the region and is welcomed by the countries concerned. Not long ago the growth of the Indian Navy was considered a "threat" by the Australian Navy. That picture has changed. To some extent, therefore, the Indian maritime capabilities have been accepted by the countries of the region. We have also started seeing the enormous possibilities of the oceans. It is in recognition of the greater responsibilities of the Indian Navy that the recent acquisition of the aircraft carrier *Admiral Gorshkov* from Russia has to be seen.

Even so, has the importance of the maritime dimensions of India's security been accepted by strategic thinkers and policymakers? Perhaps not quite. There is a mixed response to this reality. Mostly among the strategic community awareness has grown of the importance of the seas and the need to place greater emphasis on maritime activities and maritime security. Many cite the example of the Mughals, whose unawareness of the seas made it easy for the colonial powers to conquer India. Some argue that "sea blindness" still afflicts us.

Territorial outlook has continued to pervade the vision of Indian leaders post independence. They are not entirely to blame since post-independence external threats to the country originated from its land borders. The Navy, too, played a minor role in hostilities before 1971. The Indo-Pak War of 1971 brought the role of the Indian Navy into sharp focus. Since then the attitude of the policy-makers has changed slightly and the Oceans have come within the fringe of their horizon. Joining the Antarctica Treaty System in 1983 was one such step but still there is a long way to go. Take the example of the Indian ports. When foreign shipping started preferring Sri Lanka and Singapore to Indian ports, we realized the need to modernize, containerize and improve turn around time. Our poor record of creating infrastructure covers the maritime sector as well. Our shipyards have remained old and only recently schemes of modernization have begun. Indian merchant shipping tonnage too has stagnated. In the circumstances, the development of the Navy could not have been much better. Especially from the mid-1980s to the mid-1990s, depleted resources brought force levels down to alarming levels, forcing acquisition of warships from abroad. Budgetary provisions in the past few years have been near satisfactory levels. Today in naval development, the main deficiency lies in absorbing the allocated capital budget. The main problem lies in decision making at the Centre and in the shipyards, which are working at near 60 per cent idle capacity. There is still a major mismatch between our vision, planning, and its implementation. Some suggestions are made in the following paragraphs to focus on maritime security more effectively.

- There is an urgent need to evolve a policy statement on the Oceans. This should spell our vision of the Seas and their importance for not only scientific but also political, economic and security aspects.
- India should, in consultation with like-minded maritime nations, draw up a Maritime Security framework for the sealanes of communications of the North Indian Ocean against terrorism at sea.
- Terrorism at sea is an emerging threat and commonly faced by all maritime countries in the region. Sharing of intelligence and

augmented surveillance and patrolling could be instituted, in which the Indian Navy can prominently take part.

- The capabilities of the maritime forces to respond to a terrorist strike at sea need to be augmented, especially in rapid reaction response.
- The Navy and the Coast Guard are good instruments of maritime diplomacy, well endowed to build Bridges of Friendship among maritime nations in a cooperative security framework.
- Maritime cooperation among the littoral states of the Indian Ocean needs to be focused. India has a lot to offer in terms of expertise in human resource development and training, shipbuilding, anti-piracy measures, environmental protection, oceanographic survey and connected activities.
- The Navy and the Coast Guard would need to be funded adequately and self-reliance achieved in high-technology areas. Implementation of the capital schemes would have to be made more timely and effective.
- There are more than a dozen departments and autonomous bodies connected with maritime activities. These, among others, range from the ministries of Defence, Shipping, Petroleum, Department of Ocean Development, Environment, Law, Science and Technology, Fisheries, to ports, harbours, ONGC, Coast Guard and the Navy. There is a need to evolve a mechanism and coordinate their activities holistically. Setting up of a Maritime Board to guide overall security of maritime interests at the apex level is recommended.
- India has a huge coastline and thousands of remote islands. It is not possible to patrol such an extensive area continuously. However, vulnerability of the coast highlighted by the Mumbai blasts of 1992 continues to be of concern, especially since terrorism has taken front stage. Creation of Marine Police by the coastal states should be considered.
- At Independence, we had set a goal of creating Indian Flag merchant marine to carry 40 per cent of our trade in our bottoms. We are far from this objective. More resources need to be given

to the shipping sector to increase the tonnage under the Indian Flag.

- Some headway has been made towards decongesting and modernizing Indian ports but here again we are nowhere near the standards of a developed country. Our export-led growth will be greatly stunted unless modern infrastructure is created to handle goods and services with adequate security in our major and minor ports.
- We have yet to delineate maritime boundaries with Pakistan and Bangladesh. These have been vexed and complex issues but we must make an effort to resolve them.
- Patrolling by the BSF in the island waterways along our borders needs to be intensified and the water wings augmented with high-speed shallow-draught craft to operate in those areas.
- Island territories, being remote, are especially vulnerable. Poaching in the sea areas surrounding them also causes serious economic loss. The development of these island territories especially in tourism and Free Trade Zones would enable their integration into the mainstream and improve their security.
- On the subject of Maritime Law, serious apprehensions have been voiced by the maritime community. Our laws are antiquated and despite being pointed out by the Supreme Court in a judgement in 1993, not much has been done. India is also not a signatory to many useful and important international conventions. A bill has been pending for six years in Parliament for bringing amendments to our Merchant Shipping Act. Thus the area of legislation needs to be addressed urgently.
- The US, consequent to nine-eleven, is pursuing two initiatives in the war against terrorism, viz. the Proliferation Security Initiative and the Container Security Initiative. Both these measures have serious implications for us and need to be studied and debated before taking up our positions.

India has vast and growing maritime assets, which are inexorably linked to its development. The security scenario in the Indian Ocean is becoming more complex and the main threats would emanate from the oceans surrounding India. Terrorism being a common threat could also strike at sea, affecting all maritime nations of the region. There is an urgent need to organize and prepare for meeting such contingencies. Due to its location and potential, India is well suited to play a major role in providing stability and security in this area. To achieve this, India must acquire maritime capability in keeping with its size and status of a major regional power. Such capability would provide the bedrock of stability and tranquillity in the ocean areas surrounding the country, essential for the development of the entire region.

Multilateralism versus Regionalism: Challenges for India's Economic and Trade Diplomacy

*Nagesh Kumar**

Introduction

Notwithstanding the hype about globalization, the world trading system has evolved asymmetrically in the 1990s. One strong trend has been of regionalism in the western world, with more trade taking place on preferential than most-favoured nation (MFN) basis, thus undermining the very basis of multilateralism. The multilateral trade negotiations (MTNs) since the Uruguay Round have themselves been characterized by several asymmetries that do not allow all the participants to share the benefits of trade liberalization equitably. India's trade policy had to respond to these emerging challenges. This it has done effectively, with its own schemes of regional economic integration and coalition-building to protect its interests in the MTNs.

Emerging Trends in the World Trading System

The General Agreement on Tariffs and Trade (GATT) has provided a rule-based framework for international trade since its entry into force on 1 January 1948, with twenty-three countries, including India, as the founding members. The express objective of MTNs is to liberalize trade so that efficiency gains become available to the world economy at large. However, it has been recognized that there are unequal players in the game and developing countries have limited financial and physical capacities to undertake equal commitments. They need flexibility to pursue their development policy objectives that have been available to developed countries in the early stages of their development. Hence, the concept of special and differential

---

* The views expressed in this article are personal, and not necessarily those of the Research and Information System for the Non-aligned and Other Developing Countries (RIS), of which the author is the Director-General.

treatment (S&DT) to developing countries on a non-reciprocal basis was built into the process. The process of MTNs as well as making rules for governing trade in GATT is done in the rounds of trade negotiations. Between 1947 and 1980 seven rounds of trade negotiations were completed. The GATT Ministerial Meeting, held in Punta-del-Este, Uruguay, in September 1986, launched the eighth and by far the most ambitious round of MTNs, popularly called as the Uruguay Round. Due to many contentious new issues on its agenda, the Uruguay Round could be completed through protracted negotiations only in December 1993, which led to the formation of the World Trade Organization (WTO) as a successor of GATT in 1995.

The Uruguay Round proposals have led to a number of asymmetries. For instance, in this round the developing countries were made to undertake far greater commitments than their developed-country counterparts while S&DT provisions were diluted to only slightly longer transition periods. The developing countries were made to accept commitments to expand tariff bindings to cover 61 per cent of their imports compared to 13 per cent earlier and have offered US$15 billion worth of concessions by way of reducing their trade-weighted average bound tariff on imports from industrialized countries by 28 per cent. They were also made to accept commitments to liberalize their policy regimes with respect to intellectual property rights, investments, and trade in services. It has been empirically demonstrated that mercantilist balance resulting from market access commitments of the Uruguay Round has been in favour of developed countries. Furthermore, the new Agreements such as TRIPs are expected to lead to substantial income transfers from developing countries. It has been estimated, for example, that TRIPs could lead to net additional outflow of royalties from India of nearly a billion dollars a year.

Developing countries were lured into accepting these substantial commitments by the promise of additional market access to them by developed countries through liberalization of agricultural trade, textiles and clothing and movement of natural persons. However, these promises have not been delivered effectively. The developed countries while preaching the virtues of free trade to developing countries have been resistant to bringing down peak tariffs, high specific duties, and tariff escalation that affect imports from these countries. A startling example is the fact that tariffs collected by the US on $2 billion worth of imports from Bangladesh exceed those imposed on imports worth $30 billion from France. The market access commitments in textiles and clothing have been backloaded and only about 20 per cent of imports under specific quota restrictions have been liberalized in the seven years of implementation till 2002. The agriculture trade liberalization in developed countries, who are resistant to bringing down agricultural subsidies, has been undermined by dirty tariffication. The few commitments that have been made by developed countries in Mode 4 (movement of natural persons) are mostly subject to limitations, such as economic needs test, that usually render them ineffective. New barriers to movement of natural persons are being evolved in different parts of the world, such as legislation outlawing business process outsourcing, that affects India most significantly. There has been a proliferation of non-tariff barriers in the form of environmental and food safety standards much higher than the internationally agreed norms and an increased resort to contingent protection against exports of even traditional goods such as bed linen from India.

A more striking trend in the global trading system is the rise of regional trade blocs in the western world. Since the formation of single market in 1992, the EU has become a Fortress Europe that has been expanding eastward from twelve to fifteen countries and now with ten more countries joining it. North America has quickly followed the EU in building its own regional trade bloc. In 1994, the Canada-US Free Trade Agreement was expanded to cover Mexico into North American Free Trade Agreement (NAFTA). There is an ongoing agenda for expanding NAFTA southward into a Free Trade Area of the Americas (FTAA). Another grouping based on open regionalism came up in the mid-1990s, viz. Asia-Pacific Economic Cooperation (APEC). APEC combines major trading nations such as the US, Japan, China, Canada, Singapore and Australia. Subsequently, in South America another customs union, viz. Mercosur, took shape combining Brazil, Argentina, Paraguay and Uruguay. The developed countries are also pursuing bilateralism aggressively. The

United States, for instance, has recently negotiated bilateral FTAs with a number of countries in different parts of the world ranging from Chile, Jordan to Singapore.

These trading blocs in the developed world are diverting trade and investments away from developing countries. More than 60 per cent of the world trade is now conducted on preferential basis and not on MFN basis, thus undermining the multilateral trading system. Exceptions allowed under Article XXIV of GATT for Regional Economic Integration Arrangements have been effectively used by developed countries to evolve strong rules of origin to protect and build local industries while denying to developing countries flexibility to employ policies such as local content regulations phased out under TRIMs.

Empirical research has shown that these regional trade blocs have emerged as powerful factors in shaping the patterns of trade and investment flows. Countries outside such schemes face discrimination of their exports and diversion of FDI inflows, especially the efficiency-seeking FDI inflows, in favour of countries that are part of such blocs. Trade policies of affected countries have to take cognizance of these trends and respond to them appropriately by building their own regional economic integration schemes. India's trade policy over the past decade or so has evolved along these lines.

Recent Trends in India's Economic Diplomacy

India, a founder member of GATT, has faithfully pursued multilateralism all along. India has also supported economic cooperation among developing countries. As a part of this India signed the Bangkok Agreement and the Asian Clearing Union established in the 1980s under the auspices of the UN-ESCAP to promote intra-regional trade in Asia and also the Global System of Trade Preferences (GSTP) set up to promote South-South trade. India has also been an active player in the discussions on economic cooperation among developing countries in the framework of Group of 77 and the Group of 15, among others.

The growing trend of regionalism in the 1990s prompted India to take a serious look at regional economic integration as a policy. As a result of India's push towards economic cooperation in the framework of the South Asian Association for Regional Cooperation (SAARC), a South Asian Preferential Trade Agreement (SAPTA) with an eventual objective of regional free trade was signed in 1993. However, the transition from SAPTA to South Asian Free Trade Agreement (SAFTA) has been very slow as the Framework Agreement for the latter could be signed only in 2004. The slow progress of economic integration in the SAARC framework prompted India to also explore the potential of bilateral FTAs in the region. Thus, a bilateral FTA was signed with Sri Lanka in 1998 that came into force from April 2000. This FTA has produced encouraging results in terms of balanced growth of mutual trade and has prompted the partners to consider extending the scope of the agreement to cover investment and services in the framework of a Comprehensive Economic Partnership Agreement (CEPA). India already had free trading and transit links with the two land-locked neighbours, namely Bhutan and Nepal.

India has also strengthened its economic links with the South East Asian countries as a part of the Look East policy adopted in 1991. This policy was perhaps a response to the growing recognition of East Asia's potential to emerge as the centre of gravity with rapid growth and the rise of regionalism. Initially, the policy focused on engagement with ASEAN with a Sectoral Dialogue Partnership in 1992. With the entry of Myanmar, ASEAN became a contiguous neighbour and also seemed like a bridge for our economic dealings with the East Asian countries, given its vibrant economic relationship with the North East Asian countries of Japan, China and Korea. The ASEAN-India partnership culminated into an annual Summit level dialogue from 2002. At their Second Summit in October 2003, ASEAN and India signed a Framework Agreement on Comprehensive Economic Cooperation providing a FTA. This is complemented by negotiations on bilateral FTA with Thailand and a Comprehensive Economic Cooperation Agreement with Singapore. As a result of growing engagement, India-ASEAN trade has trebled since 1991 to cross US$10 billion in 2001. India is also part of a sub-regional grouping called BIMST-EC (Bangladesh, India, Myanmar, Sri Lanka,

Thailand Economic Cooperation) established in 1998 along with some South Asian and some ASEAN countries that has also adopted a Framework Agreement on FTA at its Ministerial Meeting held in February 2004.

The Look East policy is not confined to engagement with ASEAN. India is also striving to strengthen its economic links with China, Japan and South Korea. India has engaged China at a high level, with Premier Zhu Rongji visiting India in January 2002, reciprocated by the visit of Prime Minister Vajpayee to China in June 2003. The Sino-Indian trade turnover grew from about US$5 billion in 2002 to nearly US$7.5 billion in 2003, registering an average annual growth rate of about 50 per cent, much faster than the growth of trade of either country. A joint study group has been set up to study prospects of a comprehensive economic cooperation, including an FTA.

Other attempts to evolve regional cooperation schemes include the Indian Ocean Rim Association for Regional Cooperation (IOR-ARC) set up in the mid-1990s under the leadership of India, Australia and South Africa that now combines nineteen countries. IOR-ARC, however, has so far failed to adopt concrete measures to strengthen trade linkages among the member countries. India's application for membership of APEC in 1997 remains in abeyance since APEC decided to freeze the membership for ten years.

India's economic engagement with other developing countries has gone beyond Asia in recent years. A significant initiative among these is the formation of the Trilateral Commission combining India, Brazil and South Africa (IBSA) resulting from consultations of the heads of State or Government of the three countries during the G-8 Summit in Evian in April 2003 and the meetings of their Foreign Ministers in Brasilia in early June 2003 and in New Delhi in early 2004. The New Delhi Declaration notes that the areas of cooperation cover a common approach with regard to WTO and strategic cooperation besides setting a target of more than doubling the mutual trade to US$10 billion by 2007. IBSA countries have also set up a Trust Fund within the UNDP for Alleviation of Poverty and Hunger as their support towards South-South cooperation. India has also signed a Framework Agreement for Preferential Trade with Mercosur, a customs union of which Brazil is a key member. The possibility of a preferential trading arrangement is being explored with South Africa and Mauritius. India has also established a TEAM-9 Initiative to promote technical cooperation with eight West African countries. A Ministerial Meeting of TEAM-9 countries was held in New Delhi in early 2004 at which an Agreement was reached involving the offer by India of concessional credit of US$500 million and technical assistance and critical technologies to the West African countries. These engagements have brought rich dividends in the recent coalition-building processes in MTNs, as observed below.

An important challenge for India's trade policy has been to participate in the process of rule-making in the framework of MTNs effectively so as to protect its interests. India has developed some analytical capability to participate in the trade negotiations and articulate its viewpoint. However, MTNs are essentially power games. In the WTO negotiations generally the will of a handful of powerful countries, viz. Quad countries, is imposed on the entire membership in the name of "Consensus". Therefore, it is not enough to articulate our interests. We need to build effective coalitions of like-minded countries to protect our interests in these negotiations. In the Uruguay Round India had formed a coalition with Mexico and Brazil, among other countries, to resist the move of developed countries to bring the new issues, viz. TRIPs, TRIMs and GATS, on the agenda of these negotiations. However, the coalitions crumbled under pressure from developed countries and India found itself isolated towards the end and had to give in. In the Singapore Ministerial of WTO, effective coalition building by India helped in resisting a negotiating mandate on the six new issues sought by developed countries. Two of the six issues, namely core labour standards and environmental standards, were taken off the agenda while a mandate for only a study process was given on the other four issues. In the run-up to the Doha Ministerial, India had been an active member of the like-minded group in Geneva and had also helped in the coordination of positions at the SAARC level for the WTO Ministerial. Although towards the end India was isolated in its resistance for a negotiating mandate on the Singapore Issues, due to the steadfast opposition by the Indian Commerce Minister to the negotiating mandate on these issues a compromise solution was found to postpone the decision to the Fifth Ministerial Conference "by explicit consensus".

At the Fifth Ministerial Conference at Cancun and in the preparatory process leading to it, India has had considerable success in mobilizing support for its position with effective coalition-building. At Cancun the Group of 16 countries led by Malaysia (and covering China, Indonesia, Egypt, Kenya, Bangladesh, Venezuela, Zambia, Uganda, Botswana, Zimbabwe, Tanzania, Kenya, Nigeria, Cuba, Philippines) along with the group of least developed countries and ACP (African, Caribbean and Pacific) countries (in all nearly eighty countries) supported India's position of resisting a negotiating mandate. This transformation was brought about through active participation by India in the Working Groups set up on the Singapore Issues as a part of the study process. India in different submissions during the debates at these working group meetings clarified the development implications of WTO rules on investment and other issues. A breakthrough was achieved with the submission of a paper on "Investors and Home Country Obligations" (WT/WGTI/W/152, dated 19 November 2002) made by India that was co-sponsored by China and four other countries. Drawing upon detailed research done at an Indian policy think-tank, viz. RIS, this paper made a case for balancing the interests of source as well as recipient countries of investment by incorporating binding obligations for investors as well as home countries of investments along with their rights as demanded by the proponents of the multilateral rules. These proactive and constructive proposals helped in consolidating the developing-country coalition while bringing developed countries on the defensive. This submission being the first ever by India with China jointly, facilitated their coordinated position on other issues subsequently. With such a strong resistance with eighty developing countries opposing the move, the main demandeur of negotiations on these issues, viz. EU, found itself increasingly isolated at the Cancun Ministerial and towards the end of the Conference offered to drop two of the four Singapore issues from the agenda.

On agriculture, the coalition of developing countries was prompted by the US-EU proposal submitted in August 2003 that sought to extract major concessions from developing countries in terms of market access while agreeing to little reduction in their export subsidies and domestic support to their agriculture. Led by Brazil, India, South Africa, and China, a group of seventeen developing countries submitted a counter proposal in Geneva to the US-EU proposal. This group of seventeen countries grew subsequently to cover twenty countries and is called G-20. Before the end of the Ministerial ten more countries were supporting this coalition despite attempts by the US and EU to break this with both carrots and sticks. It is to the credit of the leadership of the G-20 that it has held together despite the attempt by the developed countries to break their ranks by offering to phase out export subsidies for select products of interest to some leading countries. Considering that the G-20 was led by Brazil, India and South Africa, it can be said that the trilateral IBSA framework has facilitated coalition-building on WTO issues. The Ministerial Meeting of the IBSA Trilateral Commission, held in New Delhi in early 2004, emphasized the importance of a common approach with regard to WTO, among other priorities.

Thus, although the Cancun Ministerial collapsed for failing to adopt the Ministerial Draft, for India it represented a moral victory. There was widespread support for India's principled resistance to Singapore Issues and for its position on agriculture. This contrasts well with India's virtual isolation at Doha Ministerial towards the end and was a result of the combination of its ability to put on the table proposals based on deep analysis and engaging like-minded countries to build effective issue-based coalitions. India is now well placed to play a much more important role in shaping the world trading system in the coming years by providing leadership to developing countries with its well-developed analytical capability and its skills in effective coalition-building.

Future Challenges

In the foregoing we have summarized the emerging trends in the world trading system and the recent trends in India's trade policy to respond to them. We may now discuss some challenges for the future.

In the area of world trading system, it is important to consolidate the issue-based coalitions formed at Cancun. These coalitions have been built to defend the developing countries' interests against powerful countries. Longer-term sustainability of these coalitions, however, will need some constructive proactive agenda. This agenda might cover seeking a reform of the process of decision-making in the MTNs to make it more inclusive, transparent and equitable; setting up a Developing Country Watchdog on the implementation of WTO commitments by developed countries and bringing complaints against any cases of under-compliance, strengthening the provisions of technical assistance for developing countries, strengthening the provisions for special and differential treatment with the help of a framework agreement, seeking a framework agreement on movement of natural persons, and a framework agreement on transfer of technology, among others. These coalitions could also become forums for promoting South-South cooperation such as mutual cooperation in implementation of commitments, technical assistance for compliance of emerging standards, etc., besides evolving approaches for promoting South-South trade. They could discuss ways and means for revitalizing the GSTP for promoting their mutual trade, besides addressing non-tariff barriers to it. India could take the lead in making these coalitions to pursue these proactive measures.

Another challenge for India's trade policy is to take its engagement with East Asia to its logical conclusion. The Indian economic engagement with East Asia has to be cognizant of the dynamics of economic integration in the region. Many efforts that are underway include China-ASEAN FTA signed in 2002, ASEAN-Japan FTA signed in 2003, and many bilateral pairs of FTAs. There is also growing monetary and financial cooperation between ASEAN+3 (Japan, China and Korea) since the East Asian crisis of 1997, including the Chiang-Mai Initiative. However, the widely shared expectation of eventual evolution of ASEAN+3 into an East Asian Economic Community has not taken off as yet, perhaps due to the Japanese apprehension of a possible Chinese domination of the grouping. It could be argued that the inclusion of India in a grouping like that would act as a moderating force or a balancing wheel and reduce the fears of domination by any particular country. India also brings to the grouping some unique comparative advantages and can broaden the range of complementarities such as in software and services compared to the hardware and manufacturing advantage of the East Asian countries. India can ill afford to be out of a major trade bloc that the ASEAN+3 process will finally emerge into.

The then Prime Minister Vajpayee proposed the formation of a broader Asian Economic Community covering ASEAN, Japan, China, Korea and India at the ASEAN-India Summit in Bali, based on extensive research conducted by a group of Asian think-tanks led by the RIS. The research has found a compelling case for an Asian economic community, which could be implemented in a phased manner, to begin with a core group of Japan, ASEAN, China, India and Korea (JACIK). RIS simulations show that JACIK with half of the world population, GNP comparable to the EU's, trade larger than NAFTA's and official reserves larger than NAFTA and EU combined could produce additional output of hundreds of billions of dollars and put it on a high growth path.

The idea is catching people's imagination. A survey conducted by the World Economic Forum at the New Asian Leaders Retreat held in Seoul in the middle of 2003 revealed that over 37 per cent of the New Asian Leaders view an extended Asia—ASEAN+4 including China, Japan, India and Korea—as the most desirable model of economic integration in Asia compared to just 27 per cent preferring ASEAN+3. In the coming years, India's Look East policy, therefore, should build on its highly successful track record to help evolve an Asian Economic Community along with other leading players in the region.

Imperilled Frontiers: India's North East

Jaideep Saikia

Introduction

Overarching security formulations by the State at times register a nation's bill of health in a manner that seeks to superimpose its central concerns on the periphery. Fundamentals of statecraft, too, have been known to consign fringe questions to the flames of non-visibility on the plea that hinterland issues are subject to the imperatives of heartland. Hence, the theories that sometimes characterize practice are informed by an inability to distinguish the whole from parts, erroneously decreeing that a sum of the parts makes up the whole. At other times, minutiae are dwelt upon, without an understanding of the crucial main, missing thereby the proverbial wood for the trees.

The North-East of India has, in the fifty-six years of India's independence, acquired a national nuance that seems to be characterized by comprehensions not entirely holistic. If internal security is understood as a question of law and order, the point missed is that a poor internal security situation is spawn of reasons other than those immediately manifest. While the improper development of the region is an important reason, the crucial coordinate seems to be one of insensitivity to the dynamics that administer the region. The North-East, despite its wide homogeneity, is not a composite whole, and a Lushai of Mizoram has as much in common with a Santhal of Assam as has a Kashmiri Pandit of the Valley with a Namboodiri Brahmin of Kerala. The British rulers had comprehended the diversity and kept governance of the Hills in the region to a minimum, excluding areas that did not come under the purview of their commercial cover.[1] A sensitive prognosis of the security scenario should take into account that overarching formulations do not cater for all the nooks and crannies of the enchanted frontiers. A scholar has written in a telling manner about New Delhi's perception of the region and the risks that accompany such a perception:

> The tendency of the Indian State to treat this extremely diverse region as one unit has resulted in the growth of totally incomplete and often misconceived notions about the different states that make up the northeastern part of the country. Such monolithic conceptions about a region, which stands out for its diversity of cultures and civilisations, would only help to nourish the biases and prejudices which have marked the Indian State's approach towards Assam and her neighbours since independence.[2]

This problem became evident during the crisis of 2001 when the ceasefire with the National Socialist Council of Nagalim (Isaac-Muivah) (NSCN (IM)) was sought to be extended to Arunachal Pradesh, Assam and Manipur. The extension caused a grave law and order situation in Manipur, but Assam opposed it only by way of a token protest. What occasioned the distinction? The extension of ceasefire with the NSCN (IM) in Assam was confined to a few bordering districts of the state such as Karbi Anglong and North Cachar Hills, districts which would not raise the chauvinistic hackles of mainstream caste Hindu Assamese society. Therefore, while Imphal burned in remonstration, Guwahati remained staid. Indeed, it is the same chauvinism of the Assamese mainstreamer that had estranged the Mizos, the Nagas and the Khasis, and has today raised the standard of rebellion among the Bodos and the Karbis. The socio-cultural concerns of every single sub-tribe are different from the other in the North-East. Though the separatist groups had constituted umbrella organizations,[3] the dissimilarities remain deep. For instance, though they belong to rival umbrella groups, the United Liberation Front of Asom (ULFA) was as much against the extension of the NSCN (IM) ceasefire to Assam as was the United National Liberation Front (UNLF) to Manipur. Yet, it was the NSCN (IM)—sire of a rival umbrella—that showed camaraderie to the ULFA when the latter was reeling from the Bhutanese army "Operation All Clear" in December 2003. It is also well known that the ULFA and the National Democratic Front of Bodoland (NDFB) have an alliance on the ground though they, too, belong to competing umbrella factions. Loyalties and enmity appear in the North-East most quixotically, and non-comprehension of the faultlines has its dangers. As a civil servant had warned in the early 1980s:

> In her endeavour to consolidate the unity of the nation by forcing the pace of integration of its several diverse elements, Pakistan succeeded only in losing her eastern wing and, unless she is prepared to learn from the lesson, will find the tribes of her north-western provinces similarly breaking away. This is a forewarning to India lest a similar situation develop on her strategically vital north-eastern borderlands. The movement to secede from India has hitherto been mainly confined to extremists in the Naga and Mizo hills, but it will quickly spread throughout the frontier states if the apprehension is allowed to fester that their culture is in peril.[4]

On the other hand, critics of New Delhi who accuse it of perceiving the North-East's ailments as mere law and order do little to put forward a robust policy prescription that might change such a perception. Analyses that development has to be institutionalized in the North-East, and that the opening up of the region to "dynamic Asia" will ascertain progress are only invoking statements that should have been in the forefront of policy in any event. Development cannot be relegated to a level that it must await internal dissonance before it is set in motion. Regrettably for the North-East, it has become both a sop and a reason. Development sops are put forward when there is strife, and the authors of discord in the region use conflict to attract pacifiers. The circularity of misfortune ends in the economics of expediency. To that end, not only does a sense of alienation continue to prevail, but a disservice has been done to India as a nation-state. Indeed, frontier policy seems to have abdicated responsibility towards a region that is not only strategically located[5] but one that has the potential of being further alienated as a result of the strategic encirclement. The situation in the North-East is critical,[6] that might imperil its station as an integral part of India.

Strategic Encirclement

The susceptibility to alienation that the region is heir to, although geographically mandated, has its moorings in history. India reluctantly engaged in a war with China in 1962 over territorial disputes in the region. Although recent times have witnessed fewer sabre rattles, a solution to certain disputes continues to elude the two countries. China continues to covet Arunachal Pradesh.[7] Although reports of intrusion into each other's territory are sometimes motivated by local political concerns, the fact is that the People's Republic has sought to keep the boundary issue with India alive, especially in the eastern sector (for which even maps were not exchanged unlike the central and the western sectors). This is notwithstanding that special representatives of both countries are meeting.[8] The motivation for another border war in the region, therefore, cannot be ruled out.

The strategic encirclement has also occasioned lesser neighbours like Bangladesh, Bhutan, Myanmar and Nepal to become staging grounds for sundry anti-India activities. While Bhutan has acted against the Assamese and North Bengal separatists in December 2003,[9] Myanmar's "annual jungle-bashing"[10] and its assurances to New Delhi that it will not allow its soil to be used for anti-India activities have amounted to little. Indeed, almost all the anti-India subterfuges in Arunachal Pradesh's Tirap and Changlang districts, Assam's upper districts and Nagaland's Mon and Tuensang districts are carried out from the NSCN (both factions) and ULFA camps in the Myanmar Naga Hills. Post "Operation All Clear" and the eviction of the three separatist outfits from Bhutan, Myanmar has emerged as the most important launching detachment for groups such as the ULFA.[11] Although not directly ordained by Beijing and Yangon, the existence of the Yunnan Navigational Bureau (headed by a former Chinese People's Liberation Army (PLA) officer, Brigadier Hua Binj Jao), which runs barges, mechanized boats and ships in the Irrawady river in Myanmar, is suspected to be the front for the PLA arms surplus[12] which finds its way into the hands of North-East Indian separatists.

Nepal enacts "Swiss-cheese" with myriad anti-India operations. While reports have suggested that its Jhapa, Tapegunj and Panchthar districts have in the past witnessed transit by the ULFA, the NDFB[13] and the KLO, more critically Nepal has provided a good launching pad for the Pakistani Inter Services Intelligence (ISI), and it is not inconceivable that the ISI's North-East desk (manned currently from Dhaka) has a cell functioning from Kathmandu. Nepal has also been the stage for separatist conclaves in the past. In mid-December 2000, for instance, members of almost all the separatist organizations of the region—NSCN (IM), NSCN (K), ULFA, NDFB, UNLF, PLA,

ATTF, GNLF and GLO—were in Kathmandu to meet David Patrick Ward of the London-based non-governmental organization (NGO) Naga Vigil. A Naga enthusiast, Ward met the separatists in Kathmandu's Thamel resort. The session of the United Nations Commission on Human Rights (UNHCR), which was later held in Geneva, was discussed, data on "human rights violations" collected and sponsorships for the session were applied for by the various separatist organizations. However, State support of such agendas is not evident.

Bangladesh houses camps belonging to almost all the North-East separatist groups. Sundry reports have even indicated that leaders of the ULFA, NDFB and the All Tripura Tiger Force (ATTF) are routinely chaperoned by Bangladesh's Directorate General of Field Intelligence (DGFI). Reliable sources have informed that even as General Musharraf of Pakistan was offering the olive branch to India's Prime Minister A.B. Vajpayee in Islamabad during the SAARC summit in January 2004, the DGFI spirited away the ULFA Chief of Staff, Paresh Barua from his perch in Bangladesh's Halowaghat and had kept him in a safe house in Dhaka's Mirpur Cantonment to hoodwink Indian intelligence scrutiny. Dhaka, moreover, has not been forthcoming about the extradition of the incarcerated ULFA General Secretary, Anup Chetia to India. Bangladeshi NGOs such as Odhikar are demanding not only the release of Chetia[14] but also asylum for the ULFA leader. Khaleda Zia's pronouncements that the North East Indian separatists are "freedom fighters" seem to have had an effect on the Bangladeshi populace as well.

The 4095 km long border with Bangladesh, moreover, continues to witness large-scale illegal immigration into India, an estimated 300,000 Bangladeshis illegally entering Indian territory annually.[15] Not only does Bangladesh deny the presence of a single illegal Bangladeshi in India and any North-East Indian separatist camp in Bangladesh, but has stated that India is attempting to push in Bengali-speaking Muslims into Bangladesh and that India houses "approximately ninety camps" which propagate separatist movement in Bangladesh.[16] It is groups such as the ULFA which aid the illegal immigration (in stark contrast to the ULFA's founding principles) and are even running a school in Bangladesh that reportedly teaches

Assamese to Bangladeshis who are desirous of entering Assam through the clandestine routes.[17] The ULFA has, moreover, abdicated the lofty principles by which it took birth, and is now terming the burgeoning illegal migrant population in Assam to be a consequence of movement from the rest of India. Responding to a study conducted by the Guwahati-based Omeo Kumar Das Institute of Social Change and Development on the illegal immigration into Assam, the ULFA has editorially opined:

> The Indo-Assam conflict is a classical example of the socio-political chaos created by the influx of Indian aliens of this category ... According to the recent study conducted by the Omeo Kumar Das Institute of Social Change and Development (OKDISCD), the size of the migration from India to Assam was 15,76,738 till '91 and it is continuing ... the Indian aliens have been desperately trying to establish their own culture and language taking Assam as a part of their homeland, like an extended Jamindari.[18]

An ISI-DGFI directive to the ULFA to corrupt recent history is clear.

The Islamic resurgence in Bangladesh, too, has had an effect on the North-East. Every single Muslim fundamentalist organization (MFO) of the region has active links with the erstwhile East Pakistan, with initial liaison, ideological and arms training taking place in Bangladesh, before onward dispatch to places such as Batrasi in Pakistan-occupied Kashmir. Intelligence officials in the North East are also of the view that all the MFOs of the region are now operating under the aegis of al-Qaeda,[19] which has found a haven in Bangladesh.[20]

Interior Design

If the strategic encirclement has generated the mechanics by which the North-East continues to be imperilled, the internal security situation it spawns advances the sinister design. The design may not only have escaped notice of Indian security managers, but has been sired by some of the successes achieved. The successes have been no mean feat: ceasefire with the NSCN (IM), the action in Bhutan, the diplomatic pressure for Dhaka and Yangon to oust North-East separatists, the Brajesh Mishra-led parley with China on the boundary issue and even a proactive development agenda with the institution of the Department for the Development of North Eastern Region (DONER). However, the "little wars" of the North-East continue to rage despite talk that six separatist groups from the region have expressed their willingness to enter into a dialogue with New Delhi. Although the belligerence of groups such as the Achik National Volunteer Council, the Dima Halam Daogah and the United People's Democratic Solidarity has lessened considerably, outfits such as the ULFA are pressing hard to recover both lost ground and prestige. Chauvinism, too, has received a fillip with over-ground movements in the region arraying their resentment against New Delhi in conspiratorial aid to underground aspects. The prejudices that had characterized movements in the late 1970s, too, have changed, and the ire has significantly shifted from earlier indignations like illegal immigration from Bangladesh to matters such as central authority, Hindi-speaking people and movies and for 100 per cent job reservation for the local populace. If the ear is held to the ground, it will register that both vernacular media and the general populace are increasingly becoming intolerant of the rest of India.[21] This phenomenon has been felt region-wide. Although the reasons are varied, the paper will limit its analysis to three unsettling trends in the internal security situation.

Islamic Militancy and Illegal Immigration

The author has documented sixteen Muslim fundamentalist organizations (MFO)[22] operating in the North-East. Although 90 per cent of them are silent, not by the absence of activity but by the presence of non-activity, they are ready by way of objectives and training. Although the instructions to them from their foreign minders are ambiguous (apart from directives like the assassination of leaders like Vajpayee and Deputy Prime Minister Advani),[23] they are awaiting not only a position of strength but also an opportune moment. The opportune moment will include the demise of the ethnic militant movements in the region and the demographic change that is all set to overwhelm the region. Reports indicate that new social formations called Sema Miyas have come up in Nagaland which are spawn of the Bangladeshi migrant and the Semas of Nagaland. Illegal immigration has taken on such alarming proportions that the day is not far when the immigrant constituency will not only demand a merger of some areas of the region with Bangladesh, but will also usurp seats of political power. Indeed, this has been furthered by the non-repeal of the Illegal Migrants (Determination by Tribunals) Act, which continues to be applied exclusively to Assam with serious consequences. The prognosis, therefore, is one of an attempt to Islamize the region as also that of a Greater Bangladesh. The conspiracy has grown in recent times with "modules" being formed in the state of Assam. The "modules" comprise ten to twenty illegal migrants who are to act as "sleepers". Equipped with huge sums of money, arms and ammunition, their ISI minders make trips to Assam every so often to ascertain their "readiness". According to available reports, the "modules" on being activated will start a communal riot; act as agent saboteurs in such situations, and even target members/ places of worship of the Muslim community in order to arouse communal passion.

Dialogue with the Nagas

The present stalemate in talks with the NSCN (IM)[24] has not only brought to the fore simmering discontent among the Nagas, but rumours are agog about quid pro quo which the NSCN (IM) has engineered with political parties in Arunachal Pradesh, Manipur and Nagaland. The latter development may be viewed positively—that the separatist group is increasingly being associated with the political process; but the fact that the NSCN (IM) has failed to both affirm its commitment to the Indian constitution and abjure the use of arms is disturbing. The NSCN (IM), moreover, in its bid to bring more areas under its influence is attempting to institutionalize Christianity among the Noctes and the Wanchoos in the districts of Tirap and Changlang,[25] and it seems that it is biding its time to open up new "hostilities" with the Union. The policy of attempting to "wear down" the Nagas with talks will prevent separatists such as Paresh Barua who are looking on from the sidelines from entering into similar negotiations. The suspension of hostilities will also provide the erring Nagas regrouping space. That the NSCN (IM) continues to harp on "Greater Nagalim" and "Independent Nagaland" is an important indication. The Indian agencies' insensitive dealing with the Khaplang faction could also have its repercussions. The argument that the NSCN (K) is not important because they are "Myanmarese Nagas" is facetious at best and would only keep alive the "triangle of concern" in the trijunction of Arunachal Pradesh, Myanmar and Nagaland, for future imperilment of the region.

ULFA/Assam Post-Bhutan

The Bhutan Army action should have been the precursor of not only the eviction of the separatists from the Himalayan kingdom, but also the staging ground for a determined move to root out the separatist menace from the region. Indeed, the accomplishment in Bhutan has upset the apple cart, which will have long-term consequences for India. While the Bhutanese could catch the separatists by surprise and net quite a few of their leaders, this was not followed by similar actions in Bangladesh and Myanmar. Nor could the Indian establishment, caught unawares, prepare the ground for the aftermath of the armed action.[26] Moreover, the action in Bhutan has regained sympathy for the ULFA. Intelligence reports indicate that organizations such as the Manab Adhikar Sangram Samiti, the Asom Suraksha Manch and recalcitrant aspects of the Asom Jatiyatabadi Yuba Chatra Parishad and the All Assam Students' Union are aiding the separatists in their nefarious agenda.

By all accounts, the ULFA agenda is set to experience an impetus. Even as the ULFA continues to mount sundry attacks in Assam,[27] it has been able to turn the Bhutan disorder into order inside Assam. Successful Indian security force operations have occasioned a restructuring of the organization. The Indian Army Operation Rhino II had dishevelled the ULFA, its cadres inside Assam were in disarray, and its coffers were drying up. In one fell swoop, "Operation All Clear" provided the ULFA not only sympathy, but also an important opportunity to restart its separatist agenda from within Assam. Congress-ruled Assam has not thought it wise to activate the Prevention of Terrorism Act (POTA) in the state, and it is a matter of time before the twenty-five-odd important leaders of the ULFA are released from their temporary confinement. In the past, ULFA cadres released on bail had returned to Bhutan/Bangladesh. The high-powered ULFA group now in jail will not make that mistake. Riding the sympathy wave, the over-ground engineering of the ULFA will receive a fillip. Mithinga Daimarys and Bhim Kanta Buragohains will crisscross Assam's lower and upper reaches and unite the province into a plot that has not been known since the early 1980s, when the ULFA held forceful floor in Assam. Once that is achieved, the fêted leaders of the ULFA (now heroes in battle against a "foreign" force) will arrange themselves into a council and capture the vacuum that the political leadership in the state has vacated. Indeed, the ULFA is all set to restart its agenda, this time around from within Assam and with a vigour that has not only been smelted by experience but by one that has the indirect blessing of India's democratic safeguards. Other rebel groups will possibly follow suit.

Conclusion

If the security scenario in India's North-East does not seem healthy, the primary reason—as was explicated in the introduction—is the inability to match short-term goals with long-term imperatives. Counter operations, for instance, by their very definition play black pieces in the universe of real chess—a disadvantage that determines their response. Non-sensitive solutions that do not look beyond the nose, non-comprehension of the dynamics that govern the North-Eastern mind and the failure to set into action methodologies that are more than stimulus-response will continue to beleaguer the handling of the situation along the enchanted frontiers.

Notes

1. The British came to the region primarily because of oil and tea.
2. Udayon Misra, *The Periphery Strikes Back: Challenges to the Nation-State in Assam and Nagaland*, Indian Institute of Advanced Study, Shimla, 2000, p. 3.
3. The two important separatist umbrellas in the region are the Indo-Burma Revolutionary Front sired by the NSCN (Khaplang) and the Self Defence for South East Himalayan Region headed by the NSCN (IM).
4. Nari Rustomji, *Imperilled Frontiers: India's North-Eastern Borderlands*, Oxford University Press, New Delhi, 1983, pp. 1-2.
5. The North-East of India borders Bangladesh, Bhutan, China and Myanmar. Nepal is placed slightly afield near the corridor. This is the only region in the SAARC to be situated amid five countries.
6. Improvements have marked the internal security scenario in the past couple

of years. However, this paper concentrates on aspects which continue to bedevil the region.

7. A visit by the author to China in October 2002, when he interacted with leading Chinese intellectuals, elicited the reaction that the Tawang monastery in Arunachal Pradesh is very "important" for the Tibetan people, and hence must be handed over to China. The author was also told that the People's Liberation Army (PLA) is very sensitive about the boundary and will not budge easily since it considers every point to be strategic. Most Chinese intellectuals that the author met were also of the opinion that China could entertain certain concessions in the west were India to follow suit in the eastern sector. The People's Republic had actively aided the Naga, Mizo and the Assamese separatist groups until the mid-1980s. Such aid has reportedly stopped.
8. China's exclusion of Sikkim from its official yearbook is a significant step in the direction of confidence building.
9. The Royal Bhutan Army action, "Operation All Clear" came at the end of not only six years of protracted negotiations between the separatists and the Royal government as well as considerable pressure from India, but after exacting a heavy price by way of life and property in Assam.
10. Myanmar government forces periodically "attack" the anti-India separatist camps in the Myanmar Naga Hills. However, even this annual event has not happened (at the time of writing in early February) in 2004.
11. About 150 cadres belonging to the ULFA have crossed over to Myanmar from Bhutan after the Bhutan Army action. The ULFA's Dibrugarh-based 28th Battalion HQ is also currently located in the Myanmar Naga Hills and is adjacent to the NSCN (K)'s 2nd Brigade HQ near Neansingbasti.
12. The PLA of the 1980s had to fend for itself after subsidies were withdrawn by the Deng regime. Indeed, the Chinese Army began even to produce television sets and run nightclubs to generate funds for its sustenance. Reliable sources have indicated that recalcitrant elements in the PLA have conduited its small-arms surplus to the black market in Yunnan. Lohit Deury, the renegade ULFA cadre told the author that Paresh Barua and he had visited Yunnan to liaise with a Chinese agency called the "Black House". An extensive search by the author could not unearth the provenance of an agency by such a name; it being a front for the PLA cannot be ruled out.
13. The apprehended NDFB leader, B. Swmkhr has stated that the NDFB is keen on shifting its bases to Nepal. See "NDFB Strikes Deal with Maoists, Eyes China", *The Sentinel*, Guwahati, 14 December 2002.
14. Anup Chetia was arrested in Dhaka on 21 December 1997 along with Lakhi Prasad Goswami and Babul Sarma from a rented house at Mohammadpur on charges of illegal possession of a satellite phone among other material. The ULFA's General Secretary, who had in 1997 sought to represent the organization in the United Nations Commission on Human Rights in Geneva—as a John David Salomar—has been seeking asylum in Bangladesh. On 24 September 2002, a Dhaka court sentenced Chetia and

two of his associates to a seven-year prison term.

15. Sanjay K. Jha, "Mounting Tensions over Illegal Migrants and Terror Bases", *South Asia Intelligence Review, Weekly Assessments & Briefings*, Vol. 1, No. 29, 3 February 2003. See [http://www.satp.org/satporgtp/sair/archives/archives.htm]. Jha has also written that illegal immigrants from Bangladesh can influence the electoral outcome in 25 Parliamentary and 125 Assembly constituencies in India. The Deputy Prime Minister of India in his address to the Chief Secretaries and Directors General of Police on 7 January 2003 in New Delhi had stated that there are approximately 15 million Bangladeshis illegally residing in India.
16. "90 Ultra Camps in India: BDR Chief", *Assam Tribune*, Guwahati, 7 January 2004.
17. "ULFA Schools Groom Would-be Infiltrators", *Hindustan Times* (North East), New Delhi, 6 June 2002.
18. "Indian Aliens and Demographic Collapse", *Freedom* (Newsletter of the ULFA), Vol. 5, Issue 10, 15 May 2002.
19. An umbrella organization, the Bangladesh Islamic Manch comprising nine Islamic fundamentalist groups, including the Muslim Liberation Tigers of Assam, was formed in Bangladesh's Ukhia on 10-11 May 2002. This was perhaps the precursor for a pan-Islamic group which has reportedly come into existence.
20. For an exposition of al-Qaeda's agenda in Bangladesh, see Jaideep Saikia, "Islamic Resurgence in Bangladesh", *Aakrosh*, New Delhi, October 2003, Vol. 6, No. 21.
21. The popularity of Hindi films and music and support for Indian cricket teams among a section of the people must not be read as registration of patriotism. Such outpourings are merely an urban phenomenon and have little or nothing to do with the pulse of the general populace.
22. Jaideep Saikia, *Terror Sans Frontiers: Islamic Militancy in North East India*, Program in Arms Control, Disarmament, and International Security, University of Illinois at Urbana-Champaign, USA, Occasional Paper, July 2003, Appendix 1. See http://www.acdis.uiuc.edu/homepage_docs/pubs_docs /PDF_Files/Saikia_OP
23. The author has had detailed debriefings with surrendered Harkat ul Mujahideen (HuM) cadres. The revelation about the instruction to assassinate the Indian leaders came from the HuM's General Secretary, Abu Bakr Siddiqui, on 27 December 2002 at the Special Branch HQ of the Assam Police.
24. Able attempts are being made by the Mizoram Chief Minister, Zoramthanga, to coax the NSCN (IM) to resume dialogue with New Delhi.
25. The NSCN (IM) is even operating in Tirap and Changlang under the name of "Salvation Army".
26. Apparently, Dispur was not informed of the action.
27. A new battalion, the 106 Bn has been formed by the ULFA in West Garo Hills.

Managing Diversity for Security and Stability

B.G. Verghese

Introduction

The meaning of national security in recent times has gone beyond the parameters of safeguarding the attributes of territorial and political sovereignty to include economic and cultural independence. The emphasis on an expanding list of concerns such as food, energy, health, and environmental security can no longer be divorced from national well-being.

Social instability has been the undoing of nations. India too must, therefore, pay due regard to promoting "Fraternity", which is more than secularism. It implies a sense of togetherness that "assures the dignity of the individual and the unity and integrity of the Nation".

India's extraordinary pluralism is well recognized. India is both a new nation and an ancient civilization. Even during the freedom struggle, liberal democracy was seen to provide the essential bonding for bringing together these two ideals within the framework of a modern state. Hence independent India uniquely opted for democracy as an instrument of social and economic revolution rather than as an end product of a long, slow process of transformation, as in the West.

There has been a steady and swelling upthrust from below that has leveraged cohort after cohort from "Bharat" into an Indian sunlight. With empowerment, a culture of silence is yielding to protest and a jostling for recognition of identity, entitlements, equity and justice. The transition has ended single-party and elite dominance and ushered in an era of new formations, coalitions and agendas. The vocabulary of discourse is beginning to change. "We, the sovereign People", are coming alive.

The churning will continue for another 20-30 years or more. Many worry over the din and seeming anarchy of this maturing democracy and would use the law-and-order machinery to preserve the established order. However, as India moves to achieve the goal of poverty alleviation and become a developed society by 2020, as projected, it must carefully tend the process of social change to build Fraternity or else find pent-up popular energy exploding in violence and disorder. The management of diversity is therefore going to be critical to national security in the decades ahead.

Fraternity subsumes "secularism", a word that found no mention in the Constitution until 1976. The word secularism, however, has two meanings. It implies separation of Church from State but also connotes a modernizing, worldly approach to affairs of State. The latter meaning has been somewhat clouded in India and secularism has come to be loosely defined as meaning equal respect for or equidistance from all faiths. There has also been a mistaken tendency to bracket religion with culture. The latter has, of course, a far wider compass, as evident from the Hindu cultural imprint on Indonesian and Thai societies, even though they are strongly rooted in Islam and Buddhism respectively.

The political and electoral exploitation of faith and caste has been divisive. The two-nation theory was first advocated by Savarkar in the 1920s as Hindutva or cultural nationalism and later taken up by the Muslim League. Separate electorates in turn gave weightage to numbers that tended to translate "majority" and "minority" into competing political categories. India is a land of faith and has given birth or hospitality to eight of the nine or ten extant world religions. Hinduism, Buddhism, Jainism and Sikhism were founded in India. Christianity came to the west coast in AD 52 through Thomas, an Apostle of Christ, and Islam followed it to Malabar during the lifetime of the Prophet through commerce, and not conquest, as widely believed. Jewish and Zoroastrian émigrés sought refuge on these same shores centuries ago, both representing very ancient traditions that could remain alive to this day only given an environment of tolerance. In its turn caste, an external accretion to religion, later ossified and became oppressive as a feudal class divider. Whereas the Indian tradition has been inclusive and accommodative, certain ideological groups tend to go by definitions of cultural nationalism that are exclusive.

Whereas the Indian Constitution confers complete equality on all citizens, irrespective of religion or origin (Article 15), these ideologues would differentiate between "Indian religionists" (Hindu, Buddhist, Jain and Sikh) and others (Jews, Zoroastrians, Christians and Muslims) who must per contra be assumed to be somehow non-Indian as they profess faiths of external origin. The latter category has sometimes been labelled as being made up of "foreigners" (Gujarat Class 10 Social Science textbooks) and suggestively placed on probation as though required to pass some esoteric test of "Indianness".

This apparently stems from a sense of having been rudely deprived of a glorious Indian (read Hindu) past by Islamic and, subsequently, Western (Christian) conquerors. From this follows a sense of victimhood and efforts to recreate the past. Such revivalism has been encouraged by an earlier periodization of Indian history into ancient or Hindu, medieval or Muslim and modern or Western (Christian) periods. Such categorization was perhaps implicit in a history of kings and empires, conquerors and subject peoples, tyrannical rulers and their victims. In truth, popular history was different. Kings came and went, empires rose and fell, but the common people, irrespective of faith, shared their joys and sorrows, interacting and living together. There was interdependence and a fusion of language and culture, of which Urdu is a supreme example along with Hindustani music, architecture, cuisine, dress, and much else.

Ideologues and fundamentalists of all kinds, who would revive the past selectively, rewrite history to remember what fits their theories. Hence the diligence with which an imagined past is being recreated or remoulded nearer the heart's desire. This politicization of history, unfortunately, postulates revenge for so-called earlier wrongs rather than reconciliation.

Misreading Demography

A recent book, entitled *Religious Demography of India* (A.P. Joshi, M.D. Srinivas and J.K. Bajaj, Centre for Political Studies, Chennai, 2003) seeks to show from census data that "Indian religionists" are likely to be reduced to a minority at current rates of growth of "non-Indian religious" populations. A tabulation of provincial and district data is adduced to indicate an approaching or absolute majority of "non-Indian religionists" along the land and coastal borders of the country. The inference is that India is under siege. If illicit cross-border immigration is the problem—as it is in some places—it is an autonomous issue that must be tackled irrespective of the in-migrants' religious affiliation. The ethnic tensions in Tripura and Sikkim are not caused by the in-migrants' religious faith.

Conversion is another issue that has stirred a lot of controversy, especially in recent years. The Constitution guarantees freedom of conscience and the free profession, practice and propagation of religion. "Propagation" is protected by freedom of speech and expression. However, proselytizing faiths, especially Christianity, have sought converts through missionary effort. Most of the Indian converts have been from among the Scheduled Castes, backward classes and tribal populations. Force, fraud and inducements have been alleged in procuring mass conversions. Resort to force and fraud attracts criminal liability. The principle of preventing forcible conversions is unexceptionable and the Church in India is generally averse to any such practice. However, some provisions of the recent anti-conversion enactments in some states carry the presumption that any conversion must necessarily be "forcible" or the result of "inducement" unless certified to the contrary after due official investigation. At the same time, the approach of certain so-called revivalist or charismatic churches, particularly in the United States, in seeking to "plant Bibles" and "harvest" souls is culturally arrogant and offensive.

One reason for conversion by Scheduled Castes and even Other Backward Classes is caste oppression. This is in the Ambedkarite tradition and was again manifest in the mass conversions to Islam in Meenakshipuram in Tamil Nadu in the 1980s. Tribal communities in turn feel that the slow process of sanskritization only carries them to the lowest rung of the caste ladder. Efforts are under way to overcome some of these problems through social reform. But they must be sustained and travel much further to obviate discrimination and enhance dignity.

The position in the North-East is different. Here the rival pulls of national integration and identity-assertion by communities that were treated as "totally excluded" under British rule have led to tribal communities seeking to differentiate themselves from "mainstream" traditions. So conversion often takes place by cultural osmosis as part of the modernization process in the region. But once confidence in identity is reasserted, many converted hill communities begin to search for their roots in the revival of their indigenous language, script (Kokborok in Tripura) and faith (Seng Khasi in Meghalaya and Sanamahri among the Meiteis in Manipur).

Caste has lost much of its ritual rigidity except among the lowest rungs of the ladder. But it has metamorphosed into class in a caste-feudal nexus and has been politicized for patronage and electoral constituency building. It is entrenched in the countryside, kept alive by the failure to follow zamindari abolition, especially in the Permanently Settled areas, with tenancy and wider agrarian reform. One reason for this was that records of rights were not taken over from the zamindars or properly maintained and updated. Thus, sharecroppers, marginal farmers, agricultural workers and bonded labourers continue to be cruelly exploited.

The intermediate castes were the main beneficiaries of zamindari abolition and the Green Revolution and emerged as ruling elite who were not above using the law to maintain the established order. This fuelled the Naxalite movement, which has graduated from bows and arrows to remote-controlled explosive devices and semi-automatic weapons and is spreading in several states in the Indian heartland. Political will to grapple with this problem, assuming threatening proportions, has been lacking. Dalit anger, too, is evident in urban India. Tribal India is getting restive on issues of forest and land rights and the lack of employment and development opportunities. All these communities seek partnership, not paternalism, in governance. They aspire to a life of dignity without exploitation.

India is an extraordinarily diverse country that has prided itself on maintaining unity in diversity. It is not a melting pot but a garden with varied flowers and foliage boasting myriad hues and fragrances. That has been its lasting strength. Though a civilizational entity, there is a new nation in the making as traditional Bharat evolves into modern India. The unity in 1947—in a political and social rather than in an emotional sense—was a fragile coalition of largely "Indian" elite, with a huge underprivileged and voiceless underclass resident in Bharat. Over the decades there has been a steady upthrust or upwelling from below as a result of education, growing social and political consciousness, mobility, migration, the communications revolution brought about by the chip, satellite, computer, television, and Internet, and now, a global village and instant world.

Successive cohorts are getting empowered and moving from Bharat to India. These are not neatly stratified social layers but highly segmented and differentiated boxes in terms of race, religion, caste, language, region, culture, levels of development, access to information, and so forth. Each is asserting its identity and pushing its own agenda. Hence the continuing emergence of new parties and new leaders. Though the coalition of political parties ruling at the Centre—the National Democratic Alliance (NDA)—is composed of twenty-five coalition partners and its predecessor was made up of eighteen parties, many of them regional and local, it has not made for weak and unstable governments. On the contrary, this has strengthened the federal system and made governance more consensual. Decentralization, de-regulation and a larger role for non-governmental organizations (NGOs) and civil society have reinforced this process. In consequence, despite the semblance of near-anarchy, sound and fury, the country is today stronger, more united and more democratic than it was in 1950 or 1980.

Uniform Civil Code

Sadly, however, large sections of the elite appear to be trapped in a powerful muddle. The attitude towards a uniform civil code exemplifies the confusion. Article 44, a Directive Principle, says that the State "shall endeavour to secure for its citizens a uniform civil code throughout the territory of India". The recommended "endeavour" on the part of the State has, however, not been seen since 1950. A uniform code has been demonized by extremist groups for very different reasons. In the result, Muslims fear that this will necessarily entail abrogation of their personal law, a precious identity marker for a community that has for long felt orphaned and under siege. "Secularism" therefore meant reassuring Muslim Indians that their personal law would not be touched. Legally and constitutionally, there is nothing to prevent a uniform code coexisting with personal law. The Special Marriage Act and the Indian Succession Act, flawed though some might think they are, are parts of a uniform code. Yet they have not been struck down as ultra vires. Nor indeed Goa's uniform civil code, a legacy of Portuguese rule.

The other myth is that the passage of a series of Hindu Code Bills in the 1950s has resulted in a single uniform Hindu code. Here again, the facts are otherwise. There are still several Hindu codes extant just as much as there are many personal codes among Muslims, Christians, tribal people (customary law) and others. All these need to be codified. This is best done by a consultative process among religious and community leaders of each faith so that reform in this sensitive area is brought about by group consensus rather than through majoritarian vote.

While this process takes its own course, there is every reason to go ahead with a uniform code through normal parliamentary processes, responding to informed public opinion. The country urgently needs a uniform code as Bharat increasingly becomes India. The churning and upthrust from below is forcing Indians from their little segmented community boxes towards a common citizenship, without which each group could find itself on a collision course with others. Some thirty or even twenty years ago it was common for travellers on a bus or train to ask their co-passengers to tell them their "native place". Almost everybody had a "native place" to which they belonged, from which they came and to which they would probably return. No longer. Education and information, mobility and migration have caused the world to intrude on the "native place" and take "natives" to distant lands and regions in search of education, training, employment and other pursuits. Cross-cultural tendencies are to be seen everywhere. So where do you and I belong? Increasingly to India and not to one or other of the little boxes that was our "native place" in Bharat. Marriage advertisements are startlingly different today, with caste, community, regional and linguistic barriers falling all round.

But for the Special Marriage Act, interfaith marriage might even be legally impossible, without the conversion of either party. Muslims and Christians cannot legally adopt a child in India. They are only permitted guardianship until the child attains majority. Surely this is absurd. All personal codes are male dominant, especially in terms of property. A uniform code would deliver gender justice—a hugely important goal.

Why do the State and so many elite wish to force emerging Indians back into their primordial boxes instead of promoting a common citizenship? Adoption of a uniform code—even by individual states, like Goa, for a start—would weaken the hold of orthodox clerics and hasten reforms in personal law to enable each community to face up to the more liberal citizenship standards of the uniform code.

India's age-old plurality and tradition of accommodation controverts the thesis of clash of civilizations. Yet every fundamentalism breeds an opposing fundamentalism. India must beware this danger, which has already been manifest in periodic outbursts of rage and unreason. India boasts one of the largest Muslim populations in the world—some 125 million by present count. They overwhelmingly represent a post-partition generation that can have no guilt for the past and knows no home other than India. While they have been discriminated against and ghettoized in some ways, part of the reason has been their withdrawal and inability to compete. The rise of the Taliban in Afghanistan significantly attracted no Indian mujahideen. Muslim Indians, barring some fringe elements, are of a liberal bent.

The Muslims took a dreadful beating in Gujarat after Godhra but the community is beginning to realize that its future lies in asserting its citizenship rights rather than harping on its minority character. Islam is not in danger in India. But the future of Muslim Indians lies in modernization and insisting on rights, not favours. Education is the key. Here the State must go out of its way in promoting Muslim education at all levels and assisting in the upgrading of madrasas. Any large class of citizens remaining rooted in backwardness or despondency can only be a drag on the nation. Wherever Muslims have emerged from self-imposed isolation to compete with the rest, they have excelled in every field.

Affirmative Action

The Founding Fathers were conscious of the need to protect weaker sections and assist their social and economic development.

Many provisions of the Constitution aim at this, especially those providing for affirmative action in reserving seats for Scheduled Castes and Tribes in legislatures and in public employment. These reservations were for a limited period but have been extended from time to time and have in fact been enlarged to include a small quota for Other Backward Classes for purposes of public recruitment. The list of Scheduled Castes and Tribes has also been expanded to include new categories. While the principle of reservation is well conceived, there needs to be an exit policy so that beneficiaries of reservation graduate out of the system. There has been much discussion about skimming off the "creamy layer".

Meanwhile, large sections of the Scheduled Castes live in wretched conditions. Instruments for their welfare, such as the Commission for Scheduled Castes and Tribes, remain weak. Enactments that would punish atrocities against these sections of the population have not been vigorously enforced on account of entrenched vested interests within the administration and society.

Likewise, many Scheduled Tribes live a precarious existence. India has the largest tribal population in the world, over 80 million and growing. Some of these communities are still emerging out of the hunter-gathering stage. Tribal policy, outside the North-East, has been paternalistic and somewhat laissez faire. It is certainly proper to protect and promote the best in tribal tradition and culture while helping these communities to overcome extreme poverty and backwardness. But anything that smacks of equating such backwardness with a way of life is to indulge in false romanticism.

The largest part of India's mineral wealth, bio-diversity and headwaters lies within traditional tribal homelands. These resources need to be developed in a sustainable manner in partnership with these communities so that they are prime beneficiaries. If displaced, they must be rehabilitated with generosity and compassion, with resettlement being seen as a development opportunity. Lack of development on the other hand is leading to significant distress and unplanned migration.

Far more important than a single-track reservation policy in enabling the weaker sections to compete would be the universalization of elementary education up to at least the middle level, as enjoined by the Constitution. This, combined with merit and loan scholarships for higher, technical and professional education would do more for equalizing opportunity than anything else. The country is now committed to universalization of primary education by 2010 and every effort must be made to attain this goal.

The qualitative aspects of education are no less important. Curricula and textbooks need constant upgradation to keep up with changing times and circumstances and the unceasing technological revolution. With globalization, Indians have to live in a competitive world and be able to hold their own against the best. Rewriting history and social textbooks to conform to prescribed cultural norms militates against India's proud plurality and basic unity. These tendencies must be resisted.

Apart from a liberal education, introducing studies in comparative religion and cultural appreciation at various levels would foster greater understanding and enjoyment of diversity. The United States introduced a campus diversity programme in its universities as part of its campaign to promote black-white integration. Similar programmes have been introduced in some Indian educational institutions but need to be greatly expanded.

The well-adjusted Indian, even if belonging to a numerically small faith group, need never suffer a minority complex. On the other hand, some sections of the majority community have been seen to betray an inverted minority complex, as exemplified by the language they use. Certain sections of the Sinhala majority in Sri Lanka have, for example, been seen to suffer from a similar minority complex. Great communities can sometimes frighten themselves into being less than they are.

It is not only disparities between sections of the population but regional disparities that should be cause for concern. The so-called BIMARU states of the Hindi heartland have lagged behind the rest of the country in social and economic development. Their human development indices are well below the national average, the south and west of the country being in the upper bracket. These states are characterized by rising populations, relative economic stagnation, high unemployment, feudal backwardness and gender inequality. There has been some improvement of late in Madhya Pradesh and Rajasthan, but the gap is still wide. In Bihar and Uttar Pradesh, two of the country's largest states, there has been a serious erosion of governance.

Unable to find employment and opportunity in their own states, people from this region, including Orissa, are migrating to greener pastures. This is placing an increasing burden on the host states. The murmurs of protest are growing louder. Regional tensions could grow unless ameliorative measures are put in train. Legislative representation based on population size has had to be further frozen as demographically responsible states refuse to be penalized while laggards would benefit.

Language Policy

Another matter on which there has been something of a north-south divide is language policy. Communication is vital to nation building. In view of India's multilingual nature, the Congress as far back as the 1920s resolved to adopt the principle of linguisitc states, which were brought into being after Independence. Hindi, rather than Hindustani, was adopted as the official link language alongside English. Each state adopted its own tongue as its official language and a three-language formula was adopted at the school level. Under this, every child would be entitled to be taught in his/her mother tongue at least up to the primary level, with Hindi and English being mandatory at higher levels. Provision was also made for instruction in smaller minority languages wherever enough children so opted. In Hindi-speaking states, the third language was to be any non-Hindi language or Sanskrit.

Apart from the lackadaisical manner in which the three-language formula has been implemented, language policy and propagation has faltered. There can be two views on whether it was wise to coin a pure Hindi as the link language rather than allow the existing colloquial tongue to develop in the manner of popular "film Hindi". Truly disappointing has been the failure to facilitate the learning of any Indian language, particularly Hindi, through the production and dissemination of inter-language dictionaries, keyboards, translations, children's books and simple primers and standard texts in fast-learning basic vocabulary. Dubbing and subtitling facilities have been little used and simultaneous interpreters and simultaneous interpretation facilities are rare commodities. It is easier for an Indian to learn French, German or Italian than for a Tamilian or Kannadiga to learn Hindi or Oriya. The facilities are scarce and the incentives marginal. Little has been done by way of script standardization and the production of standard, multilingual keyboards. Computerization has, however, brought about some improvement.

The centrality and importance of English as a world language and repository of knowledge has increased by leaps and bounds while the relative advantage of no Indian language has been significantly enhanced. One has only to look at the nation's libraries, bookshops, textbooks and book fairs to be hit by the painful contrast. This linguistic hiatus has slowed down pan-Indian cross-cultural fertilization. The efforts of the Sahitya Akademi, National Book Trust, translation bureaus and the rest leave much to be desired. Some hardy souls have wrestled with these problems but there has been little interest in or support for their work. The Indian language departments of our universities are at best esoteric centres of classical learning but are generally not the brightest or most intellectually stimulating. Making "official language" the centrepiece of national language policy has reduced it to the level of tedious bumbledom unable to rise above its own irrelevance.

This is an area of great importance if the elite and the masses in India are not increasingly to divide along the line of those who think in English and the rest. India's rich cultural diversity should not remain a subaltern culture.

Also evident is a huge rural-urban divide. Tenancy reform and upgradation of the rural infrastructure and its productivity must be pursued. A second green revolution can come from land and water conservation, homestead and contract farming, diversification and agro-processing that gives opportunity for higher levels of employment and income generation that will keep rural talent from migrating to the cities. At the same time, it is necessary to recognize that India is rapidly urbanizing. By 2030 a majority of the population will be urban dwellers. This too is going to be a huge challenge. Many towns are bursting at the seams and urban chaos is breeding a sullen, frustrated population that can easily be driven to violence and crime. Urban management has to be a high priority if cities are not to explode or come under the thrall of powerful mafia dons and crime syndicates.

Jammu and Kashmir

A resolution of India-Pakistan differences over Jammu and Kashmir could transform domestic community relations and set to rest ancient ghosts. In fact, such a denouement could restore the primacy of South Asian Islam not only in terms of numbers but, far more significantly, as a liberal, modernizing, democratic model for the wider Islamic world.

Pakistan refers to Kashmir as the "core" problem in India-Pakistan relations and part of the "unfinished business of Partition". However, any solution that smacks of a communal divide in Jammu and Kashmir is totally unacceptable as there can be no second partition of India. At issue is not the fact of a dispute over Jammu and Kashmir but the nature of that dispute. Pakistan's locus standi is that of an intruder in occupation of two-fifths of the state. All else is dross.

However, there is no escaping ground realities. The state is divided along the Line of Control, which is in the process of becoming an international boundary. This, incidentally, also fairly well represents an ethno-cultural divide within this plural domain.

The fact of a boundary is less important than its nature. A porous border that facilitates easy two-way movement of people, tourists, trade and investment across a divided state can transform relationships and enable the institutionalization of cross-border structures to manage them. As confidence and trust grow so could this relationship evolve to whatever limit both sides would wish to take it within the larger framework of an emerging South Asian community, progressing beyond the South Asian Free Trade Association (SAFTA). The people of Jammu and Kashmir on both sides would each have access to the other and, in fact, enjoy the best of both worlds. More important would be internal measures to persevere with a healing touch, put an end to alienation and enhance local autonomy so that self-determination is manifest on either side within the existing framework that essentially reflects twin de facto sovereignties. In Jammu and

Kashmir itself, however, wider autonomy from the Centre may have to be matched by greater regional autonomy within the state.

The North-East

The North-East provides many stages and models of sub-regional autonomy, a remarkable process of nation building. The Founding Fathers had provided a special dispensation for the hitherto constitutionally "excluded" tribal people of the region through a variety of mechanisms such as the (Fifth and) Sixth Schedule and regional and autonomous councils. These have evolved and continue to be adapted to meet a variety of local ethnic needs and aspirations over and beyond panchayati raj. The special provisions and safeguards included for specific communities, linguistic groups and territories are to be seen in the creation of new states and autonomous councils and in the varied architecture of Articles 371 A to I.

The latest Bodo Autonomous Area Council and three smaller Apex Councils for the Rabhas, Tiwas and Mishings, all small plains tribal communities in Assam, have carried the process of evolution forward in embracing the concept of non-territoriality. These communities have been provided reassurance of their cultural and linguistic identity and development within loosely defined traditional homelands, irrespective of the majority principle (Bodo Autonomous Council area) or physical contiguity (the three apex councils). These are innovative departures.

Demographic controversies have been sparked in Assam and elsewhere in the North-East in consequence of the in-migration of "outsiders" (mostly Bengalis and Nepalese) from other parts of India and that of "foreigners" or illicit immigrants from East Pakistan/ Bangladesh. This has been seen as threatening further to erode the cultural and political sway of the Assamese in their own state, with the electoral balance being held by in-migrants in an increasing number of seats. One way of overcoming the fear of being swamped by "outsiders" would be to enrol them in a given number of non-territorial constituencies. This would preclude their disfranchisement but limit their electoral influence to just those many seats. Non-territorial constituencies are not new in India. Article 171(3) provides that a sixth of the members of state legislative councils shall be elected from among a combined graduates and teachers constituency.

Many ethnic/identity problems have been resolved, most notably the Mizo insurgency. Others linger. The oldest and most stubborn of these has been the Naga uprising, now under the leadership of the National Socialist Council of Nagaland (Isaac Swu-Muivah) group. Earlier Naga settlements proved shortlived as not all Naga factions were party to the agreements reached. The movement was also fragmented on the basis of tribal loyalties, leading to fratricidal strife. This brought Church leaders, various ho-hos (tribal associations), the Naga Mothers and Youth associations and other elements of Naga civil society to introspect together and insist on an end to mindless violence and to forge Naga unity.

Thereafter, they were first able to initiate a peace process within the community and then between all the Naga underground and the Government of India. Several rounds of talks have been held in Bangkok and Amsterdam between the IM leadership and the Prime Minister's emissary.

The Naga position is that theirs is not a secessionist movement. The British conquered the Nagas as they did the Indians and for purposes of imperial convenience brought them under a single administration. So when the British departed, the Naga people became free just as did the Indian people. The Nagas therefore desire to live as an independent people in close friendship and cooperation with their Indian neighbours with whom they have no quarrel. They seek recognition of their "unique history" and unification of all claimed Naga homelands in Nagaland, north-central Manipur, Assam (Cachar) and the Tirap division of Arunachal, as well as Naga tracts in Myanmar.

The Government has acknowledged the unique history of the Naga people as free spirits within earlier village republics. But at this juncture they cannot undo the Indian state through de-accession. It should, however, be possible to assure the fullest self-determination for the Naga people within the Indian Union of which they are a free and equal, sovereign partner. Clothing this special identity with appropriate and distinctive symbols or additional devolution is feasible without jeopardy to the larger integrity of the nation.

The territorial unification of all Naga homelands across existing state boundaries is, however, infeasible. Manipur is a 2000-year-old territorial entity. Likewise, Dimapur, capital of the ancient Dimasa kingdom, is a non-Naga area that was added on to the newly formed Naga Hills district in the 1930s in order to provide it a railhead. Unscrambling political omelettes is never easy. However, it is possible to extend the guarantee to uphold Naga customary laws and way of life (Article 371-A) to all Naga areas. Economic and cultural cooperation and even non-governmental political association across borders is possible through the agency of the all-Naga Tatar Ho Ho or tribal assembly, which has been active in the current peace process. As India-Myanmar relations improve, similar cooperation and association can be conceived of across international borders among fraternal communities.

Pakistan's Strategic Thinking and Military Modernization

Arun Sehgal

Introduction

Pakistan's strategic thinking and operational concepts have been evolved both from its perception of unfinished agenda of partition and deep-seated fears of Indian hegemony aiming to undo the very concept of Pakistan. Consequently, its force development models too have been structured to ensure strategic balance with India in terms of maintaining strong dissuasive posture on its eastern border while securing the western border through political accommodation. Such an approach, together with leveraging its geostrategic location to maximize strategic advantage, is aimed at containing Indian "hegemonic" designs and getting India to concede Pakistani demands on Kashmir. Another aspect underlining the above dominant thinking has been the maintenance of special relations with the Islamic world and creation of moral and financial support of the Islamic world for its "contain India" policy.

The predominant "India threat" part of the strategy has remained ambivalent, having evolved from a genuine fear of India as a perceived early "undoer" of Pakistan to a strategy of changing the status quo against a much superior adversary. The Pakistani role as a frontline state to the US during the cold war and its close strategic ties with China have strengthened this thinking, provoking the Pakistani military elite to seek bilateral military symmetry with India.[1] Pakistan's intransigence in waging relentless proxy war in the face of strong US and international pressures has been emboldened by the above dominant thinking. Many Indians in their euphoria over improving relations with Pakistan often tend to ignore that an adversarial relationship with India provides Pakistan with a sense of regional standing both in civilizational and geostrategic terms.

Kashmir is generally perceived as the single most important cause of continued tensions between the two countries, but in fact, the

Kashmir issue is only the external manifestation of deep-seated pathological hatred for India among the Pakistani elite.[2] Pakistan has always sought strategic balance with India either by conventional means or by leveraging strategic configuration of power around its periphery to its advantage. Joining military pacts such as SEATO and CENTO, and frontline status to the US in its regional cold war engagements or strategic relationship with China are all part of this mindset. In the context of the above, the paper will, after a brief evolutionary analysis of Pakistan's strategic culture, focus on the dominant contours of current strategic thinking, what factors drive this and how it is manifesting in its force modernization programmes to deal with current and future threat paradigm.

Historical Perspective

The military's centrality in Pakistan's body politic lies in the circumstances surrounding that country's birth. Pakistan faced serious administrative, political and economic problems in the early years of its independence caused by large-scale dislocation and lack of political institutions and processes for state building. Disputes with India on evacuee property rights and sharing of common military assets such as ordnance factories, ammunition depots, air and naval assets, etc. aggravated the problem. The situation got exacerbated on transfer of Muslim-majority areas, of which the accession of Jammu and Kashmir was critical, resulting in the first Indo-Pak War of 1947. This reinforced the thinking of the Pakistani politico-military elite that survival alongside India necessitated a strong military posture. Maintaining its armed forces well beyond the requirements of self-defence or deterrence has encouraged Pakistan to seek military rather than political or diplomatic solutions to its problems with India. The sentiments for building strong defence and powerful military were shared by a large segment of the population. The strong religious furore that the events evoked also created support for this thinking. This resulted in the following:

- Virtually no governmental interference in either the parameters of defence policy or allocation of defence budget. Debate on defence or security issues was not encouraged on the plea of sensitivity and national security.

- Defence and security policy-making became the exclusive prerogative of the top bureaucrats of the Defence Ministry and the military top brass. Once the policy outlines were determined the latter enjoyed unfettered freedom on its implementation. The same applied to defence expenditure.

Formative Doctrine

Pakistan's formative strategic doctrine was shaped against the above backdrop of adversarial regional security environment, better Indian military preparedness, and initial security handicaps in terms of deficiencies in conventional strength together with overwhelming resource constraints, making it difficult to fight a protracted war.[3] Consequently, Pakistan did not aim at achieving conventional military parity with India. Its focus was twofold: one, leverage the intrusive strategic security environment, by using the prevailing cold war dynamics to enhance its own security. Second, maintenance of dissuasive posture by capitalizing on interior lines of communication backed by strong defensive deployment. The limited strategic reserves were to be employed for turning around any adverse situation or for launching counter-offensives to increase the cost of armed conflict to the adversary.

War over Kashmir and its escalation across the international border was always considered a strong possibility.[4] The strategy was to confront Indian troops as far forward as possible, and to take the war into India's territory as soon as it was tactically feasible. Lack of strategic depth and proximity of high-value targets such as the cities of Lahore and Sialkot left a slim margin of error in Pakistan's strategic perception, thus necessitating a doctrine of "dissuasive deterrence" and pro-active response right from the inception. A short fierce war was deemed more favourable than protracted conflict, in terms of raising the cost of war to unacceptable limits for the adversary. The central assumption was that if the adversary knew that the cost of war was going to be extremely high, with limited politico-military gains, he would be deterred from military initiative. Even if war did break out, it would be of short duration.[5]

This doctrine required the maintenance of a highly professional, trained, and well-equipped military force with strong firepower and mobility, backed by effective air cover. The preferred option was a J&K-centric conflict. The terrain and relative force ratios backed by assured attritional nature of such a conflict ensured maintenance of relative balance; it might even be possible to capitalize on terrain to maintain tactical advantage over the tenuous and disputed Line of Control. Extension of conflict to the international border was looked upon as a decisive disadvantage. It was this absurd assumption that led the Pakistani high command into thinking that India would not attack across the international border in 1965. Thus, when in reply to an attack in Chhamb Sector India opened up the Lahore front Pakistan was caught off guard.[6] There exists in the minds of the Pakistani military elite an element of rigidity and inflexibility based on preconceived notions, backed by a tactical mindset, a consequence of an overall tendency of being intuitive and overconfident rather than cold pragmatism. Much the same can be said for the loss of East Pakistan in 1971. Perhaps the most damning criticism of the Pakistani military high command was the way in which it drifted towards war without contemplating the consequences. The Hamoodar Rehman Commission has been most unforgiving on this point: "It is remarkable that, even in the critical months after March 1971, when war was clearly imminent, the question seems to have bothered the General Staff very little." It continues to add that it does not appear that even the Chief of Staff, much less the Commander-in-Chief, ever showed any interest in this all-important question.[7] Much the same can be said about the planning of the Kargil Operation by the Pakistani high command, led by General Musharraf.

After 1971, Pakistani strategic thinking has been centred on creating military capability to ensure strategic conventional balance with India, based on conflict avoidance. For this it adopted a twin-track approach. In organizational terms it embarked upon enhancing its conventional fighting capability by raising centralized reserves for its defensive formations in the desert (Sindh and southern Punjab) and semi-desert (Bahawalpur-Multan) sectors based on strong mechanized forces. In the LOC sector it created additional reserve by judicious combination of readjustment of defensive posture and mixing paramilitary forces with regular troops in less sensitive sectors. The Russian withdrawal from Afghanistan was a bonanza that allowed military planners the luxury of deploying predominant elements of two corps-sized forces (nearly four infantry divisions) from the Western to the Eastern Sector (against India). The creation of reserves and additional availability of forces allowed Pakistan to beef up deployments in the threatened desert and semi-desert sectors to absorb the shock of Indian strategic offensive without committing its strategic reserves for turning around any adverse situation that had the potential of threatening its sensitive heartland. It additionally allowed Pakistan to boost its offensive capability both in the Punjab and Sindh sectors in a strategy commonly referred to as "Offensive Defence". Exercise Zarbe Momin was conducted to test the efficacy of this strategy.

In addition to improving its overall military balance in quantitative terms, Pakistan simultaneously embarked upon substantially upgrading its conventional capability by qualitative upgradation in terms of inducting state-of-the-art equipment such as T-80 UD together with night-fighting capability. To enhance its surveillance capability Pakistan made a concerted effort to upgrade its intelligence, surveillance and reconnaissance capabilities by induction of force multiplier systems such as unmanned aerial vehicles (UAVs), battlefield surveillance radars, improvement in communications, and induction of electronic warfare resources, etc. Such inductions were selective and sector-specific, depending upon the threat perspective. Similarly, the PAF was modernized by selective induction of high- and medium-technology aircraft, to improve its air defence capability and to create limited strike capability in the face of the numerically and qualitatively superior Indian Air Force. Naval modernization was similarly undertaken to ensure security of its critical maritime assets in a concept called "Citadel Defence", as also protect its critical sealanes of communication by inducting Daphne-class submarines, coastal surveillance aircraft such as P3C Orion and Atlantique, and modern warships.

Power asymmetry, internal instability and inadequate domestic resource capability, deficient techno-industrial base and the urgent need to build a strong defence capability, all made Pakistan's policy-makers diligent at cultivating external linkages and connections.[8] This search for security induced Pakistan to join the US-sponsored alliance systems such as SEATO and CENTO as also sign a bilateral defence cooperation arrangement with the United States, which allowed it to obtain weapons and equipment, either as outright gift or on soft loans. Security ties with the US helped it to modernize its armed forces and provided it the confidence that it could withstand Indian military and diplomatic pressure. An important facet of American military sales to Pakistan was their relative technological superiority vis-à-vis India, e.g. Saber jet fighters, Patton tanks, etc.

The shift to China and other broad-based sources for weapon procurement began to emerge following 1962, when in response to an urgent Indian request the US started weapon supply programme to India. The final tilt towards China came about after the 1965 War when the US refused to supply arms and equipment to both the warring parties. This evenhanded attitude of the Western nations peeved Pakistan, particularly as they were members of the same military alliance and had functional security arrangements in place. It was a stark reminder that Pakistan could not totally depend upon foreign sources for its security needs and, consequently, it decided to both expand and indigenize its defence industry base. It also concurrently decided to diversify weapons and equipment procurement from abroad.

China became the all-important new source of weapon procurement towards the end of 1965 and a close politico-military relationship began to emerge. China supplied Pakistan fairly large amounts of low-to medium-technology equipment, which included MiG-19 fighters and T-59 tanks, which was crucial to the defence of Pakistan and adequate to support its defensive doctrine. Concurrent with the supply of equipment, transfer of technology and local manufacture agreement were signed, resulting in the creation of defence production facilities and complexes such as the Aeronautical Complex at Wah, Heavy Vehicles Factory and Complex at Taxila, etc. Pakistani indigenous industrial development focused upon the creation of second- and third-tier industrial infrastructure, essentially relating to transfer of technology backed by limited research and development without venturing into large-scale R&D effort in design or manufacture.[9]

Current Perspective of Strategic Thinking

Maintaining strong conventional capability underscored by robust strategic deterrence remains the cornerstone of Pakistani strategic thinking after May 1998. Its essential elements are:

- Maintenance of regional strategic balance by developing military capabilities to prevent Indian hegemony. Costs and means are of little consequence. Consequently, defence spending takes priority over all other national spending.
- Leveraging its strategic configuration of power (SCP) both for enhancing its security and sustainable development. Pakistan's constant endeavour to leverage US regional compulsions to its advantage is best exemplified in the muted US stand on the nuclear proliferation issue, rescheduling of debt to provide economic succour as also using the instrumentalities of ACSA (Acquisition and Cross Servicing Agreement) to provide defence hardware and assistance. In addition, Pakistan has now been given the exalted status of a major non-NATO ally, in recognition of its unqualified support to the US in its fight against terrorism. Additionally, it is exploiting the insecurities of China to its advantage by building greater collusive relationship in the military field.
- Third, its attempted projection as a moderate Islamic state is essentially to enhance its pan-Arab linkages and renounce the path of fundamentalism to a more moderate and progressive dispensation.

Possibility of War

An abounding belief that the current tensions would not escalate into an open all-out conflict underlies the dominant strategic mindset of Pakistan. Its first premise is that major international players like the USA, China and Russia have a common interest in maintaining regional stability in the context of prevailing geostrategic realities, and can be expected to exert strong pressure to prevent an outbreak of open hostilities with the potential of escalation to the nuclear dimension. The presence of US and other extra-regional forces in and around Pakistan is seen as curtailing the Indian options for waging a full-scale war to exploit its comparative conventional edge. Nonetheless, a limited conflict spiralling into a broader all-out conflict is not ruled out. The dominant perspective of Pakistani strategic thinking, thus, is a strategy of war avoidance through deterrence and diplomacy without compromising on the core issue of Kashmir. Pakistan also perceives the present scenario as a window of opportunity for resolution of the Kashmir issue on favourable terms, by leveraging international concerns relating to terrorism, fundamentalism and WMDs together with the larger Indian aspirations to play a dominant extra-regional role.

On terrorism per se, given Pakistan's internal compulsions, the present scenario is seen as disadvantageous to Pakistan and favourable to the US agenda of "War on Terrorism". This enables the US to exert required pressure on Pakistan to deal effectively with fundamentalist and Jehadi elements internally, while continuing to actively support ongoing counter-terrorism operations against Taliban/ al-Qaida. Such a policy is seen by Pakistan as inimical to its interests in that it forces that country to curtail its support to "Jehadi organizations" in Kashmir. India is seen as exploiting the obtaining situation by consistently projecting the Kashmir issue in terms of crossborder terrorism and linkage with al-Qaida. The dominant belief in the Pakistan military establishment is that unless the issue is tactfully handled it could impinge negatively on the Kashmir cause.

Threat Perception

While Pakistan's threat perception is centrally predicated upon India, the presence of extra-regional forces (most prominently US) in the region is also seen as potentially destabilizing, in terms of intimidation or even hostile action, should Pakistan become a threat in terms of proliferation or loss of control to fundamentalist elements.

Second and interestingly, is the dimension of growing Indo-Israeli nexus, in terms of third-party actors of high technology, and growing defence collaboration and growing convergence of Indo-US-Israeli interests on issues such as trans-border terrorism and nuclear proliferation. Transfer or sale of airborne early warning capability, such as Green Pine Early Warning radars and possible sale of Arrow-2 anti-ballistic missile system are seen as potentially negating both Pakistan's conventional capability and also the efficacy of its nuclear deterrence. President Musharraf in a recent interview highlighted that "Pakistan had to keep nuclear parity with India not perhaps in numbers but in the effectiveness of its minimum nuclear deterrent."[10]

The threat from India in the short term is based on Indian attempts at taking advantage of the international security environment to force Pakistan to regress on its Kashmir policy through politico-military coercion; failing which, achieve politico-military objectives by graduated application of force by remaining below Pakistan's perceived nuclear threshold. India's long-term objectives are looked upon as a desire to become a regional and Asian power, by ensuring significant degradation of Pakistan's economic and military potential. The manifestation of these Indian aims is seen in the following terms.

- Indian attempts at shaping the regional environment in conjunction with US and other extra-regional forces with a view to resolving the Kashmir issue on Indian terms and establishing a leadership role for India in the region.
- Undermining Pakistan's new-found relevance to the international community by accentuating economic and social problems through coercive and diplomatic/trade instrumentalities, with the potential of aggravating Pakistani difficulties.
- In a conflict scenario, cause degradation of Pakistan's military and economic potential, thereby undermining the credibility of Pakistan's government and armed forces. The aim would be to terminate the conflict on favourable politico-military terms, to negotiate peace from a position of strength.

Nature of Future War

Following the May 1998 nuclear tests by India and Pakistan, there existed for a brief period euphoria in Pakistan that its newly acquired nuclear parity largely negated the conventional edge enjoyed by India. This was reflected in an increased tempo of proxy war in Jammu and Kashmir, in the belief (or bluff) that nuclear deterrence, as part of a single-rung escalation strategy would preclude a full-scale determined Indian response. Kargil was a manifestation of this dominant military thinking in Pakistan. Supposedly chastened by the Kargil episode, the military planners in Pakistan came to believe that space exists between proxy war and nuclear end of conflict spectrum that could be exploited by India. Consequently, likely future conflicts are perceived as under:

- All future conflicts are seen as J&K-centric, in terms of incremental politico-military coercion and graduated application of military instruments to breach the national will of Pakistan. Consequently, taking off from low-intensity conflict and coercion in terms of cross-LoC strikes/operations, transcending into cross-international border hostilities, including war at sea.
- Conflict is deemed to be short and swift, pursued by economic and military coercion. International pressure and functional efficacy of strategic deterrence are looked upon as important factors in ensuring short duration of conflict allowing Pakistan to maintain credible conventional balance, particularly in Jammu and Kashmir within the constraints of existing conventional military balance.
- J&K-centric dispute is also seen as a favourable option on account of the advantage of terrain and relative force ratios.
- In any escalating conflict scenario, India will attempt to capitalize on its superior mechanized capability, in terms of mass employment, in a "space cum destruction" strategy. Superior Indian Air Force and Navy are expected to play a significant role.
- The outcome of war will be predicated upon relative degree of high-tech environment, efficacy of strategic surveillance, together with focused media and information campaign. The attempt will be to entice Pakistan's response by threatening/capturing important spaces, aimed at causing unacceptable degrading of military infrastructure and economic potential.
- War will be fought under nuclear umbrella and brinkmanship, enhancing international community stakes to play a significant role in early conflict termination.

Overall Military Strategy

Pakistan anticipates incremental politico-military coercion and graduated application of military power by India in any future conflict scenario. Indian military strategy is perceived to be based on J&K-centric initiation of hostilities graduating to deeper operations in Kashmir and Northern Areas, declaration of exclusion zones by the Indian Navy together with IAF strikes in a graduated escalation leading to a joint, synchronized conventional war. Against this backdrop, Pakistan's strategic concept aims at denying India military dominance, avoid war by credible conventional deterrence, and if imposed, terminate it at a position of relative advantage. Its strategy is based on the triad of "deterrence", "dissuasion" and "offensive LIC". The dominant strategy is likely to be "Offensive Defence", i.e. tactically offensive and strategically defensive. Pakistan's strike capability is built around strategic reserves. Offensive LIC is looked upon as a vital strand of overall military strategy, aimed at exploiting the so-called "freedom movement in Kashmir", ethnic dissensions and fissiparous tendencies in the rest of India. Yet another perspective is avoidance of double arms race by achieving balance between conventional and nuclear deterrence backed by credible and synchronized tri-service response. Realizing Indian relative advantage in conventional capabilities, Pakistan is operating at the extreme ends of the conflict spectrum, i.e. fighting low-intensity conflict below conventional war threshold backed by nuclear deterrence. Overall, Pakistani military strategy against India can be summed up as follows:

(a) *Wage offensive LIC or "proxy war"* in Jammu and Kashmir by employing regulars/irregulars together with supporting insurgencies in other parts of the country, thus tying down maximum Indian forces on counter-insurgency tasks to negate the Indian conventional edge.

(b) *Prevention of conventional war* by following a "Strategy of Deterrence by Denial". In the event of an armed confrontation, aim at confining hostilities to Jammu and Kashmir, while adopting a strategic balanced posture in other sectors. However, based on its strategic reserves, which stand greatly enhanced following reduction of threat on its Western front, retain the option of either limited offensive in Kashmir or strategic offensive across the international border in the preferred theatre.

(c) *Use the "Nuclear Card"* as a conflict avoidance or war termination strategy. Nuclear war fighting as a concept is not ruled out as an alternative to asymmetry in conventional force ratios or when conventional response leads to saturation levels. Threshold ambiguity and cultivated irrationality form an important precept of the Pakistani nuclear doctrine.[11]

(d) *Close and collusive relationship with China* as an important adjunct of its overall military strategy. Whether or not China directly assists Pakistan in preventing movement of Indian formations from the Eastern theatre, provision of critical material support is likely to continue.

(e) *Maritime Strategy*: Pakistan Navy is following a programme of modernization and self-reliance to enhance its monitoring and interdiction capabilities. Development of Gwadar port with Chinese assistance will provide it important naval facilities at the mouth of the Persian Gulf. The Pakistan Navy is unlikely to seek engagement on a force-on-force basis with the better equipped Indian Navy. Its primary focus will be to keep the sealanes of communication open and defence of important maritime assets, including vital oil installations in Karachi harbour. However, striking the Indian aircraft carrier will remain a major objective.

(f) *Air Strategy*: The Pakistan Air Force strategy too is essentially defensive. Its predominant task will be air defence, but may attempt to achieve favourable air over the Tactical Battle Area through defensive and limited offensive operations. Limited counter-air operations relative to its possible offensive options may also be expected.

Military Modernization Programme

The underlying approach in Pakistani military modernization programme is an incremental increase in military capability both by induction of high-technology weapon systems and product improvement of medium-technology equipment purchased from Chinese or ex-Soviet sources. The focus is on critical areas such as air defence, induction of hi-tech aircraft, C4ISR (command, control, computing, coordination, intelligence, surveillance, reconnaissance), precision munitions and stress on information warfare and electronic warfare. The objective of enhancing dissuasive capability and strike capability is also being achieved through its new-found relationship with the US by inducting hi-tech equipment for surveillance, command and control as also electronic warfare under the guise of counter-terrorism operations. Qualitative and quantitative medium-technology upgrades have also been undertaken primarily with help from China.

Offensive capability, including offensive LIC, command and control systems and information and intelligence systems have merited special attention. Another point of emphasis is incremental build-up of offensive capability of the air force affected due to sanctions by improving ratios between high-, medium- and low-tech, aircraft, and induction of precision weapon systems. There is also accent on development of potent platforms with long-range airborne radar and lethal missiles. In naval systems the accent is on creating naval assets that can radiate combat power with potential for offensive action. Coupled with the above is an effort being made to develop new weapon systems under the overall supervision of Strategic Plans Division.

Economies have been achieved by procuring equipment from China at 'friendship prices'. Most of ground forces and air equipment is from China, product-improved at indigenous factories. Significant upgradation of ties with the US and the new-found status of non-NATO ally will allow Pakistan to fill important voids and induct force multiplier systems. The ensuing regional military balance is likely to plunge South Asia into a counter-productive arms race.

Nuclear Perspective

The essential motivation for Pakistan to acquire nuclear weapons is almost exclusively related to its desire to maintain dissuasive deterrence capability and avoid a costly arms race with India.

Pakistani nuclear capability also needs to be seen in civilizational terms of an Islamic bomb, a perspective strengthened by the recent disclosures of proliferation by the father of the Pakistani nuclear programme, A.Q. Khan. The recent disclosures have confirmed the past suspicions about foreign linkages and funding in the development of Pakistan's nuclear programme underscored by a "cash for bomb" approach.

Pakistani nuclear policy is centred solely on maintaining credible nuclear deterrence backed by an assured second-strike capability. Use of nuclear weapons is contemplated as a doctrine in the event of an adversary (including regional/extra-regional forces) using conventional or nuclear forces, threatening Pakistan's existence, sovereignty and/or national integrity. The main thrust is on the primacy of deterrence while retaining the option for war fighting, the rationale for its First Use Policy. The broad objectives of this deterrence policy are:

- Deterrence credibility must be retained throughout the pre-, during and post-conflict periods.
- Balanced conventional and nuclear forces are necessary (including Strategic Triad) to raise threshold levels.
- Nuclear response should be configured upon the option of "*Total First Use Response*".
- Assured second-strike capability through a reliable and survivable Strategic Triad.
- *Rationality of Irrationality*: Cultivated irrationality to convince an adversary of an irrational and/or unpredictable behaviour. Functional efficacy is deemed most appropriate while dealing with both regional and extra-regional threats (read United States) particularly to its strategic assets.
- Development of robust, reliable and resilient command and control system.

  Threshold ambiguity and cultivated irrationality are perceived as important percepts to ensure the credibility of Pakistan's nuclear doctrine. The onus of determining threshold is sought to be placed on India, while Pakistan will do its best to obfuscate it with the aim of premature conflict termination on advantageous terms. The following broad deductions related to Pakistani perceived nuclear thresholds emerge from the published literature and the statements of the Pakistani leadership:

- Level of threshold will be dictated by the degree of pain and damage to its national pride and the adversity of the situation. The decision to go nuclear is likely to be based on rational calculus devoid of extraneous considerations such as Islamic pride, etc.
- Consideration of the nuclear option is likely to be dictated by the psychological and political impact of the Indian offensives. The

threshold would vary from sector to sector. Serious reverses in the Punjabi heartland may lower the threshold while losses in POK or even Sindh may not attract the same degree of response.

- Thresholds are likely to be dangerously impacted in the following scenarios:
  - — Indian attempt at bifurcation of Pakistan, pushing it into internal destabilization.
  - — A military defeat that seriously impacts on national war waging effort together with degradation of economic and strategic assets.
  - — Economic strangling of Pakistan, particularly impacting its vital energy supplies and other critical imports.
  - — Any single factor is unlikely to affect the threshold unilaterally. It would in all probability be a combination of some of the above factors.

Nuclear brinkmanship and sabre rattling are likely to be important percepts of the overall strategy. This process is likely to start quite early, including pre-emptive deployment of nuclear assets as part of a calculated strategy to prevent dangerous escalation and to draw international attention/intervention for early conflict termination. Yet another fact is the danger of premature perceptional response, particularly as the command and control is firmly in the hands of military leadership with virtually no checks and balances. As the Landau Network Report,[12] based on extensive discussions and recent statements from the Pakistani leadership points out, both the political and military establishments see nuclear deterrence as an assurance against growing Indian conventional military capability. In fact, recent Pakistani thinking alludes to enhancing the capability of its strategic assets to deal with increasing Indian conventional capability.

Conclusion

The coming shape of events in Pakistan will be dictated by three seminal perspectives—the attitude of the military establishment to Indo-Pak rapprochement, the perceptions of its ruling elite vis-à-vis India and, above all, the influences of regional players, most importantly the attitude of the US, underscored by its attempts to contain nuclear proliferation. In spite of India's positive moves Pakistan's attitude towards it continues to be a hostage to many structural factors, such as the perception that the US preoccupation with Afghanistan, rising tide of pan-Arab fundamentalism (including the blowback effect of US policies) and eliminating al-Qaida and Taliban can be leveraged to its "contain India" policy, including continuation of the proxy war in Jammu and Kashmir. In fact, there is a belief in the Pakistani establishment that given the robustness of Pakistan's strategic deterrence India is incapable of inflicting serious tactical defeat or forcing an unacceptable politico-military decision. This, coupled with nuclear deterrence will continue to limit the strategic options available to India, as long as Pakistan can manage overriding US interests and continue its overt support. It is quite likely that the current dialogue process will be used for two explicit purposes, one to ride out the storm of blatant proliferation and to cut its losses, second, to consolidate the position of President Musharraf and institutionalize the role of the military and the Presidency, after 2004, when Musharraf will have to step down from the post of the Chief of the Army Staff. The Kashmir issue will be kept on low boil, with escalation at an opportune time should it be desired.

Notes

1. Khaled Ahmed, *Friday Times*, 2 March 2001.
2. Stephen Cohen during interaction with the author in November 2003.
3. Hasan-Askari Rizvi, *Military State and Society in Pakistan*, London, Macmillan Press, 2000, p. 66.
4. Ibid., p. 66.
5. Ibid., p. 54.
6. Owen Benett Jones, *Pakistan: Eye of the Storm*, New Delhi, Viking, 2002, p. 26.
7. Ibid., p. 266.
8. Hasan-Askari Rizvi, n. 3, pp. 66-7.
9. B.M. Chengappa, "Study of Pakistani Defence Industry", monograph, p. 6.
10. *Public Opinion Trends and Analysis (POT)*, New Delhi, Vol. XXXI, No. 288, 6 December 2003.
11. See Arun Sehgal, "Comparative Analysis of Indo-Pakistan Nuclear Capabilities", *Combat Journal*, September-December 2001.
12. See Nuclear Safety, Nuclear Stability and Nuclear Strategy in Pakistan, A Concise Report of a Visit by Landau network—Centro volta.

ASEAN Ramifications and Relations with India

Sudhir T. Devare

Introduction

ASEAN (the Association of South East Asian Nations), one of the earliest regional groupings, was formed in 1967 when South East Asia was in the throes of the cold war. It was composed of key countries in the region, some of them allies of the US and others non-aligned. The primary impulse in forming the association of like-minded countries was political. Today this regional grouping of ten South East Asian countries, comprising over 500 million people with diversity of religions, ethnicity or languages, rich natural resources and strategic geopolitical importance, stands at a crossroads. The Bali Summit in October 2003 marked a milestone in ASEAN's evolution of strategic and economic thinking. Coincidentally, it was in Bali in 1976 that ASEAN held its first ever summit after being in existence as a regional organization for nine years, and the Bali Accord was signed.

Evolving Political Cohesion

ASEAN has come a long way since then. Most important, it has successfully weathered multiple challenges to its unity and integrity. After strongly opposing Vietnam's occupation of Cambodia in the 1980s and subsequently playing a leading role in the settlement of the Cambodian situation, ASEAN emerged as a credible political force and was confident enough to enlarge its membership to ten by including Cambodia, Laos, Myanmar and Vietnam (CLMV countries), thus fulfilling the dream of the founding fathers to create ASEAN 10. Pressures, both from within and outside on the territorial integrity and independence of ASEAN members have however continued to operate, as evidenced in the separatist violence in Aceh and Papua in Indonesia, the Mindanao in the Philippines, or the formation of an independent state of East Timor amidst turmoil and violence. The dispute over the sovereignty of the Spratly Islands in the South China Sea between China and four ASEAN members became acrimonious and even led to military confrontation in the mid-1990s. This difficult test for its collectivity, ASEAN handled with patience and sagacity. Although the issue remains unresolved, there is less tension among the parties concerned on this question. Today, as South East Asia faces the challenges of terrorism, Islamic radicalism and transnational crime, the ASEAN countries seek ways and means to enhance their security of the member states jointly and in a collaborative manner, and hence the adoption at the Bali Summit in October 2003 of the Indonesian proposal for an ASEAN Security Community (ASC). This was not, however, without some scepticism even within ASEAN as ASEAN declarations such as ZOPFAN (Zone of Peace, Friendship and Neutrality) or the Protocols to the SEANWFZ (South East Asia Nuclear Weapon Free Zone) have remained by and large non-operational. The concept of ASC would no doubt require to be fleshed out further with provisions for specific mechanisms for implementation of the various agreements that have been entered into within ASEAN. The announcement in the first week of February 2004 in Bali at a meeting of the US, Australian, Indonesian and ASEAN leaders of the establishment of a regional centre to deal with terrorism is a step in that direction.[1]

Economic Consolidation

On the economic side, ASEAN has by now largely recovered from the severe disruptive effects of the East Asian financial crisis of 1997-98. Except Indonesia to some extent, where political uncertainty and Islamic fundamentalism continue to engulf the country, the rest of South East Asia is on the mend as far as economic growth and employment situation is concerned. Even in Indonesia around 5 per cent GDP growth is projected next year. There is already a turnaround in the Singapore economy where growth after a recession and SARS has picked up and large-scale investments are beginning to flow. The Thai and Vietnamese economies are in boom (a little buffeted by the recent bird flu though) and Malaysia is seen to be going through political transition without any major economic fallout. As the US economy continues to pick up it will expectedly raise the overall growth in South East Asia. The main challenge for these countries is the rise of China and its competitiveness in trade or investments. Both exports from ASEAN countries as well as incoming investments have been going down even as China accounts for larger shares. ASEAN countries are beginning to express fears about competition from India as well especially in the services sector. Japan continues to be the main economic player in the region particularly as investor. Its role is unlikely to diminish for several years to come (though its profile in South East Asia at the moment is low). It is in this context the inexorable movement towards the economic integration underway in East and South East Asia that merits attention. Given the close linkage that the economies of Japan, China and Korea have with ASEAN countries the desire among the latter for policy coordination with the East Asian principal economies has led to ASEAN+3 process which seems to surpass the larger regionalism undertaking in Asia-Pacific, namely APEC (Asia Pacific Economic Cooperation) in terms of trade liberalization or investment facilitation. It also reflects the fulfilment of the interest of some of the East and South East Asian countries to have an exclusive Asia-specific grouping. Former Malaysian Prime Minister Mahathir used to describe it as the East Asian Economic Caucus. The ASEAN+3 process entails policy consultation (but very little common policy formulation so far) across a wide range of areas, including finance, trade as well as foreign affairs. There is already the Asian Swap arrangement in place involving ASEAN+3.

Search for Strategic Space

It is the strategic space that ASEAN is seeking in the current Asia-Pacific security order that will have a close bearing on ASEAN's relations with major powers, including the regional powers like India. At the end of the cold war the ASEAN countries found themselves on the winning side of the ideological divide. The Vietnamese withdrawal from Cambodia and the Cambodian settlement, in which ASEAN played a major role, had raised ASEAN's standing as a successful regional grouping. With the strong winds of globalization and liberalization blowing across Asia the South East Asian countries were able to reap benefits thanks to the infrastructural base they already had started building and the economic reforms they had undertaken. As a result, ASEAN was a much-sought-after regional organization, both as a lynchpin in the security architecture of Asia-Pacific and for economic integration. The creation of the ASEAN Regional Forum (ARF) as a confidence-building platform for all major powers of the world with ASEAN as its focal point and the emergence of APEC as a grouping to bring about trade and investment liberalization and facilitation in the vast Asia-Pacific region (as an answer to the European Union) were further high-water marks for ASEAN. The East Asian financial and economic crisis, however, dealt a blow to ASEAN's credibility and image. APEC, which still had not really taken off, was increasingly seen to be focusing (especially after 9/11) on issues other than economic. A decade-long recession and discontinuity in the political leadership in Japan already had taken their toll, resulting in reduced Japanese investments and overall presence in the region.

Prior to 9/11 US strategic interest in ASEAN also appeared to be declining. Only China seemed to loom large on the ASEAN horizon. Barely had most of the ASEAN countries recovered from the after-effects of the financial crisis came 9/11 with the spectre of terrorism and Islamic fundamentalism fast sweeping across several countries of South East Asia.

> "This region—home to radical Islamist groups such as the Jemaah Islamiah, Abu Sayyaf, Kumpulan Militan Malaysia, etc. was starting to seem like the new home base for the terrorist movement that had brought down the World Trade Centre. September 11 and its aftermath transformed U.S. relations with many South East Asian nations."[2]

The renewed US security interest in South East Asia as a result of the al-Qaida-led terrorism in this region no doubt brings back ASEAN in the US military and strategic focus, with the US troops returning to the Philippines in force and the Indonesian military being offered assistance and training facilities. The reassurance of US strategic presence, however, appears largely driven by the contingency of global terrorism.

The rise of China has in the mean time become an important factor in the power calculus of ASEAN as indeed other countries. China has also continuously striven to project itself as a partner with the countries of South East Asia. While the US agenda with South East Asia is seen to be limited to the focus on terrorism, China's approach of concentrating on the issues of trade, economic development and cooperation appears more constructive to ASEAN members. If ASEAN's overtures to China in the early 1990s through diplomatic recognition by some of the ASEAN members (till then several ASEAN countries did not have diplomatic relations with China) and subsequent bilateral or multilateral engagement through ARF, APEC, etc. led to a certain degree of "socializing" with China, thus enabling both sides to try to find solutions to outstanding issues through negotiations, it seems that China is today reciprocating the ASEAN gesture fully. It is developing close and amicable bilateral relations and through its "peace offensive" with the South East Asian neighbours, taking a series of steps such as its accession to ASEAN's Treaty of Amity and Cooperation, agreement with ASEAN for a free trade area, readiness to sign the Protocol to SEANWFZ and intensive interaction under the auspices of ASEAN+3. China through its new security concept[3] has as a policy avoided conflict with ASEAN member-states and instead sought accommodation and cooperation. Meanwhile ASEAN, which is occupied with stock-taking of the situation around and introspection over its strengths and weaknesses in the fast integrating region of East and South East Asia, gives every indication that it wishes to remain engaged with all major countries, including India.

Clearly, ASEAN does not see in the present situation a power vacuum nor does it seek any power-balancing.[4] Its primary objective seems to be to widen and intensify its engagement with as many important players as possible, which will broaden its policy options. It is against this backdrop that India-ASEAN relations call for analysis.

Changing ASEAN Perception of India

In recent years, the distance or lack of understanding that was witnessed during the cold war period between the countries of South East Asia and India has given way to greater exchanges and dialogue. The end of the cold war, the disintegration of the Soviet Union and the emergence of the US as the sole and principal power in Asia-Pacific as also the steady rise of China led to a considerable rethink in India's own policy orientation for this region. Consequently, India formulated its "Look East" policy in its extended neighbourhood, which has been pursued vigorously for a decade now. ASEAN, too, reappraised India's politico-economic position and its value as a factor for stability. As former Indonesian Foreign Minister Ali Alatas said,

> Engagement with ASEAN can give substance to India's Look East policy. A deepening of dialogue relations between India and ASEAN will certainly have a positive impact on the environment for political and economic cooperation in the Asia Pacific—and from such an eventuality all nations in the region will benefit.[5]

The ideological barrier that seemed to stand between, which was in any case not of the making by the two sides, was breaking down. The view of each ASEAN member vis-à-vis India obviously differed because of the varying level of bilateral contact and mutual stakes. But India's interaction with all South East Asian countries from historical times was benign, India never having encroached on their strategic space nor having any territorial or maritime dispute with them. On the other hand, India's military strength, population, technological development and market size had the attributes of attractive and credible options. Singapore, which perceived this potential early on spoke of an "India fever" and at the Phnom Penh summit of ASEAN and India in 2002, the Singapore Prime Minister described India as the western wing with which the ASEAN aircraft could take off.[6]

Developments in South Asia

The Muslim-majority states in ASEAN had often expressed their concern on the Kashmir issue (though Indonesia and Malaysia used to enter reservation on the Kashmir issue in international conferences, including the Organization of Islamic Conference, OIC). India's nuclear tests in May 1998 (and Pakistan's two weeks later) created a strong reaction and disquiet among ASEAN members. However, they took a balanced view of the new trend towards nuclearization in South Asia. On the one hand ASEAN expressed its unhappiness and disappointment, but chose to "deplore"[7] the tests while refusing to "condemn" them as the West, China and Japan were determined to do. India's unilateral declaration of a moratorium on further tests, no-first use of nuclear weapons and also its announcement that it would abide by the provisions of the Protocol to SEANWFZ was appreciated by ASEAN states. In the current international storm over the revelations of a Pakistani nuclear scientist's acts of passing on of nuclear technology and equipment to Libya, Iran and North Korea and persistent world-wide doubts, including those expressed by the Director General of IAEA, Mohammed el-Baradei, that Abdul Qadeer Khan's activities in the nuclear black market are "only the proverbial tip of the iceberg",[8] ASEAN members would no doubt note the nexus between China and Pakistan with respect to nuclear weapon design and equipment and the Pakistani scientists' role in nuclear proliferation. They would also note that India had consistently pointed out Pakistan's clandestine acquisition of the nuclear weapon from China as also the Pakistani connection in transfers to other countries.

The resumption of the India-Pakistan dialogue has been welcomed in South East Asia, since progress in India-Pakistan relations would augur well for peace and development in South Asia and will enhance India's capacity to play a greater role in Asia-Pacific. Pakistan has not figured as a major factor in India-ASEAN relations so far, evidently because India-ASEAN relations, dynamic and voluminous as they are, stand independently of India-Pakistan or ASEAN-Pakistan relations, though a predicament of the Muslim-majority states in ASEAN in the context of India-Pakistan differences is sometimes visible.

Terrorism—A Major Challenge and an Opportunity for Cooperation

9/11 and the Afghanistan and Iraq wars have in a dramatic way changed the contours of security in the region. The situation has brought into sharp focus the universality of al-Qaida-led terrorism, and the indivisibility or strategic integrity of the entire region stretching from the Horn of Africa and the Persian Gulf at one end to South Asia and the Andaman and Nicobar Islands and the Malacca Straits and South East Asia at the other. The salience of the Indian Ocean in the security calculus could not be more obvious in today's circumstances. India has been a target of Islamic fundamentalism and terrorism for nearly two decades. For South East Asia, too, religious radicalism and terrorism is not new. The bombings in Bali and Jakarta, Kashmir and Mumbai, or the terrorist attack on the

Indian Parliament have shown to both India and ASEAN that the evil of terrorism cannot be compartmentalized and needs to be fought jointly in close cooperation. ASEAN countries have also seen the face of Talibanism as several members of the terrorist outfits in South East Asia, namely, Jemaah Islamiah, Abu Sayyaf or Kumpulan Militan Malaysia were found to have been trained in Afghanistan or Pakistan. In the past India might not have received open support from all of ASEAN members for its concern over cross-border terrorism in Kashmir. However, the ASEAN countries are now well aware where the jihadi terror has been originating.

The threat of maritime terrorism faced by the archipelagic countries of South East Asia as also by India cannot be overemphasized. The safety of sealanes of communications in the Arabian Sea, the Bay of Bengal and the Malacca Straits and beyond through which the oil and LNG supplies vital to the economies of South East Asia, India, Japan, China, Korea and other countries of the region pass assumes critical importance. India's central geographical location in the Indian Ocean straddling the sea routes from the oil-rich Persian Gulf to the energy-starved countries of South, South East and East Asia is no less critical. The Indian Navy and Coast Guard can continue to play a useful and cooperative role in regard to energy security as also against transnational crime and piracy. This role was highlighted when Indian naval vessels escorted US ships in the Malacca Straits during the Operation Enduring Freedom in Afghanistan two years ago. Clearly, in today's changed security paradigm India seeks safety and peace in the long geopolitical curve of vulnerability across the whole northern Indian Ocean. And so does ASEAN. With Myanmar becoming part of ASEAN, India and ASEAN share a common land boundary. Developments in Myanmar are consequently of vital importance to both India and ASEAN. India shares maritime boundary with three ASEAN states—Indonesia, Thailand and Myanmar—and exclusive economic zone with Malaysia. There is also a sizeable Indian diaspora in the ASEAN region, especially in Malaysia and Singapore. These factors have led to a growing convergence between ASEAN and India on security and development issues and greater realization to evolve information sharing and coordinated action. As the then Deputy Prime Minister of India, L.K. Advani said in his address at the Institute of South East Asian Studies in Singapore in February 2003,

> South East Asia famous for its ethos of religious tolerance and spiritual-cultural fusion is sought to be replaced by calls to bigotry, exclusivism and conflict. This fear has served to crystallize and energize an emerging regional consensus on the need to counter international terrorism and on the desirability of closer cooperation among the states of the region as also closer cooperation between India and the region.[9]

India has entered into bilateral cooperative arrangements with South East Asian countries to combat terror. Their successful implementation would be reinforced by mutual legal assistance agreements, extradition treaties and basically by practical counter-terrorism regimes. At the multilateral level, India and ASEAN adopted at the Bali Summit in October 2003 the Joint Declaration for Cooperation to Combat International Terrorism.[10] The declaration "rejects any attempt to associate terrorism with any religion, race or nationality" and views "acts of terrorism in all its forms and manifestations committed wherever, whenever and by whomsoever ..." This declaration does not go into any definition of terrorism or possible cause, etc., on which, inter alia, negotiations on India's proposal before the UN for a comprehensive convention on combating international terrorism have got bogged down.

As stated earlier, security forms a basic pillar of India-ASEAN cooperative relationship. In the then Prime Minister Vajpayee's words, India's accession to ASEAN's Treaty of Amity and Cooperation (TAC) at the Bali Summit gave "formal shape to India's commitment to peace". India's actions are in no way directed against anyone nor are they in competition with any other powers. On the other hand, as ASEAN gears itself to the creation of an ASEAN Security Community without any military components unlike the European NATO, it will also require understanding and cooperation on defence with neighbours and India as a large neighbour should become an important and reliable partner of ASEAN in the latter's pursuit of stability and security in the region. As observed by the Prime Minister of Vietnam, Phan Van Khai in Bali, "India's participation in the TAC would be the basis for further peaceful, stable development between ASEAN and India in the Asia-Pacific region."[11]

India and ARF

India's membership of the ARF in 1996 marked the beginning of India's direct participation in the discussions on security and strategic issues pertaining to Asia-Pacific. Till then, India's preoccupation had principally been with South Asian affairs. Moreover, through participation in the ARF process India signalled that it was not averse to discussing issues relating to security in a multilateral setting (apart from the UN). The ARF membership provides India with new opportunities. At a time when the effectiveness of ARF as an instrument for "preventive diplomacy" or securing resolution of outstanding issues in Asia-Pacific such as the nuclear issue on the Korean peninsula is found to be limited, India through its support to ASEAN as the "core of ARF" can strengthen the credibility and utility of this fledgling but unique forum in Asia-Pacific. In recent times India has taken an active part in ARF on issues relating to maritime cooperation, anti-piracy, prevention of transnational crimes like drug trafficking, etc. India is also engaged with the Asia-Pacific region in the Track II forum, CSCAP (Council for Security and Cooperation in the Asia-Pacific) on security issues. Lack of any territorial dispute with ASEAN members and growing engagement with the US as well as China places India in a position to make significant contribution to the processes underway in the ARF (as well as in CSCAP) for maintenance of peace and stability in the region.

India-China and Indo-US Engagement

Considering that till recently India-US interactions were few and far between, and India-China interactions virtually non-existent, it is but natural that the ASEAN countries have watched India's increasing engagement both with China and the US with attention. It is already becoming evident that improved Sino-Indian relations can be a positive factor for India-ASEAN relations. India and China will need to find ways to work in coordination rather than contention in socio-economic development in South East Asia. The apprehension often aired in South East Asia these days is that India and China through their improved bilateral understanding could expand economic relations with or without ASEAN. This is unfounded. Both China and India have excellent and multi-faceted relations with ASEAN and for both the relationship with ASEAN is a cornerstone of their foreign policy. The growing Indo-US engagement, including in the military field, is a new and unexpected dimension which, by and large, is being well received in ASEAN capitals. For the first time the US, in its National Security Doctrine unveiled in 2002, displayed a new understanding of the potential of cooperation in the Indian Ocean region. According to the US Council on Foreign Relations report of 2001, "India's political, military and economic influence in South East Asia is likely to grow in the coming decades. As Washington develops its new relationship with New Delhi it should include coordinated approaches vis-à-vis South East Asia as part of its agenda."[12]

Considering that throughout the cold war period the South East Asian countries had seen major differences between India and the US especially in strategic, nuclear or other security-related issues, the intensity of India-US dialogue on these matters does cause some surprise. However, given the fact that several ASEAN countries themselves have defence cooperation arrangements with the US (and recently even Vietnam and the US exchanged high-level military visits) the increasing contacts between India and the US in military and strategic fields could be perceived as a helpful factor by the South East Asian countries in Asia-Pacific.

India-ASEAN Economic Relations

Economic relationship is another leg on which India and ASEAN can move together. Concurrent with India's economic reforms, which began in the early 1990s, the new policy orientation to the East, of which the clear focus was ASEAN countries, took place. There was a marked increase in bilateral trade (from US$2.3 billion in 1991-92 to US$7.4 billion in 2001-02).[13] Investments to and from India, however, remained small and in fact declined from 1996 to 2001. In 1996 India's approved FDI inflows from ASEAN were US$214 million. In 2001 they were US$104 million.[14] FDI in ASEAN from India remained around the same level from US$40.24 million in 1996 to US $40.27 million in 2000.[15] India, a relatively small player in international trade or investments, saw an opportunity to forge closer commercial relationship with ASEAN which had moved well ahead in these areas thanks to more liberalized trading regimes as also due to the establishment of good infrastructure. Moreover, India had virtually no experience in regional trading arrangements or free trade area agreements (the South Asia Association for Regional Cooperation (SAARC) having made little progress on account of political roadblocks) as against ASEAN's record in this respect. As India's partnership with ASEAN got continuously upgraded culminating in the annual summit-level partnership in 2002 there was increasing enthusiasm on both sides to enter into bold long-term trade and economic cooperation arrangements. After finding in 1997-98 that India was not affected by the East Asian financial crisis and viewing India's recent economic and technological performance (In the words of Singapore's Minister of State for Trade and Industry India's economic renaissance is unstoppable),[16] ASEAN has recognized the importance of closer economic partnership with India. At the Bali Summit in October 2003, India and ASEAN signed a Framework Agreement on Comprehensive Economic Cooperation, which will pave the way for a free trade area in a ten-year time-frame. (This framework agreement was negotiated in just ten months' time—much less than any of ASEAN's other partners required in respect of their FTAs.)

This will be India's first free trade area with any region in the world, thus symbolizing the importance that India attaches to its relationship with ASEAN. Simultaneously, India is engaged with Singapore for a Comprehensive Economic Cooperation Agreement (which includes an FTA) and an FTA with Thailand. Singapore is an advanced developed country and Thailand along with Vietnam is the fastest growing economy in ASEAN.

Sub-regional Economic Cooperation

India also entered into new experiments in sub-regional economic cooperation with countries in South and South East Asia, thanks mainly due to the initiative of Thailand, an ASEAN member. The sub-regional groupings, BIMST-EC (Bangladesh, India, Myanmar, Sri Lanka, Thailand-Economic Cooperation; it is now expanded with Nepal and Bhutan as additional members) and Mekong Ganga Cooperation (MGC) are the forums where India seeks closer integration between South Asia (and indeed India's own north-east region) with Myanmar and Thailand and through them with the rest of ASEAN. Such integration is planned through a free trade area under BIMST-EC by 2017, greater connectivity through a highway network across Myanmar built bilaterally with Myanmar as also with Thailand, a railway line from Hanoi to India, energy including oil and natural gas exploration and extraction, and infrastructure projects. The meeting of Ministers of BIMST-EC held in Thailand in February 2004 gave a clear expression of the political will towards the above objectives and the planned summit later in the year will formally launch the process of economic integration around the Bay of Bengal. Meanwhile, the Mekong Ganga Cooperation aims at harnessing the cooperative energies of the peoples in the Mekong basin who share with India a common civilizational and spiritual heritage. The areas of cooperation include education including Buddhist studies, human resources development, tourism, cultural exchanges and communications. As to the apprehensions voiced in the media that initiatives such as MCG might be viewed as a process directed against China, Jaswant Singh, the then External Affairs Minister put them to rest in November 2000 by underlining that "the initiative was not aimed at China, nor a means of increasing India's power projection".[17] He had termed it as "an affirmation of historical, cultural and geographical ties".

The sub-regional economic cooperation frameworks present India with very useful windows to establish and strengthen relationship with the CLMV countries which are new members of ASEAN and are also among its least developed countries. India's membership of BIMST-EC and MGC will be a useful step to assist ASEAN in narrowing the development gap between the "old" and "new" members through the implementation of the Initiative for ASEAN Integration. However, the effectiveness of India's association with this grouping will be judged by India's performance in implementation of various ideas and projects in CLMV states. India has made a good beginning with the construction of a 150 km road link from Tamu (on India-Myanmar border) to Kalemyo inside Myanmar. Additionally, a trilateral programme of action on road construction in Myanmar by India, Thailand and Myanmar has recently been agreed to.[18] So also a credit of US$57 million has been offered by India to Myanmar for upgradation of the Yangon-Mandalay railway line. India has offered unilateral trade concessions to the CLMV countries. The present volume of bilateral trade or Indian investment in these countries is, however, very small, especially when compared to their neighbours. For example, the volume of India's imports from Vietnam, a country traditionally friendly to India, is small and has actually declined over the years.[19] The level of investment has also remained stagnant. In contrast, the US with its Free Trade Area agreement with Vietnam has become its major market. China too has taken the place as Vietnam's leading economic partner.

Trade Scenario and Future Prospects

The trade between India and ASEAN increased fromUS $2.3 billion in 1991-92 to approximately US$7.4 billion in 2001-2. However, as the then Prime Minister Vajpayee said at the first ASEAN and India Business Summit in 2002, the trade of less than 10 billion dollars did not do justice to the combined population of one and a half billion people, producing a trillion and a half dollars of goods and services annually.[20] He therefore set a target of trade turnover of US$30 billion by 2007. To achieve this target major steps will be necessary on both sides. While the tariff levels have already come down to 8 per cent in Indonesia and 16.6 per cent in Thailand for non-AFTA members, the average tariff in India is around 30 per cent, even though this is a substantial reduction from a peak tariff of 300 per cent. Under the agreed ASEAN-India FTA, tariff reductions are to start from January 2006. Pending coming into force, the FTA agreement also provides for an early harvest programme, which specifies a common list of items for preferential tariff concessions.

Connectivity

As discussed earlier, the physical connectivity between India and South East Asia, be it roads, railway, telecommunications or air needs to be developed to enable a practical and sustained interaction between the two. While a road linkage including the Asian Highway network is on the drawing board (and actually undertaken to some extent within Myanmar) the railway project will be a major challenge, both financially and technologically. A high-density cable is being laid under the Bay of Bengal which will provide millions of broad-band connections between India and South East Asia very soon. In Bali last October, India offered an additional service for air carriers from all South East Asian countries to four metros in India without bilateral civil aviation talks and also services to eighteen tourist destinations in India. The air services would need a substantial expansion if tourism, business travel, and people-to-people contact in general were to develop in the coming years.

The Role of Civil Society

The time has now come that besides the central position of the governments in South East Asia and India, which so far have been largely engaged in the India-ASEAN interaction, the role of the civil society on both sides should become more active and pronounced. It is only through more frequent contact between the parliamentarians, media, academics and educationists, non-governmental organizations in the fields of environment, micro-economics, women's and children welfare, etc., entertainers and artists that the dialogue will touch various strata of the societies, thus enriching each other in the process. In the twentieth century, the world has witnessed empowerment of the common people by technology. As a result, millions of them in India and South East Asia have come out of poverty, ignorance or underdevelopment. Through education or information a sense of interdependence is growing among different parts of the world, including South East Asia and India.

ASEAN-India Vision 2020

ASEAN and India are currently working together to outline a vision for their Relationship in 2020 and beyond. It is an ambitious undertaking which will cover the whole gamut of multi-faceted relationship between the two. As both ASEAN and India look to their future as developed knowledge-based societies while retaining their values and socio-cultural identity, the contours of their interaction in the coming years will take concrete shape and India-ASEAN cooperation will inevitably become a component in the larger vision of an Asian Economic Community encompassing China, Japan and Korea.

Notes

1. "Asia-Pac Gets New Center to Fight Terror", *Straits Times*, 5 February 2004.
2. John Greshman, "Is South East Asia the Second Front?" *Foreign Affairs*,

Vol. 81, No. 4, July/August 2002.

3. Ministry of Foreign Affairs, Position Paper on the New Security Concept, 2002/08/06, Government of the People's Republic of China.
4. Rodolfo Severino, quoted in Asad Latif, "India Looks East Again", *Sunday Times*, 15 February 2004.
5. Speech by Ali Alatas, former Indonesian Foreign Minister, on "International Relations in the Era of Globalization: Challenges and Opportunities for India-ASEAN Cooperation", at the RIS (Research and Information System for the Non-aligned and Other Developing Countries), Fourteenth India-ASEAN Eminent Persons Lecture, New Delhi, 7 August 2002.
6. Speech of Goh Chok Tong, Prime Minister of Singapore, at the ASEAN-India Summit, Phnom Penh, 5 November 2002.
7. Chairman's Statement at the ARF Ministers' Meeting, Manila, 27 July 1998.
8. El-Baradei, Director General of IAEA, quoted in "Black Market for Nuclear Weapons", *Straits Times*, 6 February 2004.
9. Deputy Prime Minister of India L.K. Advani's address on "New Approaches to Security and Development" at the Institute of South East Asian Studies, Singapore, 4 February 2003.
10. ASEAN-India Joint Declaration for Cooperation to Combat International Terrorism, adopted by Heads of State/Government of ASEAN member states and India, 8 October 2003.
11. "Prime Minister Praises India's Inclusion in TAC", Vietnam News Agency (VNA), Bali, 9 October 2003.
12. Council on Foreign Relations, "The United States and South East Asia: A Policy Agenda for the New Administration", CFR 2001.
13. Calculated from "Foreign Trade and Balance of Payments", Centre for Monitoring Indian Economy, New Delhi, October 2000.
14. Secretariat for Industrial Assistance (SIA) Newsletter, January 2003.
15. ASEAN FDI Database, ASEAN Secretariat, 2003.
16. Keynote Address by Minister of State for Trade and Industry and National Development, Singapore, Vivian Balakrishnan, at the ASEAN-India Forum on ASEAN-India Economic Relations organized by the Institute of South East Asian Studies, Singapore, 9 February 2004.
17. Amit Baruah, "Mekong Initiative not Directed at China: Jaswant", *The Hindu*, 9 November 2000.
18. "1400 km Trilateral Highway Project: New Road Link for S-E Asia and India", *Straits Times*, 24 December 2003.
19. "Foreign Trade and Balance of Payments", n. 13.
20. Speech by the Prime Minister of India, A.B. Vajpayee, at the First India-ASEAN Business Summit, New Delhi, 17 October 2002.

Recent Wars and their Military Strategic Implications

Kapil Kak

Introduction

29 December 1991 was a momentous day in contemporary world history as it marked the implosion of the mighty Soviet Union and the formal end of its over half-century long ideology-based Cold War with the other superpower, the United States. It has been said,

> The end of the Cold War removed a unifying prism through which foreign policy issues could be weighted and ordered. Without such a clear and fundamental definition of national interest, foreign (and security) policy actions have tended to oscillate between the high minded and, what critics might call, high-handed.[1]

The first Gulf war (1990-91) began when the Soviet Union was in the terminal throes of its disintegration. In the absence of a power balance in the international system, an overarching Pax Americana was thus inevitable. In the West Asian context, more than a century ago, Bismarck had declared, "In international affairs, there are three wasps' nests besides the Balkans: Morocco and the Mediterranean, the Persian Gulf and the American Monroe Doctrine. God grant that we may never fall into them."[2] He made this prescient observation from a historical perspective and well before the discovery of hydrocarbons. Given the wholly one-sided character of the Gulf War, should it be a surprise that the concept of asymmetric warfare and the quest for nuclear weapons, as perceived equalizers, has received a fillip in countries that feared a similar fate?

To be sure, the air campaign in Kosovo (Yugoslavia) in 1999, without a United Nations authorization produced the first stirrings of great-power resentment, challenge and competition, howsoever anaemic, against unipolar interventionism. And the extremely complex strategic and politico-military context of the Iraq War (2003) began to get defined just as the Gulf War had concluded. In fact, the smoke of the booming guns was still to disperse when, in 1992, a group of neo-conservatives—who were later to be US President George Bush's core advisory group—conceptualized a security policy framework that would reshape the world order in conformity with American interests. It was 9/11 that tragically opened up the opportunity Bush and his powerful pro-Israel lobby were waiting to grab. America's pre-9/11 Christian right focus on missile defences abruptly shifted toward Operation Enduring Freedom directed against the long-manifest threat from Osama bin Laden, al-Qaeda and Taliban in Afghanistan followed soon thereafter to the prized objective, Iraq. In two of the conflicts—Kosovo and the Iraq War—the UN stood completely marginalized.

Significantly, technological transformations and their exploitation had substantial military strategic significance in the post-Cold War conflicts. The coalition forces were able to exploit improved space-based surveillance and intelligence gathering, information processing and stealthy long-range precision strikes and real-time connectivity at all levels of the command chain. This helped garner technological asymmetry against adversaries, reduce casualties, sustain higher levels of military effectiveness and eventually accomplish stunning victories. This paper seeks to examine the multi-dimensional components of the military-strategic implications of recent wars from the standpoint of international security and the role of technology in modern warfare.

International Security Dimensions

Gulf War

As a strategic land bridge straddling continents and located on crucial maritime trade highways, West Asia's salience remains unquestionable. Centuries-long great-power rivalry, tectonics of religious competition and later, imperatives of energy security and technological transformations have impacted not only the Gulf and its security but the regional and international security environment as well. Interestingly, drawing upon a unique military capability-oil nexus, Lord Wavell, Viceroy of India (1943-47), once remarked, "There are two main material factors in the revolutionary change that has come over the strategic face of Asia. One is air power, the other is oil."[3] Decades later the close mutuality of energy security and employment of air power led military forces to shape the military-strategic context of both the Gulf War as also the second one in Iraq, the political consequences of which the US is still confronting.

The Gulf War was triggered by Saddam Hussein's annexation of Kuwait on 2 August 1990. This was in gross violation of Article 2 of the UN Charter forbidding employment of force to alter international boundaries and constituted a flagrant challenge to the US in its strategically vital area. Twelve successive UN resolutions from August to December 1990 were of no avail. It has been alleged that the

> US made no effort to stop Iraqi invasion before it took place, and did not negotiate directly with Iraq in the aftermath of the invasion; the UN was not informed of the Iraqi threat to Kuwait before August 1990 and was never asked to act as a mediator between the parties concerned.[4]

The jury is still out on whether the US was indeed "surprised" by the Iraqi action or Saddam was trapped through a deliberate strategy. But the conflict was in accord with the transformed security construct of the "challenge to US (and international) security having shifted from global competition between the US and Soviet Union to regional conflicts and instabilities."[5]

The war tested and validated the pre-eminence of both the "hard" and "soft" side of American power—the "hard power" element being the impressive and effective demonstration of America's global power projection capabilities and its ability to overwhelm".[6] The "soft" side revolved around a painstaking effort to forge collective opposition to Iraq at the regional level, seeking cooperation from allies worldwide and obtaining financial and military support from those willing to provide. Iraq was thus unable to redraw borders militarily, a key element of the international system since 1945. "The very idea of conquest, let alone 'the right of conquest' seems to have vanished from the international vocabulary, leaving only the act of 'occupation' which is temporary by definition."[7]

In military-strategic terms, coalition force application—a 39-day air campaign and a 100-hour land forces "mop up"—was wholly one-sided. The US is said to have mobilized a force structure to fight one and a half wars simultaneously and used it to fight a half-war in near ideal conditions. It was termed a war of a historically familiar kind: "a colonial war, with an enormous imbalance of technology and casualties, more reminiscent of, say, the British occupation of Tibet in 1904, when in one of the engagements hundreds of Tibetans died with four British wounded."[8]

A new element was added to the basic fire, shock and manoeuvre triad of modern combined arms combat: "the electronic and fire strike or combination of massive electronic suppression with the destruction of the enemy by fire ... the aggregation of massed, prolonged, aerospace missiles and electronic strikes combined with strikes by naval forces."[9] Air-delivered weapons are said to have accounted for the bulk of the enemy losses on the ground. Gen. Charles Horner, the overall commander of the coalition air forces during Operation Desert Storm, drove home four lessons for the US, some of which apply to India as well:

> Surprise attacks are inevitable and must be hedged against; future adversaries will be armed with weapons of mass destruction and the means to deliver them; revolutionary combination of stealth and precision must be exploited; and, the need to minimize US casualties affects planning, decision making and operational effectiveness.[10]

Kosovo Campaign (1999)

The 78-day-long NATO air campaign in Kosovo (Yugoslavia) during 24 March-10 June 1999 involved 30,000 sorties by over 1,000 aircraft (60 per cent from the US). Unquestionably, NATO forces had favourable asymmetry in both technology and strength and employed an offensive air posture as against reactive actions by their adversary. Yugoslavia suffered 10,000 civilian casualties and small losses in its armed forces personnel. Clearly, victory through air strikes (largely like the Gulf War), without the unpalatable resort to ground troops, in what Eliot Cohen termed "immaculate coercion", led to Milosevic's capitulation, acceptance of international peacekeepers in Kosovo and complete withdrawal of Yugoslav forces from that province.

The air campaign was a logical step-up in the escalation ladder from the employment of air power in the Balkans in 1995 that created successful compellence to force the Serbs to the negotiating table. In Kosovo, despite the commonalities in overall NATO objectives, there were major differences in approach: Gen. Wesley Clark "was caught between an American desire to intensify the air strikes to include strategic bombing in and around Belgrade but avoid the threat of ground troops, and a European desire to limit the strikes to Serb forces attacking ethnic Albanians".[11] US refusal on commitment of ground troops strained the alliance: it appeared to suggest that the Americans were not willing to take casualties for the security of Europeans. "From the beginning this was a campaign where political rather than military considerations determined both strategy and tactics."[12] Winning a war may have been the easy part; it is the plethora of fundamental issues emanating from this campaign that could bedevil international security in the decades ahead. It is thus not surprising that Michael Mandelbaum, writing in *Foreign Affairs* (September/October 1999), perceptively described NATO's war against Yugoslavia as a "perfect failure". On the other hand, plaintive appeals abounded: Tony Blair pleaded, "Remove the cancer of ethnic conflict forever and build a new internationalism based on values and rule of law."[13] Jacques Chirac called it "a war in defence of law and human dignity". Some raised a relevant question: "in the future will the West be willing to make the same sort of sacrifices in defence of its values as it has made in defence of its interests?"[14]

In the Gulf War, the UN Security Council had approved employment of force against Iraq by the coalition. But Russia and China threatened to veto any repeat of that precedent in Kosovo. Many Europeans perceived the absence of a UN mandate as militating against the legitimacy of the undertaking. The NATO action violated Article 2 of the UN Charter, more so when Section 7 envisages internal disputes, as in Kosovo, as being beyond the scope of external intervention. Significantly, the actions of France and Germany, that upbraided the US no end for bypassing the UN in Iraq, reflected a selective amnesia for their own actions in Kosovo without UN authorization. Or was it another expression of "concern about what they label as US tendency to push hard for NATO to become involved in missions outside continental Europe"?[15] This trend has since become manifest. The military intervention violated NATO's own charter which permits application of force only when one of the member-countries is attacked. India's stand was doubtless unambiguous and forthright: the NATO action violated Article 53 of the UN Charter; was not authorized under Chapter VII and was, thus, completely illegal under international law.

Many believe that the actual strategic objective of the NATO intervention was to change the political character of an anti-West regime in Yugoslavia ("the last communist bulwark") on the road to an eastward expansion (since furthered with the accession of Lithuania, Latvia, Estonia, Slovakia, Slovenia, Bulgaria and Rumania in April 2004). For over a year before the attacks began, the Yugoslavs were convinced that "Western mediation was increasingly sympathetic to Kosovar Albanians and hostile to Milosevic government."[16] A Chinese scholar, possibly reflecting official thinking, ascribed Western American motives to "further squeeze Russia's space, carry out (its) preventive containment, put into practice the political aspirations of seizing Eurasia ... and shape a unipolar world under the hegemony of the sole superpower—the United States."[17]

Kosovo brought into sharp focus the imperative to resolve the dilemma between upholding the territorial integrity of sovereign states and attending to instances of genocide, ethnic cleansing and medieval-style mass murders by regimes in a way that could transcend the inviolability of nation-states. Yet might-is-right interventions in their turn could cause polarization and large-scale turbulence. Perhaps, the formulation of comprehensive criteria for humanitarian interventions and the related decision-making structures as also intervention methodologies are compulsions whose time has come. The time may also be right to undertake a root-and-branch restructuring of the UN, including enhancing its representative character so as to make it a more legitimate and effective multilateral body for overseeing international security.

Operation Enduring Freedom (2001)

Following the Taliban failure to respond to the Security Council resolutions 1267 and 1333 of 14 October 1999 and 19 December 2000 and hand over Osama bin Laden to the US for trial or close the terrorist camps, the benumbingly savage 9/11 terrorist attacks served as the catalyst to make this war inevitable. However, unlike in Kosovo, the US was able to marshal diplomatic support of a broad coalition of countries worldwide, the UN was brought on board, ground troops in limited numbers were pre-deployed in Uzbekistan and later

Tajikistan, and Pakistan's compellence for a quick flip flop on its active support to the terror machine in Kabul and grant of support bases for military operations was ensured early enough.

Significantly, the Western intervention in Afghanistan not only received widespread support, but "the antediluvian nature of the Taliban regime did not even arouse the Afghan people to resist USA, as the Vietnamese people had earlier done. The fall of Taliban was more welcome inside Afghanistan than anywhere else".[18] As the air campaign commenced, the irony of the situation was inescapable wherein the US forces were targeting the very mujahideen the CIA had funded, trained and equipped for nearly a decade during the Soviet occupation.

> This criticism recalled how after the withdrawal of the Soviet Union from Afghanistan the USA turned its back on the country forgetting its moral and political responsibility to help Afghanistan in its reconstruction and development, without which the country drifted towards a long phase of internal strife".[19]

The Pakistan government and its intelligence agencies employed the Taliban to decimate the Afghan central leadership, the educated Afghan middle class and the organs of state control, law and governance. Afghan nationalism was subsumed under a tide of Wahabi ideology, women were reduced to a stifling subhuman status and comprehensive efforts were made at mind control of an entire population.[20]

To be sure, US military planners were fully aware of the lessons of Russia's Afghan quagmire and were concerned to avoid a protracted military entanglement.[21] Consequently, technology-intensive, focused and relentless application of air power—in a military asymmetry vastly favourable to the coalition—was rightly perceived as the leading edge of military power in the conflict. Ten-week long air power-led joint operations, involving combined military operations with the United Front forces, employing real-time data access from satellites, special operations forces (SOFs) and precision-guided weapons helped the coalition to occupy Kabul. In the end, al-Qaeda-Taliban military forces were essentially neutralized, and their capacity for strong organized guerrilla resistance largely defanged. Osama bin Laden and Mullah Omar, however, remain untraced at the time of writing.

Over two years after Operation Enduring Freedom, the measures envisioned in the Bonn Agreement of December 2001 "to guarantee national sovereignty, territorial integrity and unity of Afghanistan as well as non-interference by foreign countries in its internal affairs"[22] have yet to fructify. This is despite the Security Council adopting eight or more resolutions on Afghanistan. The military-strategic scenario presents a complex picture. As a Pakistani analyst avers,

> the US is not going to leave this area in a hurry as it did in 1989 ... it is going to be a long haul indeed. They intend to remain there till all al-Qaeda cells have been eliminated. The presence of US forces in Afghanistan, Central Asia and Iraq will help in encircling the so-called rogue state of Iran. But the real reasons seem to be to keep off Russia, contain China ...[23]

Afghanistan continues to fragment politically when the country desperately needs peace, economic development and stability. Worryingly, there is already talk of the Taliban's reintegration into mainstream Afghan politics. Even US Ambassador Zalmay Khalilzad, an Afghan himself, admits that the Taliban have become more active in recent weeks and months.[24] Despite being fully aware of not a single senior Taliban leader having been apprehended in Pakistan, the Bush Administration has chosen to remain silent on the fact that Pakistan still regards the Taliban as a future ally in Afghanistan.[25]

Proposals to resolve the quagmire range from the desirability of the Afghan state reverting to its "traditional policy of neutrality guaranteed by the UN Security Council (P5)"[26] to a template of large-scale UN-led peacekeeping operation to stave off anarchy and boost Afghanistan's confidence in its ability to hold together as a nation.[27] The US is unlikely to support either such moves. Efforts towards reconciliation must inch forward even as a new constitution balances out ethno-linguistic divergences in aspirations. As one pithy assertion makes out, "Afghanistan must now reconcile state and religion, monarchism and republicanism, tradition and modernity, the centre and the periphery—all at once."[28]

Large-scale economic development and stability-enhancing political measures to counter the negative impulses generated by Pakistan and other countries that support a Wahabi footprint on Afghanistan alone can stave off anarchy. In any event Afghanistan, despite the success of Operation Enduring Freedom, is likely to remain unstable in the years ahead, with attendant security implications for the region in general and India particularly.

Iraq War (2003)

The Bush Administration opted for this war nine months before it was actually launched in disregard of international opinion voiced by alliance partners France and Germany, the UN, as also Russia and China, apart from a very large body of opinion in the Islamic world. The security strategy of the US was anchored in the Defence Policy Guidance (1992), Project for the New Century (PNAC) report (1997), the second PNAC report (2000) and Bush's National Security Document of late 2001. In essence these reports pointed towards the urgent necessity for

> "a policy of muscular military strength; enforcement of US will among nations in the world; doctrine of pre-emption in place of containment; unilateralism on core interests as part of 'American internationalism' and untrammeled military and economic dominance across the globe.[29]

The war, like the other post-Cold War coalition campaigns in the Gulf, Kosovo and Afghanistan, was a conflict of unequal adversaries marked by huge asymmetry in capabilities between the world's only superpower and a weak developing country. The inferences and lessons drawn need to be viewed and tempered in the light of this dominant reality. Iraq had been devastated by the Gulf War, followed by decade-long economic sanctions and more crucially, US-UK air attacks on its military and air defence elements. These took place over two-thirds of its territory (the northern and southern "no fly zones") for twelve years preceding the conflict. The end game of the air power-led war—marked by the coalition's speed of offensive, effective jointmanship, focused intelligence gathering, assessment and dissemination, and precision weapons—was thus a foregone conclusion. US intelligence assessment of the Iraqi Army's poor fighting capabilities was spot on, as the coalition, in disregard of the convention of having three-to-one force ratio for an offensive in the plains, fielded a near equivalent force, i.e. about five divisions against the six armoured/mechanized divisions of the Iraqi Republican Guard. A light mobile force spearheaded the rapid advance of 600 km into

Baghdad in less than two weeks. Barring some daring professional actions by one Iraqi armoured brigade near Karbala, the Iraqis fought indifferently and were let down by their higher command. Interestingly, in a repeat of the successful stratagem in Afghanistan, large numbers of key military leaders were weaned away through material inducements.

The Iraqis lacked an effective strategy to attempt to slow down the US advance. As Jasjit Singh pointed out "no attempt was made to prepare the major cities especially Baghdad for defensive urban warfare which might have raised the costs to the invading forces ...".[30] The key winning factor for the coalition was the technological-doctrinal synergy it sought throughout to provide the critically important firepower-mobility equation. Under the overarching dominance of air power, this helped deliver joint combat firepower at critical decision points of the adversary. Consequently, victory for the coalition came earlier than expected.

Was the war justified? The rationale projected by the US-UK leadership had three components: Iraq's weapons of mass destruction (WMD) that posed a threat to the West; the regime's close linkages with al-Qaeda and other terrorist groups; and a repressive dictatorial regime that needed to be changed. Over a year after the war concluded, and the US combed the nooks and corners of the country with nearly 2000 experienced inspectors, there appears no evidence of WMD capabilities. Nor is there any evidence of terrorism emanating from Iraq that could be linked to al-Qaeda and the 9/11 attacks on the US. This has justifiably raised questions on the legitimacy of this war and the credibility of the political leadership both in the US and the UK. Evidence exists to support the view that intelligence on WMDs and Iraq's terrorist linkages was doctored to meet the pre-emption decision already made in Washington and London. Besides, disregard of the UN and the international community has not only precluded their assistance in the reconstruction and nation building phase but also increased the diplomatic costs for the US and UK in cross-sectoral terms.

At the strategic level, the US blundered in launching the war in the first place. Having chosen to adopt a unilateralist mode, the coalition was unable to build a consensus, mobilize public opinion and obtain international support for employing military force for a political objective. India's successful diplomatic initiatives in the run-up to the 1971 Indo-Pak war as also during Operation Parakram (2001-2) are instances that merit study. The cardinal rule of seeking synergy between political goals of war and military strategy was also given short shrift. In the end, not surprisingly, a brilliant military success failed to achieve the political objectives set forth. As has been rightly said, "Sun Tzu never saw war as a purely military action, but instead as a combination of multiple factors—political, economic and diplomatic... a war short of legitimacy will cause negative consequences".[31] Even at the politico-military war planning levels, the need to insulate intelligence evaluation and assessment from policy-making could not have been driven home better. Intelligence assessments and analyses should shape policy and not the other way round. This is a lesson India's policy-makers have still not learned to institutionalize, notwithstanding the much-hyped initiatives on higher defence reform.

US assessments on wide-ranging support from Iraqi people for the American role as liberators of their country were weakly founded. War termination, consequence management and the stabilization process were hurriedly planned and inherently flawed. Post-conflict reconstruction—generally resented both by the State Department and the Pentagon and being handled by the latter for the first time since 1952—involves complexities and multiple dimensions. As James F. Dobbins points out,

> There should be sufficient input resources; short departure deadlines are incompatible with nation building; important hindrances to nation building include both internal fragmentation and lack of external support from neighbouring states; and, building a democracy, strong economy and long term legitimacy depends in each case on striking the balance between burden sharing and unity of command.[32]

The national reconstruction efforts in Iraq face imponderable hurdles in an insecure environment in which the coalition is perceived as occupiers rather than liberators. Remnants of the Baath party have expectedly become a major force among the Sunnis even as the coalition is understandably opposed to Shia religious leadership coming to power. The coalition is becoming more dependent on friendly Iraqi "leaders" with limited real influence and credibility. Iraq is a case example—and there will be many future cases—of the fact that victory in asymmetric and regional conflicts is directly tied to a major commitment to nation building. Victory is not defined by having a successful exit strategy, it is defined by winning the end game.[33]

Technological-Doctrinal Dimensions

Throughout history, especially over the last two hundred years, nations have pursued innovation to increase relative military effectiveness. The theoretical index of lethality is said to have improved from 1 (the arrow) to 7 (the nineteenth-century rifle) to 250 (the World War II machine gun) to 1,00,000 (the 1MT hydrogen bomb). Thanks to the sweeping advances in electronics, the technological transformation in the last two decades of the twentieth century has been dramatic indeed. The Gulf War was in many ways the prototype of the shape of wars the West would fight—and Kosovo, Afghanistan and the Iraq War conformed to the "knowledge warfare". The technological intensity facilitates targeting strategic nerve centres, combat reserves and combat support elements in depth as also "fast manoeuvre, smaller lighter units, deep battle, precision strike, coordination of land, sea, air and space and other third-wave elements."[34]

An evaluation of salient aspects of the technological transformation of recent wars would be in order. The Gulf War was the first in which cruise missiles were used, and the first in which tanks on the battlefield could communicate with headquarters in their own country via satellite. Yet the level of technology used was far less advanced than allied propaganda suggested. The most vaunted elements in the US arsenal, the Patriot missile as also the stealth bomber, were far less effective. Correctives were soon initiated. In the Gulf War, Ground Positioning System (GPS) receivers (for navigation and weapon targeting) were available at one per company (180 men); in the Iraq War the ratio was one per squad of nine men. Extreme bad weather early in the Kosovo campaign placed a premium on GPS that could punch through cloud cover.

In Afghanistan, groups of SOFs networked with 'sensors' and 'shooters', and equipped with laptops and ground target designators, were able to guide precision attacks on targets with devastating accuracy. The triumph of military strategy in the recent campaigns was founded on mastering of air power-mobility synergy intensified by space-based assets. Unmanned aerial vehicles (UAVs) and unmanned combat air vehicles (UCAVs) began to be used progressivly and extensively. It may be recalled that in the Israeli-Syrian conflict in the Bekaa valley in 1982, in the first use of UAVs in combat, along with airborne warning and control systems (AWACS) and electronic warfare, the Syrian Air Force was not routed by technological surprise alone, but by the shocking manner in which disparate elements of air power were thrown at them in combinations that were as unexpected as they were lethal.

At one level, persistence with air power and high-technology strategy was vindicated by the dramatic military victory of coalition forces in the Gulf, Kosovo, Afghanistan and Iraq. But sceptics rightly note that given the sharp asymmetry in capabilities, "both the air and ground war [in the Gulf] bore resemblance more to structured training exercises than intense combat".[35] Other conflicts too conformed to this pattern. At another level, advanced technologies provided an incentive to increase both one's striking power and distance from enemy troops and set the trend of "no contact war". Combined with enhanced firepower-mobility effectiveness and reduction of casualties to the minimum, this turned out to be a near silver bullet. That air power offers relatively low force vulnerability, high precision, low casualties and low collateral damage and can contribute to successful coercion was proved yet again in all these conflicts.

Significantly, technologically weak adversaries showed inability and unwillingness to exploit the deep vulnerability of the coalition forces' "knowledge assets", and, thus, effectively oppose coalition dominance driven by technological prowess. The emergence of thinking in China on the broad contours of "unrestricted warfare" as a countervailing strategy appears to be one strategic trend. It would be useful to recall that even at the tactical level, effective camouflage, concealment and low-cost countermeasures employed by the Iraqis in the Gulf War were soon put into practice in Kosovo by the Yugoslavs. Also, ideas in Brazil on the possibility of regional militaries inventing a few carefully selected high-technology conventional weapons that complicate the military options of an advanced power and prove decisive have their own salience. These are thought as ways and means to prevent "being Iraqed".[36]

The key technological-strategic lesson that emerged from the recent conflicts is that the US military triumphs depended less on technology per se than on achieving effective synergy between operational concepts, technology, doctrines, organizational change and force structures. Not surprisingly, decision dominance, flowing from the US Joint Chiefs of Staff paper, Vision 2020, included dominant manoeuvre, precision engagement, focused logistics and full dimension protection.[37] This offers many lessons to military powers like India. First, the nature of war the country may be required to fight needs determination in a comprehensive manner; second, in terms of fundamental principles of force employment for firepower application, the instruments of military power that would provide the most effective firepower-manoeuvre equation, especially in a nuclear environment, would need to be identified; and, finally, the type of technologies that could enhance doctrinal effectiveness or transformation, if necessary, require to be developed/procured and inducted.

It would simply be unaffordable for India to duplicate US technological capabilities across the board when budgets—either flattening out or declining—rather than military strategy constitute the decisive factor. Concentrating resources in a few technological areas instead of restructuring the entire edifice may be the optimal policy choice. As the recent conflicts have demonstrated, India would do well to reconstruct the firepower-mobility paradigm most suited to its specific war-fighting needs, evolve doctrines that reflect the altered dynamics of war and undertake a root-and-branch restructuring of its intelligence system. There would be an equally pressing compulsion to invest substantially in air power, space-based assets, network-centric warfare, UAVs/UCAVs, precision force technologies, night combat capability and additional airlift and sealift platforms so as to seek fusion of sensor-guidance-explosive force for attaining higher levels of effects-based warfare.

Notes

1. Jonathan Marcus, "Kosovo and After: American Primacy in the Twenty First Century", *Washington Quarterly*, Winter 2000, p. 89.
2. Mary Evelyn Townsend, *The Rise and Fall of the German Colonial Empire, 1884-1918*, Macmillan, New York, 1930, p. 309, cited in J.E. Peterson, "The Historical Pattern of Gulf Security", Lawrence G. Potter and Gary G. Suck (eds.), *Security in Persian Gulf*, Palgrave, New York, 2002, p. 8.
3. Olaf Caroe, *The Wells of Power: The Oil-Fields of South Western Asia*, Macmillan, London, 1951, p. 184, cited in Peterson, n. 2.
4. Pierre Salinger, "The United States, the United Nations, and the Gulf War", *Middle East Journal*, Autumn, 1995, p. 595.
5. Patrick J. Garrity, "Implications of the Persian Gulf War for Regional Powers", *The Washington Quarterly*, Summer 1993, p. 153.
6. For a comprehensive exposition on international security in a unipolar world, see Amitav Acharya, "The New World Order and International Society after the Gulf War: An assessment", *India Quarterly*, July-September 1992, pp. 1-14.
7. Martin Van Creveld, "The Persian Gulf Crisis of 1990-91 and the Future of Morally Constrained War", *Parameters*, Summer 1992, p. 26.
8. Fred Halliday, "The Gulf War 1990-1991 and the Study of International Relations", *Review of International Studies*, 1994, p. 117.
9. Charles C. Peterson, "Lessons of the Persian Gulf War: The View from Moscow", *The Journal of Strategic Studies*, September 1994, p. 240.
10. Gen. Charles A. Horner, USAF (Retd.), "What We Should Have Learned in Desert Storm, But Didn't", *Air Force Magazine*, December 1996, pp. 52-5.
11. Sean Kay, "Air Power and Allied Action: the Lessons of Modern War", Review Essay on Wesley K. Clark, *Waging Modern War: Bosnia, Kosovo and the Future of Combat*, Public Affairs, New York, 2001) in *Contemporary Security Policy*, April 2002, p. 152.
12. Marcus, n. 1, p. 81.
13. Tony Blair, "A New Moral Crusade", *Newsweek*, 14 June 1999, p. 24.
14. David Rieff, "A Just War Is Still a War", *Newsweek*, 14 June 1999, p. 25.
15. For a brief exposition on the wider ramifications of NATOs new strategic trends in intervention, see Gurmeet Kanwal, "NATO's Kosovo Intervention", *Indian Defence* Review, June 1999, pp. 50-2.
16. A.N.D. Haksar, "Kosovo Crisis: Prospects and Retrospect", *Aakrosh*, July 1999, p. 27.
17. Wang Haiyun, "Strategic Features of the War in Kosovo", *International*

Strategic Studies, October 1999, p. 10.

18. Anthony Davis, "How the Afghan War was Won", *Jane's Intelligence Review*, February 2002.
19. Babar Shah, "Geo-Strategic Patterns of a Post Talib Afghanistan", *Strategic Studies*, Spring 2002, p. 59.
20. Also see Brigadier G.D. Bakshi, *Afghanistan: The First Faultline War*, Lancer, New Delhi, 2002, p. 204.
21. See n. 19.
22. Chinmaya R. Gharekhan and Hamid Ansari, "Another Approach to Afghanistan", *The Hindu*, 24 February 2003, p. 8.
23. Lt. Gen. (Rtd.) Kamal Matinuddin, "Post 9/11 Afghanistan", *South Asian Journal*, January-March 2004, pp. 110-11.
24. Ibid., p. 108.
25. G. Parthasarathy, "Two Democracies in Poll Mode", *Indian Express*, 19 April 2004, p. 8.
26. See n. 23.
27. Kimberley Zisk Marten, "Defending Against Anarchy: From War to Peacekeeping in Afghanistan", *The Washington Quarterly*, Winter 2002-3, pp. 44-9.
28. M.K. Bhadrakumar, "Uncertain Times in Afghanistan", *The Hindu*, 9 October 2003, p. 8.
29. See Kapil Kak, "Military Strategic Dimensions of the Iraq War" in Jasjit Singh (ed.), *Military-Strategic Dimensions of Iraq War*, Knowledge World, New Delhi, 2004, pp. 36-53.
30. Jasjit Singh, "Some Pointers for Our Defence Policy", in *Military-Strategic Dimensions of Iraq War*, ibid., p. 215.
31. Wang Yanjuan, "Analysing the War", *Beijing Review*, 3 April 2003, p. 36.
32. For details of four lessons in nation-building see James F. Dobbins, "America's Role in Nation Building: From Germany to Iraq", *Survival*, Winter 2003-4, pp. 105-8.
33. For another perspective on nation building in Iraq, see Anthony H. Cordesman, *The Iraq War: Strategy, Tactics and Military Lessons*, Praeger, Connecticut, 2003, pp. 521-4.
34. Alvin Toffler, interview on "How Will Future Wars be Fought?" *USA Today* (http:/www.usatoday.com/news/opinion/columnists/toffler/toff03.htm dated 3 May 2003.
35. Gene I. Rochlin and Chris C. Demchak, "The Gulf War: Technological and Organisational Implications", *Survival*, May/June 1991, p. 260.
36. Garrity, n. 5, p. 164.
37. For more details on the importance of firepower-mobility synergy and doctrine see Jasjit Singh, n. 30, pp. 216-21.

III

Chronology of Major Events

Chronology of Major Events, 2003

UNITED STATES

Strategic Profile

28 January: In his State of the Union Address, the US President George W. Bush argued that the gravest danger facing America and the rest of the world was "outlaw regimes" that sought and possessed nuclear, chemical and biological weapons.

19 February: The 18-member Defence Planning Committee of NATO agreed to deploy AWACS early warning aircraft, Patriot air defence missile systems and chemical-biological response units in southern Turkey, a likely launch pad for any US-led strikes on Baghdad.

16 March: The US President George Bush met the Prime Ministers of Portugal, Britain and Spain at an Air Force base in the Portuguese island of Azores and sought global support to drive the Iraqi leader Saddam Hussein from power.

18 March: The US President George Bush gave a 48-hour deadline to the Iraqi President Saddam Hussein and his sons to leave Iraq.

20 March: The United States launched cruise missiles and conducted intense artillery barrages at the start of the campaign to overthrow the regime of the Iraqi leader Saddam Hussein.

7 April: The US National Security Adviser, Condoleezza Rice, met the Russian Foreign Minister, Igor Ivanov, and other officials in Moscow in a visit to mend ties frayed over the US action on Iraq.

9 April: US troops entered Baghdad, ending Saddam Hussein's 24-year rule, on the 21st day of the war.

11 April: The US Deputy Secretary of Defence Paul Wolfowitz told the Senate Armed Services Committee that the UN could not be in charge of the administration in Iraq.

14 April: The US President George Bush got a $80 billion package passed by Congress, which included $62 billion for the Pentagon for the war in Iraq and against terrorism, $4 billion for homeland security, $2.2 billion for police and emergency services, and $8 billion for foreign aid, mainly related to security concerns.

7 May: The US President George Bush appointed the former diplomat and counter-terrorism expert, Paul Bremer, as the Special Representative in Iraq.

13 May: In the deadliest attack on Americans since the 11 September 2001 attacks in New York, seven Americans were among the 91 people killed in synchronized strikes on three housing complexes in the Saudi capital, Riyadh.

2 July: The US cut off military aid to about 56 countries that refused to sign immunity deals exempting American citizens from prosecution by the International Criminal Court (ICC).

14 August: Following the resignation and departure of President Charles Taylor from Monrovia, Liberia, US Marines from the 26th Marine Expeditionary Unit arrived in Monrovia.

20 August: The US State Department spokesman, Richard Boucher, dispelled the notion that the planned military exercises in the Coral Sea were focused on North Korea. He stressed that the interdiction manoeuvres were within the agreed framework of the Proliferation Security Initiative (PSI).

27 August: The head of the IAEA, Mohammed el-Baradei, told the German weekly *Stern* that double standards were being followed by the United States on non-proliferation, with its continuing research into the so-called "mini-nukes", to be used as bunker-busters.

16 September: An anti-proliferation military exercise, the "Exercise Pacific Protector", was held off the Australian coast under the US-led "Proliferation Security Initiative" (PSI), with Australia, Japan, the US and France participating, and Germany, Italy, the Netherlands, Poland, Portugal, Spain and the United Kingdom sending observers.

20 September: At a five-day meeting of the US-Pakistan Defence Cooperation Group (DCG), which concluded in Washington on 18 September, the US gave a commitment to Pakistan to consider its requests for more security assistance, particularly in maintaining conventional capabilities and enhancing counter-terrorism capabilities.

23 September: The US President George Bush and the Russian President Vladimir Putin at Camp David called on Iran and North Korea to stop their suspected nuclear weapon programmes.

2 October: The US State Department re-designated 25 terror outfits as Foreign Terrorist Organizations. These included the LTTE, the Pakistan-based Harkat-ul-Mujahideen, al-Qaeda and Hamas.

3 October: In another blow to the Bush Administration, the Chief Weapons Inspector, David Kay, said in his initial report to Congress that there were no weapons of mass destruction in Iraq even if there was "possible evidence" of covert programmes.

16 October: The US House of Representatives voted 398-4 on the Syrian Accountability and Lebanon Sovereignty Act. The Act seeks to sanction Syria for its alleged ties to terrorist groups, among other things.

18 October: The US Congress approved overwhelmingly President George Bush's supplemental funding request for Iraq, of $87 billion he had asked for.

23 October: Concluding his tour of Asia-Pacific countries in Canberra, Australia, the US President George Bush stated that America would continue to maintain a formal military presence in Asia.

4 November: The US Senate approved an $87 billion military and reconstruction package for Iraq and Afghanistan.

12 November: The US Senate voted by a 89-4 margin in favour of punitive measures against Syria for its links to terror outfits, for its continuing troop presence in Lebanon and for pursuing programmes of weapons of mass destruction.

4 December: The US Defence Secretary Donald Rumsfeld, after talks with the newly elected President of Azerbaijan, Ilham Aliyev, confirmed Washington's resolve to expand defence cooperation with the oil-rich republic.

10 December: In a directive from the Deputy Defence Secretary Paul Wolfowitz, the Pentagon formally barred companies from countries opposed to the Iraq War from bidding on the $18.6 billion worth of reconstruction contracts.

Relations with India

6 January: The Director, Policy Planning Staff, US Department of State, Richard Haass said in New Delhi that the US would continue to consult India closely on Iraq.

16 January: The two-day talks between India and the US on missile defence concluded in New Delhi with both sides reviewing the latest developments in US missile-defence policies as well as Indian views on missile defence.

4 February: The US earmarked $53.35 million for India in the 2004 budget presented by President George Bush to Congress. This was one-sixth of what the Administration allotted to Pakistan, which amounted to $326.25 million.

6 February: The US Under Secretary of Commerce Kenneth Juster and India's Foreign Secretary Kanwal Sibal signed in Washington the Statement of Principles that would serve as the framework for advancing high-technology trade between the two countries.

14 February: Union Commerce and Law Minister Arun Jaitley met the US Trade Representative Robert Zoellick and the EC Trade Commissioner Pascal Lamy in Tokyo, on the sidelines of the WTO mini-ministerial conference, and made a commitment to phase out textile quotas and to integrate multilateral trading regimes by 31 December 2004.

25 February: Prime Minister A.B. Vajpayee, talking to reporters on the sidelines of the 15th NAM Summit at Kuala Lumpur, said that India could not support the American war moves on Iraq.

27 February: The US and India resumed cooperation on nuclear safety after the May 1998 nuclear tests, with the US Nuclear Regulatory Commission Chairman Richard A. Meserve visiting the Bhabha Atomic Research Centre (BARC) and Tarapur nuclear facilities.

21 March: The US Assistant Secretary of State for South Asia, Christina Rocca, told a Congressional Sub-Committee on Asia-Pacific that ending infiltration into Jammu and Kashmir was a key goal of the Bush Administration.

9 May: India's National Security Adviser Brajesh Mishra at the American Jewish Committee's Annual Dinner in Washington called for joint efforts by India, the US and Israel to combat terrorism and said that democratic countries should form a viable alliance against terrorism.

10 May: The US Deputy Secretary of State Richard Armitage, after meeting Prime Minister A.B. Vajpayee and Deputy Prime Minister L.K. Advani, told press persons that it was for India to assess Pakistani actions and intentions on the issue of cross-border terrorism.

22 May: According to the Israeli daily *Haaretz*, the US had dropped its objections to the transfer of the Israeli Phalcon Airborne Warning and Control System (AWACS) technology to India.

9 June: After meeting the US Defence Secretary Donald Rumsfeld in Washington, Deputy Prime Minister L.K. Advani told presspersons that the question of India contributing troops for the stabilization of Iraq was under consideration of the Government of India.

9 June: The Deputy Prime Minister L.K. Advani, accompanied by the Director, Intelligence Bureau, K.P. Singh, and the US Attorney General John Ashcroft exchanged views on issues pertaining to different aspects of terrorism, particularly the implementation aspects of the Mutual Legal Assistance Treaty and Extradition.

10 June: At a meeting between the US President George Bush and the Deputy Prime Minister L.K. Advani at the White House, issues of cross-border terrorism and the possibility of sending Indian troops to Iraq as part of the stabilization-cum-peacekeeping operations were discussed.

12 June: At the re-launch of the US-India Council Dialogue in Washington, the Union Minister for Commerce and Industry, Arun Jaitley, affirmed that there was a lot of scope for furthering cooperation in the realm of trade, investment and services.

12 June: The US Embassy, in a statement issued in New Delhi, announced that the United States Agency for International

Development (USAID) would provide $10 million technical aid for development of the Indian insurance sector over the next four years.

13 June: The US Ambassador to India, Robert Blackwill, admitted that Pakistan had not stopped cross-border terrorism against India. He also denied that Washington was putting any pressure on New Delhi to send its troops to Iraq.

13 June: The US Trade Representative Robert Zoellick gave an assurance to the Union Minister for Commerce and Industry Arun Jaitley that the Bush Administration was totally opposed to anti-outsourcing bills and would try to resist legislation coming out of some states in this regard.

1 July: The founder of the Congressional Caucus on India and Indian Americans, Democrat Frank Pallone, urged the US President George Bush to keep the proposed $3 billion aid package to Pakistan limited to the economic component and to impress upon Islamabad to move towards democracy and stopping cross-border terrorism.

3 July: The Foreign Secretary Kanwal Sibal, in Washington to attend the first meeting of the High Technology Cooperation Group, co-chaired on the American side by the Under Secretary of Commerce Kenneth Juster, told presspersons that the two sides had a robust dialogue on involving the private sector in a range of high-tech areas like information technology, life sciences, nano-technology and defence technology.

10 July: The first batch of the Rs. 800 crore deal to procure Raytheon-made Fire Finder radars arrived in New Delhi.

14 July: After a Cabinet Committee on Security meeting in New Delhi, India decided not to send its troops to Iraq under American or British command.

29 July: The Chairman of the US Joint Chiefs of Staff, Gen. Richard B. Myers, addressing presspersons in New Delhi after meeting the National Security Adviser Brajesh Mishra, and the Chief of Army Staff, Gen. N.C. Vij, said that the US was confident of militarily suppressing resistance to the Anglo-American combine in Iraq.

8 August: At the fifth meeting of the Defence Policy Group (DPG) in Washington, led by Defence Secretary Ajay Prasad on the

Indian side and Under Secretary for Defence Douglas Feith on the US side, India and the US agreed to step up cooperation in the realm of defence issues.

4 September: The US Agency for International Development (USAID) pledged a $4 million grant for community-based disaster planning and management in 20 multi-hazard-prone districts of Orissa, Gujarat, West Bengal, Uttaranchal and Assam.

9 September: India and the US reportedly began discussions on a second major defence deal involving the US Orion P-3 aircraft since sanctions were lifted in 2001.

17 September: India and the US intensified talks to expand bilateral cooperation in high-technology sectors two days before the arrival of Prime Minister Vajpayee in Washington. The talks included civilian nuclear energy, non-military space programmes and commercial technologies that could also be put to military use.

22 September: Addressing the Indian-American community at the Jacob-Javits Convention Centre in New York, Prime Minister A.B. Vajpayee asked them to set up a "political action group" that would project and lobby New Delhi's point of view on Pakistan-sponsored terrorism in Kashmir.

24 September: The US President George Bush described Prime Minister A.B. Vajpayee as a "man of peace", during a luncheon meeting between the two leaders.

7 October: The US Embassy in New Delhi announced scrapping of visa-issuance fees for students, exchange visitors, transit and crewmen of Indian nationality.

17 October: The US State Department designated Dawood Ibrahim as a global terrorist, linking the underworld don to al-Qaeda, and also pointed out his role in "funding attacks by Islamic extremists aimed at destabilizing the Indian government".

17 November: The US Under-Secretary in the Bureau of Industry and Security of the Department of Commerce, Kenneth Juster, addressing a meeting organized by the CII-Southern Region in Chennai, opined that India should fulfil its responsibility of bringing down barriers to market access faced by high-tech US goods.

24 December: The US State Department re-designated the Lashkar-e-Taiba and the Jaish-e-Muhammad as "foreign terrorist organizations". The initial designation was to expire on 26 December.

EUROPE

EUROPEAN UNION

Strategic Profile

16 January: France and Germany signed a pact on the future of the European Union and on a common approach to the European Convention, which is formulating proposals for the overhaul of the EU's institutions, ahead of the enlargement of the EU to 25 member states in 2004.

18 February: At a special meeting of the 15 EU Heads of Government in Brussels, the EU leaders delivered a tough warning to the Iraqi leader Saddam Hussein to either seize the last chance to disarm or face war.

16 April: Cyprus, Czech Republic, Estonia, Hungary, Latvia, Lithuania, Malta, Poland, Slovakia, and Slovenia became the ten new nations to sign the EU accession documents at the historic summit at Athens.

3 May: The EU Foreign Ministers meeting in Kastellorizo, Greece, agreed to draft the EU's joint common European security strategy to avoid future diplomatic rifts like the one caused by the Iraq crisis.

19 May: The EU Defence Ministers meeting in Brussels said that their new, 60,000-strong rapid reaction force was ready for a "full range" of peacekeeping operations.

20 June: EU leaders meeting in Proto Carras welcomed the draft of the EU's first-ever constitution, pledging to complete negotiations by the year-end on a final charter.

28 June: The EU at a meeting of the European Agricultural Ministers in Brussels took a decision to overhaul its Common Agricultural Policy (CAP), ensuring the removal of one of the single biggest roadblocks to global trade talks.

3 August: Turkey's Minister for Religious Affairs Mohammed

Aydin said the nation's Islamic character should not be a reason for preventing it from joining the EU.

11 August: The 22-nation western military alliance, NATO, took over the International Security Assistance Force (ISAF) in Kabul, its first such operation outside of Europe since it was established 54 years ago.

1 September: The EU's Foreign Minister Javier Solana in a blunt message to Iran said that its trade relations with the EU would suffer if it did not unconditionally open up its suspected facilities to inspections by the IAEA.

13 December: The Inter-Governmental Conference of the EU to decide on a new constitution collapsed in Brussels after members failed to agree on the percentage of voting rights allotted to each member-state.

Relations with India

11 April: The visiting Director, WTO Affairs of the European Commission, Herve Jouanjeon, held talks with Commerce Ministry officials to persuade India to discuss on the four "Singapore issues" at the Cancun Ministerial Conference of the WTO.

20 October: The External Affairs Minister Yashwant Sinha met the EU Foreign Policy Chief Javier Solana and the EU Commissioner for External Relations Chris Patten, in Brussels on 28 October, in a visit aimed at forging a common strategic foreign policy and to "expand and consolidate" bilateral relations.

28 November: Addressing the two-day India-EU Business Summit in New Delhi, the External Affairs Minister Yashwant Sinha urged the EU countries to shed the old image of India and engage with the "new India" and its new economy.

BRITAIN

Strategic Profile

21 January: Britain signalled its commitment to an expected US-led military action against Iraq when it ordered nearly 30,000 soldiers to be deployed, accounting for about a quarter of the British army.

28 January: British Foreign Secretary Jack Straw told reporters in London that the report of the UN chief weapons inspector had clearly established that the Iraqi President Saddam Hussein had reduced the inspection process to a "charade".

29 January: Taking a cue from the US President George Bush's State of the Union Address, the British Government hardened its stance on Iraq and for the first time accused the Saddam Hussein regime of sheltering al-Qaeda operatives.

28 February: The British Prime Minister Tony Blair rejected the Iraqi offer to destroy its inventory of Al-Samoud missiles. He said that in order to avert a conflict, it must comply fully and unconditionally with the UN resolution on disarmament.

17 March: The British Senior Minister Robin Cook resigned from the cabinet after the US and the UK abandoned their efforts at the UN to get approval for military action.

19 March: The British Prime Minister Tony Blair won Parliament's approval for a pre-emptive military attack on Iraq even without an explicit UN mandate.

8 April: At a summit in Hillsborough, Northern Ireland, British Prime Minister Tony Blair and the US President George Bush endorsed a limited role for the UN in Iraq.

8 June: After weeks of denial, the British Prime Minister Tony Blair's office admitted that a dossier it put out on Saddam Hussein's arms capability in February to justify an attack on Iraq was flawed and did not meet the "required standards of accuracy".

7 July: The House of Commons Foreign Affairs Committee in a report titled "The Decision to Go to War in Iraq" criticized the Blair government on the accuracy of the intelligence on which the case for war was built up.

18 July: David Kelly, a former British UN Weapons Inspector in Iraq, who emerged as a key figure in the Blair government's row with the BBC over allegations that it had "sexed up" an intelligence dossier on Baghdad's weapons capability in the run-up to the war on Iraq, was found to have died mysteriously.

20 July: The BBC admitted that the weapons expert David Kelly, who committed suicide two days earlier, was the source of its controversial report in which it had quoted an unidentified official as alleging that the government had "sexed up" a key intelligence dossier in the run-up to the war on Iraq.

28 August: The British Prime Minister, Tony Blair, said that the allegation that his government inflated intelligence to justify an attack an Iraq was so serious that if it was true it would "merit" his resignation.

19 November: The US President George Bush arrived on a state visit to London amidst unprecedented security.

20 November: The British Prime Minister, Tony Blair, and the visiting US President George Bush reiterated that the coalition forces would stay in Iraq "until the job is done".

15 December: The British Foreign Secretary Jack Straw told reporters that Britain supported the Iraqi "preference" for Mr. Hussein to be tried in Iraq rather than by the International Criminal Court (ICC).

Relations with India

17 April: The Indo-British Parliamentary Forum was launched in New Delhi by the External Affairs Minister Yashwant Sinha under the auspices of the Federation of Indian Chambers of Commerce and Industry (FICCI).

30 April: The British High Commissioner to India, Sir Rob Young, affirmed that there was no dilution of the British commitment to secure an end to cross-border terrorism against India.

16 June: While concurring with the view of the Deputy Prime Minister L.K. Advani that no dialogue with Pakistan could be meaningful unless cross-border terrorism stopped completely, the British Prime Minister Tony Blair assured Mr. Advani that he would take up the issue with the Pakistan President Pervez Musharraf, when he met him on 17 June.

10 July: India was among ten countries, the others being Pakistan, Iran, Iraq, Syria, Israel, Egypt, Cuba, Libya and North Korea, covered by a controversial British Foreign Office scheme under which post-graduate scholars from these countries were likely to be "vetted" before being accepted by a university if their research specialization contributed to proliferation of chemical or biological weapons.

28 July: On a request from the CBI, authorities in the UK froze two bank accounts of the Italian businessman Ottavio Quattrochi, worth around £3 million. The CBI believed that the accounts contained money that was part of the Rs. 64 crore Bofors payoff.

24 September: The visiting British Chief of Defence Staff, General Michael Walker, said that Britain agreed with India that Pakistan-sponsored infiltration was continuing from the LoC into Jammu and Kashmir.

29 September: The outgoing British High Commissioner, Sir Rob Young, told presspersons in Chennai that Britain fully supported India's claim to a permanent seat in the UN Security Council.

15 October: The British High Commission, in a statement in New Delhi stated that all Indian nationals travelling through UK would require a transit visa.

18 December: The newly appointed British High Commissioner, Sir Michael Arthur, told the media that Britain saw India as a strategic priority. While noting that the trade between India and Britain stood at $7 billion, an increase of 20 per cent over the last year, he added that India was the eighth largest investor in Britain.

FRANCE

Strategic Profile

4 February: At the Franco-British summit at the French town of Touquay, President Jacques Chirac told British Prime Minister Tony Blair that France was opposed to the war against Iraq.

11 February: The Russian President Vladimir Putin and the French President Jacques Chirac issued a joint declaration in Paris in which France, Russia and Germany proposed strengthening UN weapons inspections in Iraq, as part of a diplomatic initiative aimed at disarming Saddam Hussein without war. The Chinese President Jiang Zemin, in a telephone conversation with Mr. Chirac, expressed support for the declaration.

20 February: At the Franco-African Summit in Paris attended by Heads of State and representatives of 52 African states, President

Chirac stated that he was willing to step up military training and provide more equipment to help regional peacekeeping operations.

10 March: The French Foreign Minister Dominique de Villepin held talks in the Angolan capital Luanda with President Jose Eduardo dos Santos as part of the French effort to convince the three non-permanent African members of the UN Security Council to join forces with those favouring a second resolution on Iraq that would give the Iraqi leader Saddam Hussein until 17 March to disarm.

19 March: The French Foreign Minister Dominique de Villepin called the British Foreign Secretary Jack Straw to explain France's displeasure over remarks during the debate in the House of Commons that said France had blocked the possibility of a second UN Security Council resolution on Iraq.

20 March: The French President Jacques Chirac said that he regretted the US action against Iraq undertaken without the approval of the UN Security Council.

24 March: France expressed regret at calls by Washington to expel Iraqi diplomats in Paris. It also refused to freeze Iraqi assets in France, mentioning that those were questions of sovereignty that could be decided by France alone.

10 April: The French President Jacques Chirac hailed the fall of the Iraqi leader Saddam Hussein but maintained that full sovereignty should be returned to the Iraqis as soon as possible and "with the legitimacy of the United Nations".

2 June: At the G-8 meeting in Evian, France, the long-awaited tête-à-tête between President George Bush and President Jacques Chirac in the context of stiff French opposition to the war in Iraq was described as "positive and constructive".

Relations with India

24 January: A bilateral extradition treaty was signed between India and France. Home Minister L.K. Advani signed on behalf of India and the French Justice Minister Dominique Perban did so for France.

6 February: The French Prime Minister, Jean Pierre Raffarin, addressing a meeting organized by the CII, FICCI and MEDEF in

Bangalore, admitted that the economic ties between the two countries did not reflect the excellent political relations they shared. France ranked 15th as India's trading partner and 9th in countries having direct foreign investment in India.

6 February: At the Aero India 2003 show in Bangalore, Hindustan Aeronautics Limited (HAL) and the French aircraft engine manufacturer SNECMA signed four agreements for joint production, manufacture and maintenance of engines and key components to the tune of $300 million.

7 February: The French Prime Minister Jean Pierre Raffarin and Prime Minister A.B. Vajpayee, addressing a joint press conference in New Delhi, rejected the contention of US President George Bush that "the game is over for Iraq".

7 February: Bharat Dynamics Limited (BDL), India's prime agency for missile development, signed an agreement with the French company MBDA Missile Systems for designing a new anti-tank missile and also for technical cooperation in future production of air-to-air and surface-to-air missiles by India.

28 April: The visiting French Defence Minister Michelle Alliot-Marie told presspersons in New Delhi that France had offered to sell its upgraded Mirage 2000-S aircraft to India along with technology transfer, as also thermal imagers for the Army's T-72 and T-90 tanks and angular determination systems for the artillery.

24 September: French President Jacques Chirac backed India's candidature to the United Nations Security Council, adding that India's characteristics made it a natural candidate.

GERMANY

Strategic Profile

10 April: The German Chancellor Gerhard Schroeder hailed the victory of the US-led forces in Iraq but insisted that the UN should play a central role in the post-war reconstruction of the country.

11 April: The German Chancellor Gerhard Schroeder, in a television interview, warned the Bush administration against attacking the so-called "axis of evil" countries after the success of its war in Iraq.

4 September: German Chancellor Gerhard Schroeder and the French President Jacques Chirac meeting in Dresden, Germany stated that the draft US resolution seeking troops and money to rebuild Iraq did not give the UN a large enough role and fell short of the goal of turning over partial responsibility to the Iraqi people.

20 September: The leaders of Germany, France and Britain, meeting at a summit in Berlin agreed that the UN must play a significant role in Iraq and that power must be transferred as quickly as possible to Iraqi authorities.

10 October: Germany pledged $220 million to help Russia dismantle 120 atomic submarines in a six-year deal aimed at cleaning up the Kola Peninsula in the Russian far northwest.

Relations with India

3 March: The German President, Johannes Rau, addressing a meeting organized by FICCI and the CII said that India and Germany shared similar views on Iraq and added that Germany would be delighted if more Indian software exports came to his country. He also advocated the dismantling of trade and investment barriers for tapping the vast potential of trade ties between Germany and India.

28 May: Addressing a joint press conference after talks with the German Chancellor Gerhard Schroeder in Berlin, Prime Minister A.B. Vajpayee suggested that Mr. Schroeder tell the Pakistani President Pervez Musharraf, who was expected in Germany in June, to end cross-border terrorism.

28 May: The External Affairs Minister Yashwant Sinha told reporters in Berlin that after a meeting the Union Commerce and Industry Minister Arun Jaitley had with the German Federal Minister for Economy, Wolfgang Clement, Germany had assured India that it would liberalize access for Indian IT professionals.

29 May: Addressing members of the Indian and German business community, Prime Minister A.B. Vajpayee called for German expertise in the project for linking major rivers in India, both to optimize the use of water and for river transportation.

11 July: Germany extended the Green Card Scheme for overseas IT professionals to work in that country. The scheme was to expire

TURKEY

Strategic Profile

15 November: Car bombs exploded simultaneously outside two synagogues in Istanbul, killing at least twenty and injuring more than 257 people. Turkey is home to around 25,000 Jews.

20 November: Two explosions, one in front of the British Consulate and the other within the premises of the international bank, HSBC, in Istanbul killed at least 27 people and wounded more than 400. The British Foreign Secretary Jack Straw remarked in London that the attacks bore the "hallmarks of international terrorism as practised by al-Qaeda."

Relations with India

16 September: Prime Minister A.B. Vajpayee in an interview to the Turkish newspaper, *Turkish Daily News*, said that the only way to resolve the Kashmir imbroglio was through dialogue with Pakistan, which could only be meaningful when cross-border terrorism ended.

17 September: Prime Minister A.B. Vajpayee and his Turkish counterpart Tayyip Erdogan, in Istanbul, concluded three agreements that included the setting up of a Joint Working Group on terrorism, promoting joint research and development, and exchange of scientists as also of scientific and technical information.

17 September: Speaking at the Turkish think tank, the Centre for Strategic Research, Prime Minister A.B. Vajpayee identified areas of "obvious convergence of interests and objectives" between India and Turkey, which would become the basis of building "a comprehensive dialogue architecture".

EUROPE: OTHER EVENTS

17 February: The visiting Polish Prime Minister, Leszek Miller, addressing a meeting organized by the CII and FICCI, termed the current level of economic interaction with India, worth $250 million, as "insufficient" and called upon Indian businessmen to consider the opportunities Poland offered.

20 February: The Minister of State for External Affairs, Digvijay

Singh, told the Rajya Sabha that Portugal had agreed to hand over the underworld don, Abu Salem, to India, though India does not have an extradition treaty with that country.

3 March: A meeting in New Delhi of the joint committee on trade and economic cooperation between India and Slovenia agreed to finalize a bilateral investment protection agreement as well as maritime and air services agreement.

20 September: After talks with the President of the Finnish Parliament, P. Lipponen, the Lok Sabha Speaker Murli Manohar Joshi stated that Finland was in favour of a permanent seat for India in the UN Security Council.

15 October: A Lisbon Court opened extradition proceedings against Abu Salem, prime suspect in the bomb attacks in Mumbai in 1993, which killed 57 people and wounded more than 1000 people.

22 October: India and the Czech Republic signed a defence cooperation agreement in Prague during the visit of the Defence Minister George Fernandes.

23 October: The Bulgarian President Georgi Parvanov, talking to presspersons after talks with the visiting Indian President A.P.J. Abdul Kalam stated that "understanding the social roots of terrorism" was a factor that needed to be dealt with effectively for combating global terrorism.

2 November: The Hungarian Prime Minister Peter Medgyessy arrived in New Delhi on a seven-day State visit designed to augment economic ties—the first by a Hungarian Prime Minister in 29 years.

12 November: The Italian Prime Minister Silvio Berlusconi, hours after an attack at an Italian police base in Nasiriyah that killed 14 Italian armed forces personnel, affirmed that his country's forces comprising around 2400 troops would remain in Iraq.

RUSSIA

Strategic Profile

1 January: Russia, demonstrating displeasure with calls by the Organization for Security and Cooperation in Europe (OSCE) for peace talks with Chechen rebels, closed down OSCE's international monitoring in Chechnya.

7 March: The Russian President Vladimir Putin told US President George Bush, who called him up, that Moscow was determined to press for a peaceful settlement of the Iraqi crisis.

20 March: The Russian President Vladimir Putin condemned the US-led military action on Iraq and called on Washington to stop the war, calling it a "big political mistake".

24 March: Almost 80 per cent of Chechens cast votes in a referendum in which over 95 per cent approved the establishment of a new constitution that declares Chechnya an integral part of Russia.

25 March: Russia successfully test-fired an SS-22 intercontinental ballistic missile, nicknamed the "Topol", from the Plesetsk launch centre in the north-west of the country.

6 April: The Russian Ambassador to Iraq, Vladimir Titorenko, and several diplomats were wounded when their convoy came under fire from unidentified sources.

12 April: The leaders of France, Germany and Russia conducted a two-day "peace camp" summit on Iraq in St. Petersburg and stressed the primacy of the United Nations in resolving global crises.

14 April: A week after the US-British forces attacked Iraq, Russia conducted its biggest war games in the Caucasus mountains in ten years, which also included the test-firing of an intercontinental ballistic missile and Navy deployment in the Indian Ocean, its most massive since the break-up of the Soviet Union.

28 April: At a summit in Dushanbe, Tajikistan, Russia and five other former Soviet states—Kazakhstan, Kyrgyzstan, Tajikistan, Armenia and Belarus—signed accords transforming the ten-year-old Treaty of Collective Security into a regional defence pact, the Collective Security Treaty Organization (CSTO).

13 May: At the Russia-NATO Council meeting at Ambassadors' level in Moscow, Russia and NATO agreed to jointly build a missile-defence shield for Europe.

1 June: At the tercentenary celebrations of the city of St. [illegible]g, [illegible] ident

Vladimir Putin exchanged instruments of ratification of a 2002 strategic arms control treaty, which commits both countries to slash their respective nuclear arsenals by two-thirds.

24 June: President Vladimir Putin became the first Russian President in nearly 130 years to be accorded a full State visit when he arrived at the invitation of Queen Elizabeth in London. The last time a Russian leader was given this honour was in 1874, when Tsar Alexander II visited Britain.

1 July: The Russian Foreign Minister Igor Ivanov reaffirmed Russian commitment to build the $800 million nuclear reactor at Bushehr in Iran, while meeting with the visiting Iranian Vice-President and head of its atomic energy organization, Gholam Reza Aghazadeh.

12 July: The spokesman for the Russian Foreign Ministry, Alexander Yakovenko, voiced concern over NATO plans to use the territory of Georgia for aerial spying, following an AWACS plane demonstration flight in the former Soviet republic.

31 July: The Russian President Vladimir Putin, on a visit to Russia's main nuclear research centre in Sarov, remarked that Russia would honour its self-imposed ban on nuclear testing only as long as other nuclear powers did not stage nuclear blasts.

6 August: The Russian President Vladimir Putin met the Uzbek President Islam Karimov in Samarkhand in a visit meant to rebuild ties with the Central Asian Republic.

10 August: The daily *Izvestia* reported that the world's deepest and the most silent nuclear submarine, the Project 210 submarine, nicknamed "Losharik", was launched at the Severodvinsk shipyard in the Barents Sea. The submarine can sail at a depth of over 6000 metres.

27 August: Washington failed in its last-minute attempt to persuade Moscow to stop nuclear cooperation with Iran, ahead of a Russian-American summit in September. Russia not only said a firm "no" to the US demand to halt the construction of a nuclear reactor at the Bushehr power station, but has bid to build another reactor in Iran.

19 September: Meeting on the sidelines of the Commonwealth of Independent States summit in Yalta, the Presidents of Russia, Ukraine, Kazakhstan and Belarus signed an agreement to form a Single Economic Zone that provides for a Customs Union, free movement of goods, capital and labour, and a common tax, monetary and foreign trade policy.

21 September: Speaking to American media ahead of his summit with the US President George Bush, the Russian President Vladimir Putin ruled out sending troops to Iraq, saying "we are not even considering this option". He added that the UN "should play a real, not decorative role in rebuilding Iraq".

6 October: Chechnya's Moscow-backed leader Akhmad Kadyrov, who was the head of the interim administration in Chechnya, won 81 per cent of the vote in the Presidential elections, defeating seven other candidates.

22 October: The Russian Foreign Ministry, in a statement referring to the two-day Madrid International Donors Conference on the reconstruction of Iraq beginning on 23 October, stated that Russia would not make any donor contribution for the reconstruction of Iraq.

31 October: The Russian President Vladimir Putin sacked his Chief of Staff Alexander Voloshin, in a move designed to consolidate his hold on power. The change of guard was triggered by a criminal probe against Russia's biggest oil company, Yukos.

24 November: The Russian President Vladimir Putin voiced concern that the change of power in Georgia had taken place against the background of strong pressure of the use of force. The Georgian President Eduard Shevardnadze had resigned and Ms. Nino Burdzhanadze had taken over in his place in events suspected by analysts of being engineered by the United States.

19 December: At the end of the Russian-Chinese Inter-Governmental Commission for Military-Technical Cooperation in Moscow, the Russian Defence Minister Sergei Ivanov, and his Chinese counterpart, Cao Gangchuan signed a protocol for the execution of "new and ongoing contracts worth more than $2 billion".

22 December: Russia inducted six new Topol-M nuclear missiles into its arsenal. The 47-ton, 18-metre missile is capable of hitting targets more than 10,800 km away. It is also immune to electronic jamming and cannot be shot down by either existing or future anti-missile systems.

Relations with India

18 January: At the end of the third annual session of the Indo-Russian Inter-Governmental Commission (IRIGC) on Military-Technical Cooperation in Moscow, Defence Minister George Fernandes told reporters that the deal for the acquisition of *Admiral Gorshkov* as well the nuclear-capable TU-22M3 Backfire strategic bombers, and Akula-class nuclear-powered submarines would be finalized by April.

14 February: The Chairman of the Nuclear Power Corporation of India Limited, V.K. Chaturvedi, and the President of the Russian nuclear fuel corporation TVEL, Alexander Wyago, signed a $400 million contract for the supply of nuclear fuel for the Koodankulam plant in Tamil Nadu.

28 March: After talks with the visiting Foreign Secretary Kanwal Sibal, Russian Foreign Minister Igor Ivanov said that India and Russia shared a common stand on the issue of political settlement in Iraq.

6 May: The Russian Deputy Foreign Minister Yuri V. Feelotov told reporters in New Delhi that Pakistan, as the President of the UN Security Council, "cannot impose" the Kashmir issue on the agenda of the world body.

15 May: The Russian Prime Minister Mikhail Kasyanov pledged full support to the External Affairs Minister Yashwant Sinha to impart a new thrust and dynamism to trade and economic links between India and Russia and remove existing bottlenecks.

16 May: At the end of the 9th Session in Moscow of the Indo-Russian Inter-Governmental Commission (IRIGC) on Trade, Economic, Scientific and Technological Cooperation, Russia's Minister for Industry, Science and Technology, Ilya Klebanov said that Russia was willing to expand nuclear energy cooperation with India.

8 September: After talks with the Russian Foreign Minister Igor Ivanov and the first Deputy Foreign Minister Vyacheslav Trubnikov in Moscow, the Foreign Secretary Kanwal Sibal told newspersons that both sides were concerned about the "resurgence of the Taliban activity from Pakistani soil".

2 November: The Russian Atomic Energy Minister Alexander Rumyantsev said that Russia would push for lifting international restrictions on the flow of nuclear technologies to India and would impress upon the Nuclear Suppliers Group (NSG) the need to treat India as a special case as it had developed its nuclear weapon technologies indigenously and had a flawless record on nuclear non-proliferation.

12 November: After the summit meeting between the Russian President Vladimir Putin and the visiting Indian Prime Minister A.B. Vajpayee, India and Russia signed a declaration calling for a "consistent and uncompromising" approach and giving up the "double standards" to tackle terrorism. The two sides also issued a Declaration on Global Challenges and Threats to World Security and Stability.

12 November: The Indian Space Research Organization (ISRO) and the Russian Aviation and Space Agency Rosaviakosmos signed a Memorandum of Understanding (MoU) to pool efforts for an unmanned space mission to the moon and the setting up of a space navigation system.

JAPAN

Strategic Profile

14 January: The visit of the Japanese Prime Minister, Junichiro Koizumi, to the controversial Yasukuni shrine evoked serious displeasure from China and South Korea, who reacted by saying that this visit, the third in less than two years, was a further manifestation of Japan's insensitivity to the strategic concerns of its neighbours.

28 January: Japan, which said it would play a hands-on role in the Sri Lankan conflict resolution process, extended Rs. 35 million grant for the Subcommittee on Immediate Rehabilitation and Humanitarian Needs (SIRHN), comprising members of the government and the LTTE (Liberation Tigers of Tamil Eelam).

4 April: Japan outlined five principles that would govern its participation in the reconstruction of Iraq after the conclusion of the ongoing US-led war, which in Tokyo's view would be decisively won by Washington.

24 May: In a blunt message issued in Crawford, Texas, the US President George Bush and the Japanese Prime Minister Junichiro Koizumi warned North Korea of "tougher measures" in the event of escalation of its nuclear weapon programme.

7 June: Japan and South Korea agreed at a bilateral summit in Tokyo that they would make common cause to resolve the issue of North Korea's perceived nuclear brinkmanship through peaceful means.

18 July: Japan hinted that it might accept the resumption of trilateral talks on the North Korean nuclear parleys that would include Tokyo, Seoul and possibly Moscow. North Korea was believed to have strong reservations about Japan as an interlocutor on the issue.

26 July: Japan enacted a legislation that would authorize the deployment of the Self-Defence Forces (SDF) in Iraq on a humanitarian mission, even in the absence of an explicit UN mandate for the presence of international military personnel.

13 November: Japan formally announced its decision not to send its combat troops to Iraq. This followed the latest incident at Nasiriya that claimed the lives of at least 26 persons, including 16 Italian military personnel.

9 December: Japan announced that it would send its Self-Defence Forces to Iraq in small contingents on a non-combat mission of "reconstruction" activities. The move signalled the deployment of Japanese military personnel in a war zone for the first time since the end of the Second World War.

Relations with India

9 January: The Japanese Foreign Minister, Yoriko Kawaguchi, in a meeting with the Indian Prime Minister remarked that "terrorism by whatever means" was unacceptable and called upon Islamabad to dismantle the "terrorist bases" on its territory.

18 April: Following an intensive round of consultations in Tokyo, between India's National Security Adviser Brajesh Mishra and Japan's Foreign Minister Yoriko Kawaguchi, India and Japan launched the framework for a strategic dialogue between the two countries. The areas of convergence would include international terrorism, cooperation with the United Nations and the development of advanced technologies.

CHINA

Strategic Profile

3 January: China suffered a major setback in its plan to acquire the Phalcon early warning radar system after Israel, complying with a new American demand, suspended all contracts on the export of arms and military equipment to China.

15 March: The General Secretary of the Communist Party of China (CPC), Hu Jintao, was elected as the sixth President of China, succeeding Jiang Zemin.

27 March: Mr. Shaukat Aziz, Adviser on Finance to the Pakistani Prime Minister Mir Zafarullah Khan Zamali, disclosed at a news conference in Islamabad that China had agreed to help Pakistan build a second nuclear-based power plant.

1 April: Lashing out at the "double standards" of the United States in judging the human rights situation of other nations, China urged Washington to stop interfering in "others' affairs". Earlier, the State Department had said that China"s "human rights record throughout the year remained poor".

26 May: The Chinese President, Hu Jintao, left China on his first foreign trip as state leader. He was expected to meet Russian President Vladimir Putin, US President George Bush and the Japanese Prime Minister Junichiro Koizumi during the trip to the G-8 Summit in the French spa town of Evian on 1 June.

1 August: Marking the 76th Anniversary of the founding of the People's Liberation Army, China's Defence Minister, Cao Gangchuan, said that his country "must build the armed forces on the basis of advanced science and technology by applying the latest research and development achievements in all fields of army-building".

8 September: Dismissing the notion of "Taiwan independence" in the wake of pro-independence demonstrations in Taiwan, China said that there were no "forces that could prevent the final reunification of China".

25 September: In a joint communiqué issued after talks between the Chinese Prime Minister, Wen Jiabao, and his Russian counterpart, Mikhail Kasyanov, in Beijing, the two agreed to deepen and diversify their strategic partnership, expand trade ties and strengthen the authority of the United Nations and the Security Council.

8 October: China signed a "strategic partnership for peace and prosperity" agreement with ASEAN in Bali and also acceded to the ASEAN Treaty of Amity and Cooperation (TAC).

15 October: China successfully put an astronaut in orbit around the earth. The astronaut, Yang Liwei, launched in the spaceship Shenzou V was expected to return to earth the next day after making 14 orbits and performing scientific studies.

6 November: At a conference on restructuring military academies, Jiang Zemin, the Chairman of the Chinese Central Military Commission, announced that China was embarking on a scientific process of military reform to wage successful battles in the emerging era of "information war".

19 November: Wang Zaixi, the Vice-Minister in the Taiwan Affairs Office of China's State Council, said at a seminar in Beijing that if the Taiwan authorities openly engaged in pro-independence activities and challenged the "One China" principle, the use of "force may become unavoidable".

3 December: The Chinese President, Hu Jintao, commenting on the recent elections said that the people of Hong Kong should be able to reach a "broad consensus" on shaping their political system and reaffirmed China's basic policy of "one country, two systems" in regard to Hong Kong.

4 December: The Chinese Government, for the first time, issued a White Paper reaffirming a strategic policy of non-proliferation.

21 December: The Chinese President, Hu Jintao, in a telephonic conversation assured his US counterpart, George Bush, of Beijing's willingness to make a sustained effort to convene the second round of multilateral talks on the North Korean nuclear issue.

Relations with India

21 April: In talks between the visiting Indian Defence Minister, George Fernandes, and the Chinese leadership in Beijing, the two agreed to sustain the ongoing process of clarifying the Line of Actual Control (LAC), to formulate additional confidence-building measures with a military focus and to enhance bilateral cooperation to combat terrorism.

2 May: India and China agreed to exchange military officials for training in military institutes in both countries. The agreement was concluded in Shanghai with the visiting Indian Defence Minister, George Fernandes.

23 June: The visiting Indian Prime Minister, A.B. Vajpayee, and his Chinese counterpart, Wen Jiabao, in Beijing signed a memorandum on opening border trade through Sikkim. A separate "Declaration on Principles for Relations and Comprehensive Cooperation" was also signed.

24 July: The Prime Minister, A.B. Vajpayee, in a statement in the Lok Sabha said that there has been no change in the decades-old policy on Tibet. He said that India had never doubted that the Tibet Autonomous Region (TAR) was part of the territory of the People's Republic of China.

24 July: Wang Jiarui, Minister in the International Department of the CPC Central Committee, speaking to the Indian CPI (M) goodwill delegation who called on him in Beijing, said that China had identified New Delhi as a partner for "increased coordination in world affairs" so as to promote "democratization and multi-polarization of international relations".

25 July: The External Affairs Minister, Yashwant Sinha, admitted in the Lok Sabha that there had been an incursion by a Chinese patrol on 26 June in the Asaphila area of Upper Subansiri district of Arunachal Pradesh across the Line of Actual Control (LAC).

25 July: Kong Quan, a Chinese Foreign Ministry spokesman, stated in Beijing that China had "not recognized" Arunachal Pradesh as part of India and added that "Indian people" crossed the eastern sector of the LAC, and not China's forces, as claimed by New Delhi.

8 October: Beijing removed Sikkim as an "independent country" from its official Foreign Ministry website. Kanwal Sibal, the Indian Foreign Secretary, said at a resort in Bali that the development was the outcome of the meeting between the Indian Prime Minister, A.B. Vajpayee and his Chinese counterpart, Wen Jiabao.

23 October: The Chinese Vice-Foreign Minister, Dai Bingguo, and the Indian National Security Adviser, Brajesh Mishra, held their first meeting four months after they were appointed as Special Representatives to address the contentious border dispute.

13 November: Heralding the possibility of a new chapter of confidence-building cooperation, India and China held a historic naval exercise off Shanghai along the East China Sea. Official sources said from Shanghai that the conventional three-part search-and-rescue naval exercise was successfully completed.

17 December: *The Hindu* quoted "informed diplomatic sources" as saying that the Chinese Foreign Ministry's 2004 Year Book would not show the state of Sikkim as an independent country.

PAKISTAN

Strategic Profile

8 March: Pakistan declared that it had received "direct compensation" to the tune of over $891 million from different countries in recognition of its "active cooperation" in the fight against international terrorism after 11 September 2001.

15 March: The US President, George Bush, waived sanctions against Pakistan, making it eligible to receive millions of dollars in economic assistance, a move that was expected to further improve bilateral relations.

30 March: Abdul Qader Khan, known as the "father of Pakistan's nuclear programme" claimed that his country had made the atomic bomb as early as 1984 but continued to deny its existence till May 1998.

31 March: Pakistan decided to legally declare the al-Qaeda network as a terrorist organization to help prosecute suspected supporters of the group. In the past year and a half, Pakistan had handed over 480 al-Qaeda suspects to the US.

2 April: Pakistan's state-controlled news agency Associated Press of Pakistan (APP), in a report from Beijing said that the visiting Pakistani Minister of State for Defence Production, Habibullah Khan Waraich, and his Chinese counterpart, Zhung Wei Min, signed a charter on bilateral cooperation in the field of defence industry and technology.

16 April: Praising Pakistan's "strong and sustained" support in counter terrorism matters, particularly the arrest of suspected terrorist Khalid Shaikh Mohammed, the United States promised an additional $40 million to help Pakistan in its efforts.

30 April: A three-member team of inspectors of the Hague-based Organization for the Prohibition of Chemical Weapons (OPCW) conducted a much-publicized inspection of a fertilizer plant on the outskirts of Karachi. While there was anxious speculation that it was a "chemical weapons" inspection, the Pakistan Foreign Office issued an explanation that the inspection was only "routine".

7 May: In a meeting convened to reassure the international community of the soundness of its nuclear command and control structure, Pakistan's President, Pervez Musharraf, presided over a meeting of the National Command Authority (NCA), the body entrusted with the task of development and deployment of nuclear weapons. The NCA declared that "minimum deterrence" was the "cornerstone" of Pakistan's nuclear policy.

11 June: The Lahore High Court delivered a judgement saying that the continuation of Pakistan President, Pervez Musharraf, as Army Chief did not violate any provision in the Pakistan Constitution.

19 June: Portraying an alarming picture of India's growing defence capability, the Pakistan President, Pervez Musharraf, called for a Western arms "embargo" on India. General Musharraf urged Britain and America not to allow New Delhi to develop a military superiority over Pakistan or else his country would be forced to rely on its nuclear weapons as the only real deterrence.

25 June: The Pakistan President, Pervez Musharraf, in a meeting with the US President, George Bush, at Camp David, announced that Islamabad was committed to a "hundred per cent effort" in trying to stop "cross-border incidents". He also agreed "in principle" to send troops to Iraq on the condition that Islamabad would not have to finance such a force and it would go under the cover of the United Nations, the Organization of Islamic Conference or the Gulf Cooperation Council.

2 July: The Pakistan President, Pervez Musharraf, announced in Berlin that Germany had lifted all sanctions on the supply of defence equipment to Pakistan and was willing to provide a state-of-the-art radar system to the Pakistan Air Force.

16 August: The former Prime Minister of Pakistan, Nawaz Sharif, claimed that more than 4000 Pakistani troops and officials were killed in the Kargil conflict. It was for the first time that he had come out with figures of casualties on the Pakistani side.

20 August: The US Ambassador to Pakistan, Nancy J. Powell, called on the Pakistan Chief of Air Staff, Kaleem Saadat, to announce the sale of six C-130 aircraft to Pakistan as part of the defence cooperation between the two countries.

26 September: The Pakistan President, Pervez Musharraf, addressing members of the Canadian Institute of Strategic Studies (CISS) in Ottawa, where he was on a two-day official visit, admitted that North Korea had provided surface-to-air missiles to his country.

8 October: For the second time in less than a week, Pakistan conducted its second test of a missile capable of carrying a nuclear warhead. The surface-to-surface ballistic missile, Half-IV/Shaheen 1, reportedly can carry any type of warhead up to 700 km.

4 November: General Pervez Musharraf paid a five-day State visit to China. The two sides signed a number of documents, including a joint declaration on the future direction of bilateral interactions. China affirmed "support" for the "process of reconciliation" between New Delhi and Islamabad.

9 November: In a further setback for Pakistan in its efforts to convince the West on the restoration of democracy, the European Union decided to block approval of third generation trade and cooperation agreement. The decision came close on the heels of the visit of the Pakistani Foreign Minister, Khurshid Mehmood Kasuri, to Brussels to convince the EU for early ratification of the pact.

15 November: Pakistan banned three militant groups, including the Jaish-e-Mohammad — which was functioning under a new name after it was proscribed in January 2001.

20 November: Pakistan banned three more militant outfits, including the Jamat-ul-Furqun, a breakaway organization of the Jaish-e-Mohammed, blamed for the attack on the Indian Parliament on 13 December 2001. The other two outfits proscribed under the Anti-Terrorism Act were the Hizb-ul-Tahreer and the Jamat-ul-Ansar.

12 December: The Pakistan President, Pervez Musharraf, speaking after a ceremony to commission the first indigenously built Agosta 90B submarine Saad at the Pakistan Navy Dockyard in Karachi said that his country faced danger from within—from "terrorism, extremism and sectarianism".

14 December: In what appeared to be an attempt on the life of the Pakistan President, Pervez Musharraf, a powerful blast rocked a bridge in Rawalpindi minutes after the convoy of the President passed it.

25 December: The Pakistan President, Pervez Musharraf, escaped an attempt on his life when suicide bombers rammed two cars into his motorcade, killing 14 persons and injuring over 40 others in the high security zone of the Rawalpindi cantonment.

Relations with India

20 January: Pakistan raised the Kashmir issue at the United Nations Security Council meeting on terrorism and accused India of "misusing" the campaign against terror to "denigrate and suppress the right of the people of Jammu and Kashmir".

27 January: The Defence Minister of India, George Fernandes, said in London that Pakistan would be "erased from the world map" if it used nuclear weapons against India.

8 February: New Delhi expelled Pakistan's Chargé d'Affaires, Jalil Abbas Jilani, and four other staffers over allegations that the Pakistani diplomat provided money to representatives of the All Party Hurriyat Conference (APHC). Pakistan responded in kind a few hours later by asking Sudhir Vyas, India's Chargé d'Affaires in Pakistan, and four other staffers to leave Islamabad.

18 April: The Indian Prime Minister announced in Srinagar that India would like to "again" extend a hand of friendship to Pakistan. He said that this was the time to change the map of Indo-Pak relations and that Delhi was busy working towards that.

21 April: Pakistan, while welcoming the offer of talks by the Indian Prime Minister, responded by announcing that "preconditions" were not necessary for the commencement of the dialogue process. The Indian Prime Minister had earlier said that the dialogue was contingent on Pakistan ending cross-border infiltration and closing alleged militant camps.

28 April: In a direct bilateral political contact at the highest level, Mir Zafarullah Khan Jamali, Prime Minister of Pakistan, called up the Indian Prime Minister and invited him to visit Pakistan.

2 May: India's Prime Minister, Atal Bihari Vajpayee, announced that a High Commissioner would return to Islamabad and that civil aviation links would be restored with Pakistan on a reciprocal basis. Responding to the initiative by India, Islamabad also announced that it would reappoint a High Commissioner to India.

8 May: A 13-member Pakistani Parliamentary delegation visited India on a week-long peace overture. The objective of the visit, according to the delegation, was to bring a message of peace.

12 June: The Deputy Prime Minister of India, L.K. Advani, in a talk on "Indo-US Relations in a Strategic Perspective" in Los Angeles, said that India and the US had to work in tandem to defeat the menace of jehadi terrorism fuelled by religious extremism, the "epicentre" of which was Pakistan. Pakistan later in the night denounced the statement and said that the statement was "uncalled for and unhelpful" and was against the spirit of Prime Minister A.B. Vajpayee's recent peace initiative.

26 June: The Pakistan President, Pervez Musharraf, addressing a meeting organized by the United States Institute for Peace in Washington, dismissed the idea that the Line of Control (LoC) could be turned into an international border as a way of achieving permanent peace. He said that the LoC was the dispute itself and argued that the "dispute" could not become a solution.

26 June: India rejected the Pakistan President Pervez Musharraf's suggestion for a US-sponsored road map, on the lines of West Asia, to resolve the Kashmir issue, saying that there was no place for third-party mediation. India also expressed concern over the military component of the $3 billion economic package announced by the US for Pakistan during the meeting between President Musharraf and US President George Bush at Camp David.

30 June: The Pakistan High Commissioner-designate to India, Aziz Ahmed Khan, arrived in New Delhi.

4 July: The Pakistan President, Pervez Musharraf, in Paris, pursued his push for a four-step West Asia-style peace road map on the Kashmir issue that would include third-party mediation, despite India's rejection of this approach.

6 July: The Pakistan Prime Minister, Mir Zafarullah Khan Jamali, dubbed the suicide attack in Quetta, in which 53 people were killed, as a "preplanned foreign conspiracy to undermine the highly successful foreign visit" of President Pervez Musharraf and pointed the finger at India. He said that the government could not "overlook the opening" of Indian Consulates in Kandahar and Herat in Afghanistan and Zehadan in Iran, bordering Baluchistan, in the context of the incident in Quetta.

12 July: The Lahore-bound Indian bus crossed over into Pakistan at the Wagah border, signalling the reopening of the direct passenger transportation links between the two countries.

15 July: India's new High Commissioner-designate, Shiv Shankar Menon, crossed over the Wagah border to take up his position at the High Commission in Islamabad after a gap of nearly 19 months.

11 August: The Pakistan Prime Minister, Mir Zafarullah Khan Jamali, speaking to a visiting group of Indian Parliamentarians, security experts and journalists called on India as the bigger country to demonstrate "flexibility" in the resolution of the Kashmir issue.

12 August: In a 90-minute interactive session with a visiting delegation of Indian Parliamentarians, the Pakistan President, Pervez Musharraf, offered a conditional cease-fire along the Line of Control if India was willing to reciprocate and reduce the strength of its forces in the Kashmir valley and cease "atrocities" in Jammu and Kashmir.

14 August: Speaking at the official function to mark the 56th Independence Day of Pakistan, the Pakistan Prime Minister, Mir Zafarullah Khan Jamali, said that the resolution of the "core issue" of Kashmir held the key to peace in South Asia and normalization of relations with India.

15 August: Speaking on the occasion of Independence Day at the Red Fort, the Prime Minister, A.B. Vajpayee, invited Pakistan to "walk together" with India on the road to peace and to abjure its "anti-India" outlook because the people of both countries wished to live in peace.

18 August: The Pakistan Foreign Office spokesman, Masood Khan, said the biggest external threat to Pakistan's stability was from India. Mr. Khan said that there were more than 55 terrorist training camps in India across the Line of Control and Pakistan-India border that targeted Pakistan.

20 August: In an exclusive interview to *The Hindu*, the new Pakistani High Commissioner to New Delhi, Aziz Ahmed Khan, said that Pakistan was ready to discuss Indian concerns about terrorism, as part of the composite dialogue structure that was agreed upon by the Foreign Secretaries of the two countries in June 1997.

14 September: The Pakistani Interior Minister, Faisal Saleh Hayat, told correspondents at his office that India through its Research and Analysis Wing (RAW) was using its consulates in Afghanistan for "terrorist activities" inside Pakistan.

23 September: India offered to Pakistan an increase in the strength of their respective High Commissions in New Delhi and Islamabad on a reciprocal basis.

24 September: The Pakistan President Pervez Musharraf, addressing the UN General Assembly, invited India to join his country "in a sustained dialogue" to resolve the Kashmir dispute, which he termed as the "most dangerous dispute", and a just solution of which held the key to peace and security in the region.

25 September: The Prime Minister of India, A.B. Vajpayee, stated in the UN General Assembly that New Delhi would not have any dialogue with Islamabad as long as Pakistan continued to sponsor terrorism in Jammu and Kashmir.

23 October: In an attempt to break the India-Pakistan logjam, New Delhi proposed to Islamabad a new bus service between Srinagar and Muzaffarabad, a Mumbai-Karachi ferry, restoration of the Khokrapar-Munabao (Sind-Rajasthan) link by rail and bus and crossing of the Wagah border by persons above the age of 65.

29 October: Pakistan responded to the Indian proposal made on 23 October to improve people-to-people relations by giving a go-ahead to the restoration of cricketing ties, setting up of links between the Coast Guards of the two countries and allowing of persons above 65 years to cross the Wagah border on foot, but rejected the restoration of rail and air links and increase of bus services.

1 November: Speaking at a conference of India's top military commanders in New Delhi, Prime Minister A.B. Vajpayee said that India had taken the lead in restoring bilateral ties with Pakistan through a number of initiatives. He, however, ruled out a dialogue with Islamabad till it displayed sincerity in stopping cross-border infiltration and dismantling terrorist training and launch pads in its territory.

25 November: In what was described as the first substantial agreement of its kind, India and Pakistan agreed to a formal ceasefire from midnight along the International Border, the Line of Control and the Actual Ground Position Line in Siachen. Officials from both the countries said that the ceasefire accord was arrived at "pursuant to the understanding between the governments of India and Pakistan".

1 December: India and Pakistan in a joint statement issued after "technical level" talks between civil aviation officials in New Delhi agreed to resume simultaneous airlinks and overflights from 1 January on a reciprocal basis.

13 December: In the first such admission by a Pakistani leader, the former Pakistan Prime Minister, Benazir Bhutto, speaking at a conference in New Delhi, said that Islamabad had backed a low-intensity conflict in Jammu and Kashmir during her first tenure. She said that this had been done to "hype" the Kashmir issue and was a joint decision taken by the military and the political leadership.

18 December: In an interview to Reuters in Islamabad, the Pakistan President, Pervez Musharraf, said that his country had "left aside" the UN Security Council resolutions on Kashmir and was prepared to meet India "half way" in a bid to resolve the 56-year-old issue.

19 December: In an agreement between the railway delegations of India and Pakistan in New Delhi, it was decided that the Samjhauta Express, the only rail link between India and Pakistan, would restart the service from 15 January 2004.

21 December: In an interview to NDTV (New Delhi Television), the Pakistan Prime Minister, Mir Zafarullah Khan Jamali, said that the UN resolutions calling for a plebiscite in Jammu and Kashmir remained the basis of finding a solution to the issue.

NEPAL

30 January: The Nepalese Information Minister Ramesh Nath Pandey said in Kathmandu that the Nepal Government had reached a ceasefire agreement with the Maoist rebels and that cessation of hostilities would begin immediately.

29 March: The head of the Maoists' parallel government, Baburam Bhattarai, returned to Kathmandu after a gap of seven years. Bhattarai along with his military strategist, Ram Bahadur Thapa, politburo members Krishna Bahadur Mahara, Deb Gurung and Matrika Prasad came out of their hideouts to hold talks with the Government.

16 April: The Nepalese government set up a six-member committee under Deputy Prime Minister Badri Prasad Mandal to hold peace negotiations with Maoist rebels.

17 April: The Nepal Water Resource Minister Deepak Gwayali at the end of his three-day visit to India told presspersons in Patna that India and Nepal were exploring joint venture projects to use water resources in the two countries to combat the scourge of floods and to increase power generation and irrigation potential.

22 April: The Indian Army Chief, General N.C. Vij, began a four-day visit to Nepal to boost the traditional military ties between the two countries.

27 April: The Nepalese government and the Maoist rebels began the first round of peace talks in Kathmandu. The government side was led by the Deputy Prime Minister, Badra Prasad Mandal, and the Maoist team by the second-in-command of the organization, Baburam Bhattarai.

30 May: The Palace-nominated Prime Minister Lokendra Bahadur Chand stepped down to enable King Gyanendra to form a new government. This decision was taken after Nepal's major political parties threatened to end the monarchical system if the King failed to set up a democratic government.

4 June: Nepal's King Gyanendra appointed the veteran politician and pro-monarchist Surya Bahadur Thapa as the kingdom's new Prime Minister.

27 July: Maoist insurgents gave the Nepalese government a five-day ultimatum to fulfil their five major demands, which included abrogation of the US-Nepal anti-terrorism agreement, the expulsion of all US military advisers from Nepal, and implementation of the agreement to limit patrols by the Nepalese army.

5 August: China and Nepal agreed to open two new transit points connecting the latter with Tibet. A 31-member delegation led by the Tibetan Autonomous Region Vice-Chairman arrived at Kathmandu to sign the MoU on opening the Nangpa and Shahrubensi exit points.

24 August: Nepal expelled a Pakistan Embassy official, Mohammad Masood, who was recently apprehended with counterfeit Indian currency worth Rs. 45,000.

27 August: Nepal's fragile peace collapsed with the Maoists calling off the seven-month-old ceasefire. A statement issued by Maoist chief Pushpakamal Dahal said that "the justification for the talks and the ceasefire ended after the government shut the way to a negotiated settlement".

28 August: The Government declared the Communist Party of Nepal (Maoist) a "terrorist organization".

11 October: In one of the fiercest clashes since the seven-month-old ceasefire collapsed, at least fifty Maoists were killed in an encounter with the armed police force in Banke district in western Nepal.

2 November: The Maoists in a statement issued in Kathmandu alleged that the US move to list them as terrorists was "a ploy" to make Nepal a "military base to target India and China", and for "interference in Nepal's internal affairs".

4 November: The Nepalese Prime Minister, Surya Bahadur Thapa, told the media that the Government had ruled out international mediation in its struggle against the Maoist insurgents.

8 November: The Joint Secretary in the Nepalese Commerce Ministry, Purushottam Ojha, told reporters in Kathmandu that India would open a rail link to Nepal from Kolkata. He added that the train would make the 800-km journey in 36 hours as against six days by road and help in reducing transport costs by $16.2 million a year for the people of the two countries.

25 November: Prime Minister A.B. Vajpayee and his Nepalese counterpart Surya Bahadur Thapa, in a meeting in New Delhi, agreed to advance the regional cooperation agenda, including a framework free trade treaty at the upcoming SAARC Summit in Islamabad in January 2004.

13 December: Nepal decided to send 800 soldiers of the Fifth battalion to be a part of the UN peacekeeping mission in the West African nation of Sierra Leone. King Gyanendra, in a statement, stated that it was "a matter of pride" to be "contributing to the task of establishing peace "in different parts of the globe".

BANGLADESH

7 January: Deputy Prime Minister L.K. Advani, addressing a conference of Chief Secretaries and Directors-General of Police in New Delhi, said that half-a-crore Bangladeshis who resided in India without proper documents posed a serious threat to the country's internal security.

27 January: The Bangladesh State Minister for Foreign Affairs, Reaz Rahman, alleged that India's Border Security Force (BSF) tried to push in 400 Bangla-speaking Indian nationals from India into Bangladesh.

31 January: The Bangladesh Deputy High Commissioner to New Delhi, Shahadat Hussain, was called to the Foreign Office and presented with an aide-memoire expressing India's concern with regard to illegal immigration of Bangladeshis into India.

6 February: The six-day-long standoff between the Border Security Force (BSF) and the Bangladesh Rifles (BDR) ended with the 213 Bangladeshi snake-charmers returning to their country. The BDR had earlier refused entry to them at the Satgachi outpost of Coochbehar district of West Bengal.

14 February: The visiting Bangladesh Foreign Minister Mohd. Morshed Khan held talks with the Minister for External Affairs, Yashwant Sinha, and reviewed the entire gamut of bilateral relations between the two countries. New Delhi expressed concern at Pakistan's ISI (Directorate of Inter-Services Intelligence) operations in Bangladesh as well as the presence of anti-India insurgents on Bangladeshi territory.

14 February: The Bangladesh Foreign Minister M. Morshed Khan, after meeting Prime Minister A.B. Vajpayee, stated that the Beijing-Dhaka defence cooperation was not aimed at any "third country". He added that both the ISI of Pakistan and RAW (Research and Analysis Wing) of India had their presence in Bangladesh and as per information available to him, no anti-India insurgents were present.

2 March: A European Parliamentary delegation to Bangladesh warned that if the state of democracy, human rights and the rule of law in the country deteriorated, the EU might block many of its programmes envisaged in the Cooperation Agreement signed with Bangladesh on 22 May 2000.

29 April: At the end of the talks between the Bangladesh Foreign Secretary Shamsher Mobin Chowdhury and the Indian Foreign Secretary Kanwal Sibal in Dhaka, India and Bangladesh agreed to remove major irritants in their bilateral relations, including problems of border demarcation, illegal cross-border movement of people, duty-free access of more Bangladeshi items and establishment of transportation limits.

1 June: The US Secretary of State Colin Powell, in Dhaka on an official visit, invited Bangladesh to participate in the reconstruction of Iraq. He added that any decision on sending troops would be taken by Dhaka.

15 July: The Bangladesh Prime Minister Begum Khaleda Zia, after meeting India's Minister of External Affairs, Yashwant Sinha, in Dhaka—who had come to attend the India-Bangladesh Joint Economic Commission meeting—underscored the need for reducing the "huge trade imbalance" between the two countries.

6 September: The Bangladesh Foreign Secretary, Shamsher Mobin Chowdhury, told presspersons in Dhaka that Bangladesh had singed an agreement with Washington under which no US soldier or officer charged with criminal offences can be tried in Bangladesh or extradited to the International Criminal Court (ICC) for prosecution.

25 September: The Bangladesh Water Resources Minister, Hafizuddin Ahmed, urged the World Bank Country Director in Bangladesh, Christina Wallich, not to extend support to India for the implementation of the proposed $112 billion Inter-River Link Projects, as the diversion of water from the Brahmaputra would have a catastrophic impact on Bangladesh.

30 September: The Bangladesh Water Resources Minister, Hafizuddin Ahmed, told presspersons after the meeting of the 35th Joint Rivers Commission in New Delhi that he accepted India's assurances that the proposed river-linking scheme was at conceptual stage. India assured Bangladesh that the Tipaimukh dam project for irrigating Assam and Tripura would be implemented only after discussions with Bangladesh.

8 October: Bangladesh was ranked for the third successive year as "the most corrupt country", among 133 nations by the Transparency International (TI). In TI's Corruption Perception Index (CPI), 2003, Bangladesh was rated 1.3 on a scale of 10.

SRI LANKA

6 January: The fourth round of talks between the LTTE (Liberation Tigers of Tamil Eelam) and the Sri Lankan government began in the Thai town of Nakorn Pathorn.

8 February: The fifth round of talks between Colombo and the LTTE ended in Berlin. The two parties decided to appoint three committees representing both the Muslim population and the Tamils to address issues of concern in eastern Sri Lanka.

16 February: The Sri Lankan Prime Minister, Ranil Wickremasinghe, addressing the concluding session of the 33rd convention of the Ceylon Workers Congress (CWC), promised to bring in legislation to provide citizenship for nearly one lakh disenfranchised estate Tamils who had opted to stay on the island.

21 March: The sixth round of talks between the Sri Lankan government and the LTTE was held in the northern Japanese city of Hakone. Both sides devised ways to strengthen the Sri Lanka Monitoring Mission (SLMM), a multi-member Nordic team overseeing the truce since February 2001.

10 April: The visiting Sri Lankan President Chandrika Kumaratunga met the President A.P.J. Abdul Kalam and held talks with the Prime Minister A.B. Vajpayee on the progress of the peace process.

14 April: The US Deputy Secretary of State, Richard Armitage, while speaking at an international seminar on "Sri Lanka's Reconstruction and Development" held at the State Department said that while he was encouraged by the role of the LTTE in the Sri Lankan peace process, the Bush administration did not yet see a rationale for the lifting of that organization from the list of foreign terrorist organizations (FTO).

22 April: The LTTE announced its unilateral suspension of negotiations with the Sri Lankan government. Expressing "deep dissatisfaction" over the move, the Sri Lankan President Chandrika Kumaratunga ordered the military to be on maximum alert.

6 May: The Sri Lankan Prime Minister Ranil Wickremasinghe told Parliament that his government had "obtained the services" of the retired Indian Vice-Chief of Naval Staff, Vice Admiral P.J. Jacob, to "advise" it on "issues relating to the sea".

9 May: The Adviser to the Sri Lankan Government, Lt. Gen. (Retd.) Satish Nambiar, in an eight-page report on the High Security Zones (HSZs) proposed linking the delineation of Sri Lanka's northern HSZs to the "simultaneous dismantling of operational military positions" held by the LTTE.

13 May: The visiting US Assistant Secretary of State for South Asia, Christina Rocca, called on the Sri Lankan President Chandrika

Kumaratunga and "exchanged views" on the "current status of the negotiations" with the LTTE.

15 May: The deadlock in the Sri Lankan peace process continued, with the Norwegian Foreign Minister, Jon Peterson, failing to convince the leader of the LTTE, V. Prabhakaran, on the need for LTTE's participation in the next month's Tokyo Donors' Conference.

28 May: The Sri Lankan Government, through the Norwegian facilitator, Prof. G.L. Peiris, formally offered a "development-oriented structure" as an alternative to the LTTE demand for an interim administration.

30 May: The LTTE rejected the offer of a "development-oriented structure" as an unacceptable alternative to its demand for an interim administration for the North-East. LTTE's Anton Balasingham said that the Government's offer would create an "apex bureaucracy linked to several other inefficient and defunct state agencies".

9 June: At the Tokyo Donors' Conference, the Sri Lankan Prime Minister Ranil Wickremasinghe made a proposal for a "provisional administrative structure" for Tamil-majority areas in north-eastern Sri Lanka. The conference was, however, boycotted by the LTTE. The donors also pledged more than $2 billion for reconstruction purposes.

27 June: A massive public rally, calling itself the "Pongu Tamil" (Tamil Resurgence), was held in Jaffna, the third in as many years. The rally reiterated one of the key demands of the LTTE, the de-escalation of Sri Lanka's northern High Security Zones (HSZs).

28 June: In its verdict on the 14 June sinking of an LTTE tanker MT *Shoshin*, suspected to be "smuggling arms" off eastern Sri Lanka, the Sri Lanka Monitoring Mission (SLMM) ruled that the LTTE broke the UN Convention on the Law of the Sea (UNCLOS) "by not flying an appropriate flag" and not having "an official visible identification".

17 July: The Sri Lankan Government formally handed over to the LTTE its proposals for an "administrative structure" through the former Norwegian envoy to Sri Lanka, Jon Westborg, at Killinochi.

28 July: The LTTE's leader, S.P. Tamilchelvan, termed Colombo's

Provisional Administration Council offer as one that "fails to meet expectations". He added that the LTTE would send its own "counter proposals".

7 September: The leader of the LTTE, V. Prabhakaran, inaugurated the "headquarters" of the "Tamil Eelam Police Service" in Killinochi. The LTTE established this force as part of its "permanent administration" but the Sri Lankan Government has not recognized this force.

7 October: Sri Lanka decided to grant citizenship to 1,68,141 Tamils of Indian origin. These included the 84,141 people who were issued Indian passports but had to stay back due to the ethnic riots in July 1983 and the 84,000 people, who had not been issued Indian passports and were residing in the Central Province of Sri Lanka.

15 October: The External Affairs Minister Yashwant Sinha signed an agreement with Sri Lankan Foreign Minister Tyronne Fernando releasing $30 million as the second tranche of a $100 million Indian Line of Credit to rebuild the island nation.

21 October: In the joint statement issued at the end of the visit of the Sri Lankan Prime Minister Ranil Wickremasinghe, India said that it would permit "daily air services" between Colombo and New Delhi, Mumbai, Chennai, Bangalore, Hyderabad and Kolkata. While stating that the solution to the Sri Lankan ethnic issue had to "emerge purely through political processes", India affirmed its commitment to the sovereignty and territorial integrity of Sri Lanka.

1 November: The LTTE in its counter-proposals for an interim administrative structure for the Tamil-majority North-East, demanded an "Interim Self-Governing Authority for the North-East", with full control over the regional administration till a final settlement was reached.

4 November: The Sri Lankan President Chandrika Kumaratunga prorogued Parliament and took over the portfolios of Defence, Interior, and Mass Communication, citing "national interest". Prime Minister Ranil Wickremasinghe in Washington called the move "opportunistic".

7 November: In a television address to the nation, the Sri Lankan

President Chandrika Kumaratunga called for a "grand alliance" of all the "national and patriotic forces" to form a "government of national reconstruction and reconciliation". She added that the LTTE's counter-proposals had not addressed the core issue as the LTTE had not given up its demand for a separate state.

13 November: The LTTE chief, V. Prabhakaran, sought "guarantees" from the Norwegian facilitators led by the Deputy Foreign Minister Vidar Helgessen that the Sri Lankan Government "will continue with the ceasefire agreement". Mr. Helgessen conveyed to the LTTE chief the assurances of President Kumaratunga and Prime Minister Wickremasinghe that the peace process would not be affected by the political stand-off.

25 November: The EU Commissioner in Charge of External Relations, Chris Patten, after meeting the Sri Lankan President Chandrika Kumaratunga and her Senior Advisor Lakshman Kadirgamar, stated that the LTTE would "have to show" its commitment to the Oslo Agreement, wherein it had pledged to find a solution to the ethnic conflict within a united Sri Lanka.

8 December: The chief negotiator of the LTTE, Anton Balasingham, speaking in London to mark the annual "Heroes Day" on 6 December, criticized the efforts of the Sri Lankan Government to internationalize the peace process as a "containment strategy".

BHUTAN

8 May: The Indian Army Chief, Gen. N.C. Vij, held talks with the Bhutanese military officers on the issue of getting terrorist camps of ULFA (United Liberation Front of Asom) and other insurgent groups of North-East India vacated from that country.

15 September: The King of Bhutan, Jigme Singye Wangchuk, stated in New Delhi that the National Assembly of Bhutan had taken a decision to invite the ULFA, National Democratic Front of Bodoland (NDFB), and the Kamtapur Liberation Organization (KLO) for talks.

16 September: The King of Bhutan, Jigme Singye Wangchuk, assured the Deputy Prime Minister L.K. Advani, that his country's territory would not be used for anti-India activities.

15 December: The Royal Bhutan Army launched a massive crackdown on anti-India militants camping on its soil. The outfits included the United Liberation Front of Asom (ULFA), the National Democratic Front of Bodoland (NDFB), and the Kamtapur Liberation Organization (KLO).

16 December: The Bhutanese Foreign Secretary, Neten Zangmo, told PTI (Press Trust of India) that the Royal Bhutan Army had captured the central command headquarters of ULFA located at Phukatong in Sandrup Jongkhar district bordering Assam.

17 December: The Royal Bhutan Army (RBA) captured top leaders of militant organizations of North-East India in its operations against them. The arrested included Mithinga Daimary, Publicity Secretary of ULFA, B. Irakdao, Publicity Secretary of NDFB, Tom Adhikari and Dalton Burman of the KLO. More than a hundred militants were killed in the flush-out operations.

MALDIVES

20 October: The Maldivian President, Maumoon Abdul Gayoom, won a referendum that gave him five more years in power. Mr. Gayoom, Asia's longest serving leader having been about fifteen years in power, was first elected in 1978.

MAJOR GLOBAL DEVELOPMENTS

1 February: The US Space Shuttle Columbia, carrying among others mission specialist Indian-born Kalpana Chawla as one of the seven astronauts, disintegrated over the State of Texas, minutes before its scheduled landing in Florida.

25 February: The 15th Summit of Non-aligned Countries (NAM), attended by 63 Heads of State and Government, in Kuala Lumpur, called upon all countries to cooperate in resolving issues that had held up efforts at the UN for the "conclusion of a comprehensive convention for combating international terrorism".

12 March: The International Criminal Court was formally launched at The Hague, when 18 judges took their seats in the presence of Queen Beatrix and the UN Secretary General Kofi Annan. Mr. Annan appealed to the 11 men and 7 women to "act without fear or favour" and to demonstrate "unimpeachable integrity and impartiality" in their decisions.

20 May: At the Commonwealth Ministerial Action Group (CMAG) meeting in London, the Group decided to keep Pakistan suspended from the Commonwealth until the deadlock over the status of President Pervez Musharraf's controversial constitutional amendments was resolved.

31 May: Trade representatives of 49 least-developed countries (LDCs) began talks in Dhaka aimed at drafting a common strategy for airing concerns in the upcoming ministerial meeting of the WTO (World Trade Organization) in Cancun, Mexico in September.

1 June: At the "extended dialogue" of the G-8 plus 12 developing countries in Evian, France, Prime Minister A.B. Vajpayee remarked that it was "quite clear that the developing countries were deeply disappointed by the progress so far on the Millennium Development Round since the Doha meeting nearly two years ago".

2 June: At the G-8 Summit in Evian, France, the leaders warned Iran and North Korea against pursuing programmes of mass destruction weapons and described international terrorism as the "pre-eminent threat to international security".

10 September: The Fifth Ministerial Conference of the WTO began at Cancun with the Director-General of WTO, Supachai Panitchpakdi, calling on Ministers to show "flexibility and understanding to reach an agreement that could take forward the Doha round of trade negotiations".

15 September: The Fifth Ministerial Conference of the WTO was abandoned without reaching an agreement on the next step after the Doha round of trade talks.

16 October: The UN Security Council unanimously adopted the US-drafted resolution on Iraq's future, with a 15-0 vote. The resolution, among other things, asked the Iraqi Governing Council to draw up a plan for a new constitution and elections by 15 December and created a UN-authorized multinational force in Iraq under US supervision.

17 October: In a declaration issued at the conclusion of its 10th

Summit, the Organization of Islamic Conference (OIC) called upon India to allow international human rights organizations to verify the human rights situation in Kashmir. The OIC "reaffirmed the need to establish an independent Palestinian State" and reminded the "occupying forces" in Iraq of their "obligations" under international law.

20 October: At the APEC (Asia-Pacific Economic Cooperation) Forum Summit in Singapore, leaders highlighted the need for multinational cooperation to "combat security threats and promote economic growth", especially in the Asia Pacific zone. Concerns over North Korea's nuclear weapon programme and the global anti-terror war were discussed as matters of priority.

1 November: The UN General Assembly adopted a landmark 71-article Anti-Corruption Convention that makes it mandatory for countries ratifying it to return stolen assets, outlaw bribery, and requires politicians to declare campaign finances. The Assembly also decided to raise awareness of corruption by deciding to designate 9 December as International Anti-Corruption Day.

MAJOR REGIONAL DEVELOPMENTS

EAST ASIA

10 January: North Korea announced its "immediate" withdrawal from the Nuclear Non-Proliferation Treaty (NPT). Blaming the "hostile policy of the United States" for this step, it maintained that it had no intention to produce nuclear weapons.

12 February: The IAEA (International Atomic Energy Agency) in a report to the UN Security Council said that North Korea's nuclear activities had violated its international obligations. This set the stage for possible sanctions against the country.

26 March: In yet another case of diplomatic brinkmanship, North Korea threatened to walk out of the Armistice Agreement, which had brought the Korean War to a close nearly fifty years ago. North Korea alleged that the US military continued to "violate" the Armistice Agreement and "bring the political situation on the Korean Peninsula closer to war".

23 April: The highly sensitive tripartite talks on the strategic standoff between the US and North Korea concerning Pyongyang's suspected nuclear weapons programme began in Beijing at an undisclosed location.

15 May: In a joint statement issued after the visit of the South Korean President, Roh Moo-Hyun, to Washington, the two countries reaffirmed that they would not tolerate nuclear weapons on the Peninsula.

31 July: The US Under-Secretary of State for Arms Control and International Security, John Robert Bolton, on a mission to East Asia delivered a blunt message to North Korea saying that it "must" be part of the process to resolve the issue arising out of its possession of nuclear weapon capabilities.

27 August: The six-party (China, US, Russia, South Korea, North Korea and Japan) talks on the Korean nuclear issue began in Beijing, with China setting the tone for the deliberations as both the host and the principal interlocutor.

30 August: The Democratic People's Republic of Korea (DPRK) dubbed the six-party talks, which concluded in Beijing, as a "useless" exercise. China and the US, however, said that the parleys had been a "beneficial" process.

19 October: The US President, George Bush, in Bangkok, ruled out any bilateral non-aggression pact with North Korea saying that the "burden" was on North Korea and not on America. He said that it was not only the US but also other countries such as China, South Korea, Japan and Russia who had given the "same message" asking Pyongyang to disarm.

27 October: Singapore announced a military-logistics contribution towards the reconstruction of Iraq in the context of the UN Security Council Resolution 1511 that authorized the deployment of a multinational force for the maintenance of security in Iraq.

27 November: Taiwanese lawmakers defied China's threats of war and passed a historic proposal, giving the President the power to call for an independence vote if the Island was threatened by a Chinese attack.

9 December: The Bush Administration issued in uncharacteristically blunt language a warning against "any unilateral decision by either China or Taiwan to change the status quo". The warning came ahead of the visit of the Chinese Premier to the United States.

SOUTH EAST ASIA

31 May: Myanmar's pro-democracy leader, Ms. Aung San Suu Kyi, along with 19 members of the National League for Democracy (NLD), was taken into what the military junta called "protective custody" after her supporters and pro-government protesters clashed in northern Myanmar, leaving more than a dozen people dead.

6 June: The UN Special Envoy to Myanmar, Razali Ismail, arrived in Yangon on his tenth visit to bring about substantive dialogue between the State Peace and Development Council (SPDC) and Ms. Suu Kyi and her National League for Democracy (NLD). The visit acquired significance in the context of the "detention" of Ms. Suu Kyi.

12 June: The US Senate voted overwhelmingly (97-1) to approve economic penalties against Myanmar following the military government's arrest of the pro-democracy leader Aung San Suu Kyi. The sanctions would ban US import of goods from Myanmar, freeze the assets of the ruling junta, and require the US to oppose loans to Myanmar from international financial institutions.

17 June: ASEAN ended its Annual Ministerial Meeting in Phnom Penh on the unusual note of having taken cognizance of the internal political affairs of a member state, Myanmar. There was a consensus on the demand for the early release of Aung San Suu Kyi.

29 July: The US President George Bush signed a bill, the Burmese Freedom and Democracy Act 2003, which bans import of Myanmarese products and freezes the assets of senior officials and bans virtually all remittances to the country.

5 August: Ten persons were killed and over 90 injured when a bomb blast, suspected to have been carried out by a "suicide terrorist", shook a luxury hotel in Jakarta, Indonesia.

2 November: India and Myanmar signed two agreements on enhancing joint education and research programmes and exempting visa requirements for diplomatic and official passport holders, after the arrival of the Vice-President Bhairon Singh Shekhawat to Yangon on a five-day visit.

CENTRAL ASIA

29 May: At a summit in Moscow, leaders of the six-member Shanghai Cooperation Organization (SCO) issued a joint declaration denouncing the misuse of the anti-terror war to target any religion, country or ethnic group. They maintained that the fight against terrorism must be conducted on the basis of norms and principles of international law.

23 September: Russia and Kyrgyzstan signed a formal agreement on the establishment of a Russian airbase in Kyrgyzstan. The Russian President, Vladimir Putin, at the signing ceremony held in the Kremlin along with the Kyrgyz President, Askar Akayev, said that Central Asia was a key region and Russia needed a military presence there in partnership with other partners in the Commonwealth of Independent States.

WEST ASIA

19 January: The Israeli Prime Minister, Ariel Sharon, rejected the "road map" to Palestinian statehood, formulated by the United States, the United Nations, the European Union and Russia and said that it was unrealistic and would not possibly be implemented.

27 January: The Chief UN Weapons Inspector, Hans Blix, submitting his report to the UN Security Council on 60 days of weapons inspection in Iraq, told the Council that Iraq was not fully accepting the UN resolution on disarmament.

14 February: The Chief UN Weapons Inspector Hans Blix told the UN Security Council that after more than 400 inspections at 300 sites with about 250 UN personnel, no Iraqi weapons of mass destruction (WMD) were found.

14 February: The Iraqi President Saddam Hussein issued a decree banning the import and production of chemical, biological and nuclear weapons in Iraq.

22 February: The UN Chief Weapons Inspector Hans Blix

ordered Iraq to verifiably destroy missiles with ranges that violated UN limits and gave Baghdad a 1 March deadline to begin the demolition. These included the Al-Samoud missiles and warheads, SA-2 missile engines and other components.

1 March: An Iraqi official said his country destroyed four Al-Samoud 2 missiles as ordered by United Nations weapons inspectors. On condition of anonymity, the official said the destruction occurred at 1 pm local time (06.00 IST) near the Al-Taji area, which has several factories involved in missile production. Meanwhile, the United States dismissed the Iraqi claim and declared that only full disarmament coupled with a regime change was what the United States would be satisfied with.

7 March: The UN Weapons Inspector, Hans Blix, informed a "deeply divided" Security Council that Iraq's cooperation with regard to disarmament might be termed as "substantial" and "active or even proactive". He also said that Iraq had furnished additional documentation on anthrax and the VX nerve gas agent.

25 April: Syria denounced US accusations that it was developing chemical weapons as "threats and falsifications" designed to further Israeli interests. The country's Cabinet in a statement said that the "escalated language of threats and accusations" by some American officials against Syria were aimed at damaging its "steadfastness and influencing its national decisions and (Arab) national stances".

30 April: The first Palestinian Prime Minister, Mahmoud Abbas, took office in what was considered a key step towards a US-backed "road-map" for peace in West Asia.

10 May: The US Secretary of State, Colin Powell, arrived in Israel to seek Tel Aviv's endorsement of the "road map" that envisaged creation of an independent Palestinian state based on a series of confidence-building measures that Israel and Palestine should implement.

25 May: The Israeli Cabinet, headed by the Prime Minister, Ariel Sharon, conditionally endorsed the internationally brokered "road map" for peace, formally accepting the creation of an independent Palestinian state by 2005.

13 July: The Iraqi Governing Council announced the formation of an "effective" Government with necessary powers to achieve security, revitalize the economy and provide public services although final control of Iraq would still be with Paul Bremer, the US Administrator for Iraq.

19 August: A suicide attacker set off a truck bomb outside a hotel housing the UN headquarters in Baghdad. At least 20 Iraqis and UN workers, including the Chief UN official in Iraq, Sergio Vieira de Mello, were killed and 100 others were injured.

25 August: The Palestinian leader Yasser Arafat appointed Gen. Jibril Rajoub, a former security chief in the West Bank, as the National Security Adviser in an apparent move to outflank his US-backed Prime Minister in a power struggle over control of security forces.

29 August: The visiting Palestinian Foreign Minister, Nabil Sha'ath, called on the President, A.P.J. Abdul Kalam, the Prime Minister, A.B. Vajpayee, and held delegation-level talks with the Minister of State for External Affairs. Dr. Sha'ath briefed his Indian interlocutors on the current state of the West Asian peace process.

9 September: The Israeli Prime Minister, Ariel Sharon, paid a state visit to India—the first ever by an Israeli Prime Minister. He called on the President, A.P.J. Abdul Kalam, and the Prime Minister, A.B. Vajpayee, and had delegation-level talks. The leaders identified "counter-terrorism" as the key area of cooperation between the two countries.

10 September: In a joint statement issued at the end of the visit of the Israeli Prime Minister, Ariel Sharon, to India, the two countries called for the establishment of a "just and durable peace" in West Asia.

17 September: The US vetoed a Security Council resolution that sought to protect the Palestinian leader, Yasser Arafat, from an Israeli threat to "remove" him. Washington said that while it was against the elimination of Mr. Arafat or forcing him into exile, it opposed the resolution as it failed to explicitly condemn Palestinian terror outfits such as the Hamas, the Islamic Jihad or the Al-Aqsa Martyrs Brigade.

9 November: A string of explosions carried out by suspected al-Qaeda extremists in a residential compound in Riyadh, Saudi Arabia, killed 11 people and injured 120 others. The Saudi Interior Ministry said that the dead included nationals from Saudi Arabia, Lebanon, Sudan and Egypt.

12 November: At least 22 persons, including 14 Italian armed forces personnel and 8 Iraqis were killed in a car bomb attack by Iraqi resistance forces in the southern city of Nasiriya. The explosion occurred outside the headquarters of the Italian military police base.

26 November: Iraqi resistance forces fired rockets at the compound where the visiting British Foreign Secretary, Jack Straw, was staying. Mr. Straw arrived in Baghdad on an unannounced visit.

27 November: The US President, George Bush, paid a surprise visit to Baghdad in what was described as a visit to boost the troops' morale in the face of increasing Iraqi resistance. Mr. Bush spent two and a half hours at the Baghdad international airport meeting troops.

14 December: In what was seen as a major boost to the US operations in Iraq, Saddam Hussein, the former and deposed President of Iraq, was captured from a narrow hiding hole, during a raid on a farm outside the town of Adwar, 15 km from his hometown Tikrit.

20 December: The Libyan leader, Muammar Qadhafi, said that his country was taking a "wise decision and a courageous step" to rid itself of weapons of mass destruction. Col. Qadhafi's statement followed talks with the United States and Britain.

SOUTH WEST ASIA

5 January: India, Iran, and Afghanistan concluded a trilateral meeting in Tehran after discussing alternative transit routes to Afghanistan as Pakistan refused to allow India access to the overland route to Afghanistan.

6 March: The visiting President of Afghanistan, Hamid Karzai, was assured a grant of $70 million by India for the construction of the Zaranj-Dilaram road linking Afghanistan to Iran and a deal for the handover of 300 trucks, jeeps and ambulances for the fledgling Afghan National Army.

14 March: Accusing Iran of supporting international terrorism, undermining the peace efforts in West Asia and acquiring weapons of mass destruction, the United States reimposed sanctions that would bar US citizens and firms from oil dealings with Iran.

20 April: Addressing a press conference along with the Pakistani Prime Minister, Mir Zafarullah Khan Jamali, the Afghan President, Hamid Karzai, urged Pakistan to step up vigil on its border to ensure that the remnants of al-Qaeda and the Taliban did not escape the US-led coalition forces' dragnet.

16 June: The Foreign Ministers of the European Union, meeting in Luxembourg, called on Iran to "urgently and unconditionally" accept tougher inspections by the IAEA (International Atomic Energy Agency) on its nuclear facilities.

8 July: Relations between Pakistan and the Karzai Government in Afghanistan plunged to a new low as Islamabad lodged a strong protest with Kabul over the attack of its Embassy by a mob.

20 July: Iran equipped its elite Revolutionary Guard with the locally made ballistic missile, the Shahab-3 with range of about 1,296 km.

27 August: The *Washington Post* reported that Iran had received substantial foreign assistance in building a secret nuclear facility south of its capital. It mentioned that the needle of suspicion pointed to Pakistan.

13 September: The IAEA Board gave Iran until 31 October to disprove suspicions about its nuclear programme, setting the stage for a possible UN Security Council intervention if it did not comply.

21 October: Iran, after discussions with the visiting Foreign Ministers of Britain, France and Germany in Tehran, agreed to sign the Additional Protocol to the Non-Proliferation Treaty (NPT) and fully cooperate with the IAEA.

26 October: In a report to the UN Security Council, the Under Secretary-General for Peacekeeping, Jean-Marie Guehenno, said that deteriorating security due to Taliban resurgence in Afghanistan remained a significant obstacle to the country's reconstruction.

11 November: The International Atomic Energy Agency (IAEA) in a confidential report said it had not found evidence of an atomic bomb programme in Iran, but said that Tehran was associated with activity connected with plutonium production.

14 December: Afghanistan's 500-strong Loya Jirga began a crucial meeting to approve a constitution, which would take the war-battered country to its first free elections in 2004.

17 December: Iranian representative, Ali Akbar Salehi, and Head of the IAEA, Mohamed el Baradei, signed an agreement in the IAEA's headquarters in Vienna that envisaged opening up of Iran's nuclear facilities to intrusive and unannounced inspections.

SAARC

10 July: At the SAARC Standing Committee meeting in Kathmandu, member countries endorsed by consensus the Pakistan government's proposal to host the SAARC Summit from 4-6 January 2004.

11 November: Inaugurating the Third SAARC Information Ministers Conference in New Delhi, Prime Minister A.B. Vajpayee called on the participating countries to learn from the examples of ASEAN and the post-Cold War Europe to set aside political differences and strive towards evolving arrangements for regional and sub-regional cooperation.

14 November: At the first-ever meeting of the Health Ministers of SAARC countries in New Delhi, Union Health Minister Sushma Swaraj emphasized the need for region-wide strategies to deal with the introduction of a product patent regime in the drugs sector on 2005.

24 December: The meeting of the Commerce Secretaries of the member states of the SAARC ended after a two-day discussion in Islamabad, with failure to finalize draft on the South Asian Free Trade Area (SAFTA).

AFRICA

16 October: The visiting South African President, Thabo Mbeki, and Prime Minister Atal Bihari Vajpayee, in New Delhi, signed a number of agreements that included, among others, an extradition treaty, a mutual legal assistance treaty, an agreement for cooperation in the field of power and a cultural exchange programme.

21 October: While addressing the Parliament of Sudan at Khartoum, the President A.P.J. Kalam suggested a partnership between India and Sudan in building capabilities for oil exploration, refining and marketing of value-added oil-based products.

LATIN AMERICA

20 October: India and Brazil underlined the need for WTO negotiations, which collapsed at the Cancun meeting of Ministers in September, to resume at an early date. The call came after visiting Brazilian Minister of External Relations Celso Amorin met Commerce Minister Arun Jaitley in New Delhi.

21 October: The visiting Brazilian Minister of External Relations, Celso Amorin, told the media in New Delhi that India, Brazil and South Africa were three "natural candidates" to enter the United Nations Security Council as permanent members. He said that the three countries working together would be important for reforming the Security Council.

IV

Select Documents

India's Statement on 'Operationalisation' of Nuclear Doctrine, 4 January 2003

[Editor's Note: This statement was issued by the Government of India on the basis of a decision taken by the Cabinet Committee on Security on 4 January 2003.]

The Cabinet Committee on Security (CCS) met today to review the progress in operationalising of India's nuclear doctrine. The Committee decided that the following information, regarding the nuclear doctrine and operational arrangements governing India's nuclear assets, should be shared with the public.

2. India's nuclear doctrine can be summarized as follows:

(i) Building and maintaining a credible minimum deterrent.

(ii) A posture of "No First Use": nuclear weapons will only be used in retaliation against a nuclear attack on Indian territory or on Indian forces anywhere.

(iii) Nuclear retaliation to a first strike will be massive and designed to inflict unacceptable damage.

(iv) Nuclear retaliatory attacks can only be authorised by the civilian political leadership through the Nuclear Command Authority.

(v) Non-use of nuclear weapons against non-nuclear weapon states.

(vi) However, in the event of a major attack against India, or Indian forces anywhere, by biological or chemical weapons, India will retain the option of retaliating with nuclear weapons.

(vii) A continuance of strict controls on export of nuclear and missile related materials and technologies, participation in the Fissile Material Cutoff Treaty negotiations, and continued observance of the moratorium on nuclear tests.

(viii) Continued commitment to the goal of a nuclear weapon free world, through global, verifiable and non-discriminatory nuclear disarmament.

3. The Nuclear Command Authority comprises a Political Council and an Executive Council. The Political Council is chaired by the

Prime Minister. It is the sole body which can authorise the use of nuclear weapons.

4. The Executive Council is chaired by the National Security Advisor. It provides inputs for decision making by the Nuclear Command Authority and executes the directives given to it by the Political Council.
5. The CCS reviewed the existing command and control structures, the state of readiness, the targeting strategy for a retaliatory attack, and operating procedures for various stages of alert and launch. The Committee expressed satisfaction with the overall preparedness. The CCS approved the appointment of a Commander-in-Chief, Strategic Forces Command, to manage and administer all Strategic Forces.
6. The CCS also reviewed and approved the arrangements for alternate chains of command for retaliatory nuclear strikes in all eventualities.

[*Source:* Indian Ministry of External Affairs, http://meadev.nic.in/news/official/ 20030104/official.htm]

The New Delhi Declaration between the Republic of India and the Islamic Republic of Iran, 25 January 2003

The Republic of India and the Islamic Republic of Iran:

Conscious of the vast potential in the political, economic, transit, transport, energy, industries, science and technology and agricultural fields and of the benefits of cooperative endeavour,

Determined to build a strong, modern, contemporary and cooperative relationship that draws upon their historical and age-old cultural ties, the advantage of geographical proximity, and that responds to the needs of an interdependent world of the 21st century,

Aware that their strengthened bilateral relations also contribute to regional cooperation, peace, prosperity and stability,

Recalling and reaffirming the Tehran Declaration issued on April 10, 2001 jointly by H.E. Shri A.B. Vajpayee, Prime Minister of India and H.E. Hojjatoleslam Seyyed Mohammad Khatami, President of the Islamic Republic of Iran, which resulted in further strengthening of dialogue aimed at strategic cooperation,

Declare as follows:

1. International developments since the adoption of the Tehran Declaration have reinforced their faith in and reconfirmed the values of pluralism, diversity and tolerance within and between societies.
2. International peace and stability, harmony between different religions, ethnic and linguistic groups, cultures and social systems can best be promoted through dialogue and acceptance of the right to one's own beliefs and values expressed and exercised without injury or slight to those of others and without a desire to impose them on others. In this context, they positively assessed the contribution made by the concept of Dialogue among Civilizations to address discord and differences in international relations.

3. They evaluate positively the consolidation of Indo-Iranian bilateral relations since the Tehran Declaration. Meetings of the Joint Commission, the Strategic Dialogue, interaction between the Security Councils of the two countries, discussions on energy and security, and cooperation based on existing complementarities and diverse possibilities, including supplies, exploration, investment, exchange of technical expertise, and other interaction at government and private sector levels have all contributed to deepening of mutual understanding and confidence, which has provided, in turn, the basis for further consolidation.
4. The two sides welcome the fresh impetus given to Science and Technology cooperation as also to cooperation in education and training since last year. They also note the potential of technologies, such as IT, to improve the lives of people in developing societies and agree to promote cooperation efforts to exploit this potential. They agree to promote fuller utilisation of available capabilities for human resource development.
5. The two sides affirm that their growing strategic convergence needs to be underpinned with a strong economic relationship, including greater trade and investment flows. The Ministerial-level Joint Commission, the Joint Business Council and economic and commercial agreements signed recently in this regard will play a critical role in this regard. They exhort the entrepreneurs in both countries to harness each other's strengths for mutual benefit and promote the process of economic rapprochement actively, including through expert studies on trade and investment facilitation, holding of exhibitions and seminars, promotion of business travel, and joint ventures.
6. They note that the enabling legislations to promote vigorous trade and economic exchanges are primary requirements to promote business confidence between the entrepreneurs of the two countries. Many arrangements have already been concluded in this field. To consolidate the bilateral business environment further, they agree on the need to undertake expeditious negotiations, inter alia, for the conclusion of the Bilateral

Investment Promotion and Protection Agreement, Double Taxation Avoidance Agreement and MoU on Energy Cooperation.

7. India and Iran have a complementarity of interests in the energy sector which should develop as a strategic area of their future relationship. Iran with its abundant energy resources and India with its growing energy needs as a rapidly developing economy are natural partners. The areas of cooperation in this sector include investment in upstream and downstream activities in the oil sector, LNG/natural gas tie-ups and secure modes of transport.

8. They also decided to explore opportunities for cooperation in defence in agreed areas, including training and exchange of visits.

9. They agreed to explore mechanisms to preserve and maintain the common cultural heritage, rooted in history, of the two countries. As part of efforts dedicated to preservation of this heritage, they agreed to release a commemorative postage stamp.

10. Terrorism continues to pose a serious threat to nation States and international peace and security and should be eradicated. States that aid, abet and directly support international terrorism should be condemned. The international community should intensify its efforts to combat the menace of terrorism. They reiterate their resolve to strengthen the international consensus and legal regimes against terrorism, including early finalization of a Comprehensive Convention against International Terrorism. They agree that the combat against international terrorism should not be selective or based on double standards. Iran and India agree to continue joint cooperation to address the issues of international terrorism and trafficking in narcotic and psychotropic substances.

11. Both sides stressed that the interests of peace and stability in the region are best served by a strong, united, prosperous and independent Afghanistan. They assess highly the past and continuing cooperation between India and Iran in support of a united, sovereign and independent Afghanistan. They urge the international community to remain committed on long-term basis to the reconstruction and development of Afghanistan, to

controlling re-emergence of terrorist forces, and spread of narcotics from Afghanistan. They agree that stability of Afghanistan is vital for the stability of the region. The recent trilateral agreement between the Governments of India, Iran and Afghanistan to develop the Chahbahar route through Melak, Zaranj and Delaram would facilitate regional trade and transit, including to Afghanistan and Central Asia, contributing thus to enhanced regional economic prosperity.

12. The two sides note with satisfaction the operationalisation of the North South transit arrangement and the growing interest among other States in the region to participate in it. They reaffirm their commitment to develop the full potential of the North South arrangement, its infrastructure, desired certification and customs harmonisation, expert studies and regular evaluation to aid its growth.

13. India and Iran support efforts to resolve the situation relating to Iraq peacefully through political and diplomatic means under the auspices of the United Nations.

14. The two sides reiterated their commitment to commence multilateral negotiations for nuclear disarmament under effective international control. They expressed their concern about restrictions imposed on the export of materials, technology and equipment to developing countries and acknowledged the right of these countries to research, production and use of technology, material and equipment for peaceful purposes.

15. The two countries are resolved to exploit the full potential of the bilateral relationship in the interest of the people of the two countries and of regional peace and stability, and recognising that the 21st Century holds unbound promises of welfare and progress through peaceful application of science and technology, promoting knowledge based societies, and tackling fundamental problems such as disease, hunger and environmental degradation.

16. They directed that a time bound framework be worked out in agreed areas of cooperation, through the existing mechanisms of Joint Commission and Joint Working Groups, so that a firm and substantial economic and political underpinning would be

provided for a strategic and long-term orientation to the bilateral relationship.

Signed on the 25th Day of January 2003 at New Delhi in two originals, each in Hindi, Persian and English languages.

Prime Minister Republic of India President Islamic Republic of Iran

[*Source:* http://meaindia.nic.in]

Statement of Principles for U.S.-India High Technology Commerce, 6 February 2003

During their November 2001 meeting in Washington D.C., Prime Minister Vajpayee and President Bush affirmed their commitment to qualitatively transform India-U.S. relations. They further agreed that the two sides should discuss ways to stimulate bilateral high technology commerce as a step toward enhancing the new relationship between the United States and India.

In pursuit of this goal, the Governments of the United States and India decided in November 2002 to work expeditiously toward developing a new statement of principles regarding bilateral cooperation in high technology trade, including trade in "dual-use" goods and technologies, in a way that broadly advances the relationship between the two countries in this area and reinforces their mutual interest in stemming the proliferation of sensitive goods and technologies.

The two Governments have set forth the principles to further promote and facilitate bilateral high technology commerce in its broadest sense:

1. The two Governments note that there is immense untapped potential for India-U.S. high technology commerce and recognize the importance of taking steps to remove systemic tariff and non-tariff barriers, identify and generate awareness of market opportunities, and build additional confidence in the two countries for such trade, in a way that reflects their new relationship and common strategic interests.
2. The two Governments recognize that the private sectors in India and the United States are important partners in this endeavor.
3. The two Governments should focus on steps to create the appropriate environment for successful high technology commerce. The Government of India appreciates the importance that the Government of the United States attaches to a supportive regulatory and institutional environment in India for robust bilateral high technology commerce, including easing barriers to

such commerce. The Government of India intends to do its utmost in this regard.

4. The two Governments should seek to identify market opportunities in high technology commerce and related regulations that affect such commerce.
5. The two Governments, in partnership with the private sector, should consider steps for trade promotion efforts to generate awareness about market potential, relevant regulatory issues, collaboration opportunities, and financing possibilities.
6. The two Governments understand the importance of enhancing trade between India and the United States in "dual-use" items, including controlled "dual use" goods and technologies, while protecting the national security and foreign policy interests of both countries, and intend to take steps to facilitate such trade, which is a component of high technology commerce.
7. The two Governments should encourage outreach and educational activities to ensure that the private sectors in India and the United States have full and accurate information regarding the export control laws, regulations, and policies of the two countries.
8. The two Governments attach the highest importance to preventing the proliferation of sensitive goods and technologies. They further recognize the importance of continuing their export control cooperation program and activities to achieve the shared goal of strengthening export control systems through laws, regulations, and enforcement, in accordance with modern export control standards.
9. The Government of the United States appreciates the importance that the Government of India attaches to the widest possible access to U.S. "dual-use" goods and technologies and to efficiency, continuity, stability, and transparency in the export license application process. The Government of the United States intends to do its utmost in this regard, consistent with its laws and national security and foreign policy objectives, including compliance with international commitments.

10. The two Governments recognize that U.S. "dual-use" export controls currently apply to only a very small fraction of total U.S.-India high technology commerce, and that a broad range of "dual-use" goods and technologies is currently available to India.
11. The Government of the United States should seek to identify and review licensing processes and policies for exports to India of goods and technologies controlled for reasons of anti-terrorism (AT), crime control (CC), encryption (EI), national security (NS), regional stability (RS), and short supply (SS), in a manner that seeks to facilitate further trade in these "dual-use" goods and technologies.
12. For authorized transfers of "dual-use" goods and technologies controlled for missile technology or nuclear proliferation reasons, including exports to entities in civilian space and civilian nuclear energy fields, the Government of India will consider a mutually satisfactory system of assurances regarding end use, diversion, transfers and retransfers within and outside India, re-export, and, where necessary, physical protection and access to the controlled items by third parties.
13. The two Governments should examine cooperative steps to ensure that all parties adhere to license conditions for "dual-use" goods and technologies and should outline the manner in which suspected violations and infractions are to be addressed. The Government of India will cooperate with the Government of the United States in verifying Indian end users and end uses.
14. The two Governments should seek to keep each other informed about changes in their export control laws, regulations, and policies; exchange information on export licenses that are approved, denied, or returned without action; and establish a mechanism for prompt discussion of any bilateral "dual-use" export control issues.
15. This Statement of Principles constitutes the basis for further steps to enhance high technology commerce between the two countries.
16. The two Governments plan to convene as soon as possible the India-U.S. High Technology Cooperation Group (HTCG), decided upon in November 2002, to further this Statement of

Principles and develop a schedule of meetings and activities for this purpose.

(Signed)

Kenneth I. Juster
Under Secretary
U.S. Department of Commerce

Kanwal Sibal
Foreign Secretary
Indian Ministry of External Affairs

[*Source:* http://www.bxa.doc.gov/news/2003/IndiaStatePrinciples.htm]

Statement by Mr. Brajesh Mishra, National Security Adviser, Government of India, on "Global Fight Against Terrorism: Status and Perspectives", at the 39th Munich Conference on Security Policy, 9 February 2003

I thank you for this opportunity to be here once again, to participate and share my views in this Conference.

In this same forum, we discussed last year the threat to democratic societies from the globalisation of terror. That was a few months after the gruesome terrorist attacks of September 11, when the world was still coming to terms with their implications for all of humanity. Nearly a year and a half later, it is worthwhile to assess where we have reached in the global war against terrorism, which we declared through an international coalition and codified through UN Security Council Resolution 1373.

One truth, which is now generally accepted, is that global terrorism did not start on September 11, 2001. That date does, however, mark the dawn of a global recognition of this monster of international terrorism. It also heralded the declaration of the global war against terrorism. The international coalition against terrorism is the broadest group of countries outside of the United Nations and the Nonaligned Movement.

One knows when a war begins but it is more difficult to know where or when it ends. After 16 months of the global fight against terrorism, we can only be certain about the fact that it is far from over. The headquarters of Al-Qaeda may have been destroyed, but its leaders are still at large. Its patron, the Taliban government has been ousted from Kabul, but we already see a regrouping of Taliban elements in areas of southern and South-eastern Afghanistan.

In any case, we should have grasped by now that international terrorism will not die with the Al-Qaeda. As the variety and scale of incidents over the past year in Bali, Moscow and many other places indicate, its networks are still operational, and a very large number of Al-Qaeda's allied, subordinate and "like-minded" organizstions are still flourishing. Arrests in different parts of UK, France, Spain, Italy and Germany, repeatedly remind us of the extensive nature of the linkages. There is also today the real danger that terrorists might get access to weapons of mass destruction and high technology in the pursuit of their endeavours.

An important lesson to us from the past 16 months, therefore, is that the fight against terrorism is a long haul, and not a swift surgical operation. The instrument of this fight has to be an internally self-consistent international regime, with the broadest possible participation and genuine cooperation in its strict compliance.

In this global cooperative effort, the international community is still at the beginning of the learning curve. In Security Council Resolution 1373, we have a comprehensive and powerful statement of intent, which has been further reinforced in the recent Resolution 1456. But we have not as yet translated their provisions into effective mechanisms for monitoring and enforcing compliance.

So far, the Counter-Terrorism Committee has restricted itself to scrutinising reports of Member States and helping them to identify gaps in their national anti-terrorist legislation. However, it is also crucially important to fully implement the provisions for punishing those who finance, sponsor and harbour terrorists. We have to seriously consider how to give more teeth to the Counter-Terrorism Committee to enforce implementation and to deal with non-compliance.

It is most unfortunate that some diversionary arguments are still blocking a consensus on important anti-terrorist conventions and continue to impede efforts for a united and coherent international anti-terrorist strategy.

Sixteen months after the worst terrorist actions in the world, an agreed definition of terrorism still eludes the international community. Distinctions between freedom fighters and terrorists propagate a bizarre logic, which glorifies massacres of one set of innocent civilians, while condemning killings of others. We have to settle this argument, once and for all, on the civilised principle that the right to life of innocent people cannot be superseded by a right to kill them for some political cause, or to redress some real or imagined historical wrong.

Another red herring is the fallacy that terrorism can only be eradicated by addressing its "root causes". This is nonsense. Terrorism is defined by the act, not by the attributes or the description of its perpetrators. Moreover, democratic societies, which address the root causes of alienation and anger, through pluralism, tolerance and socio-economic justice, are precisely the targets of terrorism.

While we indulge in such tortured searches for definitions and first causes, we gravely risk condoning—and even promoting—the destruction of the political harmony, economic structure and social balance of our societies by terrorism.

These are views and concerns, which India has repeatedly expressed, but I am recalling them because they are of vital significance to us. We see a contradiction in attempts to insulate developments across the Pakistan-Afghanistan border from the cross-border terrorism we face. If the perpetrators of the latter are different from the Al-Qaeda groups which targeted the World Trade Centres, it is only in their names and bank account numbers—not in their ideology, objectives or sponsors. The novel version of democracy, which Pakistan recently unveiled, has brought in more religious extremist forces into the polity, particularly on the Afghanistan border. The safe havens for Al-Qaeda and Taliban elements may expand in consequence. If you also remember that Pakistan's nuclear assets are believed to be stored in tunnels and caves in the Chagai Hills of Baluchistan, our concerns should be obvious. Persistent reports of the freelance activities of some Pakistani nuclear scientists only add to our disquiet.

A larger-than-life obsession with the "global" Al-Qaeda group results in inadequate political consultations and selective intelligence sharing on the global terrorist threat. This has led to some costly gaps in the campaign against international terrorism. The international terrorist today has a network of wide geographical spread, instant communications through the internet, and a well-oiled machinery for movement of his lethal equipment, evading national customs, tariffs and non-tariff barriers. He can only be thwarted by international counter-terrorist coordination.

I had drawn attention to this in my presentation here last year. What we have to recognise is that in terrorism, the democratic world today faces the greatest existential threat to its ideology and its way of life. Compartmentalised national approaches cannot deal with the seamless web of international linkages which terrorism has developed. Real-time information sharing and operational intelligence co-operation can help to integrate diversely collected bits of data into an interlocking coherent jigsaw. Analysis of data can be enriched by involving those who are familiar with the cultural subtleties and the local idiom of its origin.

If we look back over the development of a global response to international terrorism, it is a mixed picture. Obviously, September 11, 2001 shocked the world out of complacency and jolted it into a series of immediate and strong actions—seeking a broad-based international coalition, passing a Security Council Resolution, militarily pursuing the Al-Qaeda, etc. It was a process during which the world gradually absorbed the ugly reality of global terrorism, and responded as it went along, groping for the right answers.

If we agree—as I think most would today—that the fight against terrorism is a long haul, we then need a coherent conceptual framework within which its objectives can be defined and pursued. That is what I meant when I said earlier that we need an internally self-consistent regime.

During the Cold War, the Western countries had fashioned a grand strategy to counter and roll back communism. Of course, India did not subscribe to that strategy. I am using the analogy here only to highlight that the objective of countering and rolling back terrorism requires the same level of single-minded commitment and conceptual clarity. As you did during the Cold War days, we need to understand the nature of the adversary, build a homogeneous alliance to counter it, determine the doctrine of engagement and plan for the required instruments of that engagement.

International terrorism is neither definable within geographical boundaries nor within the traditional moulds of rationality. The global terrorist does not owe loyalty to a national flag, does not defend a people, claims innocent lives as legitimate victims and seeks martyrdom in suicide missions. The threat from him is magnified by the very real prospect of non-state actors acquiring weapons of mass destruction. It is a situation of asymmetry in which normal deterrence—which is predicated on rational behaviour—is unlikely to be credible. Defences against such an adversary are necessarily imperfect; hence pragmatic justification can be advanced for counter-attack and even pre-emption.

We have recognised that the targets of international terrorism are democratic societies. There is, therefore, no conceptual ambiguity in identifying a group of democratic countries in the world as a viable alliance against terrorism.

In the immediate aftermath of September 11, there was the understandable urge to form as broad a coalition against terrorism as possible to display overwhelming superiority and to impose a decisive defeat on the adversary. This immediate expediency necessarily meant that the coalition can only be a short-term alliance to deal with a particular manifestation of terrorism. If international terrorism is defined as the adversary, the coalition contains members who are part of the problem.

To define the component elements of a natural alliance against terrorism, we recognise that three core principles define the strategic paradigm of the 21st century world: peaceful co-existence and dialogue as the basis of relations between countries and resolution of differences; democracy as the optimal means of organising internal affairs of countries; and liberal market structures to harness the forces of globalisation for economic development. Countries subscribing to these principles form a natural alliance with the shared aspirations to safeguard peace, promote pluralism and maximise economic growth with social justice. These are the very objectives which global terrorism attacks—by spreading disorder, generating fear, promoting exclusivism and intolerance, rejecting modernity and diminishing human life.

Such a group of like-minded countries with a genuine commitment to democracy would also more naturally develop the multi-lateral institutions and the multi-national coordination required to counter terrorism. They would not get bogged down in definitional and causal arguments of the kind we witness today. Blocking financial supplies, disrupting networks, sharing intelligence, simplifying extradition procedures—these are preventive measures which can only be effective through international cooperation based on trust and shared values.

It is an alliance of this nature which will have the political will and moral authority to take bold decisions on pre-emption and retribution which may be required in extreme cases of terrorist provocation. Multilateral legitimisation of such pre-emption would carry a special validity.

I am not ignoring the fact that any strategy in the real world requires a balance between values and interests. Excessive realism produces untenable quick-fixes; excessive idealism leads to crusades and disillusionment. My point is that while we work within a coalition against international terrorism with a heterogeneous composition pursuing differing and even clashing objectives, a core has to gradually emerge within this coalition which exerts a persistent pressure for creation of an eventual alliance which will take on international terrorism in a holistic, focused manner. The partners in that alliance would be those countries which have a stake in defending the core principles of the 21st century. Regimes promoting policies which breed radicalism and extremism can never be long-term allies in this battle. It is the liberal, progressive and moderate societies, which can qualify.

The balance between values and realpolitik has to shift more towards values, if this has to happen. Short-term pragmatism should not obscure a long-term vision.

Thank you.

[*Source:* http://www.meadev.nic.in/speeches/NSA-39thMunich.htm]

Speech by Mr. Yashwant Sinha, External Affairs Minister of India on India's Foreign Policy Today, at the Diplomatic Academy, Moscow, 20 February 2003

Your Excellency Mr. Yuri Fokin, Rector of the Academy, Distinguished Guests, Ladies and Gentlemen,

I am delighted to be here amongst you today. Having been Co-Chairman of the Inter Governmental Commission for almost five years, I am no stranger to Russia. It is always a pleasure to return to this beautiful city. I understand that the bi-centennial of the Russian Foreign Ministry was celebrated on 8th February as the Day of the Russian Diplomat. I am aware that this Academy which was set up in 1938 has played an extremely important role in grooming generations of Russian diplomats over the years. I am, therefore, honoured that the Academy has provided me this opportunity to share some thoughts on India's foreign policy today.

The foreign policy of any major country is a direct reflection of its overall national policies, its goals for the future, and self-perception of its role and destiny in the world. Permit me therefore to begin with a few words on where India is today and the future it sees for itself. India is the fourth largest economy in the world on the basis of Purchasing Power Parity. The Indian economy has grown at an average rate of around 6% for over a decade and has emerged as one of the fastest growing economies in the world. At the time of independence, India was a food deficit country dependent on imports from outside. Today India has nearly 50 million tonnes of surplus food grains and exports grain to many parts of the world. In 1991, India faced a severe macro economic deficit. Today, our foreign exchange reserves have crossed US$73 billion. As opposed to policies aimed at conserving foreign exchange in the past at any cost, we are now encouraging Indian companies to go abroad and establish permanent stakes in the rest of the world. A good example in this regard is the Oil & Natural Gas Commission (ONGC) of India which with a view to advancing India's energy security, has invested not only in Russia but also in Libya, Syria, Iran, Myanmar and Vietnam. The ONGC is also seeking similar opportunities in Sudan, Kazakhstan, Qatar, Indonesia and Venezuela. It is widely acknowledged that India's human resources are among the best in the world. Our space, nuclear science, bio-tech and other high-tech capabilities are a matter of pride. India's success in the field of software development is also well known.

Friends, all the above has been achieved by India within a democratic framework and without any dilution in our commitment to the building of an open, free and pluralistic society. India's democracy is an article of faith for the over one billion people of our country and we have successfully welded together within this democratic framework, a nation of extraordinary linguistic, cultural, religious and ethnic diversity. India today faces the future and the world with confidence and optimism.

Ladies and gentlemen, this self-assurance and a sense of achievement also permeate India's foreign policy. It is not easy to spell out within one single speech all aspects of India's foreign policy. Permit me, therefore, to briefly outline some of our recent efforts vis-à-vis three groups of countries—major powers, India's immediate and extended neighbourhood and our traditional friends and allies. I would also like to discuss the subject of terrorism which both Russia and India believe is one of the most important challenges confronted by the world in the 21st century. India's relations with Russia have over the last decade graduated to a level of close strategic partnership. We have institutionalised annual summits between our leaders. India understands Russia's security concerns in Europe, Central Asia and the Caucasus. At the same time, we have received understanding from Russia on our concerns. Neither country perceives a threat from the strength of the other and each perceives a stake in the increased political and economic power of the other. Our cooperation in combating terrorism is older than the coalition created after September 11. As President Putin pointed out in his address to the Indian Parliament in October 2000 itself, "the same individuals, the same terrorist and extremist organisations are involved in terrorist acts from the Philippines to Kosovo, including in Jammu & Kashmir, Afghanistan and Chechnya". India and Russia have together created a sound legal basis for cooperation in combating international terrorism. Among our common challenges is also one relating to WMD proliferation and its linkages to terrorism. In fact, there is much we can do together as partners against proliferation.

Our extensive relations encompass today intense political dialogue at various levels, close cooperation in the areas of defence, science and technology, atomic energy, space, culture, etc. During the visit of President Putin to India in December 2002, both sides accorded special emphasis and attention to economic, scientific and technical cooperation. It was noted that this has not kept pace with the political relationship. A document on enhancing trade and investment was signed, which lays down the direction of bilateral interaction in this area for the foreseeable future. As two large and modernising economies, we share similar perspectives on the pace and direction of the globalisation process. We also have the complementarities to exploit opportunities created by economic liberalisation and technology diffusion to our mutual advantage.

India and Russia have identified high value and hi-tech items for cooperation like information technology, diamonds, energy etc. The Oil and Natural Gas Commission (ONGC) of India is investing nearly US$1.7 billion in the Sakhalin-I project. This is the highest overseas investment ever by an Indian company. We are interested in further expansion of cooperation in oil and gas sector to include joint activities in third countries also. Under the framework of energy security, India and Russia are also cooperating in nuclear energy. The ongoing construction of the Kudankulum Nuclear Plant with Russian participation is an example. This year the two sides will organise trade fairs in each other's countries. As we speak, an Indian trade fair is being held in Moscow with the participation of around 300 Indian companies.

India and Russia have had substantial military-technical cooperation over many decades. A significant proportion of the military equipment of India's three armed services is of Russian (or Soviet) manufacture. Our cooperation in this field already includes joint design, development and production of new weapons systems. The historical perspective of defence relations between our two countries is being advanced further through the successful development of the Brahmos cruise missile. We will also be jointly developing a fifth generation fighter aircraft.

My current visit to Russia has been extremely rewarding. We have had wide ranging and open exchange of views on a number of bilateral and economic issues, in the spirit of strategic partnership that exists between our two countries. We have also exchanged views on a number of issues confronting the global community today.

Let me now turn to India's relations with other major countries. Our relations with the U.S. have undergone a sea-change in the last decade. Over 15 institutional forums have been established which meet regularly. Special attention is being paid to security and defence cooperation as well as trade and investment. The US is our largest trading partner (US$23 billion in goods and services in 2002), the predominant destination of our IT services exports (US$5.7 billion last year) and the major source of foreign investments. The European Union is another key trading partner of India and an important investor of capital. The strategic partnership between India and the EU is based on shared values such as democracy, pluralism and liberalism. We have had annual Summit-level interaction with the EU since the year 2000. India also has warm and friendly relations with the entire range of Central and Eastern European countries, many of whom are now hopeful of entry into the European Union. Our trade ties with these countries have been on the up-swing for the past few years and Indian firms have participated in their disinvestment and privatisation process.

In August 2002, India and Japan agreed on a Global Partnership in the 21st century. During her recent visit to Delhi, Japanese Foreign Minister Kawaguchi spoke of Japan's strategic partnership with India and India's pivotal role in their vision to create a pan-Asian economic area extending from East to South Asia. There is also cooperation amongst the two countries to ensure the security of sea lanes.

Our relations with China are following a positive course. There is steady effort to overcome past differences and build a convergence of interests. Bilateral trade between India and China last year was over US $4.5 billion. India's relations with China are and will remain forward looking and infused with a sense of optimism. They will be based on the conviction that a prosperous India is inevitable. So is a strong and prosperous China. Our objective is to sustain the steady expansion and strengthening of relations in diverse fields even as we attempt to resolve the border issue and address other issues of concern.

India has achieved rapid growth in understanding with Iran. Both countries are interested in forging a long-term strategic relationship built around energy security and transit arrangements. Iran is ready to work with India to provide viable and rapid access to Afghanistan, Central Asia and Russia and some projects have already been agreed upon. We believe that India and Iran have shared geo-political interests in the pursuit of which our region can be knit into networks of economic cooperation.

Turning to India's neighbourhood, let me begin with the South Asian Association for Regional Cooperation (SAARC). It is a matter of disappointment that despite having come formally into existence 17 years ago, SAARC is still to make progress with regard to its primary objective of economic cooperation between its members. Pakistan denies India even the most elementary MFN treatment. Further between India and Pakistan, there are only 18 items out of over 7000 tariff lines where we give each other preferential tariff. Similarly, with Bangladesh, there are 2672 items where India gives preferential tariff. India gets preferential tariff from Bangladesh in only 484 items. India has expressed its readiness to enter into a free trade arrangement in SAARC with immediate effect. We have also suggested that countries of South Asia should move forward and think of a South Asian Union in future. India is willing to go to any length to improve relations with her immediate neighbours. All she asks in return is that they respect and remain sensitive to her security concerns.

India is a member of the ASEAN Regional Forum, where we have excellent cooperative relations with Russia. We are also a summit partner with the ASEAN since last year. Recognising the positive role India can play in the region, ASEAN countries have actively engaged India. We have responded with efforts to craft special trade and investment arrangements including through an India-ASEAN

Free Trade Area to be brought about in 10 years, a BIMST-EC (Bangladesh, India, Myanmar, Sri Lanka, Thailand-Economic Cooperation) FTA as also bilateral arrangements such as the India-Thailand FTA and India-Singapore Comprehensive Economic Cooperation Agreement. BIMST-EC and Mekong-Ganga Cooperation (involving India, Thailand, Myanmar, Vietnam, Cambodia and Laos) are other important structural frameworks of India's "Look-East" policy. We are also working on a trilateral highway project between India, Myanmar and Thailand. Connectivity, canalising resources and policy coordination among India and the countries in the region are the tasks that lie ahead. India's historical links with Central Asia provide an asset for building important relationships with these countries with whom we are exploring new avenues of cooperation and new routes by land, air and sea. India was amongst the first to establish diplomatic missions in all the Central Asian States. We have participated in the Conference on Interaction and Confidence Building Measures in Asia (CICA) process from the beginning. We are also interested in the Shanghai Cooperation Organisation. In this regard, may I also mention that India has been actively participating in the reconstruction of Afghanistan since the overthrow of the Taliban regime. We have earmarked US $100 million worth of assistance to Afghanistan of which one-third has been already provided. Our assistance includes wheat, buses, civilian airplanes and human resources training in various fields including in computers. We are negotiating a preferential trade agreement with Afghanistan and also developing transit routes to Afghanistan through the Chahbahar port of Iran. We believe that India and Russia have a commonality of strategic interests in Central Asia and Afghanistan.

As many of you would be aware, the biggest challenge to relations in India's neighbourhood comes from Pakistan which has persistently refused to shed its compulsive hostility. Pakistan is today, unfortunately, the epicentre of international terrorism. The Taliban and Al Qaeda, displaced from Afghanistan have re-emerged in the North West Frontier Province and Baluchistan in Pakistan and there is indication that efforts to destabilise the region are being resumed. India sincerely seeks good relations with Pakistan. There is however no possibility of making progress in this direction unless and until Pakistan fulfils its commitment to destroy the infrastructure on its territory which trains, finances as well as sponsors terrorism and brings to an end cross-border infiltration. Here too India and Russia have a common position. India has always maintained a high level of commitment to improving relations with traditional friends in the developing countries. We have, with the intention of modernising our relations with fellow developing countries of Latin America and Africa, launched a special drive to strengthen trade and economic relations, through special bilateral and multilateral trading arrangements. We are pursuing FTAs/PTAs with Brazil, Uruguay, MERCOSUR and other regional organisations in Latin America. A delegation from the Common Market in East and Southern Africa (COMESA), led by the Foreign Minister of Mauritius, was in New Delhi recently for the conclusion of an India-COMESA MoU spanning diverse facets of economic cooperation. We are also negotiating an FTA with South Africa, the largest African economy.

As many of you are aware, the Non-Aligned Movement is to hold its summit in Kuala Lumpur a few days from now. India continues to attach importance to this Movement which represents the collective voice of the developing world. We believe an organisation of developing countries such as NAM remains relevant even in the post-Cold War world and proof of that rests in the fact that even today, membership of NAM is growing.

Let me now turn to the issue of terrorism. Terrorism is among the greatest challenges to democratic societies and international stability. The wounds inflicted by terrorism on India and Russia went unnoticed by the world. The events of September 11 have, however, created greater awareness of this phenomenon. In the global war against terrorism, there can be no room for double standards, of distinction between terrorism that can be tolerated and one that cannot, of terrorism directed against the West and that directed against the others, of the former being untarnished evil and the latter requiring resolution of its root causes. Some progress has been made since September 11 in strengthening cooperation in the field of counter terrorism. But we still have to develop new paradigms of international cooperation based on actionable intelligence. We have to develop new technologies, systems and institutions for the protection of our people. We have to systematically target financial and communication networks of terrorists and their safe havens.

The experience of Afghanistan teaches us that we have to deal with failing or failed States not only for the suffering that their own people undergo, but to prevent terrorists from exploiting the chaos to inflict suffering on people elsewhere. Most of all, we must develop a consensus on how to deal with sovereign states, whose policies, social ethos and institutions breed the mindset that sustains international terrorism. The nexus between terrorism and weapons of mass destruction is frightening and there is today grave danger of these weapons falling into the hands of terrorist outfits. There is also growing incidence of proliferation of weapons of mass destruction and delivery systems, as a result of conscious political and strategic choice by governments. Some of these countries not only have links with terrorism, but also avowed policies to change the status quo through force or resort to nuclear blackmail. These are issues which are of particular concern to India because the best example of a conjunction between authoritarian rule, support for terrorism, weapons of mass destruction, proliferation and drug trafficking is to be found in the neighbourhood of India. These are concerns shared by Russia and the rest of the international community.

Ironically, regimes of technology denial, created in the name of non-proliferation are being maintained even in the face of mounting evidence of their failure to prevent proliferation. The case of North Korea's nuclear development programme and Pakistan's involvement is the most recent illustration. Pakistan's own clandestine acquisitions of nuclear technology and missiles as well as related technology were earlier instances. These denial regimes have neither been negotiated multilaterally nor are they effective in preventing proliferation to irresponsible regimes. However, they are used to deny developmental tools to States such as India with impeccable non-proliferation credentials. As a developing economy, there is a pressing demand in India for energy security. Nuclear power generation provides a clean, viable alternative. But, international cooperation in civilian nuclear power generation remains hostage to denial regimes such as the above insisting on "club" rules rather than genuine non-proliferation. India will continue to place emphasis on multilateral efforts to establish instruments and norms that will enhance respect for international law rather than perpetuate the concept of unilateral advantage, whether in the field of security or trade or other areas of international interaction.

Finally, a few words on a country which today is under great international focus. Iraq was once the source of 30 per cent of India's oil needs and home to 90,000 Indians working in that country. India believes that every effort should be made to avoid war and find a peaceful solution to the current crisis. For this to happen, it is imperative that Iraq complies with the UN Resolutions and extends full cooperation to UNMOVIC and IAEA, so that any lingering questions about eliminating weapons of mass destruction are removed. With over three million Indian expatriates in the Gulf region, we are concerned about military action in Iraq. India, like other developing countries also has special concern with regard to volatility of oil prices and security of oil supplies. The crisis over Iraq is one of the biggest challenges ever faced by the U.N. We hope the international community will show the wisdom to prevent an erosion of the credibility and legitimacy of the U.N. by striking a balance between the objective of achieving Iraq's full compliance with the UN Resolutions and the means adopted to reach this goal.

Friends, the decade following the end of the Cold War has been a period of extraordinary challenges for India in the realm of international affairs. Like Russia, India too was confronted with the need to rapidly adapt to a sudden and total change in the world order. Besides the political adjustment, India's economy had to gear itself to deal with the wave of globalization that has been sweeping across the world. Further, Jehadi elements turned their targets on the Indian state of Jammu and Kashmir, actively aided and abetted by our western neighbour who has sought to wage a proxy war against us. The last decade has also been a period when extraordinary pressure was mounted on India by the international community to abandon its nuclear option. India's response has been to confront these challenges head on. For this purpose, it adopted a number of strategies including the infusion of a heavy dose of pragmatism and realism into the making of foreign policy, pro-active efforts to build national strength, intensive engagement with major powers and active economic diplomacy. India can note with pride that significant success has been achieved in overcoming these challenges. We have today built close political and economic relations with a wide spectrum of countries across the world and India is widely acknowledged as an emerging power and an important player on the world stage.

Friends, pursuit of national interest is the primary foreign policy goal of all nations, including India. In the future also, India will continue to evolve and implement a foreign policy that maintains a healthy balance between her principles and tradition of idealism as well as the demands of realism.

Let me conclude, ladies and gentlemen, by stating that the world is poised at a turning point in history. Institutions we have grown up with such as the U.N., etc., appear under threat. We may soon face a world which has completely changed beyond all recognition. However, in the midst of all this turmoil and turbulence, if there is a 'constant' and one unchangeable reality, it is the friendship between India and Russia.

Whatever happens in the rest of the world, I have no doubt that our relations will continue to remain strong and robust. As is evident from the remarks I have made here today, India and Russia share common perceptions, common interests and common challenges. The building of a multi-polar world is our common goal and our world view is one. It is this mature understanding of the mutuality of interests that has inspired our Strategic Partnership which is a declaration of our solidarity in the emerging political, economic and security scenario of the new millennium. Friends, there is compelling logic for close India-Russia relations and India stands ready to work with Russia to make the world a better place for the entire humanity. Thank you.

[*Source:* http://meaindia.nic.in//speech/2003/02/20spc01.htm]

Statement by the Prime Minister of India, Mr. Atal Bihari Vajpayee, at the XIII NAM Summit, Kuala Lumpur, 24 February 2003

Mr. Chairman, Your Majesties, Your Royal Highnesses, Excellencies, Heads of State and Government, Ladies and Gentlemen,

As a number of distinguished colleagues before me have already done, I congratulate Malaysia on its assumption of the Chairmanship of the Non-Aligned Movement. We are at a critical point in international relations. Perhaps we are also at a defining moment in the life of this Movement itself. We are seeking to revitalise its agenda in a global environment profoundly different from that in which it was created.

Prime Minister Mahathir Mohamad has presided over the destinies of Malaysia, as it transformed itself from underdevelopment into an economic powerhouse of South East Asia. We hope he will bring the same sure hand and deft touch to the transformation of NAM. I would also like to warmly compliment South Africa for chairing the Movement with such distinction during a period of flux in international relations. President Mbeki has invested considerable energy in guiding the Movement towards a new equilibrium between the interests of developed and developing countries.

Mr. Chairman, The tectonic shifts in international relations over the last decade have challenged NAM to adapt itself to effectively tackle the new contemporary challenges. Even while preserving independence of judgement and autonomy of action—which are its defining characteristics—NAM should take a close, hard look at the realities of today. India has participated in the various deliberations within our Movement on the theme of its revitalisation. We believe that certain principles are fundamental to this process:

One, NAM should have a clear consensus on key issues of common concern to all of us. Multilateralism, combating global terrorism and reform of the UN system would be the political elements of this agenda. Developmental issues, democratisation of international financial institutions, constructive North-South engagement and South-South cooperation would be its main economic planks.

Two, NAM should concentrate on issues that unite, rather than divide us. In a Movement of one hundred and sixteen members, it is inevitable that there are some differences or even disputes among us. We would be losing time, energy and focus if we involved ourselves in these issues. This principle is accepted in the Charters and practice of successful organisations like the OIC and ASEAN. NAM's outlook and its agenda have to be global.

Three, in projecting our view on global issues, our tone has to be objective and pragmatic. We should position NAM as a major pole in a multi-polar configuration.

Four, we should use cooperation between ourselves as an effective tool to promote our national development. South-South cooperation has to move from the political lectern to the economic marketplace.

Five, NAM should develop a progressive agenda on the fundamental values of democracy, human rights and multiculturism. The preservation and consolidation of democracy throughout our membership is a major challenge.

Mr. Chairman, The threat of global terrorism presents our Movement with an immediate test of its commitment to its core principles. It is imperative that we take a clear and unequivocal stand on this scourge. There can be no double standards, no confusion between terrorism and freedom struggles, and no implicit condoning of terrorism through an investigation of its "root causes". There can be no justification for terrorism. No political, ideological, religious or ethnic grounds can justify the shedding of the blood of innocent people. We should finally conclude the negotiations at the UN on the Comprehensive Convention on International Terrorism. It is a matter of the greatest shame to all of us that while terrorism continues to claim its victims with one brutal act after another, we cannot conclude an international agreement because we cannot find a universally acceptable definition of terrorism!

Mr. Chairman, The world's attention—like that of this Summit—is riveted on Iraq. Like every other non-aligned country, India fervently wishes for a peaceful resolution. We also support the multilateral route of the United Nations to address this issue. But objectivity—

and not rhetoric—should govern our actions. Weapons of mass destruction do need to be eliminated. It is essential that Iraq complies fully with the obligations it has accepted, including disarmament, and that it cooperates fully in implementing Security Council Resolution 1441. As a fellow member of NAM, this is our sincere advice to Iraq. We also expect that if Iraq fully complies, the sanctions against that country should be lifted. We should also not lose sight of the humanitarian dimension of the suffering of the Iraqi people. Apart from the immediate consequences of military action, there are long-term implications for stability and security in an already volatile region.

Mr. Chairman, NAM is at a historic moment in a new century. We need to introspect, take stock of our achievements as well as our failures and take concrete steps to revitalise our Movement. India is ready to play its part in this effort.

Mr. Chairman, I had never intended to mention such matters at this forum, but I am constrained to respond to some allegations against India.

President Musharraf has referred to my country a little while ago. His strange logic masks Pakistan's territorial designs on an integral part of India. He justifies terrorism against India by talking of root causes.

Does he go into the root causes of sectarian terrorism in his country? Or does he take stern action against the perpetrators of that terrorism? He talks of the "oppressed people of Kashmir". These same people very recently cast their ballots in an election universally recognised as free and fair. They defied the bullets of the terrorists, aided and abetted by Pakistan.

Those very terrorists assassinated candidates and political activists in the elections and killed women and children because they refused to provide them food and shelter. These terrorists continue to perpetrate violence against innocent civilians every day. Yet General Musharraf talks of an international humanitarian order!

Thank you.

[*Source:* http://meaindia.nic.in//speech/2003/02/24spc01.htm]

Kuala Lumpur Declaration on Continuing the Revitalisation of the Non-Aligned Movement, XIII NAM Summit, 25 February 2003

We, the Heads of State and Government of the Non-Aligned Movement, gathered in Kuala Lumpur, Malaysia on 24-25 February 2003 for the XIII Summit Conference, reaffirmed our abiding faith in, and strong commitment to, the ideals, principles and purposes of the Movement, as laid out at the Bandung Conference of 1955, and the Charter of the United Nations, in our common and continuing pursuit of establishing a peaceful, prosperous, and a more just and equitable world order.

The Movement had played an active, even central role, over the years, on the issues of concern and vital importance to its members, such as decolonisation, apartheid, the situation in Palestine and the Middle East, disarmament, poverty eradication and socio-economic development, among others. After more than forty years of its founding, and having undergone many challenges and vicissitudes, it is timely and appropriate to comprehensively review the role, structure and work methods of our Movement in keeping with the times and the new realities, aimed at the further strengthening of our Movement. With the end of the Cold War, the emergence of unipolarity, the trend towards unilateralism and the rise of new challenges and threats, such as international terrorism, it is imperative for the Movement to promote multilateralism, better defend the interests of developing countries and prevent their marginalisation.

With increased globalisation and the rapid advance of science and technology, the world has changed dramatically. The rich and powerful countries exercise an inordinate influence in determining the nature and direction of international relations, including economic and trade relations, as well as the rules governing these relations, many of which are at the expense of the developing countries. It is imperative, therefore, that the Movement respond in ways that will ensure its continued relevance and usefulness to its members.

Globalisation presents many challenges and opportunities to the future and viability of all states. In its present form, it perpetuates or even increases the marginalisation of developing countries. We must ensure that globalisation will be a positive force for change for all peoples and will benefit the largest number of countries and not just a few. Globalisation should lead to the prospering and empowering of the developing countries, not their continued impoverishment and dependence on the wealthy and developed world.

The revolution in the Information and Communications Technology is changing the world at a rapid speed and in a fundamental way, and is already creating a vast and widening digital divide between the developed and developing countries, which must be bridged if the latter are to benefit from the globalisation process. This new technological innovation must be made more easily available to the developing countries in their efforts to modernise and revitalise their economies in pursuit of their developmental goals.

The achievement of these developmental goals requires an enabling international environment and the honouring of commitments and pledges made by states, including our partners in the developed world.

The future presents as many challenges and opportunities as the past and the Movement must continue to remain strong, cohesive and resilient. The continued relevance of the Movement will depend, in large measure, on the unity and solidarity of its members as well as its ability to adapt to these changes. In this regard, the process of the revitalisation of the Movement, begun at its previous Summit Meetings, must be given further impetus.

Consistent with our desire to translate our rhetoric into action, and in rededicating ourselves to the fundamental principles, purposes and goals of the Movement of Non-Aligned Countries, we resolve to make every effort to:

- Enhance our unity, based on our common interests and history of shared struggles, and persevere with our efforts to ensure that these interests are continuously promoted and our concerns are fully addressed.
- Uphold and adhere to the fundamental principles of the Movement and the Charter of the United Nations in the

preservation and promotion of world peace through dialogue and diplomacy among states and the avoidance of the use of force to resolve conflicts.

- Promote and strengthen the multilateral process as an indispensable vehicle in safeguarding the interests of member states of the Movement as well as those of the United Nations.
- Promote the democratisation of the system of international governance in order to increase the participation of developing countries in international decision-making.
- Be pro-active, rather than reactive, to international developments, especially those that impact on the members of the Movement, so as to ensure that the Movement is not sidelined but be at the forefront of the international decision making processes.
- Strengthen our national capacities in order to enhance our individual and collective resilience.
- Enhance South-South Cooperation in all areas of our relations, particularly in the political, social, cultural, economic and scientific fields.
- Promote a more dynamic and cooperative relationship with the developed and industrialised countries, based on constructive engagement, broad partnership and mutuality of benefits.
- Promote closer interaction and cooperation with organisations of our civil society, the private sector and parliamentarians on the recognition that they can play a constructive role towards the attainment of our common goals.

In pursuit of these goals, Member States of the Movement shall strive to implement the following concrete measures:—

- Undertake a sound review and analysis of the positions of the Movement on international issues, with a view to consolidating the common denominators among member states by focusing on issues that unite rather than divide us, thereby strengthening the unity and cohesion of the Movement.
- Review and redefine the role of the Movement and improve its structure and methodology, including the need for a more focused and concise documentation, in order to make it more effective and efficient.

- Enhance our coordination and cooperation through regular meetings of the Coordinating Bureau in New York, as well as in Geneva, Vienna, Nairobi and other centres, if necessary, with a view to responding, on a timely basis, to international developments affecting the Movement and its members.
- Utilise fully and effectively all exisiting mechanisms and institutions, such as the Troika, the Coordinating Bureau and all existing working groups, committees, the Non-Aligned Caucus of the Security Council, and establish new ones, as appropriate.
- Utilise more effectively the regular NAM Foreign Ministers Meetings through more interactive sessions as well as encourage the interaction and involvement of other relevant Ministers towards enhancing the effectiveness and profile of the Movement.
- Strengthen the role of the Chair, as spokesman of the Movement, through the establishment of appropriate mechanisms as part of the necessary backup system.
- Strengthen coordination and cooperation, and formulate common strategies on socio-economic and development-related issues, with the Group of 77 through regular and more frequent meetings of the Joint Coordinating Committee (JCC).
- Follow up on decisions made at the United Nations Millennium Assembly and other international fora, such as the Doha Meeting on international trade, the Monterrey Conference on Financing for Development and the Johannesburg World Summit on Sustainable Development as imperatives in addressing the urgent concerns of developing countries, such as poverty eradication, debt relief, capacity building and HIV/AIDS.
- Expand, deepen and enrich South-South cooperation through enhanced regional and inter-regional cooperation, undertaking concrete projects and programmes, pooling of resources, and tapping the contributions of eminent personalities and institutions of the South.
- Promote and develop mechanisms, including at relevant conferences, for international cooperation and solidarity in efforts to bridge the digital divide based on a partnership involving states, civil society and the private sector.

- Continue to strongly support international programmes for Africa, particularly through NEPAD, as well as the Least Developed Countries, Landlocked Developing Countries and Small Island Developing Countries.
- Promote constructive dialogue and interaction with our development partners, particularly the G-8, through existing and appropriate new mechanisms, including institutionalised contacts, so as to bring about greater understanding between the North and South and to ensure that the views of the Movement are fully taken into account before important decisions affecting developing countries are made.

In realising our goal of revitalising the Non-Aligned Movement, we must exert every effort towards the promotion of a multipolar world through the strengthening of the United Nations, as an indispensable international organisation for the maintenance of international peace and security, the promotion of human rights, social and economic development and respect for international law, as enshrined in its Charter.

[*Source:* http://www.meadev.nic.in/speeches/NAMdec.htm]

Statement by External Affairs Minister, Mr. Yashwant Sinha, at the 9th Session of the Indo-Russian Inter-Governmental Commission for Trade, Economic, Scientific, Technological and Cultural Cooperation, Moscow, 15 May 2003

Your Excellency Mr. Ilya Klebanov, Minister of Industry and Science & Technology of the Russian Federation, Distinguished Members of the Russian and Indian Delegations, Ladies and Gentlemen:

Excellency, Thank you for the welcome. It is indeed a pleasure to be in friendly Russian Federation once again. I wish to thank you also for the warm hospitality. Before I proceed further, let me introduce the members of my delegation. (EAM introduces the Indian delegation).

Excellency, since our last meeting in November 2002, a number of important developments have taken place which have relevance for the work of the Commission. Last year our Prime Minister and President Putin signed a Joint Declaration on Strengthening and Enhancing Economic, Scientific and Technological Cooperation, which provides a vision of qualitatively new relations between our two countries in these spheres. This Commission was entrusted with the additional responsibility to monitor the implementation of the Declaration through a Joint Task Force. On our part, the Ministry of External Affairs will head the Task Force and we will nominate the members within 30 days. I hope that it will be possible for Your Excellency also to nominate the Russian members of the Task Force.

Excellency, this Commission is also a mechanism to constantly attune our institutions to the changing needs and ever-new challenges faced by the entrepreneurs and businesspeople of the two countries. We have taken some steps in this direction since our last meeting. To cite a few instances, since November 2002, most of the working groups have held their meetings, there was an Indian exhibition in Moscow in February, which Your Excellency so kindly inaugurated, there was also a meeting of the Joint Business Council in Moscow in February, a privileged sighting of rough natural diamonds for Indian buyers was organised in April, and the delegations of the Vneshtorg Bank and the ICICI visited India and Russia, respectively.

Unfortunately, these initiatives have not resulted in very significant increase in our trade turnover. Our bilateral trade has stagnated over the past few years at about 1.3-1.6 billion US dollars. The percentage share of India's trade with Russia in the Russian Federation's overall trade is around 0.98 per cent. There is no denying that there has been some progress in improving this situation, but it has been slow in a number of priority areas. It is extremely important to implement the decisions of the IRIGC quickly without overshooting the timeframe foreseen for them.

Excellency, our entrepreneurs have been facing a serious problem in sending their delegations to Russia due to stringent rules for issue of visas. Even the public sector undertakings in India are affected, and last week two members of the Working Group on Power were initially refused visas by the Russian Embassy in New Delhi since they had no clearances from Moscow, despite the fact that the meeting of this Working Group is part of the work of this session of the IRIGC. While we will tackle visa issues separately, there is need for an administrative decision at a high level, here in Moscow, to exempt at least the IRIGC members from the stringent visa requirements.

In order to reinvigorate our trade, it would be worthwhile establishing a Sub-Group on Small and Medium Enterprises (SMEs) within the Working Group on Trade and Economic Cooperation. Our Joint Business Council could also concentrate on the SMEs of the two countries cooperating with each other.

Excellency, I would like to suggest that if future meetings of the Joint Business Council could be held alongside the meetings of the IRIGC, it will send a positive signal of necessary political support and facilitation to our business communities.

We also need to take initiatives, and continue those already taken, in the fields of natural diamonds, ad campaigns for Indian tea, export of Indian bovine meat, export of rubber, fruit, horticulture products, rice and sugar from India, setting up of joint venture banks in each other's countries, enhancement of cooperation between our insurance companies and shipping lines, etc. It would be helpful if Russia could accept the Indian certification of veterinary requirements based on EU norms, to which both countries subscribe, and not insist on higher standards. While we have yet not been able to buy natural diamonds from Russia, we are looking forward to further sightings for our businessmen this year, as agreed by the concerned Joint Working Group. We would also like that the concerned companies consider the idea of setting up joint ventures for making jewellery which will be to mutual advantage, more than the mere buyer-seller relationship.

We look forward to early operationalisation of the Joint Task Force that will look into utilising Rupee debt fund for equity in Indo-Russian joint ventures. Another outstanding issue is the resolution of claims on both sides. It is also regrettable that there has been no progress in settlement of pending claims of Indian exporters. While India has made substantial payments on account of short payments to the Russian side, not even one claim of Indian exporters has so far been settled by the Russian side. This is becoming a difficult issue since such pending claims discourage our businessmen in doing business with Russia. I welcome the understanding reached in the concerned Sub-Group and Working Group on the issue of outstanding freight payments due to Indian shipping lines for shipment of cargo in Indo-Soviet trade up to March 1992. The amount thus owed to Indian companies could be adjusted in the Rupee-debt repayment.

Excellency, since it will not be possible to rely entirely on the debt fund for joint ventures between our two countries, I propose to set up a Joint Venture Capital Fund for a modest amount. A beginning has been made in this direction by the Russian investment in Kudankulam Nuclear Power Plant and by ONGC Videsh Limited in Sakhalin-I. For investments to take off, it is also important that financial and banking links are strengthened. We hope that the joint venture between State Bank of India and Canara Bank for opening a branch in Moscow will receive quick necessary approvals, and Russian banks will also be encouraged to set up operations in India.

The North-South Transport Corridor is an important venture between India, Russia and Iran and it has already attracted interest of some other countries. For it to be a big success for the growth of bilateral trade, it is important to provide for right investments and upgradation along the route, especially in the important ports, railways, containerisation and warehousing sectors.

Excellency, the world energy scenario is changing quickly. Even though large discoveries of oil and gas reserves have been made recently in India, we are poised to import a larger share of world energy in the years to come, due to our strong economic growth. Russia, endowed with large discovered and yet-to-be discovered oil will continue to be among the top suppliers to the world market. In the emerging scenario therefore we have complementarity, which opens large opportunities for close cooperation. While we continue to discuss oil and gas related issues in the Joint Working Group on Petroleum, to monitor existing projects as well as those under consideration and to discuss development of transport, transit pipeline and trilateral projects involving Russia, we envisage transferring this exercise for the larger picture to a full fledged Energy Forum, a proposal we had made two years ago. We envisage a forum which will function somewhat like the Russian energy dialogues with the EU, the USA and China.

We are happy to note that our cooperation in hydrocarbons sector is progressing well with the participation of the ONGC Videsh in the Sakhalin-I Project. We note with satisfaction that the production is likely to commence in 2005. We look forward to Russia working in a sustained manner to ensure problem-free progress in this venture. We expect that the cooperation would expand to the Caspian Sea as well, where discussions are on to include ONGC Videsh in the exploration of Kurmangazi. As advised by the Russian side, we have asked our oil companies to initiate dialogue with their Russian counterparts. We also seek your support for faster progress in this matter. I welcome the initiative to cooperate in third countries, which emerged from the recent meeting of the concerned Working Group. I also take this opportunity to invite Russian oil and gas companies, to take a more active part in exploration ventures in India.

We have placed considerable emphasis on the growth of the power sector in our country with participation of the private sector and investments from abroad. We are aware of the strengths of the Russian Federation in this sphere and hope that Russia would be able to avail itself of the considerable opportunities available for cooperation in this important sector.

Russian expertise has contributed significantly to coal mining in India. We are interested in further expansion of cooperation in this field. The Indian side has already submitted physico-mechanical properties of the roof and floor rocks of Jhanjhara mine. We hope the Russian side will expedite detailed specification of requirements so that the cooperation in Jhanjhara mine project continues. We also invite the Russian companies to participate in the tendering processes for new mines in India. This sphere presents good scope for Russian investments in India.

India and the Russian Federation have traditionally enjoyed close cooperation in the field of metallurgy. The steel plants of Bhilai, Bokaro and Visakhapatnam are examples of this cooperation, which have contributed to the development of the Indian steel industry. The organisations in our countries are also treading new paths in the field of cooperation by forming joint ventures. Romelt-SAIL is an important symbol in this direction and we shall strive to introduce such environment-friendly processes in the field of metallurgy not only in India, but in other countries as well. We also welcome the continuing interest shown by Russian enterprises to participate in upgradation of Indian steel plants as well as in solving their maintenance/operations related problems. The outstanding issue of debts owed to SAIL needs to be addressed.

Pharmaceuticals are an important area in our commercial cooperation where we have strong trade ties and immense possibilities. It is a matter of satisfaction that the first meeting of the Working Group on Pharmaceuticals was held in Moscow earlier this year. The two sides discussed several initiatives for furthering cooperation in this field. These need to be followed up in earnest. Russian companies can also explore the profitable possibilities of supplying chemicals to the Indian bulk drug and raw material industry, which is engaged in contract manufacturing for world leaders.

We are also glad that the 2nd session of the Working Group on

Information Technology was held in Delhi on 7 April and the two sides could crystallise areas of mutual interest to collaborate in this field. The issue of supply of Indian computers to Russian schools through the Rouble-Rupee debt route for payments needs to be addressed. We would also like to suggest an area-specific agreement on mutual recognition of degrees, diplomas and certificates in IT sector to facilitate active exchange of experts and developing closer cooperation in this field.

Excellency, I will like to draw your attention to the cooperation projects highlighted during the visit of the then Minister of Information Technology Mr. Pramod Mahajan to Russia in September 2001 and reflected subsequently in a Memorandum of Understanding. These include better business interaction, e.g. joint ventures, joint marketing, Indian involvement in Russian telecommunication sector and Russia's investment in India in this sphere. There is also potential for cooperation and collaboration in areas like information security, testing and certification.

Science and technology is probably one of the most flourishing areas of our bilateral cooperation. During President Putin's visit to India in December 2002, the two sides signed a new protocol on protection and use of intellectual property rights arising out of bilateral scientific collaboration. As a follow up, interaction has been initiated with industrial houses for development of industry-oriented joint scientific collaboration. In this respect, the establishment of the Science & Technology Centre in Moscow would catalyse marketing of technologies. Unfortunately, we have been faced with the visa problems in this field also. The Indian Department of Science and Technology has informed me that the Indian scientists visiting Russia under inter-governmental programmes are now facing a lot of procedural delays in securing Russian visa. In order to strengthen cooperation in the sphere of science and technology, one suggestion could be coordinated meetings of the Ministries of science and technology and trade and economic cooperation which will provide an integrated view of the cooperation in commercialising results of joint projects in this sphere. It will also provide a forum for discussing and finding sources for funding such activity. There is need for paying attention to the functioning of the S&T related centres jointly set up in the recent years and expedite consideration of the new ones being discussed. Our cooperation in environment is progressing satisfactorily. We may explore the possibility of including study of green house effect, climate change, etc.

Cooperation between the States of India and the Regions of Russia is an important part of our multi-faceted cooperation. Last year two documents were signed on cooperation between Gujarat and Astrakhan region and between Hyderabad and Khazan city. During the visit of President Putin in December 2002, we signed a Protocol on cooperation between Karnataka and Samara Region. There has also been some follow up action on cooperation in this area by the visit of a delegation of Astrakhan to Gujarat earlier this year where they signed a set of Agreed Minutes on cooperation. There are also proposals for exchange of visits between Andhra Pradesh and Tatarstan. We welcome these exchanges which hopefully will result in concrete economic and trade relations between our regions. However, we need the Russian side to urgently nominate the co-chairman of this Group so that it can hold its meeting. Contacts between regions will also increase contacts between small and medium enterprises of the two countries.

Excellency, relations between India and Russia go beyond politics and trade. I cannot overstress the importance which should be attached to the finalisation of a new Cultural Exchange Programme between India and Russia. We also welcome the decision to hold Days of Russian Culture in India and of Indian Culture in Russia. A delegation of the Russian Ministry of Culture will visit India in the next few days to finalise the arrangements in this regard. I am sure these events will significantly promote people-to-people friendship and appreciation of each other's cultural and civilisational heritage.

Excellency, our special efforts over the last two months have resulted in an increase of the traffic of Russian tourists to India. This will have reciprocal opportunities for Russia. There is scope for more contact between good tourist operators and effective mutual facilitation.

Excellency, before I end, I would like to make a few proposals for enhancing the efficacy of the IRIGC. First of all, the Calendar of meetings of the Joint Working Groups for the entire year should be drawn up soon after an IRIGC meeting, so that these Groups do not meet in a hurry on the occasion of our IRIGC meeting. Secondly, we should agree, Excellency, that the Secretaries of the Joint Commission should meet every two months and submit joint report of progress to us. If there is any issue where progress is not satisfactory, we should be able to bring it to each other's notice.

Excellency, I am sure that our work today will be productive and mutually beneficial. I look forward to working closely with you in our joint endeavour to further consolidate our bilateral relations for mutual benefit.

Thank you for your kind attention.

[*Source:* http://meaindia.nic.in//speech/2003/05/15spc01.htm]

Singapore's Senior Minister Lee Kuan Yew's Address at the "Shangri-La Dialogue", Singapore, 30 May 2003

Introduction

When we met here for the Shangri-la Dialogue in May a year ago, the world faced many threats. Osama bin Laden's al-Qaeda warned the United States of more terror attacks. India and Pakistan had over a million troops facing each other across the line of control in Kashmir. The regime of Saddam Hussein Iraq continued to flout its disarmament obligations under binding UNSC resolutions.

A year later, although al-Qaeda has hit soft targets elsewhere, its threats to attack the United States and Britain have not materialised. India and Pakistan are restoring air and land links, and war is no longer imminent though a solution to the Kashmir problem is unlikely. The defining event was the removal of Saddam's regime in Iraq after only 21 days of fighting with few casualties.

Earlier in February, Germany, America's most loyal and steadfast European ally for 50 years since the end of the Second World War, joined Russia and France in opposing the US in a public stand-off in the UNSC; it marked the end of an era. When a German Chancellor is closer to a Russian President and at odds with an American President, this is a different world. The French and German leaders would probably have persuaded Chinese President Jiang Zemin to join them if Jiang had not been so focused on China's economic restructuring that requires stable relations with the United States to encourage more trade and investments. China is as strongly against United States unilateralism as France, Germany or Russia. The Chinese describe it as hegemony. But for a long while China needs equable relations with the United States so that it can grow its economy.

Is this a one-off breach, an accident that both sides can put behind them? Or is it something deeper, more basic? NATO now lacks a common enemy in place of the former Soviet Union. The war in Iraq highlighted this problem. It may have profound geopolitical consequences whose full impact may not be evident for many years. The war shattered the definition of 'the West; that for so long was the foundation of global stability during the Cold War. On 23 May, France and Germany supported a new UNSC resolution giving the US the lead role in administering Iraq. But can transatlantic relations ever return to the previous level of intimacy? This is not just an abstract question because terrorism by Islamic fanatics, the Israel-Palestinian conflict and the shape of the Middle East after Iraq may sharpen transatlantic differences.

For Americans after 9/11 the number one enemy is terrorism by Islamic extremists. Many American policy makers believe that the radical Islam of the extremists and the tyranny of Saddam are symptoms of a deeper malaise infecting the Arab world. Some compare the Bush Doctrine of pre-emption of terror to the Truman Doctrine of containment of communism half a century earlier. A recent *New York Times* editorial said: "The end goal is a transformed region in which autocratic governments open the windows to democracy while their moribund societies join the global economy." To achieve this goal, the US has marshalled its enormous power and influence to bear on the Middle East.

Europeans agree that terrorism is a problem, but it's one that Europe has learned to live with, ETA the Basque separatists, the Red Brigade in Germany and the IRA in Britain. They have not suffered a shock like 9/11 and do not feel so vulnerable, in part because since 9/11 al-Qaeda has concentrated its threats on America and Britain. With their long experience in the Middle East, Europeans are also more sceptical about changing the region's basic dynamics.

Europeans regard the primary cause of terrorism as the unending Israeli-Palestinian conflict and America's unqualified support for Israel. They believe that to solve terrorism this cause must be removed. They find it difficult to refute the Arab view that without unqualified American support and the use of its veto in the UNSC, Israel's policies towards the Palestinians would soon become untenable. Europe is much closer geographically to the Middle East and will suffer directly from any fallout if a war with WMD breaks out across the Mediterranean between Arabs and Israelis. Europeans are also mindful of their own substantial Muslim minorities (13/14 million Muslims in the European Union of whom 4/5 million North Africans are in France alone, and 1.5 million in Britain). They believe that a just and enduring settlement of the Israeli-Palestinian conflict is possible if America not only wills it, but also works in close partnership with a Europe that is seen by the Arabs as more even-handed than the US. Such a settlement will allow Islamic anger to subside and Europe's Muslim problems to become less difficult to manage.

The United States does not agree that the Arab-Israeli conflict is the primary cause of terrorism. It believes that terrorism by Islamic militants has to be considered in the context of the wider problems of the Middle East and the Arab/Muslim world. It sees the need to change the geo-political balance in the Middle East and reshape the political structures of Arab countries to make them more democratic and focused on development and progress.

Washington believes this will allow an Israeli-Palestinian settlement in which all Israel's neighbours, including Lebanon, Syria, Saudi Arabia, the Gulf States and Iraq, will accept Israel's right to exist in something more than the cold peace that now exists between Egypt and Israel. Furthermore placing the power of the United States-right in the heart of the Middle East, in Iraq and the Gulf States, will result in Iran and Syria being flanked by American-friendly states—Iran by Afghanistan to its east and Iraq to its west, and Syria by Israel, Turkey and Iraq. As Colin Powell told Syrian President Bashir Asad the power equation in the region has changed, and governments in the region have to adjust to the new strategic situation.

Also Saudi Arabia will no longer be so indispensable to America's strategic interests. America will be in a better position to persuade the Saudis that it would be in their interest to stop the funding and export of Wahhabism. For years many Saudis and others in the oil-rich Gulf States have bought off their extremists by funding their activities in the world beyond the Arabian Peninsula. The Saudis paid for the building of mosques and madrasahs world wide and sent ulemas to preach Wahhabism, a severe, fanatical and anti-Western version of Islam. The resulting heightened religiosity has made it easier for Islamic extremists to recruit many Muslims for their jihad of terror. The May 13 suicide bombing in Riyadh and another on May 16 in Casablanca were recent reminders of the dangers of this Saudi policy.

Whether the changes in the Middle East after the fall of Saddam's Iraq can lead to a stable balance in the longer term is not certain. Permanent peaceful co-existence between Arabs and Israelis will be difficult to achieve. A stop to this bloodletting may not dissipate Arab hatred and bitterness against Israelis and Jews. These deep visceral animosities have been socially institutionalised in Palestine and its neighbouring Arab countries. Ever since the founding of Israel, Arabs in the Middle East have been taught to hate Israelis and Jews in their schools, madrasahs and mosques, reinforced regularly by repeated media images of powerful Israeli military incursions into the occupied Palestinian territories. After 40 years of patchy economic development, many Arabs feel anger and humiliation that their once glorious Islamic civilisation has been diminished by the West, especially America, and corrupted by its licentious culture.

The source of Islamic militancy among Muslims in South East Asia has been the increasing fanaticism of extremist Muslims in the Arab world that has been exported by Arab extremists to previously moderate Muslims in South East Asia. This Islamic militancy has taken on a life and dynamic of its own. To halt this trend, a peace deal between Israelis and the Palestinians is a necessary but not a sufficient condition. Ending the Palestinian conflict will deprive extremists of a convenient rallying point. But unless militant groups in the Arab countries and Islamic theocracies are seen to fail, JI and other militant groups in the non-Arab Muslim world will continue to recruit extremists. Even if there is an Israeli-Palestinian settlement, the US and its Western allies must ensure that Islamic militancy is defeated by economic, military and other means to clearly demonstrate to non-Arab Muslims that fanaticism and militancy have no future.

Islamic Extremist Terrorism

Since last year, Jemaah Islamiyah (JI), an affiliate of al-Qaeda has committed many acts of terror in the Philippines and Indonesia and one major terrorist act, the bombing in Bali on 12 October 2002 killing 200 Western and Australian tourists. They have paid a price for it. The Indonesian government that hitherto had been neutral vis-à-vis Muslim extremists, decided to act. With technical help from the FBI and the Australian Federal special unit, the Indonesian police have arrested the actual perpetrators and their accomplices, some 30 JI operators. But there are hundreds more JI operators still in the region who will regroup and in good time can execute more suicide attacks.

The terrorist jihad is against all non-believers, especially Christians and Jews whether in America, Europe, Pakistan, or even Indonesia. Al-Qaeda's leadership has been disrupted and dispersed and they do not appear so far to have restored their ability to execute a spectacular terror attack in the US or UK. So their regional affiliates have blown up Americans and Westerners in Riyadh on 13 May and in Casablanca on 16 May. Other affiliates will attempt similar attacks wherever they can. They will certainly try to attack soft targets in South East Asia.

It is in Europe's interest to have America succeed in Iraq. The kind of government and society that emerges in Iraq will have a profound influence on all Arab nations and will have a spill-over effect on non-Arab Muslims. The present disorder delays the rebuilding of Iraq's political structures. However the possibility of a more fundamentalist Iraq is real; Iraqi Shias form 60 per cent of the population. They are well organised around their Imams in their respective mosques and the influence of the principal imams, or ayatollahs, is considerable. Therefore free voting for a representative government can produce a more Islamic government in Iraq.

East Asia and North Korea

After the demonstration of American technological military wizardry in Iraq, is it more likely that there could be less blackmailing by the North Koreans in their talks with the Americans? I believe despite all the bluster North Korea knows that there are limits to brinkmanship when blackmailing a Bush Presidency.

Beijing wants North Korea intact. An imploded North Korea and reunification will bring American troops up to the Yalu River. A nuclear North Korea is not in China's interest because Japan would then have to go nuclear. So China will have to take a stand against a nuclear North Korea.

The South Korean President Roh Moo Hyun was elected at the end of last year on an anti-American platform. The South does not want an imploded North that would be a huge burden. Peaceful reunification in the very long term is the desired outcome. Should the North have nuclear bombs, the South would then inherit them. After President Roh's meeting with President Bush, US and South Korean positions towards the North no longer seem to be so much at odds.

Japan does not want a North Korea that can threaten it with missiles and nuclear warheads. An imploded North Korea may land Japan with some refugees, but it will not be in the numbers that will flee into South Korea and China. A reunited Korea is not necessarily good for Japan.

For America, the simplest solution is an imploded North, and it does not matter if reunification is the result. If a peaceful resolution to the present impasse requires yielding to Pyongyang's blackmail for aid and a promise of non-aggression that will stick in the throats of the Americans. In any case the North is unlikely to give up its nuclear weapons whatever the deal.

Because the four parties most closely involved with North Korea—United States, South Korea, Japan, China—have different objectives, a neat solution is not obvious.

Conclusion

To conclude, British Prime Minister Tony Blair wants Europe to embrace the United States as a full partner and as such, influence the direction and policy of the United States. France on the other hand believes that Europe should be a counterweight to restrain American excessive unilateralism.

Europeans were naturally pro-American since the end of World War II, when the Marshall Plan salvaged them from the ravages of the war and NATO protected them from Soviet domination. More recently some Europeans, besides the French, have become uncomfortable when they see the US, confident of its technological supremacy, pursue what they feel are high-risk solutions to complex problems. Up to the present, Blair's policy of supporting the United

States and influencing its decisions as a partner can claim to work. But if America does not cultivate its friends and allies with more tender loving care, coalitions of the willing may become smaller.

Throughout history, every force has generated a counter-force. For the present, Russia, China and many countries in the European Union want to maintain good or friendly relations with the United States. There is reason to hope that tending to these relations can prolong US pre-eminence. Not to do so may persuade more nations that the way to restrain American unilateralism is to join a group of all those opposed to it.

[*Source:* http://www.iiss.org/shangri-la-more.php?itemID=10& PHPSESSID=b5a38b30699f7f0ba266cc5 237a94fea]

Speech of Defence Minister Mr. George Fernandes at the 'Shangri-La Dialogue' on "The Changing Strategic Environment: Impact on Security Policy and Military Doctrine", Singapore, 1 June 2003

Mr. Chairman, Director of the IISS, Excellencies and distinguished delegates to this year's Shangri-La Conference. At the outset allow me to thank our hosts for making this interaction possible and for according me this opportunity to share an Indian perspective with you. The last two days have been stimulating both inside and outside the Conference Hall. The IISS and the Government of Singapore are to be commended for sustaining this initiative begun last year. The events that have punctuated the calendar since then make the current deliberations even more relevant, and may I add, imperative.

I have been asked to speak briefly on "The Changing Strategic Environment: Impact on Security Policy and Military Doctrine". To cover these issues, which deserve individual analysis, is quite a challenge. I hope I can be forgiven for being a little discursive as I touch upon what I consider are the principal features as quickly as I can.

Two features of the evolving strategic environment stand out. The first is the contemporary phenomenon of 'jehadi' terrorism. The second is the danger of the acquisition of weapons of mass destruction and their means of delivery by deviant states and/or radical non-state formations. A third, which impacts on our political environment very differently, but nevertheless forms part of the strategic calculus, is an increasing unilateralism in the use of force.

The tragedy of 9/11 had set the stage for last year's conference. The scourge of terrorism was acknowledged as the challenge before the global community. An appropriate collective response was the need of the hour.

The emotional reaction was spontaneous but the practical experience of fighting terrorism has been more sobering. There was a very astute observation in last year's 'Strategic Survey' brought out by the IISS, that (I quote): "Containing and ultimately defeating terrorism is a formidable task, offering as much scope for disagreement as for cooperation. Yesterday's sense of emotional solidarity is today's shared political burden. It needs to be handled with economic finesse, political savvy, military firmness and moral resolve in careful balance." (Unquote). A year down the road, this holds true. The execution of the war against terrorism, while impressive, has been far from consistent, the campaign sometimes confusing, the links with the elimination of weapons of mass destruction and regime change leading to democracy unclear, and the final outcome still uncertain.

Terrorism is not a new phenomenon, but 9/11 marked the watershed between its perception as a geographically localized malady, and as a global threat. The Bombay blasts of 1993, which killed over 200 people in serial and synchronised explosions, was arguably the first major act of mass terrorism. But it went relatively unregistered in the catalogue of terrorist acts. New York, Washington, the attack on the Indian Parliament in Delhi in December 2001, Bali, Riyadh and Casablanca, among other such events, have driven home the global nature and reach of terrorism. Today's terrorism is different in scale, in its selection of targets, in the causes it espouses and in the identification of the enemy. Its roots lie in a distorted use of religion; its target is modern civilisation and democratic values. Bali, Riyadh and Casablanca show that its targets are not only the non-Muslim world but Islamic societies as well. This is a matter of particular concern to South-East Asia that, like India, has had traditions of Islam that have been moderate and syncretic, and where communities have lived peacefully for centuries. The intrusion of alien, extremist and distorted, ostensibly religious, values, with militant pan-Islamic sentiments threatens the harmony of their pluralist societies and the security of states.

Until recently, there was a sense that the end of the Cold War had left the world groping for the contours of a new threat. That threat now has a clearer face than ever. It is the threat of terrorism misguidedly inspired by, and using, religion as its raison d'être. It is typically perpetrated by non-state actors but it flourishes because of the support it receives from certain states and their institutions and sections of society. The global terrorist finds refuge in places and regions where sovereignty is weak and lacking, in failed States and States that are adrift and where governments are neither legitimate nor effective, or in repressive, authoritarian, alienated regimes propped up from outside where mechanisms for political change towards popular or representative government are restricted. Some governments even use terrorism as a convenient instrument of State policy. But though terrorism thrives in these nether regions, the networks of terrorism exist all over. Finances are raised globally, as are its recruits. The very spread of technology that underpins the current surge of globalisation and modernity has also empowered the terrorist with a new lethality. Militant religious outfits and deviant regimes have become new determinants affecting the strategic environment. The use of modern technology and the tenacious pursuit of weapons of mass destruction is coupled with suicide terrorism to raise the spectre of mass terrorism.

This then, is the challenge posed by terrorism: not just the terrorism of some misguided youth in pursuit of some lofty ideal, but the nihilism of the fanatic whose goal is not just to die for his cause but, as far as possible, to take civilisation along with him. It poses a fundamental challenge to open societies. To what extent can an open society protect itself from the malicious use of the freedoms and opportunities that it provides? To what extent can the challenge of fundamentalist, jehadi terrorism be met with military force and new military doctrines? The answers are not easy. The dictates of security often offer no alternative but military force. Afghanistan is a classic case where the infrastructure for terrorism was removed by the plain use of superior military force even though the dangers of destabilisation remain. However, force may not suffice in all cases, and every case may not be alike.

Terrorism has changed the strategic environment and the security discourse fundamentally. Its implications are likely to be every bit as serious and far-reaching as the end of the Cold War necessitating a review of force structures and doctrines. The front lines in the war against terrorism will be different from the frontlines of the Cold War. Some countries and institutions may lose their importance in the new conjuncture; others may gain in prominence. Terrorism has forced a new world where each nation will have to take sides because no nation can be immune from it.

The second major challenge to security impacting on the strategic environment, already alluded to, is the very real fear of the proliferation of weapons of mass destruction, including in crude or rudimentary forms, and their means of delivery. It is bad enough if such proliferation takes place at the level of states, of one state assisting another belligerent, hostile or deviant state in obtaining such weapons from scientific laboratories or the nuclear grey market. But it is altogether a different proposition if such capabilities fall into the hands of deviant states or terrorists, or if political parties that share a fundamentalist ideology force their way through weak or defective political structures to find a place in nuclear decision-making. This is another challenge to international security linked to, but distinct from, the challenge posed by terrorism, and even though it finds a place in our security consciousness, I do not feel that we have evolved an adequate policy to deal with it. Indeed, the complications of dealing with it are such that it may be tempting to close one's eyes to its dangers.

The last issue that I wish to flag today is the demonstration of US power in Kosovo, Afghanistan and Iraq. On the one hand, the world has witnessed the consensus with which the global community responded to the threat of terrorism in the aftermath of 9/11 as reflected in the UN Security Council Resolution 1373 and the military campaign against the Taliban-Al-Qaida. On the other hand, where a consensus has not been forthcoming, we have seen the US prepared to exercise its military power unilaterally or in "coalitions of the willing", ignoring the experience and advice of others. And yet, the problem of the longer haul after the military successes remains. I make this point only to underline that while decisive action may be necessary, such actions need a cooperative broad-based order to be sustainable. Absolute power has its own limits. If we have common objectives in confronting the threat of terrorism and proliferation, it is important that our efforts are based on a common pool of experience and that they endure.

Side-by-side with such omnipotence lurk unexplained and unknown threats. The virus has become a prominent metaphor of our times and has, through the computer 'virus', crossed over from the biological sphere to the technological. While we modify organisms by transplanting genes from one organism to another, nature displays its own ingenuity and seeks its own revenge. Viruses from the avian and animal worlds invade the human world, if some of the hypotheses about the origins of SARS or even AIDS are to be believed. As we think of the strategic environment ahead, and of the security challenges and policies and doctrines that correspond to it, it might be worth considering the hubris that mankind finds itself in.

What then is the impact of this new strategic context to security doctrine and policy? I would aver that there must be a recognition prima facie that the nature of the new challenges has response implications that go beyond the confines of domestic and regional police and para-military capability and coordination. We have to evolve security policies that will now factor the transnational and domestic terrorist dimension as the major challenge to the well-being of society and as a potential threat to the security of states and sometimes to their territorial integrity. Military capability and civilian intelligence will have to be synergised towards greater cooperation along the low intensity conflict/internal security grid. As we all know there is little of that at this point in time both at the regional and global level.

Mr. Chairman, we are here not only to deliberate upon what may be the most serious security challenges that the global community now faces but to arrive at the most effective means of dealing with it through reasoned deliberations and consensus. Our experience with terrorism and its attendant perceptions may differ. But I believe that we are united in our resolve to deal with the challenges and are equally cognisant of the need to translate thought and intent into tangible and fruitful action. I hope that when we meet again a year later, significant progress will be recorded so that, in due course, the promise of Shangri-La can be fulfilled.

[*Source:* http://www.iiss.org/shangri-la-more.php?itemID=15]

Declaration on Principles for Relations and Comprehensive Cooperation Between the Republic of India and the People's Republic of China, Beijing, 23 June 2003

At the invitation of Premier of the State Council of the People's Republic of China, H.E. Wen Jiabao, Prime Minister of the Republic of India, H.E. Atal Bihari Vajpayee paid an official visit to the People's Republic of China from 22 to 27 June 2003.

During this visit, Premier Wen Jiabao held talks with Prime Minister Vajpayee. Their Excellencies President Hu Jintao of the People's Republic of China, Chairman Jiang Zemin of the Central Military Commission, Chairman Wu Bangguo of the Standing Committee of the National People's Congress and Vice President Zeng Qinghong of the People's Republic of China held separate meetings with Prime Minister Vajpayee. The talks and meetings were held in a sincere and friendly atmosphere.

Leaders from both countries noted with satisfaction the progress made over recent years in bilateral relations. This is conducive not only to their respective development, but also to regional stability and prosperity. The two sides recalled the historical depth of their friendly contacts. India and China are the two largest developing countries of the world with centuries-old civilisation, unique history and similar objectives. Both noted that the sustained economic and social development in the two countries, representing one-third of humanity is vital for ensuring peace, stability and prosperity not only in Asia but also in the whole world.

The two sides agreed that India and China have a mutual desire for good-neighbourly relations and have broad common interests. They agreed to fully utilise the substantial potential and opportunities for deepening mutually beneficial cooperation.

Friendship and cooperation between the two countries meets the need to:

- promote the socio-economic development and prosperity of both India and China;

- maintain peace and stability regionally and globally;
- strengthen multipolarity at the international level; and
- enhance the positive factors of globalisation.

Both sides affirmed that they would abide by the following principles, promote a long-term constructive and cooperative partnership and, on this basis, build a qualitatively new relationship:

- Both sides are committed to developing their long-term constructive and cooperative partnership on the basis of the principles of Panchsheel, mutual respect and sensitivity for each other's concerns and equality;
- As two major developing countries, India and China have a broad mutual interest in the maintenance of peace, stability and prosperity in Asia and the world, and a mutual desire in developing wider and closer cooperation and understanding in regional and international affairs;
- The common interests of the two sides outweigh their differences. The two countries are not a threat to each other. Neither side shall use or threaten to use force against the other; and
- Both sides agree to qualitatively enhancing the bilateral relationship at all levels and in all areas while addressing differences through peaceful means in a fair, reasonable and mutually acceptable manner. The differences should not be allowed to affect the overall development of bilateral relations.

Both sides agreed to hold regular high-level exchanges between the two countries. This will greatly enhance mutual understanding and expand bilateral relations. With a view to deepening their coordination and dialogues on bilateral, regional and international issues, both sides agreed on the need for annual meetings between Foreign Ministers of the two countries. They also agreed that personnel exchanges and friendly contacts between ministries, parliaments and political parties of the two countries should be further enhanced.

The two sides welcomed the positive momentum of bilateral trade and economic cooperation in recent years and shared the belief that continued expansion and intensification of India-China economic cooperation is essential for strengthening bilateral relations.

Both sides shared the view that existing complementarities between their two economies provide an important foundation and offer broad prospects for further enhancing their economic relations. In order to promote trade and economic cooperation, both sides will take necessary measures consistent with their national laws and rules and international obligations to remove impediments to bilateral trade and investment. They reaffirmed the importance of the ministerial meeting of the Joint Economic Group (JEG) and agreed to hold the next (seventh) JEG meeting within the year.

The two sides will set up a compact Joint Study Group (JSG) composed of officials and economists to examine the potential complementarities between the two countries in expanded trade and economic cooperation. The JSG would also draw up a programme for the development of India-China trade and economic cooperation for the next five years, aimed at encouraging greater cooperation between the business communities of both sides. The Group should present a study report and recommendations to the two Governments on measures for comprehensive trade and economic cooperation by the end of June 2004.

The two countries will launch a financial dialogue and cooperation mechanism to strengthen their dialogue and coordination in this sector.

The two sides agreed to enhance cooperation at the World Trade Organisation, which is not only to mutual benefit but also in the broader interest of developing countries. The two sides will hold dialogues on a regular basis in this regard.

Historical and cultural links between India and China will be strengthened, inter alia, through the promotion of exchanges in culture, education, science and technology, media, youth and people-to-people relations. They agreed to set up Cultural Centres in each other's capitals and facilitate their establishment.

Both sides will work towards the enhancement of direct air and shipping links, tourism, exchange hydrological data in flood season on common rivers as agreed, cooperation in agriculture, dairy, food processing, health and other sectors.

They agreed on the need to broaden and deepen defence exchanges between the two countries, which will help enhance and deepen the mutual understanding and trust between the two armed forces. They confirmed that the exchange of visits by their Defence Ministers and of military officials at various levels should be strengthened.

The two sides exchanged views on the India-China boundary question and expounded their respective positions. They reiterated their readiness to seek a fair, reasonable and mutually acceptable solution through consultations on an equal footing. The two sides agreed that pending an ultimate solution, they should work together to maintain peace and tranquillity in the border areas, and reiterated their commitment to continue implementation of the agreements signed for this purpose, including the clarification of the Line of Actual Control.

The two sides agreed to each appoint a Special Representative to explore from the political perspective of the overall bilateral relationship the framework of a boundary settlement.

The Indian side recognises that the Tibet Autonomous Region is part of the territory of the People's Republic of China and reiterates that it does not allow Tibetans to engage in anti-China political activities in India. The Chinese side expresses its appreciation for the Indian position and reiterates that it is firmly opposed to any attempt and action aimed at splitting China and bringing about "independence of Tibet".

The Indian side recalled that India was among the first countries to recognise that there is one China and its one-China policy remains unaltered. The Chinese side expressed its appreciation of the Indian position.

India and China recognised the primacy of maintaining international peace. This is a prerequisite for the socio-economic development of all developing countries, including India and China. The world is marked by diversity. Every country has the right to choose its own political system and path to development. As two major developing countries, India and China acknowledged the importance of their respective roles in the shaping of a new international political and economic order. The international community must help the developing countries to eliminate poverty and narrow the gap between the North and the South through dialogue and cooperation so as to achieve common prosperity.

The two sides acknowledged the vital importance of the role of the United Nations in world peace, stability and development. They are determined to continue their efforts in strengthening the UN system. They reaffirmed their readiness to work together to promote reform of the UN. In reform of the UN Security Council, priority should be given to enhancing representation of the developing countries.

Both sides stood for continued multilateral arms control and disarmament process, undiminished and equal security for all at progressively lower levels of armament and for multilateral negotiations aimed at nuclear disarmament and elimination of nuclear weapons. They are firmly opposed to introduction of weapons in outer space, use or threat of force against space-based objects and support cooperation in development of space technology for peaceful purposes.

The two sides recognised the threat posed by terrorism to them and to global peace and security. They resolutely condemned terrorism in any form. The struggle between the international community and global terrorism is a comprehensive and sustained one, with the ultimate objective of eradication of terrorism in all regions. This requires strengthening the global legal framework against terrorism. Both sides shall also promote cooperation on counter-terrorism through their bilateral dialogue mechanism.

India and China face special and similar challenges in their efforts to protect the environment while simultaneously forging ahead with rapid social and economic development of their countries. In this context, the two sides agreed to work together in a practical manner to cooperate on preserving the environment and ensuring sustainable development and to coordinate positions on climate change, biodiversity and other issues in relevant multilateral fora.

The two sides supported multilateral cooperation in Asia,

believing that such cooperation promotes mutually beneficial exchanges, economic growth as well as greater cohesion among Asian countries. The two sides viewed positively each other's participation in regional and sub-regional multilateral cooperation processes in Asia.

The two sides stated that the improvement and development of India-China relations is not targeted at any third country and does not affect either country's existing friendly relations and cooperation with other countries.

The two sides agreed that the official visit of the Prime Minister of India to the People's Republic of China has been a success, has contributed to enhancing mutual understanding and trust between the Governments, leaders and peoples of the two countries, and marks a new step forward in strengthening the all-round cooperation between India and China in the new century.

Prime Minister Vajpayee invited Premier Wen Jiabao to visit India at a mutually convenient time and conveyed to President Hu Jintao an invitation from President Abdul Kalam to visit India. The Chinese side accepted the invitations with appreciation. The dates of the visits will be settled through diplomatic channels.

On behalf of the Government and the people of India, H.E. Prime Minister Atal Bihari Vajpayee thanked the Government and the people of China for the warm welcome received by him and his delegation.

Signed in Beijing on 23 June 2003 in the Hindi, Chinese and English languages.

(Atal Bihari Vajpayee)	(Wen Jiabao)
Prime Minister	Premier of the State Council
The Republic of India	The People's Republic of China

[*Source:* http://meadev.nic.in/ind-chn-decla.htm]

Memorandum between the Government of the Republic of India and the Government of the People's Republic of China on Expanding Border Trade, Beijing, 23 June 2003

The Government of the Republic of India and the Government of the People's Republic of China (hereinafter referred to as the two sides),

With a view to promoting the development of friendly relations between the two countries and two peoples,

Pursuant to the Memorandum between the Government of the Republic of India and the Government of the People's Republic of China on the Resumption of Border Trade signed on 13 December 1991, and Protocol on Entry and Exit Procedures for Border Trade signed on 1 July 1992,

Desirous of opening another pass on the India-China border and setting up an additional point on each side for border trade,

Have agreed as follows:

Article I

The Indian side agrees to designate Changgu of Sikkim state as the venue for border trade market; the Chinese side agrees to designate Renqinggang of the Tibet Autonomous Region as the venue for border trade market.

Article II

The two sides agree to use Nathula as the pass for entry and exit of persons, means of transport and commodities engaged in border trade. Each side shall establish checkpoints at appropriate locations to monitor and manage their entry and exit through the Nathula Pass.

Article III

All the provisions of the Memorandum on the Resumption of Border Trade signed between the two Governments on 13 December 1991 and the Protocol on Entry and Exit Procedures for Border Trade signed between the two Governments on 1 July 1992 under the Memorandum shall also be applicable to the border trade through the Nathula Pass.

Article IV

This Memorandum may be amended or supplemented by agreement in writing between the two sides.

Article V

This Memorandum shall come into force as from the date of its signature and shall be valid during the validity of the Memorandum on Resumption of Border Trade signed between the two Governments in New Delhi on 13 December 1991.

Done in Beijing on 23 June 2003 in two originals each in the Hindi, Chinese and English languages, the three texts being equally authentic.

(Signed)	(Signed)
For the Government of the Republic of India	For the Government of the People's Republic of China

[*Source:* http://meaindia.nic.in//speech/2003/06/23spc02.htm]

Joint Statement on the Meeting of the U.S.-India Defence Policy Group, Washington D.C., 8 August 2003

The U.S.-India Defence Policy Group (DPG) met 6-7 August 2003 in Washington, D.C. Under Secretary of Defence for Policy Douglas Feith hosted the meeting and Defence Secretary Ajay Prasad led the Indian delegation.

The strategic situation in the world has changed dramatically in recent years. Global terrorism, state sponsors of terrorism, and the proliferation of weapons of mass destruction are the key threats to international peace and security. The U.S. and India are drawn together in an effort to deal with these new circumstances. As a result, President Bush and Prime Minister Vajpayee have redefined the U.S-India relationship: democracy, common principles, and shared interest are the foundation of our new strategic partnership.

Since the last meeting of the DPG in May 2002, the U.S. and Indian defence establishments have continued to expand cooperation. The past year's accomplishments include:

- Combined special forces counter-insurgency exercise in North East India;
- Combined Air Force exercise in Alaska;
- Complex naval exercises on the East Coast of India;
- Delivery of "Firefinder" radars to India;
- Senior-level missile defence talks; and
- Conclusion of a master information exchange agreement to facilitate cooperation in research and development of defence technologies

During this year's DPG, the delegations emphasized the long-range strategic concepts that guide the new approach to the U.S.-India relationship. They agreed that the work of the two countries together during the past year and planned activities for the next year are translating that strategic vision into action.

The delegations discussed the threat posed by the proliferation of weapons and technologies of mass destruction, including the risk that terrorists will acquire such weapons. They also discussed measures to combat proliferation.

The two sides agreed to establish a high-level dialogue on defence technology security issues.

The two sides reaffirmed the shared view that missile defence enhances cooperative security and stability. They decided to hold a missile defence workshop in India in the next six months as a follow-on to an international workshop attended by U.S. and Indian delegations at the June 2003 Multinational Ballistic Missile Defence Conference held in Kyoto, Japan. The Indian delegation also accepted invitations to the July 2004 Multinational Ballistic Missile Defence Conference in Berlin and the 2005 Roving Sands Missile Defence Exercise.

The two sides welcomed the improved prospects for freedom and security in the Middle East. They underlined their commitment to furthering stability and security for the people of Iraq and the contribution that international cooperation could make to that process. They agreed to continue to seek ways for the United States and India to work together to support the people of Iraq. They also welcomed the establishment of Iraq's Governing Council and noted the important role of the U.N. Special Representative in addressing the needs of the Iraqi people.

They discussed the success of Operation Enduring Freedom and reaffirmed the ongoing commitment of both countries to the future of Afghanistan. They agreed that a permanent end to terrorism is critical to ensuring a future of peace and stability in South Asia.

The U.S. and India have continued to work together to enhance their capabilities to combat terrorism and increase interoperability. The two delegations highlighted the importance of the ongoing series of joint and combined exercises in building interoperability between U.S. and India armed forces and agreed to continue this interaction. They also agreed to continue to review counter terrorism equipment requirements for India's special operations forces.

The two delegations welcomed the reports on the recent meetings of the Military Cooperation Group (coordinating military exercises and exchanges), Security Cooperation Group (coordinating sales and licensing), and Joint Technical Group (coordinating research and development). These groups will meet again in the coming months.

In addition to the areas above, the two delegations approved a range of activities for the coming year, including:

- Specialized training programs and joint exercises to be carried out by the armed services of the two countries, including an air combat training exercise.
- India will host in coordination with the U.S. a multinational planning exercise to develop standard operating procedures.
- Continued development of a defence supply relationship, through the Government-to-Government Foreign Military Sales program. A U.S. team will travel to India in September to discuss the details of a possible sale of P-3 maritime patrol aircraft.
- U.S. sale to India of training materials and specialized equipment to support India's peacekeeping training capabilities.
- A Defence Planning Exchange to permit U.S. and Indian defence experts to conduct discussions on defence strategy and planning.

Secretary Prasad also met with U.S. Secretary of Defence Donald Rumsfeld, U.S. Deputy Secretary of State Richard Armitage, and Chairman of the Joint Chiefs of Staff General Richard Myers. These meetings emphasized the importance both sides place on the growing bilateral relationship.

Next year, the DPG will hold its meeting in New Delhi.

[*Source:* http://www.state.gov/p/sa/rls/pr/23209.htm]

Speech by External Affairs Minister, Mr. Yashwant Sinha, at the Institute of Defence and Strategic Studies, Singapore, 26 August 2003

Prof. Jayakumar, Mr. Desker, Ladies & Gentlemen,

Thank you, Mr. Chairman, for your warm words of welcome. It is a privilege to be addressing this distinguished gathering here today. Though I have chosen to use the wider term of Asia, the focus of my comments are naturally going to be on this part of the world and on India's engagement with this region. In the process, I hope to outline the changes taking place in India and to situate in the larger context, her foreign policy as well as domestic economic trends. Speaking a day after India's premier commercial centre, Mumbai has been rocked by a dastardly terrorist attack causing over 50 deaths and over a hundred wounded, I hope to also dwell on the scourge of terrorism and the need for the world to collectively address the problem.

Asia, stretching from the Mediterranean to the Pacific, is witnessing rapid expansion of its role in global economic and security affairs, despite the small setback caused by the financial crisis of the late 1990s. We have seen economic growth on a historic scale, first among the "tiger" economies and then among a wider group, including China and India. Asia is more outward looking and there is growing realisation of the importance of regional cooperation in our area which has led to emergence of new institutions like SAARC, ASEAN, and more recently, the Asia Cooperation Dialogue or ACD spearheaded by Thailand. Active discussions about new concepts such as the Asian Bond market and Asian Rating Agencies are a sign of the increasing self-awareness by Asia of its capabilities and strengths and are indicative of a thirst to regain an older, more glorious heritage and develop independent thinking on major issues affecting the region.

Asia: basic facts and figures

Let me give you some facts about Asia collated from various sources that could provide the backdrop to our discussions.

- Home to 60 per cent of the world's population, Asia encompasses extraordinary diversity in terms of religion, race, ethnicity and culture. Each of its regions, whether they be the Gulf and West Asia, Central Asia, South Asia, South East Asia and North East Asia, all have distinctive characteristics that separate them from the others. Yet Asia has civilisational commonalities that seek unity in its diversity.
- Asia accounts for about a quarter of global GDP. It is estimated that by 2025, it will contribute to 57 per cent of the global GDP. Already Japan, China, Korea and India are among the top twelve countries in terms of GDP.
- In 2000, Asian exports accounted for 31 per cent of total global trade.
- Intra-regional trade accounted for 52 per cent of exports and 63 per cent of imports and amounted to 16 per cent of total world trade.
- International reserves of developing countries in Asia accounted for 77.5 per cent of total international reserves of all developing countries of which 21 per cent was mainland China's, 13.4 per cent Hong Kong's and 12 per cent South Korea's. I understand the reserves of Singapore and India also come to around 13 pre cent each of the total reserves.
- FDI flows into Asian developing countries amounted to 11 times of those for developing countries in the Americas, 35 times those in Eastern Europe and nearly 200 times those for African countries.
- The labour force in developing countries of Asia Pacific and South Asia totalled 1.1 billion and 600 million respectively, of which over 750 million and 450 million were accounted for by China and India.
- It also accounts for the world's largest energy resources on which depends the prosperity, not only of the Asian continent but also of the rest of the world. Of this, the Middle East is the biggest source for global fuels while Central Asia has vast untapped resources. South East Asia too is a significant source of petroleum and natural gas.

- More recently, the Asia Pacific region has become a major information age hub with abundant satellite services, major teleport bases and software programming.
- In general, it has a huge competitive advantage in manufacturing because of the presence of natural and agricultural resources, inexpensive labour—skilled and unskilled, low cost of production, and a diversified market.
- Asia has some of the largest standing armies.

Today, there is a new dynamism in the region as Asian countries acquire an increasing role in global trade and capital flows. Singapore itself is one of the best illustrations of such a dynamic role. With a per capita income of US$22,000, it is on par with the older industrialised countries. It attracts US$10 billion of FDI annually. Its trade turnover is over US$300 billion. Singapore's success in these fields is a source of inspiration for others in Asia including India. It is by now widely accepted that the 21st century will be an Asian century. The fulcrum of political and economic activity in the world is clearly shifting towards Asia.

Changes and Challenges Facing Asia

What are the most important changes that can be noticed in recent times, particularly in this region? First of all, terrorism stalks Asia as never before. India, a long-standing victim of terrorism, was hit again yesterday. Mumbai was deliberately chosen because what these terrorists and their sponsors envy the most is India's success in the economic field. The relative stability that ASEAN enjoyed over the last few decades has also been shattered by the rise of extremist forces in the region. A harsh, militant, puritanical form of Islam brought in by outsiders, preying on a false sense of victimisation, is threatening to displace South East Asia's Islamic tradition of syncretism and co-existence. The bombings in Bali and Jakarta and the discovery of expansive networks of terrorist organisation in the region have revealed the scale of the new threat to Asia. Secondly, a new international order has begun to emerge in the region replacing the uncertainties of the post-Cold War era. The region is no longer marked by rivalry between superpowers. Countries of the region have more or less settled into a system where major powers are learning to co-exist peacefully. Thirdly, the after-effects of the Asian financial crisis have blown over and the region is entering a new trajectory of growth. While globalisation and the opportunities and challenges that it presents continue to be debated extensively, integration of the principal economies of the region with the world has proceeded apace. Fourthly, the remarkable success of the ASEAN experiment has prompted many others of Asia to actively strive for regional cooperation. Persisting poverty and underdevelopment, rising population, increase in migration and refugee flows, rapidly depleting natural resources including water, trafficking in small arms and drugs, transnational crimes etc.—all provide ballast for such cooperation amongst countries. Finally, proliferation with the attendant risk of nuclear weapons falling into the hands of terrorist groups is now the greatest in Asia. This is particularly so in the immediate neighbourhood of India where it is possible to find the conjunction of authoritarian rule, religious fundamentalism, terrorism, drug trafficking and weapons of mass destruction. Some of the most deliberate and well-documented instances of nuclear and missile transfers have taken place in this region.

Asia's Response

Confronted by such change, what should be Asia's response? It is a commonly shared conviction that in order to continue the march towards prosperity of our peoples, we must work towards the twin goals of enhancement of peace and security and sustained economic growth and development. While countries will continue to have a national perspective of security arising out of their own geography and history, it is increasingly accepted today that in the realm of security, we are all dealing with global threats and global challenges. It is no longer possible for any country in the world to insulate itself from developments that are taking place in an increasingly interconnected and interdependent world. The events of September 11, 2001 provide the most telling example of this. A cooperative approach to security which helps in increasing stakes of members in enduring peace and stability is therefore essential. Such an approach would be accommodative of the diversity of the region and would also be a reflection of growing strength and confidence amongst countries. The ARF plays an important role in the above regard. But it needs to be strengthened through effective bilateral and other arrangements amongst the countries of the region on issues such as counter terrorism, curbing proliferation and protection of sealanes of communication.

To effectively tackle terrorism, there must be clarity on three important issues. There are some in the world who argue that certain "root causes" are responsible for the phenomenon of terrorism and that this menace can only be addressed by dealing with the proclaimed political grievances of those indulging in violence. Others insist on a definition of terrorism before dealing with it. The emphasis on root causes and semantic exercises in defining terrorism, however, tend to play into the hands of those who resort to indiscriminate violence. No grievance and sense of historical injustice can justify the use of violence against innocent civilian populations. Those who emphasise addressing "root causes" such as poverty, absence of political freedom, territorial disputes, religious intolerance, ethnic discrimination, etc. are suggesting that we must continue to live with terrorism or rather die at its hands until all these problems are resolved. It is equally baseless to link terrorism to any particular religion and perceive its recent growth as heralding a "clash of civilisations". Also important is the issue of double standards in the fight against terrorism. I refer to the tendency by some to condone terrorism in some places while condemning it elsewhere. This is counter-productive. Such leniency will only boomerang on everyone. We collectively owe it to ourselves as well as to the world to push, prod, persuade and mobilise the international community into redoubling efforts aimed at eradicating the phenomenon of terrorism from its very roots.

Changing India

Let me now turn to India and discuss two of the most important changes of recent times, namely the success of India's economic reform programme which has brought her new confidence and strength as well as the evolution of her foreign policy particularly as it affects this region. India is today at the forefront of the many positive changes that our continent is witnessing. Our GDP growth has averaged around 6 per cent in the last decade. We are now a US$550 billion economy and will be recording close to 7 per cent GDP growth this year. This will bring us within striking distance of the US$600 billion mark or a little above the ASEAN GDP combined. We have pre-paid US$3 billion of external debt earlier this year. At the macro level, four chronic problems of the Indian economy, which had dogged us for full 50 years, have been effectively addressed and should not ever reappear. The first is balance of payments. Our foreign exchange reserves have today crossed US$85 billion and we are racing towards the US$100 billion mark. For the first time in 23 years, the current account of India's balance of payments recorded a surplus equivalent to 0.3 per cent of GDP in 2001-02. Short-term debt has also declined steadily and this has been achieved in an extremely volatile international situation where country after country has fallen prey to economic crisis caused by the external sector.

Today, India is a model of management as far as the external sector is concerned. The second chronic problem of the Indian economy was perpetual food shortages and its import. Our food stocks were 20 million tonnes in 1996. Today, they stand at 39.8 million tonnes, even though food grain production last year was sharply affected by the poor monsoon. India has emerged as the seventh largest exporter of food grains in the world today. The third problem, which has been effectively tackled, is price rise. Inflation over last five years has averaged 4.66 per cent. The fourth chronic problem of our economy has been infrastructure. In January 1998, the total number of telephones in India was 16.2 million. Today, we have more cell phones than that. In addition, the number of landlines has grown dramatically to 41.3 million as of April 2003. Prices have dropped sharply and vegetable sellers and farmers can be seen sporting mobile phones. Similar transformations have been taking place in the field of roads, ports and housing. A drop in interest rates has brought home loans within reach of the middle class and the quantum of loans given out for buying homes has gone up by roughly five times in the last five years. We have also steadfastly worked on bringing India's financial sector up to world standards of quality and robustness. The insurance sector has been opened up to private competition and we are hence seeing very rapid growth in the penetration of insurance products. The banking system has been also given a better legal foundation. Courtesy the software revolution and IT enabled services,

India's image has undergone a qualitative upgradation. After 1995 when we signed the WTO accord, Indian industry has gone through a process of transition, adjustment and change particularly after April 2001 when the last of quantitative restrictions were removed. Indian industry is emerging out of this churning lean, mean and stronger to face the challenge of global competition. This is evident both in terms of the economic recovery at home as well as in our export performance.

India is today recognised not only as one of the most important emerging economies but also as a leader in the field of science and technology, human resources development and provision of services. All this has happened in a decade that has seen a political transformation in India. After a brief spell of political instability, coalition politics in India has stabilised and the present Government is shortly due to complete its full term of five years. It will achieve the distinction of being the first non-Congress Government in India's history to do so. There is today growing empowerment of different segments of our population and a thirst for growth that manifests itself across the board. Among all political parties, there is conviction that economic growth and reform must be the mantra to guide us into the future.

The social transformation of India has been even more impressive. Indian culture has gone global. Indian fashion, film and food are now well established in practically every corner of the world. Yoga, meditation and traditional medicine have become part of the life style of Generation X. Overseas Indians and Persons of Indian Origin are moving up in their chosen careers in the countries they live in. Their contribution to the success and prosperity of Singapore is well known and needs no elaboration before this audience. In the U.S., Indians now rank first in terms of education and earnings. India is rapidly breaking out of its traditional stereotype. While we continue to face our share of problems and benefits of rapid economic growth are still to be evenly distributed, these issues are being addressed with all seriousness and with confidence.

India's Foreign Policy

In terms of foreign policy, our main concern has been to ensure stability on our borders and in the larger geographical region, which we call our neighbourhood, namely, the Persian Gulf, Central Asia, Indian Ocean region and South East Asia. In its immediate neighborhood, India continues its approach of building confidence and trust through dialogue. Given India's size and potential, this engagement imparts stability to India's extended neighbourhood. In this connection, I would like to highlight some recent developments, which are of significance.

- India has placed the utmost importance on improving relations with its immediate neighbourhood. This is an area I took up as a personal priority immediately after assuming office about a year back.
- Reflecting our commitment to the idea of regional economic integration, we have placed the idea of a South Asian Union before our South Asian neighbours.
- Pending conclusion of SAPTA and SAFTA, India has indicated its willingness to conclude bilateral free trade agreements with those countries who are willing to move faster. The bilateral Free Trade Agreement entered into with Sri Lanka has been a big success. Services sector, particularly in the tourism and travel trade, has also witnessed a boom. Indian nationals now constitute the largest number of tourists to Sri Lanka and they are also the biggest spenders. In fact, the Prime Minister of Sri Lanka in a speech recently made in Chennai called for the development of the South India-Sri Lanka sub-region as a single market.
- India's relationship with China is changing in response to the dynamics operating in both countries, regionally and globally. In the last few years, we have seen our relationship develop and diversify in many areas and at many levels. The level of mutual understanding which has been achieved is exemplified by our success in maintaining relative peace and tranquillity for nearly three decades along a border which extends for about 3500 kilometres and where there are clear differences of perception. Especially noteworthy is the increased emphasis on the economic aspect of our relationship. Our bilateral trade has shot up from around US$200 million in the early '90s to around US$5 billion in 2002, and this year we hope to reach US$7 billion. Indian

business and industry who used to talk of an invasion of India by Chinese goods have now overcome their initial cultural and commercial apprehensions of Chinese business and are strengthening linkages in a pro-active manner.

- Japan accounts for 40 per cent of the GDP of all the Asian countries together. Our trade and economic interaction with Japan is of the order of US$3.6 billion. We are also developing our political ties and have had exchanges at the level of Prime Ministers within the last three years.

Phase II of our Look East policy

India's "Look-East" policy is now over a decade old. The fact that successive governments in India continued with these policies shows the extent of consensus there is within India of the validity and importance of this policy.

With the holding of the first India-ASEAN Summit in Phnom Penh last November, we have effectively entered Phase II of our "Look East" policy. At the Summit, Prime Minister Vajpayee proposed an India-ASEAN Free Trade Area within 10 years and task forces are already hard at work to finalise a Framework Agreement by the time we hold the next Summit in October. We are also committed to supporting the Initiative for ASEAN Integration for bridging the developmental gap between old and new ASEAN, through capacity building and infrastructure development. We in fact, have a bilateral agreement with Singapore to cooperate in this sector. Another institutionalised mechanism for India-ASEAN cooperation is the India-ASEAN Business Summit being held once a year. This partnership will help in exploiting the synergies and complementarities between India and the ASEAN. India-ASEAN trade grew by 30 per cent between 1999 and 2001, i.e. from US$7.6 billion to nearly US$10 billion.

With ASEAN engaged in negotiating free trade arrangements with India, China, Japan and South Korea, we stand for the first time on the threshold of an Asian economic community. This process will be further pushed along by other initiatives at the sub-regional level such as the Mekong Ganga Cooperation as well as a trilateral initiative for a transport network between Thailand, Myanmar and India.

India and Singapore

Ladies and gentlemen, in the development of our ties with ASEAN, few countries have been as creative and pro-active as Singapore. We are grateful to our many friends here, in particular, Prime Minister Goh Chok Tong, for his vision and leadership in bringing India and ASEAN closer. This has been made possible by virtue of strong bilateral relationship that India and Singapore have built over the years. It was Prime Minister Goh who started the "India fever" back in 1992 when India first embarked on its economic liberalization programme. It is in recognition of his outstanding role that India has this year decided to award the Jawaharlal Nehru Award for International Understanding to Prime Minister Goh.

We have come a long way since. In April this year, India and Singapore launched negotiations for a Comprehensive Economic Cooperation Agreement (CECA) during the visit of Prime Minister Goh to India. Three rounds of CECA negotiations have been held and the agreement is expected to be concluded by early 2004. The CECA will lead to far-reaching benefits for both countries in trade and investment flows and in greater exchanges in professional services, especially in the Knowledge Economy. Business communities from both countries will be able to leverage each other's strengths better while achieving greater competitiveness. It's a win-win situation for both.

Ladies and Gentlemen, power in the 21st century will flow from the sinews of a well-run economy. I am convinced that the future of Asia rests in expanded economic interaction. The logic of economics is bound to inevitably overwhelm Asia just as it has happened in Europe.

The key to enhancing Asian security lies in our collective ability to build mutual economic stakes in each other. This is a process, which is already happening throughout the region. Regional infrastructure linkages in the form of roads, railway lines and pipelines are rapidly becoming a reality. They hold the potential to knit Asia together in a manner never before seen. On its part, India too has been contributing to this process by expanding connectivity with its neighbours towards the east as well as the west.

I would like to conclude by recalling the words of Prime Minister Goh Chok Tong at the first ASEAN-India Summit in Phnom Penh in November 2002 about ASEAN-India relations. He said that ASEAN was building a jumbo jet and one wing was provided by its Plus Three Summit partners to its east (China, Japan and South Korea). But the jumbo needed a second wing to take off and hence, the ASEAN-India partnership. It is a description I welcome. India would like to see ASEAN and in particular Singapore continue to be the engine of growth and of change in the region. India is happy to be part of a process of increased regional cooperation with ASEAN, China, Japan, Korea and the rest of the region. India is ready to board the jumbo jet towards greater collective security and enhanced prosperity. Thank you.

[*Source:* http://meaindia.nic.in//speech/2003/08/26spc01.htm]

Delhi Statement on Friendship and Cooperation between India and Israel, 10 September 2003

At the invitation of the Prime Minister of India, Atal Bihari Vajpayee, the Prime Minister of Israel, Ariel Sharon, paid a State visit to India from September 8-10, 2003, the first-ever by an Israeli Prime Minister.

Prime Minister Sharon was accompanied by Deputy Prime Minister and Minister of Justice, Yosef Lapid, Minister of Culture, Education and Sport, Limor Livnat (together with a cultural delegation) and Minister of Agriculture, Israel Katz. The large accompanying business delegation underscored the importance the two countries attach to expanding their economic relations.

During the visit, Prime Minister Sharon called on President Dr. A.P.J. Abdul Kalam, and held talks with Prime Minister Vajpayee. He also held separate meetings with Deputy Prime Minister and Minister for Home Affairs Lal Krishna Advani, Minister of Defence George Fernandes, Minister of Finance Jaswant Singh, Minister of External Affairs Yashwant Sinha and Leader of the Opposition Sonia Gandhi.

As ancient cultures and societies, India and Israel have left their mark on human civilisation and history. As democratic countries since their inception, both nations share faith in the values of freedom and democracy. Both countries gained independence during the same period and embarked on a course of nation building to advance the well-being of their respective peoples and to build modern democratic states able to face difficult challenges.

The two Prime Ministers discussed a range of important bilateral, regional and international issues. They reiterated their commitment to further advance the bilateral relations between the two countries and increase the scope of trade and economic exchanges.

The shared ideals draw both peoples into a natural amity in pursuit of common goals. Since the establishment of diplomatic relations in

1992, there has been rapid expansion and deepening of bilateral relations. Both sides attach great importance to strengthening their long-term cooperation in the political, defence, economic, commercial, cultural and science and technology areas.

In the presence of the Prime Ministers, Ministers from both sides signed the following agreements: a. An agreement on Environment Protection. b. An agreement on Cooperation in Combating Illicit Trafficking and Abuse of Narcotic Drugs and Psychotropic Substances. c. An agreement on Visa Free Travel for Diplomatic, Official and Service Passport Holders. d. An agreement on Cooperation in the fields of Health and Medicine. e. Exchange Program on Cooperation in the field of Education f. Exchange Program on Cooperation in the field of Culture. These agreements will further enhance the institutional framework created by those which have already been signed between the two countries.

Both sides agreed to increase the frequency of bilateral visits by Ministers and officials and to consolidate the ties between business communities of the two countries. People-to-people relations will also be encouraged, in order to increase and deepen understanding between the societies.

Both sides expressed their satisfaction with the impressive growth in bilateral economic relations. They believe that there is considerable untapped potential to enhance these relations, particularly in fields such as hi-tech and infrastructure where there are synergies, in order to encourage the private and public sectors to expand the scope of mutual trade and investments. Israel expressed its interest in and willingness to participate in key national Indian projects. Indian companies were invited to expand their activities in Israel—to encompass the field of investment—and to participate in the process of privatisation in Israel. Both sides will explore together the best ways to strengthen and implement these goals.

Both sides noted the scientific and technological cooperation between the two countries and expressed willingness to enhance participation in the joint fund for scientific research established in 1994, as well as explore the possibility of the establishment of a bi-national research and development fund in the industrial fields, particularly in bio-technology, information technology, telecommunication, agricultural research and the civilian use of outer space.

Both sides expressed satisfaction with the relations between the countries in the field of tourism, and called for the expansion of these relations as an additional tool for strengthening the bond of familiarity between their peoples.

Israel and India expressed their desire to work together, along with other countries and the international community, to create a new and better world—a world of peace, prosperity and welfare, for the benefit of all peoples and nationals.

Terrorism undermines the very foundation of freedom and democracy, endangers the continued existence of open and democratic societies and constitutes a global threat; therefore, there cannot be any compromise in the war against terrorism. Together with the international community and as victims of terrorism, Israel and India are partners in the battle against this scourge. In line with their adherence to UNSCR 1373, they strongly condemn terrorism in all its forms and manifestations and call upon the international community to take decisive action against this global menace, and condemn states and individuals who aid and abet terrorism across borders, harbour and provide sanctuary to terrorists and provide them with financial means, training or patronage.

India and Israel called for the establishment of a just and durable peace in the Middle East. The two sides expressed their respective views, and called for a complete cessation of violence, so that a conducive environment is created for continuation of the dialogue.

India and Israel share the goal of advancing peace, security and stability in their own region and respect for democracy in the entire world, and will continue efforts to encourage this trend.

Both sides paid tribute to the contribution of the Jewish community in India and the Indian community in Israel in providing a bridge of understanding and in strengthening the ties of culture and trade between the two countries. The shining example of the freedom always given to the Jews of India to practise their religion and give expression to their culture is a tribute to India's religious tolerance and secularism and sends a vital message of coexistence and harmony to the international community.

Prime Minister Sharon invited Prime Minister Vajpayee to visit Israel. Prime Minister Vajpayee accepted this invitation with pleasure.

India and Israel believe that the State visit of Prime Minister Ariel Sharon will further expand and enhance the framework of bilateral cooperation in various fields, and will contribute to strengthening the friendship between the two countries.

[*Source:* http://meaindia.nic.in//declarestatement/2003/09/10js01.htm]

Prime Minister Mr. Atal Bihari Vajpayee's Address at ASEAN Business and Investment Summit: "The India-ASEAN Partnership and Beyond", Bali, 7 October 2003

It is a great pleasure to be here among eminent business representatives from ASEAN, East Asia and India. I congratulate the organisers of this first ASEAN Business and Investment Summit. Events like these provide valuable opportunities for interaction among business and industry of our countries and for exchange of perspectives between Governments and industry.

Friends, While the 20th century economy was driven by capital accumulation, manufacturing technologies and labour power, the 21st century is defined by knowledge and human capital. It is this that gives strength to the Asian identity. There is an emerging perception that this will be the century of Asia's pre-eminence. The brain power of Asian scientists and engineers, the dynamism of our businessmen and industrialists, our intellectual and human resource capital—all these support this perception. The growing economic weight of Asia is strengthened by favourable demographic trends, and is no longer constrained by Cold War divisions.

India, ASEAN and the countries of East Asia are a part of this trend. ASEAN is already in an advanced stage of economic integration. With each of China, Japan and Korea also, ASEAN has a well-developed and diverse economic relationship. India has lagged behind, for a variety of political and economic reasons, which are now history. However, this situation is changing rapidly, and it is the exciting potential of the future India-ASEAN partnership that I propose to put before you today.

Over the last 12 years, the Indian economy has maintained an average annual growth of over 6 per cent, which is better than that of most other countries. Our interest rates are falling, inflation has been kept down, and foreign exchange reserves are growing rapidly. India remained unaffected by the Asian financial crisis a few years ago. We have targeted an 8 per cent growth over the next five years. As our economic base is large, there is considerable untapped potential for India's continued—and even accelerated—economic growth.

Friends, perceptions shape decisions. Often they are flawed. Sometimes, they are incomplete. The rich cultural diversity and spiritual traditions of India are well known, but they constitute only one aspect of India. There is another India, the India of the 21st century, which is still not so well known, with its many strengths:

- One, an inherently strong economy driven primarily by indigenous skills and domestic enterprise.
- Two, a growing and accessible domestic market, with import and investment barriers falling away. To take just one random example of the growth of the market: in the last few months, it has been absorbing about 2 million mobile phones a month. Import duties are moving towards ASEAN levels, and sectoral caps on foreign investment are rising.
- Three, a rich pool of human resources—English speaking, with R&D skills, technological training and managerial capabilities.
- Four, some special capabilities in state-of-the-art technologies. India is one of only three countries—the others are USA and Japan—to have indigenously designed and manufactured supercomputers. It is one of only six countries, which can build and launch its own satellites.
- Five, global leadership in technologies of the Knowledge Economy. India's pre-eminent position in IT and IT-enabled services has led global companies to set up captives in India or to outsource their operations to quality Indian service providers.
- Six, a sound and transparent financial system, with well-managed banking and insurance sectors, and vibrant capital markets. Our paperless, computer-driven National Stock Exchange is the third largest in the world, in terms of number of annual transactions.

India is today a country on the move. We are experiencing many revolutions simultaneously. There is, of course, the IT revolution. This in turn has unleashed a socio-cultural revolution, which has empowered hundreds of millions of our citizens, strengthening our democracy and stimulating our creativity. We are experiencing a demographic revolution, where the numbers of young people are increasing. Already, 54 per cent of our population is below 25 years of age. This has created a revolution of expectations, where a powerful new force of young people, full of optimism and ambition, fired by boundless energy, is actively seeking opportunities for wealth, success and prosperity. The combined effect of these has been a psychological revolution, in which a defensive, introverted approach has given way to an outward-looking, self-confident attitude, willing to accept challenges and take risks, rejecting fear and shunning fatalism.

It is this India that seeks to partner ASEAN in this era of globalisation. India's trade and economic interaction with the ASEAN countries has been steadily growing, but not fast enough. A year ago at the First India-ASEAN Business Summit, I had said that the India-ASEAN trade of less than 10 billion dollars does not do justice to our combined population of one and a half billion people, producing a trillion and a half dollars worth of goods and services annually. Our trade has since grown by about 25 per cent, but my comment remains valid.

We have recognised this fact in the India-ASEAN Framework Agreement for Comprehensive Economic Cooperation, which we have been negotiating over the past year. We are working on eliminating trade and investment barriers to facilitate business.

At the same time, India is conscious of the concerns of the new ASEAN members. We are offering unilateral tariff concessions on items of export interest to the CLMV countries. We are also seeking to incorporate an Early Harvest scheme to provide the incentive for a long-term engagement. If we proceed along this course, we can target a trade turnover of US$30 billion by 2007 and a Free Trade Area within 10 years.

A study, commissioned by our apex commerce and industry organizations, has highlighted five main areas with maximum promise for growth:

- Indian IT-enabled services create multiple opportunities for collaboration in embedded software or joint development of industry-specific solutions. ASEAN countries can outsource their operations to quality Indian service providers at competitive prices. Today, South East Asian countries import most of their IT products from the West. The irony is that most of these products are actually created by Indian sub-contractors. The result is a double disadvantage: you pay much more, and India gets much less.

- The Indian financial services industry is growing rapidly, driven by deregulation of insurance and investment in the banking sector by private companies and foreign banks. ASEAN investors will find attractive opportunities in personal financial services, insurance and corporate banking. India is poised to emerge as an additional global hub for financial transactions.
- The Indian pharmaceutical industry has achieved global recognition. The strength of this industry is low cost, high quality generics. Branded and patented medicines are also beginning to emerge as an important segment of the industry. ASEAN can source its imports of low cost generics from India, or shift manufacturing base to India.
- Indian entertainment business has benefited from deregulation and export opportunities. Joint ventures for TV content production and animation software exports present attractive opportunities for India and ASEAN.

India has placed special emphasis on infrastructural development to stimulate rapid economic growth. This includes deregulation of all segments of our telecom industry and upgradation of highways, bridges, ports, airports and convention centres. Many ASEAN companies are already present in these and other sectors. There are many other opportunities here for Asian business.

For free trade and open economic interaction, we must review, improve and harmonise our travel-related regulations and restrictions, including visa regimes. We have to upgrade our air, sea, road and rail links in capacity and quality, to meet new demands. To improve the profitability of business activities and tourist ventures, we should develop cross-regional links of tourist centres to enhance the synergy of Asian destinations.

I will say a brief word about India's investment regime. It is liberal and transparent, as befits a democracy like ours. We may occasionally have some problems, because of the difficulties in reconciling competing interests and concerns. This is normal in an open, democratic set-up. We are constantly trying to refine our regulations and procedures. All the same, if you analyse the experience of our foreign investors, returns on investments in India are generally higher. Repatriation of profits is also much easier than in many other countries.

Investors have to understand that India's continental size and diversity are unique. Marketing or investment strategies that may have worked well elsewhere may need to be tailored differently for India. Those who understand this do well. Companies that have taken the trouble of finding the right keys to unlock the doors of the Indian consumer's mind have done well for themselves. People tell me that successful investors often paint a deliberately pessimistic picture to discourage competitors from entering a lucrative market!

In spite of the stalemate at the Cancun Ministerial Conference, a rule-based and fair multilateral trading system should remain our goal. But while we search for this ideal, regional trading arrangements offer immediate advantages, particularly for geographically contiguous regions. They can provide our domestic industry and agriculture with a valuable learning period, before being exposed to the far greater competition of global free trade.

Friends, non-Asians view Asia as the principal market of the future. But it will also emerge as a manufacturing hub and a global provider of services. In the next fifty years, as the population of the developed world ages, a younger and better-educated work force will emerge in Asia to fill the breach. This generation will drive the future growth of the global economy. Asian countries should work towards strengthening their mutual synergies, so that they are strategically placed to derive maximum benefit from the emerging opportunities. The India-ASEAN partnership should energise this process to move us closer to our shared goal of making this truly the Asian century.

Thank you.

[*Source:* http://meaindia.nic.in//speech/2003/10/07ss01.htm]

India's CBM Proposal to Pakistan, 22 October 2003

I. External Affairs Minister Mr. Yashwant Sinha's Press Conference 22 October 2003

Friends, good afternoon. As you are aware, the Cabinet Committee on Security met this morning. Among other things, we discussed the progress of the Prime Minister's peace initiative with Pakistan. After the discussion, the Cabinet Committee has approved a number of new steps, which we have already conveyed to Pakistan. The Pakistan High Commissioner was asked to meet the Foreign Secretary this afternoon. He met the Foreign Secretary at 3:15 p.m. What I am going to tell you is something that has already been conveyed to the High Commissioner to the Government of Pakistan. We have made a number of suggestions to Pakistan.

The first is, the next round of the technical level discussion for resumption of civil aviation. You are aware that we could not reach an agreement in the first round, which was held in Islamabad. That meeting ended with the promise that the two sides will meet again. We propose to hold these talks once again, and the Director-General Civil Aviation will get in touch with his Pakistani counterpart to fix the dates for this meeting.

India is keen, though it is not a sign of our weakness mind you, that civil aviation links should be restored along with overflights, overflying rights over the air space of each country. We are keen because we feel that it is in the interest of the people of India and Pakistan that this should happen. I would also like to make it absolutely clear that there is no question of India giving any guarantees to Pakistan. So, this is the first step, resumption of talks for civil aviation.

The second is, we have offered to Pakistan to hold technical level discussions for the resumption of rail link. At the same time it has also been conveyed to Pakistan that the resumption of rail link will be undertaken after the successful completion of the technical level talks with regard to civil aviation.

The third is, we have decided to resume bilateral sporting encounters. This includes cricket also.

Fourth, in order to further benefit the people in both the countries, we propose the holding of visa camps by the respective High Commissions in different cities through a mutually agreed arrangement for the cities as well as the frequency of such camps. Details in this regard can be worked out through the diplomatic channels.

Five, senior citizens—which means persons of 65 years of age and above—would henceforth be permitted to cross Wagah checkpoint on foot. At the moment our policy is restricted to crossings by groups. We are extending this facility to individuals but restricting it to senior citizens to begin with. Anyone who travels by bus is free to cross.

(Six), We have also proposed to increase the capacity of Delhi-Lahore-Delhi bus service by running more buses in convoys on the already agreed days. The Delhi Transport Corporation, which I happened to chair at one time, would follow up on this with the Pakistan Tourism Development Corporation.

(Seven), We have proposed establishment of links between the Coast Guards of the two countries. Such links, we have suggested, could be on the pattern of the existing link between the DGMOs (Directors General of Military Operations), and could be established between their respective headquarters. Flag meetings could also be held at sea before and after the fishing season. Details could initially be tied up through diplomatic channels and subsequently followed up by the Indian Coast Guards and Pakistan Maritime Security Agency.

(Eight), We have proposed to Pakistan the non-arrest by either side of fishermen of the other country within a certain band on the sea. Details of the band on the sea again could be worked out through diplomatic channels.

(Nine), Government of India would provide free medical treatment to a second batch of 20 children from Pakistan. You are aware of the fact that after baby Noor's case we had announced that we would make this facility available to 20 children from Pakistan which will include medical treatment in India. Sixteen children have come to India. They have undergone treatment. They have either gone back or have undertaken treatment and recuperating, or waiting for treatment. Our Mission in Islamabad informs us that they have received a very large number of applications. Therefore, we have decided that we make 20 more slots available under this category.

(Ten), After all these steps are taken and the work of the Missions expands, we will be ready to look at further accretion to the strength of the two Missions—in Islamabad and Delhi. As you are aware, we have recently suggested increasing the strength by eight, which Pakistan has accepted. We are in the process of implementing it. We are prepared to increase it by another number to be mutually agreed upon once, as I said, as a result of all these steps the work increases.

(Eleven), We propose to go beyond the transportation links by air, road and rail. Therefore, we have proposed to Pakistan that we could consider a ferry service between Mumbai and Karachi. We will await the response of Pakistan.

(Twelve), Finally, but very importantly, we have proposed to Pakistan the start of two new bus services—one between Srinagar and Muzaffarabad, and the other either a bus or rail link between Khokrapar and Munabao, in Sindh and Rajasthan.

These are the steps which have been decided upon by the Cabinet Committee on Security and conveyed to Pakistan. We will await their response.

Our war against terrorism, especially cross-border terrorism, will continue. There will be no let up in dealing with terrorists who dare to infiltrate into India.

Thank you.

[*Source:* http://meaindia.nic.in//pressbriefing/2003/10/22pb02.htm]

II. Pakistan's Response 29 October 2003

The main points in Pakistan's reply to India's 22 October proposals with regard to CBMs are:

1. Welcomes Srinagar-Muzaffarabad bus proposal in principle. Wants check points along the way to be manned by UN officials and people should move with UN documents.
2. Sustained and serious dialogue needed.
3. India has proposed date for talks on technical-level talks for resumption of air links. Pakistan agrees to talks in first week of December.
4. Resumption of Samjhauta Express because bulk of traffic through rail, so we believe it will serve India's purpose of people-to-people contact.
5. No link between talks on resumption of air and rail links.
6. Welcome resumption of sporting ties.
7. Welcome (novel) idea of visa camps in various cities. But problem is how to implement? Pakistan wants restoration of number of staff in embassy to pre-December 2001 levels.
8. Senior citizens welcome to cross border on foot.
9. Instead of increase in frequency of Delhi-Lahore bus, Pakistan says it is better to resume Samjhauta Express because it will spare people a torturous 14-hour bus journey. India should have courage to restore rail links.
10. Pakistan proposes bus service between Amritsar and Lahore.
11. Work with India on release of fishermen arrested by both sides, on humanitarian grounds.
12. Heart institutes in Karachi and Punjab province have offered to treat some poor Indian children.
13. Mumbai-Karachi ship: Issue can come up when the composite dialogue is resumed.
14. Rail between Sindh and Munabao: Issue can come up when the composite dialogue is resumed.

Pakistan also made some fresh proposals:

1. It will offer 100 scholarships to Kashmiri children to take graduation and post-graduation courses in Pakistan
2. Will offer treatment to aged Kashmiris
3. Help widows and victims of rape (which, Pakistan's Foreign Secretary Riaz Khokar alleged, occurred due to the action of security forces). Wants UN agencies to identify such people.

Khokar said if India is sincere about bridging the gap between Kashmiris separated by the Line of Control, it would allow Kashmiris to accept the offers Pakistan has made.

[*Source:* http://www.rediff.com//news/2003/oct/29pak2.htm]

iii. India's Response 30 October 2003

Ministry of External Affairs Spokesman:

We welcome the fact that Pakistan has responded positively to at least some of the proposals announced by our External Affairs Minister on October 22. We are disappointed that they have attached impractical, extraneous or delaying conditions to the others.

Based on the positive responses, there would be immediate implementation of the proposals to allow senior citizens to cross at Wagah on foot. We would also initiate further steps for working out modalities for links between our Coast Guards and Pakistan's Maritime Security Agency. We also look forward to bilateral sporting encounters. We will work on the modalities of Pakistan's proposal for release of apprehended fishermen within a month, although we would have preferred to work out an arrangement for their non-arrest.

We hope that Pakistan will come to the talks on civil aviation on December 1-2, with an open mind and with the intention of finalising arrangements for their successful resumption.

We would look forward to holding of technical level talks for resumption of Samjhauta Express, in the middle of December, as proposed by Pakistan, after the successful conclusion of the talks in early December for resumption of civil aviation.

We welcome Pakistan's offer of medical treatment to 40 Indian children. Such offers and their implementation will no doubt enhance interaction and contribute, in some measure, to increasing understanding and empathy.

We are disappointed that Pakistan has, in effect, not agreed to our proposals for running extra buses on the Delhi-Lahore route, and establishing links between Mumbai and Karachi, Khokrapar and Munabao, and Srinagar and Muzaffarabad. Such links would have facilitated widening of people-to-people contacts and cooperation. They could have easily been put into effect through technical level discussions. Holding up such simple steps, and making them part of the Composite Dialogue process, in effect means delaying them. Since these measures are aimed at expanding interaction, widening areas of cooperation and building up trust, we will continue to hope that Pakistan will agree to their implementation. Our offer for a bus link between Srinagar and Muzaffarabad was motivated by humanitarian considerations. It is unfortunate that Pakistan has instead opted to politicise and disrupt this by attaching conditions that they knew would not be acceptable. In fact, even now people from these regions travel without the requirement of the kind of documents that Pakistan spoke about.

We have noted Pakistan's proposal for a bus link between Lahore and Amritsar. We can assess the requirement for this after progress on Delhi-Lahore bus, civil aviation and Samjhauta Express.

We are ready for a calibrated increase in size of Missions, as the requirement grows with the re-establishment of links, and setting up of new ones. However, there is no need to wait for this for holding of visa camps, which would ease the situation for the normal traveller who otherwise has to come all the way to Delhi or Islamabad to get visas. We would urge Pakistan to reconsider this.

As far as Pakistan's offer of 100 scholarships is concerned, we believe that the process of building trust and cooperation between India and Pakistan, and establishing lasting peace, would be facilitated if offers are not targeted on any particular region of India. India has never adopted, for instance, a selective approach for Balochistan, Sind or NWFP, or for any particular community. Our offers have been available to any Pakistani. If Pakistan were to make such non-discriminatory and general offers of cooperation, then it would no doubt contribute to taking the process further.

We are amused at Pakistan's profession of concern at the plight of disabled and negatively affected people in the state of Jammu & Kashmir. If Pakistan's concerns are really sincere, it should take immediate steps to end infiltration, dismantle the infrastructure of support to terrorism, and offer compensation to those affected by the terrorism it has sponsored. Its references to alleged repression on J&K are obviously only a ploy for its failed attempt to camouflage its sponsorship and support for terrorism.

I would also like to reiterate that Jammu & Kashmir is not a disputed territory. The only issue that remains to be resolved for a final settlement of J&K is the question of Pakistan's illegal occupation of a portion of the State.

Despite the limited positive responses from Pakistan, it is clear that our Prime Minister's initiative has gathered momentum. India would sincerely continue with the process, building on the successes achieved and the support generated, so that lasting peace is established between the two countries. We also remain committed to a dialogue process based on the premise that sustained dialogue requires an end to cross-border infiltration and terrorism. If Pakistan perceives, as it has claimed, that Composite Dialogue is in mutual interest, it must immediately put an end to its sponsorship of cross-border terrorism.

[Source: http://meaindia.nic.in//speech/2003/10/30ss01.htm]

Joint Declaration of the Republic of India and the Russian Federation on "Global Challenges and Threats to World Security and Stability", on the Occasion of the Visit of the Indian Prime Minister to Moscow, 12 November 2003

The Republic of India and the Russian Federation:

GUIDED by noble purposes and principles of the United Nations Charter,

RELYING on the provisions of the United Nations Millennium Declaration of 8 September 2000 concerning shared responsibility of States for managing threats to international peace and security and for promoting principles of human dignity, equality and justice at the global level,

NOTING the United Nations General Assembly Resolution 57/145 entitled "Responding to Global Threats and Challenges" of 16 December 2002,

RECOGNISING globalisation and interdependence in the world as natural processes in the evolution of mankind, which offer both opportunities and challenges,

TAKING into account the fact that uneven distribution of benefits and costs of globalisation have resulted in growing disparities among countries of the world,

DETERMINED to cooperate in countering global challenges and threats, which emanate from international terrorism in all its forms and manifestations, transnational organised crime, illicit drug trafficking, money laundering and environmental and developmental challenges,

PROCEEDING from an urgent need to consolidate efforts of the international community and the role of the United Nations in eliminating these global challenges and threats,

CONSCIOUS of their common values and responsibilities as pluralistic democracies,

DESIRING to continue to closely cooperate in contributing to world peace and progress,

CONFIRMING their obligations in accordance with the Treaty of Friendship and Cooperation between the Republic of India and the Russian Federation of 28 January 1993, Moscow Declaration on Protection of Interests of Pluralistic States of 30 June 1994, the Declaration on Strategic Partnership between the Republic of India and the Russian Federation of 5 October 2000, the Delhi Declaration on Further Consolidation of Strategic Partnership between the Republic of India and the Russian Federation of 4 December 2002, the Moscow Declaration by the Republic of India and the Russian Federation on International Terrorism of 6 November 2001 and the Memorandum of Understanding between the Government of the Republic of India and the Government of the Russian Federation on Cooperation in Combating International Terrorism of 4 December 2002,

Hereby declare:

India and the Russian Federation recognise that the aim of promoting global peace, security and stability through dialogue, consultation and cooperation among the countries concerned is essential. As strategic partners, India and the Russian Federation reaffirm their commitment to cooperate bilaterally and at the multilateral level on strategic issues, and to evolve a universal effective system of countering global challenges and threats of the 21st century. The UN should continue to play a leading role in this regard.

India and the Russian Federation as two large and influential democracies are to play a significant role in this context. Both countries are committed to promoting to the maximum extent, democratic values in international relations. India and the Russian Federation affirm that the future international order based on multi-polarity, should be determined by collective and multilateral processes rather than unilateral ones. Both countries stand for building a unified, just and democratic world order and a comprehensive system of collective security based on respect for rule of law and international norms, reciprocal trust, mutual benefit, equality and cooperation.

India and the Russian Federation stress that the United Nations

Organisation has a vital role in tackling major international issues. The United Nations can and should be reformed to reflect the current realities, with a view to preserve and enhance its efficacy and efficiency. India and the Russian Federation proceed from the idea that the reform of the UN should include an early expansion of the UN Security Council. The UN should continue to play an important role in the prevention and peaceful settlement of conflicts in conformity with the UN Charter and international law.

India and the Russian Federation are convinced that greater interaction and mutual respect among diverse societies and cultures will lead both to enrichment of these cultures as well as to enhanced harmony and security in the world. In this era of globalisation, it is by preserving pluralism that true multipolarity—in its political and economic as also social and cultural dimensions—will be attained. India and the Russian Federation also resolutely affirm that there is no place in today's pluralistic and diverse global village for any type of extremist ideology and intolerance. They will resist with their full might all forms of extremism, including religious extremism, which has proved to be a hot bed of terrorism in their common neighbourhood.

India and the Russian Federation are united in their fight against the evil of international terrorism. They actively cooperate with each other and with other countries in anti-terrorist activities. Both countries resolutely declare that international terrorists, whatever be their stated objectives and the causes they espouse, will never succeed in bringing the world to its knees.

India and the Russian Federation believe that most urgent and essential steps in effectively and comprehensively dealing with the threat of international terrorism should be:

- the creation of an environment for total rejection of terrorism and absolute unacceptability of any of its forms;
- consistent and uncompromising approach to terrorism and giving up "double standards";
- preventing the flow of funds for terrorist activities;
- effective implementation of the UNSC Resolution 1373 aimed against those who support, fund, or abet terrorists or provide

them shelter or asylum to engage in cross-border terrorism;

- promotion of confidence between members of the anti-terrorist coalition by, inter alia, due consideration of interests of each one of them and ensuring that the fight against terrorism is strictly based on rules of international law and principles of the UN Charter;
- reinforcing national and international legal instruments for countering terrorism, making the existing anti-terrorist Conventions genuinely universal, and earliest completion of negotiations on the draft Conventions in the UN, including the Comprehensive Convention against International Terrorism submitted by India and the International Convention on Suppression of Acts of Nuclear Terrorism submitted by the Russian Federation;
- steadfast cooperation to prevent terrorists from acquiring weapons of mass destruction, their means of delivery and materials and technology related to their manufacture;
- improvement of mechanisms of legal assistance and extradition in order to ensure the inevitability of punishment for terrorist crimes;
- efforts to promote coexistence of different religions, cultures and civilisations by stressing greater mutual understanding and respect amongst them, especially the idea that terrorism cannot be identified with any particular religion or ethnic group.

India and the Russian Federation are concerned that trafficking in illegal drugs, psychotropic substances and their precursors is assuming ever more threatening dimensions. Strong and effective measures are required by the international community to handle this threat, especially as narcobusiness serves as a source of financing to international terrorism. Both countries are taking specific practical steps to counter traffic in illegal drugs, psychotropic substances and their precursors, especially in their common neighbourhood.

India and the Russian Federation believe that one of the most urgent challenges today is strengthening multilateral cooperation for countering the global narcothreat. India and the Russian Federation underline the urgency of the need for the development of a comprehensive strategy, under the auspices of the UN, to effectively counter this problem and reiterate their commitment for close cooperation with the United Nations and other international organisations within the framework of the UN Drug Control Programme.

India and the Russian Federation support the efforts by Transitional Islamic State of Afghanistan to rebuild the nation and express full support to all international efforts aimed at promoting peace, stability, national reconciliation and economic reconstruction. It is important to adhere to the timetable, as envisaged in the Bonn Agreement, in the implementation of its provisions leading to the holding of democratic elections next year. India and the Russian Federation strongly believe that Afghanistan should emerge as a peaceful, strong, prosperous, united and independent nation that would be free from external interference and living in peace and harmony with its neighbours.

India and the Russian Federation are convinced that a concrete and time-bound plan of action under the UN aegis should be adopted for the earliest restoration of Iraq's sovereignty, stabilisation of the political and humanitarian situation in the country, and ensuring its economic growth, through broad international efforts.

India and the Russian Federation call for the prevention of the failure of the Road Map drawn to settle the Israeli-Palestinian conflict. The failure of the Road Map may result in the situation in Israel and Palestine, as also in the entire Middle East, spiralling beyond control. This may have adverse consequences not only for the region but for the whole world.

India and the Russian Federation support the efforts of the countries concerned and the international community for a peaceful settlement of the nuclear issue on the Korean Peninsula and maintaining its non-nuclear status. They also support all efforts including the continuation of six-party talks, started at Beijing, to bring about mutually acceptable solution, as well as further development of the inter-Korean dialogue and cooperation.

India and the Russian Federation are convinced that the success of the efforts aimed against contemporary global challenges and threats largely depends on adequately addressing social and economic issues, such as elimination of poverty, mass unemployment, illiteracy, and racial, ethnic and religious discrimination. Both countries believe that it is essential to promote steady and sustainable development of the world economy to ensure prosperity of all countries. One of the ways to achieve this goal, as they see it, is to ensure access of the majority of people around the world to high technology—a driving force of globalisation. Wider reach of scientific and technological achievements and benefits will bring more prosperity to a larger number of people, reduce the gap between the developed and the developing world and neutralise some of the impulses which trigger conflicts.

India and the Russian Federation, which are important partners in science and high technology, possess a vast potential for joint development of alternative technologies. They are convinced that multi-polarity in the world of high technology will make an immense contribution to the enhancement of political and economic multi-polarity in the modern world.

India and the Russian Federation declare that through their longstanding relationship as reliable, predictable and responsible strategic partners, they are dedicated to strive for finding effective and long-term solutions and appropriate responses to the aforementioned new global challenges and threats to humanity, basing their efforts on the UN Charter and principles of international law.

(Signed) Prime Minister of the Republic of India	(Signed) President of the Russian Federation

[*Source:* http://meaindia.nic.in//declarestatement/2003/11/13jd01.htm]

Admiral R.D. Katari Memorial Lecture by Mr. Yashwant Sinha, External Affairs Minister, on "The Emerging India-China Relationship and its Impact on India/South Asia", New Delhi, 22 November 2003

It is a privilege for me to be invited here today to deliver this lecture in memory of Admiral Ramdas Katari, a distinguished sailor, strategist and diplomat. The first Indian to become the Chief of the Naval Staff, Admiral Katari envisioned a modern navy for the country and did a lot to translate that vision into reality. A highly decorated soldier, he moved effortlessly to the world of diplomacy and served with distinction as India's Ambassador to Burma (now Myanmar) for four years. I would like to compliment the Indian Navy for carrying forward the fine traditions initiated by visionaries like Admiral Katari.

I have been asked to share a few thoughts with you on one of the most important bilateral relationships we have. Let me begin on a somewhat provocative note by saying that the title of this lecture—"The Emerging India-China Relationship and its Impact on India/South Asia"—represents a particular mind-set that is no longer valid. This is because first, I think that the relationship between India and China today is mature enough to be seen as having "emerged" rather than "emerging", though in a sense the relations between these two large countries will always remain a work in progress. Secondly, the impact of our relationship is global and to restrict the canvas to South Asia is to limit the scope of our understanding of India-China relations.

Let me substantiate my first contention regarding the maturity of the relationship between India and China. In recent years, relations between India and China have progressively developed and diversified. This is a process that both governments have consciously promoted. Our Prime Minister's visit to China marked the beginning of a new phase in the India-China relationship. It was a historic visit, the results of which have surprised many. During the visit, the leaders of the two countries agreed that we should qualitatively enhance the bilateral relationship in all areas, while addressing differences through peaceful means in a fair, reasonable and mutually acceptable manner. We agreed that the common interests of the two sides outweigh their differences, and that they are not a threat to each other. For the first time, the two Prime Ministers signed a Joint Declaration. It is an important document, which outlines the principles and shared perspectives that will guide the future development of our bilateral relations. The Declaration sends a signal to Asia and the world that our two countries are committed to working more closely together, including through our common desire to strengthen the trend towards multi-polarity.

I will illustrate the maturity of the present state of our relations with China with a few observations, which do not attempt to present a comprehensive picture. First, India and China have today extensive dealings in bilateral, regional and multilateral forums. We are seeking improved relations with each other without preconditions. We continue to have differences, including an unresolved boundary issue, but over the years, we have, together, evolved a remarkable matrix of relations, under which we have consciously decided to "compartmentalise" our differences and address them without letting them come in the way of the development of relations in other areas. We have not allowed our differences to define our relationship. It is a pragmatic model of inter-state relations, which has obvious relevance in other situations, including in our dealings with Pakistan.

Secondly, it is a relationship that is characterised by a strong political commitment, and indeed investment, by the leaderships of the two countries. This is evident in the pattern of high-level exchanges. There is no objective reason for discord between us. We also believe that mutual exclusion or containment is not a valid policy choice. At the same time, we are fully aware that there is a deficit of trust, which must be addressed as the two countries move towards their shared vision of a constructive and cooperative partnership. Our Prime Minister's visit to China represented a major step forward in that direction.

Thirdly, the level of mutual understanding that has been achieved is exemplified by our success in maintaining peace and tranquillity along the border. It is no mean achievement considering that we have a common border that extends for almost 3500 kilometres and where there are clear differences of perception, both in terms of the boundary and the Line of Actual Control (LAC). You are aware that in the late 1980s, there was tension along the border, particularly after the Wangdung incident, but the two countries responded in a sensible manner and have over the years carefully put in place an edifice of CBMs, of dialogue and interactions at the diplomatic and border commanders levels, of service-to-service exchanges, including the first-ever joint search and rescue exercise conducted by our Navies only a week ago. This has helped preserve and reinforce peace, tranquillity and indeed amity in border areas. We are engaged in clarifying the LAC, a process that must be expedited. During the Prime Minister's visit to China, the two Prime Ministers appointed their Special Representatives to explore the framework of a boundary settlement from the political perspective of the overall bilateral relationship. It is an issue I will return to a little later in my talk.

Fourthly, bilateral economic and commercial interactions have acquired an altogether new dimension now. Possibly for the first time in the exchanges between India and China since our independence, we have now a significant economic aspect to this relationship. Our bilateral trade has shot up from around US$200 million in the early nineties to around US$5 billion in 2002, and this year we hope to reach US$7 billion. Indian business and industry have overcome their initial cultural and commercial apprehensions of Chinese business and are strengthening their linkages in a pro-active manner. Enhanced trade and investment linkages not only make great economic sense but also provide ballast to the political relationship; mutual economic stakes will be a factor of stability in a relationship, which has seen many ups and downs in the past.

Finally, the India-China dialogue already transcends bilateral relations to encompass international issues such as security, environment and sustainable development. These are being discussed through dialogue mechanisms which have recently been extended to new subjects such as counter-terrorism and policy planning. Our deliberations in these forums have revealed a growing convergence of views on key issues, including on terrorism. We have an increasing commonality of interests within the WTO and overlapping concerns on globalisation, as was evident at the recent ministerial meeting at Cancun. Our coordination and collaboration in various multilateral institutions is expanding into newer and newer areas. Both countries seek to reinforce multilateralism and multi-polarity. The concept of multi-polarity must not, however, be mistaken for creating poles in opposition to each other. We do not want to reinvent the confrontationist model of the Cold War. Both India and China look upon the next twenty years as a window of strategic opportunity to raise the living standards of their peoples.

It is clear that as in India, there is also a need felt in China to improve the bilateral relations. This is not only because together we represent one-third of humanity. This has much to do with the changing perceptions about India, her economic success, her achievements in the field of science and technology, and global reach and dynamism of her foreign policy. It is also a factor of our steadily improving relations with the United States, the continued strategic partnership with Russia, our comprehensive partnership relations with the EU and its constituents, and our initiatives in West Asia, CIS countries, Africa and Latin America. It also has to do with our improving relations with other Asian countries, particularly ASEAN. It has to do with the increasing scope of potential cooperation between India and China in regional and multilateral forums, as we face new global challenges such as terrorism, drugs and piracy, as well as dangers in the fields of public health, environment, etc. It has to do with the fact that we are both in the forefront of developing countries and have similar approaches to many global and regional issues. It is clear that both India and China respect each other's independent foreign policies and are adjusting their relationship to take into account the new global realities, each other's growth as vibrant nations and economies and also in response to the dynamics operating regionally and globally.

Let me also clarify here what does not drive our relations with China. There are some who argue that India's relations with the United States could be used as a counterforce against China. We categorically reject such notions based on outmoded concepts like balance of power. We do not seek to develop relations with one country to "counterbalance" another. We value our relations with both China and the USA and both relationships have their own compelling logic. We must also debunk the theory that India's "Look East" policy of greater engagement with ASEAN is somehow aimed at containing China. Indeed, as I have stated at other forums recently, we have now entered Phase-II of the "Look East" policy, which encompasses not only the ASEAN Ten but also China, Japan, and other countries of East Asia, including Australia and New Zealand.

I would also like to reiterate what I have said earlier, that we reject the theory that a conflict between India and China is inevitable. India neither pursues nor makes policy towards China based on the belief that conflict between the two is inevitable. India's approach to China is and will remain forward-looking and full of optimism. It will not be driven by a sense of either fear or envy. We are convinced that both countries can grow strong and prosperous in partnership rather than in conflict, and maintain their independence and national character in the process. While it is undeniable that China and India are in some sense competitors, it is also clear that, just as the US and Europe, we can be both partners and competitors at the same time. All that is required is that this competition be healthy. This also relates to the level and rate of success achieved by the different development paradigms followed by India and China. While China may be seen by some as currently being ahead in this competition, India's success is clearly recognised and better understood now nationally and internationally than before. The management of this competition is the challenge and the Joint Declaration signed during the Prime Minister's visit to China provides an agreed via media for that.

Likewise, the argument that the dominant theme of China's South Asia policy is to prevent the rise of a potential rival or competitor in the form of India is a defeatist argument. There are probably some in our neighbourhood who seek to play their "China connection" or "China card" to "counter" or even "contain" India. The bankruptcy of this approach is however becoming increasingly evident. China cannot objectively be a competitor for India in South Asia. Destinies of the countries of South Asia are interlinked by the overwhelming logic of history, geography and economics. I believe the current relationship between India and China is certainly beneficial for each other and for South Asia. That India and China have succeeded in maintaining peace and tranquillity on their borders, and are steadily increasing the lines of communication between them, brings a large measure of stability to the region. We do not and should not judge our relationship with China in the context of our bilateral relations with any other country, whether in the region or outside the region. It also means that other countries need to adjust their own equations with both India and China to factor in the reality that it is no longer a matter of playing one against the other. It must also be recognised that increasing cooperation between India and China in the multilateral arena, which is a sub-set of our current relationship, will also have a positive cascading effect on the region, especially on issues relating to the interests of developing countries.

As I have stated earlier, during the Prime Minister's visit to China in June this year, both countries agreed to qualitatively enhance their bilateral relationship in all areas and also charted out a roadmap for doing so. Let me share with you some of my thoughts on what can be done by India and China to bring about a quantum jump in the relationship.

While the basic paradigm of the relationship—of seeking improved relations at all levels and in diverse areas while addressing differences—remains valid, the time has perhaps come to deal with some of those outstanding issues in a determined manner, without postponing tough decisions for the next generation. We believe the relationship has reached a level of maturity where we can discuss those issues with a greater sense of urgency. This updated paradigm of relationship is both desirable and sustainable. The initiative on the appointment of the Special Representatives flows from such an assessment. As the Prime Minister stated recently, a final resolution of the boundary question is a strategic objective and both countries should be ready to take some pragmatic decisions to achieve it. While India and China agree that their differences should not be allowed to affect the overall development of bilateral relations, there is little doubt that a boundary settlement will give a major boost to the relationship. It will also send a powerful signal to the rest of the world that India and China have broken out of the shackles of the past.

Secondly, the two countries must pay closer attention to each other's sensitivities and aspirations. This has been agreed to in the Joint Declaration signed by the two Prime Ministers. We have taken a principled position on issues like Tibet and Taiwan, and our position is appreciated by China. We are happy that the understanding reached during the Prime Minister's visit to China started the process by which Sikkim will soon cease to be an issue in India-China relations. Some aspects of China's relations with Pakistan, including their nexus in nuclear and missile proliferation, however, continue to cause serious concern in India as they have a direct and negative bearing on our national security environment. We regard China as a friend and we expect friends to show greater sensitivity to our security concerns. It is also important that both countries acknowledge each other's strengths and aspirations, and try to ensure that each has sufficient strategic space in keeping with the principle of multi-polarity to which both India and China subscribe.

Thirdly, we must be far more pro-active and ambitious in developing our economic partnership by exploiting more fully our complementarities and the new opportunities created by globalisation. Though our bilateral trade has shown an impressive increase in recent years, the turnover is still less than one per cent of China's overall trade, which is expected to reach US$800 billion this year. India-China trade is quite inadequate when compared to the complementarities that exist. For the first time, the business communities of the two countries are seriously looking at each other, with optimism and not with anxiety, and the two Governments must encourage this process with appropriate policy initiatives. Our economic engagement must be commensurate with the fact that India and China have two of the fastest growing economies in the world. A recent report by Goldman Sachs projects that India's economy will overtake that of France, Germany and Japan in less than thirty years and emerge as the third largest economy in the world in US dollar terms (and not just in Purchasing Power Parity), next only to that of the USA and China.

I believe that we in India must be ambitious, and not excessively cautious. Our experience during the last two-and-a-half years has shown how our apprehensions regarding Chinese goods overwhelming our manufacturing sector, following the lifting of quantitative restrictions on imports, were greatly exaggerated. This is a matter of some personal satisfaction to me because, as Finance

Minister, I was at the receiving end of all this criticism. I do expect that the India-China Joint Study Group, agreed upon during the Prime Minister's visit, will examine the feasibility of an upgraded bilateral framework for relationship, including a Free Trade Area. I know that some will receive this suggestion with disbelief and regard it as premature, as they did when the Prime Minister proposed a framework agreement for a Free Trade Area between India and ASEAN just over a year ago. But the fact is that we have already concluded a framework FTA with ASEAN. An Asian FTA, including China, Japan and South Korea, apart from ASEAN and India should therefore be within the realm of possibility. Indeed, I am also inclined to believe that in the years to come, India and China will be key partners in regional economic arrangements transcending Asia.

Finally, it is in the interest of both India and China to continue to raise the level of mutual trust and understanding. We must upgrade the quality of our dialogue and continuously address each other's concerns in a frank but constructive manner, not as adversaries but as friends, convinced that there is no fundamental contradiction in our basic interests. The degree of positive or negative influence which the actions of other countries can have on the bilateral relationship between India and China is proportional to the level of mutual trust and understanding that exists between us. It is important to continue in the conflict resolution mode that now exists between India and China, and indeed accelerate this process, not only because it is beneficial to us but also because it is beneficial to the region, and to the world. The risk of conflict or even divisive rivalry, open or covert, between two of the largest countries in the world, with huge and steadily growing economies, with nuclear weapon capabilities, with geographical contiguity and unresolved territorial issues, is a spectre that should never be allowed to haunt us or affect our search for peace and stability in this world.

Friends, India's fundamental national goal is the pursuit of a better quality of life for its people. What we seek the most is, economic progress and prosperity, the development of art, culture, literature and sports, and the emergence of a plural and multifaceted society that utilises the natural talents and versatility of our people to the full. I believe China also has a similar motivation. Peace and stability in the neighbourhood is of critical importance to both of us, in order to be able to pursue these goals and it is in this context that we must see India-China relations over the long term.

[Source: http://meaindia.nic.in//speech/2003/11/22ss01.htm]

White Paper on China's Non-Proliferation Policy and Measures, 3 December 2003

[Editor's Note: The Information Office of the State Council of China issued a White Paper on "China's Non-Proliferation Policy and Measures" in Beijing on 3 December 2003. The following is the full text of the White Paper]

Foreword

To prevent the proliferation of weapons of mass destruction (WMD) and their means of delivery is conducive to the preservation of international and regional peace and security, and compatible with the common interests of the international community. This has become a consensus of the international community. Through protracted and unremitting efforts, the international community has established a relatively complete international non-proliferation regime, which has played a positive role in preventing and slowing down the proliferation of WMD and their means of delivery, and in safeguarding peace and security both regional and global.

Economic globalization and the rapid advancement of science and technology have provided the international community good opportunities for cooperation and development, and also many new challenges. At present, traditional and non-traditional security factors are inter-woven, with the latter being steadily on the rise. Countries are linked more closely to each other in security matters, and their interdependence is continually deepening. It is an inevitable demand of the times to strengthen international cooperation and seek common security for all countries. The non-proliferation efforts of all countries and the development of the international non-proliferation mechanism are mutually complementary and inseparably linked with each other. Given the new international security situation, it is particularly important and urgent to step up international cooperation in the field of non-proliferation, and develop and improve the international non-proliferation mechanism.

The purpose of China's foreign policy is to help safeguard world peace and promote common development. A developing China needs both an international and a peripheral environment of long-term peace and stability. The proliferation of WMD and their means of delivery benefits neither world peace and stability nor China's own security. Over the years, with its strong sense of responsibility, China has step by step formulated a whole set of non-proliferation policies and put in place a fairly complete legal framework on non-proliferation and export control. It has taken positive and constructive measures to accelerate the international non-proliferation process with concrete actions, thus making significant contributions to safeguarding and promoting international and regional peace and security.

I. China's Basic Stand on Non-Proliferation

China has always taken a responsible attitude toward international affairs, stood for the complete prohibition and thorough destruction of all kinds of WMD, including nuclear, biological and chemical weapons, and resolutely opposed the proliferation of such weapons and their means of delivery. China does not support, encourage or assist any country to develop WMD and their means of delivery.

China holds that the fundamental purpose of non-proliferation is to safeguard and promote international and regional peace and security, and all measures to this end should be conducive to attaining this goal. The proliferation of WMD and their means of delivery has its complicated causes; it has everything to do with the international and regional security environment. To pursue the universal improvement of international relations, to promote the democratization of such relations and to accelerate fair and rational settlement of the security issues of regions concerned will help international non-proliferation efforts to proceed in a smooth manner. China resolutely supports international non-proliferation efforts, and at the same time cares very much for peace and stability in the region and the world at large. China stands for the attainment of the non-proliferation goal through peaceful means, i.e. on the one hand, the international non-proliferation mechanism must be continually improved and export controls of individual countries must be updated and strengthened, and on the other hand, proliferation issues must be settled through dialogue and international cooperation.

China maintains that a universal participation of the international community is essential for progress in non-proliferation. To gain an understanding and support of the overwhelming majority of the international community, it is highly important to ensure a fair, rational and non-discriminatory non-proliferation regime. Either the improvement of the existing regime or the establishment of a new one should be based on the universal participation of all countries and on their decisions made through a democratic process. Unilateralism and double standards must be abandoned, and great importance should be attached and full play given to the role of the United Nations.

China believes that given the dual-use nature of many of the materials, equipment and technologies involved in nuclear, biological, chemical and aerospace fields, it is important that all countries, in the course of implementing their non-proliferation policies, strike a proper balance between non-proliferation and international cooperation for peaceful use of the relevant high technologies. In this connection, China maintains that, while it is necessary to guarantee the rights of all countries, especially the developing nations, to utilize and share dual-use scientific and technological achievements and products for peaceful purposes subject to full compliance with the non-proliferation goal, it is also necessary to prevent any country from engaging in proliferation under the pretext of peaceful utilization.

II. Actively Participating in International Non-Proliferation Efforts

Over the years, China has participated extensively in the construction of the multilateral non-proliferation mechanism and actively promoted its constant improvement and development. China has signed all international treaties related to non-proliferation, and joined most of the relevant international organizations.

In the nuclear field, China joined the International Atomic Energy Agency (IAEA) in 1984, and voluntarily placed its civilian nuclear facilities under IAEA safeguards. It acceded to the Treaty on the Non-Proliferation of Nuclear Weapons (NPT) in 1992. It took an active part in the negotiations of the Comprehensive Nuclear Test-Ban Treaty (CTBT) at the Conference on Disarmament in Geneva and made important contributions to the conclusion of the treaty. China was also among the first countries to sign CTBT in 1996. China became a member of the Zangger Committee in 1997. China signed the Additional Protocol to the Agreement between China and IAEA for the Application of Safeguards in China in 1998, and in early 2002 formally completed the domestic legal procedures necessary for the entry into force of the Additional Protocol, thus becoming the first nuclear-weapon state to complete the relevant procedures. China actively participated in the work of the IAEA, the Preparatory Commission for the CTBTO and other related international organizations. It supported the IAEA's contribution to the prevention of potential nuclear terrorist activities, and took an active and constructive part in the revision of the Convention on the Physical Protection of Nuclear Materials.

China has energetically backed up countries concerned in their efforts to establish nuclear-weapon-free zones. It has signed and ratified the protocols to the Treaty for the Prohibition of Nuclear Weapons in Latin America and the Caribbean (Treaty of Tlatelelco), the South Pacific Nuclear-Free Zone Treaty (Treaty of Rarotonga), and the African Nuclear-Weapon-Free Zone Treaty (Treaty of Pelindaba). China has expressly committed itself to signing the protocol to the South East Asia Nuclear-Weapon-Free Zone Treaty (Treaty of Bangkok) and supported the initiative for the establishment of a Central Asian nuclear-weapon-free zone.

In the biological field, China has always strictly observed its obligations under the Convention on the Prohibition of the Development, Production and Stockpiling of Bacteriological (Biological) and Toxin Weapons and on Their Destruction (BWC) since its accession in 1984. As from 1988, it has, on an annual basis, submitted to the United Nations the declaration data of the confidence-building measures for the BWC in accordance with the decision of its Review Conference. China has also enthusiastically contributed to the international efforts aimed at enhancing the BWC effectiveness, and actively participated in the negotiations on the protocol to the BWC and in international affairs related to the BWC.

In the chemical field, China has made a positive contribution to the negotiation and conclusion of the Convention on the Prohibition of the Development, Production, Stockpiling and Use of Chemical Weapons and on Their Destruction (CWC). It signed the Convention in 1993 and deposited its instrument of ratification in1997. Since the CWC came into force, China has stood firmly by the Organization for the Prohibition of Chemical Weapons (OPCW) in carrying out its work, and earnestly fulfilled its obligations under the CWC. China has set up the National Authority for the performance of its obligations envisaged in the CWC, and submitted initial and annual declarations of all kinds on schedule and in their entirety. By the end of October 2003, China had received 68 on-site verifications by the OPCW.

In the missile field, China supports the international community in its efforts to prevent the proliferation of missiles and related technologies and materials, and adopts a positive and open attitude toward all international proposals for strengthening the missile non-proliferation mechanism. China has constructively participated in the work of the UN Group of Governmental Experts on Missiles, as well as the international discussions on the draft of the International Code of Conduct Against Ballistic Missile Proliferation and the proposal of a Global Control System.

III. Non-Proliferation Export Control System

Effective control of materials, equipment and technologies that could be used in the development and production of WMD and their means of delivery is an important aspect in a country's implementation of its international non-proliferation obligation, and an important guarantee for the success of the international non-proliferation efforts. As a country with some sci-tech and industrial capabilities, China is well aware of its non-proliferation responsibility in this field. For a long time, the Chinese government has adopted rigorous measures both for the domestic control of sensitive items and technologies and for their export control, and has kept making improvements in light of the changing situation.

For a fairly long time in the past, China practised a planned economy, whereby the state relied mainly on administrative measures for import and export control. This proved to be effective for implementing the non-proliferation policy under the then prevailing historical conditions. But with the deepening of China's reform and opening-up, and especially following the country's entry into the World Trade Organization (WTO), the environment of China's domestic economy and foreign trade has undergone a tremendous change. So far, China has initially established a socialist market economy, and its non-proliferation export control pattern has shifted from an administrative control to a law-based control.

In recent years, the Chinese government has constantly strengthened the work of building a legal system to bolster non-proliferation on the principle of rule of law to ensure the effective enforcement of its non-proliferation policy. China has attached great importance to studies on the current international standards of non-proliferation export control. Integrating the multinational export control mechanism and the valuable experience of other countries with its own national conditions, China has widely adopted the current international standards and practices, vigorously strengthened and improved the system for ensuring non-proliferation export control, and formulated and enacted a number of laws and regulations, which form a complete system for the export control of nuclear, biological, chemical, missile and other sensitive items and technologies, and all military products, and provide a full legal basis and mechanism guarantee for the better attainment of the non-proliferation goal. This export control regime has embraced the following practices:

Export Registration System: All exporters of sensitive items or technologies must be registered with the competent departments of the Central Government. Without the registration, no entity or individual is permitted to engage in such exports. Only designated entities are authorized to handle nuclear exports and the export of controlled chemicals and military products. No other entity or individual is permitted to go in for trade activities in this respect.

Licensing System: It is stipulated that the export of sensitive items and technologies shall be subject to examination and approval by the competent departments of the Central Government on a case-by-case basis. No licence, no exports. The holder of an export licence must engage in export activities strictly as prescribed by the licence within its period of validity. If any export item or contents are changed, the original licence must be returned and an application made for a new export licence. When exporting the above-mentioned items and technologies, an exporter shall produce the export licence to the Customs, go through the Customs formalities as stipulated by the Customs Law of the People's Republic of China and the relevant control regulations and control measures, and be subject to supervision and control by the Customs.

End-User and End-Use Certification: An exporter of sensitive items and technologies is required to provide a certificate specifying the end-user and the end-use, produced by the end-user that imports them. Different kinds of certificates must be produced, depending on the circumstances and particularly the sensitivity of the exported items or technologies. In some cases, the certificates must be produced by the end-user and authenticated by the official organ of the end-user's country and the Chinese embassy or consulate in that country, while in others, they must be produced by the relevant government department of the importing country. The end-user must clarify the end-user and end-use of the imported materials or technologies in the above-mentioned certificates, and definitely guarantee that without permission from the Chinese government, it shall not use the relevant item provided by China for purposes other than the certified end-use, or transfer it to a third party other than the certified end-user.

List Control Method: China has drawn up detailed control lists of sensitive materials, equipment and technologies. In the nuclear, biological and chemical fields, the relevant lists cover virtually all of the materials and technologies included in the control lists of the Zangger Committee, the Nuclear Suppliers' Group, the Chemical Weapons Convention (CWC), and the Australian Group. In the missile field, the scope of the Chinese list is generally the same as the Technical Annex of the Missile Technology Control Regime (MTCR). In the arms export field, the Chinese government also drew on the experience of the relevant multilateral mechanism and the relevant practice of other countries when it first formulated and issued the arms export control list in 2002. The Chinese government will make timely adjustments to the above lists in light of actual conditions.

Principle of Non-Proliferation-Oriented Examination and Approval: Before making a decision on whether to issue an export licence, the competent department will give overall consideration to the possible effect of the relevant exports on national security and the interests of general public, as well as its effect on international and regional peace and stability. The specific factors for reference in the examination and approval process include China's incumbent international obligations and international commitments, whether the export of the sensitive items or technologies will directly or indirectly jeopardize China's national security or public interests, or constitute a potential threat, and whether it conforms to the international non-proliferation situation and China's foreign policy. An assessment of the degree of proliferation risk of exporting a sensitive item or technology shall be made by an independent panel of technical experts organized by the examination and approval department.

The assessment will serve as an important reference in the examination and approval process. The examination and approval department shall also make an overall examination of the situation of the country or the region where the end-user is located. It shall give special consideration to whether there is any risk of proliferation in the country where the end-user is located or any risk of proliferation to a third country or region, including: whether the importing country will present a potential threat to China's national security; whether it has a program for the development of WMD and their means of delivery; whether it has close trade ties with a country or region having a program for the development of WMD and their means of delivery; whether it is subject to sanctions under a UN Security Council resolution; and whether it supports terrorism or has any links with terrorist organizations. Moreover, the examination and approval department shall also pay attention to the ability of the importing country in exercising export control and whether its domestic political situation and surrounding environment are stable. The focus of examination of the end-user and end-use is to judge the ability of the importing country to use the imported items or technologies, and to assess whether the importer and the end-user are authentic and reliable, and whether the end-use is justified.

"Catch-all" Principle: If an exporter knows or should know that there is a risk of proliferation of an item or technology to be exported, the exporter is required to apply for an export licence even if the item or technology does not figure in the export control list. When considering an export application or deciding on whether to issue an export licence, the export examination and approval departments shall make an overall assessment of the end-use and end-user of the item or technology to be exported and the risk of proliferation of WMD. Once such a risk is identified, the competent departments have the right to immediately refuse the requested export licence, and terminate the export activity. Moreover, the competent departments may also exercise, on an ad hoc basis, export control on specific items not contained on the relevant control list.

Penalties: Exporters who export controlled items or technologies without approval, arbitrarily export items beyond the approved scope, or forge, alter, buy or sell export licences shall be investigated for criminal liability in accordance with provisions in the Criminal Law of the People's Republic of China (PRC) on smuggling, illegal business operation, disclosure of state secrets or other crimes. For cases that do not constitute crimes, the competent government department shall impose administrative sanctions, including warning, confiscation of illicit proceeds, fines, suspension or even revocation of foreign trade licences.

IV. Concrete Measures for Non-Proliferation Export Control

In the nuclear field, China has persisted in exercising stringent control over nuclear exports and nuclear materials. In nuclear materials control, since its accession to the IAEA, China has established a "State System for the Accountancy and Control of Nuclear Materials," and a "Nuclear Materials Security System" that measures up to the requirements of the Convention on the Physical Protection of Nuclear Materials. In 1987, the Chinese government issued the Regulations on the Control of Nuclear Materials. Under the regulations it instituted a licensing system for nuclear materials. It designated the department for supervision and control over nuclear materials and defined its duties, the measures for nuclear materials control, the application for, and examination and issuance of, nuclear materials licences, the management of nuclear materials accounts, the accountancy of nuclear materials, the physical protection of nuclear materials, and relevant rewards and punishments.

China's nuclear export is handled exclusively by the companies designated by the State Council. China adheres to the following three principles: guarantee for peaceful use only, acceptance of the safeguards of the IAEA, and no retransfer to a third country without the prior consent of the Chinese government. The Chinese government issued the Regulations of the PRC on the Control of Nuclear Export in 1997. Apart from the above-mentioned three principles, the regulations also expound on China's policy of not advocating, not encouraging and not engaging in the proliferation of nuclear weapons, not helping other countries develop nuclear weapons, not providing any assistance to any nuclear facility not placed under IAEA safeguards, not providing nuclear exports to it, and not conducting personnel and technological exchange or cooperation with it. The regulations also provide for a rigorous examination system for nuclear export, severe violation punishments and a comprehensive and detailed control list.

In 1998, the Chinese government promulgated the Regulations of the PRC on the Control of Nuclear Dual-Use Items and Related Technologies Export. Therein it reaffirms its determination of strictly performing its international nuclear non-proliferation obligations and exercising strict control over the export of nuclear dual-use items and related technologies, and it instituted a licensing system for related exports. It established a registration system for exporters and the procedures for the examination and approval of exports, and defined punishments for violations of the regulations. The Amendments to the Criminal Law of the PRC adopted in December 2001 designate as criminal offences such acts as illegally manufacturing, trafficking and transporting radioactive substances, and stipulate corresponding punishments for such offences.

In the biological field, China has promulgated and implemented a series of laws, rules and regulations in the past two decades and more, including the Criminal Law of the PRC in 1979, the Tentative

Measures on the Stockpiling and Management of Veterinarian Bacteria Culture in 1980, the Regulations on the Management of Veterinary Medicines in 1987, the Law of the PRC on the Prevention and Control of Infectious Diseases in 1989, the Law on the Quarantine of Animals and Plants Brought into or Taken Out of the Chinese Territory in 1991, the Measures for the Control of Biological Products for Animal Uses and the Procedures for the Safe Administration of Agricultural Biological Gene Engineering in1996, and the Standards for the Quality of the Biological Products for Animal Uses in 2001. These laws, rules and regulations have made strict provisions on the production, control, use, stockpiling, carriage and transfer of relevant bacteria (viruses), vaccines and biological products. The Amendments to the Criminal Law of the PRC adopted in December 2001 designate as criminal offences such acts as illegally manufacturing, trafficking, transporting, stockpiling or using infectious pathogens, and stipulate corresponding punishments for such offences.

In October 2002, the Chinese government promulgated the Regulations of the PRC on the Export Control of Dual-Use Biological Agents and Related Equipment and Technologies, and the control list. It instituted a licensing system for the export of dual-use biological agents and related equipment and technologies and a registration system for the exporters, and established the principle that the relevant exports shall not be used for biological weapon purposes, that without prior consent of the Chinese government, the dual-use biological agents and related equipment and technologies supplied by China shall not be used for purposes other than the declared end-use, or be retransferred to a third party other than the declared end-user. Besides, the regulations also provide strict procedures for export examination and approval and punishments for violations of the regulations.

In the chemical field, the Chinese government promulgated between 1995 and 1997 the Regulations of the PRC on the Administration of the Controlled Chemicals, the Controlled Chemicals List and the Detailed Rules for the Implementation of the Regulations of the PRC on the Administration of the Controlled Chemicals, designating the department in charge of the supervision of the controlled chemicals and defining its duties, making a detailed classification of the controlled chemicals and exercising strict control over the production, sale, use, import and export of sensitive chemicals. Under the regulations, the import and export of the controlled chemicals must be handled by the designated departments. No other department or individual is permitted to engage in import and export of these items. In 1998, the Chinese government added 10 controlled chemicals to the Controlled Chemicals List. The Amendments to the Criminal Law of the PRC adopted in December 2001 designate as criminal offences such acts as illegally manufacturing, trafficking, transporting, stockpiling or using toxic materials, and stipulate corresponding punishments for such offences.

In October 2002, the Chinese government further promulgated the Measures on the Export Control of Certain Chemicals and Related Equipment and Technologies, and the control list. The measures are a substantive supplement to the Regulations on the Administration of the Controlled Chemicals, not only adding 10 chemicals to the list, but also providing for the export control of the related equipment and technologies. The measures provide a licensing system for the export of the materials and technologies on the control list. They require importers to guarantee that the controlled chemicals and related equipment and technologies supplied by China shall not be used for stockpiling, processing, producing or handling chemical weapons, or for producing precursor chemicals for chemical weapons, and that, without the prior consent of the Chinese government, the related materials and technologies shall not be used for purposes other than the declared end-use or be retransferred to a third party other than the declared end-user. The measures also provide a registration system for exporters and corresponding rules for the examination and approval of such exports, as well as punishments for violations of the regulations.

In the missile field, China has always taken a prudent and responsible attitude toward the export of missiles and related technologies. The Chinese government declared in 1992 that it would act in line with the guidelines and parameters of the MTCR in its export of missiles and related technologies. In 1994, it committed itself not to export ground-to-ground missiles featuring the primary parameters of the MTCR—i.e. inherently capable of reaching a range of at least 300 km with a payload of at least 500 kg. In 2000, China further declared that it had no intention to assist any country in any way in the development of ballistic missiles that can be used to deliver nuclear weapons, and that it would formulate and publish regulations on the missile export control and the relevant control list.

In August 2002, the Chinese government promulgated the Regulations of the PRC on Export Control of Missiles and Missile-Related Items and Technologies, and the control list. The regulations and the list, in light of the actual conditions in China and the prevailing international practice, adopt a licensing system for the export of missiles, items and technologies directly used for missiles, and missile-related dual-use items and technologies. The regulations provide that the receiving party of the export shall guarantee not to use missile-related items and technologies supplied by China for purposes other than the declared end-use, or retransfer them to a third party other than the declared end-user without the consent of the Chinese government. They also provide for strict procedures for the examination and approval of such exports, and the punishments for violations of the regulations.

In the arms export field, in addition to the above-mentioned special regulations, the Chinese government promulgated the Regulations of the PRC on the Administration of Arms Export in 1997, and revised them in 2002 in order to strengthen the administration of arms export and to regulate arms export. The regulations reaffirm the three principles that China has always adhered to in its arms exports: being conducive to the capability for just self-defence of the recipient country, no injury to the peace, security and stability of the region concerned and the world as a whole, and no interference in the internal affairs of the recipient country. The regulations also stipulate that arms export can only be handled by arms trading companies which have obtained the business operations right for arms export; that arms export shall be subjected to a licensing system; and that dual-use products whose end-use is for a military purpose shall be regarded as military products and be placed under control. In November 2002,the Chinese government issued the Military Products Export Control List as a supplement to the Regulations on the Administration of Arms Export, exercising, for the first time, arms export control according to the list. The list contains a detailed classification of conventional weapons and armaments, constituting a framework with the main body of four levels of weapon components, weapon categories, main systems or components of weapons, and the parts and components, technologies and services directly related to the weapon equipment, thus providing a scientific and powerful legal guarantee for strengthening the control of the arms trade and arms export.

In addition, the Regulations on the Import and Export Control of Technologies issued by the Chinese government in 2001 also stipulate that strict control shall be exercised over the export of nuclear technologies, technologies related to dual-use nuclear products, the production technologies of controlled chemicals, and military technologies. The Customs Law of the PRC and the Administrative Punishments Law of the PRC also provide a legal basis for non-proliferation export control.

V. Strictly Implementing the Laws and Regulations on Non-Proliferation Export Control

Through the past years, China has steadily improved and developed its laws and regulations on non-proliferation, providing a solid legal basis and strong guarantee for the better attainment of the government's non-proliferation goals and, at the same time, setting a new demand for law-enforcement capability of the relevant functional departments of the government. In order to ensure the effective implementation of these laws and regulations concerning non-proliferation export control, the departments concerned of the Chinese government have devoted a great deal of effort to improving non-proliferation export control organs, publicizing the relevant policies and regulations, conducting education for enterprises, and investigating and handling cases of violations.

Export Control Organs: China's non-proliferation export control involves many of the government's functional departments. So far, a mechanism for a clear division of responsibility and coordination has been established among these departments.

China's nuclear export comes under the control of the Commission of Science, Technology and Industry for National

Defence (COSTIND), jointly with other relevant government departments. Arms export, including the export of missiles, and facilities and key equipment used directly for the production of missiles, is under the control of COSTIND and the relevant department under the Ministry of National Defence, jointly with other government departments concerned.

The export of nuclear dual-use items, dual-use biological agents, certain chemicals, and the missile-related dual-use items and technology for civilian use is under the control of the Ministry of Commerce (MC), jointly with other government departments concerned. Among them, the export of nuclear dual-use items and missile-related dual-use items and technologies is subject to examination by the MC, jointly with COSTIND. The export of dual-use biological agents and technologies related to animals and plants is subject to examination by the MC, jointly with the Ministry of Agriculture if needed. The export of dual-use biological agents and technologies related to humans is subject to examination by the MC, jointly with the Ministry of Health if needed. The export of equipment and technologies related to dual-use biological agents and of equipment and technologies related to certain chemicals is subject to examination by the MC, jointly with the State Development and Reform Commission if needed. The export of controlled chemicals is subject to examination by the State Development and Reform Commission, jointly with the MC.

The export of sensitive items and related equipment and technologies that relate to foreign policy is subject to examination by the above-mentioned competent departments, jointly with the Ministry of Foreign Affairs. Where the export items entail significant impact on national security and public interests, the competent departments shall, jointly with other relevant departments, submit the case to the State Council and the Central Military Commission for approval.

The General Administration of Customs of the PRC shall be responsible for the supervision and control of the import and export of the above-mentioned items and technologies.

Special organs, staffed with specialists, have been set up in the above-mentioned ministries and commissions to take charge of the export control work.

Publicity of Laws and Regulations and Education for Enterprises: Immediately after the non-proliferation export control regulations were issued, a news release was announced through the national media, and the full text of the regulations and control lists was published in the professional publications and on the web sites of the government departments, foreign trade enterprises and research institutes concerned. The publicity has provided favourable conditions in informing the concerned exporters of the regulations and control lists. Competent departments concerned have also taken positive steps to ensure earnest implementation of the regulations by relevant enterprises and institutions, and to make export enterprises familiarized with the contents of the regulations and procedures for export examination and approval by organizing lectures and training courses on these regulations.

Building of the Export Examination System: In order to effectively implement the export control regulations, China has established a system involving application, examination and approval, certificate issuance and Customs control, inspection and clearance, and this system applies to all interested exporters. The Ministry of Commerce and other competent departments are formulating the Export Licensing Catalogue of Sensitive Items and Technologies (i.e. the commodities on the lists attached to relevant export control regulations bearing Customs HS codes), and are doing their best to ensure compliance by export enterprises at all stages of export, and enhance the government's capability to exercise supervision on export control.

To make it more convenient for export enterprises to apply for export licences, the Ministry of Commerce plans to provide an online service for licence application, examination and approval geared to the needs of the general public once the operation system is available. The Chinese government will also establish a corresponding export control information exchange network among the examining, approving and licence-issuing organs and the Customs office.

Investigation and Handling of Law Violations: The Chinese government attaches great importance to the investigation and handling of cases of law violations relating to non-proliferation. After being informed of possible illegal exports, concerned competent departments will make earnest investigations and administer corresponding administrative punishments, or transfer the cases to the judicial organs for ascertaining criminal responsibility, depending on the seriousness of the law-breaking acts. In recent years, China has dealt with a number of law-breaking export cases and administered corresponding punishments to the units and individuals involved according to law.

Strengthening the ability of law enforcement and effectively implementing the non-proliferation export control regulations is a complex system engineering project that involves many aspects and requires coordination and cooperation among different government departments. At the same time, understanding of the relevant state policies and regulations by domestic enterprises, their increased consciousness of the importance of non-proliferation, and the establishment of a self-discipline mechanism among them also have a direct bearing on the implementation of the non-proliferation laws and regulations. The concerned departments of the Chinese government are summing up their experience, constantly strengthening the training of the law-enforcing personnel, intensifying publicity and further improving the domestic non-proliferation export control system.

Conclusion

While sparing no effort to implement the non-proliferation policy, to strengthen and to improve the non-proliferation laws and regulations and the export control mechanism, the Chinese government is fully aware that the above efforts should proceed in a systematic way and advance step by step.

The international non-proliferation effort is inseparable from the policies and measures of the countries involved, and the building of the domestic mechanisms in various countries is inseparable from the establishment of international non-proliferation standards. China will continue to take an active part in international non-proliferation endeavours, and exert great efforts to maintain and strengthen the existing non-proliferation international legal system within the UN framework. It will constantly increase consultations and exchanges with the multinational non-proliferation mechanisms, including the "Nuclear Suppliers' Group", the MTCR, the "Australia Group" and the "Wassenaar Arrangement", and continue to take an active part in international discussions related to non-proliferation.

The Chinese government will continue to keep in touch and hold consultations with other countries on non-proliferation issues, and is willing to strengthen its exchange and cooperation with all sides in the fields related to non-proliferation export control to keep improving their respective non-proliferation export control systems.

Confronted with the complicated and changeable international security situation, China stands for fostering of a new security concept of seeking security through cooperation, dialogue, mutual trust and development. Non-proliferation is an important link in maintaining international and regional peace and security in the new century. China will join the members of the international community who love peace and stability in making contributions to accelerating the development and improvement of the international non-proliferation mechanism and to promoting world peace, stability and development through unremitting international efforts and cooperation and by persisting in the settlement of the issue of proliferation of WMD and their means of delivery through peaceful means.

[*Source:* http://www1.chinadaily.com.cn/en/doc/2003-12/03/content_287062.htm]

V

Basic Statistics

Table 1. India's Selected Socio-Economic Indicators

Population	1.027 billion (March 1, 2001)
Birth Rate	25.4 per 1,000 (2001)
Death Rate	8.4 per 1,000 (2001)
Life Expectancy at Birth (Year)	Male—62.3, Female—65.3 (2001)
Infant Mortality Rate (per thousand live births)	Rural—72, Urban—42, Total—66 (2001)
Morbidity Rate (per 1000 pop.)	55 (1999)
No. of hospitals per million pop.	16 (1998)
Doctor-Population Ratio	888 (1998)
Urban Population	27.8% (2001)
Density of Population	324 persons per sq. km (2001)
Sex Ratio	933 Females per 1,000 Males (2001)
Poverty—Numbers	260 million
Poverty Ratio	26.10% (1999-2000)
India's Ranking in UNDP Human Development Index (HDI)	127/175 (2003)
Literacy Rate	65.38% (2001)
GDP at factor cost (current prices)	Rs. 2,516,912 crore (2003-04, Advance Estimate), $549,184 million
GDP at factor cost (constant prices)	Rs. 1,424,507 crore (2003-04, Advance Estimate) $310,824 million
Per Capita GDP (current prices)	Rs. 23,457 (2003-04, AE)
Per Capita GDP (constant prices)	Rs. 13421 (2003-04, AE)
Gross Domestic Capital Formation (Current Prices)	23.3% of GDP (2002-03)

(Continued)

Table 1 Continued

Gross Domestic Savings (Current Prices)	24.2% of GDP (2002-03)
Consumption Expenditure (Current Prices)	76.9% of GDP (2002-03)
Gross Domestic Investment (Current Prices)	24% of GDP (2000-01)
Average Rate of Inflation (WPI)	4.4 (April 2002-January 18, 2003)
Electricity Generated	499.6 billion KWh (2001-02)
Towns Electrified	100% (2001-02)
Villages Electrified	86.76% (2001-02)
Foodgrains Production	210.0 million tonnes (2003-04 est.)
Gross Irrigated Area	40.2% (1999-2000)
Fertilizer Consumption	95.2 kg/ha (1999-2000)
Per capita Foodgrain Availability	151.1 kg/per annum (2000-01)

Source: Man Power Profile 2003, IAMR, New Delhi; UNDP, *Human Development Report 2003; Economic Survey 2002-3, Government of India; Handbook of Statistics on the Indian Economy 2002-3, RBI; Monthly Review of the Indian Economy*, CMIE; April 2004 Ministry of Statistics and Programme Implementation, Government of India website (22.05.2004).

Table 2. Area, Population and Electorate by States in India

State/ Union Territory	Area in Sq. km.	Population (2001 Census) (2004 General Election)	% of Rural Population (2001)	No. of Lok Sabha Constituencies	No. of Electors (2004 General Election)
Andhra Pradesh	275,045	75,727,541	72.92	42	51,142,162
Arunachal Pradesh	83,743	1,091,117	79.59	2	684,019
Assam	78,438	26,638,407	87.28	14	15,014,874
Bihar	94,163	82,878,796	89.53	40	50,553,503
Chhatisgarh	136,034	20,795,956	79.92	11	13,719,235
Goa	3,702	1,343,998	50.23	2	941,167
Gujarat	196,024	50,596,992	62.65	26	33,675,054
Haryana	44,212	21,082,989	71.00	10	12,320,377
Himachal Pradesh	55,673	6,077,248	90.21	4	4,181,995
Jammu & Kashmir	222,236	10,069,917	75.12	6	6,369,963
Jharkhand	79,714	26,909,428	77.75	14	16,812,338
Karnataka	191,791	52,733,958	66.02	26	38,673,910
Kerala	38,863	31,838,619	74.03	20	21,099,334

(Continued)

Table 2. continued

State/ Union Territory	Area in Sq. km.	Population (2001 Census) (2004 General Election)	% of Rural Population (2001)	No. of Lok Sabha Constituencies	No. of Electors (2004 General Election)
Maharashtra	307,713	96,752,247	57.60	48	62,992,047
Manipur	22,327	2,388,634	76.12	2	1,536,508
Meghalaya	22,429	2,306,069	80.37	2	1,289,374
Mizoram	21,081	891,058	50.50	1	549,959
Nagaland	16,579	1,988,636	82.26	1	1,041,433
Orissa	155,707	36,706,920	85.03	21	25,652,789
Punjab	50,362	24,289,296	66.05	13	16,615,391
Rajasthan	342,239	56,473,122	76.62	25	34,711,594
Sikkim	7,096	540,493	88.90	1	281,937
Tamil Nadu	130,058	62,110,839	56.14	39	47,255,649
Tripura	10,486	3,191,168	82.98	2	1,978,222
Uttar Pradesh	240,927	166,052,859	79.22	80	110,630,632
Uttaranchal	53,484	8,479,562	74.41	5	5,562,637
West Bengal	88,752	80,221,171	71.97	42	47,436,050

Union Territory					
Andaman and Niocbar Islands	8,249	356,265	67.32	1	241,645
Chandigarh	114	900,914	10.22	1	527,684
Dadra and Nagar Haveli	491	220,451	77.11	1	122,681
Daman and Diu	112	158,059	63.74	1	79,232
Delhi	1,483	13,782,976	6.99	7	8,764,524
Lakshadweep	32	60,595	55.53	1	39,033
Pondichery	492	973,829	33.43	1	636,667
INDIA	3,287,263	1,027,015,247	72.22	543	671,524,934

Source: *Statistical Abstract, India, 2002*, CSO, New Delhi; *India 2004*: *A Reference Manual*, Government of India; Election Commission of India website (22.05.2004).

Table 3. India's GDP: Total and Growth Rates

Year	GDP at Factor Cost (at 1993-94 prices) Rs. crore	Growth Rate(%)	GDP at Factor Cost (at 1993-94 prices) Million $*
1993-94	781,345	5.9	249153
1994-95	838,031	7.3	266889
1995-96	899,563	7.3	268928
1996-97	970,083	7.8	273494
1997-98	1,016,594	4.8	273867
1998-99	1,082,748	6.5	257307
1999-2000	1,148,442	6.1	265352
2000-01	1,198,685	4.4	276960
2001-02	1,267,833	5.8	292937
2002-03	1,318,321 (Quick Estimate)	4.0	273114
2003-04	1,424,507 (Advance Estimate)	8.1	310824

*Values in dollar are calculated as per the exchange rate in respective years as given in Table 10.

Source: *Economic Survey 2002-3*, Government of India; Ministry of Statistics and Programme Implementation, Government of India website (22.05.2004).

Table 4. Percentage Change in Value Addition (Constant Prices) in India's Economy

Year	Agriculture	Industry	Service
1996-97	9.6	7.1	7.2
1997-98	-2.4	4.3	9.8
1998-99	6.2	3.7	8.4
1999-2000	0.3	4.8	10.1
2000-01	-0.1	6.5	5.5
2001-02	6.5	3.4	6.7
2002-03	-5.2	6.4	7.1
2003-04 (Est.)	12.6	6.5	8.3

Source: Monthly Review of the Indian Economy, CMIE, April 2004.

Table 5. India's Agricultural Production (In Million Tonnes)

Item	1996-97	1997-98	1998-99	1999-2000	2000-01	2001-02	2002-03	2003-04
Foodgrains	199.4	192.3	203.6	209.8	196.8	212	174.2	210
• Cereals	185.2	179.3	188.7	196.4	195.7	198.8	163.1	195.8
• Pulses	14.5	13	14.9	13.4	11.1	13.2	11.1	14.2
Oilseeds	25	21.3	24.7	20.7	18.4	20.8	15.1	24.9
Sugarcane	277.6	279.5	288.7	299.3	296	300.1	281.6	275
% Change in Production of Total Foodgrains	9.6	-3.1	6.1	2.7	-6.3	8	-18.3	20.4
% Change in Production of Total Non-Foodgrains	7.2	-9.4	10.5	-4.7	-6.6	5	-10.3	18.6

Source: Monthly Review of the Indian Economy, CMIE, April 2004.

Table 6. Industrial Production in India (Percentage Change)

Industry	1996-97	1997-98	1998-99	1999-2000	2000-01	2001-02	2002-03	2003-04 (Est.)
Index of Industrial Production	6.1	6.6	4.1	6.6	5.1	2.6	5.8	7.0
Manufacturing	7.3	6.6	4.4	7.2	5.4	2.9	6.0	7.6
• Spun Yarn	12.4	6.4	-5.6	8.5	3.8	—1.9	-0.9	
• Fertilizers	-1.7	17.8	4.0	4.7	2.5	—1.0	-0.8	
• Finished Steel	6.1	2.9	1.9	12.1	9.6	2.6	7.6	
• Cement	7.4	2.8	6.2	15.4	0.7	9.7	8.7	
Mining & Quarrying	-1.9	7.0	-0.8	1.0	3.7	0.5	5.8	5.0
Electricity	4.0	6.6	6.4	7.3	4.0	3.1	3.2	4.0
Automobiles	15.6	- 4.4	-1.2	12.0				
Basic Goods	3.0	6.8	1.7	5.5	3.9	2.4	4.8	
Capital Goods	11.4	5.8	12.6	7.0	1.7	-3.4	10.5	
Consumer Goods	6.2	5.5	2.2	5.7	8.0	6.0	7.1	
Intermediate Goods	8.1	8.0	6.1	8.8	4.7	1.6	3.9	

Source: Monthly Review of the Indian Economy, CMIE, April 2004.

Table 7. Production and Import of Energy in India

Item	Unit	1996-97	1997-98	1998-99	1999-2000	2000-01	2001-02	2002-03
Coal Production	mln. tns.	289.3	300.4	296.5	304.1	313.7	327.8	341.3
Coal Imports	mln. tns.	13.2	23.0	16.5	19.7	20.9	20.5	
Elect. Generation	bln. kwh	395.9	421.7	448.5	481.1	501.2	513.1	
• Thermal & Nuclear	bln. kwh	327	374.2	365.6	400.3	426.8	439.9	
• Hydel	bln. kwh	68.9	74.6	82.9	80.8	74.4	73.1	
Crude Oil Production	mln. tns.	32.9	33.9	32.7	31.9	32.4	32	33.0
Crude Oil Imports	mln. tns.	33.9	34.5	39.8	57.8	74.1	78.7	82.0
Natural Gas Production	bln.cu. mtrs	23.3	26.4	27.4	28.4	29.5	29.7	31.4
Petroleum Products Imports	mln. tns.	22.2	24.0	23.8	16.6	9.3	7.0	6.7
Consumption of Petroleum Products	mln. tns.	82.7	87.8	94.3	102.6	107	111	111.1

Source: Monthly Review of the Indian Economy, CMIE, April 2004.

Table 8. Finances of Central Government in India (Rupees Billion)

Item	1996-97	1997-98	1998-99	1999-2000	2000-01	2001-02	2002-03	2003-04 (Est.)
Revenue Receipts	1,263	1339	1495	1815	1926	2013	2317	2630
Tax Receipts	1,288	1392	1438	1718	1886	1871	2163	2549
• Direct Tax	388	482	464	578	682	691	829	1033
• Indirect Tax	900	911	974	1139	1204	1180	1333	1517
Expenditure	2,010	2321	2793	2981	3256	3623	4004	4743
• Plan Exp.	535	591	668	762	827	1012	1115	1215
• Non-plan Exp.	1,475	1730	2125	2219	2429	2611	2889	3527
Subsidies	155	185	236	245	268	312	435	447
Defence	295	353	399	474	496	453	557	603
Interest	595	656	779	902	993	1075	1178	1246

Source: *Monthly Review of the Indian Economy*, CMIE, April 2004.

Table 9. India's External Transactions

Item	Units	1996-97	1997-98	1998-99	1999-2000	2000-01	2001-02	2002-03	2003-04(Est.)
1. Exports	$mn	33,498	35,049	33211	36,760	44,147	43976	52,370	58,900
% of GDP)		10	9.5	9.2	9.1	10.4	10	11.1	
• Agro Products	$mn	6,869	6,634	6033	5,615	5,983	5921	6,429	
• Ores and Minerals		1,173	1,062	893	917	1,155	1267	1,905	
• Manufactured goods		24,634	26,579	25786	29,751	34,391	33483	38,452	
2. Imports	$mn	39,165	41,535	42379	49,799	50,056	51588	61,445	75,000
% of GDP)		11.7	11.3	11.7	12.4	11.8	11.7	13	
• POL	$mn	10,045	8,174	6397	12,627	15,676	14048	17,685	20,000
• Non-POL	$mn	29,121	33,361	35982	37,172	34,381	37540	43,760	55,000
3. Foreign Capital Inflow (Net)	$mn	11,031	9,226	8042	10,184	9,992	10573	12,113	
• Net Foreign Aid	$mn	1,101	885	799	891	410	1,117	—2460	

(Continued)

Item	Units	1996-97	1997-98	1998-99	1999-2000	2000-01	2001-02	2002-03	2003-04(Est.)
• Net External Borrowing	$mn	2,856	4,010	4,367	333	3,737	-1576	-2344	
• Net NRI Deposits	$mn	3,350	1,125	960	1540	2,317	2,754	2976	
• Foreign Direct Investment	$mn	2,841	3,562	248	2167	4,029	6,131	4660	
• Portfolio Investment	$mn	3,312	1,828	-68	3024	2,760	2,020	979	
4. Debt Servicing	$mn	12,657	11,404	11,204	11543	12,821	10,862		
• Repayments	$mn	8,229	6,901	6,723	7059	8,359	6,776		
• Interest Payments	$mn	4,428	4,503	4,484	4484	4,462	4,086		
5. Outstanding External Debt	$mn	93,470	93,531	96,886	98,263	97,504	96,016	104551	
(As % of GDP)		24.5	24.3	23.6	22.1	21.8	20.5	20.1	
6. Debt Service Ratio	%	23	19.5	18.7	17.1	16.2	13.6		
7. Foreign Exchange Reserve (Excl. gold and SDRs) March end	$mn	22367	25,975	29,522	35,058	39,954	51,049	71890	118628*
8. Rupee Exchange Rate	Rs/ Dollar	35.47	37.12	42.08	43.28	45.61	47.53	48.27	45.83

*As on 14 May 2004 as given in Reserve Bank of India website (22.05.2004)

Source: Monthly Review of the Indian Economy, CMIE, April 2004

Table 10. India's Share in World Power Structure

Items	Share in Percentage	Reference Year
Military Expenditure	1.55	2002
Gross National Income	1.59	2002
Manufacturing Value Added	1.11	2000
Commercial Energy Production	4.21	2000
Trade	0.75	2001
Merchandise Exports	0.71	2001
High Tech Exports	0.21	2001
FDI Outflow	0.12	2001
Scientific Journal Articles	1.74	1999
Patent Applications Filed	0.65	2000

Source: The Military Balance 2003-2004, IISS; *World Development Report 2004*, The World Bank; *World Development Indicators 2003*, The World Bank; *World Investment Report 2003*, UNCTAD.

Table 11. Achievements of Selected Countries in Science and Technology

Country	Scientists and Engineers in R&D (per million people) 2000	Scientists and Technical Journal Article 1999	Expendture for R & D (%of GDP) 2000	High Technology Export (% of Manufacturing exports) 2001	Royalty and Licence Fees, 2001		Patent Application Filed 2000		Trademark applications filed 2000
					Receipts ($mn)	Payments ($ mn)	Residents	Non-residents	
Australia	3353 (4)	12525 (9)	1.51 (10)	10 (11)	298 (12)	868 (13)	10367 (9)	70354 (13)	71496 (8)
Brazil	323 (16)	5144 (15)	0.77 (15)	18 (9)	112 (13)	1245 (12)	41 (20)	64645 (18)	-
Canada	2985 (6)	19685 (6)	1.84 (9)	15 (10)	1499 (7)	3474 (5)	5518 (11)	80408 (12)	46252 (10)
China	545 (15)	11675 (11)	1.00 (13)	20 (8)	110 (14)	1938 (8)	25592 (6)	96714 (11)	6252 (17)
France	2718 (7)	27374 (5)	2.15 (6)	23 (6)	2504 (5)	1879 (9)	21471 (8)	138707 (6)	111781 (3)
Germany	3161 (5)	37308 (4)	2.48 (5)	18 (9)	3149 (4)	5243 (4)	78754 (3)	183796 (3)	97325 (6)
Greece	1400 (13)	2241 (19)	0.67 (16)	8 (12)	14 (18)	225 (18)	59 (19)	140481 (5)	10583 (16)
India	157 (20)	9217 (13)	1.23 (11)	6 (13)	83 (15)	306 (17)	90 (17)	60852 (19)	66378 (9)
Israel	1563 (12)	5025 (16)	3.62 (1)	25 (5)	432 (10)	457 (14)	2460 (14)	65398 (17)	11730 (14)
Italy	1128 (14)	1714 (7)	1.04 (12)	10 (11)	443 (9)	1312 (11)	3667 (13)	138248 (7)	11392 (15)
Japan	5095 (1)	47826 (2)	2.98 (2)	26 (4)	10462 (2)	11099 (2)	388879 (1)	97325 (10)	145834 (2)
Korea Rep.	2319 (10)	6675 (14)	2.68 (4)	29 (3)	668 (8)	3221 (6)	73378 (4)	98806 (9)	110073 (4)
Kuwait	212 (19)	260 (21)	0.20 (19)	1 (15)	0 0	- -	-		

(Continued)

Table 11 continued

Country	Scientists and Engineers in R&D (per million people) 2000	Scientists and Technical Journal Article 1999	Expendture for R & D (%of GDP) 2000	High Technology Export (% of Manufacturing exports) 2001	Royalty and Licence Fees, 2001		Patent Application Filed 2000		Trademark applications filed 2000
					Receipts ($mn)	Payments ($ mn)	Residents	Non-residents	
Mexico	225 (18)	2291 (18)	0.43 (18)	22 (7)	40 (17)	419 (15)	451 (15)	66465 (15)	46146 (11)
Netherlands	2572 (9)	10441 (12)	2.02 (7)	32 (1)	1723 (6)	2319 (7)	7528 (10)	136813 (8)	-
Russia	3481 (3)	15654 (8)	1.00 (13)	8 (12)	60 (16)	343 (16)	23658 (7)	65771 (16)	42806 (12)
Saudi Arabia	-	528 (20)	- 0	0 0	72 (18)	1114 (20)		-	
Spain	1921 (11)	12289 (10)	0.94 (14)	8 (12)	365 (11)	1678 (10)	3813 (12)	198626 (2)	98739 (5)
Turkey	306 (17)	2761 (17)	0.63 (17)	5 (14)	0	119 (19)	333 (16)	67289 (14)	33731 (13)
UK	2666 (8)	39711 (3)	1.87 (8)	31 (2)	7910 (3)	5909 (3)	33658 (5)	199565 (1)	85570 (7)
USA	4099 (2)	163526 (1)	2.69 (3)	32 (1)	38660 (1)	16360 (1)	175582 (2)	156191 (4)	292464 (1)

Note: Figures in brackets are ranks among the 21 countries given in the table.
Source: World Development Indicators, 2003.

Table 12. GDP and Defence Expenditures of India, Pakistan, and China

Year	GDP (In US$ bn)	Defence Expenditure (In US $ bn)	Defence Expen-diture as % of GDP	GDP (In US $bn)	Defence Expenditure (In US$ bn)	Defence Expend-iture as % of GDP	GDP (in US$ bn)	Defence Expenditure (In US$ bn)	Defence Expenditure as % of GDP
1993-94	269.73 (92)	8.07 (91)	2.99	44.06 (92)	3.55 (92)	8.05	434.08 (92)	21.76 (92)	5.01
1994-95	290.4 (93)	7.0 (93)	2.41	50.8 (93)	3.3 (93)	6.49	507.5 (93)	27.4 (93)	5.39
1995-96	270.2 (94)	7.43 (94)	2.74	51.2 (94)	3.3 (94)	6.44	509 (94)	28.5 (94)	5.59
1996-97	330 (95)	8.3 (95)	2.51	56 (95)	3.6 (95)	6.42	560 (95)	31.7 (95)	5.66
1997-98	371 (96)	10.4 (96)	2.8	64 (96)	3.7 (96)	5.78	616 (96)	38 (96)	6.16
1998-99	385 (97)	12.2 (97)	3.16	61 (97)	3.4 (97)	5.57	639 (97)	36.6 (97)	5.72
1999-2000	469 (98)	14.1 (98)	3	61 (98)	4.0 (98)	6.55	703 (98)	37.5 (98)	5.33
2000-01	440 (99)	14.2 (99)	3.22	61.6 (99)	3.5 (99)	5.68	732 (99)	39.5 (99)	5.39
2001-02	471 (2000)	14.7 (2000)	3.12	62.8 (2000)	3.65 (2000)	5.81	794 (2000)	42 (2000)	5.28
2002-03	490 (2001)	14.3 (2001)	2.91	55.8 (2001)	2.4 (2001)	4.3	1200 (2001)	47 (2001)	3.91
2003-04	505 (2002)	13.8 (2002)	2.73	68 (2002)	2.7 (2002)	3.97	1300 (2002)	51 (2002)	3.92

Source: IISS, The Military Balance, 1993-94 to 2003-2004, London.

Note: Figures in parentheses indicate the year of the given data.

Table 13. Defence Expenditure, Manpower, Weapons and Equipment of Major Military Powers

Country	Defence Expenditures (In US $ mn)	Manpower	Weapons and Equipment								
		Active/ Reserves	Army			Navy			Air Force		
			MBT	Combat Vehicles (Recce., AIFC, APC, Light Tanks)	Artillery	Submarines	Principal Surface Combatants	Amphibious Vehicles	Fighter Ground Attack/ Bomber Aircraft	Fighter Aircraft	Reconnaissance Aircraft
US	329,616	1,427,000 1,237,700	7,620	21,715	5,540	72	118	40	203 (B-52H, B-1B, B-2A)	3,513 (F-4 D/E/G, F-15 A/B/C/D, F-16 A/B/C/D, F-22A, F-111, F-117, among others) (Tactical)	32 (U-2S, TU-2S, E-8C, E-9A RC- 135S among others)
China	48,380	2,250,000/ 500-600,000	7,180	6,000	15,200	69	63	56	700 (J-6/A, Q-5C/D, Su30 MKK), 180 Bomber Aircraft (H-6E/F/H, H- 6H, H-5	1000 (J-7 II/ IIA, J-7 IIH, 27SK/UBK, among others)	290 (HZ-5, JZ-6/7/8

Russia	48,040	960,600/-20,000,000	21,870	28,125	20,746	53	32	22	801 (Tu-95, Tu-160, Su-24 Su-25)	908 (MiG-25 MiG-29, Su-27 MiG-31)	214 (MiG-25 Su-24)
France	38,005	259,050/-100,00	614	6,030	794	10	34	9	6 sqn *(Mirage 2000D, Jaguar A, Mirage F1-CT)*	5 sqn *(Mirage 2000C/B/5F)*	2 sqn *(Mirage F1-CR)*
Japan	37,070	239,900/-47,000	780	990	750	16	54	8	3 sqns (F-4EJ, F-1, F-2)	9 sqns (F-15J, F-4E)	1 sqn (RF-4E EJ
UK	35,249	212,660/-272,550	543	5,228	407	15	34	6	10 sqns (Tomado GR4, Harrier GR7/ Jaguar GR3/3A	4 sqns (Tamodo F3)	4 sqns GR4A, CanberraPR-9 Jaguar GR3/ 3A)
Germany	31,465	284,500/-358,650	2,398	5,901	1,682	12	13		5 Wings with sqns (Tomado, ECR Tomado	4 Wings with 7 sqn F-4F	1 Wing with 2 sqn Tornado
Italy	24,210	200,000/-63,200	1,183	2,970	1,439	6	18	3	8 sqn (Tornado IDS, AMX)	5-6 sqn (F-104 ASA, Tornado ADV, F-16)	1 sqn Maritime Reconnaiss-ance (BR 1150 Atlantic),

(Continued)

Table 13 continued

Country	Defence	Manpower	Weapons and Equipment								
	Expenditures (In US $ mn)	Active/ Reserves	Army			Navy			Air Force		
			MBT	Combat Vehicles (Recce., AIFC, APC, Light Tanks)	Artillery	Submarines	Principal Surface Combatants	Amphibious Vehicles	Fighter Ground Attack/ Bomber Aircraft	Fighter Aircraft	Reconnaissance Aircraft
											ECM/Recce sqn (G-222 VS, PD-808 P-180, P-166 DL-3
Saudi Arabia	20,981	124,500	1,055	4,460	408		8	8	4 sqns (F-5B/F/RF, Tornado IDS)	9 sqns (Tornado ADV, F-15)	1 sqn (E-34) (Airborne Early Warning)
India	13,073	1,325,000/- 535,000/-	3,898	2,107	4,355	19	29	7			
South Korea	12,615	686,000/- 4,500,000	2,330	2,520	4,589	20	39	12	7 Fighter Wings (F-16C/D, F-5E/F, F-4D/E)		1 Group (RF-4C, RF-5A, Hawker 800 RA)

Brazil	9.651	287,600/-1,340,000	178	1,498	599	4	20	3	254 Combat Aircraft (Mirage (*Mirage* F-103 E/D, F-5E/F, AT-27, AT-29, among others)		
Israel	9,437	167,600/-358,000	3950	13,070	2,660	3	53	2	1 sqn (A-4N)	13 sqns(F-4E-2000, F-4E, F-15, F- 16	49 (Recce, AEW EW, MR)
Turkey	8,727	514,850/-378,700	4,205	4,543	1,553	13	19	8 F-16C/D)	11 sqns (F-5A/B, F-4E, F-16C/D)7	7 sqns (F-5A/B, E-4E,	2 sqns(RF-4E)
Spain	8,253	150,700/-328,500	552	2484	984	6	16	4	1 sqn with EF 18 (F-18 Hornet	8 sqns (F-18 Hornet, *Mirage* F1, CE/BE)	
Canada	7,771	52,300/-36,900	114	2711	502	2	16		140 Combat Aircraft (CF-18, CP-140, among others)		
Australia	7,549	53,650/-20,300	71	619	385	6	11	3	2 sqns (F-111, F-111C, F-111A(C), F-111G)	3 sqns (F/A-18)	2 sqns (EP-3C, EC-130 H)

(Continued)

Table 13 continued

Country	Defence Expenditures (In US $ mn)	Manpower Active/ Reserves	Weapons and Equipment								
			Army			Navy			Air Force		
			MBT	Combat Vehicles (Recce., AIFC, APC, Light Tanks)	Artillery	Submarines	Principal Surface Combatants	Amphibious Vehicles	Fighter Ground Attack/ Bomber Aircraft	Fighter Aircraft	Reconnaissance Aircraft
Taiwan	7,479	290,000/- 1,657,500	926	2,080	1,465	4	32	18	20 sqns (F-5E/ F, F-16A,/B AT -3, Ching-Kuo)	3 sqns (Mirage 2000-5)	1 sqn (RF-5E)
Nether-lands	7,330	53,130/- 32,200	283	663	367	4	15	1	6 sqns of F-16 M (FTR/ FGA/Recce)		
Indonesia	6,245	302,000/- 400,000		999	125	2	1	26	4 sqns (A-4, F-16, *Hawk* Mk 109/209)	1 sqns (F-5)	1 sqn (Boeing 737-200 OV-10F
Greece	6,154	177,600 291,000	1,723	2,316	1,900	8	14	6	14 sqns (A-7 H, F-16CG/ DG, F-4E, F-5A/B, *Mirage* F-1CG, Mirage 2000 EG/BG)		2 sqns (RF-4E, Saab 340 H *Erieye*)

Mexico	5,319	192,770 300,000	1,26	199		11	3			1 sqn (F-5E, 2-F) 500S, SA-237A, C-26)	1 photo sqn (*Commander*
Pakistan	2,541	620,000 513,000	2,368	1,251	1,617	10	8		6 sqns (*Mirage* IIIEP/DP, Mirage 5, Q-5)	12 sqns (F-7PG, F-7P/FT-7, F-16A/B/, Mirage IIIO/7-OD)	1 sqn (*Mirage* IIIRP)

Note 1: The countries included in the table are all those whose defence expenditure exceeds $5 billion.
Note 2: Pakistan has been included as a special case.
Source : IISS, *The Military Balance, 2003-4*, London.

Table 14. Operational Nuclear Warheads

Country	Strategic					Sub-Strategic				
	ICBM	IRBM	SLBM	Delivery System (ALCM/ Bombs)	Strategic Total	SSM	Navy/SLCM	Delivery System (Aircraft)	Sub-Strategic Total	Grand Total
United States	1,700		3,168	1,106	5,974		320	800	1,120	7,094
Russian Federation	3,072		1,732	632	5,436		450	1,1540	3,190	8,626
France			288	50	338			10	10	348
People's Republic of China	20	108	12	120	260	120		30	150	410
United Kingdom			185		185					185
Israel					90+	Some	100	200	200	
India							40+	40+	40+	
Pakistan						Some		40+	40+	40+
Democratic People's Republic of Korea								±2	±2	±2

Notes 1: ICBM (Inter-Continental Ballistic Missile), IRBM (Intermediate Range Ballistic Missile), SLBM (Sea-Launched Ballistic Missile), ALCM (Air-Launched Cruise Missile), SSM (Surface-to-Surface Missile), SLCM (Sea-Launched Cruise Missile).

2: Strategic (Missiles with a range of over 5,000km, or air-launched from long-range aircraft); Sub-strategic (Missiles with a range less than 5,000km).

Source: IISS, *Military Balance, 2003-4*, London, p. 229.

Table 15. Operational Offensive Nuclear Delivery Systems of Major Military Powers

Country	Land Ballistic Missiles		SLBM		Aircraft		SLCM		ALCM	
	Designation/ aka	Range (km)	Designation/ aka	Range (km)	Designation /aka	Range (km)	Designation/ aka	Range (km)	Designation/ aka	Range (km)
United States	LGM-30 G/ *Minuteman III*	13,000	UGM-96/ *Trident* I C-4	7,400	B-52H/ *Stratofortress*	16,000	Tomahawk/ TLAM-N	2,500	AGM-86B	2,500
	LGM-118/MX/ Peacekeeper	9,600	UGM-133/ Trident II D-5	12,000	B-2/Spirit	12,200			AGM-129	3,500
					F-15 E/ *Strike Eagle*	2,500				
					F-16A/B/C/D/ Fighting Falcon	2,500				
					F-117A	2,100				
Russian Federation	SS-18/*Satan*	15,000	SS-N-8/*Sawfly*	9,100	Tu-95M/*Bear*	12,000	SS-N-9/*Siren*	110	AS-4/Kh-22 Kitchen	310
	SS-19/*Stilleto*	10,000	SS-N-18/ *Stingray*	6,500	Tu-160/ *Backfire*	4,000	SS-N-12/ *Sandbox*	550	AS-15A/ KH-55 Kent	2,500
	SS-24/*Scalpel*	10,000	SS-N-20/ *Sturgeon*	8,300	Tu-22M-3/ *Backfire*	4,800	SS-N-19/ *Shipwreck*	550	AS-15B/Kh-55SM *Kent*	3,000
	SS-25/*Sickle*	10,000	SS-N-23/*Skiff*	8,300	Su-24M/ *Fencer*	2,100	SS-N-21/ *Sampson*	2,400	AS-16/Kh-15 *Kickback*	150

(Continued)

Table 15. Continued

Country	Land Ballistic Missiles		SLBM		Aircraft		SLCM		ALCM	
	Designation/ aka	Range (km)	Designation/ aka	Range (km)	Designation /aka	Range (km)	Designation/ aka	Range (km)	Designation/ aka	Range (km)
	SS-27/Topol-M	10,500					SS-N-22/ Sunburn	120		
Peoples Republic of China	CSS-2/DF-3A	2,800	CSS-N-3/JL-1	2150	H-6/Tu-16	5,000				
	CSS-3/DF-4	4,750			Q-5/MiG-19	400				
	CSS-4/DF-5A	13,000								
	CSS-5/DF-21	2,150								
	CSS-5/DF-21A	2,500								
	CSS-6/DF-15/ M-9	600								
	CSS-7/DF-11/ M-11	300								
	CSS-8/DF-7	150								
	CSS-9/DF-31	8,000								
Pakistan	Ghauri 1/Hatf 5	1,500			F-16A/B/ *Fighting Falcon*	2,500				
					Mirage 5	1,200				
					Q-5/MiG-19	1,200				

Israel	Jericho 1	500			F-4E-200/ *Kurnass*	2,200	Turbo-Popeye 3	1,500		
	Jericho 2	1,800			F-16A/B/C/D/ Fighting Falcon	2,500				
					F-151/ Thunder	2,500				
United Kingdom			UGM-135/ Trident II D-5	12,000						
France			M-4	4,000	Super Etendard	650			ASMP	250
			M-45	4,000	Mirage 2000N	1,200				
					Rafale	1,200				
India					Jaguar S(1)/ Shamsher	1,600				
					MiG-27M/ Bahadur	1,000				
					Mirage 2000H/Vajra	1,200				
DPRK					H-5/IL-28	2,100				

Notes 1: SLBM (Sea-Launched Ballistic Missile), SLCM (Sea-Launched Cruise Missile), ALCM (Air-Launched Cruise Missile).
2: aka (also known as).

Source: IISS, *The Military Balance, 2003-4*, London, p. 228.

Index